The College Cost Book, 1994

COLLEGE COSTS AND FINANCIAL AID HANDBOOK 1994

Fourteenth Edition

College Scholarship Service

College Entrance Examination Board
New York

The College Scholarship Service (CSS) is an activity of the College Board concerned with improving equal educational opportunity. The CSS, through the determination of financial need, assists in the equitable distribution of financial assistance to students. Its services are offered to students and their parents, to secondary schools, to noncollegiate sponsors of financial aid programs, and to all institutions of postsecondary education.

The College Board is a nonprofit membership organization committed to maintaining academic standards and broadening access to higher education. Its more than 2,800 members include colleges and universities, secondary schools, university and school systems, and education associations and agencies.

This publication contains material related to Federal Title IV student aid programs. While the College Board believes that the information contained herein is accurate and factual, this publication has not been reviewed or approved by the U.S. Department of Education.

Copies of this book may be ordered from your local bookseller or from College Board Publications, Box 886, New York, New York 10101-0886. The price is $16.

Editorial inquiries regarding this book should be addressed to the College Scholarship Service, The College Board, 45 Columbus Avenue, New York, New York 10023-6992.

Photo credits: page 4, left, University of New Mexico; page 4, right, and page 25, Bill Sublette and the University of Virginia Alumni Association; pages 67, 68 and 73, Monkmeyer Press; pages 69 and 74, Michael Paras, Columbia High School, New Jersey; pages 20 and 37, Hugh Rogers.

Copyright © 1993 by College Entrance Examination Board. All rights reserved.

College Board, Advanced Placement Program, College-Level Examination Program, CLEP, College Scholarship Service, CSS, FAF, SAT, *College Explorer,* and the acorn logo are registered trademarks of the College Entrance Examination Board. CollegeCredit, ExtraCredit, *College Cost Explorer FUND FINDER,* and *College Planner* are trademarks owned by the College Entrance Examination Board.

Library of Congress Catalog Number: 80-648095

International Standard Book Number: 0-87447-481-7

Printed in the United States of America

Contents

Preface ix

Part I. Paying for college

1. What does college cost? 3
The components of college costs. 3
    Tuition and fees 3
    Books and supplies 4
    Room and board. 4
    Personal expenses. 5
    Transportation. 5
    Total expense budget 5
Questions and answers about college costs 6

2. How much will you be expected to pay? . 7
Evaluating a family's income 7
Evaluating a family's assets 7
Evaluating a student's ability to pay 8
Estimating your expected family contribution ... 8
Setting a goal. 9
Special note on independent (self-supporting)
    students 9
Questions and answers about how much you
    will be expected to pay 10

3. How to make time work for you 11
What does "expected family contribution"
    actually mean?. 11
Financing the parents' contribution. 11
Questions and answers about making time
    work for you 13

4. Making the most of your own resources 14
Strategies for stretching your resources 14
    Rearranging your personal finances 14

The long-range approach 15
More immediate options. 15
Federal Parent Loan for Undergraduate Students . . 15
Privately sponsored supplemental loans. 16
Combination savings/loan plans. 16
College-sponsored financing programs 16
Strategies for cutting costs 17
    Reducing the time involved in earning a degree . . 17
    Reducing indirect costs 17
    Guaranteed or stabilized tuition plans 18
Strategies for working your way through college . . 18
    Part-time employment. 18
    Cooperative education. 19
    Deferred enrollment 19
    Employee fringe benefits 19
    Managing your time if you work 19
Questions and answers about making the
    most of your resources. 20

5. How financial aid can help. 22
Who gets financial aid?. 22
Types of financial aid. 22
Eligibility for financial aid 23
Financial aid from the federal government 23
    Federal Pell Grant Program 24
    Federal Supplemental Educational
    Opportunity Grant Program 24
    Federal Perkins Loan Program 24
    Federal Work-Study Program 24
    Federal Stafford Loan Program 24
Military options. 25
    Service academies 26
    Reserve Officers' Training Corps 26
Assistance from the Bureau of Indian Affairs 27
Assistance from benefit programs 27

Assistance for military personnel and veterans ... 27
Vocational rehabilitation benefits ... 27
Financial aid from state governments ... 28
Financial aid from colleges ... 28
Financial aid from private sources ... 28
Scholarship search services ... 29
Questions and answers about financial aid ... 30
Further reading ... 32
General ... 32
Specific population groups ... 33
Fields of study ... 34
Graduate study ... 35
Study abroad ... 35

6. Applying for financial aid ... 37
What do you need to do? ... 37
When do you need to do it? ... 38
How do you do it *right*? ... 39
Questions and answers about applying for financial aid ... 40

7. Borrowing for education ... 42
Keep borrowing in perspective ... 42
How serious are you? ... 42
Credit where credit is due ... 42
Educate yourself about loans ... 43
Learn the language ... 43
Evaluate how much you need ... 44
Estimate how much you can repay ... 44
A special note to parents about borrowing ... 45
Understand what you're doing ... 46
Questions and answers about borrowing for education ... 48

8. Pulling it all together ... 49
Understanding financial aid awards ... 49
Comparing award offers ... 49
Accepting a financial aid award ... 50
Appealing your award package ... 50
Loans and your aid award package ... 50
Sample financial aid award statement ... 51
Work and your aid award package ... 52
Private scholarships and your aid award package ... 52
Your rights and responsibilities ... 53
Student rights ... 53

Student responsibilities ... 54
Questions and answers about pulling it all together ... 54
Financial aid checklist ... 55

9. Long-range planning: A special message to parents ... 57
The purpose of planning ... 57
The Smiths and the Joneses ... 57
How to plan ... 59
Setting realistic goals ... 59
Developing a timetable ... 60
Strategies for paying your fair share ... 60
Evaluating savings and prepayment plans ... 61
Finding extra outside help ... 61
A closing note ... 61
Questions and answers about planning ... 62

10. Tables, sample cases, and worksheets ... 63
Sample cases and worksheets ... 63
Tables of average student expenses and estimated parents' contribution ... 64
Carlos, Beth, and Andrea plan for college costs ... 66
Your personal plan ... 74

Glossary ... 79

Part II. College costs and financial aid ... 85

Table of college information ... 87

Sources of information about state grant programs and Federal Stafford Loans ... 212

Part III. College indexes

Colleges that offer academic, music or drama, or art scholarships ... 224
Academic ... 224
Music or drama ... 232
Art ... 237

Colleges that offer athletic scholarships ... 241
Archery ... 242
Badminton ... 242

Baseball 242
Basketball 244
Bowling 248
Cross-country 248
Diving 250
Fencing 251
Field hockey 251
Football (tackle) 251
Golf 253
Gymnastics 255
Horseback riding 255
Ice hockey 255
Lacrosse 255
Rifle 256
Rowing (crew) 256
Sailing 256
Skiing 256
Soccer 256
Softball 258
Squash 260
Swimming 260
Table tennis 261
Tennis 261
Track and field 263
Volleyball 265
Water polo 268
Wrestling 268

Tuition and/or fee waivers and special payment plans 270

For adult students 270
Children of alumni 270
Senior citizens 271
Minority students 276
Family members enrolled simultaneously 277
Unemployed, or children of
unemployed workers 279
Credit card 279
Installments 286
Discount for prepayment 292
Deferred payments 293

Alphabetical list of colleges 298

Mission Statement

The College Board champions educational excellence for all students through the ongoing collaboration of member schools, colleges, universities, educational systems, and organizations. It promotes—by means of responsive forums, research, programs, and policy development—universal access to high standards of learning, equity of opportunity, and sufficient financial support so that every student is prepared for success in college and work.

The College Board

Educational Excellence for *All* Students

Preface

This book starts out from a simple premise: without advance planning, almost no one can afford to pay for college. But with planning, *anybody* can. It's true for families whose children are already high school juniors and seniors—and even truer for families whose children are still quite young.

You may have doubted that education or training after high school is within your family's reach. *That's probably not true.*

You may have assumed that there's nothing you can do to help yourself or improve your chances of finding the outside help you need. *That's definitely not true.*

This book is designed to help students and their families meet college costs. If you're worried about your family's ability to pay future educational expenses, early planning *can* help. The *purpose* of planning is twofold:
- to get as much mileage as you can out of your own resources, and
- to secure the additional outside help—the "financial aid"—you may need.

Planning ahead to meet college costs involves several different kinds of activities. This book will:
- show you how to estimate the full costs of attending the colleges you're considering,
- help you to estimate what share of those costs you and your family will probably be expected to bear,
- prove that you can make time work *for* you in covering your share of the costs,
- describe different ways that families can make their costs more manageable,
- help you estimate your own probable need and eligibility for financial aid,
- explain the various types and sources of financial aid available and what you need to do to apply, and
- assist you in developing a personal financing plan and timetable for gathering the resources *you* need.

Next to buying a home, the money that you and your family pay toward college costs may well be the largest financial investment you ever make in your lifetime. You owe it to yourself to investigate all your options beforehand, and then to manage that investment as carefully as you would any other.

The author gratefully acknowledges the contributions of the many individuals who assisted in the development of the 1994 edition of *College Costs and Financial Aid Handbook*. Data in Parts II and III were collected by the editorial staff of Guidance Publishing under the direction of Nica Ganley and Dorothy Siegfried, using information collected through the College Board's Annual Survey of Colleges. The book was edited by Renée Gernand.

Jim Anderson, Jack Joyce, Laura Greene-Knapp, Sheila Kokidko, Kathleen Payea, and Mary Gaffney provided valuable assistance in various aspects of research and statistical analysis.

At the time this book went to press, several aspects of financial aid delivery for academic year 1994-95 had not yet been finalized. Changes in program, application, and eligibility rules are possible, starting in academic year 1995-96. As is always the case in times of change, it is very important that students seeking aid for the fall of 1994 take steps, early on, to ensure that they fully understand and comply with all application requirements.

To improve your chances of getting the help you need, you must know *what* you have to do, *when* you have to do it, and *how* to do it right—the first time. Missed deadlines, incomplete or inaccurate answers, and messy or illegible forms can hurt you. *If you have any doubts at all about which forms to file or which questions to complete, contact the financial aid offices at the colleges to which you are applying.*

Kathleen Brouder
Director
CSS Information Services
The College Scholarship Service

Part I. Paying for college

1. What does college cost?

Some of the best things in life may be free, but unfortunately, college isn't one of them.

In fact, it costs even more than you may think. High as the prices may seem to the family that's facing them, the truth is, they represent only part of the real costs. Only a very few colleges charge you the *full* costs of providing an education.

Public colleges and universities receive large operating subsidies from state and local taxes. Most independent or private colleges and universities meet at least some of their operating expenses through endowments, contributions from graduates, and government or foundation grants. Virtually all of them invest money and use the return to help pay for their activities. The influx of federal and state institutional aid for research, facilities, and special programs is an important part of most colleges' operating budgets, helping to hold down the amounts that must be charged to students and their families.

However, all of this may not be much consolation to students and parents like you who actually have to find a way to pay the bills. Average annual costs of attendance continue to climb for virtually every postsecondary educational option, from commuting to a low-cost community college to living on campus at a high-cost private institution.

The purpose of this book is to help you plan to meet college costs. Because every family's personal and financial circumstances are different, each family's plan for meeting college costs will be different, too. The worksheets in Chapter 10 follow three sample students from different family and financial backgrounds—Andrea, Beth, and Carlos—as they plan to meet college costs. Space is also provided for you to make some preliminary plans.

Your first step in planning is to learn what college costs. Part II of this book lists the average student expenses at 3,000 colleges and universities for the 1993-94 academic year (AY). The average expenses at different kinds of colleges for 1992-93 (the most recent year for which averages are available) are listed in Chapter 10.

The components of college costs

Regardless of where you enroll, your expenses include both direct educational expenses *and* living expenses, and typically consist of five parts:
- tuition and fees
- books and supplies
- room and board
- personal expenses
- transportation

Many students have additional expenses not covered under any of these categories, such as costs arising from medical care or a disability. Be sure to include these extra expenses in estimating the costs of attending the particular colleges you're considering.

Don't let the costs scare you! As this book explains, you may not have to pay the whole amount yourself, *and* there are ways of making more manageable the part you do have to pay.

Tuition and fees

Tuition is the charge for instruction. Fees may be charged for services such as the library, student activities, or the health center. The amount of tuition and fees charged by a particular college depends on many factors, but the most significant factor is what kind of college it is.

Because they receive funds from taxes, tuition and fees at public institutions are generally the lowest, particularly for legal residents of the state or district in which they are located. Most two- and four-year public colleges charge higher tuition for nonresidents, however. This "out-of-state" tuition (or "out-of-district"

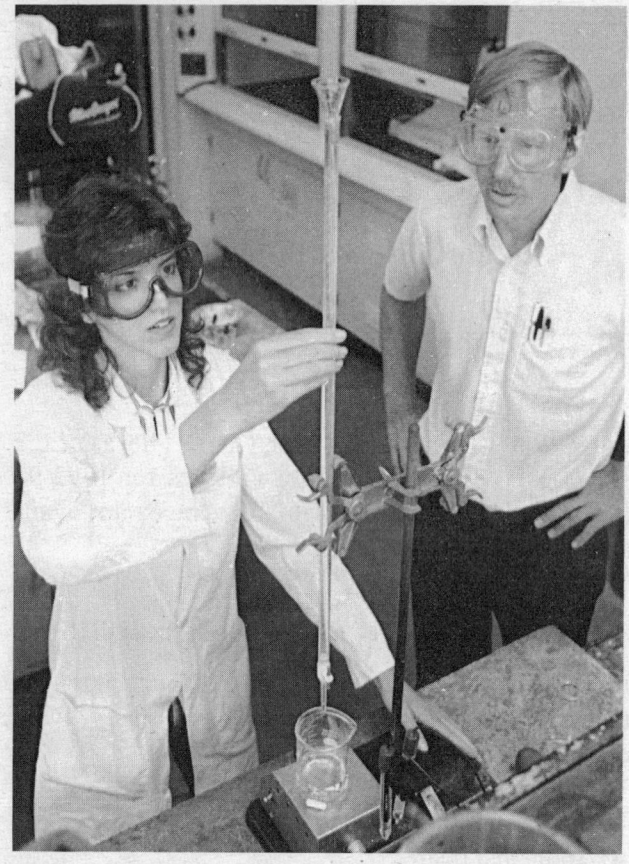

The budget for maintaining, staffing, and operating college facilities is met by federal and state aid, endowments, and investments in addition to charges to students.

tuition, in the case of two-year community colleges) often can make the cost of attending a public institution as high as the cost of attending many private institutions. (In rare instances, religiously affiliated colleges may add a surcharge for students who are not members of that religious group.) Tuition at private colleges is usually much higher than at public institutions because private colleges must charge a larger percentage of the real costs. Tuition at proprietary or profit-making institutions (such as many trade and technical schools) is usually set at a level to recover all of their operating costs plus a profit.

The tables in Part II of this book show the tuition and fees charged to most first-time, full-time students. Part-time charges, usually set by credit or semester hour, may work out to be higher per unit. Tuition and fees for upperclassmen and graduate or professional students may also vary.

Books and supplies

Every college student has to buy books, pencils, paper, and other supplies. The amount you spend for books and supplies will vary only slightly by type of institution but is generally related to the curriculum or courses you select. In some academic fields, for instance, students may have to spend a good deal more than the averages cited in Part II of this book.

Art students, for example, may need more extensive supplies such as canvases, paints, brushes, and clay. Engineering students may need calculators or slide rules. Students in the sciences may have additional expenses for lab work. Computer science students may need to buy more computer time, or even purchase personal computers. In some programs, the textbooks are more expensive simply because the "information explosion" causes rapid changes in the field.

Room and board

Room and board means basic living expenses for food and housing. Regardless of the kind of institution you choose, you will have to consider these expenses.

You may choose to live in a dormitory on campus or in other college-operated housing located near campus (such as college-owned apartments). Although some private two-year colleges have college-operated housing available, most public community colleges do not.

Or you may want to live in privately owned housing, such as an apartment or rooming house near campus. At many large colleges and universities where on-campus housing is limited, students often live in dormitories for the first year or two and then shift to off-campus private housing.

Or you may choose to live at home with your parents and commute to campus.

The terms "resident student" and "commuter student" can be confusing. In this book, students who live in dormitories or in off-campus, college-owned housing away from their families are called "resident students" (not to be confused with the term "legal resident" used in the discussion of tuition and fees). "Commuter students" are those who live at home with their families. Many colleges have additional budget categories designed to cover students who live off campus in private housing; information about estimated expenses for such students is available in college catalogs and financial aid bulletins. Students who live off campus in private housing generally have expenses that are more like the resident budgets in this book than the commuter budgets.

Colleges with their own housing typically charge residents on a nine-month basis for room rental and most meals, excluding holiday and vacation periods. The room and board charge is built into the student expense budget. Colleges also expect that students living in privately owned, off-campus housing have a similar level of expense (although this is sometimes estimated as somewhat higher or lower than the college's own room and board costs, depending on the local housing market).

Commuter students, on the other hand, are generally assumed to have somewhat lower expenses than resident students because they do not have to pay for housing. However, families should remember that they will still need to buy food for the student and pay for other normal living expenses. For example, if classes start early in the morning and go on until late at night, commuter students will need to buy at least one meal a day, and possibly additional snacks, in the student union or coffee shop. Therefore, the estimated cost of food and other expenses at home is usually built into commuter student expense budgets for financial aid purposes. Take these costs into account in your planning.

Personal expenses

No matter what kind of institution you choose, you will have some personal expenses for such things as clothing, laundry, toiletries, recreation, medical insurance and care, and perhaps incidental furnishings for your dormitory room. This is an area in which you can economize, but colleges usually estimate that students spend at least $950 to $1,250 per academic year on such items.

Transportation

All students spend some money for travel. Resident students who live on or near campus must travel to get there at the start of the academic year and return home at the end; most also go home at least once during the year. If you plan to live at college but expect to travel home frequently, your transportation costs may be considerably higher than the averages shown in this book or reported by individual colleges. Include estimated travel costs in your planning. For financial aid purposes, colleges often budget students for two round-trips home per year by the lowest-cost means of travel possible.

Commuter students who travel to and from campus daily also have travel expenses, whether they use public transportation or a private car. The costs of gasoline and daily parking can add up quickly, so estimate carefully. These costs, too, are built into student expense budgets by colleges for financial aid purposes.

Total expense budget

The total expense budget for a particular college is determined by adding up these five categories of expenses. "Tables, sample cases, and worksheets" in Chapter 10 reflect sample total expenses for resident and commuter students. For your own estimates, remember to consider any additional costs that might result from medical bills or other extraordinary personal expenses.

The total budgets at public colleges are lower than those at private colleges largely because tuition and fees tend to be lower at the former. There is not, however, a lot of difference in the other costs. So don't rule out a private college because of its higher tuition. Private institutions often have more financial aid resources that can help you make up the difference between costs and financial aid. *The greater your overall expense, the greater is the possibility of your demonstrating need for financial aid.*

Questions and answers about college costs

Q All of these costs look greater than anything we can afford. How can we possibly manage to pay for college?

A First, you may be eligible for some financial aid to help you meet part of the costs. What *you* pay for college is not necessarily what the price tag says. Second, you may be able to cut your costs and stretch your resources, as described in later chapters, but be prepared to contribute *something*. In very rare cases, parents are judged too poor to contribute anything toward the costs. Third, remember that you and your family are already paying some of these expenses right now—your food, clothing, and personal expenses, for example.

That's not to say that your expenses as a member of the household aren't putting a strain on the household budget; they may well be. If you can manage it now, however, ask yourself seriously if your family can't manage it for another two or four years.

Q With college costs so high, as well as the rising cost of living in general, shouldn't I just look for the cheapest alternative?

A Not necessarily. Higher cost colleges often have more financial aid to help families bridge the gap between the costs and what they can afford to pay.

Q How do I know that the costs at a particular college won't keep going up during the years I'm enrolled?

A You don't. In fact, they probably *will* continue to rise. However, your family's income will probably rise, too. Whether your family's ability to pay will increase at the same rate as college costs depends on a lot of factors, including the overall state of the economy.

2. How much will you be expected to pay?

You should regard your family as the first—and probably primary—source of funds for education. Virtually all colleges, government agencies, and private student aid programs expect you to pay *something* toward college costs, according to your ability. Financial aid often makes up the difference between the costs of attendance and what a family can afford to pay. You may not have to pay as much as the prices listed in a college's catalog if you are eligible for financial aid. Thus, estimating how much your family can reasonably be expected to pay toward educational expenses is a major part of understanding financial aid—and a critical aspect of goal setting.

Whether your family's share of the total costs amounts to 5 percent or 100 percent, you have a better chance of achieving the goal if you know how much you are aiming for.

To help them evaluate a family's financial strength, most college financial aid administrators and aid sponsors use a set of federal formulas that take into consideration income, assets, expenses, family size, and other factors.

In addition, many colleges use an alternate set of formulas for awarding their own *institutional* student aid funds. This alternate guideline, informally known as the "Institutional Methodology," differs from the "Federal Methodology" in several respects. (For instance, the Institutional Methodology takes home equity into account and includes a minimum expected contribution from students in calculating a family's ability to pay, but also permits more generous treatment of medical/dental expenses, elementary and secondary school tuition payments, and child support paid.) In Chapter 10, you will see how the formulas actually work. But the two methodologies share some common general principles.

Evaluating a family's income

A family's total income for the previous calendar year is added up. Parents' wages and all other income (such as dividends, social security, or welfare benefits) are included, but not all of this income can be used to pay for college. For most families, the largest part of its annual income must be used to provide for basic living expenses—housing, food, medical care, clothing, and so forth.

In evaluating a family's financial strength, aid administrators also take into account other demands on the parents' income, such as taxes or unusually large medical or dental bills. Even the costs of working must be taken into consideration—clothing, transportation, meals away from home, and so forth. Elementary and secondary school tuition payments for other children may also be considered.

After all these family expenses are taken into account, the amount remaining to a family for other uses is quite a bit smaller than its original income. This remaining amount is called "available income." A family would be expected to use some of this remaining income to help pay college costs. The more available income a family has, the more would be expected of them.

Evaluating a family's assets

Many family's assets are considered, too, because a family with assets is in a stronger financial position than a family with similar income but no assets. All of the assets are added up—the value of a business or farm, cash, savings and checking accounts, stocks and bonds, and so forth. At lower income levels, home equity is not considered in the *federal* aid formulas.

In the same way that a family can't be expected to spend all its income on education, neither is it expected to use all its assets to pay for college. The system "protects" a portion of parents' assets for their use in retirement. The amount parents are allowed to protect gets larger as the age of the primary wage earner increases, because an older worker has fewer years to save for retirement than a younger one. The system also "protects" a substantial portion of family assets tied up in a business or farm, since a business or farm is also a source of income. If it were all used up to pay for college, there would be nothing left to generate income in the future.

Even when the various allowances are subtracted from total assets, a family is not expected to convert all its remaining assets into cash for college—only a portion called "income supplement from assets."

Available income (the discretionary part of a family's annual income) is added to the income supplement from assets to get a dollar amount called "adjusted available income." Not all the adjusted available income is tapped for educational expenses, only a percentage. A family with a higher adjusted available income is expected to pay a greater share of college costs than is a family with a lower adjusted available income.

If more than one family member is attending college at the same time, the amount parents are expected to pay is divided by the number attending, in order to find the expected contribution per student. This means that sometimes a family is not eligible for aid when the first child goes to college, but becomes eligible in subsequent years when a younger brother or sister starts college.

Evaluating a student's ability to pay

A student is usually expected to contribute toward college expenses, too, from savings and summer earnings. While *federal* student aid rules do not prescribe a minimum expected contribution from students, many colleges expect a freshman to contribute at least $700 a year from summer job earnings when it comes to awarding their own private funds. Upperclassmen are often expected to contribute even more from summer and part-time jobs—upwards of $900 a year at most colleges, and more than that at many.

Estimating your expected family contribution

Your family's "share" is the sum of what your parents can contribute from their income and assets *and* what

Table 2.1. Sources for educational expenses

Resources	Percentage of students having resource	Percentage of students receiving $1,500 or more from resource
Parents' assistance	78%	49%
Federal Pell Grant	23	6
Federal Supplemental Educational Opportunity Grant	6	1
State scholarship or grant	14	3
College scholarship or grant	24	11
Other scholarship or grant	10	3
Federal Stafford Loan	23	11
Federal Perkins Loan	8	2
College loan	6	3
Other loan	6	3
Federal Work-Study Program	12	1
Part-time job on campus	20	2
Part-time employment	26	2
Full-time employment	3	1
Savings from summer work	51	6
Other savings	30	6
Student's spouse	2	*
Other government aid	2	2
Other aid	3	1

Note: Asterisk indicates less than 1 percent.
Source: *The American Freshman: National Norms for Fall, 1992* (Los Angeles: American Council on Education and University of California at Los Angeles, 1992).

you can contribute from your earnings, savings, and so forth. In the financial aid process, this amount is also referred to as the "expected family contribution":

    What parents can contribute from income
+ What parents can contribute from assets
+ What a student can contribute from income
+ What a student can contribute from assets
= Expected family contribution.

If you're simply curious about what magnitude of expense this represents, the Parents' Contribution table in Chapter 10 gives you a sense of what is expected of *parents* at different income and asset levels, assuming they meet the specifications as to age, family size, and other characteristics. Pick the combination of annual income and asset figures that most resembles your own, and you will have a *very* crude approximation of how your parent's share might work out.

You can make a much closer estimate of what might be expected of you and your family by fully completing the worksheets in Chapter 10. By subtracting your expected family contribution from the average costs of attendance at different kinds of colleges, you can get a sense of your remaining financial need. (In addition, computer software, such as the College Board's *College Cost Explorer FUND FINDER*, can be helpful when you're trying to determine how to pay for college. It provides a scholarship data base, detailed information about costs at 2,700 colleges and also explains how expected family contribution is calculated and then translated into eligibility. Check to see if your guidance office or library has a copy of *FUND FINDER* for you to use.)

You are usually eligible for financial aid equal to the amount of your demonstrated financial need. (Whether you are able to obtain all of the financial aid you're eligible for depends on a variety of factors, such as the availability of funds in any given year.)

Setting a goal

Your estimate of your expected family contribution—be it 5 percent or 100 percent of college costs—should be your goal. Your plan should be organized to help you achieve, or even exceed, that goal. If the goal seems too *big* in relation to your household budget, don't panic! Chapters 3 and 4 give some ideas about ways to finance your share of the costs. If your goal seems too *small* in relation to actual college costs, don't worry! Chapters 5 and 6 demonstrate how financial aid can bridge the gap. Whatever your goal, write it down on a piece of paper and refer to it occasionally. *Writing goals down on paper helps to make them real.*

Special note on independent (self-supporting) students

So far the discussion has focused on students who are dependent on their parents for financial support. If you are truly financially independent of your parents, you are called an "independent," or "self-supporting," student. This does not mean that your resources are always sufficient to pay your direct educational costs as well as living expenses (for yourself and your family).

What it *does* mean is that, in considering your need for financial aid, colleges and other aid providers assume that your parents will not provide you with any support. (When it comes to awarding their own *institutional* funds, some colleges will expect parents to supply *information*, however, regardless of the student's dependency status.)

Your ability as a self-supporting student to contribute toward college costs is evaluated on the basis of your own income, assets, and expenses. Expenses are typically higher than a dependent student's because self-supporting students must provide for maintenance and living expenses year-round. You may also have extra expenses, such as child care, which may be considered in the student expense budget developed by a college for self-supporting financial aid applicants. Because they do not get help from their parents and because their expenses are usually higher than dependent students' expenses, self-supporting students often have a greater financial need. (They may also be expected to contribute more toward their own educational expenses.)

Who is considered self-supporting and who is not? There are certainly many students who really are self-supporting, such as younger students who no longer have financial support of their parents, or older students with families of their own. The problem is defining what really constitutes self-supporting status.

At the time this book went to press, it was assumed that for the 1994-95 academic year the federal definition of independence, as outlined in the Higher Education Amendments of 1992, will be used to determine eligibility for the Federal Pell Grant, Federal Stafford Loan, and campus-based programs. Most state, institutional, and private aid sponsors are expected to use a similar definition.

Under the new definition, if you are receiving federal aid for the first time, you are *automatically* considered to be self-supporting if:
- you are at least 24 years old by December 31 of the award year (e.g., by December 31, 1994, for the 1994-95 award year),
- you are a veteran of the United States Armed Forces, regardless of age,
- you are an orphan or a ward of the court,
- you have legal dependents of your own *other than* a spouse,
- you are married, or
- you are a graduate or a professional student.

Financial aid administrators can make exceptions for students who do not meet these criteria but are nonetheless self-supporting. Contact the financial aid offices at the colleges you're considering if you need more information about dependency status.

Even if you meet the federal criteria for self-supporting status, however, you may be required to submit parents' financial data as part of the aid application process at some colleges. Some colleges may also ask you to provide additional documentation of your income and expenses if you claim self-supporting status. Also, some private sponsors may use different definitions than the federal government for determining self-supporting status. Contact the financial aid offices at the colleges from which you are seeking help if you think you may qualify as a self-supporting student and wish further information.

Questions and answers about how much you will be expected to pay

Q We have special expenses that aren't talked about in this chapter that affect our ability to pay (for example, a handicapped child who requires special medical care or education). Does anybody take this into account?

A Colleges try to take into account the unique circumstances of each applicant. In Chapter 6, where applying for financial aid is discussed, you will learn about ways in which you can make sure that the colleges you're considering at least understand your situation fully. Whether they will be able to give you extra help depends on a variety of factors, one of the most important being how much money they have available to help students in any given year.

Q We live in a big city and the rents for apartments are very high. Does the need analysis system take this into account?

A The formulas do take housing costs into account, along with food, clothing, and other family living expenses. Financial aid administrators at some colleges also may consider the high cost of living in your particular residential area.

Q I've calculated our expected family contribution, and it's more money than we can possibly afford. How can we pay this out of our current earnings?

A You aren't necessarily expected to pay it out of your current earnings alone. The next chapter will explain that no matter how large that expectation may appear to you, it can be made smaller if you break it into monthly amounts. The earlier you start planning, the more choices you have about how to finance your share of the costs.

3. How to make time work for you

If you had estimated how much you may be expected to pay toward college costs, you may wonder how you can possibly squeeze that much out of current income.

In fact, you probably *can't* squeeze it all out of current income. Few people are wealthy enough to pay cash for houses, cars, or major appliances. Most of us save or borrow, sometimes both, to finance the purchase of "big-ticket" items. In fact, we may not even be able to figure out whether we can afford something until we see how it breaks down in terms of monthly payments.

The more time you give yourself, the more choices you will have about how to finance your share. If you still have several years left before enrollment, you have many more options than families who are facing enrollment within the next year or two. But even if you were to enroll next month, you would still have some choices.

What does "expected family contribution" actually mean?

Your expected family contribution is *not* a prediction of how much extra cash you actually have on hand, or even an assumption of how much you "ought to" be able to pull from current income. Rather, the expected family contribution is a measure of your family's overall capacity to absorb some portion of educational expenses, and you can cover your share in any number of ways.

If you start early enough, you may be able to *save* your entire share, and more. One of the advantages of starting early is that you *earn* interest toward your goal. If you start late, you may have to *borrow*. The downside is that you're *paying* interest, not earning it. You could use a combination of saving *and* borrowing—or even "leverage" your money by borrowing against your own savings. The toughest way to cover your share of educational expenses, though, is to force them into your current household budget. Some families do it, but it's not easy.

Financing the parents' contribution

Students can get summer or part-time jobs to help finance their portion of the expected family contribu-

Table 3.1. Relationship of family income to parental contribution (1993-94 Federal Methodology)

Annual family income	Net income (after tax)	Parents' contribution (annual)	Percentage of total	Percentage of net
$ 5,000	$ 4,218	$ 0	0.0%	0.0%
10,000	8,435	0	0.0	0.0
15,000	12,653	0	0.0	0.0
20,000	16,150	40	0.2	0.2
25,000	19,618	800	3.2	4.1
30,000	23,085	1,560	5.2	6.8
35,000	26,553	2,360	6.7	8.9
40,000	30,020	3,320	8.3	11.1
45,000	33,488	4,540	10.1	13.6
50,000	36,955	6,070	12.1	16.4
55,000	39,903	7,450	13.5	18.7
60,000	42,999	8,910	14.9	20.7
65,000	46,126	10,380	16.0	22.5
70,000	49,254	11,850	16.9	24.1
75,000	52,381	13,320	17.8	25.4
80,000	55,509	14,790	18.5	26.6
85,000	58,636	16,260	19.1	27.7
90,000	61,764	17,730	19.7	28.7
95,000	64,891	19,200	20.2	29.6
100,000	68,019	20,670	20.7	30.4

Note: Estimated parents' contributions in Tables 3.1-3.4 assume four family members; one family member in college as an undergraduate; older parent (age 45) is employed; the other parent is not employed; income only from employment; no unusual circumstances; standard deductions on U.S. income tax; asset neutrality (assets equal to Asset Protection Allowance). Values are approximate.

Table 3.2. Parents' contribution related to monthly net income (1993-94 Federal Methodology)

Annual family income	Monthly net income (after tax)	Amount of monthly net required to pay parents' contribution
$ 5,000	$ 352	$ 0
10,000	703	0
15,000	1,054	0
20,000	1,346	3
25,000	1,635	67
30,000	1,924	130
35,000	2,213	197
40,000	2,502	277
45,000	2,791	378
50,000	3,080	506
55,000	3,325	621
60,000	3,583	743
65,000	3,844	865
70,000	4,105	988
75,000	4,365	1,110
80,000	4,626	1,233
85,000	4,886	1,355
90,000	5,147	1,478
95,000	5,408	1,600
100,000	5,668	1,723

Values are approximate.

Table 3.3. Financing parents' contribution (PC) under four different scenarios: percentage impact on monthly budgets

Percentage of gross income required each month to finance PC

Annual family income	Expected parents' contribution	Pay from current income (0-4-0)	Borrow in full (0-4-10)	Borrow and save (4-4-4)	Save in full (8-4-0)
$ 20,000	$ 40	.2%	0.1%	0.1%	0.1%
25,000	800	3.2	1.2	1.0	0.9
30,000	1,560	5.2	1.9	1.7	1.5
35,000	2,360	6.7	2.5	2.2	2.0
40,000	3,320	8.3	3.1	2.7	2.4
45,000	4,540	10.1	3.7	3.3	3.0
50,000	6,070	12.1	4.5	4.0	3.6
55,000	7,450	13.4	5.0	4.4	4.0
60,000	8,910	14.9	5.5	4.9	4.4
65,000	10,380	16.0	5.9	5.2	4.7
70,000	11,850	16.9	6.2	5.5	5.0
75,000	13,320	17.8	6.5	5.8	5.2
80,000	14,790	18.5	6.8	6.0	5.4
85,000	16,260	19.1	7.1	6.3	5.6
90,000	17,730	19.7	7.3	6.4	5.8
95,000	19,200	20.2	7.5	6.6	5.9
100,000	20,670	20.7	7.6	6.8	6.1

Values are approximate.

tion. Accommodating the parents' portion, or "par-ents' contribution," in the current household budget can be much harder, simply because the amount represents a large portion of annual income, as Table 3.1 illustrates.

At any point on the chart, you can see that the expected parents' share would require a pretty large percentage of income—*if* you were trying to take it all out of current income. At the $45,000 annual income level, for example, the expected parents' contribution would require *10 percent* of gross income, and a whopping *14 percent* of net (after-tax) income. As Table 3.2 demonstrates, that translates into a pretty big chunk of the monthly household budget.

You don't have to finance your share that way. You can if you want to and are able to, but spreading the expense out over time has a much smaller impact on your monthly budget. This is true whether you save, borrow, or both.

By way of illustration, consider these four very different scenarios for financing the *same* parents' contribution:

- Pay the entire contribution out of current income during the four years of enrollment.
- Borrow the full amount of the same contribution, starting at the point of enrollment and spreading repayment out over the four years of enrollment and the 10 years following graduation.
- Save some of the amount during the four years preceding enrollment, and then borrow the balance, with repayments spread out over the four years of enrollment and the four years following graduation.
- Save the full amount in the eight years preceding and the four years of enrollment.

The four approaches yield the same parents' contribution, but their respective effects on a household's monthly budget differ. Table 3.3 displays parents' contributions as constant percentages of total (pre-tax) income under each of the four scenarios.

To get a feel for how the percentages in Table 3.3 work out in dollar terms, see Table 3.4.

Look at the $45,000 annual income band again. Paying the parents' contribution entirely from current income would require modifying consumption by approximately $378 a month. Spreading the expense over time by any of the other scenarios could reduce the effect on the monthly budget by more than half.

Table 3.4. Financing parents' contribution under four different scenarios: dollar impact on monthly budgets

Annual family income	Expected parents' contribution	PC in monthly scenarios			
		Pay from current income	Borrow in full	Borrow and save	Save in full
$ 20,000	$ 40	$ 3	$ 2	$ 2	$ 2
25,000	800	67	25	21	19
30,000	1,560	130	48	43	38
35,000	2,360	195	73	64	58
40,000	3,320	277	103	90	80
45,000	4,540	379	139	124	113
50,000	6,070	504	188	167	150
55,000	7,450	614	229	202	183
60,000	8,910	745	275	245	220
65,000	10,380	867	320	282	255
70,000	11,850	986	362	321	292
75,000	13,320	1,113	406	363	325
80,000	14,790	1,233	453	400	360
85,000	16,260	1,353	503	446	397
90,000	17,730	1,478	548	480	435
95,000	19,200	1,599	594	523	467
100,000	20,670	1,725	633	567	508

Values are approximate.

The other important point about Tables 3.3 and 3.4 is that it is *never too late* to plan. If you were to enroll tomorrow and hadn't yet saved any money, you could still make time work for you by borrowing. The differences in the monthly payouts between the borrowing, saving, and borrowing/saving options in Tables 3.3 and 3.4 are nowhere near as large as the difference between all three of them and the pay from current income options.

However, when you are actually at the point of determining what your family should do, analyze the total *costs* associated with each option. Depending on the length of time you will be making loan payments, the amount of interest you will be paying, the rate of inflation, and the general state of the economy, some borrowing options may be a lot more expensive than others.

NOTE: The values in Tables 3.3 and 3.4 are calculated by a computer model using standard annuity formulas to create a monthly "outlay" computed as a constant percentage of family income. The model also assumes a 7 percent yield on investments, an 11 percent interest rate on borrowed money, and 5 percent annual increases in income and parents' contributions over the period of years associated with each scenario. Note that the model is designed to compare the relative effects of various financing scenarios on a monthly household budget. It cannot be used to compare the relative *costs* associated with those scenarios; borrowing, for instance, typically costs more than saving (except when inflation is high). Furthermore, the model deliberately fixes the monthly outlay as a constant percentage of income for comparison purposes, and thus Tables 3.3 and 3.4 cannot be used as amortization tables.

Questions and answers about making time work for you

Q My child will start college in less than a year. Isn't it too late to start saving?

A It is *never* too late to make plans. First of all, check your current finances to ensure you're getting as high a rate of return as possible. Second, take steps to make sure that you are creditworthy. If you are going to have to borrow, make sure that your credit history is accurate and that you have not exhausted your borrowing capacity. Third, look at the next chapters for some ideas about ways to finance your share—and reduce your costs. Fourth, investigate financial aid. Remember, even if your child *does* start college next year, he or she will be enrolled for four or more years. You don't just have one year to plan ahead; you have several.

Q Is it wise to borrow for education?

A Borrowing is an honorable way of paying for education; many students *and* parents take out loans to cover college costs. The important thing is not to get in over your head. Chapters 5 and 6 describe some current loan programs designed to help students and parents cover expenses, and Chapter 7 includes consumer advice about responsible borrowing.

Q How do I actually start saving for future educational expenses?

A The worksheets in Chapter 10 will help you estimate probable future college costs and what might be expected of your family toward paying those expenses. Once you have set an overall goal, break it down into annual, monthly, or even weekly goals.

The next chapter describes a variety of approaches to financing your share of the costs. If you have many resources already, you may wish to consult your financial adviser to make sure that your savings and investment programs are achieving your objectives.

4. Making the most of your own resources

Are you concerned that your family can't come up with enough cash to cover the contribution a college believes you should be able to make? What if a college can't give you any aid or can't give you enough to meet your need fully? What if you decide to attend college late in the year, and financial aid has already run out by the time you apply for admission?

Remember that colleges and most other student aid sponsors regard the student and his or her family as the primary source of funds for meeting the cost of education or training after high school. (There are rare instances where parents are considered unable to contribute anything whatsoever toward college costs, but even then, the student would be expected to contribute something from savings and summer earnings.)

This chapter will review some of the strategies that students and families have used to meet their share of college costs. Not all of these ideas will be applicable to your unique family situation, of course, but perhaps one or two will provoke some creative thinking. (Several commercial and not-for-profit organizations' programs are described in this chapter. Their inclusion is intended to illustrate the wide and growing array of options available to families in meeting college costs but does not imply any endorsement whatsoever.) The next chapter will describe how financial aid—grants and scholarships, loans, and jobs—can cover the gap between your best efforts and the costs of attendance.

If there is a "silver lining" to the rising costs, it is that colleges are working harder than ever not only to contain the costs but also to develop new mechanisms to assist students and families in meeting the costs. This chapter also describes some of the ways that colleges are trying to help families finance education after high school. Not all of these approaches will be available at the particular colleges you're considering, but they're worth asking about. Make sure that you review the lists in Part III of this book; you'll find the names of many colleges that offer special kinds of help to families in financing educational expenses.

Strategies for stretching your resources

Many students and families have used a variety of strategies for getting the most out of the resources they *do* have for meeting college costs. Some of these ideas may work for you, and some may make you angry! This section describes some possible strategies for getting more mileage out of family resources. Remember, the point is to do your share, *not* necessarily to cover the whole expense.

Rearranging your personal finances

Few families can cover their expected share from current earnings only, never mind bridge the gap that could be created by insufficient financial aid resources. To minimize the impact on your household budget when the time comes to start paying college bills, you should start planning as early as possible.

For instance, you might want to think about how your current assets can be resources for paying educational bills. Ask yourself, What are they worth now? What are they most likely to be worth when I want to use them? You may want to talk to your banker, a financial adviser, or an investment specialist about the best way of "saving" for college, given your financial situation. These professionals can offer you advice on financial planning for college based on your present situation, how much time you have left to save, and the risks involved in selecting certain financing alternatives.

The long-range approach

The earlier you start, the more time you have to arrange your personal finances to the greatest advantage. Families with young children, for instance, should think about creating a regular savings plan against the day when their children start college. Starting earlier rather than later really does make a difference. Deposited funds accrue interest, and the effect of compounding can be astonishing over a long period of time.

Many banks, savings and loan organizations, credit unions, investment firms, and other financial institutions market programs designed to help families accumulate resources for their children's future education. Under some programs, families make regular deposits to a savings account at interest rates that increase with the amount of the balance in savings; other programs provide for one-time or periodic payments into various kinds of investment funds or other financial products. Sometimes counseling and financial planning services are included as part of the program.

The Tax Reform Act of 1986 changed some of the rules governing ways in which families can accumulate money for college. Consumer guides to the tax law are widely available in bookstores, and you can also pose questions directly to the local office of the Internal Revenue Service (IRS). Or you may want to seek the help of a professional adviser, such as a Certified Financial Planner (CFP), a Certified Public Accountant (CPA), or a tax attorney. In any case, carefully investigate all the features of the programs offered by banks and investment firms. There is considerable variety in the safety, the yield, and the requirements of college savings programs and products now on the market. Shop around before you invest your hard-earned dollars.

More immediate options

Even if you have to start paying bills within the next year, it is worth your time to talk to your banker about your current savings and investment arrangements. Banks, savings and loan associations, credit unions, and investment firms never have been more eager for your money or have offered so many varieties of plans. The family with several thousand dollars in a passbook savings account is almost certainly not getting the most mileage out of its money.

No college expects you to sell the family homestead to pay for education, but when it comes to awarding their own institutioal funds, some colleges *are* quite explicit about their expectations of families with assets. The Higher Education Amendments of 1992 eliminated consideration of home equity in the case of families at lower income levels for purposes of determining eligibility for federal Title IV student aid. You may find that a college financial aid office wants to know your net return on investments, for instance. Others may suggest that you refinance the mortgage on your home. Others may inquire about the contribution that other members of the extended family (such as grandparents) might make to a student's educational expenses. Such observations from colleges may startle or even anger you, but they reflect a renewed emphasis on the family's central responsibility for financing education or training after high school.

There are some respects in which the family homestead has taken on potential new importance in paying educational expenses. Under the Tax Reform Act of 1986, the consumer interest deduction was phased out over a period of five years, effective December 31, 1986. One important exception is interest on indebtedness securing a taxpayer's principal residence or a second residence, up to the amount of the original purchase price plus improvements. (Taxpayers can't take out home equity loans on the appreciated value to make consumer purchases and deduct the interest, except in strictly limited cases where loans are to be used for education, medical expenses, or home improvements. Make sure you understand how the IRS rules are applied before you act.)

Many banks are marketing new loans and lines of credit based on home equity. Some of the new programs are geared specifically to educational expenses. As with most financial services, there is considerable variation in the terms of such programs, so you will want to shop both widely and cautiously. Make sure you understand all the implications of using your home this way, not just the tax-related ones.

Here are some other ideas.

Federal Parent Loan for Undergraduate Students

The Higher Education Amendments of 1992 expanded an important financial resource for families—the Federal Parent Loan for Undergraduate Students Program. (The Federal Stafford Loan Program will be described in the next chapter.)

As of July 1, 1993, parents may borrow up to the total cost of education *minus* any student aid awarded, per child. (There is no longer an annual limit or aggregate total.) The interest rate on a Federal PLUS Loan is variable, based on the 52-week T-Bill (treasury-bill) rate plus 3.1 percent, and is capped at 10 percent. Monthly repayment begins within 60 days of disbursement (although some lenders may permit borrowers to make interest-only payments while the child is still enrolled.) Federal PLUS loans are made without regard to financial need, but borrowers must demonstrate that they do not have an adverse credit history.

Because repayment generally must begin within 60 days, Federal PLUS loans are primarily assistance in meeting the cash-flow problems caused by college bills. Some parents borrow under the Federal PLUS program to meet all or part of the expected parental contribution, while others may borrow to make up the difference between costs and their contribution plus available financial aid.

Federal PLUS loans are widely available through programs like CollegeCredit™, sponsored by the College Board, as well as many banks, credit unions, and savings and loan associations.

There is a similar program for self-supporting undergraduate students and graduate and professional students called Federal Supplemental Loans for Students.

Privately sponsored supplemental loans

Many organizations, banks, and credit unions sponsor special education loan programs that have more favorable interest rates and/or other special features that make the loans more attractive than other consumer borrowing options. Eligibility generally relates more to demonstrated creditworthiness than demonstrated financial need, and parents rather than students are generally the borrowers under such programs (although creditworthy students may be eligible as well).

For example, the College Board sponsors two privately insured supplemental loan programs as part of its CollegeCredit™ Program. The ExtraCredit™ Loan works like a line of credit for families who want to plan ahead for meeting up to four full years of college costs. Borrowers have up to 15 years to repay; competitive interest rates, high loan limits, fixed monthly payments, and a one-time application process afford families both convenience and control. The ExtraTime™ Loan provides funds for families who need help in paying for up to the total costs of attendance for a single year of college. Borrowers have up to 10 years to repay. A key feature of ExtraTime Loans is that the borrower pays only the *interest* while the student is enrolled, so that monthly payments are lower when the parents' expenses are the highest. (For more information about ExtraCredit and ExtraTime Loans, call 1-800-874-9390.)

A few private supplemental loan programs permit students and parents to borrow *jointly*. For instance, under the MassPlan™ sponsored by the Massachusetts Educational Financing Authority, parents *and* students (from any state) may jointly borrow up to 100 percent of the costs of attendance (minus any financial aid) at 56 participating Massachusetts colleges and universities. Two options are available: a 15-year, fixed-interest-rate plan and a 10-year, variable-interest-rate plan. Borrowers who secure their loans with a home mortgage option may be able to take advantage of the tax deductibility of interest payments. (For information about MassPlan, call 1-800-842-1531 or 1-617-261-9760.)

Chapter 7 contains extensive information about responsible borrowing, and includes some advice about evaluating the terms and features of private supplemental loan programs.

Combination savings/loan plans

This approach to financing a child's education is becoming more widely available. Under such plans, a participating bank will "leverage," or multiply, a customer's balance to give a family a line of credit for meeting college costs that is, in effect, a long-term loan, with the interest on savings offsetting to a substantial degree the interest on the loan.

Terms and conditions of these and similar programs can vary considerably from sponsor to sponsor, so prospective users will want to shop around. Inquire about the availability of programs at banks in your community.

College-sponsored financing programs

Many institutions of higher education participate in a tuition budgeting plan that permits families to spread out their payments over a longer period of time. Some colleges finance the programs themselves, while others participate in commercially available options. Because of the interest, insurance, and service fees involved in such programs, a family will typically end up spending more money than if the charges had been paid outright. However, for families with cash-flow problems or insufficient reserves, as well as for families who prefer to preserve their capital, such programs can be very helpful. Information about the options available at a particular college usually can be found in its catalog or financial aid bulletin; if you don't find it, ask.

Some insurance companies offer tuition budgeting programs to families. Insurance features on plans like these generally guarantee that the tuition will continue to be paid in the event of a parent's death or total disability. Some colleges offer variations on plans like this, financed through their own resources.

In evaluating these approaches to stretching your resources, get all the facts before you sign any contracts, promissory notes, or loan agreements. You should evaluate both what you pay and what you get back to ensure that you are getting the best possible deal.

Don't assume that you can always find financing plans or tuition installment plans at every college and university. Some public institutions, for instance, are prohibited by state law from extending credit to anyone. However, they may be able to direct you to commercial budgeting or installment plans offered by outside companies. Information about programs designed to help you manage educational expenses at a particular college can usually be found in the college's catalog or financial aid bulletin.

Strategies for cutting costs

In the absence of sufficient personal resources and financial aid, one obvious approach to financing a college education is to reduce the overall costs. There are many different ways to cut expenses, and your personal situation and ambitions will determine whether any of these approaches can work for you.

Reducing the time involved in earning a degree

By reducing the length of time involved in earning a degree, you can reduce the overall costs. (Reducing the amount of time you spend in education or training may also reduce your "forgone income," or the amount of money you could otherwise have earned if you were employed.) There are several approaches to cutting time and thus cutting costs.

For instance, many colleges award advanced placement and/or academic credit to students who can demonstrate proficiency in college-level studies through examinations such as those sponsored by the Advanced Placement (AP) Program and the College-Level Examination Program (CLEP) of the College Board. Credit-by-examination means the number of courses required to earn a degree is reduced, so the overall costs are cut. As you investigate colleges, you may want to ask about credit-by-examination policies.

Some colleges also grant advanced placement and/or academic credit to students who can demonstrate proficiency because of prior independent study and "life experience." A student might demonstrate particular competencies or skills, for example, by compiling a portfolio that documents prior learning experiences. College requirements for documenting prior learning tend to be quite rigorous, but if you can meet them, you can reduce both your time and your financial investment. (You may find that the approach is less commonly available than credit-by-examination options. You may also find that some colleges offering such opportunities restrict their use to older, "nontraditional" students who have spent several years working or raising a family.)

Some students also compress the time required to earn their degrees by taking more courses than the average student and/or attending summer school. (Obviously, attending summer classes will cut down on your ability to work during the summer to earn money for college.) Some students successfully complete a bachelor's degree in less than four years, thus reducing their overall costs, but this clearly requires a high degree of motivation. You may want to ask colleges you're considering whether it's possible to earn a degree in less than four years, since some colleges have policies limiting the number of credits a student can carry per semester.

Sometimes students can earn some college credit without actually attending classes, thus reducing transportation and possibly some living expenses. (This approach would also allow a student to work and save for full-time attendance later.) Check with the colleges you're considering if this appeals to you.

Reducing indirect costs

Living at home instead of on campus has helped many students reduce their overall costs. Some students live at home and commute to campus for the entire course of their studies, while others alternate between living in college housing (or off-campus private housing) and living at home with their families. Other students elect to attend a local, lower cost college (such as a community college) for the first two years and then transfer to a higher cost public or private college to complete their degrees.

Dormitory residents at some colleges have also discovered that savings can be achieved in the choice of college-sponsored meal plans. Investigate carefully the options open to you before you select a particular meal plan.

Some students work in return for room and board in private homes. Information about such opportunities is often available through a college's placement or student affairs office.

Students at many colleges have banded together to provide services for each other that can reduce both their direct educational expenses and their living expenses. The range of student-sponsored services is enormous and well worth investigating as part of your college-search process. Secondhand bookshops enable students to reduce textbook expenses. Food co-ops enable residents in private, off-campus housing to cut their food bills and still get adequate nutrition. Daycare programs provide help to students with dependents of their own. Revolving emergency loan funds can provide short-term financial assistance. Housing referral services or guides can help students to locate private housing, while tenant organizations protect and advocate their rights with landlords. Entertainment programs are specifically designed to provide free or low-cost recreation to students living on a budget.

College administrators, too, have instituted programs at many institutions, usually in conjunction with the student affairs or financial aid offices. The financial aid office may conduct workshops on money management, for instance, or the student activities office may issue guides to low-cost housing and shopping in the community. As the effects of rising costs and declining aid begin to be felt more widely, the number and range of such programs to help students live on a tight budget can be expected to grow.

Guaranteed or stabilized tuition plans

You can expect increases in tuition charges at least once, and probably annually, during your enrollment at a particular college. A few colleges guarantee their tuition for four years at the time of enrollment, at no obligation to the student. Under other plans, families can prepay tuition for four years in one lump sum and escape subsequent tuition increases.

Taking advantage of such programs could reduce your overall expenses, although you may want to consider whether you can get a return on your investments that's equivalent to or better than the rate of tuition increases, while still having the use of your money. For families who do not have enough disposable income to pay the entire sum at once, some colleges offer a borrowing option whereby payment is made in monthly installments over a period of years. However, with the gradual phaseout of consumer interest deductibility, you may want to make some calculations to ensure that this option still makes financial sense for you.

Strategies for working your way through college

Working your way through college is certainly possible, but it's not easy, particularly if you want to attend college on a full-time basis. The problems include both money and time. Educational and living expenses are sufficiently high to make it difficult to earn enough money to cover them fully while maintaining a full course load, but here again, there are a variety of approaches to working your way through. One or more of them may work for you. An estimated half of all college students now hold jobs of some sort.

Part-time employment

Some students find that they can earn enough money through part-time employment to meet their costs. Many students work part-time while enrolled full-time, and find that a part-time job does not hamper their studies. The Federal Work-Study Program described in Chapter 5 provides employment opportunities for many students with demonstrated financial need. Other students work in jobs, on or off campus, that they find themselves.

Some colleges have made a special commitment to helping students pay some of their educational expenses through working. For example, Cornell University in New York has two distinctive programs that assist students in meeting their educational costs. The Cornell Tradition, a loan forgiveness fellowship program, recognizes students committed to the work ethic and service. Tradition Fellows receive awards that reduce the amount of their student loans up to $2,500 per year. Since the program's inception, over $10 million has been awarded in recognition of student work and service; in 1990-91, 600 students were recognized. Summer Job Network students are referred to career-related summer jobs, many of which have been identified or created by alumni. Through the 1991-92 academic year, the SJN program has served over 15,000 student applicants; their positions have generated more than $9.5 million in earnings for Cornellians.

To find out about employment opportunities, contact the job placement office or consult the job bulletin board.

At Babson College in Massachusetts, students are encouraged to own and operate their own businesses, both to earn needed funds and develop hands-on business skills. A student Chamber of Commerce serves as a forum for exchanging ideas and sharing skills, while the Babson Entrepreneurial Exchange links students with alumni and nonalumni business people.

Some colleges have instituted special programs to help students find part-time employment. Check with the financial aid and student employment offices at the colleges you're considering.

You should begin lining up summer job prospects as soon as you are old enough to work. You might also think about acquiring and cultivating skills that will be useful in finding part-time jobs to help finance your education. As you investigate colleges, you may want to inquire about the availability of part-time jobs on and off campus. Admissions recruiters, financial aid counselors, and job placement counselors may be able to give you some clues about the kinds of jobs most frequently available. If you're visiting a college, pick up copies of the student newspaper as well as local newspapers to check out the help-wanted ads.

You might be able to tailor some of your precollege courses or summer job experiences to improve your chances in the job market once enrolled. For example, if there's a typically heavy demand for typing term papers at the college you're aiming for, it may be worth your while to take a word processing course. If there are usually openings on campus and in the community for experienced waiters and waitresses, that might be useful to know when you're looking for summer and part-time jobs in high school.

Unless you have truly unusual and marketable skills, part-time work is not likely to earn you enough money to cover all your expenses, but, depending on your overall costs and your family's ability to contribute toward your education, plus financial aid, you may be able to cover the difference through part-time employment.

Cooperative education

Some students have found that alternating periods of full-time employment and full-time enrollment works best for them. Many colleges have even formalized such arrangements through cooperative education programs. In cooperative education programs, students alternate semesters of academic enrollment with semesters of full-time employment, usually in jobs directly related to their field of study. In addition to helping them finance their studies, cooperative education programs give students a chance to develop concrete job skills and experience that enhance their employability after graduation. About 1,000 colleges and universities across the country offer some form of cooperative education opportunities; inquire about the possibility at the colleges you're considering.

Deferred enrollment

Some students take a year or two off before going to college to get some money in their pockets. Some colleges have formalized this, too—it's called "deferred enrollment." You're accepted, but you don't actually start going to college until the following year. You might keep this in mind as a question to ask about the various colleges you investigate.

Employee fringe benefits

Some students decide to work full time and attend college part time at their employer's expense. Many employers offer educational opportunities as fringe benefits. Sometimes workers are reimbursed, in whole or in part, for successfully completed course work; other programs pay tuition expenses up front. (Check with the Internal Revenue Service for the most current tax treatment of employee educational expense benefits.)

Keep in mind, too, that some unreimbursed educational expenses may be considered tax deductible. However, under the Tax Reform Act of 1986, they can be deducted only if they meet specific criteria. Check with the IRS for more information.

Managing your time if you work

There have not been many studies of students who combine work and school. The information that does exist, however, tends to show that students who work part time do not usually seem to suffer academically for the time they put into their jobs. Some studies have indicated, in fact, that students who work part time achieve higher grade-point averages than their nonemployed fellow students. For most students who work, the discipline required to juggle their responsibilities and manage their time effectively pays off in academic work, too. (At the same time, some colleges try to minimize the necessity of part-time work for some groups of students, particularly freshmen, in order to ease their transition into college life.) Some students also like the opportunity to develop employment experience in anticipation of job hunting after graduation.

Questions and answers about making the most of your resources

Q My parents have scrimped and saved for my college education, but because we have savings, we won't have as much eligibility for financial aid. Aren't we being penalized for being thrifty?

A You and your parents *will* be expected to contribute something toward the cost of college from the money you and they have saved, but as subsequent chapters will illustrate, the system *also* takes into account your parents' ages and corresponding need to save for retirement. Remember, too, that a student whose parents have no savings must rely much more heavily on financial aid than you. That family may have a heavier work or loan burden than yours will have to carry. In a time when public appropriations for student aid programs are not keeping pace with increases in college costs, your reduced reliance on financial aid may give you a wider range of choices.

Q Didn't tax reform knock out all the incentives for college saving?

A The Tax Reform Act of 1986 affected many of the "income transfer" strategies that some parents have used in the past to accumulate college savings and shelter some assets from taxation by putting them in their children's names. "Clifford Trusts," for instance, were eliminated entirely, and new restrictions were imposed on "generation-skipping" bequests from grandparents.

The experts still have lots of ideas about how families can build up money for college, with or without tax advantages. The more time you give yourself to study the various ideas, the better off you'll be. The important thing is to take advantage of whatever time you and your family have before enrollment. The loss of a specific tax break that may have existed in previous years is no reason to stop saving for college.

Q Is the interest on educational loans tax-deductible?

A The Tax Reform Act of 1986 initiated a gradual phaseout of the deductibility of consumer interest on all nonmortgage loans, including loans assumed by students and parents to pay for education, such as Federal Stafford Loans (formerly Guaranteed Student Loans) and Federal PLUS loans. However, interest on home mortgages, including second mortgages up to the fair market value of the house, is still deductible, and interest on debt *in excess* of a house's value may still be deductible if used for educational or medical expenses. Always check with the IRS or your tax adviser before making any personal financial decisions on the basis of tax treatment. Laws change and so do regulations.

Since the passage of the Tax Reform Act of 1986, legislation that would *reinstate* the tax deductibility of student loans has often been contemplated, but is not yet enacted. This could change.

Q Is it better to borrow a Federal PLUS Loan or a private supplemental loan?

A Like many financial questions, this one does not have a black-and-white answer.

The interest rate on Federal PLUS Loans will sometimes be lower than supplemental loans, and the rate is always capped by law, making it a better choice for some borrowers.

Other borrowers may prefer the comfort of fixed monthly payments and/or the security of a four-year credit line, available with some private loans such as ExtraCredit. "Shop around" before you borrow. Terms and conditions vary widely from program to program. (See Chapter 7 for more advice on responsible borrowing.)

5. How financial aid can help

Financial aid is help for meeting college costs: both direct educational costs (such as tuition, fees, and books) and personal living expenses (such as food, housing, and transportation). People are sometimes surprised that students can get financial aid to help them pay for living expenses. Even colleges with comparatively low tuition, such as community colleges, can give qualified students some help in paying for food, rent, commuting, and other personal expenses.

Many students don't realize that financial aid is available to pay for noncollegiate education and training programs, too. If you are thinking about vocational or trade school after high school, financial aid could be a possibility for you.

Who gets financial aid?

While many scholarships are based on criteria other than demonstrated need, most financial aid today is awarded on the basis of need. (Sometimes factors such as academic performance, career plans, or special abilities are considered in addition to demonstrated need.) Chapter 2 explained that "need" is the difference between what it costs to attend a particular college and what you and your family can afford to pay toward those costs. Students are usually eligible for aid equal to the amount of their demonstrated financial need.

Since the amount a family can afford to pay stays the same whether the costs are high or low, you can see that you would be eligible for different amounts of aid at different colleges. In fact, if you get all the financial aid you're eligible for, you could end up paying the same amount at a high-cost college as you would at a low-cost one.

That's a pretty big "if." In 1992-93, more than 5 million students received an estimated $30 billion in various forms of student assistance to help them meet the costs of education or training after high school. Large as that amount may seem, it still wasn't enough to fully meet the need of all the students who could have used some help.

You can improve your chances of getting the outside help you need. Financial aid doesn't just happen to you. You have to take an active part in the process—by identifying all possible sources of assistance for which you might be eligible (the topic of this chapter) and by applying in the right way at the right time (discussed in Chapter 6).

Types of financial aid

There are three types of financial aid generally offered to undergraduate students in college.

Grants and scholarships are sometimes called gift aid, because you don't have to repay them or work to earn them. Grants are usually awarded on the basis of need alone, while scholarship recipients may have to meet criteria other than or in addition to need (academic achievement, for example).

Educational loans are a form of self-help aid. These are usually subsidized by the state or federal government or by colleges themselves and carry lower interest rates than commercial loans. They have to be repaid, generally after you have graduated or left college.

Student employment or work aid is another form of self-help aid. The Federal Work-Study Program is perhaps the best known example of this kind of assistance. Students work, usually 10 to 15 hours a week, to "earn" their aid.

Financial aid comes from a variety of sources: the federal government, the state government, colleges themselves, and a wide range of private organizations.

Most students get a combination of gift aid and

self-help aid from a variety of sources. This is called a financial aid package. The financial aid administrator at the college you attend or apply to will help you put your package together.

Eligibility for financial aid

While each program has its own special criteria, certain basic eligibility requirements are common to almost all programs. For instance, to be eligible for many programs, you must be at least a half-time student (usually defined as six semester hours of courses per semester or the equivalent). In some cases, less-than-half-time students may be eligible for some federal funds but other programs, such as those sponsored by colleges and private organizations, require recipients to attend on a full-time basis, usually at least 12 hours per semester.

You must be enrolled in an eligible program at an eligible institution, according to the aid program's definition. For some federal student aid programs, you can receive aid to attend more than 9,500 eligible institutions, including colleges, universities, and vocational and technical schools. State aid programs are sometimes limited only to accredited colleges and universities. Some programs have restrictions on providing aid to students in certain fields of study (for example, religious studies) or in vocational or technical courses (those that are shorter than six months in duration). Most programs require that you maintain satisfactory academic progress toward a degree or certification and that you be in good standing with the institution you attend.

Federal student aid programs require that a recipient be either a United States citizen, or a noncitizen who is a permanent resident; refugees or persons granted political asylum may be eligible, too. State student aid programs are usually restricted to legal residents of their particular state, although exceptions to this rule do exist, especially in loan programs. College-sponsored and private assistance programs usually require recipients to be citizens of the United States, too, except for a few programs designed for foreign students.

Financial aid from the federal government

The federal government is the largest single source of student assistance, providing over $23 billion—or about 74 percent of all available financial aid

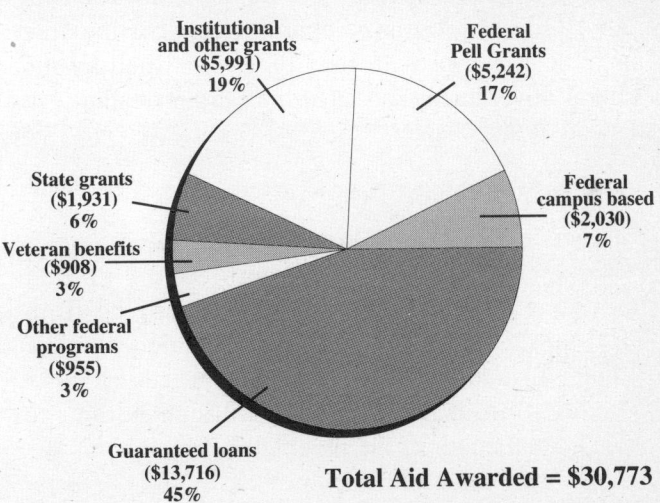

Figure 5.1. Estimated student aid by source for academic year 1991-92 (current dollars in millions)

Note: "Other federal programs" include State Student Incentive Grants, Income Contingent Loans, military, other grants, and other loans.

dollars—in academic year 1991-92 (see Figure 5.1). About 60 percent of federal dollars were concentrated in Guaranteed Student (now Stafford) loans, and another 23 percent in the Pell Grant Program.

This massive commitment of taxpayer dollars to financial aid reflects the bipartisan national commitment to equalizing postsecondary educational opportunity that has prevailed in the United States since the 1950s—a commitment unparalleled anywhere in the world.

Despite real growth over the past decade, however, federal funding of student aid programs has not kept pace with educational costs. There are many reasons why: the rate at which college costs have been increasing annually, competing demands on the federal budget, the downward pressure of the federal deficit, and the effects of a recessionary economy on families' ability to contribute to educational expenses. But the net result is that federal funds—and indeed, *all* student aid funds—are being stretched further and further to meet growing needs.

In the summer of 1992, the Congress "reauthorized" the Higher Education Act. The configuration of federal Title IV student aid programs remained fundamentally the same, but the authorized maximums for some programs were increased. (Whether the authorized maximums will actually be available in any given year depends on whether the Congress subsequently appropiates more funds.)

The Higher Education Amendments of 1992 also modified the formulas for determining eligibility for federal Title IV funds. The result is expanded eligibility for many families.

For the most current and detailed information about federal programs, obtain a copy of the free pamphlet, *The Student Aid Guide,* published by the federal government and cited in "Further reading" at the end of this chapter.

Federal Pell Grant Program

The Federal Pell Grant Program is the largest need-based student aid program. An estimated 4 million undergraduates received Pell Grants ranging from $100 to $2,200 for the 1991-92 academic year. The amount a student receives depends on need, the costs of education at the particular college he or she attends, the length of the program in which he or she is enrolled, and whether enrollment is full- or part-time. Graduate students are not eligible, nor are students who have previously received a bachelor's degree.

Federal Supplemental Educational Opportunity Grant Program

The Federal Supplemental Educational Opportunity Grant Program is one of three federal campus-based programs. "Campus-based" means that while the money comes from the federal government, the colleges distribute the money to students who demonstrate need. Recipients must be United States citizens enrolled at least half-time in an undergraduate program at an accredited college or university. Grants of up to $4,000 a year are awarded on the basis of need. About 728,000 students received Federal SEOGs in 1991-92.

Federal Perkins Loan Program

The Perkins Loan Program is another federal campus-based program administered by colleges and universities. Undergraduate and graduate students enrolled at least half-time may borrow up to $4,500 a year for the first two years of undergraduate study, to a total of $9,000 for an undergraduate degree and $18,000 for graduate and professional study (including any amount borrowed as an undergraduate). Approximately 660,000 students borrowed Perkins Loans in 1991-92.

Federal Perkins Loans carry the lowest interest rate of any educational loans (5 percent) and repayment is deferred until a student graduates or leaves school. Nine months after a student leaves school, regular repayments are required over a maximum period of 10 years until the total amount (including interest) is repaid. A minimum monthly payment of $30 is usually required, unless the college agrees to a lower amount.

Repayment can sometimes be further deferred for up to three years for service in the military, the Peace Corps, or approved comparable organizations, or if study is resumed on at least a half-time basis. (In such instances, however, the student does not get another six-month grace period in which to defer payment.) A student who wants to have repayment of a Perkins Loan deferred for any reason must complete a request form and submit it to the college from which the loan was originally borrowed. Perkins Loans are cancelled outright in the event of a student's death or total disability. (See Chapter 7 for more information about borrowing money from this and other programs, including legal requirements and advice.)

Federal Work-Study Program

The Federal Work-Study Program (FWSP) is also a federal campus-based program. Participating colleges provide employment opportunities for students with demonstrated need who are enrolled for at least half-time study at either the undergraduate or graduate level. Students are almost always employed on campus, although occasionally jobs are arranged off campus. In assigning work-study to aid recipients, financial aid administrators typically take into account their employable skills, class schedule, and academic progress.

Students are generally paid at least the prevailing federal minimum wage. Students may work as many as 40 hours a week under the program, although 10 to 15 hours is far more typical. The only limitation on Federal Work-Study is a student's demonstrated financial need.

Examples of on-campus jobs for students are faculty aide, dining hall worker, library assistant, grounds keeper, office secretary, and financial aid peer counselor. About 841,000 students received help under the Federal Work-Study Program in 1991-92.

Federal Stafford Loan Program

The Stafford Loan Program (formerly called the Guaranteed Student Loan Program) permits students with demonstrated need to borrow money for educational expenses from private sources such as banks, credit unions, savings and loan associations, and educational organizations. For example, the new CollegeCredit™ program sponsored by the College Board is a coordinated array of subsidized and unsubsidized educational loans available through participating colleges and universities. In some states, a public agency also acts as a lender; some colleges also participate in the program as lenders.

Because Stafford Loans are subsidized by the government, the interest rate is lower than most commercially available loans (although higher than Perkins Loans). The government pays the interest while the student is enrolled—another big advantage. For new borrowers after October 1, 1992, the interest rate is variable, based on the 91-day Treasury-bill rate plus 3.1 percent, capped at 9 percent. Repayment on both interest and principal is deferred until a student graduates or leaves school. In most states, a state government guaranty agency (or a private organization authorized by the state government) insures the loans; in those states where there is no guaranty agency, the federal government insures them, in which case they're called Federally Insured Student Loans. An estimated 3.85 million students borrowed under the Stafford Loan Program in 1991-92.

Although some states permit half-time students to borrow under the Stafford Loan Program, most states require that borrowers be full-time students. Freshmen may borrow up to $2,625 a year, and upperclassmen may borrow larger amounts annually, to a maximum of $23,000. Graduate and professional students are currently eligible to borrow a maximum of $65,500, including any undergraduate loans.

If you borrow money under the Stafford Loan Program, you are charged an origination fee or service charge of about 5 percent. Your guaranty agency may also charge you an insurance premium of up to 3 percent. This amount is subtracted from the amount of your loan money before you receive payment.

Stafford Loans are insured against the student's death or total disability, but there are no provisions for cancellation of any part of a loan for other reasons. Under certain circumstances (such as full-time study or service in the military or Peace Corps), repayment can be deferred temporarily. The schedule for repayment is worked out between the student and the lender; the borrower usually has between 5 and 10 years to repay, with the amount of monthly payments and the length of the repayment period depending on the total amount borrowed.

The Higher Education Amendments of 1992 created a new resource for students—the *unsubsidized* Federal Stafford Loan Program. Unsubsidized Stafford Loans are intended for use by students who *don't* qualify for a Federal Stafford Loan and/or who need additional funds. The amounts, interest rates, and terms are generally the same as for subsidized Federal Stafford

ROTC offers college scholarships with a commitment of military service after graduation.

Student Loans, with a couple of important differences. For example, repayment begins when the loan is disbursed instead of when the student borrower graduates or leaves school; the borrower may opt to postpone payments until leaving school, but interest begins to accrue immediately. Borrowers are also charged a 6.5 percent origination/insurance fee paid to the United States Department of Education.

For more information about Stafford Loans, contact the financial aid office at the colleges you're considering, your guidance counselor, or the guaranty agency for your state listed in Part II of this book. (See Chapter 6 for information about applying and Chapter 7 for advice on responsible borrowing.)

Military options

Military service options are a way of paying for education as you go. Service academies offer a college education at no cost to students, while the Reserve Officers' Training Corps (ROTC) programs help pay for your education at participating colleges and universities. (Still another approach is described elsewhere in this chapter under the heading "Assistance from Benefit Programs.")

Service academies

The United States service academies prepare both men and women for careers in the military, merchant marine, or coast guard. Students attending one of the academies have all expenses paid by the federal government and receive a monthly stipend for incidental expenses as well. Appointments to the academies (with the exception of the Coast Guard) are made through nominations from members of Congress. If you are interested, contact your senator or congressional representative early in the spring of your junior year in high school. Appointments to the Coast Guard Academy are based on national competition for admission. For more information write:

Director of Admissions
United States Air Force Academy
Colorado Springs, Colorado 80840-5651

Director of Admissions
United States Military Academy
606 Thayer Road
West Point, New York 10996-1797

Dean of Admissions
United States Naval Academy
117 Decatur Road
Annapolis, Maryland 21402-9156

Director of Admissions
United States Merchant Marine Academy
Kings Point, New York 11024

Director of Admissions
United States Coast Guard Academy
15 Mohegan Avenue
New London, Connecticut 06320-4195

Reserve Officers' Training Corps

Reserve Officers' Training Corps (ROTC) programs are located at approximately 600 colleges and universities across the country; in addition to the institutions that serve as hosts or extensions, there are about 1,800 other institutions in which an ROTC student can cross-enroll. Graduating high school seniors may qualify for competitive four-year ROTC scholarships that typically cover the costs of tuition, fees, and books, and provide a monthly stipend. Students who receive ROTC scholarships must meet certain physical and academic requirements and agree to accept appointment as commissioned officers in the military after graduation. (A minimum of four years' active and two years' reserve duty is required.)

In addition, some ROTC in-college scholarships may be available for students who decide to join as sophomores or even juniors, as well as for students who originally joined ROTC units as nonscholarship students. The requirements and obligations are somewhat different than for four-year scholarship students.

There are different procedures, requirements, and benefits associated with the ROTC programs operated by the different military services. In addition to ROTC programs, there are also other special programs providing financial assistance for education to students who promise to fulfill a term of military service after graduation; the officer training occurs during summer vacations or after college. A good source for students interested in exploring the various military-related options for college assistance is *How the Military Will Help You Pay for College*, by Don M. Betterton (see "Further reading"), which describes each service's ROTC program, the service academies, and several other programs available to military personnel who want to continue with their education. The book also contains a comprehensive list of host and cross-enrollment institutions. Contact the ROTC units at the colleges you are considering, or write:

Air Force ROTC Four-Year Scholarship Branch
HQ AFROTC/RREC
551 East Maxwell Boulevard
Maxwell Air Force Base
Montgomery, Alabama 36112-5001

Army ROTC Scholarship Program
HQ—Cadet Command
Building 56/Scholarship Branch
Fort Monroe, Virginia 23651

Navy-Marine Corps NROTC Scholarship Program
Chief of Naval Education and Training
Code N-1/081
Naval Air Station
250 Dallas Street

Pensacola, Florida 32508-5100
Telephone: (800) NAV-ROTC

Assistance from the Bureau of Indian Affairs

Students who can demonstrate financial need and are registered as being at least one-fourth Native American or Alaskan native of a federally recognized tribe are eligible for assistance through the Bureau of Indian Affairs (BIA). Scholarship assistance may be used at any accredited postsecondary institution. For more information, contact your tribal education officer, BIA Area Office.

Assistance from benefit programs

Benefit programs are not quite the same as financial aid programs, but they provide many students with assistance in meeting college costs.

Assistance for military personnel and veterans

There are several programs designed to help servicemen and women pursue higher education, as well as to assist veterans. Defense Activity for Non-Traditional Education Support (DANTES) permits military personnel to demonstrate job proficiency, qualify for college admission, or earn college-level credits by taking correspondence courses and/or examinations. Each of the services operates programs in which active duty personnel can take courses on an off-duty basis, and you also may be able to translate some of your on-the-job technical training into college credits later on. If you are thinking about enlisting, carefully explore the educational possibilities associated with the various services, including the requirements and obligations of each.

If you think you may want to go to college eventually but are also interested in the military, investigate the major initiative launched on July 1, 1985, called the New G.I. Bill, which replaced the former Veteran's Educational Assistance Plan (VEAP). Although an enlisted service person could use the plan to pay for college work while on active duty, it is more likely that people will use the New G.I. Bill to accumulate benefits for use after discharge. Under the terms of the New G.I. Bill, $100 per month would be automatically deducted from your paycheck during your first year of active duty for a total initial deposit of $1,200 in your "education account." (You can choose not to participate when you enlist, in which case the deduction would not be made.) Depending on how many years you serve on active duty, the government would add between $7,800 and $9,600 more to your account for later use in paying for education.

The New Army College Fund currently offers additional benefits beyond those cited above to men and women who enlist in the army. Men and women serving in the reserves can also participate in New G.I. Bill benefits in return for a service commitment. Because these programs are still new and subject to modification, they may be changed by the time you are ready to go to college; the most current information can be obtained from military recruiting offices.

If you are already a veteran and want to know whether you or your spouse or dependents qualify for educational assistance, contact your local Veterans Administration (VA) office.

Vocational rehabilitation benefits

Since 1977 the federal Rehabilitation Act has prohibited discrimination on the basis of a handicap and has provided for equal participation by handicapped people in programs and activities of postsecondary educational institutions that receive federal funds. The intent of the law is to assure qualified handicapped students of access to educational programs, including financial aid. Many colleges have tried to expand opportunities, particularly in the Federal Work-Study area.

State vocational rehabilitation agencies in most states can help students with handicaps meet the costs of education or job training after high school. In many states, these agencies are working with groups of financial aid administrators to develop cooperative agreements about financial aid and other assistance for handicapped students enrolled in postsecondary institutions. In developing an aid package for a handicapped student, the financial aid administrator at the college typically will consider both the amount of assistance and type of services provided by the vocational rehabilitation agency. A handicapped student's expense budget may be larger than a nonhandicapped student's budget, in order to take into account their greater expenditures for such things as special equipment, noninsured and nonroutine medical expenses, assistants or attendants, and special transportation. To find out about special help for handicapped students, contact your state department of vocational rehabilitation.

Financial aid from state governments

Every state has a scholarship or grant program that provides some form of financial aid to eligible students who are legal residents of the state. Eligibility criteria vary from state to state. Most state programs award aid to students with demonstrated need, although a few states have some funds available to assist students who meet criteria other than or in addition to need (such as academic performance). Most programs require that students attend a postsecondary institution within the state. (A few states have reciprocal agreements with other states, meaning that students can use their state grants in other states, but this practice may decline as funds become more limited.) Over 1.6 million students received some form of state grant or scholarship in 1991-92.

Your high school guidance counselor can provide you with additional information about the programs and requirements in your state. Part II of this book contains summaries of the major scholarship and grant programs in each of the 50 states, with an address to which you may write for additional information.

Financial aid from colleges

Assistance programs sponsored and administered by colleges and universities themselves are another important resource. College-sponsored financial aid usually comes from one of two sources: tuition revenues and contributions from private donors.

Some scholarships and grants-in-aid are based on demonstrated need, while others are awarded to students who meet criteria other than or in addition to need (such as academic performance, proposed field of study, or special talents or abilities). See Part III of this book for lists of colleges offering various types of scholarships.

Student employment programs are also provided on many campuses to supplement employment provided through the Federal Work-Study Program. These college-funded job programs usually are not based on financial need but on the special skills of the student employees. Examples include laboratory assistant, business office aide, and dormitory resident adviser. At some colleges, need is also considered in addition to skills and experience.

Short-term and emergency loans usually are available to all students. The repayment period generally is confined to an academic year, and interest is either quite low or not charged at all.

The criteria and application procedures for college programs vary considerably, and your best source of information is the catalog or financial aid bulletin published by the college you're considering. Private colleges often have more college-sponsored aid available to assist students than do public institutions; proprietary or profit-making institutions generally have very little or none at all.

Financial aid from private sources

While aid from the federal government, state governments, and colleges and universities constitutes most of the financial assistance received by students, private student aid programs can offer important assistance. The total amount of funds available through such private programs is comparatively small. For an individual student, however, these programs can mean the difference between attending the college one likes best and the college one can afford. So it's well worth investigating the private programs for which you may be eligible.

There are literally thousands of private student aid programs in the United States that award grants, scholarships, and low-interest loans to students to help them further their education or training after high school. One of the best programs is the National Merit Scholarship Program, which awards over $35 million each year to about 7,800 students. High school juniors compete for these awards by taking the Preliminary SAT/National Merit Scholarship Qualifying Test (PSAT/NMSQT) each October at nearly 20,000 high schools around the country that offer the test.

Eligibility criteria, application procedures, number of awards given annually, and average award amounts vary tremendously from program to program. Some programs base their awards on financial need, others on need plus other criteria, and still others don't consider need at all. You might qualify because of your:

- academic achievement
- religious affiliation
- ethnic or racial heritage
- community activities
- artistic talents
- leadership potential
- athletic ability
- career plans
- proposed field of study
- hobbies and special interests
- parents' employers or union membership
- parents' membership in a civic or fraternal group.

Since virtually everyone can claim to meet one of these general criteria, some perspective on the subject seems important. Frequently, stories appear in the press about the "millions of scholarship dollars that go begging every year." Strictly speaking, that's true, but that doesn't mean that if *you* go begging for some of them, you'll necessarily get any!

Many of the scholarships are tied to particular colleges and universities, or programs of study within those institutions. For instance, there actually may be an obscure little scholarship fund for students with a particular last name, but it has to be used at the particular college that administers that bequest. That means you have to be admitted to that college before you can claim any of the funds. If that happens to be a college you have been accepted to and want to attend anyway, terrific! But trying to finance your education in this way is a little like using coupons to get a discount on a product you don't really want and would never buy under normal circumstances.

Many of the scholarships have very detailed and restrictive eligibility requirements—you might, for instance, have to live in a certain state or region, attend a particular college, pursue a particular course of study, meet certain high academic standards, and demonstrate financial need. If you don't meet them all, you don't qualify.

Nevertheless, it makes good sense to investigate all possible sources of assistance for which you might be eligible. Check with your guidance counselor, and periodically look for notices on your school bulletin board. If you are not yet a senior, read your hometown newspapers (especially in April, May, and June) for the names of scholarships given to graduating seniors in your area. If you think you might qualify, check with the sponsor.

Contact your church or synagogue to see if either the local unit or national organization offers any student aid programs. Contact local civic and fraternal organizations, religious groups, and veterans' posts; many local, state, and national units sponsor some scholarship programs, especially for members' children.

Ask your parents to check with their employers. Many employers have some form of scholarship or grant aid available to help employees' children meet educational expenses; sometimes these programs are competitive, with awards based on academic achievement, while others are based on demonstrated need alone. Some employer programs are even offered as employee fringe benefits, particularly in educational institutions and nonprofit organizations.

If your parents are members of labor unions or trade and professional associations, they may discover that these organizations have some type of aid available to assist members' children. If one of your parents is a military veteran, you might also qualify for some help.

Investigate programs that may be underwritten by local businesses and industries. Community-based Education Opportunity and Upward Bound programs sometimes can assist you in identifying private sources of aid, too.

Scholarship search services

The microcomputer is a powerful tool that can help you in your search for financial aid. Should you use the services of a company that matches you to appropriate scholarships? The Student Advisory Committee of the College Scholarship Service looked at that question in 1985. Here are the questions that the committee suggests you ask when evaluating a service:

- If the company suggests that large amounts of aid currently are not being used, how does it document the statement?
- How many financial aid sources exist in the company's computer file? Does the company maintain its own file of sources, or does it use the file of some other company or service?
- Is there a minimum number of sources provided by the company? Are the listings in the form of scholarships, work, loans, or contests? Do they include federal and state programs for which the student will be considered through the regular financial aid application process?
- How often does the company update its list of aid sources? Does the company check to confirm that the source still exists, and that data concerning application deadlines and eligibility criteria are current?
- Can the student apply directly to the aid sources provided by the company, or must he or she be recommended for consideration by some other person or group? Are there application fees for the sources provided?
- How long will the student have to wait for the information? Will the list of aid sources be received prior to application deadlines?
- What characteristics are used to match students with aid sources?
- How successful have previous participants been in

obtaining funds from aid sources identified by the company?
- Will the company refund the program fee if aid sources are incorrectly matched with the student's qualifications, if aid sources no longer exist or fail to reply to the student, or if application deadlines for aid sources have already passed when the information is received?

The College Board, in the interest of enabling families to get scholarship information *without* paying a fee, developed a new software program that includes a scholarship search. *College Cost Explorer FUND FINDER*, annually updated software, enables you to:
- Search a data base of private and public scholarships for ones you are eligible for
- Get detailed cost and scholarship information at 2,900 undergraduate institutions
- Calculate your family's Expected Family Contribution to college costs under the federal methodology.

Students cannot be charged for using *FUND FINDER*. Check with your library or guidance office to see if they have the program.

You could be pleasantly surprised to discover that there is a local, regional, or national scholarship program aimed specifically at someone with your particular experiences talents, part-time employment history, career plans, or proposed field of study. Realize that there is no guarantee that you will receive any funds, even if through reputable sources you find and apply for scholarships that you are eligible for.

There are also many helpful publications that describe sources of financial aid. (Some are listed at the end of this chapter.)

Questions and answers about financial aid

Q With fewer scholarship and loan dollars available and jobs so hard to find, is financial aid available only to people with very low incomes?

A No. You don't have to be poor to receive financial aid, but you have to prove you need it. You are eligible for financial aid equal to the difference between college costs (tuition, living expenses, and so forth) and what you and your family can afford to contribute toward those costs.

Q I've done an estimate of my expected family contribution and financial need on the worksheets in Chapter 10. Can I count on getting this much money to help me?

A Not necessarily. You may be eligible for a certain amount, but you may not be able to get all you're eligible for simply because there's not enough to go around. If you've done the estimate, you've got a rough idea of your financial need, but you should be aware of some important limitations on this estimate.

The methods and formulas used in analyzing a family's financial need can and often do change from year to year.

Family situations change. Your family may have unusual personal or financial circumstances that could not be taken adequately into account in these calculations, but would affect your family's ability to pay for education. (An example might be unusually high expenses associated with an illness or a disability.) When the time comes for you to actually apply for financial aid, you can provide more detailed information than you used in completing these worksheets. At that time, you can explain your financial situation in more detail, and note any special family circumstances.

You should be aware that financial aid administrators at colleges can—and often do—adjust the family share calculated by CSS if a change in circumstances or additional information about your situation warrants a revision. This is because a national need analysis system can never accommodate all the special circumstances that make each family's situation unique. For any of these reasons, your expected family contribution and financial need could be different from your current estimate when the time actually comes for you to apply for financial aid. Use the estimates as a tool for planning, but count on doing as much as you can to help yourself.

Q If I am awarded aid, when will I actually get my money?

A You should get your money when you enroll (although not necessarily "on the spot") or at the start of the term or semester for which you enroll. The financial aid officer can tell you exactly when you will receive your award. Note that awards are not necessarily cash grants but may also be in the form of loans and jobs; most students get a combination or "package."

Q I plan to attend school half time, but I'll still need help with expenses. Will going to college part-time lessen my chances of receiving aid?

A In awarding aid, many institutions give priority to full-time students; however, you may be eligible for some aid on a half-time basis. Depending on the priorities and availability of funds at a particular college, half-time students could be eligible for virtually all forms of federal aid. Depending on your financial situation, you could be eligible for a Pell Grant. Ask the financial aid office at the colleges you're considering whether part-time students are given any assistance.

Q Are noncitizens eligible for financial aid?

A In most cases noncitizens are not eligible for tax-supported financial aid (such as federal or state assistance). Usually, however, noncitizens who are permanent residents are eligible, as are some refugees. Some colleges may have limited private funds to assist foreign students.

Q Will I receive special consideration if I have brothers and sisters who are continuing their education beyond high school?

A Generally speaking, yes. Your parents will not be expected to contribute as much to your college costs if you have brothers and sisters whom they are also assisting.

Q My older brother was turned down for financial aid last year. Is there any point in my trying for financial aid?

A Definitely! College costs, institutional policies, and your family's financial circumstances change from one year to the next. The only way to know for sure whether you're eligible for financial aid is to apply for it. (See the next chapter for details.)

Q My older sister and my next-door neighbor both applied for financial aid at the same school last year. Their house is bigger than ours, and they make more money than our parents, so why did my neighbor get more financial aid than my sister?

A The formulas used to assess family financial strength are designed to treat families in similar circumstances equally. There are many reasons why your neighbor may have received more money than your sister:

1. Although her family has a larger house and a greater total income, they may also owe substantially more money on their home mortgage. If so, they would be able to contribute less to college costs and would be eligible for more aid.

2. The family might have financial circumstances of which you are unaware (more family members, extraordinary medical expenses, and so forth).

3. Your neighbor may have met the criteria for some financial aid award that your sister did not meet. For instance, the college may have been able to award her some aid because of her proposed academic major or because of her past academic achievement.

4. The college didn't have enough money to fully meet the needs of all the students who needed some assistance. Unfortunately, when the overall student need at a college exceeds the funds available, the financial aid administrator has to make difficult choices in deciding how much to give each recipient.

But *you* are not your sister. The only way to find out if you're eligible and how much you can receive is to apply for financial aid.

Q Do I have to pay income tax on my student aid award? How about FICA tax on my earnings from work-study jobs?

A The Tax Reform Act of 1986 included some new provisions related to the taxation of scholarships and fellowships. Under the new law, grants, scholarships, and fellowships *in excess of* the amount needed for tuition and fees plus related expenses must be included in taxable income. The Internal Revenue Service has ruled that this means that amounts of awards used for tuition, fees, and required books, supplies, and equipment are nontaxable, but amounts used for other indirect expenses—such as room and board—are subject to taxation.* (However, remember that even these portions of your student aid package would be taxable only if you make enough money overall that you are required to pay income taxes.) Ask at your financial aid office or local IRS office if you have questions about the taxability of your aid award.

Under current law, students are *not* required to pay social security (FICA) tax on wages they earn in jobs provided by the colleges and universities they attend, such as jobs in the Federal Work-Study Program. (Jobs with *other* employers are subject to FICA tax withholding.)

---

*Deparment of the Trasury, Internal Revenue Service, Public Affairs Division, News Release IR-87-55, April13, 1987, page 1.

Further reading

Many of these publications are available in public and/or school libraries.

General

Annual Register of Grant Support, 1993. 26th ed. New Providence, N.J.: R.R. Bowker. Lists over 3,000 programs providing grant support in the humanities, international affairs, race and minority concerns, education, environment and urban affairs, social sciences, physical sciences, life sciences, technology and other areas. Revised annually. $165 plus $11.55 shipping and handling. R.R. Bowker, 121 Chanlon Rd., New Providence, NJ 07974. Order ISBN 0-8352-3293-X.

Chronicle Financial Aid Guide, 1992-93. Moravia, N.Y.: Chronicle Guidance Publications, Inc., 1992. Information on more than 1,600 financial aid programs for students at high school and undergraduate levels of study, including those offered by noncollege organizations, labor unions, and federal and state governments. Revised annually. $19.97 plus $2 postage and handling. Available September 1993. Contact Chronicle Guidance Publications, 66 Aurora St., P.O. Box 1190, Moravia, NY 13118-1190.

College Blue Book: Scholarships, Fellowships, Grants, and Loans. 24th ed. New York: Macmillan Publishing Co., 1993. Lists sources of financial aid assistance for high school seniors through students in advanced professional programs. One of a set of five volumes, $48 per volume. Macmillan Publishing Company, Inc., Attn: Order Dept., 100 Front St., Box 500, Riverside, NJ 08075.

College Costs and Financial Aid Handbook, 1994. 14th ed. New York: College Board Publications, 1993. This how-to reference for students and parents outlines major aid programs, discusses how financial need is determined, and lists current costs and scholarship opportunities at 3,200 two- and four-year public, private, and proprietary institutions. Indexes to colleges that award scholarships for achievement in academics, visual and performing arts, and sports. Revised annually. $16 plus $3.95 handling. Order item #004817 from College Board Publications, Box 886, New York, NY 10101-0886.

Financial Aids to Higher Education, 1993. Keeslar, Oreon, ed. 15th ed. Dubuque, Ia.: Wm. C. Brown Company, 1990. Updated biennially. Lists more than 3,000 programs for students entering as college freshmen. Information includes title, sponsor, nature of program, monetary value, rules for eligibility, basis for selection, application procedures, deadline dates, and addresses. $35 plus $3.50 shipping and handling. Order from Brown & Benchmark, a division of Wm. C. Brown Communications, 2460 Kerper Blvd., Dubuque, IA 52001.

Foundation Grants to Individuals. Mills, Carlotta, R., ed. 8th ed. New York: The Foundation Center, 1993. Lists undergraduate and graduate scholarship sources by general and specific requirements. Also includes fellowships, residencies, internships, and grants by U.S. foundations to foreign nationals and citizens and company-sponsored aid. $55 plus $4.50 postage and handling for first copy, $1.50 for each additional copy. Order from The Foundation Center, 79 Fifth Ave., 8th Floor, New York, NY 10003.

Fulbrights and Other Grants for Study Abroad, 1992-93. New York: Institute of International Education, 1992. Information on Mutual Educational Exchange, Fulbright, and other grants offered by foreign governments, universities, and private donors. Free. Write U.S. Student Programs Division, IIE, 809 United Nations Plaza, New York, NY 10017-3580.

Need A Lift? Educational Opportunities, Careers, Loans, Scholarships, Employment. 43rd ed. Indianapolis: The American Legion Education Program, 1993-94. Updated annually. Sources of career, scholarship, and loan information for all students, with emphasis on scholarships for veterans, their dependents, and children of deceased or disabled veterans. $2 prepaid. Order from Emblem Sales, Attn.: Need A Lift, P.O. Box 1050, Indianapolis, IN 46206.

The Official Handbook for the CLEP Examinations. New York: College Board Publications, 1992. Information about earning college credit for college-level learning acquired elsewhere. Includes questions from general and subject CLEP exams, a description of each examination, test preparation advice, and a list of 1,200 CLEP test centers by city and state. $15 plus $3.95 shipping and handling. Order item #004558 from College Board Publications, Box 886, New York, NY 10101-0886.

The Scholarship Book: The Complete Guide to Private Sector Scholarships, Grants, and Loans for Undergraduates. 4th ed. Cassidy, Daniel J., and Michael J. Alves. Englewood Cliffs, N.J.: Prentice Hall, Inc., 1993. Lists over 50,000 private-sector scholarships, grants, loans, fellowships, internships, and contest prizes covering major fields of study.

Includes sample form letters requesting information on scholarship application requirements and tips on applying for scholarship money. $19.95 plus postage and sales tax where applicable. Order from Order Processing Center, P.O. Box 11071, Des Moines, IA 50336-1071. For charge card orders call 1-800-947-7700.

The Student Guide. 1993-94. Washington, DC: U.S. Department of Education, Office of Student Financial Assistance, 1993. Detailed information on federal student aid programs, eligibility rules, application procedures. Free. Order from Federal Student Aid Programs, P.O. Box 84, Washington, DC 20044, or call 1-800-433-3243.

Specific population groups

Bureau of Indian Affairs Higher Education Grants and Scholarships. Washington, D.C.: Bureau of Indian Affairs. Free. Lists sources of assistance for students who are native American or Alaskan natives of a tribal group recognized by the Bureau of Indian Affairs for certain benefits. Order from Office of Indian Education Programs, Code 522-Room 3516, 18th and C Streets NW, Washington, DC 20240.

The College Board Guide to Going to College While Working. Hawes, Gene. New York: College Board Publications, 1985. Advice and strategies for fulfilling college goals while holding down a full- or part-time job. Includes tips from educators and counselors as well as adult college students on organizing the process of applying for financial aid, plus worksheets for step-by-step planning. $9.95 plus $2.95 postage and handling. Order item #002075 from College Board Publications, Box 886, New York, NY 10101-0886.

Directory of Financial Aids for Minorities, 1993-95. 5th ed. Schlacter, Gail Ann. San Carlos, Ca.: Reference Service Press, 1993. Biennial. Over 2,100 references and cross-references to scholarships, fellowships, grants, loans, awards, and internships set aside for ethnic minorities. $47.50, plus $4 for shipping. Order from Reference Service Press, 1100 Industrial Rd., Suite 9, San Carlos, CA 94070.

Directory of Financial Aids for Women, 1993-95. Schlacter, Gail Ann. San Carlos, Ca.: Reference Service Press, 1993. Over 1,750 scholarships, fellowships, grants, loans, awards, and internships set aside for women. $45 plus $4 postage and handling. Order from Reference Service Press, 1100 Industrial Rd., Suite 9, San Carlos, CA 94070.

Educational Assistance and Opportunities Information for Army Family Members. Alexandria, Va.: Department of the Army. A general guide available to the Department of the Army on educational financial assistance of particular interest to dependents of active duty, retired, or deceased Army personnel. Free. Order from Commander U.S. Army Pers. Comm., Attn: TATC-POE, 2461 Eisenhower Ave., Alexandria, VA 22331.

Federal Benefits for Veterans and Dependents. Washington, DC: Veterans Administration, 1993. Comprehensive summary of benefits, updated every January. $3.25, prepaid. Order Fact Sheet IS-1 from Superintendent of Documents, U.S. Government Printing Office, Washington, DC 20402.

Financial Aid for the Disabled and Their Families. 1992-94, Schlacter, Gail Ann, & R. David Weber. San Carlos, Ca.: Reference Service Press, 1992. Lists hundreds of scholarships, fellowships, loans, grants-in-aid, and awards established for the disabled and their children or parents. 750 entries. Also identifies state educational offices and agencies concerned with the disabled. $37.50 plus $4 for shipping. Order from Reference Service Press, 1100 Industrial Rd., Suite 9, San Carlos, CA 94070.

Financial Aid for Minorities in Business and Law. Garrett Park, Md.: Garrett Park Press, 1992. Lists financial aid sources for minority students specifically in business and legal fields. Other books in the *Financial Aid for Minorities* series cover allied health, education, engineering, science, mass communications and journalism, and sources available regardless of major. $4.95 each *or* $27 for the series. Order from Garrett Park Press, P.O. Box 190, Garrett Park, MD 20896.

Financial Aid for Veterans, Military Personnel and Their Dependents, 1992-94. Schlacter, Gail Ann, and R. David Weber. San Carlos, Ca.: Reference Service Press, 1992. Identifies scholarships, fellowships, loans, grants-in-aid, awards, and internships for military-related personnel. More than 850 references to programs open to applicants at all levels (from high school through postdoctoral) for education, research, travel, training, career development, or emergency situations. $37.50 plus $4 postage and handling. Order from Reference Service Press, 1100 Industrial Rd., Suite 9, San Carlos, CA 94070.

Higher Education Opportunities for Minorities and Women. Washington, D.C.: U.S. Government Printing Office, 1991. Select listing of opportunities for minorities and women in higher education, including some information on scholarships, fellowships, and loans. $8. Order document #065-000-00458-5 from Superintendent of Documents, U.S. Government Printing Office, Washington, DC 20402-9325.

How the Military Will Help You Pay for College. Betterton, Don M. 2nd ed. Princeton, N.J.: Peterson's Guides, 1990. Information about scholarship and financial aid for students going directly to college after high school, including the service academies, ROTC, and other special programs, as well as scholarship and tuition-payment programs for members of the armed forces. $9.95. Available in bookstores.

Fields of study

Allied Health Education Directory. 21st ed. Chicago: American Medical Association, 1993. Contains a section on financial aid and a listing of allied health education programs. $45.00. Order from American Medical Association, P.O. Box 10946, Chicago, IL 60610-9050.

Directory of Grants in the Humanities, 1993. 7th ed. Phoenix, Az.: Oryx Press, 1993. $84.50 plus $8.50 postage and handling. Contains more than 3,500 current funding programs that support research and performance in literature, language, anthropology, philosophy, ethics, sculpture, crafts, mime, etc. Order from Oryx Press, 4041 N. Central, Suite 700, Phoenix, AZ 85012-3397.

Fellowships and Grant Opportunities of Interest to Philosophers, 1993-94. Newark, Del.: American Philosophical Association, 1992. Updated annually and included as a section in the association's *Proceedings and Addresses*. $10.00 prepaid. Order from American Philosophical Association, University of Delaware, Newark, DE 19716.

Financial Assistance for Library Education, Academic Year 1993-94. Chicago: American Library Association, 1992. Produced by Office of Library Personnel Resources. Lists assistance administered by state library agencies and associations, local libraries, and academic institutions. $1 (postage and handling). Order from Office for Library Personnel Resources, American Library Association, 50 East Huron St., Chicago, IL 60611.

Graduate Study in Psychology and Associated Fields, 1992, with 1993 addendum. Washington, D.C.: American Psychological Association, 1992. Information about financial assistance and foundations and agencies accepting fellowship applications, as well as information about graduate programs in psychology. $15.95 to members, $19.95 to nonmembers, plus $3.50 for shipping and handling. For charge card orders call 202-336-5570. Order from American Psychological Association, 750 First St. NE, Washington, DC 20002-4242.

Grants and Awards Available to American Writers. 17th ed. New York: PEN American Center, 1992. Updated annually. Lists awards granted to American writers to use in the United States or abroad. $8.00. Order from PEN American Center, 568 Broadway, New York, NY 10012.

Grants, Fellowships and Prizes, 1992-93. Washington, D.C.: American Historical Association, 1991. Lists over 400 history-oriented sources of humanities grants, fellowships, prizes, internships, and awards from undergraduate to senior postdoctoral level. Includes section on article, book, and essay prizes. $8 to members; $10 to nonmembers. Updated annually. Order from American Historical Association, 400 A St. SE, Washington, DC 20003.

A Journalist's Road to Success: A Career and Scholarship Guide (formerly, *Journalism Career and Scholarship Guide*). Princeton, N.J.: Dow Jones Newspaper Fund, 1993. Updated annually. Information on journalism programs, scholarships, and minority grants. $3.00. Order from Dow Jones Newspaper Fund, P.O. Box 300, Princeton, NJ 08543-0300 or call 1-800-DOW-FUND.

Medical School Admissions Requirements, U.S. and Canada, 1994-95. 43rd ed. Washington, D.C.: Association of American Medical Colleges, 1993. Updated annually. Describes U.S. and Canadian medical schools, detailing entrance requirements of each school, selection factors, and curriculum features. It includes up-to-date information on medical education, premedical planning, choosing a medical school, the Medical College Admission Test (MCAT), the American Medical College Application Service (AMCAS), financing a medical education and other aspects of the medical school application and admissions process. Information for minority students, high school students, and applicants not admitted to medical school. $10 plus $4 for shipping and handling. Order from Association of American Medical Colleges, 2450 N St. NW, Washington, DC 20037. Attn: Membership and Publication Orders.

The National Directory of Grants and Aid to Individuals in the Arts. Fandel, Nancy A. 8th ed. Des Moines, Ia.: Washington International Arts Letter, 1993. Lists grants, prizes, and awards for professional work in the United States and abroad. Includes information about universities and schools offering aid to students in the arts, as well as retreats and residencies. $30. Order from Washington International Arts Letter, Box 12010, Des Moines, IA 50312.

Scholarships and Loans for Nursing Education, 1993-94. New York: National League for Nursing, 1993. Lists fellowships, scholarships, traineeships, and loans for nursing education, including public funding—federal and state scholarships and loans and work study programs. Outlines packages offered by selected schools and universities; scholarships from community groups and membership organizations for specific purposes and constituencies; fellowships, traineeships, and grants for research and postdoctoral studies; and aid for minority students. Includes tips on how to apply for aid. Bibliography. Appendix of state boards of nursing and brief explanation of the licensing process and types of nursing programs. $14.95 plus $3.50 postage. Order from National League for Nursing, Publications Order Unit, 350 Hudson St., New York, NY 10014. Order No. 41-1964.

Scholarships for Architecture Students. New York: American Institute of Architects, 1993. Poster. Lists major scholarship programs in architecture; accredited schools of architecture; programs for minorities, postgraduates, and professionals. Free. Order from the American Institute of Architects, 1735 New York Ave. NW, Washington, DC 20006.

Student Financial Aid: Speech-Language Pathology and Audiology. Rockville, Md.: American Speech and Hearing Association, 1986. Mimeographed list of general information about grants, scholarships, and loans at the graduate level and aid for graduate education in the field. Free. Order from American Speech and Hearing Association, 10801 Rockville Pike, Rockville, MD 20852.

Graduate study

Graduate Guide to Grants. Verba, Cynthia. Cambridge, Mass: Harvard University, 1993. Annual publication prepared by the Harvard Graduate School of Arts and Sciences. Designed to help graduate students locate grants and fellowships applicable to a wide range of fields in the arts and sciences. Most grants listed are to support specific research projects—usually dissertation research—but some support earlier stages of graduate study during course work. $25, including postage. Order from Harvard University, Byerly Hall, 8 Garden St., Cambridge, MA 02138.

Grants Register, 1993-95. New York: St. Martin's Press, 1993. Updated biennially. Lists scholarships and fellowships at all levels of graduate study. Includes specific awards for refugees, war veterans, minorities, and students in unexpected financial difficulties. $89.95 plus $6 postage and handling from St. Martin's Press, Attn.: Cash Sales, 175 Fifth Ave., New York, NY 10010.

Selected List of Fellowship Opportunities and Aids to Advanced Education for U.S. Citizens and Foreign Nationals. Washington, DC: The National Science Foundation, 1988. 59 pages. Prepared by the National Research Council of the National Academy of Sciences. Lists organizations, federal and private, offering fellowships at advanced levels of education. International sources included. Free. Order NSF 88-119 from the Publications Office, National Science Foundation, 1800 G St. NW, Washington, DC 20550.

Study abroad

Financial Aid for Research and Creative Activities Abroad, 1992-1994. San Carlos, Ca.: Reference Service Press, 1992. Approximately 1,100 entries. $40. Order from Reference Service Press, 1100 Industrial Rd., Suite 9, San Carlos, CA 94070.

Financial Aid for Study and Training Abroad, 1992-1994. San Carlos, Ca.: Reference Service Press, 1992. Approximately 1,100 entries. $40. Order from Reference Service Press, Suite 9, 1100 Industrial Rd., San Carlos, CA 94070.

Fulbrights and Other Grants for Graduate Study Abroad, 1994-95. New York: Institute of International Education, 1993. Mutual Educational Exchange, Fulbright and other grants offered by foreign governments, universities, and private donors. Free. Order from U.S. Student Programs Division, Institute of International Education, 809 United Nations Plaza, New York, NY 10017-3580.

Funding for U.S. Study: A Guide for Foreign Nationals. New York: Institute of International Education, 1989. Information resource on grants and fellowships available to foreign nationals from public and private sector organizations. $39.95. Order #87206-181-7 from Institute of International Education, 809 United Nations Plaza, New York, NY 10017-3580.

The International Scholarship Directory. Cassidy, Daniel J. 4th ed. Available fall 1993. Santa Rosa, Ca.: National Scholarship Research Service. Guide to financial aid for worldwide study. Lists scholarships, fellowships, grants, internships, and loans available for graduates and undergraduates in every major field of study. Can be used in many countries by both Americans and international students seeking educational opportunities anywhere in the world. $24.95 (subject to change) plus postage and sales tax where applicable. Order from National Scholarship Research Service, 2280 Airport Blvd., Santa Rosa, CA 95403 or call 1-707-546-6781.

6. Applying for financial aid

If you have estimated your expenses at the colleges that interest you, evaluated your family's financial situation, and concluded that you will need some extra help in meeting educational expenses, then you should apply for financial aid. Even if you are not certain that you will qualify, you should apply—that's the only way to find out if you are eligible. Simply applying for admission to college is not enough. If you think you need financial aid, you *must apply* for aid.

The process of applying for financial aid can be confusing and time-consuming, especially to the first-time applicant. (Yes, you must reapply for aid every year, but it really does seem a lot simpler and less confusing the second time around.) In Chapter 5, you learned about the various types and sources of financial aid. Application requirements differ from college to college (and program to program), but the good news is that you don't really have to file separate applications for each and every one.

In order to improve your changes of getting the aid you need, you must know *what* you have to do, *when* you have to do it, and how to do it right—the first time.

What do you need to do?

Financial aid doesn't just *happen* to you. You have to provide information about yourself and your family as the first step in the application process.

The process begins with identifying which form or forms you need to complete in order to meet the requirements of the various sources from which you are seeking financial aid. Don't guess! Find out for sure.

All applicants for *federal* student aid, including Federal Stafford Loans, *must* complete the Free Application for Federal Student Aid (FAFSA). The FAFSA is available from high school guidance offices and college financial aid offices, generally in the late fall. Depending on where you are applying for admission, this may be the *only* form you need to complete.

Your high school counselor can probably tell you what form you need to complete to apply for assistance from your *state* scholarship or grant program. In some states, your FAFSA information is enough to establish your eligibility; in other states, a separate form may be required. If your counselor doesn't know what's required in your state, contact the appropriate agency at the address listed in Part II of this book.

The FAFSA may also be sufficient to apply for aid at many colleges and universities. However, many other colleges and most private scholarship programs require the completion of *additional* forms. Check with each college and private scholarship program from which you are looking for assistance.

Details about the form requirements for both colleges and private scholarship programs are generally found in the descriptive material they send to applicants, such as college catalogs and special financial aid information packets or brochures. If you do not see the information in these materials or are not certain what it means, contact the college or program and ask.

What other kinds of forms might you be instructed to complete? Many colleges and private scholarship programs require their applicants to complete the Financial Aid Form (FAF), distributed and processed by the College Scholarship Service (CSS) of the College Board, *in addition* to the Free Application for Federal Student Aid. The FAF collects additional data beyond that collected on the FAFSA, and colleges use it to award *nonfederal* student aid funds, such as institutionally or privately

Applying for aid usually begins with completion of a "need analysis" form. Find out about the forms required by the colleges that interest you, and be sure to meet the financial aid deadlines.

funded grants and scholarships. The FAF is available from high school guidance offices and college financial aid offices, also in the late fall.

Some colleges and private scholarship programs also ask students to complete a separate student aid application that they create and distribute to applicants themselves. Private programs sometimes have other requirements as well, such as personal essays or biographical statements.

Later in the process, you may receive requests from colleges or other aid sponsors for clarification of information you provided on your original forms. For example, you may be asked to provide copies of your own or your parents' most recent tax return. Or you may receive a letter asking for additional information about some aspect of your application.

Respond to any such inquiries promptly and in as much detail as is requested. Don't assume that something is "wrong" with your application just because you're asked for additional detail. Colleges that administer federal funds are required to verify information from at least a portion of their applicants; some routinely request tax returns from all their aid applicants.

When do you need to do it?

Here again the key is to find out what colleges and programs want from you, and to follow their instructions as closely as possible. Some colleges have deadlines for the receipt of all application materials; others have preferred filing dates; still others will accept applications at any time.

For most types of aid, you start the application process in the late winter or early spring *preceding* the fall term for which help is needed. If you can, submit your FAFSA (and your FAF, if your college requires it) at least four weeks *before* the earliest deadline you need to meet. Do *not* file before January 1, however.

Many private scholarship programs have *earlier* deadlines than colleges and government programs. Check the material they provide to ensure that you know what deadlines you need to meet.

After you have started the application process, the important thing is to respond promptly to any follow-up requests for information that you receive from a college or a program.

Generally speaking, it's unwise to wait until you've found out whether you're *admitted* to a college before you apply for financial aid. There are two reasons for not waiting.

First, most colleges try to tell you what financial aid is available before you have to accept their offers of admission; if you *need* financial aid, the colleges understand that you need information about what's available before you can make informed decisions about where to enroll.

Second, if you wait until after you've heard from colleges about your admissions applications, their grant and scholarship funds may be exhausted. Colleges don't have enough money to meet fully the needs of all the students who could use some help, and grants and scholarships usually run out first.

How do you do it *right*?

The forms you complete as part of the application process collect information about your family and finances much like that reviewed in Chapter 2—information about income, assets, family size, unusual circumstances, and so forth. Detailed step-by-step instructions are provided.

Read the instructions. Then read them again. If you don't understand what an instruction means, ask your counselor or call the financial aid office. Enough said.

Get organized. Before you sit down to complete your forms, gather together your most recent income tax returns, W-2 forms, pay stubs, interest statements, home mortgage debt information, records of medical and dental expenses, business or farm records, notices of social security payments for veterans benefits, and other financial records. You will need the records for the calendar year preceding the academic year for which you are seeking assistance. For example, for the 1994-95 academic year, you will need to collect information for calendar year 1993.

Know which federal income tax forms you plan to file, and draft your responses. The tax form you are eligible to file—an IRS 1040, 1040A, or 1040EZ—is one of the factors that influences how your eligibility for federal aid programs will be determined. You don't actually have to *file* your income tax return before you complete financial aid applications, but it's a good idea to at least rough it out. Some questions on the FAFSA and the FAF are cross-referenced to the most common IRS forms in order to make them easier to complete. Besides, figuring out your answers to your IRS forms in advance—even if you don't actually file your tax return until later—increases the likelihood that if your case is verified, the answers on the financial aid applications will match up with the answers on your tax forms.

Complete all forms accurately, completely, and legibly. Inaccurate or missing information, or unreadable answers, could cause costly delays in the processing of your documents.

Provide all the information requested in the form it's requested. For instance, if the answer calls for a zero, enter a zero. Don't just leave the question blank. (A blank and a zero and a "not applicable" may seem like the same thing to you, but the computers may not interpret them the same way.)

At the same time, don't provide more information than you're asked for. If there's something you want to communicate to a college, for example, and there doesn't appear to be any place to enter it on the form you're completing, don't try to *force* the information into another answer. Send the college a letter. (If you are completing a FAF, a blank space is provided in which you can explain special circumstances.)

Keep photocopies of every form you complete. If you are asked for follow-up information, you may need to refer to your original answers. Don't trust your memory.

Identify yourself consistently on all forms you complete. Don't call yourself "John James Doe" on one form and "Jack Doe" on another. Take special care to check that you always write social security numbers correctly. Colleges and programs sometimes need to match up records from multiple sources in order to complete your file, and incorrect social security numbers and variations on your name can slow the process down.

Review carefully all the communications that you receive back from programs and colleges. For example, within a few weeks of completing a FAFSA, you will receive back a Student Aid Report (SAR). If there are errors in the information, make corrections directly on the special page provided, and mail it back to the processor; within another few weeks, you will get a revised SAR. If you complete a FAF, within a few weeks you will receive from CSS an Acknowledgment. Check the Acknowledgment carefully and follow the instructions provided about correcting information or adding more listings to your original request. You may also receive letters from colleges or private programs requesting additional information.

Respond promptly. If additional information is needed, send it as soon as possible. If you find errors, fix them quickly. When it comes to applying for aid, time *is* money.

Chapter 8—*"Pulling It All Together"*—describes what happens to your forms in the final stages of the application process. Don't skip it! It includes some important information about what *you* need to do to nail down your financial aid award.

Questions and answers about applying for financial aid

Q Must I be accepted for admission before I apply for financial aid?

A You should apply for financial aid at the time you apply for admission. Remember, too, that simply applying for admission is not the same as applying for financial aid. To receive aid, you must *apply* for aid; this means that you must file the appropriate form(s). In some cases, you may also be required to submit a separate institutional or state application as well. You will not actually receive aid until you have enrolled.

Q Is it necessary for me to apply for financial aid every year?

A Yes. At most colleges you must apply each academic year, but applying is almost always easier the second time around because there is less paperwork and you are familiar with the process.

Q I want to apply for a scholarship only. Do I have to fill out the FAFSA or the FAF or both?

A Check with the sponsor of the scholarship and/or the financial aid office at the institution to which you are applying. Find out what forms should be completed and when they are due.

Q How can I find out what the deadline is for applying for aid at the college I am interested in?

A Look for the deadline in Part II of this book or in the college's catalog. If you cannot find it there, ask the college's financial aid office. Be aware that many institutions have "priority filing dates," which you should meet if you possible can. After that date, some aid may still be available; check with the financial aid office if you are applying later than the deadline or priority date given.

Q One college I'm applying to *requires* the FAFSA plus the FAF and another *requires* only a FAFSA. What should I do?

A List the college that requires the FAFSA plus the FAF on both forms. List the college that requires *only* the FAFSA on the FAFSA only.

Q My parents are divorced. Who should complete the form?

A The parent with whom you lived for the longest period in the last 12 months should fill out the form. If you didn't live with either parent, or lived with each parent for an equal number of days, the form should be filled out by the parent who provided things such as housing, food, clothes, car, medical and dental care, and college costs.

Q Can a college legally require each of my divorced or separated parents to fill out forms?

A To be considered for financial aid, you need to provide FAFSA information only from the parent with whom you live. However, an aid administrator at a particular college can make his or her decision about whether to require both parents to file the FAF or other need analysis forms when you are being considered for institutional aid. The current marital status and other obligations of the parent who doesn't have custody would be considered in this situation.

Q My parents are divorced, but the parent who qualifies and who must complete the form doesn't want to provide the necessary data. However, the parent who doesn't qualify is willing. What should I do?

A According to criteria established by federal programs, the qualifying parent *must* provide information unless an exception is made by a financial aid administrator. However, for purposes of qualifying for aid administered by colleges, the aid administrator at the college may resolve the problem. The administrator may determine, for instance, that there are sufficiently adverse home circumstances that information from the responsible parent cannot be obtained and that information from the other parent is acceptable. This situation should be explained in a letter to your college's financial aid administrator (and on your FAF, if your college requires you to complete it).

Q My parents refuse to file any forms. What should I do?

A In order to be considered for financial aid, you must file a need analysis form. However, aid administrators will sometimes consider special circumstances if they are documented by your clergyman, counselor, or social worker. You must realize that resources will be limited because no state or federal funds can be distributed without documented financial need. (You also may be asked to provide a notarized statement of parent nonsupport.)

Q I plan to start college in the fall of 1994. So why do all the forms ask questions about my parents' income from *this* year when I need the money next year?

A 1993 is the last complete year for which your parents' income can be verified through tax returns. If your parents' income in 1994 will differ substantially from their 1993 income, explain this situation. The financial aid administrator may be able to take these special circumstances into consideration in making your award.

Q Will anyone else see the information we provide on a FAFSA or FAF?

A Information is shared with the colleges and programs you list as recipients because you are seeking financial aid from them. (You should be aware, however, that the federal government *does* routinely perform some data base matches of federal student aid applicants' records with the Selective Service and Immigration and Naturalization Service, for instance.)

Q Should I attach receipts? Will anyone ever ask for receipts? Should I attach my IRS Form 1040 to my FAFSA or FAF?

A No. Don't enclose receipts. However, financial aid offices at colleges at which you apply may ask for documentation of unusually high expenses that occur during the academic year. It is more likely that they will request a copy of your tax returns to verify expenses that occurred in the prior calendar year. More and more colleges are requesting tax returns to validate information reported on applicants' forms. Do *not* attach a copy of your tax returns to the FAF or other need analysis document. If a college or program wants to see your tax returns, send them directly to the address indicated.

7. Borrowing for education

As costs rise and financial aid resources get tighter, fewer and fewer students will be able to escape the necessity of borrowing some amount of money to complete their education.

Almost half of the student aid dollars available today are in the form of loan dollars, predominantly in the Federal Stafford Student Loan Program. Other federal loans available to students include Federal Perkins Loans and Federal Supplemental Loans for Students. (See Chapters 4 and 5.)

Parents, too, are increasingly turning to public and private loan programs to help finance some or all of their "expected contribution." Federal PLUS Loans and private supplemental loans are among the options available to parents of college students. (See Chapter 4.)

Keep borrowing in perspective

The idea of borrowing to pay for college makes some students and parents anxious. This is especially understandable among people who have never before borrowed money, or who have had a negative experience with borrowing.

But without borrowing, few people could afford houses or cars or major appliances—*or* college. Borrowing can be a useful and appropriate way to help meet college expenses.

If you are worried about your ability to repay a student loan, remember that education usually makes people more employable and thus increases their earning power. U.S. Census data make it clear that the average lifetime earnings of *college* graduates far exceed the average lifetime earnings for high school graduates. By earning a degree or certificate, you will be better prepared to find a job that allows you to repay your student loan.

At the same time, remember that a loan *is* a loan, and not a gift. You are legally responsible for *repaying* student loans when you graduate or leave school, and you will have to repay both the *principal*—or the total amount you borrow—and *interest,* which is a fee that you pay for using someone else's money. (There are provisions for certain loans that allow the fulfillment of some or all of the obligation through specific kinds of service.)

How serious are you?

When you borrow, you commit a portion of your *future* income to pay for a *current* expense. That makes it a serious business, so it's important to know how serious *you* are about your education.

If you have grave doubts about your ability to do college-level work, or if you're honestly not sure you're interested in education or training after high school, you might want to hold off on borrowing until you have a clearer sense of what you really want. Taking out a large student loan just to "see how you like college" may not be as sensible as taking courses part time at a low-cost institution or working for a while to save the first semester's tuition.

On the other hand, if you *are* sure about your desire for education, a student loan can be a wise investment in your own future. The education that you purchase with your student loan dollars is something that you'll have forever—not a product that will wear out or get used up.

Credit where credit is due

Thinking of your loan as "credit," rather than as "debt," may ease your mind a little. When people lend you money, they extend credit to you because they believe you will be willing and able to repay the money, with interest. That makes it a good deal on both sides of the transaction—and it's why the federal government has put so much money into subsidized student loans.

And, contrary to the headlines, the vast majority of citizens *do* repay their student loans. Furthermore, they go on to participate fully in the social and economic life of the country in a way that justifies the nation's investment in them.

Repayment of student loans *does* leave borrowers with less money in their pockets than they'd like, especially in the first few years out of college—but they manage. And as their salaries grow over time, repaying their student loans becomes less burdensome. If financial setbacks occur, they can and do take steps to arrange for temporary relief of student loan payments until their financial situations improve again.

Educate yourself about loans

Your student loan may be the first big legal obligation you've assumed. And it may well be the largest single financial obligation you ever take on, short of a home mortgage. Many students borrow during their undergraduate years, and then borrow more funds for graduate or professional school as well.

Protect yourself by becoming an informed consumer. Take the time to educate yourself about loans in advance of applying for them. Familiarize yourself with the key terms and concepts, and know what questions you should ask *before* you sign on the dotted line.

Learn the language

Know your terms. The amount of money you borrow is called the *principal*. When you pay back a loan, you pay both principal and the *interest*—which is the fee you pay for using someone else's money. Interest is expressed as a percentage.

When you investigate the interest rates on different loans, look for the annual percentage rate (APR). (This is also sometimes called the *simple interest rate*.) Your lender is required by law to tell you what this rate is. Don't be confused by a description that talks about *compound monthly interest*. A 1 1/2 percent monthly compounded interest rate may sound like a better deal than a 10 percent annual interest rate, but spread out over one year, that 1 1/2 percent compounded monthly amounts to nearly 18 percent (12 x 1 1/2 = 18).

How much you pay each month is called the *minimum monthly payment*. Your lender or your financial aid office can help you estimate your minimum monthly payment, which varies by the amount borrowed and the number of years for which you've borrowed it.

The *term* of a loan is how long you have to repay the obligation. This can vary substantially, up to 10 years or more. Some loan programs, such as the Federal Stafford, Federal PLUS, and Federal SLS Programs, permit you to *prepay* your loan, or pay it off early; that can save you considerable interest. (In other programs, you may pay a penalty if you pay off early.)

The *grace period* is how long you can wait before you have to *start* repaying; this, too, varies by program. With Federal Stafford Loans, for example, you have a grace period of six months after you graduate, leave school, or drop below half-time status. With some supplemental loans, including several privately sponsored loan programs, the borrower (usually the parent) has to begin making payments within 30 to 60 days of the date the loan is *disbursed* (made available).

An *origination fee* is a charge deducted from a loan to pay for the costs of making the loan; some programs have an origination fee and others do not. Some programs also charge an *insurance premium* or a *guaranty fee* to insure your loan, while others may charge an *application fee*, which may or may not be refundable, depending on whether you qualify for the loan. Read the lender's literature carefully to make sure you understand what costs you may be incurring.

Subsidized loans—such as Federal Stafford, Perkins, PLUS, and SLS Loans—are loans backed by a guarantor; they usually have a lower interest rate and/or other more favorable features than *commercial* loans. A *guarantor* (or *guarantee agency*) is an organization that agrees to pay the loan if the student doesn't; state agencies, the federal government, and authorized private organizations are the most typical guarantors for student loans. Some loans are *privately insured* rather than backed by a guarantor.

A *lender* may be a bank, a savings and loan association, a credit union, a finance company, a college or university, a public or quasi-public agency, or a private organization.

Check out several lenders before you make a decision about where to borrow. Even in the case of the government-backed loans, there are some important differences among lenders, such as what kind of *repayment options* they offer. Repayment options can include *graduated repayment*, where payments are smaller in the first few years after you leave school (when earning power is less), and increase later on; and *consolidation,* where you combine multiple loans

43

into a single obligation for smaller monthly payments but a longer repayment term. (Knowing that these *options* are available is important. You should also be aware, however, that exercising such repayment options can add to the *overall* cost of borrowing.)

Regardless of where you borrow or from what loan program you borrow, you will have to provide some information about yourself on a *loan application*; this information may be checked before a loan is actually made to you. A *promissory note* is another name for a legal agreement or contract you sign when you borrow money.

A *cosigner* or *cosignatory* is a person who signs for your loan with you. You don't need a cosigner for Federal Stafford or Perkins Loans, but you may be asked for one if you borrow from other loan programs, particularly if you are a minor.

If you *default*, or fail to repay your loan when it comes due, a cosigner is legally responsible for your debt. There are other things that can happen, too, if you default on a loan. Your *credit record* (or *credit history*) will most likely be damaged, which will create problems for you if you want to borrow money for other purchases, like a car or a house (or more education). Your salary may be *attached* (or *garnished*), which means that your employer is legally required to turn over part of your earnings to your lender; your federal income tax refund may also be withheld.

People sometimes default because they don't know that other options are available to them—options that would protect their credit records and help them meet their obligations. Under certain circumstances, for example, you may qualify for *deferment*, or temporary postponement of payments (*forbearance*); interest may or may not continue to *accrue* (or add up) during this time.

Evaluate how much you need

Make a realistic but conservative estimate of how much you really *need* to borrow. Remember, you don't have to borrow the maximum amount available. Have you exhausted other alternatives for meeting your expenses? Could you cut your expenses a little, or perhaps work a bit more and borrow a bit less?

Borrowing *more* than you really need just because the yearly or aggregate maximums are higher than your immediate need can be risky. It could impede your eventual ability to repay your loans, or at least reduce your borrowing capacity at a point in the future when you genuinely need more money.

At the same time, borrowing *less* than you really need can also be risky, but in a different way. You

Table 7.1. Average annual salary of bachelor's degree recipients employed full time one year after graduation, by field of study, 1987

	Average salary of 1985-86 degree recipients in June 1987
Total	$20,300
Engineering	26,600
Business and management	21,100
Health professions	22,600
Education	15,800*
Public affairs and social services	17,700
Biological sciences	16,400
Physical sciences, mathematics, and computer sciences	22,500
Psychology	17,300
Social sciences	20,300
Humanities	16,200
Communications	**
Miscellaneous	17,600

*Most educators work 9- to 10-month contracts
**Fewer than 75 respondents
Source: U.S. Department of Education, National Center for Education Statistics, "Recent College Graduates" surveys.

don't want to jeopardize your enrollment by trying to get by on a lot less money than is really required to meet your educational expenses. For one thing, if you drop out of school *before* achieving your degree, you'll be at a disadvantage in the job market, but you'll still have a loan to repay!

Estimate how much you can repay

Estimating how much debt you can manage becomes more critical every time you borrow (and many students borrow more than once, and from more than one program). Take into account the amounts you've already borrowed, how much more you'll need to complete your education (including graduate or professional school, if that's in your plans), your estimated monthly payments, and starting salaries for the kinds of jobs you're likely to get once you graduate.

According to the U.S. Census Bureau, the average monthly income for persons with a bachelor's degree is $2,109, while monthly incomes for persons with professional degrees average $4,323. Of course, those figures are for all workers with degrees. A somewhat better frame of reference for estimating your own future earnings are the data in Tables 7.1 and 7.2,

Table 7.2. Income, earnings, and work activity of persons who held a bachelor's or advanced degree, by field of study: Spring 1984

	Mean monthly income[1]		Mean monthly earnings[2]		Number of months worked during previous 4 months	
	Bachelor's degrees	Advanced degrees	Bachelor's degrees	Advanced degrees	Bachelor's degrees	Advanced degrees
All degree recipients	**$1,841**	**$2,711**	**$1,540**	**$2,341**	**3.08**	**3.35**
Agriculture and forestry	1,945		1,559		3.25	
Biology	1,559		1,201		2.73	
Business and management	2,381	3,564	2,179	3,192	3.48	3.64
Economics	2,846		2,280		3.36	
Education	1,290	2,062	1,012	1,695	2.76	3.23
Engineering	2,833	3,308	2,282	2,886	3.38	3.55
English and journalism	1,477	1,945	1,095	1,567	2.66	3.48
Home economics	1,065		525		2.12	
Law		4,060		3,624		3.57
Liberal arts and humanities	1,400	1,720	1,072	1,466	2.87	3.17
Mathematics and statistics	2,116		1,809		3.20	
Medicine and dentistry		4,234		3,797		3.53
Nursing, pharmacy, and health	1,424	1,804	1,196	1,610	2.99	2.98
Physical and earth sciences	2,529	2,913	2,068	2,431	3.08	3.21
Psychology	1,251	2,282	1,166	1,881	2.91	3.28
Religion and theology		1,584		1,211		3.36
Social sciences	1,610	2,124	1,371	1,745	3.00	3.20
Other	1,840	2,101	1,656	1,717	3.24	3.15

[1] Includes money wages and salary and net income from farm and nonfarm self-employment and all other income.
[2] Includes money wages or salary and net income from farm and nonfarm self-employment.

Note—Data are based on sample surveys of the civilian noninstitutional population. Data not shown where base is less than 200,000 persons.

Source: U.S. Department of Commerce, Bureau of the Census, *Current Population Reports*, Series P-70, No. 11, "Educational Background and Economic Status: Spring 1984." (This table was prepared October 1987.)

---

which highlight *starting* salaries. (If you want to check out the job and salary prospects for the career field you're thinking about, a good place to start is the *Occupational Outlook Handbook* published by the U.S. Department of Labor Bureau of Labor Statistics and available in many public libraries.)

Note that these averages are based on information that is almost a decade old. Average salaries when you start loan repayment will probably be higher (but so too will be many of the other expenses you face).

Repaying your student loans may seem far in the future when you're first starting college, but a loan *is* a loan. Student loan payments may become difficult to manage if they exceed 8 to 15 percent of your available income once repayment begins. That's why it's not smart to borrow any more than you really need—particularly if graduate or professional school is in your future.

It's also why you should find out *before* you borrow whether your lender makes available any special plans for graduated repayment (with lower payments in the first few years, when earnings tend to be lower) or other financial incentives for making on-time payments.

A special note to parents about borrowing

Many parents find that they must borrow to help their children meet college costs. While many families elect to use privately insured supplemental loans or lines of credit, many other families turn to the Federal PLUS Loan Program, which was dramatically expanded by the 1992 reauthorization of the Higher Education Act. But before you take out a Federal PLUS loan or any other private supplemental loan, it's important to understand your cash flow so that you know exactly how much you can afford to repay each month.

The worksheet on the next page was prepared by the College Board's CollegeCredit Education Loan program to help parents calculate their monthly expenses.

Financial planners generally recommend that a family's *total* outstanding debt should not exceed 38 to 40 percent of its *net* annual income. That's why you need a close approximation of your cash on hand after monthly expenses before you can assess your ability to manage monthly loan payments under the Federal PLUS Loan Program or any other program.

In chapter 4, the Federal PLUS Loan Program was described as having a variable interest rate, capped at 9 percent. The following chart from the CollegeCredit Program illustrates repayment over 10 years for various loan amounts at various interest rates.

Amount of loan	Interest rate (%)		Repayment factor		Monthly payment
$ 10,000	7.00	x	.011611	=	$ 116.11
	7.25	x	.011740	=	$ 117.40
	7.50	x	.011870	=	$ 118.70
	7.75	x	.012001	=	$ 120.01
	8.00	x	.012133	=	$ 121.33
	8.25	x	.012265	=	$ 122.65
	8.50	x	.012399	=	$ 123.99
	8.75	x	.012533	=	$ 125.33
	9.00	x	.012668	=	$ 126.68
$ 20,000	7.00	x	.011611	=	$ 232.22
	7.25	x	.011740	=	$ 234.80
	7.50	x	.011870	=	$ 237.40
	7.75	x	.012001	=	$ 240.02
	8.00	x	.012133	=	$ 242.66
	8.25	x	.012265	=	$ 245.30
	8.50	x	.012399	=	$ 247.98
	8.75	x	.012533	=	$ 250.66
	9.00	x	.012668	=	$ 253.36
$ 30,000	7.00	x	.011611	=	$ 348.33
	7.25	x	.011740	=	$ 352.22
	7.50	x	.011870	=	$ 356.10
	7.75	x	.012001	=	$ 360.03
	8.00	x	.012133	=	$ 363.99
	8.25	x	.012265	=	$ 367.95
	8.50	x	.012399	=	$ 371.97
	8.75	x	.012533	=	$ 375.99
	9.00	x	.012668	=	$ 380.04

To calculate a monthly payment for a Federal PLUS Loan amount other than those on the chart, multiply the amount borrowed by the repayment factor for your interest rate. (For example, if you borrowed $12,500 at 7.5 percent, your monthly payment would be $148.38 ($12,500 x .011870.)

If you are considering a private supplemental loan program or line of credit, ask your lender for sample monthly repayment schedules.

Understand what you're doing

Make sure you know what you're doing before you sign on the dotted line. Sometimes students borrow without even realizing that they're doing it; they fail to read award letters carefully and aren't paying attention when they sign a promissory note. Some students also have borrowed from more than one program on the mistaken assumption that their loan will automatically be consolidated in a single obligation later on; that's not the case, although sometimes it may be possible.

Whether you are considering a subsidized government loan or a commercial loan, you should know the answers to all of these questions before you commit yourself:

- What is the simple interest rate?
- When will you have to begin repayment?
- How large will the monthly payments be, and how long will you be paying back the loan?
- Are there any extra charges involved in borrowing the money? (For instance, you may have to pay an origination fee, service fee, or insurance charges up front.)
- Are there any restrictions?
- Can the lender terminate the loan, and under what conditions?
  Do you have to be notified before cancellation?
- Can you terminate the loan before the contract is up? How much notice must you give the lender? Are there any prepayment penalties, such as additional costs for paying the loan off early?
- Does the loan agreement contain a "balloon clause"—one payment, usually larger than the rest, that is tacked onto the end of the contract? (Sometimes borrowers can't afford to pay this larger sum when the time comes and must get their loans refinanced.)
- Does the contract include a clause allowing wage assignments or garnisheeing? Such a clause allows the lender to ask your employer to take out a specified sum from your monthly earnings and send it to the lender if you default on your loan for any reason, and without any legal procedure. Most

Monthly family expenses

Housing and Maintenance

- ❏ Mortgage or rent payment $ _____
- ❏ Electricity _____
- ❏ Gas _____
- ❏ Water and sewer _____
- ❏ Telephone _____
- ❏ Property taxes _____
- ❏ Homeowner's insurance _____
- ❏ Household help _____
- ❏ Furniture and appliances _____
- ❏ Other household items _____
- ❏ Home maintenance _____
- ❏ Other _____

Family

- ❏ Groceries $ _____
- ❏ School lunches _____
- ❏ Clothing _____
- ❏ Laundry and dry cleaning _____
- ❏ Toiletries _____
- ❏ Prescription drugs _____
- ❏ Child care _____
- ❏ Education expenses _____
- ❏ Children's camp expenses _____
- ❏ Children's allowances _____
- ❏ Gifts _____
- ❏ Medical expenses _____
- ❏ Medical insurance _____
- ❏ Dental expenses _____
- ❏ Dental insurance _____
- ❏ Life insurance _____
- ❏ Other _____

Transportation

- ❏ Automobile payments $ _____
- ❏ Gasoline _____
- ❏ Auto insurance _____
- ❏ Auto maintenance _____
- ❏ Other _____

Subtotal Monthly Expenses $ _____

Subtotal from previous column $ _____

Leisure

- ❏ Movies and theater $ _____
- ❏ Cable television _____
- ❏ Books/magazines/newspaper _____
- ❏ Vacations _____
- ❏ Restaurants _____
- ❏ Club memberships _____
- ❏ Other _____

Other

- ❏ Installment loans $ _____
- ❏ Credit card debt not accounted for above _____
- ❏ Investment expenses _____
- ❏ Accountant's fees _____
- ❏ Attorney's fees _____
- ❏ Charitable and political contributions _____
- ❏ Other _____

TOTAL Monthly Expenses $ _____

Monthly Income

- ❏ Net monthly income after taxes and payroll deductions $ _____
- ❏ Rent paid to you _____
- ❏ Alimony received _____
- ❏ Interest and dividend income _____

TOTAL Monthly Income $ _____

TOTAL Monthly Income $ _____
Minus
TOTAL Monthly Expenses $ _____
Equals
Cash on Hand After Monthly Expenses $ _____

banks have eliminated such clauses from their loan contracts, and you should avoid any contract with such a clause.

- What kind of repayment options does the lender offer? Can you count on graduated repayment and/or consolidation options later on?
- Have you borrowed other loans from this lender already? If you plan to borrow under the Federal Stafford Student Loan Program for each of your years in school, it makes sense to borrow from a single lender. That will make it easier for you to manage your obligations when you go into repayment, as well as to request consolidation if you decide you want it.

Before you sign any contract or promissory note, make sure you understand what it is all about. If something is unclear, don't be embarrassed to ask for an explanation. You have the right to seek outside counsel and advice before entering into any binding legal agreement.

Questions and answers about borrowing for education

Q Our family didn't qualify for need-based aid. Is any help available?

A A Federal PLUS Loan is a possibility, because you don't have to demonstrate financial need. A Federal PLUS Loan is a government-sponsored loan for *parents* of dependent students. Parents at all income levels may apply; these are "signature loans" that require no collateral. You may borrow from any lender approved by the U.S. Department of Education.

If you are creditworthy, you may also be able to qualify for a privately insured supplemental loan. These programs take many forms, from lines of credit and tuition budgeting plans to more conventional installment loans for students and/or parents. (See Chapter 4 for some examples, or ask your financial aid office for suggestions.)

Q My child is taking out a Federal Stafford Loan. May I take out a Federal PLUS Loan, too?

A Yes. In many families, both students and parents help to pay for college. Your child is legally responsible for Federal Stafford Loan repayment, and you are legally responsible for Federal PLUS Loan repayment. (You may also borrow under a supplemental loan program, if you are creditworthy.) In some loan programs, both the student and the parent(s) are actually co-signatories on the loan, and legally share the obligation for repayment.

Q How much should I borrow?

A Ask yourself two questions: How much do I really need, and how much can I eventually repay?

Estimating how much debt you can manage becomes more critical each time you borrow. Take into account amounts you've already borrowed, how much more you'll need to complete your education (including graduate or professional school, if that's in your plans), your estimated monthly payments, and starting salaries for the kinds of jobs you're likely to get. (If you're a *parent*, and you're thinking about a Federal PLUS Loan or a privately sponsored supplemental loan, you may want to consider how much you've already borrowed for education as well as for other purposes, how much more you're likely to need to educate other children, other family needs and goals, your current salary and your prospects over the next several years, and how much debt you can handle for a sustained period.)

Q Can I borrow more than once, or from more than one program?

A Yes, many students borrow under the Federal Stafford Loan Program for each year in school; many also borrow from other loan programs.

Keep in mind, though, that each time you borrow from a new loan program, you create a new repayment obligation. Unless you eventually consolidate your loans, you may have separate minimum monthly payments to make on *each* loan program.

Q What is consolidation?

A Once you've entered your grace period or actually started repayment, you may be able to combine your Federal Stafford Loans and most other government-sponsored student loans into one debt. The result is a single monthly payment for the consolidated debt, which is smaller than the total of the separate monthly payments, at least in the initial years. You generally get more time to pay off the consolidated debt, but you'll also pay more in interest.

Investigate consolidation options before you borrow. The option is not available with all lenders.

8. Pulling it all together

Most of this book has been about how you interact with other people and agencies and institutions in the process of planning to pay for college. (That's partly because most of this book has been about getting other people's help for meeting college costs!) You have read about *guidelines*—for estimating costs, for demonstrating need, for determining eligibility. You've learned about *questions* you'll be asked—questions about your income and your assets, your hopes, and your needs. You've heard about *decisions*—how colleges, the federal government, state student assistance agencies, and private scholarship programs make them.

In the end it comes down to the student and his or her family. There are a lot of people who will help you to pull together a personal financing strategy, get financial aid, or offer you advice. But advice is cheap—college isn't. At some point in the process (the earlier the better), you need to develop your own guidelines, ask yourself some questions, and make some personal decisions.

Understanding financial aid awards

Elsewhere in this chapter you'll see a sample financial aid award letter. In mid-spring of your senior year of high school, you will begin to receive notices from financial aid administrators at the colleges to which you applied. Most selective institutions tell you about their admissions and aid decisions at the same time, often around April 15. Other institutions may have a "rolling" admissions schedule—that is, they make admissions decisions as soon as applications are complete—and use either a rolling or a fixed schedule for telling admitted students about their financial aid awards.

Sometimes financial aid administrators will not know exactly how much money is available in the aggregate to help their applicants; uncertainty about state or federal student aid appropriations, for example, can make estimating difficult. Many colleges issue tentative or preliminary award notices in the spring, which are subsequently confirmed in the summer when more information becomes available. In such a circumstance, a college will try to meet its original commitment to a student, but if government funds are reduced, the college may have to adjust the original award offer. The colleges find this process just as frustrating as do families, but in a time of uncertainty, it may simply be unavoidable.

Comparing award offers

If you are considering more than one college, you may want to compare the financial aid awards offered by the colleges. Resist the temptation to look only at the amount of the awards! College A may offer you $1,500 and College B may offer you $3,000. You need to look at the total student expense budgets at College A and College B before you can determine which award comes closer to meeting your need. The smaller award from College A may be all the extra help you need to attend, while the award from College B may not be enough to bridge the gap.

Here are some points to consider in comparing financial aid awards:

- What is the budget that the college used in determining your award offer? Does it coincide with your estimated budget for that college?
- What is the amount determined by the college that you and your family can be expected to pay toward college costs?
- How much of your need is met at each college—costs minus family contribution?
- What portion of each financial aid package is made up of gift aid (scholarships and grants) and

what portion consists of self-help aid (loan and work)?
- Which college would you most like to attend from an educational standpoint? From a financial standpoint, is this college also your best choice? If not, is the aid offered sufficient to permit you to attend?

Worksheet 6 in Chapter 10 provides a simple framework in which to analyze and compare your financial aid awards from various colleges. Remember, the point is not so much how many dollars you are awarded as how much of your need is met.

Accepting a financial aid award

After you have received award letters from the colleges to which you applied and have compared the offers, accept the award at the college you choose by signing the award letter. Complete and return any additional forms that were sent with the award letter. Also notify the other colleges that you are declining their aid offers, so that the funds can be distributed to other students.

If you have any questions about your award, contact the financial aid office at the college. Sometimes revisions in the composition of your award package are possible. For example, you may be able to shift a loan to a work opportunity. You are usually not required to accept the entire financial aid package as offered. If you decide not to accept a part of your aid offer, it may not be possible for the financial aid office to restore that aid later, should you change your mind.

Particularly in a time of declining resources, you should understand that if you need financial aid to meet college costs, you will almost certainly have to accept some of that aid in the form of self-help aid—that is, loans and/or jobs—during the course of your education. Many colleges gradually increase the self-help portion of a student's financial aid package over the four years he or she is enrolled, so you cannot necessarily expect the same package every year, even if your need is the same. For instance, some colleges try to minimize the Federal Work-Study awards offered to freshmen so that they can devote more time to studying and adjusting to college life, but colleges that do this may replace some of the grant aid in the freshman packages with jobs in subsequent years.

Appealing your award package

If you believe that your financial aid package is insufficient to meet your needs, you may want to contact the financial aid office at the college. Inquire about how your expense budget was put together and how your family contribution and financial need were determined. If there are special circumstances that you think have been overlooked, bring these to the aid administrator's attention. It may be that the aid administrator can take your particular situation into account and adjust your award offer.

After visiting with the aid administrator, if you still feel that you have unmet needs or that you have been treated unfairly, you may want to consider appealing your award. Some colleges have a formal administrative procedure with a review board to hear your appeal. Others have a much less formal process: usually the award decision is reviewed by the aid administrator's superior to see that institutional policies have been followed. Contact the financial aid office to find out what the appeal procedures are, and follow them.

Understand, though, that a college's inability to meet your full need probably reflects nothing more than insufficient funds. There has never been enough aid to fully meet the needs of all the students who could use some extra help, and when this book was written, resources were shrinking, not expanding. You have a right to a full explanation of a college's policies and practices with regard to determining need, eligibility, and priorities for distribution of funds, and a college will probably be happy to provide you with this information. The answers to your questions will not necessarily provide the answers to your financial problems. (You may want to review Chapter 4 for some ideas on getting the most mileage out of your own resources.)

Loans and your aid award package

Your financial aid award letter may include the recommendation that you borrow from the Federal Stafford Student Loan Program as part of your aid package.

You will need to complete a separate application for the Federal Stafford Student Loan Program. Your award letter will tell you how to proceed. Some colleges send applications directly to their students; in other situations, you may receive a loan application from your state guaranty agency or be directed to pick one up from your local bank.

The processing of Federal Stafford Student Loan applications varies somewhat from state to state, but the basics are the same. As the borrower, you complete

BROOKDALE COLLEGE

Ms. Juanita L. Student
21 Cornwall Lane
Centerville, CA 95007

Date 06/28/93

ID# 123-45-6789

Dear Juanita:

We have completed our review of your application for financial assistance from Brookdale College. Listed below is the financial aid that we can offer to you at this time, showing how it will be paid to you during the year.

SOURCE:	FALL	WINTER	SPRING	TOTAL
Jacobson Family Grant	667	667	666	2,000
Federal Work-Study Employment	779	778	778	2,335
Federal Pell Grant (ESTIMATED)	284	283	283	850
State Award: Cal Grant	367	367	366	1,100
	2,097	2,095	2,093	6,285

Our decision was based on an analysis of your estimated costs and projected family and other resources. In addition to the awards listed above we recommend that you apply for a Federal Stafford Loan in the amount of $2,625. For information or an application for the loan, contact the Financial Aid Office.

The Jacobson Family Grant was provided by Mr. E.C. Jacobson. If you wish to write him a thank you letter, it should be addressed to him care of my office. We will forward it to him with our annual accounting for the fund.

Please read the enclosed financial aid brochure carefully. If you wish to accept these awards, please complete and return the form enclosed within 30 days. If you have any questions or would like further information, please telephone my office.

Kathleen M. Brouder
Dean of Admissions and Financial Aid

A Fictional, Non-Degree-Granting Institution

one section of the application. Your financial aid administrator completes another, certifying that you are enrolled or have been admitted and providing other information about the cost of education and financial one section of the application. Your financial aid administror completes another, certifying that you are enrolled or have been admitted and providing other information about the cost of education and fincial aid awarded. The application is sent to your lender, and once the loan has been made, the application is sent on (either by mail or electronically) to your guarantor for approval.

Read carefully any information about how to borrow from the Federal Stafford Student Loan Program that accompanies your award letter. Follow the instructions completely and promptly. If you are uncertain how to proceed, call or write the aid office for additional details.

Your aid package may also contain an award of a Federal Perkins Loan. If you are awarded a Federal Perkins Loan, you will not have to complete a separate loan application. However, you will be required to sign a promissory note for each loan advance. A copy of the promissory note and other loan information is provided to recipients in accordance with federal loan disclosure laws. Recipients may also have to provide additional information at some point in the process, such as a list of personal references.

When you review your award letter, make sure you understand exactly what kind of aid you are being offered and what you must do to receive it. Take particular notice of any loans you are awarded, and whether you need to file separate applications in order to get the funds. (And remember the advice in Chapter 7 about borrowing only as much as you *really* need.)

Work and your aid award package

Many students receive a work-study job as part of their aid packages, generally through the Federal Work-Study Program (although some colleges also sponsor work-study programs of their own). Your aid award will tell you how much of your package you are expected to earn through your work-study job, but will not typically tell you what kind of job you'll get. The aid award notice will explain to you how to find out about and apply for eligible jobs, usually on campus.

A student who receives funding under the Federal Work-Study Program will be required to file a federal income tax witholding form (Form W-4) or witholding exemption form (Form W-4E) with the college before he or she can earn any funds. The financial aid office will provide you with full information and copies of the necessary forms.

Private scholarships and your aid award package

Thousands of organizations other than colleges and universities and state and federal governments provide scholarships to thousands of students every year. The way that these outside awards "fit" into a financial aid package can sometimes cause confusion—or even bad feelings—among recipients *and* donors. Often students receive outside scholarships *after* they have already received notification about colleges' financial aid awards. If a student's package was designed to fully meet demonstrated financial need, as discussed earlier in this book, then the college *must* make adjustments in the original award to comply with federal regulations that prohibit recipients of federal aid from getting *more* money than they need. Even if their original awards from colleges did not fully meet their demonstrated need, outside scholarship winners sometimes find that their packages are nonetheless reduced; this might occur because the colleges have a policy of reducing packages to maximize limited resources.

A few years ago, the New England Regional Office of the College Board asked an advisory committee of college financial aid administrators, high school guidance counselors, and foundation personnel to look at some of the problems that were occurring in that particular region of the country. The advisory committee discovered wide differences in colleges' policies regarding financial aid packaging, the percentage of demonstrated financial need met, and how outside awards were treated—a diversity repeated across the country. The committee helped create a pamphlet addressed to high school students who were applying for or had received outside scholarship assistance. Here is some of the good advice included in that pamphlet:

> Organizations other than colleges, universities, and state and federal governments routinely award scholarships to worthy students to help them pay college expenses. These "outside" scholarships come from various sources including business and industry, church and civic organizations, unions, local scholarship boards, or school-related groups. Such scholarships vary in value anywhere from one hundred to several thousand

dollars and are often renewable. Students fortunate enough to be awarded both an outside scholarship and financial aid from a university, college, or government source may encounter reductions of or revisions to their institutional aid because of the outside scholarships. And, if federal funds are involved, federal regulations forbid over-awards, thereby requiring institutional adjustments in cases where a student's full need has been met by an institution before knowledge of an outside scholarship. A review of the institution's policy in advance can prevent disappointment or surprise about the nature of the reduction.

Q. *If I receive financial aid from the college I'm planning to attend, and then I am awarded a scholarship from a civic group or business organization, how do I know if the college will change its financial aid award?*

A. The only way to be sure if your financial aid award will be adjusted is to check the policy of the institution you plan to attend. The financial aid officer at the college or university is your best source of information. A quick review of the institution's financial aid materials might also provide the answers. Remember, policies differ greatly from one institution to another. What may be true for your classmate's college may not be true for yours.

Q. *Is it true that my institutional financial aid can be reduced by as much as the full amount of any outside scholarship I receive? That seems really unfair.*

A. The answer depends primarily on whether or not your institution has already met your financial need (as measured by the institution). The answer: probably yes if your need has been met; probably no if your need has not been met.

Q. *What if I decide to avoid all this and don't report an outside scholarship to my college?*

A. That's a bad idea. Institutional policies and state and federal regulations require that, if you are a candidate for financial aid, you must report your outside scholarships to the financial aid office of the institution you're planning to attend. Remember, the information you and your parents provide about your financial situation and your outside scholarships must be complete and accurate. If it is not, you risk losing your entire financial aid package.

So what happens if a student's need has already been fully met and he or she receives an outside scholarship? The advisory committee noted that different colleges have different ways of handling the situation. Some reduce the gift aid (grants or scholarships) in the institutional offer by the same amount as the outside award. Others reduce the self-help (work and/or loan) portion of the package, while still others adjust both the gift and the self-help portions. If a student's need has *not* been fully met, however, the committee noted that many colleges would apply the amount of the outside award against the student's remaining unmet need, and not reduce the aid package until the student's need was fully met.

The advisory committee noted that students were still better off receiving outside scholarships even if their institutional awards were reduced, simply because "only a small number of New England institutions will reduce your institutional gift aid by the full value of your outside scholarship," a situation that holds true in most areas of the country. Investigating institutional policies in advance is certainly advisable, as the committee recommended, and high school counselors and college financial aid administrators continue to be good sources of information and advice on this subject.

Your rights and responsibilities

Education or training after high school requires an investment of time, money, and energy. Some people think of students as consumers, and feel that students, like other consumers, have both rights and responsibilities. The federal government has outlined a series of rights and responsibilities that you may want to keep in mind as you develop a personal financial plan and pursue financial aid opportunities.

Student rights

You have a right to receive the following information from a college:
- what financial aid is available, including information about federal, state, and institutional programs
- what the deadlines are for applying for each kind of aid
- what the cost of attendance is, and what the refund policies are if you withdraw
- what criteria the college uses to select aid recipients
- how the college determines your financial need, including how student expenses are figured in your budget

- what resources, such as parents' contribution, other financial aid and benefits, assets, etc., are considered in determining your need
- how much of your financial need has been met
- what aid resources make up your financial package
- what part of the aid received must be repaid and what part is grant aid
- if you receive a student loan, what the interest rate is, what the total amount is that must be repaid, what the procedures are for paying back the loan, how long you have to repay, and when repayment is to begin
- what the procedures are for appealing a financial aid decision if you feel you have been treated unfairly
- how the college determines whether or not you are making satisfactory academic progress, and what happens if you are not.

Student responsibilities

You have a responsibility to:
- review and consider all information about a college's program before you enroll
- pay special attention to your application for student financial aid, including completing it accurately and submitting it on time to the right place. (Errors can delay your getting aid, and intentional misreporting of information is a violation of law subject to penalties under the United States Criminal Code.)
- return all additional documentation, verification, corrections, and/or new information requested either by the financial aid administrator or the agency to which you submitted your application, read and understand all forms that you are asked to sign and keep copies of them, accept responsibility for all agreements signed by you
- if you receive a loan, notify the lender of any change in your name, address, or school status
- if you are assigned student employment, perform in a satisfactory manner the work that is agreed upon in accepting the aid
- know and comply with the deadlines for applying and for reapplying for aid
- know and comply with your college's refund policies and procedures.

Questions and answers about pulling it all together

Q If I accept a college's financial aid offer, how can I be sure of getting the same amount of money next year? How do I renew my award?

A The terms and conditions of your award will be spelled out in your award letter and/or accompanying literature from the aid office. Review this information carefully to make sure you understand exactly what you have to do to maintain your eligibility.

For several reasons, you may not receive exactly the same financial aid package next year. Your parents' income could go up (or down), or the college's tuition and room and board charges could increase. The college may have more or fewer aid dollars to distribute, or government funding could increase or decrease. Factors like these could influence the amount for which you qualify.

It's also possible that the *contents* of your financial aid package may change somewhat, even if its overall value stays approximately the same. Some colleges don't like to give first-year students too much work-study, for example, lest jobs distract them from academics in the critical first year. Others try to minimize loans until students have demonstrated their persistence by successfully completing a year or two.

The important thing to remember is that the financial aid office is there to *help* you. The staff are as anxious to see you make it—academically and financially—as you are. If you're worried about getting help for future years, or have any questions at all about what your package means or what you need to do to maintain your eligibility, call the aid office and *ask*.

Q I decided really late in the school year that I want to go to college in the fall. Is there any chance that I can still get some financial aid?

A It's possible, but you'll have to act quickly!

If you've already initiated the *admissions* application process, call the aid office to find out what you need to do to apply for assistance. If you haven't taken any action whatsoever yet, call the admissions office and explain that you need information about applying for admissions and financial aid.

If you are eligible for a Federal Pell Grant and/or a Federal Stafford Student Loan, you can still apply. However, you are likely to find that you've missed the deadline for state aid, college scholarships, and other programs administered by the college, like work-study. (You *may* be able to get consideration for some of these during the second semester.)

Q My parents say they just can't (or won't) come up with the amount of the expected contribution, and the aid offer from the college I like best just doesn't go far enough. What should I do?

A You can call or write the aid office to explain your situation and see if the staff have any suggestions. Some colleges have installment payment programs or tuition budgeting plans that might make it easier for your parents to finance their contribution. You could also investigate Federal PLUS Loans (for parents) or one of the privately sponsored supplemental loan programs.

If you truly have extenuating circumstances that affect your family's ability to contribute to your educational expenses, the aid office *may* be willing to reconsider your application. Just keep in mind that an aid administrator is likely to be more interested in factors that influence your family's *ability* to pay, not its *willingness* to do so.

It's not always easy—for the aid administrator or the family—to tell the difference between ability and willingness. Another child with exceptional needs or continuing medical expenses, or a parent who's lost a job, affect ability. Not wanting to "spend down" a child's educational trust fund, or wanting more grants in order to avoid borrowing, may reflect more on willingness than on ability. Be prepared to answer some questions.

Q I didn't get nearly as much aid as I needed to attend the college I like best. What now?

A You still have options. Find out if your preferred college will defer your enrollment for a year, giving you time to earn some money. Or consider enrolling in a less expensive college for a year or two, and transferring to your preferred college later on.

You could also go to college part time while you work. Look for an employer that offers tuition payment or reimbursement as a fringe benefit. (As a matter of fact, colleges and universities often give their staffs free or reduced tuition as a benefit of employment. The advantage is, you're already on campus.)

Financial aid checklist

❏ **Develop a list of colleges that interest you** and that seem to match your educational and career goals. You may want to use a comprehensive guide, such as *The College Handbook* or *Index of Majors and Graduate Degrees*, to help you do this. Software packages like *College Cost Explorer FUND FINDER* can also help; see if it's available in your counselor's office, or obtain a copy to use at home.

❏ **Write to the admissions office** at each college on your list for an admissions application form. Remember also to inquire about financial aid opportunities and application procedures. It is best to do this early in the fall of your senior year of high school.

❏ **Make certain you know what need analysis form to file.** You can usually get forms from your high school guidance office or a college financial aid office. The documents are generally first available in November, but they should not be filed until *after* January 1.

❏ **Mail your completed form(s) as soon after January 1 as possible.** The form should be sent for processing at least four weeks before the earliest financial aid deadline set by the colleges or state scholarship or grant programs to which you are applying (but no earlier than January 1). Carefully follow the instructions for filling out the form. Make sure your answers are complete and correct.

❏ **Apply for all forms of student financial aid.** Determine early on whether you must fill out additional application forms. Find this out well in advance and make certain you file the appropriate forms by the deadlines.

❏ **Supply additional information promptly.** If you or your parents receive requests for additional information about your need analysis form, respond promptly so that there will be no further delay in processing your request for aid.

❏ **Review the acknowledgment you get back.** After submitting your need analysis form, you will receive some type of acknowledgment from the processor. Make certain that all entries on the acknowledgment are correct.

❏ **Review your award letters carefully.** The director of financial aid at each college and scholarship program is responsible for determining a student's need, knowing which funds a student is eligible for, and making a decision about who will receive financial aid and how much. Once that decision is made, you will receive an award letter describing the contents of your financial aid package and outlining any conditions attached to the award.

❑ **Check to see if other financial aid application forms are required** by the colleges to which you are applying and find out the deadline dates for each. Complete these forms as early as possible.

❑ **Check with your guidance counselor, high school library, and public library** for books and pamphlets about other aid sources. Follow the directions for applying. You may qualify for a private scholarship, grant, or loan program because of your:

 academic achievement
 religious affiliation
 ethnic or racial heritage
 community activities
 hobbies or special interests
 organizational memberships
 artistic talents, athletic abilities, or
  other special skills
 career plans or proposed field of study

❑ **Find out if your parents' employers, professional associations, or labor unions** sponsor any aid programs.

❑ **Investigate community organizations and civic, cultural, and fraternal groups** to see if they sponsor scholarship programs at the local, state, or national level. Also check with local religious organizations, veterans' posts, businesses, and industries.

❑ **If you or either of your parents is a military veteran,** you may be eligible for special assistance. Contact the nearest office of the Veterans Administration for information.

❑ **Ask about benefits from vocational rehabilitation or other social service agencies** if you think you qualify for assistance.

❑ **Pay close attention to award notices from state and federal student financial aid programs.** Review your federal Student Aid Report (SAR) carefully.

❑ **Learn how the payments from each aid source will be made.** Generally, payment of financial aid awards is made at the time you actually enroll. Also find out if there are additional procedures you should be aware of or forms you must fill out in order to receive aid.

❑ **Explore alternatives.** Some colleges offer tuition and/or fee waivers to certain categories of students, such as adults, children of alumni, or family members enrolled simultaneously. If you qualify, you may want to take advantage of this type of discount. (See Part III of this book for lists of colleges that offer tuition and/or fee waivers.) Colleges that offer special tuition payment plans—installment, deferred, or credit card—or tuition discounts for prepayment also are listed in Part III of this book.

❑ **Educate yourself about loans.** Investigate all the options before you borrow, and make sure that you understand the interest rates, repayment requirements, and other terms and conditions for each loan program you're considering. Give yourself plenty of time—at least six weeks—before the start of the semester to have your loan application processed.

❑ **Make a decision about which college to attend on the basis of your education and career goals.** Remember to notify the college whose offer you are accepting and to communicate your decision to other colleges so that the financial aid they reserved for you can be freed for other applicants.

9. Long-range planning: A special message to parents

If your child will not be enrolling in college for several years, or if you have one enrolling now but others coming up. you have more time to plan. This chapter is written especially for you.

If you have not already done so, turn now to the tables in the next chapter showing average costs, or look up the average expenses for a few colleges with which you are familiar. And then think about this question:

When it is time to enroll in college, will you have enough ready cash to cover these expenses, in a single lump-sum payment, at the start of the semester?

Most people don't. Even what is generally regarded as the *least* expensive of the various educational options—living at home and commuting to a nearby community college—requires nearly $5,300 a year on average. The budget for students living on campus now averages about $8,000 per year at an in-state public college or university and over $17,000 at a private one. And no one is sure how much higher the costs are going to go.

If your family saves little or no money before enrollment, it will be almost impossible to change your household budget fast enough or radically enough to pay for all your college expenses out of current income alone. People with low or fixed incomes don't have the extra money to spend. Even people with high incomes can't afford to divert large chunks of current income to make big payments once or twice a year. However, if you do the best you can for yourself, you may be able to get enough outside help to cover the difference between what you can afford and what college costs.

The purpose of planning

Remember that the purpose of financial planning to meet educational costs is twofold:
- to get as much mileage as you can out of your own resources, and
- to secure the additional outside help—the "financial aid"—you may need in order to make up the difference between what you can afford and what it costs to attend the college of your choice.

The two objectives are inseparable. The entire financing system for American postsecondary education is based on the assumption that you and your family have the *primary* responsibility for meeting college costs, to the extent of your ability.

You may wonder, Why should we use *our* resources at all if financial aid is available? Why not "plan" to have financial aid pay for it all?

The answer is that the bulk of financial aid awarded in the United States is, and always has been, based on "demonstrated need"; that is, it comes into play only after a family has done as much as it can reasonably be expected to do for itself, according to formulas that are applied to all aid applicants. Also, every dollar that you save in advance is probably one less that your child will have to borrow.

Some students come from families that have few or no resources to contribute toward college expenses. Others come from families that can easily foot the bill for even the most expensive educational options. But most students come from families that fall somewhere between the two extremes.

The Smiths and the Joneses

Imagine two families whose overall income pictures have been very similar over time and whose current

The Smiths

Two parents, both working outside the home, older parent age 45. Two children, one in junior high school, the other starting college in the fall. No unusual expenses; standard U.S. income tax deductions and exemptions

The Smiths saved $75,000.

Income before taxes	$50,000
Total assets	75,000
Expected from parents	
from income:	$4,850
from savings:	2,115
First-year costs	$15,000
− Expected from parents	6,965
= Demonstrated need	$8,035

The Joneses

Two parents, both working outside the home, older parent age 45. Two children, one in junior high school, the other starting college in the fall. No unusual expenses; standard U.S. income tax deductions and exemptions

The Joneses saved $15,000.

Income before taxes	$50,000
Total assets	15,000
Expected from parents	
from income:	$4,850
from savings:	0
First-year costs	$15,000
− Expected from parents	4,850
= Demonstrated need	$10,150

*Parental expectations are based on the Congressional Methodology formulas for the 1992-93 academic year. Values are approximate.

incomes are identical. Both the Smiths and the Joneses have two children, one of whom will be in college, and the parents are of the same age.

The one big difference between the families is that the Smiths have done a much better job of saving over the years. They started saving a portion of both incomes each month when their children were very young, in anticipation of needing some of those assets to pay for college. They have accumulated $75,000 in savings while the Joneses have spent more of their current income each year and have saved only $15,000.

It is obvious that when the time comes for their respective children to enroll in college, the Smiths will have more money available to put toward college costs than the Joneses. But, won't the Joneses simply qualify for more financial aid?

The answer is, to a degree, yes—but the Smiths will be much better off than the Joneses. Here's why.

Assets, such as savings, *are* considered in the formulas for estimating a family's ability to pay for educational expenses. A family with assets is considered to be in a much stronger financial position than a family without assets. Despite this, the contribution from *income* has a much greater influence on the expected contribution, as demonstrated with the Smiths and Joneses.

As shown above, the Federal Methodology will assume that the Smiths will be able to contribute $2,115 from their assets for the first year of their child's college expenses. That's only $2,115 out of the $75,000 saved! The Joneses, however, are not expected to make a contribution from assets since their assets are so low. Both families will be expected to contribute $4,850 toward educational expenses from their current incomes.

While some might argue that the Smiths are being "penalized" for saving, let's take a closer look. The Smiths have options the Joneses don't have.

Many families find it difficult to contribute the amount assumed available from current income. Families often accumulate financial obligations related to choices they have made in selecting a home or car, or in acquiring more consumer debt than they would like. These obligations can make it difficult to divert enough current income to educational expenses.

Because they have saved, the Smiths have the option of substituting some of their savings for part of the contribution expected from income, thus freeing up current income and lessening their need to borrow to meet educational expenses. This is a choice the Joneses can make for a year or two for their first child's college expenses, but doing so would leave them without that option for their second child and would leave the parents with very little savings toward their retirement.

In addition, both the Smiths' and Joneses' college-bound children will be asked to take out student loans to meet part of their expenses. The Smiths are in a much better position to use more of their savings to reduce the need for their child to go into debt.

If the families do find it difficult to contribute the amounts expected from their incomes, the availability of assets can make the difference between selecting a college on the basis of *educational value* rather than on the basis of *cost*.

Saving for college makes good sense. It puts a family in a strong position when decisions about college are to be made. It provides a family with options that might not otherwise be available. And as far as being "penalized" for saving is concerned, it's important to note that under the current Federal Methodology, the maximum amount that parents can be expected to contribute from their assets in a given year is *less than six percent of their total assets*. And, home equity is excluded. That leaves a great deal of a family's wealth unassessed by the formula, giving the family a real chance for receiving financial aid while leaving them with the ability to make sound educational decisions.

How to plan

The *basics* are the same for long-range planning as for short-range planning, and have been described earlier in this book: educating yourself about college costs, estimating what you will be expected to pay toward those costs, developing a timetable, choosing strategies to get the most mileage out of your family resources, and finding out about financial aid programs.

The details of your plan to meet college costs will necessarily be very different from a family whose child will enroll within the next few months. If your children are still quite young, time is on your side—a big advantage. On the other hand, you also have the disadvantage of uncertainty about what circumstances will influence both college costs and your ability to pay between now and enrollment. However, you still can—and should—plan.

Setting realistic goals

Setting realistic goals is the first step. A goal is not a wish but a statement of purpose, a description of an objective to be achieved. It should be as concrete and specific as possible.

Reviewing Chapters 1 and 2 will help you:
- learn what college costs today, and
- estimate what share of those costs *you* would be expected to pay if your child were enrolling in the near future.

Once you have done so, you will have to make some *additional* assumptions about what college costs and family expectations will look like when it's time for your children to enroll.

No one is really sure what college will cost in 5 or 10 or 15 years, and the further into the future you look, the murkier becomes the crystal ball. In the short run, at least, the prices charged by institutions for tuition, room, and board are *not* likely to go down, because operating costs continue to rise. Although colleges and universities are working harder than ever to achieve economies in their operating budgets, higher education continues to be very labor intensive. That means that one of their largest continuing expenses is salaries and benefits for employees —faculty members, administrators, librarians, cafeteria and maintenance workers, health service and security personnel, etc.

Does that mean that the costs charged to students and parents will continue to rise at the same rate as they have in recent years? For the last several years, overall increases have averaged 6 to 8 percent, a somewhat slower rate of increase than the double-digit annual increases that characterized the early 1980s.

A family whose children will start college in the fall of 1994 will probably not be too far off in their estimates of total expense if they add 7 or 8 percent *per year* to the 1992-93 averages in Chapter 10. Beyond that, you will have to keep track of annual increases and revise your own projections.

Nor is anyone certain that the formulas for assessing a family's ability to contribute will remain stable over time. However, the basic *principles* embodied in the current methodology have been in place for over 30 years. The same kinds of factors will probably continue to be considered in evaluating a family's financial strength as are discussed in this chapter, although they may be treated or weighted differently.

If you are trying to make some ballpark estimate of what will be expected of you when the time comes, you might want to complete the worksheets in Chapter 10, estimating what you think your income, assets, etc., will be at the time of enrollment. Subtract that estimate from your estimate of future college costs. Alternately, use current figures for estimating both total costs and family share, and inflate the resulting goal statement by your assumption of annual inflation between now and the point of enrollment.

Update your assumptions and goals annually. Revise your estimates of probable future expenses by incorporating new data about actual college costs and periodic changes in the formulas for assessing family ability to contribute. Keep your eye on changes in other leading economic indicators, too.

Developing a timetable

Developing a realistic timetable is closely related to goal-setting. The amount of time—in months or years—that's left before your children *start* college is an important factor. It represents the period in which you can *save* money and *look* for extra outside help. However, your plans could also include assumptions about the periods of time *during and after* college in which you may *spend* money to repay loans. Developing a timetable also lets you translate big goals into more manageable terms. To save $1,200 in one year you have to put aside $100 a month or $25 a week or $3.50 a day—actually a little less, assuming your money earns some interest.

Review Chapter 3 to prove to yourself that time really *is* on your side. It demonstrates that the longer the time period over which you finance any purchase, the smaller its impact will be on your monthly budget. For most families, the hardest possible way to finance their fair share of college costs—whether that share is 5 percent or 100 percent—is by cramming it into their household budget during the four-year period of enrollment. Don't assume, however, that you can, or should, defer saving with the intention of relying on loans when your children are ready to enroll.

Under some economic conditions, borrowing is certainly a feasible and even sensible way of making major purchases, but planning to borrow may not be your wisest strategy. The farther into the future you look, the harder it is to be sure about credit availability, your borrowing capacity, the state of the economy, etc.

If you are fortunate enough to have many years before your children enter college and considerable discretionary income, consult your financial adviser for recommendations about various savings and investment strategies to achieve your goals for meeting college costs. A lot is going to be expected of you. Even if you don't have much to spare, plan to save as much as you can in advance. Regular, systematic savings—even of small amounts—add up, and compounding of interest multiples your money powerfully.

Strategies for paying your fair share

Deciding how to pay your fair share is the next step, once you've established goals and timetables. Review Chapter 4 for descriptions of many of the options that are available today. Some are used far in advance of enrollment to save money, while others are designed to make the burden more manageable at the time of enrollment. To keep education affordable, many colleges and universities have instituted new financing programs in the last several years.

Not every choice is appropriate for—or even available to—every student and family. But the earlier you start, the more choices you'll have, and the more time to investigate the potential benefits and risks.

The dilemma, of course, is that other concerns and expenses may push college savings to the back burner. In particular, you may not feel as though there's much to be saved at the end of the month, once the basic bills have been paid.

Financial planning to meet college costs *isn't* just for wealthy people. It's true that particular financial accounts or products may be appropriate for (or even available only to) families at higher income levels. But financial planning itself isn't a product. It's a *process*, a way of thinking about how to organize whatever resources you do have—including your own time and energy—to meet college costs. In fact, the fewer financial resources you have, the more you need to plan the most effective way of using those you do.

- If you can afford to invest several hundred dollars a month to cover future college costs, *do it*. You'll need every penny of the principal *and* interest when the time comes.
- If you can carve $50 or $75 a month out of your household budget to save toward future college costs, *do it*. You may not be able to finance the whole amount that way, but you'll be able to man-

age a good piece of it. If you cover your fair share, then financial aid may be available to cover the rest.
- If your best effort is only $2 or $5 a week, *do it*. Even a few dollars a week in the jar beside the kitchen sink is important, not just in a financial sense, but as a statement of faith in the future. The important thing is to make it *regularly*.

Evaluating savings and prepayment plans

Should you use one of the many new public and private plans that have recently been developed to help families engage in long-term saving for college costs? The answer will be different for each family, depending on its resources and its goals.

To help families assess the strengths and weaknesses of the different options, the College Board issued a set of guidelines, some of which are cited below.*

1. Is there a minimum contribution required to enter the program? Are incremental additions possible?
2. Is there a maximum annual amount that can be contributed? Will any such maximum restrict the accumulation below a realistic projection of future college costs?
3. Can anyone in the family, or an agent of the family, contribute to the plan? Are there exclusions?
4. Can the proceeds from the plan be transferred to another family member if educational plans change?
5. Are there eligibility restrictions to a particular class of institutions, either within a state or within an institutional sector, such as independent colleges? Are there penalties associated with these restrictions?
6. Is the yield from the plan guaranteed? How is it guaranteed? How is the family protected from investment deficits below college cost levels?
7. Is the plan insured? Can the investment be recovered if the plan sponsor ceases to exist?
8. Does the plan cover all college costs, or just tuition?
9. Are there any residency requirements for eligibility? What happens if the family moves during the plan years?
10. Are there age restrictions or time limits on use? Do proceeds from the plan have to be used within a certain number of years after high school?
11. How many years of study are covered by the proceeds? Undergraduate only? Is graduate study possible? Full time only? Is part-time attendance possible?
12. Are there restrictions as to who might match funds contributed to the plan? Could an employer or state contribute?
13. What are the refund conditions in the event of a student's nonadmission to college, disability, or death?
14. Does the family benefit from any investment surplus over the necessary cost levels, or is that a profit to the sponsor?
15. Will the plan benefits be taxable, either for federal or state taxes? Will any tax accrue to the contributor, plan sponsor, or student?

Finding extra outside help

Will financial aid continue to be available to help families cover the gap between their best efforts and the costs of attendance? Probably, although its form may change over time. Federal funding of student assistance programs has not kept pace with rising costs in recent years, but Congress has consistently resisted proposals to reduce the level of federal support. Many colleges, states, and private organizations actually have increased their support of student aid programs.

There is not very much you can do in advance of your child's senior year in high school about finding financial aid, beyond educating yourself about it (and expressing your continuing support of it to your legislators). The vast majority of federal, state, and institutional programs do not permit you to apply before January 1 of the year in which your child will actually enroll in college.

Private scholarship programs constitute one exception to this general rule. Review the section on private aid sources in Chapter 5. Competition for some of these private awards begins in the junior year of high school, or even earlier. One of the things you *can* do in advance of your child's senior year is check out the terms, conditions, and application procedures of any private aid source for which you think he or she might be eligible.

A closing note

A college education *is* within the reach of every qualified student in the United States. Paying for it is hard—but planning for it makes the paying easier.

---

*The *College Board Review*, spring 1988, No. 147, p.11.

If you do as much as you can for yourself, chances are you will find the extra outside help—the financial aid—you need to take care of the rest.

The other kind of planning you should do is academic. Watch what courses your children are taking in school, and make sure that they're on a college preparatory "track." This can save time and money in the future—the curricular choices that children make, as early as the seventh grade, can either open doors or close them.

The College Scholarship Service wishes you well in your planning, and looks forward to serving you when the time comes to apply for financial aid.

Questions and answers about planning

Q Isn't educational financial planning complicated?

A A little. Certainly some savings and investment programs can be pretty complicated! The more money you have, the more sophisticated are the options that may be open to you, and the more you may want to get professional advice.

The basic principles are simple. Dr. Karl E. Case, a professor of economics at Wellesley College who has done a lot of thinking about how families can prepare themselves to meet future educational expenses, cites three important ideas:

1. if you pay over more years, your payment is lower
2. if you decide to pay early, you will earn some interest on this investment
3. compound interest can yield surprisingly large gains (8% compounded annually doubles your money in nine years).*

Besides, educational financial planning isn't as complicated as figuring out how to pay for college when you *haven't* done any planning at all.

Q I've done some calculations, and I don't think we're going to be able to save our full share between now and the time of enrollment. Can we count on loans being available?

A Review Chapter 4 for some insight into the kinds of financing options available today. You'll note that most of the loan programs aimed at parents (as distinct from many of the student loan programs) require a credit check. So it's important that you not arrive at the point of enrollment with your borrowing capacity already exhausted.

Also, don't assume that installment payment plans are necessarily going to be available at all colleges; state laws may even prohibit them at some public institutions. (Remember that installment plans and budgeting plans typically carry some additional costs, too.)

---

*Case, Karl E. "The Office of Family Finance and Planning" (formerly "The Financial Aid Office") in *Educational Financial Planning: A New Concept for the Financial Aid Office*. Columbus, Ga.: Southern Association of Student Financial Aid Administrators, 1986, page 34.

10. Tables, sample cases, and worksheets

The first table in this chapter provides average college costs for the 1992-93 academic year. These costs are based on information from all colleges that provided data for two consecutive years. Average tuition and fees are weighted by total undergraduate enrollment; room and board charges for resident students are weighted by the percentage of undergraduates living in college housing. Additional out-of-state tuition and fees are the mean charges reported by public institutions; they are not weighted by enrollment. (Private colleges rarely have additional nonresident tuition and fees.)

All other figures are average student expenses in each category. Average costs for books and supplies are weighted by total undergraduate enrollment; transportation and other expenses for resident students are weighted by the percentage of undergraduates living in college housing; and board, transportation, and other expenses for commuters are weighted by the percentage of undergraduates who commute.

This table is followed by sample expense budgets based on these average 1992-93 costs for resident students and commuters at different types of colleges.

By the time that *you* are ready to enroll in college, these costs will almost certainly be higher, but the patterns will probably be similar.

The table on estimated parents' contribution shows estimates used to determine how much parents would be expected to pay based on income and family size according to the 1993-94 Federal Methodology. See Chapter 3 for a discussion of how you can use this in your early financial planning.

Sample cases and worksheets

Meet our three sample students—Carlos, Beth, and Andrea—whose family backgrounds, financial situations, and educational goals have been made up from many of the characteristics of students who are facing the choices of a college education and how to pay for it. Following them through the process of determining financial need and applying for aid may help you develop your own financial plan.

All three begin their planning by estimating on Worksheet 1 their probable expenses at the colleges that interest them. Carlos, Beth, and Andrea come from families with very different financial situations. Before they can tell how much they will be expected to pay toward these educational expenses, they need to evaluate their own circumstances in relation to the costs of attending the particular colleges they're interested in. You will see that Worksheets 2-5 have been completed to help in this process. Worksheet 6 is a record of financial aid they are offered.

You can use Worksheets 1-6 for your personal plan.

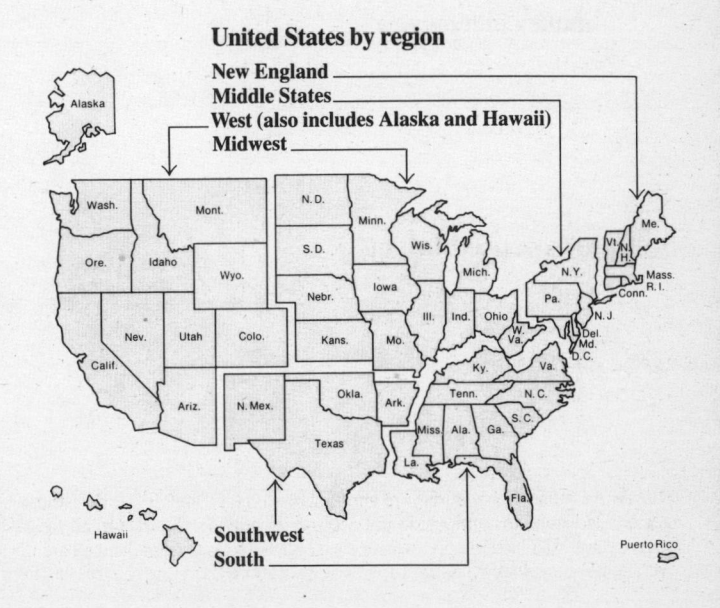

United States by region
New England
Middle States
West (also includes Alaska and Hawaii)
Midwest
Southwest
South

Average student expenses, 1992-93

	Tuition and fees	Add'l out-of-state tuition	Books and supplies	Resident Room and board	Resident Transportation	Resident Other costs	Commuter Board only	Commuter Transportation	Commuter Other costs
National									
2-year public	1,292	2,440	502				1,592	926	970
2-year private	5,621		512	3,750	517	866	1,558	812	941
4-year public	2,315	3,668	528	3,526	497	1,205	1,549	843	1,238
4-year private	10,498		531	4,575	487	936	1,762	794	1,036
New England									
2-year public	1,891	3,053	474				1,931*	—	—
2-year private	8,216		415	5,248	448	622	1,862	793	709
4-year public	3,650	4,492	528	4,102	337	1,101	1,524	1,032	1,076
4-year private	14,095		529	5,592	384	817	1,668	843	958
Middle States									
2-year public	1,915	2,887	526				1,393	912	1,014
2-year private	7,684		503	4,368	1,006	434	1,769	893	957
4-year public	3,129	3,244	546	3,991	1,213	454	1,476	790	1,324
4-year private	11,079		526	5,164	906	373	1,913	712	1,015
South									
2-year public	907	2,168	474				1,636	974	849
2-year private	4,961		461	3,478	919	526	1,684	967	1,188
4-year public	2,027	3,239	516	3,161	996	511	1,601	958	1,057
4-year private	8,996		525	3,915	927	628	1,571	853	975
Midwest									
2-year public	1,400	2,610	502				1,687	963	1,084
2-year private	5,663		599	3,096	734	420	1,333	858	822
4-year public	2,523	3,317	495	3,236	1,315	419	1,424	781	1,268
4-year private	10,075		520	3,818	900	485	1,804	855	1,045
Southwest									
2-year public	701	1,314	487	2,451*	1,045	448*	1,599	965*	994*
2-year private	—		363	2,437*	—	—	—	—	—
4-year public	1,411	3,262	499	3,106	1,144	801	1,432	1,021	1,137
4-year private	7,542		520	3,607	1,113	643	1,594	839	1,055
West									
2-year public		2,826	—				1,599	762	801
2-year private	2,781		—	—	1,094	920	—	—	—
4-year public	1,973	5,213	577	4,215	1,446	574	1,708	739	1,384
4-year private	10,252		595	4,977	1,229	590	1,647	798	1,181

Sample expense budgets

	Resident	Commuter
2-year public		$5,282
2-year private	$11,266	9,444
4-year public	8,071	6,473
4-year private	17,027	14,621

Note on the table: Calculations are enrollment-weighted and utilize only those institutions for which two consecutive years' worth of price and enrollment data are available. Institutions do not necessarily provide cost data in all fields. A dash (—) indicates that the number of institutions reporting data on this item was too small to support an analysis. A blank indicates that the data are not generally applicable for the type of institution. An asterisk (*) following an average indicates that while the number of institutions reporting data on this item was large enough to support an analysis, the sample size was marginal.

1993-94 Estimated parents' contribution

Net assets	$20,000				$40,000			
Family size	3	4	5	6	3	4	5	6
1992 income before taxes								
$12,000	$0	$0	$0	$0	$0	$0	$0	$0
16,000	64	0	0	0	356	0	0	0
20,000	787	0	0	0	1,037	83	0	0
24,000	1,510	422	0	0	1,718	693	129	0
28,000	2,256	1,070	471	0	2,443	1,304	739	103
32,000	3,143	1,719	1,119	443	3,305	1,914	1,350	713
36,000	4,212	2,408	1,768	1,091	4,376	2,587	1,960	1,323
40,000	4,171	3,221	2,463	1,739	4,333	3,380	2,639	1,933
44,000	6,958	4,186	3,285	2,431	7,150	4,349	3,451	2,609
48,000	8,413	5,322	4,269	3,248	8,604	5,514	4,432	3,410
52,000	9,665	6,565	5,421	4,221	9,857	6,757	5,612	4,384
56,000	10,889	7,639	6,574	5,354	11,081	7,831	6,766	5,545
60,000	12,216	8,815	7,750	6,530	12,407	9,007	7,942	6,721
64,000	13,542	9,991	8,926	7,706	13,734	10,183	9,117	7,897
68,000	14,868	11,167	10,102	8,882	15,060	11,358	10,293	9,073
72,000	16,195	12,343	11,278	10,057	16,387	12,534	11,469	10,249

Net assets	$60,000				$80,000			
Family size	3	4	5	6	3	4	5	6
1992 income before taxes								
$12,000	$174	$0	$0	$0	$702	$0	$0	$0
16,000	884	1	0	0	1,412	529	0	0
20,000	1,565	611	47	0	2,096	1,139	575	0
24,000	2,270	1,221	657	20	2,902	1,749	1,185	548
28,000	3,103	1,832	1,267	631	3,874	2,400	1,795	1,159
32,000	4,110	2,493	1,878	1,241	5,058	3,161	2,452	1,769
36,000	5,370	3,269	2,545	1,851	6,498	4,069	3,222	2,422
40,000	5,320	4,199	3,330	2,515	6,448	5,163	4,140	3,187
44,000	8,278	5,338	4,283	3,295	9,406	6,466	5,261	4,099
48,000	9,732	6,642	5,437	4,234	10,860	7,770	6,565	5,204
52,000	10,985	7,885	6,740	5,380	12,113	9,013	7,868	6,508
56,000	12,209	8,959	7,894	6,673	13,337	10,087	9,022	7,801
60,000	13,535	10,135	9,070	7,849	14,663	11,263	10,198	8,977
64,000	14,862	11,311	10,245	9,025	15,990	12,439	11,373	10,153
68,000	16,188	12,486	11,421	10,201	17,316	13,614	12,549	11,329
72,000	17,515	13,662	12,597	11,377	18,643	14,790	13,725	12,505

NOTE: The figures shown are estimated parents' contributions, assuming the older parent (age 45) is employed; the other parent is not employed; income only from employment; IRS form 1040 filed with standard deductions claimed; no unusual circumstances; net assets do *not* include home equity; and one undergraduate family member in college. Values are approximate.

Carlos, Beth, and Andrea plan for college costs

Worksheet 1: Estimating student expenses

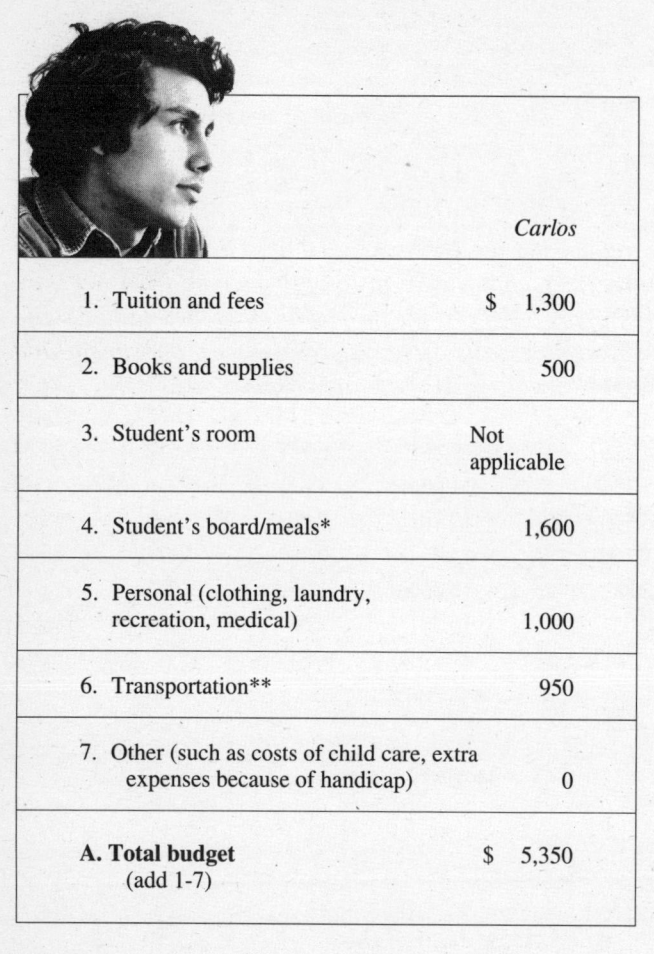

		Carlos
1.	Tuition and fees	$ 1,300
2.	Books and supplies	500
3.	Student's room	Not applicable
4.	Student's board/meals*	1,600
5.	Personal (clothing, laundry, recreation, medical)	1,000
6.	Transportation**	950
7.	Other (such as costs of child care, extra expenses because of handicap)	0
A.	**Total budget** (add 1-7)	$ 5,350

* You will want to consider these expenses to your family if you live at home.

** If you are planning to live on campus, estimate the costs of the round-trips you will have to make to your home. Colleges usually estimate a student makes two or three round-trips during the year. Students living at home should figure the costs of daily tranportation to college.

Carlos Fernandez age 18, graduated from high school in June 1993. He plans to live with his family and attend a nearby community college to pursue an Associate of Arts degree in chemistry. He hopes to transfer to a four-year college of engineering when he completes his AA degree and eventually to become a chemical engineer.

Carlos' father, age 42, earns $19,700 per year as a maintenance worker; his mother, age 41, earns $8,500 as a part-time beautician at a local salon. His younger brother, age 16, is a junior in high school and also hopes to attend college after he finishes high school. The family owns a cooperative apartment and files IRS form 1040. They earn about $50 a year in interest from their savings of $5,320. Carlos earned $2,750 in 1992 working as a grocery clerk after school and full time during the summer. He expects to continue working part time at the grocery store while enrolled in college. He has saved $1,500 toward his college education.

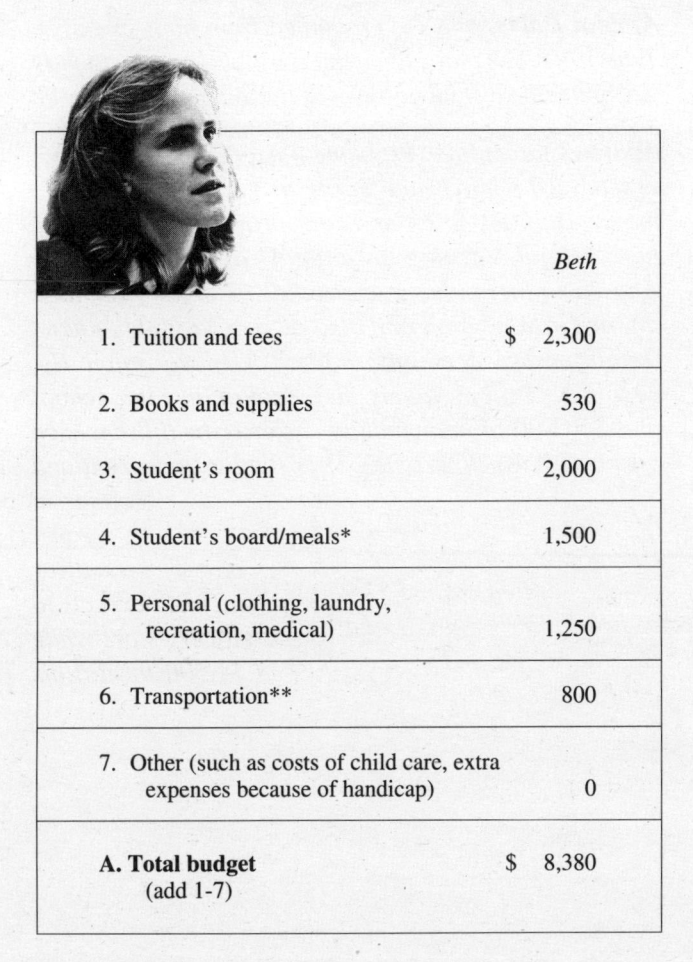

	Beth
1. Tuition and fees	$ 2,300
2. Books and supplies	530
3. Student's room	2,000
4. Student's board/meals*	1,500
5. Personal (clothing, laundry, recreation, medical)	1,250
6. Transportation**	800
7. Other (such as costs of child care, extra expenses because of handicap)	0
A. Total budget (add 1-7)	$ 8,380

* You will want to consider these expenses to your family if you live at home.

** If you are planning to live on campus, estimate the costs of the round-trips you will have to make to your home. Colleges usually estimate a student makes two or three round-trips during the year. Students living at home should figure the costs of daily tranportation to college.

Beth Edwards *is 17 and graduated from high school in June 1993. She hopes to attend the state university to study journalism and plans to live on campus.*

Beth's mother, age 45, does not work outside the home, but is kept busy looking after Beth's 5-year-old twin sisters. Beth's father passed away unexpectedly in December, 1991. The family is now supported by social security benefits of $16,500 (which will be reduced when Beth starts college). Her mother also receives about $950 in interest income from her savings of $30,000, the proceeds of Beth's father's life insurance policy. The family rents an apartment and Beth's mother files IRS form 1040A.

Beth earned $1,500 during the summer of 1992 as a summer camp counselor and spent the school year doing volunteer work. She has been unable to save since she has contributed most of her earnings to her mother for household expenses.

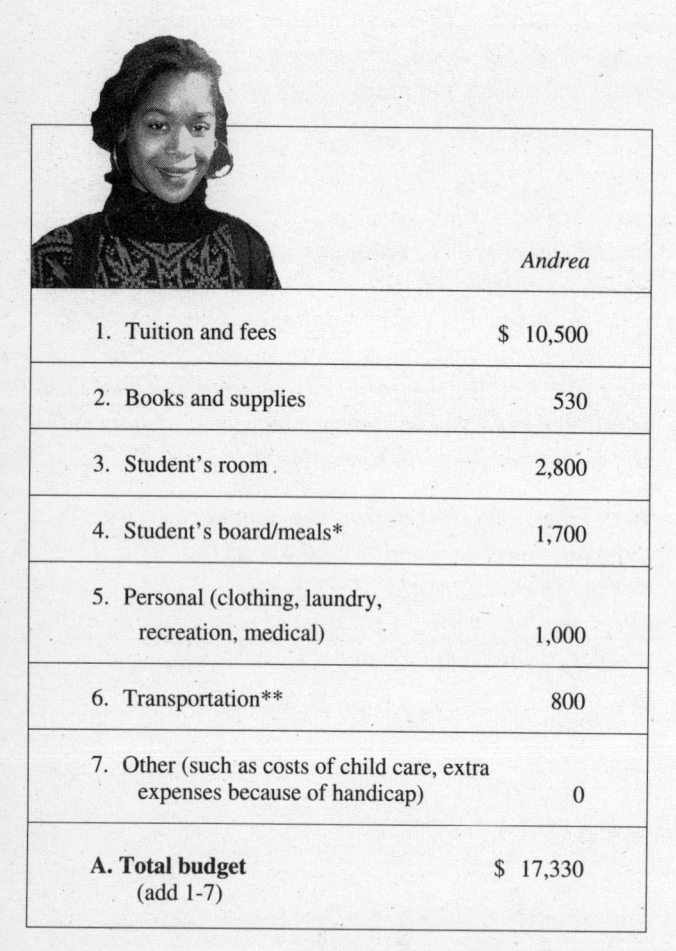

		Andrea
1.	Tuition and fees	$ 10,500
2.	Books and supplies	530
3.	Student's room	2,800
4.	Student's board/meals*	1,700
5.	Personal (clothing, laundry, recreation, medical)	1,000
6.	Transportation**	800
7.	Other (such as costs of child care, extra expenses because of handicap)	0
A.	**Total budget** (add 1-7)	**$ 17,330**

* You will want to consider these expenses to your family if you live at home.

** If you are planning to live on campus, estimate the costs of the round-trips you will have to make to your home. Colleges usually estimate a student makes two or three round-trips during the year. Students living at home should figure the costs of daily tranportation to college.

Andrea Daley, *age 18, graduated from high school in June 1993. She plans to attend a private college to pursue premedical studies. She will live on campus.*

Andrea's father, age 49, is the pastor of the community's Baptist Church and earns $18,000 per year. Her mother, age 50, is an assistant principal at the local high school, earning an annual salary of $46,000. Andrea's parents have additional income of $750 in interest from savings and also receive $1,000 per year from a part-ownership in a family dry-cleaning business. The Daley's assets include $25,000 in savings and $55,000 in home equity. Their part of the family business is worth $62,500. They file IRS form 1040.

Andrea has a sister, age 20, who is a junior in college. Her younger brother, age 14, is a freshman in high school. Andrea earned $1,050 in 1992 as the organist at her father's church and has saved $500. She has also been selected to receive two local scholarships totalling $1,000.

Worksheet 2: Parents' expected contribution (Federal Methodology)

		Carlos	Beth*	Andrea
A.	**1992 income:**			
1.	Father's yearly wages, salaries, tips, and other compensation	$19,700	$ 0	$18,000
2.	Mother's yearly wages, salaries, tips, and other compensation	8,500	0	46,000
3.	All other income of mother and father (dividends, interest, social security, pensions, welfare, child support, etc.) Include IRA/Keogh payments and 401(K) and 403(B) contributions.	50	17,450	1,750
4.	IRS allowable adjustments to income (business expenses, interest penalties, alimony *paid*, etc.) *Do not include IRA/Keogh payments.*	0	0	0
B.	**Total income** (Add 1, 2, 3 and subtract 4.)	28,250	17,450	65,750
Expenses:				
5.	U.S. income tax parents paid on their 1992 income (not amount withheld from paycheck)	$ 1,950	$ 0	$ 8,850
6.	Social Security (FICA) tax (See Table for 6.)	2,157	0	4,896
7.	State and other taxes (Enter 8% of B.)	2,260	1,396	5,260
8.	Employment allowance. If 2-parent family and both parents work, allow 35% of lower salary to a maximum of $2,500; if 1-parent family, allow 35% of salary to a maximum of $2,500. No allowance for a 2-parent family in which only one parent works.	2,500	0	2,500
9.	Income Protection Allowance (See Table for 9)	16,180	16,180	17,290
C.	**Total allowance against income** (Add 5, 6, 7, 8, 9.)	25,047	17,576	38,796
D.	**Available income** (Subtract C from B.)	3,203	(126)	26,954
Assets:				
10.	Other real estate equity (value minus unpaid balance on mortgage)	0		0
11.	Business or farm (Figure total value minus indebtedness and then take percentage shown in Table for 11.) If your family is only part owner of the farm or business, list only your share of the net value.	0		25,000
12.	Cash, savings, and checking accounts	5,320		25,000
13.	Other investments (current net value)	0		0
E.	**Total assets**	5,320		50,000
Deductions:				
F.	Asset protection allowance (See Table for F.)	34,100		44,300
G.	Remaining assets (Subtract F from E.)	(28,780)		5,700
H.	Income supplement from assets (Multiply G by 12%, if negative, enter 0.)	0		684
I.	Adjusted available income (Add D and H.)	3,203	126	27,638
J.	Parents' expected contribution (Multiply I by taxation rate amount given in Table for J.)	705	28	9,200
K.	Parents' expected contribution if more than one family member is in college (Divide J by number of family members in college at least half-time.)	705	28	4,600

*Federal need analysis provisions provide a "simple needs test" treatment for families with total Adjusted Gross Income or earned income of $50,000 or less, who file the 1040A or 1040EZ federal income tax return or do not file taxes. Therefore, if neither Beth nor her parent filed a Form 1040 federal tax return, family assets would not be considered in the "simple needs test," and only available income ($126) shown in line D would be used to compute a $28 expected contribution for line J.

Tables used for completion of Worksheets 2 and 3

Table for Social Security (FICA) Tax Allowance (Items 6 and 19)

When individual's yearly wage total equals	Allowance per wage earner for Social Security (FICA) tax is:
$ 1 to $ 55,500	7.65% of income earned by each wage earner (maximum $4,246 per person)
$ 55,501 or more	$4,246 + 1.45% of income earned above $55,500, up to $130,200, by each wage earner (maximum $5,329 per person)

Table for asset protection allowance (Item F)

Age	Two-parent family	One-parent family
39 or less	$ 30,200	20,500
40–44	34,100	24,700
45–49	38,800	27,600
50–54	44,300	31,100
55–59	51,300	35,200
60–64	60,300	40,300
65 or more	66,800	44,000

Table for income protection allowance (Item 9)

Family size* (including student)	Number in college**				
	1	2	3	4	5
2	$10,520	$ 8,720			
3	13,100	11,310	9,510		
4	16,180	14,380	12,590	10,790	
5	19,090	17,290	15,500	13,700	11,910
6	22,330	20,530	18,740	16,940	15,150

* For each additional family member, add $2,520.
** For each additional college student, subtract $1,790.

Table for parents' expected contribution (Item J)

Adjusted available income (AAI) (Item I)	Total parents' contribution
Less than $ 3,409	$ -750
$ 3,409 to 9,400	22% of AAI
$ 9,401 to 11,800	$ 2,068 + 25% of AAI over $ 9,400
$ 11,801 to 14,200	$ 2,668 + 29% of AAI over $11,800
$ 14,201 to 16,600	$ 3,364 + 34% of AAI over $14,200
$ 16,601 to 19,000	$ 4,180 + 40% of AAI over $16,600
$ 19,001 or more	$ 5,140 + 47% of AAI over $19,000

Table for business or farm adjustments (Item 11)

Net worth (NW)	Adjusted net worth
Less than $ 1	$ 0
$ 1 to 75,000	$ 0 + 40% of NW
$ 75,001 to 225,000	$ 30,000 + 50% of NW over $ 75,000
$225,001 to 375,000	$105,000 + 60% of NW over $225,000
$375,001 or more	$195,000 + 100% of NW over $375,000

Worksheet 3: Student's expected contribution	Carlos	Beth	Andrea
L. Student's 1992 income:			
14. Student's yearly wages, salaries, tips, and other compensation	$ 2,750	$ 1,500	$ 1,050
15. Spouse's yearly wages, salaries, tips, and other compensation	0	0	0
16. All other income of student (dividends, interest, untaxed income, and benefits)	30	0	21
M. Total income (Add 14, 15, and 16.)	2,780	1,500	1,071
Allowances:			
17. U.S. income tax student (and spouse) paid on 1992 income (not amount withheld from paychecks)	0	0	0
18. State and other taxes (enter 4% of M.)	111	60	43
19. Social security (FICA) tax (See Table for 19.)	210	115	80
20. Dependent student offset	1,750	1,750	1,750
N. Total allowances against student's income (Add 17, 18, 19, and 20.)	2,071	1,925	1,873
O. Available income (Subtract N from M.)	709	0	0
Resources:			
21. Contribution from income (Line O x 50%) cannot be less then $0	355	0	0
22. Contribution from assets (Multiply the total savings and other assets—such as stocks and bonds excluding home equity by 35%.)	525	0	175
23. Other gifts and scholarships already received	0	0	0
Q. Total student resources (Add 21, 22 and 23.)	$ 880	$ 0	$ 175

Worksheet 4: Total family contribution	Carlos	Beth	Andrea
J. Parents' expected contribution (Use figure for K instead of J if there is more than one family member in college.)	$ 705	$ 28	$ 4,600
Q. Student's expected contribution from resources	880	0	175
R. Total family contribution (Add J and Q.)	$ 1,585	$ 28	$ 4,775

Worksheet 5: Student need	Carlos	Beth	Andrea
S. Total college expense budget	$ 5,350	$ 8,380	$ 17,330
R. Total family contribution	1,585	28	4,775
T. Student need (Subtract R from S.)	$ 3,765	$ 8,352	$ 12,555

Worksheet 6: Financial aid awards

	Carlos
A. Total student budget	$ 5,350
M. Total family contribution	1,585
N. Demonstrated financial need	3,765
1. Federal Pell Grant	750
2. State scholarship	500
3. Institutional grant	0
4. Federal Work-Study	0
5. Federal Perkins Loan	0
6. Federal Supplemental Educational Opportunity Grant	500
7. Federal Stafford Loan	2,015
8. Private scholarships	0
Total resources for college	$ 5,350

	Beth
A. Total student budget	$ 8,380
M. Total family contribution	28
N. Demonstrated financial need	8,352
1. Federal Pell Grant	2,250
2. State scholarship	1,500
3. Institutional grant	0
4. Federal College Work-Study	977
5. Federal Perkins Loan	0
6. Federal Supplemental Educational Opportunity Grant	1,000
7. Federal Stafford Loan	2,625
8. Private scholarships	0
Total resources for college	$ 8,380

Carlos *received a financial aid award from the community college that fully met his need. He received a Federal Pell Grant and a Federal Supplemental Educational Opportunity Grant along with a state scholarship The combined total of his grants was enough to cover his tuition and books. Since Carlos has an off-campus job at the grocery store, the college did not offer him a campus job, instead recommending that he take out a Federal Stafford Loan to meet his remaining need. Before applying for the loan, Carlos planned to carefully evaluate how much he might need to borrow. He might decide to increase his hours at the grocery store in an effort to mimimize his borrowing.*

The financial aid award offer **Beth** *received met her demonstrated need and included a wide variety of sources. Beth received a Federal Pell Grant from the federal government, a scholarship from her state student assistance agency, and—because her family income is quite low—a Federal Supplemental Educational Opportunity Grant. In addition, like almost all financial aid recipients, Beth will be expected to assume some "self-help" aid. In her case, she borrowed a Federal Stafford Loan, which she will repay after she graduates or leaves college, and she accepted the offer of a campus job through the Federal Work-Study Program.*

	Andrea	
	Federal Methodology	*Institutional Methodology*
A. Total student budget	$ 17,330	$ 17,330
M. Total family contribution	4,775	8,298
N. Demonstrated financial need	12,555	9,032
1. Federal Pell Grant	0	0
2. State scholarship	0	0
3. Institutional grant	3,500	3,500
4. Federal Work-Study	900	900
5. Federal Perkins Loan	1,000	1,000
6. Federal SEOG	0	0
7. Federal Stafford Loan	2,625	2,625
8. Private scholarships	1,000	1,000
Total resources for college	$ 13,800	17,323

*included in M (above).

*Even though **Andrea's** family has the greatest resources of the three students, she also has the greatest need because the college she wanted to attend has the highest costs. The financial aid award Andrea received included awards from three federal programs, a scholarship from the college's own scholarship fund, as well as two local scholarships from her hometown. The federal funds Andrea received included a campus job through the Federal Work-Study program, and two loans including a Federal Perkins Loan and a Federal Stafford Loan. Because Andrea's parents' income was higher than average, she was not eligible for the Federal Pell Grant or a state scholarship, and the college was unable to offer her a Federal Supplemental Educational Opportunity Grant.*

All colleges awarding federal financial aid funds must determine need by using a mandatory Federal Methodology. Although this methodology establishes eligibility for federal funds, most colleges, particularly higher cost schools, do not have enough federal funds to meet their students full federally determined need. Many colleges that award substantial amounts of their own funds use a need analysis methodology that differs from the Federal Methodology. Colleges using an institutional methodology to award institutional funds do so because they feel that it is a better means of assessing a family's true ability to pay for college costs. In Andrea's case, her eligibility for a scholarship from the college was based on an institutional methodology, which unlike the Federal Methodology, took into account her parents' home equity and depreciation-based business losses. Under the institutional methodology, her parents' contribution to costs is higher and the college also assumes that Andrea will make a minimum contribution of $900 from her summer savings.

Based on the college's own assessment of Andrea's need, Andrea received a scholarship from the college, which in addition to her awards from the federal programs and her local scholarships, met her institutionally determined need in full. Because Andrea's college uses an institutional methodology in awarding its own scholarship funds, two breakdowns of need are shown above.

Your personal plan

Now that you've followed Carlos, Beth, and Andrea through the financial aid application process, complete your own need analysis estimate. You can begin to make your own plans by filling in Worksheet 1 for the colleges you are considering. You can use the college cost information in Part II of this book, but *remember* that these costs are for the 1993-94 academic year. If you will be starting college in September 1994 you should make a somewhat higher estimate. (Some colleges will have a greater increase, others a smaller one.) When you are actually applying for aid, the college catalog or financial aid bulletins for the colleges to which you are applying are the most authoritative sources of information about costs that will apply to you.

You can begin to get a sense of your need at these colleges by completing your own Worksheets 2-5. These will take you through the steps of estimating parents' expected contribution (Worksheet 2 and table of parents' contribution), estimating your own contribution (Worksheet 3), combining the total family contribution (Worksheet 4), and finding the difference between the contribution and the costs at each of the colleges you are considering (Worksheet 5)—that is, your financial need.

Worksheet 1: Estimating student expenses	College A	College B	College C
1. Tuition and fees	$	$	$
2. Books and supplies			
3. Student's room			
4. Student's board/meals*			
5. Personal (clothing, laundry, recreation, medical)			
6. Transportation**			
7. Other (such as costs of child care, extra expenses because of handicap)			
A. Total budget (Add 1–7.)	$	$	$

*You will want to consider these expenses to your family if you live at home.

**If you are planning to live on campus, estimate the costs of the round-trips you will have to make to your home. Colleges ususally estimate a student makes two or three round-trips during the year. Students living at home should figure the costs of daily transportation to college.

See Worksheet 2 for Carlos, Beth and Andrea, and use the tables following their worksheet to help you estimate parents' expected contribution.

Worksheet 2: Parents' expected contribution (Federal Methodology)	
A. 1992 income:	
1. Father's yearly wages, salaries, tips, and other compensation	$
2. Mother's yearly wages, salaries, tips, and other compensation	
3. All other income of mother and father (dividends, interest, social security, pensions, welfare, child support, etc.) *Include IRA/Keogh payments and 401(K) and 403(B) contributions.*	
4. IRS allowable adjustments to income (business expenses, interest penalties, alimony *paid*, etc.) *Do not include IRA/Keogh payments.*	
B. Total income (Add 1, 2, 3 and subtract 4.)	
Expenses:	
5. U.S. income tax parents paid on their 1992 income (not amount withheld from paycheck)	$
6. Social Security (FICA) tax (See Table for 6.)	
7. State and other taxes (Enter 8% of B.)	
8. Employment allowance. If 2-parent family and both parents work, allow 35% of lower salary to a maximum of $2,500; if 1-parent family, allow 35% of salary to a maximum of $2,500. No allowance for a 2-parent family in which only one parent works.	
9. Income Protection Allowance (See Table for 9.)	
C. Total allowance against income (Add 5, 6, 7, 8, 9.)	
D. Available income (Subtract C from B.)	
Assets:	
10. Other real estate equity (value minus unpaid balance on mortgage)	
11. Business or farm (Figure total value minus indebtedness and then take percentage shown in Table for 11.) If your family is only part owner of the farm or business, list only your share of the net value.	
12. Cash, savings, and checking accounts	
13. Other investments (current net value)	
E. Total assets	
Deductions:	
F. Asset protection allowance (See Table for F.)	
G. Remaining assets (Subtract F from E.)	
H. Income supplement from assets (Multiply G by 12%, if negative, enter 0.)	
I. Adjusted available income (Add D and H.)	
J. Parents' expected contribution (Multiply I by taxation rate amount given in Table for J.)	
K. Parents' expected contribution if more than one family member is in college (Divide J by number of family members in college at least half-time.)	

*Federal need analysis provisions provide a "simple needs test" treatment for families with total Adjusted Gross Income or earned income of $50,000 or less, who file the 1040A or 1040EZ federal income tax return or do not file taxes. Therefore, if neither Beth nor her parent filed a Form 1040 federal tax return, family assets would not be considered in the "simple needs test," and only available income ($126) shown in line D would be used to compute a $28 expected contribution for line J.

Student's expected contribution

Students, too, are expected to contribute toward college costs when they are employed and or have accumulated assets. Worksheet 3 will allow you to estimate what your contribution will be for your first year in college based on the Federal Methodology. It is important to note, however, that many colleges will expect a minimum contribution, such as $900 for a freshman and $1,100 for an upperclassman, when consideration is given for nonfederal funds.

Worksheet 3: Student's expected contribution	
L. Student's 1992 income:	
14. Student's yearly wages, salaries, tips, and other compensation	$
15. Spouse's yearly wages, salaries, tips, and other compensation	
16. All other income of student (dividends, interest, untaxed income, and benefits)	
M. Total income (Add 14, 15, and 16.)	
Allowances:	
17. U.S. income tax student (and spouse) paid on 1992 income (not amount withheld from paychecks)	
18. State and other taxes (enter 4% of M.)	
19. Social security (FICA) tax (See Table for 19.)	
20. Dependent student offset	
N. Total allowances against student's income (Add 17, 18, 19 and 20.)	
O. Available income (Subtract N from M.)	
Resources:	
21. Contribution from income (Line O x 50%. Cannot be less than 0.	
22. Contribution from assets (Multiply the total savings and other assets, such as stocks and bonds, excluding home equity, by 35%.)	
23. Other gifts and scholarships already received	
Q. Total student resources (Add lines 21, 22, and 23.)	$

Total family contribution

Use *Worksheet 4: Total Family Contribution* to transfer figures from Worksheet 2 (line J, or line K if there will be more than one family member in college) and from Worksheet 3 (line Q). By adding together these two figures, you can determine your total estimated family contribution.

Worksheet 4: Total family contribution	
J. Parents' expected contribution (Use figure for K instead of J if there is more than one family member in college.)	$
Q. Student's expected contribution from resources	
R. Total family contribution (Add J and Q.)	$

Estimated financial need

Are you potentially eligible for financial aid? Use *Worksheet 5: Student Need* to compare your family contribution with the cost of going to college. Record the student expense budgets at the colleges that interest you. Enter your total family contribution (from line R in Worksheet 4) and subtract it from each of the student expense budgets. If your family contribution is less than the student expense budget, you have demonstrated financial need and may be eligible for financial aid equal to this estimate of your need.

It is important to remember that the figure you arrive at in line T is only an estimate, and you should consider this figure to be only a rough approximation of your eligibility for financial aid. It is also important to remember that this estimate of need is based on a need analysis methodology for *federal* financial aid programs. Colleges that award significant amounts of nonfederal funds may use a different methodology, as demonstrated in Andrea's case.

Your eligibility for financial aid, and the amount and type of aid you receive, will be determined by the financial aid administrator at each college. Many colleges lack sufficient funds to meet the need of all needy students, regardless of the methodology used. So it is most important that you apply for financial aid as early as possible and meet all deadlines. The only way you can find out how much you might receive is to apply for financial aid!

Worksheet 5: Student need	*College A*	*College B*	*College C*
S. Total college expense budget	$	$	$
R. Total family contribution			
T. Student need (Subtract R from S.)	$	$	$

Worksheet 6:
Financial aid awards

	College A	College B	College C
A. Total student budget	$	$	$
M. Total family contribution			
N. Demonstrated financial need			
1. Federal Pell Grant			
2. State scholarship			
3. Institutional grant			
4. Federal Work-Study			
5. Federal Perkins Loan			
6. Federal Supplemental Educational Opportunity Grant			
7. Federal Stafford Loan			
8. Private scholarships			
Total resources for college	$	$	$

Glossary

The definitions given here of terms commonly used by colleges to describe their programs, admissions procedures, and financial aid policies are necessarily general. Students should consult the catalogs of specific colleges and financial aid programs to get more detailed and up-to-date descriptions of their programs and procedures.

Accelerated program. A college program of study completed in less time than is usually required, most often by attending in summer or by carrying extra courses during the regular academic terms. Completion of a bachelor's degree program in three years is an example of acceleration.

ACT. *See* American College Testing Program Assessment.

Advanced placement. Admission or assignment of a freshman to an advanced course in a certain subject on the basis of evidence that the student has already completed the equivalent of the college's freshman course in that subject. In some cases, the college also grants academic credit for the college-level work that has been completed.

Advanced Placement (AP) Program. A service of the College Board that provides high schools with course descriptions in college subjects and Advanced Placement Examinations in those subjects. High schools administer the examinations to qualified students, who are then eligible at many colleges for advanced placement, college credit, or both on the basis of satisfactory grades.

American College Testing Program. Sponsor of the ACT, a test battery given in test centers in the United States and other countries on specified dates throughout the year, that includes tests in English, mathematics, reading, and science reasoning. Also, a federally approved Multiple Data Entry (MDE) contractor, one of several organizations authorized to process the Free Application for Federal Student Aid (FAFSA).

Bachelor's degree. The degree given for completing undergraduate college programs that normally take four years. Also called the baccalaureate degree.

Campus-based programs. The three federally funded student financial aid programs that are directly administered by colleges. Federal Supplemental Educational Opportunity Grant Program, Federal Perkins Loan Program, and Federal Work-Study Program.

Candidates Reply Date Agreement (CRDA). A college subscribing to this agreement will not require any applicants offered admission as freshmen to notify the college of their decision to attend (or to accept an offer of financial aid) before May 1. The purpose of the agreement is to give applicants time to hear from all the colleges to which they have applied before they have to make a commitment to any one of them.

Certificate. An award for completing a particular program or course of study, sometimes given by two-year colleges or vocational or technical schools.

College-Level Examination Program (CLEP). A service of the College Board that provides examinations in undergraduate college courses so that students and other adults may demonstrate achievement at the first- and second-year college levels. The examinations are used by colleges to award credit by examination to adult applicants who have not attended college (or have not done so recently), students transferring from other colleges, and entering freshmen. They are also used by business, industries, government agencies, and professional groups to satisfy education requirements for advancement, licensing, admission to further training, and other purposes.

College Scholarship Service. A service of the College Board that assists postsecondary institutions, state scholarship programs, and other organizations in the equitable distribution of student financial aid funds by measuring a family's ability to contribute to college costs. CSS sponsors the Financial Aid Form (FAF), a need analysis form required by many colleges in awarding nonfederal funds. CSS is also a federally approved Multiple Data Entry (MDE) contractor, one of several organizations authorized to process the Free Application for Federal Student Aid (FAFSA). CSS additionally offers services in education financing through the CollegeCredit Program.

College Work-Study Program. *See* Federal Work-Study Program.

Consumer Price Index (CPI). A measure of inflation or deflation at the consumer level, updated monthly by the U.S. Bureau of Labor Statistics. The index is determined by comparing the current price of a "market basket" of goods to the price at which the same "basket" could have been purchased during a given base year. The goods include food, shelter, clothing, transportation, and other items.

Cooperative education. A college program in which a student alternates between periods of full-time study and full-time employment in related work. Students are paid for their work at the prevailing rate. Typically, five years are required to complete a bachelor's degree program, but graduates have the advantage of having completed about a year's practical experience in addition to their studies. Some colleges refer to this sort of program as work-study, but it should not be confused with the federally sponsored Federal Work-Study Program.

CRDA. *See* Candidates Reply Date Agreement.

Credit by examination. Academic credit granted by a college for a student's having demonstrated proficiency in a subject as measured by an examination.

CSS. *See* College Scholarship Service.

Dependent student. A student dependent on his or her parents for financial support. A student's dependency status is determined by guidelines established by the federal government.

Early decision. Early decision admission plans are offered for applicants who are sure of the college they want to attend and are likely to be accepted by the college. An early decision admission application is initiated by the student, who is then notified of the college's decision earlier than usual—generally by December 15 of the senior year.

Early Decision Plan (EDP-F, EDP-S). Colleges that subscribe to this plan agree to follow a common schedule for early decision applicants. Colleges may offer either of two plans. A student applying under the first-choice plan (EDP-F) must withdraw applications from all other colleges as soon as he or she is notified of acceptance by the first-choice college. A student applying under the single-choice plan (EDP-S) may not apply to any colleges other than his or her first choice unless rejected by that institution. If a college follows either type of plan, applications (including those for financial aid) must be received by a specified date no later than November 15, and the college agrees to notify the applicant by a specified date no later than December 15.

FAF. *See* Financial Aid Form.

FAFSA. *See* Free Application for Federal Student Aid.

Family contribution. The total amount a student and his or her family are expected to pay toward college costs from their income and assets. The amount is derived from a need analysis of the family's overall financial circumstances. A Federal Methodology is used in determining a student's eligibility for federal student aid. Colleges, state agencies, and private aid programs may use a different methodology in determining eligibility for nonfederal sources of financial aid.

Federal Parent Loan for Undergraduate Students. Federal PLUS loan program permits parents of undergraduate students to borrow up to the full cost of education less any other financial aid the student may have received. The interest rate is variable, set at 3.1 percent above the one year Treasury-bill, capped at 10 percent. The current rate at press time was 6.64 percent; however, the rate is adjusted annually each July 1. (At press time, the U.S. Congress was considering changes to the loan limits in the Federal PLUS Program.)

Federal Pell Grant Program. The largest need-based student aid program. Congress annually sets the dollar range. The amount received depends on need, college costs, the length of the program of study, and whether enrollment is full- or part-time. Students apply using the Free Application for Federal Student Aid (FAFSA).

Federal Perkins Loan Program. A federally funded program that provides loans of up to $3,000 per year during the undergraduate years and up to $15,000 for the total undergraduate program. Repayment need not begin until the student graduates or leaves school; service in the military, Peace Corps, VISTA, or comparable organization may carry other special provisions for deferment or cancellation. Repayment terms are favorable, and repayment may be partially or wholly waived for certain kinds of employment.

Federal Stafford Student Loan Program. A federal program that allows students to borrow to meet educational expenses. Funds are borrowed directly from banks or other lending institutions, or, for colleges participating in the Federal Direct Loan Program, from the U.S. Government.

The federal government pays the full interest on loans while students are enrolled in college if the loan is made on the basis of demonstrated need. For students who have not demonstrated need, unsubsidized Federal Stafford Loans are available. For unsubsidized loans, students will usually be asked to make interest payments while enrolled in school. Following a grace period, all students borrowing in the Federal Stafford Loan Program must begin repaying principal and interest after graduating or leaving school.

Federal Stafford Loans have a variable interest rate set at 3.1 percent above the federal 91-day Treasury-bill. The current rate at press time was 6.22 percent; however, the rate is adjusted annually on July 1.

The amounts that may be borrowed depend on the student's year in school. The undergraduate loan limits are as follows: first year, $2,625; second year, $3,500; third and fourth years, $5,500; to a total amount as an undergraduate of $23,000. Graduate students may borrow $8,500 per year to an aggregate limit, including undergraduate borrowing, of $65,000. Loan limits are the same for borrowers of unsubsidized Federal Stafford Loans, or borrowers of combination subsidized/unsubsidized loans.

Federal Supplemental Educational Opportunity Grant Program. A federal program administered by colleges to provide need-based aid to undergraduate students. Grants of up to $4,000 a year may be awarded.

Federal Supplemental Loan for Students. Self-supporting undergraduate students and graduate students are eligible to apply for these loans in addition to the Federal Stafford Loan. Effective July 1, 1993, loan limits in the Federal SLS program are $4,000 per year for the first two years of undergraduate study, $5,000 per year for the third and fourth year of undergraduate study, and $10,000 per year for graduate study. Aggregate borrowing is limited to $23,000 for undergraduate study and $73,000 for undergraduate and graduate study combined.

Federal Work-Study Program. A federally sponsored campus-based program. Participating colleges provide employment opportunities for students with demonstrated need who are enrolled for study at either the undergraduate or graduate level. Students are usually employed on campus, although occasionally jobs are arranged off campus. In assigning work-study to aid recipients, financial aid administrators typically take into account the recipient's employable skills, class schedule, and academic progress.

Financial aid award letter. A notice from a college or other financial aid sponsor that tells a student how much aid is being offered. The award letter also usually explains how a student's financial need was determined, describes the contents of the financial aid package, and outlines any conditions attached to the award.

Financial Aid Form (FAF). A need analysis form processed by the College Scholarship Service. (*See also* Need analysis form.)

Financial aid package. The total financial aid award received by a student. It may be made up of a combination or "package" of aid that includes both gift aid and self-help. Many colleges try to meet a student's full financial need, but availability of funds, institutional aid policies, and the number of students needing assistance all influence the composition of a financial aid package.

Financial need. The amount by which a student's family contribution falls short of covering the student expense budget. Assessments of need may differ depending on the need analysis methodology used. (See Family contribution.)

Free Application for Federal Student Aid (FAFSA). A form distributed by the federal government for use by students applying for Federal Pell Grants and other federal financial aid programs. All students applying for federal financial aid must file the FAFSA.

Gift aid. Student financial aid, such as scholarships and grants, that does not have to be repaid and that does not require a student's being employed.

Independent student. *See* Self-supporting student.

Multiple Data Entry (MDE). This refers to three organizations approved to process the Free Application for Federal Student Aid (FAFSA): American College Testing, College Scholarship Service, and the Pennsylvania Higher Education Assistance Authority.

Need analysis. The method for determining how much a family can reasonably be expected to pay toward a student's college education costs. Need analysis is based on the assumption that parents and students have the major responsibility for paying college costs to the extent they are able. Formulas used in need analysis are updated annually to reflect changes in the economy and are approved by the federal government and most colleges and other organizations that award financial aid.

Need analysis form. The starting point in applying for financial aid. All students must file the federally sponsored Free Application for Federal Student Aid (FAFSA) to apply for the federal financial aid programs. For many colleges, this may be the only need analysis form you will need to file. For other schools, particularly private colleges, the Financial Aid Form (FAF) may also be required. To apply for state financial aid programs, the FAFSA may be all that you will need to file, but you should check with your state agency to learn if any other application forms need to be submitted.

The forms that will be most commonly required are the following:

- Free Application for Federal Student Aid (FAFSA) of the U.S. Department of Education
- Financial Aid Form (FAF) of the College Scholarship Service
- PHEAA Aid Information Request (PAIR) of the Pennsylvania Higher Education Assistance Authority (Pennsylvania applicants only)

Open admissions. The college admissions policy of admitting high school graduates and other adults generally without regard to conventional academic qualifications, such as high school subjects, high school grades, and admissions test scores. Virtually all applicants with high school diplomas or their equivalent are accepted.

Parents' contribution. The amount a student's parents are expected to pay toward college costs from their income and assets. The amount is derived from need analysis of the parents' overall financial situation. The parents' contribution and the student's contribution together constitute the total family contribution, which, when subtracted from the student expense budget, equals financial need. Generally, students are eligible for financial aid equal to their financial need.

Pell Grant Program. *See* Federal Pell Grant Program.

Perkins Loan Program. *See* Federal Perkins Loan Program.

PHEAA Aid Information Request (PAIR). Need analysis form sponsored by the Pennsylvania Higher Education Assistance Authority (PHEAA) for use in applying for assistance from the State of Pennsylvania. The PAIR form is required by most colleges in Pennsylvania. PHEAA is also a federally approved Multiple Data Entry (MDE) contractor, one of several organizations authorized to process the Free Application for Federal Student Aid (FAFSA).

Parent Loan for Undergraduate Students (PLUS). *See* Federal Parent Loan for Undergraduate Students.

Preliminary SAT/National Merit Scholarship Qualifying Test (PSAT/NMSQT). A shorter version of the College Board's SAT administered by high schools each year in October. The PSAT/NMSQT aids high schools in the early guidance of students planning for college and serves as the qualifying test for scholarships awarded by the National Merit Scholarship Corporation.

Reserve Officers' Training Corps (ROTC). Reserve Officers' Training Corps programs conducted by certain colleges in cooperation with the U.S. Air Force, Army, and Navy. Local recruiting offices of the services themselves can supply detailed information about these programs. Information is also available from participating colleges.

SAR. *See* Student Aid Report.

SAT. The College Board's test of verbal and mathematical reasoning abilities, given on specified dates throughout the year at test centers in the United States and other countries. Required of substantially all applicants by many colleges and sponsors of financial aid programs. In March 1994, the new SAT I: Reasoning Test will replace the SAT.

Self-help. Student financial aid, such as loans and

jobs, that require repayment or a student's being employed.

Self-supporting student. For financial aid purposes, a student who is independent of support from his or her parents.

Stafford Loan Program. *See* Federal Stafford Student Loan Program.

Student Aid Report (SAR). A report produced by the U.S. Department of Education and sent to students who have applied for federal student financial aid. The SAR must be submitted to the college that the student attends to certify his or her eligibility for Federal Pell Grants and other federal financial programs such as the Federal Work-Study Program, Federal Perkins Loan Program, Federal Supplemental Educational Opportunity Grants, and the Federal Family Education Loan Programs.

Student expense budget. The annual cost of attending college that is used in determining a student's financial need. Student expense budgets usually include tuition and fees, books and supplies, room and board, personal expenses, and transportation. Sometimes additional expenses are included for students with special education needs, students who have a disability, or students who are married or have children.

Student's contribution. The amount students are expected to pay toward college costs from their income, assets, and benefits. The amount is derived from need analysis of the student's resources. The student's contribution and parents' contribution constitute the total family contribution, which, when subtracted from the student budget, equals financial need. Generally, students are eligible for financial aid equal to their financial need.

Supplemental Educational Opportunity Grant Program. *See* Federal Supplemental Educational Opportunity Grant Program.

Supplemental Loan for Students. *See* Federal Supplemental Loan for Students.

Tuition and fee waivers. Some colleges waive the tuition or tuition and fees for some categories of students, such as adults, senior citizens, or children of alumni. Colleges with such plans are listed in a separate section in this book.

Part II. College costs and financial aid

Table of college information

Introduction

This section provides detailed lists of expenses and financial aid at 2,900 colleges, universities, and proprietary schools. The data were compiled from information supplied by the institutions themselves on the College Board's Annual Survey of Colleges, 1993-94. The lists are alphabetical by state, and include the information provided by all participating institutions through the end of May 1993. Every effort is made to insure that the data are as complete and accurate as possible. However, students are urged to contact institutions directly to confirm the information.

Institutions were asked to give expense figures for the academic year beginning fall 1993. If the 1993-94 tuition and fees were not yet set but a reliable forecast was available, the estimated tuition and fees are given with a single dagger next to them. If these figures were not yet available, the 1992-93 tuition and fees are listed with a double dagger next to them.

Details on each category of expenses and financial aid and what these figures can mean to applicants are explained here.

In an effort to collect comparable cost information, the College Board asked institutions to provide data for specifically budgeted items. The figures supplied under each column heading represent the following.

Educational costs

Tuition and fees

This figure indicates the annual tuition and general fees an institution charges most first-year, full-time students. Colleges were asked to report these costs based on a nine-month academic year of 30 semester hours or 45 quarter hours.

Additional out-of-state/district tuition

This item represents only the *additional* charges made to students who do not meet state or district residency requirements. The figure to the left of the diagonal mark shows additional charges for out-of-state students; the figure to the right shows additional out-of-district charges. These charges added to the tuition and fees in the first column will give you the total tuition and fees for out-of-state and out-of-district students, respectively.

Books and supplies

This figure is the average cost of books and supplies for the normal course load for full-time students. Supplies may be more expensive for students in certain areas of study (art, architecture, or engineering, for example) and institutions did not include these special costs unless the majority of their students are in these fields.

Living costs: Campus residents

Room and board for campus residents

For resident students, room and board includes the charge for living and eating for nine months in facilities operated by or for the college. These are average charges based on double-room occupancy and 21 meals a week in college facilities.

Transportation for campus residents

These figures include typical costs for two round-trips between home and campus during the nine-month academic year. If you anticipate more frequent trips between home and campus during the academic year, you should adjust this figure accordingly.

Other costs for campus residents

This column shows typical costs for miscellaneous

personal expenses, such as clothing, laundry, entertainment, snacks, medical insurance, and furnishings.

Living cost: Students living at home

Board for students at home
This column shows average costs for dependent students living at home, including three meals a day, seven days a week.

Transportation for students at home
The figures in this column represent the typical costs for daily travel to and from college for students who commute.

Other costs for students at home
This column shows miscellaneous personal expenses for students living at home. These include clothing, laundry, entertainment, and medical insurance.

Financial aid information

Total freshmen enrolled
This is the total freshman enrollment for fall 1992 on which the percentage of freshman students receiving aid is based.

Percentage receiving aid
This figure represents the percentage of enrolled freshmen (preceding column) who received some form of financial aid in fall 1992. The aid could be based on financial need or on other criteria such as talent or athletic ability. The financial aid could be in the form of grants, scholarships, loans, or jobs.

Freshmen judged to have financial need
This column shows the number of freshmen in fall 1991 who were judged to have financial need.

Percent offered aid
This figure is the percentage of freshmen with financial need (preceding column) who were offered aid. The financial aid could be grants, loans, or jobs.

Grants and scholarships

Need-based scholarships
An X in these columns indicates that the college awards scholarships on the basis of financial need combined with exceptional academic ability or talent in music or drama, art, or athletics.

Non-need scholarships
An X in these columns indicates that the college awards scholarships, without regard for financial need, on the basis of exceptional academic ability or talent in music or drama, art, or athletics.

Financial aid deadlines

Priority deadline for financial aid
The priority deadline is the date by which the college prefers you submit your financial aid application. Missing this deadline may mean that most or all financial aid may have already been awarded, but it does not necessarily mean that *all* aid has been given. It is best to meet the college's priority deadline in order to have the best chance of receiving aid if you qualify.

Closing deadline for financial aid
This is the final date by which the college will accept your application for financial aid.

Institutional aid form
An X in this column indicates that the college has its own financial aid form that you will have to complete if you are applying for aid. This requirement is in addition to the FAFSA or any other financial aid form the college might require. Be sure to verify with the college what it requires. (See "Need analysis form" in the Glossary for more information.)

Notes
Use this column to make notes about the colleges that interest you.

Part II. College costs and financial aid

	Tuition and fees	Add'l out-of-state/ district tuition	Books and supplies	Costs for campus residents			Costs for students at home		
Institution				Room and board	Trans-portation	Other costs	Board only	Trans-portation	Other costs
Alabama									
Alabama Agricultural and Mechanical University	1,550	1,600/—	500	2,675	990	835	1,442	990	835
Alabama Aviation and Technical College	‡ 855	608/—	1,625		1,000	1,300	2,700	1,000	1,000
Alabama Southern Community College	‡ 1,035	608/—	600				1,100	300	400
Alabama State University	‡ 1,608	1,500/—	600	2,110	900	1,500	1,500	1,500	1,500
Athens State College	† 1,590	1,440/—	450		564	971	1,783	989	1,021
Auburn University									
Auburn	1,950	3,900/—	600	3,873	633	1,275	1,590	633	1,275
Montgomery	1,800	3,600/—	600		900	1,260	1,650	1,650	1,260
Bessemer State Technical College	† 858	608/—	618				1,500	900	800
Bevill State Community College	‡ 936	668/—	450				1,200	1,150	800
Birmingham-Southern College	‡ 10,306		400	4,090	500	900	1,500	1,500	900
Bishop State Community College	‡ 1,026	668/—	400				1,500	610	738
Central Alabama Community College									
Alexander City Campus	‡ 1,116	668/—	300				1,800	600	500
Childersburg Campus	‡ 1,116	668/—	450					150	675
Chattahoochee Valley Community College	‡ 1,135	668/—	500				1,900	600	500
Community College of the Air Force	‡ 0								
Concordia College	4,186		550	2,600	1,700	3,375	1,800	800	2,925
Douglas MacArthur State Technical College	‡ 855	608/—	400				1,800	800	668
Draughons Junior College	‡ 4,525		400						
Enterprise State Junior College	‡ 1,035	675/—	345				1,900	650	550
Faulkner University	5,250		600	3,050	650	1,000	800	704	840
Gadsden State Community College	† 1,125	743/—	525	2,025	150	525	1,500	785	525
George C. Wallace State Community College									
Dothan	‡ 1,125	743/—	300				2,000	700	300
Selma	† 1,035	608/—	600		568	962	1,500	568	962
Harry M. Ayers State Technical College	‡ 903	576/—	400				2,400	1,200	
Huntingdon College	7,640		500	3,760	500	600		300	400
International Bible College	3,370		400		350	1,500	1,500	900	1,500
J. F. Drake State Technical College	‡ 900	608/—	500					550	
Jacksonville State University	† 1,680	1,680/—	600	2,600	900	1,200	1,400	1,500	1,200
James H. Faulkner State Community College	† 1,125	743/—	450	2,025	550	800	1,500	950	700
Jefferson Davis State Junior College	‡ 900	608/—	525				1,500	300	600
Jefferson State Community College	‡ 1,215	743/—	450				2,199	750	525
John C. Calhoun State Community College	‡ 1,035	608/—	500				1,900	700	774
John M. Patterson State Technical College	‡ 1,125	743/—	400				1,500	300	200
Judson College	† 5,450		650	3,275	376	1,520		650	1,896
Lawson State Community College	1,134	1,557/720	400				1,550	725	700
Livingston University	† 1,827		570	2,340	900	1,200	1,500	1,500	1,200
Lurleen B. Wallace State Junior College	† 1,145	742/—	375				1,800	600	600
Marion Military Institute	5,926		644	3,790	625	1,822		400	1,253
Miles College	4,150		400	2,400	500	1,000		500	800
Northeast Alabama Community College	† 909	547/—	400				1,000	750	1,500
Northwest Alabama Community College	‡ 1,035	608/—	400				2,700		
Oakwood College	‡ 6,216		600	3,663	1,845	1,500		400	615
Phillips Junior College: Birmingham	10,425		325				1,962	421	
Reid State Technical College	990	675/—	400						

†Figures are projected for 1993-94. ‡Figures are for 1992-93.

Alabama: Reid State Technical College

All aid		Need-based aid		Grants and scholarships								Financial aid deadlines		Inst aid form	Notes
Total freshmen	Percent receiving aid	Freshmen judged to have need	Percent offered aid	Need-based				Non-need-based							
				Acad	Music/drama	Art	Athl	Acad	Music/drama	Art	Athl	Priority	Closing		
992	88	872	100	X				X	X		X	4/1	6/1	X	
								X					none	X	
				X	X	X	X	X	X	X	X	7/15	none	X	
1,512	90							X	X	X	X	4/1	none	X	
							X	X	X	X	X	6/1	none		
3,129	55	1,389	100	X				X	X	X	X	4/15	none	X	
833	40							X	X		X	4/15	none	X	
420	65	500	96	X				X				9/1	none		
681	43							X	X		X	8/1	none		
321	83	130	100	X	X	X	X	X	X	X	X	3/31	none	X	
1,960	40			X	X	X	X	X	X		X	6/15	none	X	
								X	X	X	X	7/15	none		
													none		
574	41	320	100					X	X	X	X	7/15	none		
													none		
143	98			X	X								none	X	
47	90							X				6/1	none		
													9/26	X	
				X				X	X	X	X	4/1	none	X	
929	90							X			X	5/1	none	X	
2,886	36	900	100					X	X		X	4/1	none	X	
900	65							X	X		X		none		
999	60							X	X		X	6/1	none	X	
													none		
169	92	96	100	X	X	X	X	X	X	X	X	6/1	none	X	
25	100			X									none		
141	75			X									none		
1,102	45	500	100					X	X	X	X	4/1	none		
2,514	63							X	X	X	X	7/1	8/1	X	
								X	X	X	X		none		
1,125	40			X				X	X		X	5/1	none		
5,223	21							X	X	X	X	5/1	none		
175	50							X					none		
109	94	70	100	X	X	X		X	X	X	X	4/1	none	X	
873	85			X	X						X	6/1	none		
400	65							X	X	X	X	4/20	none	X	
678	70			X	X	X	X	X	X	X	X	6/1	none		
10	60			X				X	X		X	6/15	none		
398	84			X			X	X				4/15	none		
1,201	45			X	X	X		X	X	X			5/1		
				X	X		X						none		
352	90											4/15	9/11		
125	90						X						none	X	
294	70												none		

Alabama: Samford University

Institution		Tuition and fees	Add'l out-of-state/ district tuition	Books and supplies	Room and board	Trans-portation	Other costs	Board only	Trans-portation	Other costs
Samford University		7,770		524	3,838	700	1,650	1,500	990	1,650
Selma University		4,200		200	3,700		600			600
Shelton State Community College	†	1,095	675/—	450		500	200	1,000	500	200
Shoals Community College	‡	1,116	668/—	405				1,500	800	900
Snead State Community College	†	1,101	720/—	450	1,643	540	700	1,500	925	700
Southeastern Bible College		4,050		300	2,700	500	1,500	2,000	900	1,500
Southern Christian University		5,420		633		1,602	3,602	6,267	1,602	3,602
Southern Union State Junior College	†	1,116	693/—	435	1,950	600	1,100	1,800	600	600
Sparks State Technical College	‡	1,056		790						
Spring Hill College		11,425		550	4,590	900	900	1,500	900	900
Stillman College		4,460		500	2,629	300	1,000	1,500	300	1,000
Talladega College		5,584		600	2,664	800	500	878	800	500
Trenholm State Technical College	†	1,125	675/—	575				2,350	850	350
Troy State University										
Dothan		1,697	1,187/—	600				2,940	1,740	1,380
Montgomery	‡	1,485	1,485/—	625						
Troy	‡	1,620	1,125/—	500	3,021	500	600	1,400		
Tuskegee University		6,735		600	3,395	600	1,125	2,000	250	250
University of Alabama										
Birmingham	†	2,238	2,010/—	720	4,380	750	1,200	2,700	1,500	1,200
Huntsville	†	2,400	2,400/—	600	4,200	900	1,200	1,800	1,350	900
Tuscaloosa	‡	2,008	3,008/—	501	3,288	773	1,323	1,498	1,323	1,103
University of Mobile	‡	5,090		500	3,180	250	1,000	1,500	450	400
University of Montevallo	‡	2,164	2,040/—	500	2,986	800	1,500	800	900	1,000
University of North Alabama	‡	1,368	600/—	550	2,580	950	2,000	1,484	2,375	2,375
University of South Alabama	†	2,349	900/—	470	3,378	990	1,023	1,986	702	1,023
Virginia College	‡	5,460		300				1,700	100	100
Walker College	†	2,354		354	1,988	2,300	4,040	2,500	4,072	2,700
Wallace State Community College at										
Hanceville	†	900	608/—	450		675	2,650	1,500	1,155	900
Alaska										
Alaska Bible College		2,670		250	3,200	120	400	1,800	600	300
Alaska Pacific University	‡	6,930		600	4,050	750	1,200	1,500	750	1,200
Prince William Sound Community College		1,172	3,024/—	500		936	1,125	2,520	936	1,125
Sheldon Jackson College		9,116		500	4,800	2,000	1,000	2,700	500	1,000
University of Alaska										
Anchorage		1,788	3,328/—	490		980	1,180	3,600	980	1,180
Fairbanks		2,214	3,328/—	550	3,220	1,710	1,980	1,500	1,710	1,980
Southeast		1,698	3,328/—	500		625	1,000	2,250	225	1,000
Arizona										
American Indian Bible College		3,012		450	2,800	1,100	1,400		1,100	1,400
Arizona College of the Bible		4,830		450		670	1,400	2,100	2,750	1,200
Arizona State University		1,844	5,506/—	700	4,850			1,650		
Arizona Western College	‡	720	4,230/—	350	2,590	350	952	1,100	924	950
Central Arizona College	‡	594	4,230/—	400	2,690	700	1,500	1,500	700	1,500
Cochise College		750	3,810/—	600	2,950	680	1,125	1,800	800	675
DeVry Institute of Technology: Phoenix		5,580		525				1,792	2,257	1,928
Eastern Arizona College		628	3,252/—	400	2,748	950	900	1,700	950	900
Embry-Riddle Aeronautical University:										
Prescott Campus		7,460		490	3,230	1,640	1,120	1,600	1,780	1,120
Gateway Community College	‡	870	3,750/—	400						3,228
Glendale Community College		960	3,750/—	700				4,850	1,105	1,105

†Figures are projected for 1993-94. ‡Figures are for 1992-93.

Arizona: Glendale Community College

Total freshmen	Percent receiving aid	Freshmen judged to have need	Percent offered aid	Acad	Music/drama	Art	Athl	Acad	Music/drama	Art	Athl	Priority	Closing	Inst aid form	Notes
687	70	423	100	X				X	X	X	X	3/1	none		
125	95											9/15	none		
3,386	30	875	99	X	X	X	X	X	X	X	X	6/30	none		
1,036	40	350	100					X	X		X	6/1	none		
426	65							X	X	X	X	4/15	none	X	
23	81			X				X	X			5/30	9/8		
		7	100	X				X				5/30	7/30	X	
965	49			X	X	X	X					4/1	none		
300	76	177	100	X				X			X	3/1	none		
253	90			X	X			X	X			6/15	none		
344	82			X		X		X			X	4/1	6/10	X	
595	20			X								8/18	none		
4	15			X				X				5/1	8/1	X	
													none		
1,100	50											5/1	none	X	
734	90	111	100	X				X	X		X	3/15	3/31		
1,134	50	450	100	X			X	X	X	X	X		none	X	
598	31							X	X	X	X	4/1	none		
2,461	35	576	93	X				X	X	X	X	3/15	none		
242	96							X	X	X	X	3/31	none	X	
522	57						X	X	X		X	4/15	none		
755	44	270	100	X				X	X	X	X	4/1	none	X	
1,240	35			X				X	X		X	4/1	none	X	
100	75												6/15		
357	61	230	100			X	X	X		X	X	7/1	none	X	
1,346	50							X	X	X	X		none	X	
9	67	9	100	X				X	X			5/31	8/5	X	
58	69			X				X				3/15	none		
24	55			X				X					none	X	
84	91			X			X	X	X		X	4/1	none		
1,299	34			X				X	X	X	X	5/15	none	X	
				X	X	X			X	X	X	5/15	none		
125	75	45	100	X	X	X		X	X	X		6/1	none	X	
27	100			X				X				4/1	8/23		
30	44	16	100	X	X		X	X	X			4/15	9/15	X	
3,357	65			X	X			X	X	X	X	3/1	none		
2,027	70							X	X	X		3/15	none		
2,100	60	375	100	X	X	X	X	X	X	X	X	4/15	none		
713	45			X			X	X			X	3/15	4/15		
663	77							X					none		
539	74							X	X	X	X	4/15	none		
296	54			X				X				4/15	none		
				X				X				4/15	none		
4,606	25			X				X	X	X	X	5/15	none		

Arizona: Grand Canyon University

Institution	Tuition and fees	Add'l out-of-state/ district tuition	Books and supplies	Costs for campus residents			Costs for students at home		
				Room and board	Trans- portation	Other costs	Board only	Trans- portation	Other costs
Grand Canyon University	6,730		600	2,950	612	1,125	1,530	612	1,125
ITT Technical Institute: Phoenix	‡ 11,768		1,100				1,842	546	1,308
Mesa Community College	‡ 870	3,750/—	400					350	
Mohave Community College	520	2,930/—	600				1,800	900	900
Navajo Community College	620		450	2,740					
Northern Arizona University	1,844	4,752/—	690	3,300	900	1,350	1,800	650	1,125
Northland Pioneer College	600	1,650/—	500		680	1,120		900	1,120
Paradise Valley Community College	‡ 885	3,750/2,670	400						
Phoenix College	960	3,750/—	400						2,016
Pima Community College	700	3,630/—	450					1,794	638
Prescott College	9,545		353				1,820	729	807
Rio Salado Community College	‡ 870	3,750/2,820	400					1,038	800
Scottsdale Community College	‡ 870	3,750/—	400						
South Mountain Community College	960	3,750/—	700				1,200	740	
Southwestern College	5,220		400	2,350	350	2,200			3,900
University of Arizona	1,854	5,506/—	620	3,820	900	1,750	1,500	1,200	1,750
University of Phoenix	4,448		500					500	200
Western International University	6,120		720						500
Yavapai College	666	4,450/—	500	2,720	600	1,050	700	600	900
Arkansas									
Arkansas Baptist College	‡ 1,670		600	2,200	860	850	1,100	860	860
Arkansas College	8,040		500	3,536	750	500	1,500	1,440	300
Arkansas State University									
Beebe Branch	‡ 984	660/—	500	1,780	560	500		800	500
Jonesboro	‡ 1,920	1,830/—	500	2,420	780	630	1,500	1,200	400
Arkansas Tech University	‡ 1,560	1,500/—	450	2,410	350	875	2,200	700	750
Capital City Junior College	‡ 5,520						1,200		
Central Baptist College	2,610		500	2,152	600	800	1,264	600	800
East Arkansas Community College	‡ 552	372/168	200				1,200	500	400
Garland County Community College	792	1,128/216	450				3,000	844	795
Harding University	† 5,790		600	3,380	900	930	1,828	900	930
Henderson State University	1,660	1,560/—	600	2,490	1,300	1,800	1,245	1,200	1,400
Hendrix College	† 8,610		400	3,060	500	625	1,500	562	563
John Brown University	6,520		500	3,360	900	1,400	1,500	700	1,300
Mississippi County Community College	‡ 720	1,200/144	250				900	917	2,416
North Arkansas Community/Technical College	792	1,128/216	300		1,003	3,958	2,957	1,003	1,001
Ouachita Baptist University	6,230		400	2,760	600	900	1,500	600	900
Philander Smith College	‡ 2,620		400	2,415	700	750		700	750
Phillips County Community College	‡ 696	552/192	450				1,350	841	1,925
Rich Mountain Community College	‡ 580	1,242/160	300					600	470
Shorter College	‡ 2,456		300	2,400	200	200		200	300
South Arkansas Community College	744	504/144	450				1,500		450
Southern Arkansas University									
Magnolia	1,500	840/—	350	2,240	300	600		500	600
Technical Branch	912	408/—	400		500	900		700	800
University of Arkansas	1,838	3,024/—	650	3,300	1,250	950			950
University of Arkansas									
Little Rock	1,996	3,024/—	500				2,100	800	800
Medical Sciences	1,812	2,718/—	470		831	1,600	3,874	1,152	2,413
Monticello	1,464	1,920/—	450	2,200	475	850	1,150	950	850
Pine Bluff	1,464	1,920/—	500	2,194	950	800		800	700

†Figures are projected for 1993-94. ‡Figures are for 1992-93.

Arkansas: University of Arkansas at Pine Bluff

All aid		Need-based aid		Grants and scholarships								Financial aid deadlines		Inst aid form	Notes
Total freshmen	Percent receiving aid	Freshmen judged to have need	Percent offered aid	Need-based				Non-need-based							
				Acad	Music/ drama	Art	Athl	Acad	Music/ drama	Art	Athl	Priority	Closing		
173	85			X	X	X		X	X	X	X	3/15	none	X	
279	97												9/20		
3,863	15	4,831	100	X			X	X			X	5/15	none		
2,952	30			X	X			X	X			3/1	none		
310	75			X				X			X	4/15	none		
2,156	65							X	X	X	X	4/15	none		
2,500	10	1,000	95					X	X	X	X	6/1	none		
				X				X					none		
								X	X	X	X	4/15	none		
5,127	20										X	4/1	none		
50	75			X				X				4/15	none	X	
7,852	2											4/15	none		
3,046	20											4/15	none		
2,934	50			X	X	X	X	X	X	X	X	5/1	none		
36	89	29	100									4/15	7/15		
4,026	24	1,207	95	X	X	X	X	X	X	X	X	3/1	none		
													none		
18	56												none		
1,761	44	720	90	X	X	X	X	X	X	X	X	4/15	none		
47	43			X			X	X			X		5/1		
211	94			X				X	X	X	X	4/1	none		
1,343	60	365	96					X	X		X	5/1	none	X	
1,712	60			X				X	X	X	X	5/1	none	X	
1,698	51			X	X		X	X	X		X		none		
139	64												none		
103	56	71	100	X	X		X	X	X		X		none		
431	50			X								4/15	none		
2,192	68			X	X	X		X	X	X	X	4/1	none	X	
847	85							X	X	X	X	4/1	none	X	
725	55			X				X	X	X	X	4/15	none		
346	78	184	100	X				X	X	X	X	4/1	none	X	
238	83	142	99	X				X	X	X	X	4/1	none		
		400	100	X				X	X	X	X	4/15	none		
433	65							X	X	X	X	5/1	none	X	
302	90	250	92					X	X		X	5/1	none		
434	90											5/1	none		
								X	X		X	4/1	5/1		
227	46			X				X				7/1	none		
72	33	19	100	X							X	5/1	none		
680	54			X				X	X		X	7/1	none		
534	70							X	X		X	6/1	none		
								X	X	X		7/15	none		
2,382	66	1,200	100	X	X			X	X	X	X	4/1	none	X	
1,339	60			X				X	X	X	X	5/1	none		
													none		
603	78			X				X	X		X		none		
718	88			X	X	X	X					4/15	none	X	

95

Arkansas: University of Central Arkansas

Institution	Tuition and fees	Add'l out-of-state/ district tuition	Books and supplies	Room and board	Trans- portation	Other costs	Board only	Trans- portation	Other costs
				Costs for campus residents			*Costs for students at home*		
University of Central Arkansas	‡ 1,546	1,420/—	500	2,420	500	1,000	1,800	1,000	1,000
University of the Ozarks	4,920		600	2,850	1,800	2,700	1,400	1,300	1,215
Westark Community College	‡ 778	1,032/240	400				1,500	600	450
Williams Baptist College	‡ 3,262		500	2,332	350	600	500	900	450
California									
Academy of Art College	9,060		700		576	4,905	684	1,998	
Allan Hancock College	† 300	3,120/—	612				1,980	268	950
American Academy of Dramatic Arts: West	7,975		460					532	1,204
American Armenian International College	12,910		500	4,980			1,200		
American College for the Applied Arts: Los Angeles	9,090		750		800		800		4,042
Antelope Valley College	‡ 120	3,120/—	384					720	1,340
Antioch Southern California at Los Angeles	8,100		300						
Armstrong University	7,470		450						1,200
Art Center College of Design	13,430		3,312		856	1,696		856	1,696
Art Institute of Southern California	8,850		1,185		1,293	2,263	4,471	1,293	2,263
Azusa Pacific University	‡ 10,292		600	3,700	700	1,250		1,000	
Bakersfield College	‡ 145	3,120/—	500	3,636	450	900		750	900
Barstow College	‡ 120	3,120/—	600				1,700	500	1,250
Bethany College	6,520		700	3,120	600	2,000	1,500	650	2,000
Biola University	11,388		612	4,736	576	1,350	999	684	1,548
Brooks College	‡ 5,790		1,000	5,490	1,300	1,100	1,100	900	1,100
Brooks Institute of Photography	‡ 7,600		3,500				800	1,400	
California Baptist College	7,848		612	5,352	576	1,350	1,566	684	1,548
California College of Arts and Crafts	13,080		600	5,526	684	1,728	1,998	684	1,548
California Institute of the Arts	13,910		1,000	5,966	576	1,680		680	1,480
California Institute of Technology	16,110		700	6,117	700	2,670	1,800		1,350
California Lutheran University	12,040		612	5,200	576	1,548	1,998	684	1,548
California Maritime Academy	‡ 2,006	4,590/—	550	4,770	640	1,900			
California Polytechnic State University: San Luis Obispo	‡ 1,553	7,380/—	576	4,416	429	1,119	1,512	675	1,119
California State Polytechnic University: Pomona	† 1,523	7,380/—	612	5,526	576	1,728	1,998	684	1,728
California State University									
Bakersfield	‡ 1,439	7,380/—	576	3,635	510	1,242	1,512	500	1,111
Chico	‡ 1,468	7,380/—	576	4,008	526	1,368	1,688	644	1,435
Dominguez Hills	† 1,959	7,380/—	612		576	1,464	1,998	684	1,464
Fresno	† 1,446	7,380/—	612	4,287	576	1,242	558	684	1,138
Fullerton	‡ 1,480	7,380/—	574		576	1,728	1,512	700	1,728
Hayward	‡ 1,423	7,380/—	612		576		1,998	684	1,401
Long Beach	‡ 1,423	7,380/—	576	4,800	576	1,728	1,512	684	1,728
Los Angeles	† 1,428	5,904/—	612		576	1,728	1,649	684	1,728
Northridge	† 2,002	7,380/—	612	5,340	576	1,384	1,998	676	1,384
Sacramento	‡ 1,420	7,380/—	576	4,618	522	1,251	1,512	684	1,251
San Bernardino	‡ 1,440	7,380/—	612	4,266	576	1,728	1,548	684	1,728
San Marcos	† 1,854	5,904/—	612				1,998	684	1,406
Stanislaus	‡ 1,434	7,380/—	576	4,119	550	1,170	1,512	684	1,280
Canada College	‡ 135	3,390/—	500					650	1,450
Central California Commercial College	‡ 6,600		600						
Cerritos Community College	† 240	2,808/—	612					684	1,000
Cerro Coso Community College	‡ 120	3,120/—	480				1,500	580	765

†Figures are projected for 1993-94. ‡Figures are for 1992-93.

California: Cerro Coso Community College

All aid		Need-based aid		Grants and scholarships								Financial aid deadlines		Inst aid form	Notes
Total fresh-men	Percent receiving aid	Freshmen judged to have need	Percent offered aid	Need-based				Non-need-based							
				Acad	Music/ drama	Art	Athl	Acad	Music/ drama	Art	Athl	Priority	Closing		
2,031	58	1,080	100						X	X	X	4/15	8/1	X	
210	65	66	100	X				X	X		X	5/1	none		
				X				X				6/1	none		
213	82			X	X	X	X					6/1	none		
				X		X		X		X			none	X	
				X	X	X	X	X	X	X	X		5/1		
71	63				X							7/1	none	X	
34	72			X				X				3/2	3/28	X	
140	22											3/2			
2,122	20	850	100	X	X	X		X	X	X		3/2	none	X	
													none		
223	61	187	100									3/1	none	X	
22	47	13	100	X		X		X		X		4/20	none		
475	80			X	X		X	X	X		X	3/1	none	X	
3,275	19	1,513	63	X				X				5/1	none	X	
750	80	208	100	X				X					5/1		
206	82			X				X				6/1	none		
472	70							X	X	X	X	3/2	none		
426	52							X					none		
42	35			X		X		X		X		4/15	none		
252	89	207	100	X				X	X			4/1	none	X	
65	42	47	100	X		X		X		X		3/2	none	X	
					X	X			X	X		3/2	none		
232	70	180	100	X				X				2/1	none		
424	85	200	100	X	X			X	X			3/2	none		
157	38	55	91	X				X				3/2	none		
1,331	15			X		X		X		X	X		3/1		
1,542	47			X	X	X	X	X			X	3/2	none		
429	63			X	X	X	X	X	X	X	X	3/2	none	X	
1,364	24			X	X	X	X					3/1	none		
518	70							X	X	X	X	4/15	none		
1,580	33			X	X	X	X	X	X	X	X	3/2	none		
2,070	17	1,099	93	X				X	X	X	X	3/2	none		
607	27			X				X				3/2	none		
1,790	33	1,051	88					X	X	X	X	3/2	none		
1,268	48			X				X	X	X	X	3/1	none		
				X	X	X	X	X	X	X	X	3/2	none		
1,451	28			X	X	X						3/2	none		
832	30			X	X	X		X				3/2	none		
				X				X				3/2	none	X	
348	25			X				X	X	X		3/2	none		
				X	X							5/8	none		
													none		
4,119	10							X				5/10	none	X	
1,192	6			X	X	X		X	X	X		5/1	none		

97

California: Chabot College

Institution	Tuition and fees	Add'l out-of-state/ district tuition	Books and supplies	Room and board	Trans-portation	Other costs	Board only	Trans-portation	Other costs
				Costs for campus residents			*Costs for students at home*		
Chabot College	‡ 123	3,150/—	750				2,700	750	500
Chaffey Community College	‡ 135	3,150/—	576				1,512	684	1,000
Chapman University	16,328		600	5,780	650	1,300	2,000	650	1,300
Charles R. Drew University: College of Allied Health	‡ 2,500		2,268		1,683	2,832	1,440	720	1,460
Christian Heritage College	† 7,900		576	3,900	486	1,638	1,200	576	1,638
Citrus College	‡ 167	3,120/—	450					640	1,000
City College of San Francisco	† 300	3,420/—	600					550	3,880
Claremont McKenna College	16,400		600	5,750		850	3,380		850
Coastline Community College	‡ 136	3,060/—	432				1,512	594	1,386
Cogswell Polytechnical College	‡ 6,640		600					620	1,232
Coleman College	6,403		425					1,000	1,000
College of the Canyons	295	3,120/—	612		684	1,551	1,551	684	1,551
College of Marin: Kentfield	† 320	3,690/—	500				1,100	680	1,710
College of Notre Dame	11,750		612	5,832	576	1,350	1,998	684	1,548
College of Oceaneering	13,550						750	300	750
College of the Redwoods	† 280	3,510/—	612	4,001	684	1,724	1,998	684	1,536
College of San Mateo	‡ 135	3,390/—	576				1,512	684	1,000
College of the Sequoias	† 620	3,480/—	612				1,512	684	900
College of the Siskiyous	320	3,120/—	612	3,660	684	1,548	1,998	684	1,548
Columbia College	374	3,300/—	650		400	1,200	850	500	900
Columbia College: Hollywood	‡ 5,490		550					700	1,800
Compton Community College	‡ 120	3,060/—	410						
Concordia University	‡ 9,315		540	4,230	540	900	1,800	750	900
Contra Costa College	† 302	3,420/—	612				1,998	684	1,548
Cosumnes River College	‡ 120	3,210/—	500					900	3,000
Crafton Hills College	‡ 135	3,120/—	550					750	550
Cuesta College	† 350	3,120/—	612				1,566	684	1,548
Cuyamaca College	‡ 145	3,120/—	450				1,500	600	700
Cypress College	‡ 150	3,300/—	500				1,100	750	750
DeVry Institute of Technology: City of Industry	5,580		500				1,777	2,320	1,911
Diablo Valley College	† 332	3,300/—	612		684	1,548	3,528	684	1,548
Dominican College of San Rafael	12,180		612	5,680	576	1,350		684	1,548
Dominican School of Philosophy and Theology	‡ 5,065		522				1,998	1,260	1,872
D-Q University	3,800		500	4,352	517	1,622	1,680	550	1,402
Evergreen Valley College	† 300	2,640/—	612				1,998	684	1,548
Fashion Institute of Design and Merchandising									
Los Angeles	‡ 9,545	150/—	1,050						
San Francisco	‡ 9,545	150/—	975				1,410	612	1,512
Feather River College	† 279	2,640/—	550		700	1,638	1,998	700	1,638
Foothill College	† 315	3,060/—	750				600	750	1,000
Fresno City College	295	3,459/—	612				1,600	684	1,449
Fresno Pacific College	9,462		612	3,510	576	1,350	1,998	684	1,548
Fullerton College	‡ 135	3,300/—	550						
Glendale Community College	‡ 185	3,120/—							
Golden Gate University	7,010		504				1,575	2,115	
Golden West College	† 320	2,568/—	612		684		1,998	684	1,548
Grossmont Community College	† 360	3,120/—	600				1,800	650	1,200
Harvey Mudd College	16,410		600	6,440		900			

†Figures are projected for 1993-94. ‡Figures are for 1992-93.

California: Harvey Mudd College

All aid		Need-based aid		Grants and scholarships								Financial aid deadlines		Inst aid form	Notes
Total freshmen	Percent receiving aid	Freshmen judged to have need	Percent offered aid	Need-based				Non-need-based							
				Acad	Music/drama	Art	Athl	Acad	Music/drama	Art	Athl	Priority	Closing		
9,145	25			X				X				8/1	none		
												5/1	none		
330	48	187	100	X	X	X		X	X	X		3/2	none		
92	99	18	100	X				X					2/28		
80	85			X	X		X	X	X		X	6/1	none		
				X	X	X	X	X	X	X	X	5/1	none		
				X	X	X	X	X				3/2	5/21	X	
207	73	114	100					X				2/1			
2,419	10	90	100										none		
56	29			X				X				5/1	none	X	
125	87							X					none		
				X			X	X			X	6/15	none		
2,961	10			X		X						3/1	none		
88	85			X				X	X	X	X	3/2	none	X	
237	80												none	X	
1,289	50			X				X		X		4/15	none	X	
2,008	38	200	100									5/10	none		
2,400	31	1,825	100	X	X		X	X				3/2	none	X	
435	25							X				5/2	none		
2,543	13	161	89	X	X	X		X	X	X		3/2	none		
92	35			X								4/15	none		
1,515	75			X				X	X	X	X		5/15	X	
114	84			X	X		X	X	X		X	4/30	6/30	X	
2,625	37	1,011	74									3/2	none	X	
				X	X							5/15	none		
				X				X				5/1	none		
				X				X				2/19	none		
846	8			X								7/28	none	X	
2,412	15			X	X					X		5/31	none		
574	78							X					none		
12,232	10			X				X				3/2	none		
68	76			X	X		X	X	X		X	2/1	none	X	
													none		
103	70			X									none		
				X					X	X	X	5/31	none		
675	74											3/2	none	X	
												3/2	none		
470	25	100	90	X				X				3/2	none		
3,100	11	280	100	X	X	X	X	X	X	X	X	4/30	none	X	
4,000	11			X				X	X	X		4/15	none	X	
170	90	93	100	X	X	X	X	X	X	X	X	1/31	none	X	
3,056	3			X				X	X	X	X	5/1	none		
1,353	20											7/1	none		
76	33			X				X				3/1	none		
2,670	20			X	X			X		X		6/30	none		
5,111	10			X	X	X	X	X	X	X	X	4/1	none	X	
171	78							X				2/15	none		

California: Heald Business College: Concord

Institution	Tuition and fees	Add'l out-of-state/ district tuition	Books and supplies	Room and board	Trans-portation	Other costs	Board only	Trans-portation	Other costs
Heald Business College									
Concord	6,300								
San Jose	5,850		450						
Hebrew Union College: Jewish Institute of Religion	‡ 6,000		750						
Holy Names College	10,834		612	4,876	576	1,350	1,998	684	1,548
Humboldt State University	‡ 1,468	7,380/—	576	4,201	529	1,277	1,600	512	1,277
Humphreys College	4,724		812		1,009	1,920	3,436	1,068	1,920
ITT Technical Institute: Sacramento	‡ 7,400		750				2,043	2,000	1,143
John F. Kennedy University	‡ 6,948		504					675	
Kelsey-Jenney College	8,088		612				1,998	684	1,548
La Sierra University	11,592		450	3,780	522	1,314	1,512	612	1,458
Lake Tahoe Community College	† 321	3,510/—	612				1,512	594	1,386
Laney College	† 304	2,808/—	612				1,998	684	1,548
Lassen College	† 295	2,912/—	612	3,290	576	1,350	1,588	684	1,548
LIFE Bible College	4,450		375	2,900		450	200		450
Lincoln University	‡ 5,250		400				360		
Long Beach City College	† 312	2,736/—	684					612	1,535
Los Angeles City College	‡ 120	3,690/—	576					684	1,728
Los Angeles Harbor College	‡ 120	3,690/—	558					684	
Los Angeles Mission College	‡ 120	3,510/—	612				599	684	1,548
Los Angeles Pierce College	‡ 120	3,690/—	576				1,512	684	1,728
Los Angeles Trade and Technical College	‡ 120	3,510/—	504				1,512	630	1,548
Los Angeles Valley College	‡ 120	3,540/—	450					600	1,500
Los Medanos College	† 152	3,150/—	520				1,800	800	2,000
Louise Salinger Academy of Fashion	‡ 12,180		1,000						
Loyola Marymount University	13,060		530	6,093	50	1,350	1,566	684	1,350
Marymount College	11,714		612	5,940	576	1,350	2,233	684	1,548
Master's College	8,394		612	4,472	576	1,350	1,998	684	1,548
Mendocino College	† 300	3,096	612				3,960	684	1,548
Menlo College	14,175		600	6,200	700	1,625	1,500	250	1,625
Merced College	† 240	3,120/—	612				1,998	684	1,548
Merritt College	‡ 120	3,510/—	450					240	2,000
Mills College	14,100		420	6,000		1,275	1,200	580	1,330
MiraCosta College	333	3,060/—	576				1,512	684	1,080
Mission College	† 305	3,300/—	612				1,998	684	1,548
Modesto Junior College	† 830	3,300/—	612				1,926	684	1,548
Monterey Institute of International Studies	13,245		500					700	1,400
Monterey Peninsula College	‡ 155	3,240/—	576				1,512	684	1,728
Moorpark College	‡ 135	3,300/—	576				1,512	684	1,000
Mount St. Mary's College	‡ 10,800		558	4,700	576	1,638	1,512	648	1,638
Mount San Antonio College	‡ 153	3,150/—	576				1,512	684	1,728
Mount San Jacinto College	‡ 120	3,690/—	576				1,512	684	1,198
Napa Valley College	‡ 122	3,390/—	576				1,512	684	1,500
National University	‡ 5,985		500				650		
New College of California	‡ 6,500		600				800		2,268
Occidental College	16,188		558	5,325		1,152			2,796
Otis School of Art and Design	‡ 11,990		1,650		550	1,375		550	1,375
Pacific Christian College	6,710		612	4,584	576	1,350	1,998	684	1,548
Pacific Oaks College	‡ 10,400		450				2,475	1,575	1,350
Pacific Union College	11,400		612	3,675	576	1,350	1,500	576	1,350

†Figures are projected for 1993-94. ‡Figures are for 1992-93.

California: Pacific Union College

All aid		Need-based aid		Grants and scholarships								Financial aid deadlines		Inst aid form	Notes
Total freshmen	Percent receiving aid	Freshmen judged to have need	Percent offered aid	Need-based				Non-need-based				Priority	Closing		
				Acad	Music/drama	Art	Athl	Acad	Music/drama	Art	Athl				
												3/2	none	X	
50	80			X								6/1	none	X	
				X									none		
68	75	35	100	X	X	X		X	X	X		3/2	none	X	
796	44			X	X	X		X	X	X		3/2	none		
73	60	67	100									4/4	none	X	
				X				X				4/1	none		
161	85			X				X					none	X	
310	65			X	X	X	X	X	X	X	X	5/1	none		
				X				X	X	X		5/1	none		
												4/15	none		
874	85			X								7/1	none		
48	25	14	100	X				X				6/1	none	X	
													none		
4,998	20	3,400	100	X	X	X		X	X	X		5/1	none		
3,884	20			X	X	X	X						6/26		
2,392	14	186	100	X				X				3/14	none	X	
								X				8/1	none		
2,308	1			X				X				7/7	none		
		2,250	67									7/7	none		
3,107	5											6/12	none		
2,316	13			X				X				3/2	8/1		
21	60												none	X	
674	63			X	X	X	X	X	X		X	2/15	none		
376	40	227	94	X	X			X					3/2	X	
162	90	162	96						X	X	X	3/31	7/31		
		184	45									5/31	11/1		
137	53	73	100	X				X				3/2	none		
2,101	35			X				X				6/1	none		
1,297	28			X								4/1	none		
149	67			X	X	X		X	X	X			2/15	X	
6,524	10	500	100					X	X	X		5/28	none		
		800	88	X				X				5/1	none	X	
1,985	30							X	X	X		3/2	none	X	
				X				X				3/1	none	X	
				X	X	X		X	X	X	X	3/2	none		
2,531	5											5/16	none	X	
215	75	142	99	X	X	X		X				3/1	none		
				X			X	X			X	5/22	none		
5,843	40	507	81	X				X	X	X	X		none	X	
				X		X	X	X	X	X	X	5/5	none		
342	80			X								3/2	none	X	
36	85											3/1	none	X	
435	55			X				X	X			2/1		X	
				X		X						3/1	none	X	
94	99	72	100	X	X			X	X			3/2	none	X	
				X				X				3/1	none	X	
452	70	390	100					X	X			3/2	none	X	

California: Palomar College

		Tuition and fees	Add'l out-of-state/ district tuition	Books and supplies	Room and board	Trans-portation	Other costs	Board only	Trans-portation	Other costs
Institution										
Palomar College	‡	135	3,240/—	560				1,610	500	1,235
Pasadena City College	‡	180	4,200/—	450				1,200	275	900
Patten College		4,920		550	3,980	440	1,100	1,650	330	1,595
Pepperdine University		17,260		800	6,530	660	660	2,450	1,450	726
Phillips Junior College: Fresno Campus		4,644		992					684	1,638
Pitzer College		18,198		650	5,582		900			900
Point Loma Nazarene College		9,542		612	3,990	576	1,350	1,998	684	1,548
Pomona College		16,900		750	6,920		1,000	2,000	750	
Porterville College	‡	140	3,120/—	480					350	630
Queen of the Holy Rosary College		2,500		100						
Rio Hondo College	‡	135	2,970/—	400						
Sacramento City College	‡	120	3,210/—	558				1,350	684	1,206
Saddleback College	†	260	2,520/—	612				2,261	1,040	1,800
St. Mary's College of California		12,738		612	6,110	684	1,350	1,998	684	1,548
Samuel Merritt College		11,890		865	5,520	700	3,348	1,998	700	3,348
San Diego City College	†	315	3,150/—	612				1,382	684	1,548
San Diego Mesa College		315	3,150/—	450					890	935
San Diego Miramar College	‡	125	3,180/—	576				1,525	684	1,728
San Diego State University	‡	1,490	7,380/—	612	4,365	576	1,728	1,998	684	1,728
San Francisco Art Institute		12,900		1,100				2,000	684	1,512
San Francisco College of Mortuary Science		8,525		600				3,600	1,800	1,200
San Francisco Conservatory of Music		12,250		600				2,000	700	1,800
San Francisco State University	‡	1,424	7,380/—	612	4,474	684	1,728		684	1,454
San Joaquin Delta College	†	600	3,210/—	612				1,512	650	1,300
San Jose Christian College	‡	5,205		450	3,240	522	1,314	1,512	612	1,458
San Jose City College		310	2,900/—	612					684	
San Jose State University	‡	1,502	7,380/—	612	4,872	684	1,548		684	1,548
Santa Barbara City College	‡	135	3,120/—	558				1,584	639	1,440
Santa Clara University		12,879		558	5,904	576	1,638	1,512	684	1,638
Santa Monica College	‡	155	3,600/—	400					585	
Santa Rosa Junior College	†	316	3,510/—	612		684	1,548	1,998	684	1,548
Scripps College	†	16,536		600	7,077		800			3,546
Shasta College	‡	126	3,300/—	434		500	1,200	1,500	500	900
Sierra College	†	315	3,360/—	600	3,934	300	1,500	1,500	800	1,500
Simpson College		6,938		612	3,690	576	1,350	1,998	684	1,548
Skyline College	‡	135	3,390/—	384				1,300	576	1,332
Solano Community College	‡	131	3,210/—	450				1,595	594	1,386
Sonoma State University	†	1,534	5,904/—	612	5,062	291	1,370	1,998	535	1,096
Southern California College		8,836		612	3,820	576	1,350	530	684	1,548
Southern California Institute of Architecture	‡	10,050		1,400					1,390	
Southwestern College		180	2,970/—	612				1,998	684	1,728
Stanford University		17,775		815	6,535		1,315			1,315
Taft College		365	3,060/—	250	2,300	684	1,548	1,998	684	1,548
Thomas Aquinas College	†	12,480		275	5,410	600	700		650	900
United States International University		11,115		612	3,900	756	1,773	1,998	882	1,773
University of California										
Berkeley	†	4,330	7,699/—	600	5,992	300	1,582	1,786	300	1,582
Davis	†	3,975	7,699/—	827	5,822	670	1,507	1,500	792	1,381
Irvine	‡	3,074	7,699/—	690	5,383	576	1,728	1,512	684	1,728
Los Angeles	†	3,899	7,699/—	640	5,410	165	135	2,600	2,580	135

†Figures are projected for 1993-94. ‡Figures are for 1992-93.

California: University of California: Los Angeles

Total freshmen	Percent receiving aid	Freshmen judged to have need	Percent offered aid	Need-based Acad	Need-based Music/drama	Need-based Art	Need-based Athl	Non-need-based Acad	Non-need-based Music/drama	Non-need-based Art	Non-need-based Athl	Priority	Closing	Inst aid form	Notes
15,394	12	450	100	X				X				4/1	none		
4,987	15							X	X	X	X	6/24	none	X	
61	80	15	100	X				X				3/2	none	X	
594	63			X	X	X	X	X	X	X	X	2/15	3/1	X	
171	43												2/1		
374	72			X	X	X	X	X			X	4/10	none	X	
363	52											2/11	none	X	
676	50	400	52	X				X				6/1	none		
3	100											3/1	7/1		
1,135	11			X	X	X	X	X	X	X	X	7/15	none	X	
2,283	35			X	X	X						3/2	none	X	
3,855	6			X				X	X	X		3/2	5/2		
487	46							X			X		3/2		X
13	100	6	100	X				X				3/2	none	X	
								X	X	X	X	5/1	none		
				X				X				5/1	none		
2,048	7	463	100									5/1	none	X	
2,194	49	965	100	X	X	X	X	X	X	X	X	3/2	none		
93	65								X			4/1	none	X	
73	85												9/5		
17	63	10	100		X				X			4/1	none	X	
				X				X	X			3/1	none		
4,273	22	1,516	68	X	X	X		X	X	X		4/15	none		
22	80			X	X		X	X	X		X	3/2	none	X	
3,291	6											5/31	none		
1,543	30										X	3/1	none		
2,132	20			X				X				5/15	none		
899	53			X	X	X		X	X			2/1	none		
3,774	23			X	X	X	X	X	X	X	X	5/15	none	X	
				X				X	X	X	X	3/2	none		
165	48			X				X				2/1	3/2	X	
2,997	27			X	X	X	X	X	X	X	X	3/2	none		
2,546	5			X	X	X	X	X	X	X	X	6/15	none		
43	96			X	X		X	X	X		X	3/31	none	X	
6,341	8			X								5/13	none	X	
2,300	10											6/1	none		
601	50	236	95	X				X	X			3/2	none		
172	80	160	100	X	X		X	X				3/2	none	X	
47	49	24	100	X		X		X		X		3/2	none	X	
4,133	29											3/2	none		
1,593	69			X	X	X	X				X	2/1		X	
				X				X				8/1	none		
68	79	54	100									3/1	9/1	X	
								X				4/15	none	X	
3,420	41			X				X			X		3/2		
		1,862	100	X				X				3/2	none		
								X	X	X	X	3/2	5/1		
3,460	52			X				X	X	X	X		3/2	X	

California: University of California: Riverside

Institution		Tuition and fees	Add'l out-of-state/ district tuition	Books and supplies	Room and board	Trans- portation	Other costs	Board only	Trans- portation	Other costs
Riverside	‡	2,923	7,699/—	700	5,430	575	1,100	1,000	1,200	1,100
San Diego	†	4,008	7,699/—	612	6,562	957	1,598	1,613	936	1,531
San Francisco	†	4,147	7,699/—	3,187	7,470	675	1,935	1,755	675	1,935
Santa Barbara	‡	2,953	7,699/—	576	5,780	340	1,284	1,512	684	1,284
Santa Cruz	‡	3,023	7,699/—	570	5,805	425	1,509	1,620	425	1,509
University of Judaism	‡	8,950		700	5,850	750	1,680	1,600	645	1,540
University of La Verne		12,890		612	4,910	684	1,584	612	684	
University of the Pacific		15,800		565	5,300	840	1,050	1,500	840	1,050
University of Redlands		15,760		600	5,999					
University of San Diego		12,990		550	6,400	560	1,350	1,980	680	1,500
University of San Francisco		12,578		725	6,174	600	1,800	1,935	600	1,800
University of Southern California		16,810		600	6,244	580	1,630	1,602	940	1,630
University of West Los Angeles	‡	4,640		250					1,000	1,500
Ventura College	†	300	3,300/—	600				1,700	700	1,300
Victor Valley College	‡	120	2,910/—	576				1,512	684	1,000
West Coast University		9,155		500						
West Hills Community College	†	268	3,360/—	576		684	1,728	1,512	684	1,728
West Valley College	‡	159	3,120/—	504					648	1,548
Westmont College		13,660		480	5,072	800	600		800	600
Whittier College		16,181		500	5,480	548	1,450	1,636	662	1,607
Woodbury University		12,120		612	5,490	576	1,350	1,998	684	1,548
Yuba College	†	340	3,420/—	612	4,500	600	5,588	1,998	600	1,590
Colorado										
Adams State College	‡	1,649	2,890/—	500	2,950	800	1,200	750	800	1,200
Aims Community College	‡	753	3,582/630	290					580	1,050
Arapahoe Community College	‡	1,571	4,320/—	450				2,385	900	274
Bel-Rea Institute of Animal Technology	‡	4,550		800				1,584	195	1,053
Beth-El College of Nursing	‡	4,435								
Colorado Christian University		6,350		500	3,400		2,070			3,600
Colorado College		15,942		450	4,096	200	900	1,580	200	900
Colorado Institute of Art	‡	7,925		1,200					675	1,250
Colorado Mountain College										
Alpine Campus		1,030	4,500/840	700	3,600	400	1,000	1,500	200	900
Spring Valley Campus		1,030	4,500/840	700	3,600	400	1,000	1,500	200	900
Timberline Campus		1,030	4,500/840	700	3,600	400	1,000	1,500	200	900
Colorado Northwestern Community College	‡	260	2,850/770	450	3,050	400	2,250			3,105
Colorado School of Mines	†	4,504	7,260/—	700	4,050		1,200	1,600	1,000	1,200
Colorado State University	‡	2,510	5,166/—	470	4,140	300	1,500			1,850
Colorado Technical College	‡	6,240		700				800	800	200
Community College of Aurora	‡	1,510	4,320/—	400						
Community College of Denver	‡	1,609	4,320/—	415				1,115	720	916
Denver Technical College	†	6,600							750	450
Fort Lewis College	†	1,765	4,750/—	500	3,540	800	1,384	900	800	1,384
Front Range Community College	‡	1,572	4,320/—	395				1,000	570	675
Lamar Community College	‡	1,720	2,880/—	400	3,138	200	400	1,700	450	375
Mesa State College	‡	1,684	2,922/—	425	3,256	350	800	650	360	750
Metropolitan State College of Denver	‡	1,595	3,648/—	482				3,165	896	1,096
Morgan Community College	‡	1,500	4,320/—	475				1,200	855	750
Naropa Institute		8,100		450						
National College	‡	4,765		300						
Nazarene Bible College	†	3,405		490				1,500	720	500
Northeastern Junior College		709	3,131/859	430	3,468	720	800	1,500	565	800

†Figures are projected for 1993-94. ‡Figures are for 1992-93.

Colorado: Northeastern Junior College

Total freshmen	Percent receiving aid	Freshmen judged to have need	Percent offered aid	Acad	Music/drama	Art	Athl	Acad	Music/drama	Art	Athl	Priority	Closing	Inst aid form	Notes
1,303	50			X				X	X	X	X	3/2	none		
2,650	40	1,107	100	X				X				3/2	5/3		
				X				X				7/1	none	X	
3,218	35	730	100	X	X	X	X	X	X	X	X	3/2	none		
1,810	33	740	100	X	X	X		X	X	X		3/2	none		
19	81	4	100					X				3/2	none	X	
619	63			X	X		X	X		X	X	3/2	none	X	
299	86			X	X	X		X	X	X		3/1	6/30		
930	61	457	100	X	X		X	X			X	2/20	none		
499	37	236	96	X			X	X			X	3/2	none		
2,429	58			X	X			X	X	X	X	2/15	8/15	X	
				X								6/1	none		
12,200	15			X	X	X			X	X		3/2	5/1		
		480	100	X				X					none	X	
				X									6/1		
900	68			X	X	X						3/2	none		
2,434	15			X				X			X	5/31	none		
411	70	259	100					X	X	X	X	3/1	none	X	
338	83	238	100	X	X	X		X	X	X		2/15	none		
134	76	265	91	X				X				3/2	none	X	
2,417	12			X				X				3/2	none		
569	84	496	100	X				X	X	X	X	4/15	none		
				X				X				6/1	none		
2,800	24							X				3/15	none		
83	55							X				8/31	none	X	
													none		
197	80			X	X		X	X	X		X	3/1	4/1	X	
523	50	254	100	X				X			X	2/15	none		
475	80			X	X	X		X	X	X			none	X	
237	46							X			X	3/31	none		
268	46							X			X	3/31	none		
108	46							X			X	3/31	none		
188	95	103	100	X			X	X			X	5/1	none	X	
502	85	375	100	X	X		X	X	X		X	3/1	none	X	
2,225	92							X	X	X	X	3/1	none		
225	45			X				X					none		
1,000	12			X				X				6/1	none		
3,133	28	1,056	100					X	X	X		6/1	none	X	
350	97												none		
1,705	61	612	100	X	X	X	X	X	X	X	X	4/15	none		
1,600	36			X				X				5/15	none	X	
300	80	190	100	X			X	X		X	X	5/1	none	X	
990	70	630	95	X	X	X	X	X	X	X	X	3/1	none		
1,479	67	1,400	81	X				X	X		X	3/1	none		
265	90			X				X				3/1	none		
				X				X				3/31	none		
				X				X					none	X	
59	95			X				X				6/1	none		
1,033	35							X	X	X	X	4/1	none		

Colorado: Otero Junior College

Institution	Tuition and fees	Add'l out-of-state/ district tuition	Books and supplies	Room and board	Trans-portation	Other costs	Board only	Trans-portation	Other costs
				Costs for campus residents			*Costs for students at home*		
Otero Junior College	‡ 1,562	2,880/—	400	3,464	600			800	1,200
Pikes Peak Community College	‡ 1,514	4,320/—	400					900	1,350
Pueblo Community College	‡ 1,666	4,320/—	500						
Red Rocks Community College	‡ 1,548	4,320/—	450				2,000	805	875
Regis University	11,980		520	5,300	350	1,400	1,580	700	1,415
Rocky Mountain College of Art & Design	5,880		1,000				2,920	800	1,067
Trinidad State Junior College	‡ 1,564	2,880/—	470	3,598	600	1,125	1,800	450	900
United States Air Force Academy	0								
University of Colorado									
Boulder	‡ 2,540	8,792/—	520	3,664	900	2,334	1,581	900	2,334
Colorado Springs	‡ 2,143	4,678/—	454				1,575	794	330
Denver	‡ 1,917	6,148/—	450				2,835	765	830
Health Sciences Center	‡ 3,748	7,166/—	865				1,575	100	2,340
University of Denver	‡ 13,572		400	4,302		1,350		540	1,887
University of Northern Colorado	‡ 2,027	4,861/—	500	3,814	350	1,730	1,700		520
University of Southern Colorado	‡ 1,834	4,552/—	500	3,720	950	1,200	800	800	550
Western State College of Colorado	† 1,924	3,556/—	500	3,744	750	1,250	1,500	500	1,000
Yeshiva Toras Chaim Talmudical Seminary	‡ 4,050			4,400					
Connecticut									
Albertus Magnus College	† 11,420		400	5,240	420	847	1,600	642	847
Asnuntuck Community-Technical College	1,398	2,808/—	600				2,000	1,500	950
Briarwood College	8,847		500		945	1,400	2,296	945	1,400
Bridgeport Engineering Institute	5,780		400						
Capital Community-Technical College	1,398	2,808/624	400				2,000	820	1,700
Central Connecticut State University	2,976	3,924/—	500	4,324	159	1,023	1,550	639	1,097
Connecticut College	18,130		500	6,030		500	1,800		500
Eastern Connecticut State University	‡ 2,764	3,568/—	500	3,826	400	1,100	1,700	1,000	600
Fairfield University	14,590		450	5,900	300	900	1,500	700	600
Gateway Community-Technical College	1,398	2,808/—	600				1,800	950	1,460
Housatonic Community-Technical College	1,398	2,808/—	750				1,800	925	960
Middlesex Community-Technical College	1,398	2,808/—	500				3,645	1,425	650
Mitchell College	11,100		500	4,890	500	500	1,100	1,000	500
Northwestern Connecticut Community-Technical College	1,398	2,808/624	500				700	1,100	1,000
Norwalk Community-Technical College	1,398	2,808/624	400				900	1,800	1,600
Paier College of Art	10,120		600					600	1,200
Quinebaug Valley Community-Technical College	1,398	2,808/624	600				2,000	1,200	1,000
Quinnipiac College	11,810		500	6,077	300	800	1,500	500	800
Sacred Heart University	10,525		475	5,300			1,600		
St. Joseph College	11,600		550	4,625	200	900	1,500	1,000	900
Southern Connecticut State University	‡ 2,646	3,568/—	700	4,104	300	976	1,854		1,690
Teikyo-Post University	11,110		600	5,450	700	400	2,750	1,000	700
Three Rivers Community-Technical College	1,398	2,808/624	450				550	644	400
Trinity College	18,700		500	5,420		680	2,000		710
Tunxis Community-Technical College	1,398	2,808/—	420				4,500	1,300	1,210
United States Coast Guard Academy	‡ 0								
University of Bridgeport	‡ 12,375		550	6,150	400	500	778	500	500
University of Connecticut	4,290	7,120/—	600	4,878	200	1,332	2,100	200	1,310
University of Hartford	14,260		400	5,598	400	424	1,400	1,000	516
University of New Haven	10,180		500	4,990	200	1,000	1,600	720	1,000

†Figures are projected for 1993-94. ‡Figures are for 1992-93.

Connecticut: University of New Haven

Total freshmen	Percent receiving aid	Freshmen judged to have need	Percent offered aid	Acad	Music/drama	Art	Athl	Acad	Music/drama	Art	Athl	Priority	Closing	Inst aid form	Notes
426	70			X			X				X	5/1	none		
								X				7/1	none	X	
1,293	51			X				X				3/15	5/1		
5,448	18							X				6/1	none	X	
309	76			X				X			X	3/15	none	X	
59	80			X		X		X		X		7/31	none	X	
526	68							X	X	X	X	5/1	none	X	
				X	X	X	X		X	X	X	4/1	none		
331	40	127	91	X			X	X			X	4/1	none		
				X				X	X	X		3/30	none	X	
								X				3/15	none	X	
751	54	275	100					X	X	X	X	2/21	3/1		
1,474	68	950	92	X				X	X	X	X	3/1	none		
695	58	470	84	X				X	X	X	X	3/1	4/15	X	
745	70	500	70	X	X	X	X	X	X	X	X	4/1	none		
74	74	56	100	X				X				2/15	none	X	
653	20	250	100									8/1	none	X	
135	70							X				4/30	none		
				X									none	X	
1,540	21	360	89	X				X				7/1	none		
964	35							X			X	3/15	none		
443	43	186	100										2/15	X	
567	50			X				X					3/15		
870	65	411	100										2/1		
1,089	19							X					none	X	
		485	100									7/1	none	X	
				X								8/15	none		
294	58											3/1	7/15		
455	33	75	100					X				6/15	none		
1,333	25			X								4/15	none	X	
55	39											5/1	none		
356	18	131	100					X	X				11/1	X	
979	50			X				X			X	3/1	none	X	
505	86			X			X	X		X	X	3/1	none		
147	79	70	100	X				X					3/1	X	
944	33							X				3/16	none	X	
311	85	210	100	X			X	X			X	3/15	none	X	
1,103	40												none	X	
475	46	231	100										2/1	X	
527	20			X				X				7/1	none	X	
72	100			X			X	X			X	4/1	none	X	
2,188	33	1,238	87	X	X	X	X	X	X	X	X	2/15	3/1		
954	54	730	93	X				X	X	X	X	3/1	none		
424	65							X			X	3/15	none	X	

Connecticut: Wesleyan University

Institution	Tuition and fees	Add'l out-of-state/ district tuition	Books and supplies	Room and board	Trans-portation	Other costs	Board only	Trans-portation	Other costs
Wesleyan University	18,780		500	5,390		850		850	
Western Connecticut State University	2,887	3,924/—	700	3,722	280	1,149	900	650	1,149
Yale University	18,630		620	6,480	522	1,400			1,400
Delaware									
Delaware State College	‡ 1,788	880/—	400	3,454	750	1,250		500	1,500
Delaware Technical and Community College									
Southern Campus	‡ 1,119	1,566/—	450				1,500	500	300
Stanton/Wilmington Campus	‡ 1,119	1,566/—	450				1,500	500	300
Terry Campus	‡ 1,119	1,566/—	450				1,500	500	300
Goldey-Beacom College	5,820		485		600	6,035	1,634	850	974
University of Delaware	‡ 3,721	5,660/—	530	3,756		1,300			1,300
Wesley College	9,645		500	4,100	600	695	1,950	757	1,345
Wilmington College	5,290		700				1,800	2,000	1,500
District of Columbia									
American University	15,386		450	6,154	700	600	1,600	700	600
Catholic University of America	13,644		480	6,220	500	1,100	850	500	1,100
Corcoran School of Art	10,480		1,700		1,050	1,785	1,650	1,050	1,785
Gallaudet University	4,570		630	5,110	947	2,232	741	947	1,945
George Washington University	16,988		600	5,482		950		600	950
Georgetown University	17,586		630	6,824	400	1,170	820	500	1,170
Howard University	7,535		700	4,100	250	2,250	2,000	967	2,250
Mount Vernon College	13,250		500	6,918		600			600
Oblate College	4,250		500					200	
Southeastern University	8,250		400				1,000	600	850
Strayer College	‡ 4,860		450				2,625	1,150	2,100
Trinity College	11,230		500	6,430	600	800		500	
University of the District of Columbia	‡ 800	2,880/—	600					800	1,400
Florida									
Art Institute of Fort Lauderdale	‡ 8,014		953				1,000	1,260	750
Barry University	† 10,770		500	5,600	650	800	700	800	800
Bethune-Cookman College	5,165		500	3,396	490	1,520	1,500	775	840
Brevard Community College	‡ 990	2,719/—	450				1,800	600	600
Broward Community College	† 960	2,778/—	640				1,620	1,552	1,080
Caribbean Center for Advanced Studies:									
Miami Institute of Psychology	5,660		600						
Central Florida Community College	‡ 1,044	2,870/—	540				1,620	1,125	666
Chipola Junior College	‡ 893	2,550/—	375		700	500	1,400	1,020	500
Clearwater Christian College	5,300		500	3,200	800	800	2,000	1,800	2,000
Daytona Beach Community College	† 1,040	2,868/—	464				1,630	1,000	1,000
Eckerd College	14,930		575	3,925	780	590	1,500	450	345
Edison Community College	‡ 910	2,355/—	450				1,500	876	732
Edward Waters College	‡ 3,930		400	3,400	500	750		600	550
Embry-Riddle Aeronautical University	7,430		540	3,400	1,860	1,200	1,500	1,240	1,200
Flagler College	4,920		500	3,070	700	1,360	1,680	800	1,360
Florida Agricultural and Mechanical University	1,829	4,903/—	315	4,903	680	1,050	1,010	680	1,050
Florida Atlantic University	† 1,550	3,800/—	600	4,090	1,150	1,120	1,700	1,770	1,120
Florida Baptist Theological College	2,050		485		1,000	600	1,800	1,000	
Florida Bible College	4,090		350	2,050	600	2,973	1,500	650	975
Florida Christian College	3,695		625		825	1,440	2,215	1,030	1,440

†Figures are projected for 1993-94. ‡Figures are for 1992-93.

Florida: Florida Christian College

All aid		Need-based aid		Grants and scholarships								Financial aid deadlines		Inst aid form	Notes
Total freshmen	Percent receiving aid	Freshmen judged to have need	Percent offered aid	Need-based				Non-need-based							
				Acad	Music/drama	Art	Athl	Acad	Music/drama	Art	Athl	Priority	Closing		
706	51	363	100										1/15	X	
384	65							X					3/15	X	
1,327	46	639	100										2/1	X	
								X	X		X	5/1	none		
610	33			X			X	X					none		
1,513	25							X			X	7/1	none		
376	25											5/30	none		
317	60			X				X			X	4/1	none	X
3,007	63	1,259	98	X				X	X		X	3/15	5/1		
306	70	254	100					X	X			4/15	none	X	
199	47							X			X	6/1	none		
1,059	60	530	100	X			X	X			X	3/1	none		
499	80			X	X			X	X			2/15	none	X
75	64			X		X		X		X		3/15	6/15	X
366	68	253	99	X								4/15	none	X
1,233	80			X				X	X		X	2/1			
1,391	50	541	100	X			X					2/1	none		
				X				X	X	X	X	3/1	4/1		
89	60	30	100	X				X	X			3/1	none		
													none	X	
112	45							X				6/1	none		
936	64			X				X				7/1	none		
89	81			X				X				3/1	none		
1,534	4	300	83					X	X		X	3/15	none	X
778	51												none	X	
1,165	75			X			X	X	X		X	4/1	none	X
603	84	519	97	X	X		X	X	X		X	3/1	none	X
2,253	27	1,470	100	X	X	X	X	X	X	X	X	5/8	none	
								X	X	X	X	4/15	none	X
													6/1		
				X				X	X		X	5/1	none	X
1,357	62	700	100					X	X	X	X	6/15	none	X
103	51			X	X			X				5/1	none		
								X	X	X	X		none		
349	79	197	100	X	X	X	X	X	X	X	X	4/1	none	
1,765	35							X	X	X	X	6/1	none	
197	83												none		
608	75	430	99	X				X			X	4/15	none	
300	75	150	100	X	X	X	X	X	X	X	X	3/15	4/1	X
								X	X		X	4/1	none		
893	50			X				X	X		X	4/15	none	
51	85			X	X							5/1	none	
50	65	10	100					X	X			5/31	none	
54	87	39	100					X	X			4/15	7/15	X

109

Florida: Florida College

Institution	Tuition and fees	Add'l out-of-state/ district tuition	Books and supplies	Costs for campus residents			Costs for students at home		
				Room and board	Transportation	Other costs	Board only	Transportation	Other costs
Florida College	4,350		800	3,100	1,250	950	1,800	500	
Florida Community College at Jacksonville	† 990	2,610/—	450				804	727	1,149
Florida Institute of Technology	13,205		750	4,300	1,150	1,452	1,600	1,150	1,452
Florida International University	† 1,870	5,234/—	750	5,820	1,320	1,708	1,552	1,810	1,336
Florida Memorial College	4,750		550	2,950		900	1,170	2,140	1,100
Florida Southern College	7,610		500	4,600	600	600	1,950	600	600
Florida State University	1,780	4,902/—	500	3,880	600	850		600	850
Fort Lauderdale College	‡ 4,511		150			360	1,600	1,075	360
Gulf Coast Community College	† 910	2,440/—	600				2,395	750	900
Hillsborough Community College	† 848	2,317/—	600				1,800	1,640	2,000
Hobe Sound Bible College	4,000		400	2,475	800	2,000	1,400	400	2,000
Indian River Community College	‡ 900	2,664/—	450					350	400
Jacksonville University	10,080		700	4,250	600	800	1,000	600	800
Jones College	3,900		750					950	1,700
Lake City Community College	† 900	2,460/—	350	2,774					
Lake-Sumter Community College	‡ 1,043	2,685/—	370				1,600	980	500
Lynn University	13,200		500	5,100	1,100	1,100	1,500	550	550
Manatee Community College	† 967	2,296/—	535				6,300	1,100	1,020
Miami-Dade Community College	‡ 996	2,469/—	920				2,146	2,566	2,726
National Education Center: Bauder Campus	‡ 5,717		450					522	1,206
New College of the University of South Florida	† 1,855	5,705/—	600	3,612	490	2,100	1,664	1,720	2,100
New England Institute of Technology	‡ 6,300		265				1,500	850	1,190
North Florida Junior College	† 773	2,227/—	400				1,700	300	475
Nova University	† 8,320		700	4,600	1,900	1,950		1,900	1,950
Okaloosa-Walton Community College	† 966	2,718/—	496				2,456	824	900
Palm Beach Atlantic College	† 7,200		500	3,000			1,200		
Palm Beach Community College	† 939	2,355/—	600					1,061	800
Pasco-Hernando Community College	‡ 1,044	2,838/—	600				1,500	792	1,480
Pensacola Junior College	‡ 1,035	2,838/—	500				1,920	640	1,100
Phillips Junior College: Melbourne	† 4,995							113	
Polk Community College	† 1,045	2,869/—	350					1,000	500
Ringling School of Art and Design	10,350		1,500	5,400	500	500	2,000	500	500
Rollins College	15,950		400	4,925	750	550	1,500	350	51
St. John Vianney College Seminary	6,500		550	3,500	900	990			
St. Johns River Community College	† 900	2,700/—	550				1,500	600	781
St. Leo College	9,370		500	4,200	900	640		950	
St. Petersburg Junior College	‡ 1,001	2,677/—	500				2,100	1,015	915
St. Thomas University	9,680		550	4,600	1,250	2,000	2,200	1,250	2,000
Santa Fe Community College	† 990	2,835/—	690					800	800
Schiller International University	10,740		350	2,800	972	2,527			
Seminole Community College	‡ 996	2,580/—	500				1,705	720	918
South College: Palm Beach Campus	‡ 4,525		650						
South Florida Community College	† 1,035	2,700/—	700	1,978				1,300	1,000
Southeastern College of the Assemblies of God	‡ 3,600		600	2,860					
Southern College	4,722		565					608	210
Stetson University	11,995		600	4,440	540	825			
Tallahassee Community College	‡ 900	2,475/—	500					775	1,000
Tampa College	5,225							600	700

†Figures are projected for 1993-94. ‡Figures are for 1992-93.

Florida: Tampa College

All aid		Need-based aid		Grants and scholarships								Financial aid deadlines		Inst aid form	Notes
				Need-based				Non-need-based							
Total fresh-men	Percent receiving aid	Freshmen judged to have need	Percent offered aid	Acad	Music/ drama	Art	Athl	Acad	Music/ drama	Art	Athl	Priority	Closing		
196	80	103	100	X	X			X	X		X	6/1	none	X	
								X	X	X	X	3/1	none	X	
474	70			X				X			X	2/1	none	X	
1,105	40			X	X	X		X	X	X	X	3/15	5/1	X	
557	95			X			X	X	X			4/1	none		
396	82			X	X	X	X	X	X	X	X	4/15	none	X	
2,941	52	1,033	100					X	X	X	X		3/1	X	
289	45							X					none		
966	59			X				X	X	X	X	4/1	none	X	
								X	X	X	X	4/15	none	X	
44	55	30	100										none		
								X	X	X	X		none		
338	63			X	X	X	X	X	X	X	X	3/15	none		
200	80												none		
872	12			X	X		X	X			X	6/1	none		
								X	X	X		5/1	none		
454	51	105	99	X			X	X			X	2/15	none		
1,220	33			X	X	X	X	X	X	X	X	6/1	7/1		
8,359	47			X	X	X	X	X	X	X	X	4/15	none	X	
141	85			X									none		
111	76	48	92	X	X			X			X	2/1	6/1		
450	70							X					none	X	
448	25	308	100	X				X	X	X	X	7/1	none		
311	90	100	100	X				X			X	4/1	none	X	
879	40							X	X	X	X	4/1	none	X	
283	90			X				X	X		X	5/1	none		
				X				X	X		X		none		
1,124	43			X			X	X	X		X	6/1	none	X	
1,926	30			X				X	X	X	X	4/1	none		
210	52			X									none	X	
3,200	45	650	100	X	X	X	X	X	X	X	X		5/15		
240	70					X				X		3/15	none	X	
400	61			X		X	X	X	X	X	X	3/1	none	X	
11	50	4	100										none	X	
								X	X	X	X	5/15	none		
200	75			X	X	X	X	X	X	X	X	3/1	none	X	
3,440	60			X				X	X	X	X	4/15	none		
390	81											5/1	none		
1,709	55			X	X	X	X	X	X	X	X	3/1	4/1		
408	35			X				X				3/30	none		
				X	X	X	X	X	X	X	X	5/1	none	X	
102	97												none		
381	30			X	X		X	X	X		X	4/1	none	X	
								X	X			4/1	none	X	
280	87	282	100										none		
503	80	276	99	X	X		X	X	X		X	3/15	none	X	
5,821	18			X				X	X			6/1	none		
485	75			X									none		

111

Florida: Trinity College at Miami

Institution	Tuition and fees	Add'l out-of-state/district tuition	Books and supplies	Room and board	Trans-portation	Other costs	Board only	Trans-portation	Other costs
				\multicolumn{3}{c}{Costs for campus residents}	\multicolumn{3}{c}{Costs for students at home}	
Trinity College at Miami	6,450		700	3,240	540	900	2,250	540	1,800
University of Central Florida	† 1,820	5,000/—	660	4,990	1,640	1,630	1,580	1,640	1,630
University of Florida	† 1,770	5,120/—	600	4,080	510	1,130	1,500	750	1,130
University of Miami	15,700		600	6,227	968	924	1,800	1,004	880
University of North Florida	1,722	4,903/—	450	4,200				720	540
University of South Florida	† 1,820	4,759/—	500	3,626	400	2,180	1,750	1,640	2,180
University of Tampa	12,280		775	4,450		1,100		1,200	1,100
University of West Florida	† 1,667	4,760/—	523	3,859	519	1,352	1,666	968	1,397
Valencia Community College	† 1,043	2,706/—	500					2,200	700
Warner Southern College	6,750		600	3,270	500	1,200	2,500	500	1,200
Webber College	5,950		500	2,900	800	100	1,200	300	100
Georgia									
Abraham Baldwin Agricultural College	† 1,311	939/—	675	2,820	648	1,146	1,011	648	1,146
Agnes Scott College	12,135		450	5,000	850	500	1,500	850	500
Albany State College	1,773	1,380/—	675	2,475	486	726	1,683	369	726
American College for the Applied Arts	‡ 7,440				560	960			
Andrew College	4,590		600	3,780	700	1,200	950	200	1,100
Armstrong State College	† 1,569	1,380/—	450	3,306	500	750	1,575	800	1,425
Art Institute of Atlanta	‡ 7,900		1,500		500	500	1,100	200	500
Athens Area Technical Institute	‡ 740	740/—						3,174	
Atlanta Christian College	4,000		400	2,900		500			500
Atlanta Metropolitan College	1,164	939/—	500						
Augusta College	† 1,593	1,380/—	480		975	4,206	975	975	975
Bainbridge College	1,089	939/—	600				1,800	1,734	450
Bauder College	‡ 6,120		650		1,000	1,100	1,100	1,000	1,100
Brenau University	8,823		600	5,911	575	800	1,500	775	800
Brewton-Parker College	‡ 3,885		575	2,295		1,000	1,140	500	1,000
Brunswick College	1,179	939/—	600				1,600	1,000	500
Chattahoochee Technical Institute	‡ 654	360/—	850						
Clark Atlanta University	7,460		630	4,200	840	945	1,970	378	945
Clayton State College	† 1,440	1,341/—	555				1,700	945	1,080
Columbus College	1,602	1,380/—	650				1,500	600	600
Covenant College	9,200		470	3,744	560	200	1,980	560	200
Dalton College	1,074	939/—	600				2,100	741	200
Darton College	1,119	939/—	300				1,100	450	600
DeKalb College	1,160	630/—	400						
DeKalb Technical Institute	840	180/—	400				2,000	660	600
DeVry Institute of Technology: Atlanta	‡ 5,249		500				1,777	2,226	1,911
East Georgia College	1,089	939/—	400				1,800	700	350
Emmanuel College	4,360		550	2,990	600	800	1,970	680	700
Emory University	16,820		570	5,110		1,100	1,800		1,100
Floyd College	† 1,089	939/—	495				2,400	600	450
Fort Valley State College	† 1,779	1,380/—	630	2,460	1,145	1,386	1,600	1,890	900
Gainesville College	1,104	939/—	500					1,600	1,000
Georgia College	† 1,695	1,380/—	400	2,829	721	1,352	1,446	721	1,228
Georgia Institute of Technology	‡ 2,277	2,610/—	795	4,308		1,164	2,265	1,062	1,050
Georgia Military College	‡ 3,270		475	3,654		1,025		550	1,025
Georgia Southern University	1,827	1,380/—	552	2,700	525	735	1,800	705	735
Georgia Southwestern College	† 1,704	1,380/—	600	2,570	400	750	1,500	650	770
Georgia State University	2,019	4,433/—	980				2,150	324	800
Gordon College	1,164	939/—	379	2,430	750	700	590	750	700
Gwinnett Technical Institute	756	360/—	500						

†Figures are projected for 1993-94. ‡Figures are for 1992-93.

Georgia: Gwinnett Technical Institute

Total freshmen	Percent receiving aid	Freshmen judged to have need	Percent offered aid	Acad	Music/drama	Art	Athl	Acad	Music/drama	Art	Athl	Priority	Closing	Inst aid form	Notes
38	80			X	X		X	X				4/1	none	X	
								X	X	X	X	3/15	none	X	
3,187	30	899	99	X				X	X		X	4/1	4/15	X	
1,790	83	1,483	100	X	X			X	X		X	3/1	none		
493	30			X				X	X		X	4/1	none	X	
		776	94	X				X	X	X	X	4/9	none		
305	70	225	100					X	X	X	X	3/15	none		
462	44			X				X	X			4/1	none	X	
3,130	37			X	X	X	X	X	X	X	X	4/1	none	X	
96	83			X			X	X			X	4/1	none		
82	73	55	100	X			X				X	3/31	7/15		
932	76	600	100	X	X	X	X	X	X	X	X	5/1	none	X	
133	94	92	100	X	X			X	X			3/15	none		
1,249	88			X	X		X	X				6/1	none	X	
285	70							X				6/1	none		
203	90			X	X	X	X	X	X	X	X	6/1	none	X	
378	25			X	X	X	X	X	X	X	X	5/31	none		
													none		
320	25			X											
64	65			X	X			X	X			6/1	8/1		
726	25			X	X							8/20	none		
		607	100	X	X	X		X	X	X	X	5/1	none	X	
114	39											7/1	none	X	
310	55												none		
133	55	71	100	X				X	X	X	X	5/15	none		
710	96							X	X	X	X	4/1	none	X	
111	50			X				X			X	5/1	none	X	
1,079	15	296	100	X				X					none		
797	78	561	100	X	X		X	X	X		X	4/1	4/15	X	
2,710	25	179	100	X				X	X	X	X	4/1	none	X	
358	37	161	100					X	X	X	X	6/1	none		
179	86	111	100		X	X		X	X		X	3/31	none	X	
				X				X				8/1	none	X	
				X				X	X	X		9/1	none	X	
				X			X						7/1	X	
				X				X				4/15	none	X	
858	86							X					none		
164	18			X				X					none		
294	95			X	X		X	X	X		X	3/15	none		
1,200	61	571	100	X				X	X			2/15	4/1		
289	45			X	X	X		X	X	X		4/30	6/30		
715	96	412	96	X	X		X	X	X		X	4/15	5/1	X	
1,981	17							X	X	X		4/15	none	X	
798	62	527	90	X	X	X	X	X	X		X	4/15	none	X	
2,391	39			X				X					3/1	X	
803	50											4/1	none		
2,858	22			X				X	X		X	3/1	4/15	X	
485	98	182	98					X	X	X	X	4/1	none	X	
1,553	25			X				X	X	X	X	5/1	none		
645	44							X	X	X	X	6/22	none	X	
													none		

113

Georgia: Kennesaw State College

Institution	Tuition and fees	Add'l out-of-state/ district tuition	Books and supplies	Costs for campus residents			Costs for students at home		
				Room and board	Trans-portation	Other costs	Board only	Trans-portation	Other costs
Kennesaw State College	† 1,560	1,380/—	600				2,265	900	935
LaGrange College	6,375		600	3,480	900	900		600	600
Macon College	1,113	939/—	500				1,500	800	950
Meadows College of Business	‡ 2,775								
Medical College of Georgia	2,085	1,845/—	700	3,807	315	1,170	1,773	495	1,170
Mercer University									
Atlanta	‡ 6,435		450				1,607	675	800
Macon	11,160		450	3,963	400	600	1,500	600	600
Middle Georgia College	† 1,284	939/—	515	2,520	288	515	1,515	309	515
Morehouse College	8,000		500	5,224		2,500	1,500		1,700
Morris Brown College	7,796		600	4,438	500	650		500	650
North Georgia College	1,662	1,380/—	525	2,445	750	1,191	1,545	1,530	640
Oglethorpe University	11,990		600	4,330	1,850	2,390	1,500	1,720	2,390
Oxford College of Emory University	12,350		450	4,348	350	750		750	750
Paine College	‡ 5,468		400	2,739	1,525	485			485
Piedmont College	‡ 4,430		600	3,320	600	900	1,500	800	900
Reinhardt College	‡ 4,140		500	3,375	70	1,000	1,200	600	400
Savannah College of Art and Design	9,180		1,200	5,250	900	6,000	2,580	316	600
Savannah State College	† 1,743	1,380/—	575	2,310	650	650	1,275	650	
Savannah Technical Institute	‡ 744	756/—							
Shorter College	6,670		500	3,600	600	1,400	1,750	1,350	1,400
South College	† 4,525		450				2,115	1,109	1,260
South Georgia College	† 1,152	939/—	600	2,880	600	750	2,100	600	750
Southern College of Technology	1,650	1,380/—	650	2,775		750	2,000	1,000	750
Spelman College	7,702		600	5,250	800	1,300	2,625	800	1,300
Thomas College	3,084		525		750	651	2,500	750	651
Toccoa Falls College	‡ 5,436		500	3,264	1,108	1,354		982	1,354
Truett-McConnell College	‡ 3,885		450	2,475	400	600		650	600
University of Georgia	2,250	1,845/—	525	3,165		1,230	1,725		1,650
Valdosta State College	† 1,731	1,380/—	600	2,913	636	636	830	636	636
Waycross College	1,134	939/—	500				1,500	600	900
Wesleyan College	11,195		515	4,250	412	957	2,150	412	957
West Georgia College	† 1,497	1,380/—	450	2,436	750	1,000	1,800	1,200	1,000
Young Harris College	† 5,000		500	3,605	450	900	1,500	750	600
Hawaii									
Brigham Young University-Hawaii	2,225		450	4,200		1,000			1,000
Hawaii Pacific University	5,900		600	5,600	1,000	900	1,950	400	900
University of Hawaii									
Hawaii Community College	510	2,290/—	554	4,151	207	914	2,414	207	914
Hilo	510	2,340/—	687	4,151	207	1,074	2,414	207	914
Honolulu Community College	470	2,340/—	554					207	914
Kapiolani Community College	475	2,800/—	554				2,011	207	777
Kauai Community College	470	2,340/—	554				2,414	207	914
Manoa	‡ 1,437	2,730/—	540	3,186	207	1,342		207	892
West Oahu	870	1,940/—	687				1,463	207	1,865
Windward Community College	480	2,340/—	554				2,414	207	914
Idaho									
Albertson College	‡ 10,750		400	2,850	400	675	1,850		675
Boise Bible College	‡ 3,261		400	2,840	600	895	1,500	609	417
Boise State University	1,480	3,050/—	400	3,240	550	928	1,300	600	603
College of Southern Idaho	900	1,200/—	800	2,870	1,300	1,530	2,000	1,300	1,100
Idaho State University	1,386	3,614/—	500	2,970	360	1,575	1,800	360	1,575

†Figures are projected for 1993-94. ‡Figures are for 1992-93.

Idaho: Idaho State University

All aid		Need-based aid		Grants and scholarships								Financial aid deadlines		Inst aid form	Notes
Total freshmen	Percent receiving aid	Freshmen judged to have need	Percent offered aid	Need-based				Non-need-based							
				Acad	Music/ drama	Art	Athl	Acad	Music/ drama	Art	Athl	Priority	Closing		
1,184	15	213	100	X	X		X	X	X	X	X	4/15	5/1	X	
200	75	115	100	X				X	X	X		5/1	none	X	
1,116	25							X				4/1	none	X	
101	90												none		
				X				X				3/2	none	X	
				X				X				5/1	none	X	
667	80			X				X	X	X	X	5/1	none	X	
698	28			X				X	X		X	7/1	none	X	
660	70			X				X	X		X		4/1	X	
628	95			X			X	X	X	X	X	4/15	6/15	X	
492	70	361	100	X			X	X	X	X	X	5/15	none		
238	81	144	100	X	X			X	X				5/1		
335	78	130	100	X				X				4/1	none		
225	90				X				X			5/15	none	X	
161	88	80	100	X				X	X	X	X	6/1	7/1		
				X	X	X	X						5/1		
777	55	315	100	X		X		X		X		4/1	none	X	
686	85			X	X		X	X	X		X	5/1	8/1		
460	36	183	100					X					none		
224	100			X	X	X	X	X	X	X	X	4/1	none	X	
83	85							X					none		
411	68							X			X		7/12	X	
346	38			X			X	X			X	3/15	5/31	X	
548	81	375	81	X	X			X	X				4/15	X	
78	66			X	X			X				9/1	none		
300	75	165	100					X	X			4/1	none	X	
732	95							X	X		X		none	X	
3,231	30			X	X		X	X	X			3/1	none	X	
924	36	575	100					X	X	X	X	5/1	none	X	
				X				X	X	X	X		9/19	X	
135	86	111	74	X				X	X	X		4/1	none	X	
1,260	45	513	100	X				X	X	X	X	3/15	none		
				X				X	X	X	X	5/1	7/1	X	
550	80	400	100	X					X	X	X	X		7/31	
1,799	25	171	100					X	X		X	3/15	none		
345	33	375	100	X				X				3/1	none	X	
307	49			X	X	X	X	X	X	X	X	3/1	none	X	
1,058	7							X				5/1	none		
1,389	20			X				X				5/1	none		
				X	X			X	X			5/1	none	X	
				X				X	X		X	3/1	none		
								X	X	X		5/1	none	X	
594	10							X				4/1	none		
176	80			X	X	X	X	X	X	X	X	3/1	none	X	
49	81							X					none	X	
1,869	60			X	X	X		X	X	X	X	3/31	none		
1,027	65			X	X	X	X	X	X	X	X	3/1	none	X	
1,137	80			X	X	X	X	X	X	X	X	3/15	none		

Idaho: Lewis Clark State College

Institution	Tuition and fees	Add'l out-of-state/ district tuition	Books and supplies	Room and board	Trans- portation	Other costs	Board only	Trans- portation	Other costs
				Costs for campus residents			*Costs for students at home*		
Lewis Clark State College	1,320	2,920/—	560	3,026	852	1,116	1,864	756	796
North Idaho College	942	1,602/1,000	500	3,064	500	830	1,700	500	830
Northwest Nazarene College	9,105		675	2,645	630	788	1,575	579	723
Ricks College	‡ 1,550		550	2,760	1,000	1,000	1,335	700	1,000
University of Idaho	1,426	3,900/—	770	3,400	860	1,650	1,800	860	1,650
Illinois									
American Academy of Art	‡ 8,380		800						
American Conservatory of Music	7,000		500					800	1,200
Augustana College	‡ 12,009		480	3,849	300	250	600	1,750	1,000
Aurora University	9,700		600	3,681	1,142	1,415	2,285	1,305	870
Barat College	9,830		700	4,300	1,000	1,500		1,500	1,500
Belleville Area College	1,060	3,030/2,130	500				1,500	1,200	1,320
Black Hawk College									
East Campus	1,500	4,110/1,740	500				1,334	677	1,418
Moline	1,500	4,110/1,740	500				1,334	677	1,418
Blackburn College	8,120		500	1,000	250	800	1,500	50	800
Blessing-Reiman College of Nursing	7,850		400	3,075	250	500	1,725	500	500
Bradley University	10,408		480	4,310	200	1,322	500	600	1,902
Carl Sandburg College	‡ 1,350	4,310/1,678	450				1,600	1,400	500
Chicago State University	2,198	3,696/—	825		1,200	3,000	2,000	1,200	2,000
City Colleges of Chicago									
Harold Washington College	‡ 985	2,940/1,895	600				1,500	540	1,761
Kennedy-King College	‡ 985	2,940/1,895	600				1,500	540	1,761
Malcolm X College	‡ 985	2,940/1,895	600				1,500	540	1,761
Olive-Harvey College	‡ 985	2,940/1,895	600				1,500	540	1,761
College of DuPage	‡ 990	3,285/2,070	860				1,968	1,435	1,065
College of Lake County	1,181	5,206/3,931	400						
College of St. Francis	9,100		400	3,970	340	900	1,500	710	900
Columbia College	‡ 6,654		500				1,560	700	1,612
Concordia University	8,576		450	4,035	400	600	1,750	310	600
Danville Area Community College	† 1,150	3,107/1,830	800				1,600	1,000	1,400
De Paul University	10,590		480	6,723	660	1,300	1,500	400	1,100
DeVry Institute of Technology									
Addison	5,580		525				1,792	2,007	1,928
Chicago	5,580		525				1,792	2,007	1,928
Eastern Illinois University	2,600	3,696/—	120	2,948	400	1,280	1,800	800	1,790
East-West University	6,282		600				1,200	500	1,800
Elgin Community College	‡ 1,110	3,210/2,220	550				2,400	1,100	700
Elmhurst College	9,676		550	3,964		2,000	1,500	1,150	1,600
Eureka College	11,105		330	3,450	160	510	1,840	675	295
Gem City College	3,150		400					400	1,800
Governors State University	1,978	3,696/—	450				1,600	800	800
Greenville College	10,030		400	4,360	500	500	1,685	300	500
Harrington Institute of Interior Design	‡ 8,025		925			2,000		1,000	2,000
Highland Community College	1,050	2,997/2,012	550				1,500	1,500	1,045
Illinois Benedictine College	10,080		650	4,067		1,500	2,460		1,500
Illinois Central College	1,350	3,330/2,170	500	3,225			2,225	1,344	2,335
Illinois College	7,550		600	3,650	300	700		700	200
Illinois Eastern Community Colleges									
Frontier Community College	820	3,234/2,224	600				1,500	1,200	800
Lincoln Trail College	820	3,234/2,224	600				1,500	1,200	800

†Figures are projected for 1993-94. ‡Figures are for 1992-93.

Illinois: Illinois Eastern Community Colleges: Lincoln Trail College

Total freshmen	Percent receiving aid	Freshmen judged to have need	Percent offered aid	Acad	Music/drama	Art	Athl	Acad	Music/drama	Art	Athl	Priority	Closing	Inst aid form	Notes
529	64	256	91	X			X	X	X		X	3/1	none	X	
1,146	43			X				X	X	X	X	4/15	none	X	
290	85							X	X	X	X	3/1	none	X	
2,843	78							X	X	X	X		none	X	
1,353	65			X	X	X	X	X	X	X	X	2/15	none	X	
185	45									X			none	X	
7	69								X			6/1	none		
538	88	404	100					X	X	X		4/1	none	X	
				X				X				5/1	none		
111	70	95	100	X	X	X	X	X	X	X		3/15	none	X	
9,986	50			X				X	X	X	X	5/31	none	X	
291	60			X				X			X	6/1	none		
1,778	62			X	X	X	X	X	X	X	X	5/15	none		
203	89			X				X				4/1	none		
				X				X						X	
1,193	82	595	100	X				X	X	X	X	3/1	none		
2,000	60			X	X	X	X	X	X	X	X	5/1	none	X	
698	75	478	100	X					X	X	X	4/15	none	X	
2,515	42			X								5/1	none		
				X									none		
				X								5/1	none		
1,946	72							X			X	8/10	none	X	
6,123	10			X	X	X		X	X	X		6/15	none		
									X	X	X		none	X	
160	95	117	100	X			X	X			X	5/1	none		
				X				X				5/1	none		
252	81			X	X			X	X			6/1	none		
950	80	900	100					X			X	6/1	none		
961	69			X	X	X	X	X	X	X	X	5/1			
765	71							X					none		
1,014	77							X					none		
				X				X	X	X	X	4/15	none	X	
								X					none		
2,497	28	378	65	X				X	X	X	X	7/1	none	X	
235	59	144	100	X	X			X	X			4/15	none	X	
118	90							X	X	X		5/1	none		
													none		
				X				X	X	X		5/1	10/1	X	
228	94			X				X				6/1	none	X	
89	39											6/1	none		
1,108	40			X	X	X	X	X	X	X	X	6/1	none		
231	94							X	X	X		4/15	none	X	
2,546	18	1,000	95	X		X		X			X	4/15	none	X	
261	85			X				X	X			5/1	none		
				X	X	X		X					none		
				X	X	X	X	X					none		

Illinois: Illinois Eastern Community Colleges: Olney Central College

| | | | | Costs for campus residents ||| Costs for students at home |||
Institution	Tuition and fees	Add'l out-of-state/district tuition	Books and supplies	Room and board	Trans-portation	Other costs	Board only	Trans-portation	Other costs
Olney Central College	820	3,234/2,224	600				1,500	1,200	800
Wabash Valley College	820	3,234/2,224	600				1,500	1,200	800
Illinois Institute of Technology	13,750		800	4,540	100	800	1,500	800	1,000
Illinois State University	‡ 2,791	4,322/—	500	2,910	430	1,867	1,800	900	1,937
Illinois Valley Community College	1,004	2,760/1,800	450				1,500	1,152	1,044
Illinois Wesleyan University	13,295		400	3,985	100	550	800	310	600
International Academy of Merchandising and Design	8,000		500					525	1,500
ITT Technical Institute: Hoffman Estates	‡ 7,402		1,100						
John A. Logan College	‡ 748	4,896/2,192	450				1,320	1,240	550
Joliet Junior College	1,080	3,400/2,780	400				1,727	1,097	1,274
Judson College	9,284		450	4,422	200	1,000	2,500	400	1,000
Kankakee Community College	1,216	4,320/720	480				1,008	768	855
Kaskaskia College	‡ 1,013	3,270/1,050	500				900	672	648
Kendall College	7,880		400	4,851			2,005	300	
Kishwaukee College	‡ 1,040	2,857/1,936	400				1,500	1,152	943
Knox College	15,132		350	3,858	200	600	2,142	200	
Lake Forest College	16,175		500	3,785	300	140		775	1,500
Lake Land College	† 1,209	2,850/990	205				1,800	1,530	830
Lakeview College of Nursing	5,775		400						
Lewis and Clark Community College	1,035	4,011/1,875	600				2,000	800	1,000
Lewis University	10,112		400	4,340	600	1,200	1,700	1,350	1,200
Lexington Institute of Hospitality Careers	† 4,800		600	3,000	720	360		720	360
Lincoln Christian College and Seminary	4,304		500	2,750	400	1,530	1,000	400	1,530
Lincoln College	8,205		450	3,650	200	1,000	2,300	500	1,000
Lincoln Land Community College	1,033	2,910/1,380	450					650	500
Loyola University of Chicago	10,680		700	5,230		1,500	1,650		1,500
MacCormac Junior College	6,300		600				1,650	444	1,200
MacMurray College	9,120		625	3,680	350	500		350	500
McHenry County College	‡ 1,156	4,740/3,810	440				1,600	1,160	1,400
McKendree College	7,010		500	3,600	200	800	250	600	800
Mennonite College of Nursing	7,560		450	2,240	220	600	1,500	220	600
Millikin University	11,331		450	4,168	200	765	2,000	200	765
Monmouth College	13,000		400	3,800	90	150	1,500	200	
Montay College	5,630		500				1,620	810	990
Moody Bible Institute	754		400	3,750	200	500		500	500
Moraine Valley Community College	‡ 1,172	3,180/2,520	405				1,500	1,031	1,256
Morrison Institute of Technology	† 6,500		800	2,000	400	1,200	1,000	800	1,200
Morton College	1,320	3,115/2,200	400				2,000	1,000	900
National College of Chiropractic	8,352		830		950	1,945		1,160	2,130
National-Louis University	9,090		645	4,500	360	1,116	2,124	1,251	1,116
North Central College	11,286		450	4,212	320	1,180	1,500	1,050	1,180
North Park College	11,990		650	4,290	550	515	1,500	550	600
Northeastern Illinois University	2,340	3,696/—	515				1,663	564	2,150
Northern Illinois University	3,343	4,950/—	450	3,086	350	1,376	2,116	350	1,376
Northwestern University	15,804		723	5,289		1,059		984	1,059
Oakton Community College	948	3,798/3,750	400				1,750	1,100	1,000
Olivet Nazarene University	7,836		500	4,140	400	900		400	900
Parks College of St. Louis University	8,510		450	4,020	250	800		840	800
Principia College	12,567		375	5,232		750			

†Figures are projected for 1993-94. ‡Figures are for 1992-93.

Illinois: Principia College

All aid		Need-based aid		Grants and scholarships								Financial aid deadlines		Inst aid form	Notes
Total freshmen	Percent receiving aid	Freshmen judged to have need	Percent offered aid	Need-based				Non-need-based							
				Acad	Music/drama	Art	Athl	Acad	Music/drama	Art	Athl	Priority	Closing		
				X	X	X	X	X					none		
				X	X	X	X	X					none		
409	96			X			X					5/1	none	X	
								X	X	X	X	3/1	none	X	
								X	X	X		5/1	none	X	
553	85	358	100	X	X	X		X	X	X		3/1	none		
170	35	91	100					X					none	X	
131	95												none	X	
1,430	65			X				X	X	X	X	5/1	none		
2,599	25	1,200	83					X	X	X		7/1	none		
133	94	102	100	X				X	X	X	X	5/1	none		
1,300	55			X				X	X	X	X	6/1	none	X	
1,898	19	313	96					X	X		X	7/1	none		
158	62			X				X				6/1	none	X	
				X			X	X			X	6/1	none	X	
292	89	212	100	X	X	X		X	X	X		3/1	none		
235	58											3/1	none	X	
1,438	46			X			X	X	X	X	X	5/1	none	X	
														X	
2,003	52							X	X		X	6/1	none	X	
651	80							X	X	X	X	4/1	none		
26	76	14	100	X				X				6/1	none		
129	90			X				X				8/10	none	X	
1,140	84			X	X	X	X	X	X	X	X		none	X	
								X	X	X	X	5/1	none	X	
1,080	75			X				X	X	X	X	4/1	none		
350	80												none		
204	92			X	X	X		X	X	X		1/1	8/1		
2,000	20	300	83					X		X	X	7/1	none	X	
143	85			X			X	X			X	6/1	none		
				X				X				4/1	none	X	
521	91	459	100	X	X	X		X	X	X		6/1	none	
124	86	93	100	X	X	X		X	X	X			3/1		
118	56	26	100	X	X	X		X	X	X		6/1	none	X	
388	2			X	X								none	X	
								X				6/1	none	X	
91	60							X					none		
								X		X	X	6/1	none	X	
				X				X				8/1	none	X	
273	85			X				X			X	6/15	none		
295	85			X				X	X	X		4/1	none	X	
211	85			X	X	X		X	X	X		4/1	8/1	X	
791	22							X	X	X	X	4/1	none	X	
2,759	68			X					X	X	X	3/1	5/1		
1,888	60	953	100						X		X	2/15			
								X	X	X	X	6/1	none		
388	86	317	100	X	X	X	X	X	X	X	X	4/1	8/1	X	
138	80			X				X				1/1	none	X	
121	82	104	100					X				3/1	none	X	

119

Illinois: Quincy University

Institution	Tuition and fees	Add'l out-of-state/ district tuition	Books and supplies	Costs for campus residents			Costs for students at home		
				Room and board	Trans- portation	Other costs	Board only	Trans- portation	Other costs
Quincy University	9,742		400	3,904	460	620	1,500	460	620
Ray College of Design	8,330		1,000				2,241	540	1,260
Richland Community College	1,035	3,041/2,083	400					1,000	
Robert Morris College: Chicago	8,100		525				1,125	450	1,020
Rock Valley College	1,204	4,785/2,673	600					1,080	2,400
Rockford College	11,500		800	3,800	140	1,080	1,500	756	1,080
Roosevelt University	8,640		528	4,950	600	1,456	1,580	600	1,456
Rosary College	10,550		500	4,490	50	900	1,500	500	900
Rush University	† 9,434		325		235	1,100		510	1,100
St. Augustine College	5,800		835				1,570	650	750
St. Francis Medical Center College of Nursing	6,343		600	3,750	350	1,257	1,500	350	1,257
St. Joseph College of Nursing	7,460		750				1,800	750	1,350
St. Xavier University	† 10,340		450	4,410	284	779	1,764	814	779
Sangamon State University	2,539	4,522/—	600		740	1,454	1,500	1,220	854
Sauk Valley Community College	† 1,110	2,375/1,301	500					1,000	900
School of the Art Institute of Chicago	13,380		1,860				2,472	450	1,080
Shawnee Community College	694	4,296/1,453	300				1,500	1,632	540
Shimer College	11,200		650			1,300			
Southeastern Illinois College	750	3,570/3,150	500				1,500	1,300	855
Southern Illinois University									
Carbondale	3,052	4,500/—	575	3,182	700	1,900	1,500	700	1,208
Edwardsville	2,199	3,454/—	215	3,300	1,146	1,146	1,500	1,146	1,016
Spoon River College	1,170	4,170/300	500						
Springfield College in Illinois	5,540		400		276	3,225	390	1,700	878
State Community College	‡ 918	4,620/—	200				1,550	425	1,300
Trinity Christian College	9,460		600	3,800	700	1,050	1,850	800	900
Trinity College	9,750		600	4,110	400	900	2,030	400	900
Triton College	† 1,146	4,470/2,550	450				1,100	1,020	
University of Chicago	18,207		652	6,130		556			
University of Illinois									
Chicago	3,317	4,194/—	630	4,988	702	3,100	1,800	702	2,526
Urbana-Champaign	3,388	4,252/—	500	4,358	400	1,600			
VanderCook College of Music	8,930		400	4,610	450	400	3,300	500	250
West Suburban College of Nursing	8,576		350	4,035	200	525	2,000	525	600
Western Illinois University	2,548	3,696/—	595	3,043	620	1,317	925	1,050	1,277
Wheaton College	10,640		500	4,070		1,300	1,710		1,100
William Rainey Harper College	‡ 1,030	3,630/2,670	450				1,150	800	1,325
Indiana									
Ancilla College	2,460		400				950	800	700
Anderson University	9,520		500	3,400	400	700	1,600	400	700
Ball State University	‡ 2,464	3,408/—	500	3,376	352	1,100	1,500	1,078	1,100
Bethel College	8,500		600	2,900	600	700	1,900	1,000	700
Butler University	12,280		500	4,245	340	1,260	2,500	340	1,260
Calumet College of St. Joseph	† 4,250		400				1,545	775	1,130
DePauw University	13,700		550	4,830	250	700	1,500	670	280
Earlham College	15,326		550	4,056	600	600	2,079		600
Franklin College	10,090		525	3,870	450	895	2,520	675	895
Goshen College	8,770		560	3,590	360	960	1,503	360	960
Grace College	8,450		400	3,670	425	800	1,600	975	700
Hanover College	7,750		500	3,200	400	800	2,000	450	800
Holy Cross College	4,950		500				1,902	2,088	1,441

†Figures are projected for 1993-94. ‡Figures are for 1992-93.

Indiana: Holy Cross College

All aid		Need-based aid		Grants and scholarships								Financial aid deadlines		Inst aid form	Notes
				Need-based				Non-need-based							
Total freshmen	Percent receiving aid	Freshmen judged to have need	Percent offered aid	Acad	Music/drama	Art	Athl	Acad	Music/drama	Art	Athl	Priority	Closing		
317	98			X				X	X	X	X		none		
360	86	66	100	X				X		X		1/1	none	X	
1,479	28			X			X	X			X		none		
2,343	82							X				6/1	none		
2,536	48							X	X			6/1	none		
143	80			X	X	X		X	X	X		4/15	none		
256	60			X	X	X		X	X	X		5/1	none		
145	75	107	100	X				X			X	5/1	none		
				X								4/15	none		
509	97							X					none	X	
								X					none		
				X									6/1	X	
221	34	142	100	X	X		X	X	X		X	3/1	none		
				X				X			X	4/1	none	X	
1,585	35							X	X		X	5/1	none	X	
203	72			X		X				X		4/1	none	X	
669	72			X				X	X	X	X	9/1	none	X	
42	80	10	100	X	X	X		X	X	X		6/1	7/31	X	
2,200	68			X	X	X	X	X	X	X	X	8/19	none		
2,689	90							X	X	X	X	4/1	none		
1,027	70			X	X	X	X	X	X	X	X	4/1	none		
1,600	80			X	X	X	X	X	X	X			none		
130	89			X			X	X	X	X		5/1	none	X	
400	85											7/1	none	X	
148	87							X	X	X	X	2/15	8/15		
203	87							X	X		X	4/1			
6,785	44			X				X				4/15	none	X	
910	67							X	X	X	X		2/1	X	
2,667	86			X			X	X	X		X	3/1	none		
5,504	78	2,411	97	X				X	X	X	X	3/15	none		
12	81								X			3/1	6/1		
													4/1	X	
1,634	85							X	X	X	X	3/1	none	X	
549	69	302	100					X	X			3/15		X	
3,814	12			X				X	X	X		5/1	none	X	
497	60	145	100	X		X	X	X			X	5/1	none	X	
577	87			X	X	X		X	X	X		3/1	none		
3,262	60	1,729	97			X		X	X		X	3/1	none		
								X	X		X	3/1	none	X	
758	80	520	100				X	X	X		X	3/1	none		
330	62	99	100	X				X					10/5		
566	59	243	100					X	X	X			2/15		
286	72	209	100	X	X	X		X				3/1	4/1	X	
309	95	223	100	X				X	X	X		3/1	none		
226	97	130	100	X	X	X	X	X	X		X	3/1	none	X	
167	85	144	100					X	X	X	X	4/1	none	X	
334	70			X				X				4/15	none		
200	47											3/1	none		

121

Indiana: Huntington College

Institution		Tuition and fees	Add'l out-of-state/ district tuition	Books and supplies	Costs for campus residents			Costs for students at home		
					Room and board	Trans-portation	Other costs	Board only	Trans-portation	Other costs
Huntington College		9,490		500	3,730	560	800	1,950	1,030	700
Indiana State University	‡	2,452	3,508/—	530	3,468	600	1,100	1,700	968	600
Indiana University										
Bloomington	†	2,828	5,712/—	584	3,630	398	1,486	1,500	936	1,394
East	†	2,354	3,450/—	587				1,892	1,080	1,052
Northwest	‡	2,156	3,195/—	500				2,050	1,705	1,436
South Bend	‡	2,255	3,195/—	574				1,810	1,356	1,356
Indiana University—Purdue University										
Fort Wayne	†	2,330	3,324/—	500				1,800	810	900
Indianapolis	‡	2,611	4,863/—	528	2,925	378	1,359	1,827	1,233	1,359
Indiana Vocational Technical College										
Central Indiana	‡	1,509	1,236/—	484					1,474	1,340
Columbus	‡	1,509	1,236/—	484					1,474	1,340
Eastcentral	†	1,509	1,236/—	515					640	1,236
Kokomo	‡	1,509	1,236/—	484					1,474	1,340
Lafayette	‡	1,509	1,236/—	484					1,474	1,340
Northcentral	‡	1,509	1,236/—	484					1,474	1,340
Northeast	†	1,610	1,380/—	515		640	2,800		640	5,800
Northwest	‡	1,509	1,236/—	484					1,474	1,340
Southcentral	†	1,674	1,371/—	515					1,780	1,975
Southeast	‡	1,509	1,236/—	484					1,474	1,340
Southwest	†	1,674	1,371/—	515					640	1,109
Wabash Valley	†	1,509	1,236/—	515					640	1,109
Whitewater	†	1,675	1,384/—	515					1,196	
Indiana Wesleyan University		8,660		640	3,672	400	528	800	400	550
Lutheran College of Health Professions		4,914		486			1,800	1,170	1,697	1,800
Manchester College		9,600		425	3,640	350	900	1,860	350	900
Marian College		9,360		450	3,616	650	900	1,500	640	900
Martin University		6,060		400			2,400		100	2,400
Oakland City College		7,026		700	2,840	900	1,350	2,500	900	1,800
Purdue University										
Calumet	†	2,269	3,339/—	490				1,860	1,086	1,169
North Central Campus	†	2,200	3,200/—	485				1,860	1,250	1,200
West Lafayette	†	2,720	6,130/—	570	4,450	640	1,060	1,840	1,770	1,060
Rose-Hulman Institute of Technology		12,495		500	3,984	300	600	1,550	800	600
St. Francis College		8,300		450	3,630	250	1,000	2,200	1,000	500
St. Joseph's College		10,830		500	3,900	320	500		1,760	2,960
St. Mary-of-the-Woods College		10,670		775	4,130	750	900	2,470	1,000	700
St. Mary's College		12,890		500	4,252	275	1,250	1,700	404	1,430
St. Meinrad College		6,003		500	4,227	1,100	900			
Taylor University		10,650		400	3,800		1,100	1,700		1,100
Tri-State University		9,642		469	4,200	412	850	1,550	320	320
University of Evansville		11,330		600	4,170	350	450	1,650	1,150	450
University of Indianapolis		10,590		515	3,920	410	975	1,585	820	925
University of Notre Dame		16,010		550	4,150	500	1,165	2,000	500	1,165
University of Southern Indiana	†	2,118	3,062/—	500		500	925	1,660	900	925
Valparaiso University		11,720		500	3,090	400	600	750	750	800
Vincennes University	†	2,220	3,270/1,110	500	3,480	700	550	550	1,000	500
Wabash College		12,450		500	4,000		635	2,000		635

†Figures are projected for 1993-94. ‡Figures are for 1992-93.

Indiana: Wabash College

All aid		Need-based aid		Grants and scholarships								Financial aid deadlines		Inst aid form	Notes
Total fresh-men	Percent receiving aid	Freshmen judged to have need	Percent offered aid	Need-based Acad	Music/ drama	Art	Athl	Non-need-based Acad	Music/ drama	Art	Athl	Priority	Closing		
155	89	119	100	X				X	X	X	X	3/1	9/1	X	
2,349	76							X	X	X	X		3/1	X	
6,086	70	1,914	92	X	X	X	X	X	X	X	X	3/1	none	X	
785	55	307	96	X				X				3/1	none	X	
1,250	40							X				3/1	none	X	
523	40							X	X	X		3/1	none	X	
								X	X	X	X	3/1	none		
2,964	65							X		X	X		3/1	X	
925	25							X				3/1	none	X	
594	60							X				3/1	none	X	
727	35			X								3/1	none	X	
517	45			X				X				3/1	none	X	
382	64			X				X				3/1	none	X	
								X				3/1	none	X	
768	56			X				X				3/1	none	X	
													none	X	
639	70											3/1	none		
207	66			X								3/1	none	X	
804	65			X				X				8/31	none	X	
735	80											3/1	none	X	
391	80											3/1			
415	82	286	100	X				X	X	X	X	4/1	none	X	
56	51			X				X				4/15	none	X	
247	82			X	X	X		X				5/1	none		
278	89	165	100	X	X	X	X	X	X	X	X	8/15	none	X	
251	80	60	100					X				3/1	none	X	
206	97	140	100	X				X	X	X	X	3/1	none		
2,942	41			X				X			X	3/1	none		
980	25	675	100					X				3/1	none		
5,492	60	3,400	85	X				X			X	3/1	none	X	
364	90	285	100					X				12/1	3/1		
84	80	92	100	X				X		X	X	3/1	none	X	
200	93	148	100	X				X	X		X	5/1	8/1	X	
341	82							X	X	X		3/1	none		
393	52	200	100	X	X	X						3/1	none		
29	100							X				3/1	none		
493	75	284	100	X				X	X		X		3/1		
225	90	164	100				X	X			X	3/1	none		
703	95	529	100					X	X	X	X	3/1	none		
365	76	252	100	X				X	X	X	X	3/1	none	X	
1,882	67	813	100	X							X		2/28		
1,399	53	807	86	X				X	X	X	X	3/1	none	X	
630	80							X	X		X	3/1	none		
3,529	60			X	X	X	X	X	X	X	X	3/1	none	X	
219	90	180	100					X	X	X		3/15	none		

Iowa: American Institute of Business

Institution	Tuition and fees	Add'l out-of-state/ district tuition	Books and supplies	Costs for campus residents — Room and board	Costs for campus residents — Transportation	Costs for campus residents — Other costs	Costs for students at home — Board only	Costs for students at home — Transportation	Costs for students at home — Other costs
Iowa									
American Institute of Business	5,000		720	2,760	480	990	930	855	1,620
American Institute of Commerce	‡ 5,095		850					1,008	1,206
Briar Cliff College	9,930		600	3,445	500	1,000	2,000	500	1,000
Buena Vista College	12,565		450	3,585	450	950	1,642	450	950
Central College	10,365		650	3,660	550	52	2,021	550	52
Clarke College	10,455		400	3,500	300	600	2,500	300	300
Clinton Community College	‡ 1,455	645/—	900				1,500	900	900
Coe College	12,805		500	4,280	500	1,200	890	500	1,200
Cornell College	14,228		550	4,197	200	1,000		200	1,000
Des Moines Area Community College	† 1,377	1,230/—	500				1,360	1,200	640
Divine Word College	‡ 5,535		400	1,200	800	800			
Dordt College	9,200		610	2,490	1,100	1,700	1,990	1,500	1,700
Drake University	12,780		550	4,520	175	1,500	1,500	500	1,500
Ellsworth Community College	‡ 1,865	1,750/—	400	2,700		1,800		1,000	1,800
Emmaus Bible College	1,820		400	3,900	800	1,770	2,000	504	1,770
Faith Baptist Bible College and Theological Seminary	‡ 4,436		345	2,964	800	1,000	1,800	800	1,000
Graceland College	8,680		550	2,920	370	880	1,870		880
Grand View College	9,870		450	3,360	400	625	1,333	543	656
Grinnell College	15,404		400	4,386	500	400		1,000	400
Hamilton Technical College	‡ 5,010						1,400	350	750
Hawkeye Community College	‡ 1,643	1,575/—	700				1,577	975	2,182
Indian Hills Community College	‡ 1,330	600/—	675	2,115	1,361	750	2,016	1,361	750
Iowa Central Community College	† 2,040	910/—	500	2,860	630	1,240	1,500	630	945
Iowa Lakes Community College	‡ 1,557	605/—	405	2,205	820	455	1,645	820	455
Iowa State University	‡ 2,228	4,768/—	520	3,044	366	1,690	1,564	366	1,690
Iowa Wesleyan College	9,850		500	3,400	432	1,448	2,500	757	1,569
Iowa Western Community College	† 1,800	810/—	325	3,000	300	900	1,500	675	900
Kirkwood Community College	‡ 1,410	1,230/—	400					1,000	850
Loras College	10,580		600	3,660	300	450	720	300	450
Luther College	12,375		600	3,525	400	400	1,700		400
Maharishi International University	10,736		400	2,760	450	660	1,696		660
Marshalltown Community College	‡ 1,865	1,760/—	425					630	690
Morningside College	10,376		500	3,520	500	1,000	1,760	500	1,000
Mount Mercy College	9,900		500	3,330	700		1,800	700	
Mount St. Clare College	9,280		600	3,600	350	700	2,000	400	500
Muscatine Community College	‡ 1,455	645/—	900				1,500	900	900
North Iowa Area Community College	1,620	735/—	600	2,570	300	1,125	2,000	700	1,125
Northeast Iowa Community College	1,943	1,695/—	1,000				1,500	1,155	945
Northwest Iowa Community College	‡ 1,575	675/—	525				900	1,200	675
Northwestern College	9,300		450	2,950	450	950	1,400	450	950
St. Ambrose University	9,850		500	3,830	510	940	2,830	940	510
Scott Community College	‡ 1,455	645/—	900				1,500	900	900
Simpson College	10,825		550	3,810	300	1,100			2,500
Southeastern Community College									
North Campus	‡ 1,302	600/—	300	2,392				500	
South Campus	‡ 1,302	600/—	500				1,350		
Southwestern Community College	‡ 1,590	690/—	500	2,400	440	968	1,240	660	825
Teikyo Marycrest University	9,800		525	3,400	630	700	1,600	630	700
Teikyo Westmar University	9,780		560	3,350	800	880	1,740	800	880
University of Dubuque	10,530		500	3,620	600	600	1,845	600	600

†Figures are projected for 1993-94. ‡Figures are for 1992-93.

Iowa: University of Dubuque

Total freshmen	Percent receiving aid	Freshmen judged to have need	Percent offered aid	Acad	Music/drama	Art	Athl	Acad	Music/drama	Art	Athl	Priority	Closing	Inst aid form	Notes
277	77	200	100					X				4/1	none		
140	80												none		
159	94			X	X	X	X	X	X	X	X	3/1	none		
297	95			X	X	X		X	X	X		4/20	none		
431	98	363	100	X	X	X		X	X	X		3/1	none		
198	89			X				X	X	X		3/1	none		
480	50			X		X	X	X		X	X	4/20	none	X	
303	85	287	100	X	X	X		X	X	X		3/1	none	X	
383	80	352	100	X	X	X		X	X	X			3/1	X	
3,008	60			X				X			X	3/1	none		
9	100	9	100	X								8/31	none		
327	98	280	100					X	X	X	X	4/1	none	X	
				X				X	X	X	X	3/1	none		
595	70			X	X		X	X	X		X	4/1	none		
89	65	30	90	X				X				5/15	8/1	X	
58	87			X	X			X				2/15	none		
230	85	166	99					X	X	X	X	3/1	none		
244	98			X	X	X	X	X	X	X	X	4/20	none		
297	79							X				2/1		X	
356	90												none		
870	75			X				X				4/20	6/30		
1,163	80			X				X	X	X	X	4/1	none		
1,834	75			X	X	X	X	X	X		X		none		
594	80			X	X	X	X	X	X	X	X		none	X	
3,384	75			X	X	X	X	X	X	X	X	3/1	none		
151	85			X	X	X	X	X	X	X	X	7/1	none		
1,414	76							X			X	5/1	none	X	
3,354	65			X	X		X					3/15	none		
440	80			X				X	X	X	X		4/15		
604	83	424	100	X	X	X		X	X	X		3/1	6/1	X	
73	79			X								2/28	none	X	
739	50	480	85	X		X	X	X				3/15	none	X	
197	88	157	100					X	X	X	X	3/1	none		
279	85				X	X		X	X	X		3/1	none		
270	90							X	X	X	X	4/1	8/1		
407	40			X	X		X	X	X		X	4/20	none	X	
1,790	60	960	95	X	X		X	X	X	X	X	3/1	none		
2,283	76			X				X				4/1	none	X	
280	78							X				4/20	none	X	
334	95	260	100	X	X	X	X	X	X	X	X	4/1	none		
258	92	175	100	X	X	X	X	X	X	X	X	3/15	none	X	
1,382	49			X				X				4/20	none	X	
284	90	236	100	X	X	X		X	X	X		4/20	none	X	
1,610				X				X					none		
557	63			X				X					none		
634	75			X	X		X	X	X		X	4/15	none		
268	90			X	X	X	X	X	X	X	X	3/1	none	X	
85	99	77	100					X	X		X	4/1	none		
177	85	136	100	X				X	X			4/1	none		

125

Iowa: University of Iowa

Institution		Tuition and fees	Add'l out-of-state/district tuition	Books and supplies	Room and board	Trans-portation	Other costs	Board only	Trans-portation	Other costs
University of Iowa	†	2,352	5,388/—	610	3,306	400	1,854	1,800	590	1,612
University of Northern Iowa	‡	2,228	3,342/—	565	2,620	415	1,735	1,300	515	1,735
University of Osteopathic Medicine and Health Sciences		7,870		1,100					200	
Upper Iowa University		8,840		500	3,060	400	600	660	675	440
Vennard College		5,590		448	2,680	690	1,280	1,250	800	1,280
Waldorf College		9,620		495	3,250	515	940	1,550	515	940
Wartburg College		11,080		300	3,450	430	520	1,500	250	700
Western Iowa Tech Community College	‡	1,365	1,290/—	425		150	800		825	660
William Penn College		10,290		500	3,100	500	750	1,130	1,000	800

Kansas

Institution		Tuition and fees	Add'l out-of-state/district tuition	Books and supplies	Room and board	Trans-portation	Other costs	Board only	Trans-portation	Other costs
Allen County Community College	†	1,088	1,429/—	200	2,600	500	1,620	1,200	500	1,670
Baker University		8,234		586	4,050	730	1,350	2,200	1,280	1,350
Barclay College		3,400		300	2,650	350	600	1,500	600	600
Barton County Community College	†	896	1,456/—	500	2,000	800	1,000	1,500	800	1,000
Benedictine College		9,080		550	3,750	570	1,250	2,000	570	1,250
Bethany College		8,105		550	3,225	600	1,092	550	2,500	1,474
Bethel College		8,180		475	3,500	550	925	1,600	760	925
Brown Mackie College		6,870		700				1,500	1,071	1,008
Butler County Community College	‡	878	1,470/—	500	2,748	600	1,200	1,700	600	900
Central College		7,250		400	3,050	500	500	1,400	400	500
Coffeyville Community College	†	960	1,536/—	350	2,400	300	1,200		200	900
Colby Community College	‡	870	1,395/—	400	2,500	400	500	1,000	500	500
Dodge City Community College	‡	975	1,275/—	400	2,600	400	900	1,080	400	900
Donnelly College		2,600		500						
Emporia State University	‡	1,584	2,880/—	450	2,790	500	1,018	1,180	500	1,018
Fort Hays State University	†	1,711	3,052/—	500	2,941	1,200	1,250	750	400	1,000
Fort Scott Community College	†	750	2,430/—	500	2,480	700	2,100	1,450	700	1,800
Friends University		8,230		575	2,890		2,300			2,300
Garden City Community College	‡	894	1,305/—	420	2,500	450	500	1,160	550	500
Haskell Indian Junior College	‡	70		70		600	989		600	
Hesston College		7,500		600	3,450	500	1,000		200	1,000
Highland Community College	‡	930	1,410/—	350	2,600	350	400	900	650	300
Hutchinson Community College	‡	840	1,335/—	500	2,200	600	900	1,800	1,388	900
Independence Community College	‡	780	1,455/—	400	2,500	400	700	800	800	700
Johnson County Community College	‡	990	1,980/—	400				2,025	1,170	1,620
Kansas City Kansas Community College	†	672	1,080/—	750				1,850	1,800	
Kansas Newman College	†	7,380		586	3,486	1,198	1,458		1,636	1,458
Kansas State University	‡	1,841	4,172/—	572	2,840	375	1,710	1,704	472	1,710
Kansas Wesleyan University		8,020		500	3,200	400	500	1,500	400	500
Labette Community College	‡	690	1,800/—	320	2,160	400	425	1,300	750	425
Manhattan Christian College		4,140		600	2,670	600	800		400	
McPherson College		7,810		550	3,550	450	1,560	1,975	450	930
MidAmerica Nazarene College		6,656		600	3,614	220	1,000	1,500	800	1,000
Neosho County Community College	†	705	1,440/—	300	2,400	350	350		350	350
Ottawa University		7,290		600	1,620	950	1,780	1,940	900	1,780
Pittsburg State University	‡	1,564	2,880/—	450	2,704	500	1,000	1,600	700	1,000
Pratt Community College	†	900	1,560/—	400	2,500	600	1,125		800	1,125
St. Mary College		7,550		500	3,700	535	910	2,000	535	910
Seward County Community College	†	960	1,440/—	600	2,700	900	700		900	700
Southwestern College		6,500		550	3,532	600	900	1,500	600	900

†Figures are projected for 1993-94. ‡Figures are for 1992-93.

Kansas: Southwestern College

All aid		Need-based aid		Grants and scholarships								Financial aid deadlines		Inst aid form	Notes
Total freshmen	Percent receiving aid	Freshmen judged to have need	Percent offered aid	Need-based				Non-need-based				Priority	Closing		
				Acad	Music/ drama	Art	Athl	Acad	Music/ drama	Art	Athl				
3,253	75			X				X	X	X	X		none		
2,607	65	899	90	X				X	X	X	X	2/15	none	X	
													none		
226	99	156	100	X	X	X		X				4/20	none		
41	85			X	X			X	X			5/1	8/1	X	
324	95	209	100		X	X	X	X	X	X	X	4/20	8/1		
492	89	266	100	X	X	X		X	X	X		3/1	none	X	
1,000	75												none		
197	98			X	X	X		X	X	X		8/1	8/15		
673	48							X	X		X		none		
245	92	149	100	X				X	X	X	X	3/1	none		
				X	X			X	X			5/15	none		
1,894	40			X	X	X	X	X	X	X	X	3/1	none	X	
233	90			X	X		X	X	X		X	4/15	none		
198	97	162	100	X				X	X	X	X	3/15	none		
106	57							X	X	X	X	1/1	none		
		530	100	X			X	X			X		none	X	
							X	X	X		X	5/1	none		
177	90	128	100					X	X		X	6/1	none		
752	66							X	X	X	X		none	X	
								X	X	X	X	6/1	none		
				X	X	X	X	X	X		X		none		
97	85			X				X				6/1	8/1		
668	85			X	X	X	X	X	X	X	X	3/15	none		
806	70			X	X	X	X	X	X	X	X	3/15	none	X
1,243	40	500	100	X	X	X	X					5/1	none		
194	87							X	X	X	X	4/15	none		
506	75			X	X	X	X	X	X	X	X	7/15	none		
509	65			X				X	X	X	X	5/15	none		
188	92	153	100					X	X	X	X	5/1	none	X	
873	39			X	X	X	X	X	X	X	X	4/1	none		
2,739	28	919	64	X	X	X	X	X	X	X	X	3/1	none	X	
				X	X	X	X	X	X	X	X		none		
2,010	25			X				X	X	X	X	4/15	none		
1,144	17	841	71				X	X	X		X	4/15	none	X	
100	88	55	100	X	X		X					3/15	none		
3,100	38	1,450	100	X	X	X	X	X	X	X	X	3/15	Closing		
141	97			X	X		X	X	X	X	X	3/1		X	
522	44			X	X	X	X						none		
61	70			X	X			X				4/1	none		
131	91			X	X	X	X	X	X		X	4/15	none		
225	87			X	X			X	X		X	3/1	none	X	
694	65			X	X	X	X	X	X	X	X		none		
136	92	109	100	X	X	X						4/1	none	X	
945	71	329	100	X	X	X	X	X	X	X	X	3/15	none		
480	65							X	X	X	X	5/1	none	X	
250	80	48	100	X			X	X	X	X	X	3/16	none		
844	91	301	100	X	X	X	X					5/1	none		
106	83							X	X	X	X	4/1	none		

127

Kansas: Sterling College

Institution		Tuition and fees	Add'l out-of-state/ district tuition	Books and supplies	Costs for campus residents			Costs for students at home		
					Room and board	Trans-portation	Other costs	Board only	Trans-portation	Other costs
Sterling College		7,890		475	3,100	850	650		1,250	
Tabor College	‡	7,520		550	3,290	750	2,500	1,200	750	2,500
University of Kansas										
Lawrence	†	1,914	4,506/—	700	3,376	770	1,600	2,214	825	1,500
Medical Center	†	1,696	4,506/—	500				1,500	990	2,025
Washburn University of Topeka	‡	2,762	1,380/—	450	2,995	640	755		640	525
Wichita State University	†	2,018	4,506/—	600	3,005	800	900	1,425	800	900

Kentucky

Institution		Tuition and fees	Add'l	Books	Room/board	Trans.	Other	Board	Trans.	Other
Alice Lloyd College	‡	270	3,360/3,960	450	2,480	320	500	1,350	800	500
Asbury College		8,445		500	2,660	750	750	1,500	950	
Ashland Community College	†	840	1,680/—	450					460	848
Bellarmine College		8,172		750	4,505	473	750	1,200	608	700
Berea College		183		400	2,700	230	788	1,386	944	788
Brescia College		6,760		650	3,100	650	650	1,800	755	1,000
Campbellsville College		5,720		600	3,000	300	1,000	1,700	900	1,000
Centre College		11,600		600	4,200	250	600	1,500	150	300
Cumberland College		6,230		400	3,526	600	500		600	500
Eastern Kentucky University	‡	1,460	2,680/—	250	3,046	450	600	1,700	600	600
Elizabethtown Community College		840	1,680/—	450				2,348	460	
Georgetown College		7,390	100/—	550	3,600	650	550	1,800	885	550
Henderson Community College	†	840	1,680/—	475						
Hopkinsville Community College	†	840	1,680/—	450						2,808
Institute of Electronic Technology		4,975		100				1,500	500	1,000
Jefferson Community College	†	840	1,680/—	450				1,500	460	848
Kentucky State University	†	1,600	3,000/—	510	2,682	300	800		350	800
Kentucky Wesleyan College		7,600		500	3,950	300	750	1,280	725	750
Lees College		3,900		400	2,700	300	650	800	720	400
Lexington Community College	†	1,938	3,240/—	450	3,534				223	
Lindsey Wilson College		6,080		450	3,450	210	960	1,600	910	960
Louisville Technical Institute	‡	6,360		500			1,830		810	
Madisonville Community College	‡	840	1,680/—	450				1,700	500	250
Maysville Community College	†	840	1,680/—	450				1,500	460	848
Mid-Continent Baptist Bible College		1,740		250	3,382	250	600		900	600
Midway College		6,660		600	3,850	320	500	1,100	640	500
Morehead State University	†	1,790	3,000/—	500	2,800	200	800	1,500	950	800
Murray State University	†	1,780	3,000/—	500	3,022	350	600	1,770	340	600
Northern Kentucky University	†	1,720	3,000/—	500	3,240	700	800	1,500	700	800
Owensboro Junior College of Business		3,668		600					380	
Paducah Community College	†	840	1,680/—	375				1,300	950	400
Pikeville College		5,500		600	3,000	400	800	1,800	800	800
Prestonburg Community College	†	840	1,680/—	450					400	2,808
RETS Electronic Institute	‡	6,065						2,608	750	896
Southeast Community College	†	840	1,680/—	450				1,500	425	425
Spalding University		7,896		600	2,600		1,000	1,280	480	800
Sue Bennett College		4,800		500	3,580	1,000	700	2,000	2,000	1,000
Thomas More College		9,182		500	3,680	800	1,800	750	1,100	1,800
Transylvania University		10,670		500	4,300	200	800	700	600	800
Union College		7,000		500	2,790	900	600	1,500	900	600
University of Kentucky	†	2,290	3,920/—	450	4,190	460	850	1,500	460	850
University of Louisville	†	2,080	3,920/—	510	3,426	474	1,680	1,500	1,104	2,136
Western Kentucky University	†	1,704	3,000/—	500	3,096	400	1,100	898	1,400	1,998

†Figures are projected for 1993-94. ‡Figures are for 1992-93.

Kentucky: Western Kentucky University

All aid		Need-based aid		Grants and scholarships								Financial aid deadlines		Inst aid form	Notes
Total freshmen	Percent receiving aid	Freshmen judged to have need	Percent offered aid	Need-based				Non-need-based							
				Acad	Music/drama	Art	Athl	Acad	Music/drama	Art	Athl	Priority	Closing		
127	90			X	X	X	X	X	X	X	X	5/1	none		
130	100			X	X		X	X	X		X	4/15	none		
3,553	43	1,876	100	X				X	X	X	X	3/1	none		
		281	100	X				X				4/15	none		
906	80			X	X	X	X	X	X	X	X	3/15	none		
1,211	27	580	100	X				X	X	X	X	3/15	none		
240	100							X			X	2/15	8/31		
268	92	202	100	X	X	X		X	X	X		3/15	none	X	
689	40	376	100	X				X				4/1	none	X	
391	90	181	100					X	X	X	X	4/1	none		
397	100											2/28	none		
93	39			X	X	X	X	X	X	X	X	4/1	none		
270	88			X	X	X	X	X	X	X	X	4/1	none	X
288	79	169	100	X				X					3/15	X	
340	85	298	100					X	X	X	X	3/15	none		
2,499	71							X	X	X	X	4/15	none	X	
951	60							X				4/1	none		
326	85	227	100	X	X	X	X	X	X	X	X	4/1	none		
626	55							X			X		none	X	
								X				4/1	none	X	
89	80												none	X	
2,088	35							X				4/1	none	X	
421	82							X	X		X	3/15	4/15		
152	85	180	100	X				X	X	X	X		4/1		
352	90	290	100					X			X	4/1	none	X	
942	5							X				4/1	none	X	
306	96			X	X	X	X	X	X	X	X	4/15	none		
244	82							X					none		
1,656	54			X				X				4/1	none		
246	51			X				X				4/1	none		
17	65	9	100									5/1	none	X	
235	80							X	X	X	X		8/1		
1,393	68			X				X	X	X	X	4/1	none	X	
1,145	60	535	89					X	X	X	X	4/1	none	X	
1,636	21	568	100					X	X	X	X	4/1	none	X	
175	96			X				X					none		
		493	100	X				X			X	4/1	Close		
200	80			X			X	X			X	3/15	none	X	
657	60			X				X				4/1	none	X	
138	85												none	X	
609	70			X				X				4/15	none	X	
110	95			X	X	X		X	X	X		3/15	none	X	
173	93												none	X	
265	70	190	84					X	X	X		3/1	none		
255	94	220	100	X				X	X	X	X	3/15	8/1	X	
201	85	152	100					X	X		X	4/1	none		
2,567	48			X				X	X	X	X	4/1	none		
1,815	49	1,228	95					X	X	X	X	4/15	none		
2,417	41	1,076	94					X	X	X	X	4/1	none	X	

Louisiana: Bossier Parish Community College

| | | | | Costs for campus residents ||| Costs for students at home |||
Institution	Tuition and fees	Add'l out-of-state/ district tuition	Books and supplies	Room and board	Trans-portation	Other costs	Board only	Trans-portation	Other costs
Louisiana									
Bossier Parish Community College	‡ 605	600/90	575				1,600	900	1,000
Centenary College of Louisiana	8,400		600	3,420	700	1,200	1,900	1,050	1,200
Dillard University	6,400		600	3,750	442	1,166	1,882	1,076	1,166
Grambling State University	‡ 2,088	1,650/—	576	2,612	428	1,259	1,480	1,034	1,259
Grantham College of Engineering	2,050								
Louisiana College	4,770		535	2,984	410	1,040		970	1,040
Louisiana State University									
Agricultural and Mechanical College	‡ 2,170		576	2,900		1,544			2,153
Alexandria	924	1,472/—	520				1,630	934	1,011
Eunice	‡ 960	1,200/—	650						
Medical Center	‡ 1,802	2,400/—	1,658		385		880	979	2,492
Shreveport	‡ 1,480	2,190/—	575				1,500	859	1,025
Louisiana Tech University	† 2,256	1,455/—	600	3,654	442	1,166	1,883	1,076	1,166
Loyola University	10,625		600	5,190	800	750	1,100	350	750
McNeese State University	† 1,864	1,550/—	600	2,412	442	1,166	1,882	1,076	1,166
Nicholls State University	† 1,862	1,800/—	520	2,650	400	1,000		859	930
Northeast Louisiana University	‡ 1,626	1,584/—	520	1,980	384	1,011	1,630	859	1,011
Northwestern State University	‡ 1,772	1,800/—	550	2,093	981	1,051	1,696	981	
Nunez Community College	‡ 520		300				500	100	300
Our Lady of Holy Cross College	4,694		600				1,882	1,076	1,166
Phillips Junior College: New Orleans	‡ 4,665								
St. Joseph Seminary College	‡ 5,530		780	4,200	680				
Southeastern Louisiana University	‡ 1,615	1,800/—	520	2,200	898	972	295	898	972
Southern University									
New Orleans	‡ 1,456	1,558/—	400						
Shreveport	‡ 910	1,130/—	500				1,700	1,000	1,420
Southern University and Agricultural and Mechanical College	‡ 1,588	1,522/—	500	2,865	425	500	750	200	275
Tulane University	18,760		350	5,700		800	735	650	555
University of New Orleans	‡ 2,024	2,792/—	600	2,972	401	1,055	1,702	975	1,055
University of Southwestern Louisiana	‡ 1,598	1,800/—	500	2,136	353	930	1,500	859	930
Xavier University of Louisiana	6,760		576	3,800	1,034	1,119	1,806	1,034	1,119
Maine									
Andover College	4,700		700				2,860	1,050	1,000
Bates College	23,990	(Comprehensive)	610		200	900			
Beal College	‡ 3,610		750		350	1,400	1,200	1,500	700
Bowdoin College	18,300		620	5,855		875			875
Casco Bay College	† 5,370		650	3,200			800	400	800
Central Maine Medical Center School of Nursing	5,066		879			700	1,500	459	700
Central Maine Technical College	1,950	1,980/—	500	3,200	1,000	1,000	2,500	1,050	1,000
Colby College	18,690		500	5,540	200	800			
College of the Atlantic	13,287		420	3,860		430	1,400		430
Eastern Maine Technical College	1,880	1,980/—	600	3,200	500	1,200	1,700	1,000	1,200
Husson College	‡ 7,630		375	3,880	650	1,100		1,200	1,400
Maine College of Art	10,645		1,490	5,020	500			1,935	
Maine Maritime Academy	‡ 4,210	2,720/905	400	4,245	200	1,000	600		1,000
Northern Maine Technical College	1,950	1,980/—	750	3,200	500	3,285	1,600	1,050	900
St. Joseph's College	9,670		550	4,850	300	1,200	550	1,000	1,200
Southern Maine Technical College	1,840	1,980/—	600	3,200	423	832	1,700	714	950
Thomas College	9,050		600	4,450	800	1,000	800	1,500	1,000

†Figures are projected for 1993-94. ‡Figures are for 1992-93.

Note: Comprehensive fees include tuition, fees, room, and board.

Maine: Thomas College

All aid		Need-based aid		Grants and scholarships								Financial aid deadlines		Inst aid form	Notes
Total freshmen	Percent receiving aid	Freshmen judged to have need	Percent offered aid	Need-based				Non-need-based							
				Acad	Music/ drama	Art	Athl	Acad	Music/ drama	Art	Athl	Priority	Closing		
1,266	10	150	100	X			X	X			X	6/1	none		
236	86	134	100	X				X	X	X	X	3/15	none	X	
133	85			X			X	X			X	4/15	6/1		
1,404	95							X	X		X	4/15	none	X	
308	75							X			X		5/15		
3,564	50	1,911	89	X				X	X		X	4/1	none	X	
466	43			X				X	X	X		6/15	none		
744	60			X				X				7/1	none	X	
				X				X				5/1	none		
								X					none	X	
1,596	77	635	100	X				X	X	X	X	4/1	none	X	
661	50	372	98					X	X	X		5/1	8/1		
1,522	60	791	100	X				X	X	X	X	5/1	none	X	
1,303	59			X				X	X		X	2/14	5/29	X	
1,885	65	1,000	100	X				X	X	X	X	4/1	none	X	
1,528	70	1,030	99	X	X		X	X	X	X	X	4/1	none		
122	5			X			X						6/30		
138	65			X				X				4/15	none	X	
													none	X	
12	72	6	100										none		
2,551	55			X	X			X	X		X	5/1	none		
550	80												5/1		
231	90	136	100	X	X	X		X					none	X	
2,095	90			X	X		X	X			X	4/15	none	X	
1,213	56	594	100	X				X			X	3/1	none		
1,675	49	596	86	X	X		X	X	X		X	5/1	none		
2,513	75	1,260	83					X	X	X	X	3/1	none		
744	90							X	X	X	X	5/1	none	X	
232	70							X					none		
404	50	178	100										2/12	X	
165	70	85	100	X				X				5/1	none		
410	55	175	100										3/1	X	
340	80	142	100										none	X	
40	68	31	100									3/15	7/1		
				X								5/1	none	X	
455	75	179	100									1/15	2/1	X	
33	66											2/15	5/1		
428	76											4/1	none		
360	88			X			X	X				3/15	none		
87	75	38	100			X		X		X		3/1	none	X	
250	82	154	97					X				4/15	none		
538	83			X				X				4/1	none	X	
233	88	177	100	X				X				3/15	none	X	
815	55	250	100	X				X				4/15	8/15		
157	92			X				X				2/15	none		

131

Maine: Unity College

| | | | | Costs for campus residents ||| Costs for students at home |||
Institution	Tuition and fees	Add'l out-of-state/ district tuition	Books and supplies	Room and board	Trans-portation	Other costs	Board only	Trans-portation	Other costs
Unity College	7,910	1,100/—	450	4,660	400	600		225	600
University of Maine									
Augusta	† 2,715	3,720/—	520				800	1,100	600
Farmington	† 2,823	3,717/—	450	3,790	500	1,400	1,690	1,100	100
Fort Kent	† 2,730	3,720/—	500	3,600	800	1,000	900	1,000	1,000
Machias	† 2,755	3,717/—	460	3,530	800	1,100	1,970	800	1,100
Orono	† 3,286	5,130/—	500	4,580	400	1,150	1,455	1,100	650
Presque Isle	† 2,820	3,720/—	400	3,494	700	975	750	875	975
University of New England	11,200		850	4,870	400	600		775	1,300
University of Southern Maine	† 2,978	5,135/—	500	4,450	362	1,533	1,500	900	1,533
Westbrook College	11,000		550	4,900	450	800		800	800
Maryland									
Allegany Community College	† 1,865	1,290/540	500				1,530	1,056	966
Anne Arundel Community College	‡ 1,720	3,960/1,320	500				1,700	950	1,200
Baltimore City Community College	1,320	3,210/—	500					400	2,000
Baltimore Hebrew University	‡ 3,230		800					500	100
Baltimore International Culinary College	12,255		650		510	3,627	3,312	510	
Bowie State University	2,736	2,392/—	600	3,799	650	1,300	2,500	850	950
Capitol College	8,013		600		800	1,175	1,475	1,575	1,175
Catonsville Community College	‡ 1,510	3,090/1,290	500					1,500	900
Cecil Community College	† 1,674	2,640/1,590	660				1,800	900	900
Charles County Community College	† 1,580	3,000/1,500	650				2,000	600	400
Chesapeake College	1,502	4,480/1,820	475				500	950	1,720
College of Notre Dame of Maryland	10,650		450	5,400	250	700	1,600	300	700
Columbia Union College	9,760		750	3,450	1,000	1,000	1,200	750	1,000
Coppin State College	2,605	2,072/—	500				1,500	2,050	1,031
Dundalk Community College	† 1,570	3,090/1,290	600				1,500	1,500	1,000
Essex Community College	‡ 1,418	2,738/1,162	500					1,500	
Frederick Community College	2,003	3,990/1,800	600				1,650	1,100	775
Frostburg State University	2,666	2,628/—	550	4,198	210	750	1,750	600	600
Goucher College	14,525		500	5,995	350	1,100	1,500	700	400
Hagerstown Business College	‡ 3,560		650		325	325	925	725	325
Hagerstown Junior College	1,950	1,530/750	480				1,500	380	200
Harford Community College	1,814	2,310/1,020	600				1,800	1,200	800
Hood College	13,258		400	5,752		700	2,172	745	2,300
Howard Community College	† 1,663	1,368/696	450				1,500	675	700
Johns Hopkins University	17,900		450	6,460		1,050	1,500		1,050
Johns Hopkins University: Peabody Conservatory of Music	‡ 13,000		450	5,450	1,500	700	1,700	870	700
Loyola College in Maryland	12,465		550	6,060	200	650	1,700	650	650
Maryland Institute College of Art	13,080		1,400	5,300	500	600	600	1,000	1,000
Montgomery College									
Germantown Campus	1,911	2,880/1,560	560				1,100	1,700	1,000
Rockville Campus	1,911	2,880/1,560	560				1,100	1,700	1,000
Takoma Park Campus	1,911	2,880/1,560	560				1,100	1,700	1,000
Morgan State University	2,526	2,536/—	1,000	4,840	300	1,600	750	450	2,350
Mount St. Mary's College	11,725		450	6,100	300	525	2,875	625	750
Ner Israel Rabbinical College	3,200		500	4,000	685	1,600	2,500	550	1,600
Prince George's Community College	‡ 2,290	4,490/2,040	500					800	800
St. John's College	16,350		275	5,450	350	700	2,000	200	700
St. Mary's College of Maryland	4,400	2,300/—	650	4,500	200	1,000	1,650	750	1,000

†Figures are projected for 1993-94. ‡Figures are for 1992-93.

Maryland: St. Mary's College of Maryland

All aid		Need-based aid		Grants and scholarships								Financial aid deadlines		Inst aid form	Notes
Total freshmen	Percent receiving aid	Freshmen judged to have need	Percent offered aid	Need-based				Non-need-based							
				Acad	Music/drama	Art	Athl	Acad	Music/drama	Art	Athl	Priority	Closing		
160	73	105	100					X			X	4/15	none	X	
204	50							X	X	X		4/1	none		
443	65			X				X				3/15	none	X	
104	75	78	100	X				X				3/15	none		
186	65											5/1	none		
1,500	60			X				X	X	X	X	3/1	none		
246	72	141	99	X		X		X	X	X	X	5/1	none	X	
249	85	193	100					X				3/1	none		
889	40	455	93					X	X			3/1	none		
61	86	59	100	X								5/1	none		
852	54			X			X	X				3/15	none	X	
				X		X	X	X			X	4/15	none		
2,477	75			X			X	X			X	6/1	none	X	
													7/1	X	
134	90	134	100					X					none	X	
444	64			X		X	X	X	X		X	6/1	none	X	
47	39	37	100	X				X				3/15	none		
2,369	10							X			X	3/1	none		
				X	X	X	X	X	X	X	X	8/1	none		
1,832	24	325	92	X				X		X	X	4/1	none		
596	33			X				X			X	6/1	none		
165	90	128	100	X				X	X	X		2/15	none		
112	85							X	X		X	3/31	5/31		
449	48	353	100	X							X	4/1	none	X	
				X		X		X			X	4/15	none	X	
								X	X		X	7/1	none		
1,362	15			X				X	X	X	X	6/15	none	X	
861	58	400	100	X				X	X	X		4/1	none	X	
223	53	150	100	X				X	X	X		2/15	none	X	
266	92	160	100					X				10/3	none		
844	50	550	100	X		X		X			X	6/15	none	X	
				X				X	X		X	5/1	none	X	
150	80	104	100	X				X				3/31	none		
				X	X							3/1	none		
856	50	367	100					X	X		X	1/15	2/1	X	
47	97				X				X			2/17		X	
792	62	396	98					X			X	2/15	3/1	X	
201	65			X		X		X		X		3/1	none	X	
												2/15	none	X	
												2/15	none	X	
												2/15	none	X	
1,242	79	933	96	X				X			X	4/1	none	X	
				X				X			X		3/15		
42	28	17	100	X				X				6/1	none	X	
2,730	57	1,200	100	X			X	X	X		X	6/15	none		
107	48	55	100	X				X				3/1	none	X	
235	53	61	92	X				X	X				3/1		

133

Maryland: Salisbury State University

Institution	Tuition and fees	Add'l out-of-state/ district tuition	Books and supplies	Costs for campus residents			Costs for students at home		
				Room and board	Trans- portation	Other costs	Board only	Trans- portation	Other costs
Salisbury State University	3,026	2,668/—	550	4,490	750	750	1,045	850	850
Sojourner-Douglass College	5,265		450				1,400	600	1,400
Towson State University	3,123	2,502/—	600	4,400	330	922	2,500	330	582
United States Naval Academy	0								
University of Baltimore	2,874	2,240/—	550				1,775	1,185	1,776
University of Maryland									
Baltimore	3,006	5,390/—	1,145		1,116	1,200		1,116	1,200
Baltimore County	3,338	5,256/—	494	4,556	464	1,085	1,500	2,156	1,085
College Park	3,179	5,604/—	550	5,003	515	1,550	1,360	515	1,550
Eastern Shore	2,674	4,727/—	500	3,580	500	1,000	1,800	1,000	1,000
University College	4,850	450/—	800				771	806	1,159
Villa Julie College	6,860		500				1,100	1,000	1,000
Washington College	13,952		500	5,318		300	750		300
Western Maryland College	13,750		400	5,240	400	500	1,500	600	500
Wor-Wic Community College	† 1,615	2,760/2,130	450				1,700	1,000	450
Massachusetts									
American International College	9,414		535	4,553	575	900	1,475	675	600
Amherst College	19,152		660	5,000		1,358			
Anna Maria College for Men and Women	10,800		513	4,835	481	995	1,787	1,070	1,048
Aquinas College at Milton	‡ 7,400		400				1,900	2,450	1,000
Aquinas College at Newton	‡ 6,950		375				1,900	1,000	1,600
Assumption College	11,595		500	5,670	400	715	1,500	400	715
Atlantic Union College	10,700		500	3,550	500	800		500	800
Babson College	16,445		450	6,715		1,000	1,500	1,000	1,000
Bay Path College	9,600		550	6,100	300	900	600	1,000	900
Bay State College	7,825		500	5,900	630	1,460	2,200	810	1,250
Becker College									
Leicester Campus	7,935		500	4,210	300	600	1,500	700	600
Worcester Campus	7,935		500	4,210	300	600	1,500	700	600
Bentley College	12,880		400	5,200	420	850	1,500	1,320	1,350
Berklee College of Music	11,070		500	6,790	750	1,000	2,500	950	1,000
Boston Architectural Center	‡ 3,084		1,210				1,800	1,430	935
Boston College	16,006		500	7,400	500	800	1,500	1,300	700
Boston Conservatory	11,980		475	5,925	450	1,000	1,500	450	1,000
Boston University	17,650		465	6,480	270	735	900	1,050	735
Bradford College	13,220		425	6,120	450	950	1,650	550	950
Brandeis University	17,726		410	6,505		1,000	1,800	2,950	1,000
Bridgewater State College	‡ 3,000	3,864/—	500	3,590	500	1,250	2,490	1,250	1,250
Bristol Community College	‡ 2,040	3,822/—	500				2,525	1,000	1,175
Bunker Hill Community College	‡ 1,800	3,822/—	400				1,000	500	1,000
Cape Cod Community College	‡ 1,865	3,822/—	500				2,000	960	1,000
Clark University	17,000		500	4,500	100	700	1,760	250	700
College of the Holy Cross	17,550		400	6,300	100	960	1,500	300	1,630
Curry College	13,550		650	5,500	300	800		1,400	800
Dean Junior College	‡ 9,460		400	5,700	500	500	1,000	1,000	500
Eastern Nazarene College	8,765		450	3,400	350	700		350	700
Elms College	10,974		450	4,665	400	800	1,500	700	850
Emerson College	14,831		500	7,662		937	1,500		1,577
Emmanuel College	11,973		500	5,800	350	900		350	900
Endicott College	11,110		400	5,890	600	1,000		1,000	1,000
Essex Agricultural and Technical Institute	1,785	—/3,700	500				2,000	1,500	

†Figures are projected for 1993-94. ‡Figures are for 1992-93.

All aid		Need-based aid		Grants and scholarships								Financial aid deadlines		Inst aid form	Notes
Total fresh-men	Percent receiving aid	Freshmen judged to have need	Percent offered aid	Need-based				Non-need-based				Priority	Closing		
				Acad	Music/drama	Art	Athl	Acad	Music/drama	Art	Athl				
637	19	310	89	X				X				3/1	none	X	
72	48			X				X					none	X	
1,348	22	330	88	X	X	X	X	X	X	X	X	3/15	none	X	
								X				4/1	none	X	
												3/15	none	X	
933	66	615	82	X	X		X	X	X	X	X	3/1	none		
3,283	34	1,176	93	X	X	X	X	X	X	X	X	2/15	none		
508	80							X	X	X	X	3/1	none		
				X		X		X					5/1		
242	82			X				X				3/1	none		
300	80	189	100	X				X		X			2/15	X	
301	78	181	100	X	X	X		X				3/1	none	X	
440	30	140	100					X					none		
264	70			X			X	X			X	4/15	none		
394	55	157	100										2/1	X	
659	78	66	100	X	X			X	X			3/1	none	X	
103	73	75	100	X				X				3/1	none	X	
100	64			X				X						X	
454	60			X							X		3/1	X	
220	95							X	X		X	4/15	none		
437	48	194	100	X				X					2/1		
278	75	157	100					X	X			2/28	none		
422	75							X				3/1	none		
220	71	145	97								X	2/15	none	X	
398	87	390	66				X	X			X	2/15	none	X	
789	66	450	100	X			X	X			X		2/1		
667	45	393	82	X	X			X	X				3/31	X	
119	47	55	100					X		X			none	X	
2,215	61			X				X			X		2/1	X	
84	79	62	90		X			X					3/1	X	
3,788	75	2,088	99	X	X	X		X	X	X	X	3/1	none		
150	71	87	100					X				3/1	none	X	
761	49	375	100	X				X				2/15	4/15	X	
974	52							X				5/1	none	X	
948	48			X	X	X		X		X		4/15	none	X	
												5/1	none	X	
1,109	47											4/1	none		
533	51			X	X	X		X					2/1		
769	61	475	100					X				2/1	none		
214	48												4/15	X	
1,196	48	279	100	X	X	X	X					1/31	none	X	
168	80	118	100	X	X			X	X			3/1	none	X	
112	80	80	100	X				X				2/15	none	X	
505	80	272	100	X	X			X	X			3/1	none	X	
165	80			X		X		X				3/1	none		
307	57	283	100									3/15	none		
368	25	90	83									5/1	none	X	

Massachusetts: Fisher College

Institution	Tuition and fees	Add'l out-of-state/district tuition	Books and supplies	Room and board	Trans-portation	Other costs	Board only	Trans-portation	Other costs
Fisher College	10,300		600	6,000	800	900	1,500	1,000	
Fitchburg State College	‡ 3,206	3,864/—	450	3,232	350	1,538	1,600	1,000	1,538
Forsyth School for Dental Hygienists	12,111		400	6,905	175	450		675	450
Framingham State College	‡ 3,017	3,864/—	475	3,466	500	1,200	900	1,200	1,200
Franklin Institute of Boston	8,231		600	7,300	500		660	600	1,390
Gordon College	12,720		400	4,070	400	400	1,300		400
Greenfield Community College	‡ 2,006	3,882/—	550				2,153	1,030	1,351
Hampshire College	19,490		375	5,160		1,120	1,665		1,120
Harvard and Radcliffe Colleges	18,745			6,135	1,600	1,820			5,045
Hellenic College	7,135		500	4,920	700	1,300	2,000	400	1,300
Holyoke Community College	‡ 2,112	3,822/—	480				2,500	800	1,600
Katharine Gibbs School	‡ 7,545		450						
Lasell College	11,675		600	6,000	450	1,700	1,600	450	1,700
Lesley College	12,450		550	5,300	350	850	1,800	735	850
Marian Court Junior College	6,850		450				750	1,054	1,393
Massachusetts Bay Community College	‡ 1,980	3,822/—	400				2,015	800	860
Massachusetts College of Art	‡ 4,318	4,740/—	1,700	5,827	600			600	2,200
Massachusetts College of Pharmacy and Allied Health Sciences	‡ 10,630		500	6,495	320	1,600	1,700	750	1,600
Massachusetts Institute of Technology	19,000		700	5,800	450	1,550	210	500	1,470
Massachusetts Maritime Academy	‡ 3,203	4,740/—	450	3,710	350	1,250		1,300	1,200
Massasoit Community College	‡ 1,804	3,822/—	400				2,250	900	900
Merrimack College	11,700		600	6,200	1,000	450	1,600	1,000	450
Middlesex Community College	‡ 1,924	3,822/—	405				1,500	1,677	936
Montserrat College of Art	8,700		800				1,800	800	600
Mount Holyoke College	18,110		700	5,520		700			3,000
Mount Ida College	10,025		715	6,890	580	525		990	525
Mount Wachusett Community College	‡ 2,190	3,822/—	500				1,500	1,305	1,165
New England Banking Institute	‡ 1,782		300						
New England Conservatory of Music	15,290		400	6,990	550	1,350	1,700	800	1,800
Newbury College	9,825		500	5,750	500	900	350	250	900
Nichols College	9,040		500	5,160	250	650		500	650
North Adams State College	‡ 3,361	3,279/—	500	3,920	262	1,150	1,800	1,127	1,150
North Shore Community College	‡ 2,044	3,822/—	600				1,745	1,034	1,056
Northeastern University	† 12,359		600	7,155	750	900	2,250	750	900
Northern Essex Community College	‡ 1,813	3,822/—	500				1,700	1,175	1,400
Pine Manor College	15,865		500	6,460	500	450	1,500	315	450
Quincy College	‡ 1,880		400				500	200	400
Quinsigamond Community College	‡ 2,104	3,822/—	400				2,475	720	1,448
Regis College	11,850		450	5,600		700	1,500	900	700
Roxbury Community College	‡ 1,400	3,822/—	525				1,575	1,065	1,470
St. Hyacinth College and Seminary	3,795		425	4,500	400	725	1,300	800	700
St. John's Seminary College	‡ 4,400		400	2,600	400	600			
Salem State College	‡ 3,073	3,864/—	450	3,514	450	900	1,422	1,233	900
School of the Museum of Fine Arts	13,285		1,000					1,000	1,500
Simmons College	15,794		482	6,740		1,124	1,500	550	1,494
Simon's Rock College of Bard	18,120		400	5,620	400	450	2,740	250	400
Smith College	18,136		400	6,100		700			700
Springfield College	10,368		400	4,832		1,000		350	1,000
Springfield Technical Community College	‡ 1,856	3,822/207	400				1,450	800	1,500
Stonehill College	11,440		480	5,996	350	724	2,500	1,550	820
Suffolk University	9,860		500	5,600	700	2,400	1,500	700	2,400

†Figures are projected for 1993-94. ‡Figures are for 1992-93.

Massachusetts: Suffolk University

All aid		Need-based aid		Grants and scholarships								Financial aid deadlines		Inst aid form	Notes
Total freshmen	Percent receiving aid	Freshmen judged to have need	Percent offered aid	Need-based				Non-need-based							
				Acad	Music/ drama	Art	Athl	Acad	Music/ drama	Art	Athl	Priority	Closing		
249	76											3/1	none		
564	53	139	100	X				X	X	X		3/30	7/1	X	
42	22	28	60	X				X				3/1	none	X	
582	50	136	100	X				X				3/1	none	X	
174	90	126	100	X								4/1	none	X	
294	86			X	X			X	X			3/15	6/15		
532	76			X								4/15	none	X	
339	52							X				2/15	none	X	
1,606	74	797	100									2/15	none	X	
23	80	17	100	X				X					4/1	X	
				X				X	X	X	X	5/15	none	X	
393	58	87	100	X									none	X	
263	76	144	100					X				5/1	none		
124	65	104	100					X				3/1	none		
75	58			X								4/1	none		
1,593	12	567	100	X				X	X	X	X		5/1		
167	41	92	100									5/1	none		
113	75	92	97					X				4/1	none	X	
1,139	62	731	100									2/1	none	X	
260	77	58	100	X				X				5/1	none	X	
1,195	65			X		X		X			X	4/15	none	X	
467	70			X		X					X		3/1		
3,093	40	249	83									3/31	none		
77	60	39	100	X		X				X		4/15	none		
514	64	320	100										2/1	X	
				X		X						5/1	none	X	
1,200	63	850	88										none	X	
74	70				X				X			1/15	none	X	
3,171	60	216	100					X				8/1	none	X	
187	80			X				X				4/1	none		
204	36	230	95									5/1	none	X	
932	30											3/1	none	X	
2,508	76	1,893	100	X				X			X	3/1	none		
1,657	50											4/1	none	X	
136	41	64	100	X								3/15	none	X	
1,425	75											5/1	6/15	X	
959	25							X	X	X	X	5/1	none	X	
138	70	106	93	X				X				2/15	none	X	
666	85											5/1	none	X	
4	60			X				X				6/1	none		
5	60	4	100										7/1		
1,010	55	618	74	X	X	X		X	X	X		4/15	none		
87	60	78	100									3/15	none	X	
292	80	225	100					X					2/1	X	
141	70	89	100										none		
641	51	317	100										1/15	X	
494	70	331	100	X									4/1	X	
								X	X	X	X	4/1	none	X	
514	69	310	99	X				X	X		X	2/15	none		
393	60			X				X					3/1	X	

Massachusetts: Tufts University

	Tuition and fees	Add'l out-of-state/district tuition	Books and supplies	Room and board	Trans-portation	Other costs	Board only	Trans-portation	Other costs
Institution									
Tufts University	19,269		600	5,693		938			3,031
University of Massachusetts									
Amherst	5,467	6,346/—	500	3,828	400	1,000	1,800	600	1,000
Boston	‡ 4,087	6,103/—	540				1,912	978	1,182
Dartmouth	‡ 3,153	4,886/—	500	4,471	400	1,000	1,500	1,250	1,000
Lowell	‡ 4,513	4,911/—	400	4,223	200	1,160	1,500	900	1,010
Wellesley College	17,725		500	6,090	435	700	1,000		700
Wentworth Institute of Technology	9,250		800	5,950	400	450	1,900	800	500
Western New England College	9,354		475	5,400	300	800	1,625	925	1,140
Westfield State College	‡ 3,026	3,864/—	450	3,542	400	1,280	750	1,350	1,280
Wheaton College	17,790		660	6,050		800	1,550		800
Wheelock College	12,640		300	5,360	150	700	2,500	150	700
Williams College	18,795		500	5,795	250	800			
Worcester Polytechnic Institute	15,290		520	5,060		905	1,500		905
Worcester State College	‡ 2,536	3,864/—	500	3,690	500	1,150	1,250	1,000	1,150
Michigan									
Adrian College	10,700		400	3,540	300	694	1,650	300	694
Albion College	13,676		500	4,588	400	400	2,304		
Alma College	12,046		700	4,334	400	625	1,200	700	700
Alpena Community College	† 1,460	1,260/630	300				1,500	840	600
Andrews University	11,250		1,050	3,990					
Aquinas College	10,402		350	4,124	515	700	1,700	915	700
Baker College									
Auburn Hills	‡ 4,815		600					900	
Cadillac	5,040	1,575/—	750				1,675	2,000	
Flint	5,376		650		1,000	2,500	1,575	900	2,494
Mount Clemens	‡ 5,136								
Muskegon	5,040		750		1,675	2,000	1,675	2,000	1,750
Owosso	‡ 5,136		700	1,575		400			
Port Huron	‡ 4,815		500				1,575	1,825	2,000
Bay de Noc Community College	‡ 1,364	1,620/510	400		409	586	1,500	818	586
Calvin College	9,450		390	3,570	520	660	1,800	1,080	660
Center for Creative Studies: College of Art and Design	‡ 9,853		1,926	4,100	530	636	2,332	1,484	477
Central Michigan University	‡ 2,653	3,836/—	600	3,724	500	1,000	495	1,188	1,000
Charles Stewart Mott Community College	‡ 1,420	1,230/570	550					600	600
Cleary College	‡ 5,790		800				2,000	1,500	1,000
Concordia College	9,548		500	4,126	154	1,000	2,350	154	1,032
Davenport College of Business	6,890		675	3,023	915	785		915	785
Delta College	‡ 1,440	1,470/570	420					900	600
Detroit College of Business	‡ 6,095		575				2,500	955	825
Eastern Michigan University	‡ 2,529	3,585/—	450	3,850	100	1,200	2,000	800	1,200
Ferris State University	† 3,210	3,306/—	540	3,924	400	650	1,800	640	650
Glen Oaks Community College	‡ 1,170	420/120	460				1,000	760	773
GMI Engineering & Management Institute	11,000		575	3,166	2,980	2,205	1,325	2,980	2,205
Gogebic Community College	‡ 900	—/360	350		750	750	800	750	750
Grace Bible College	4,850		300	3,100	915	650	1,800	915	650
Grand Rapids Baptist College and Seminary	‡ 5,920		500	3,738	792	1,150	3,300	1,230	1,150
Grand Rapids Community College	1,384	1,120/672	420					720	460
Grand Valley State University	† 2,658	3,202/—	600	3,930	550	450		950	550
Great Lakes Christian College	4,037		500	3,635	500	1,500		500	1,500

†Figures are projected for 1993-94. ‡Figures are for 1992-93.

Michigan: Great Lakes Christian College

All aid		Need-based aid		Grants and scholarships								Financial aid deadlines		Inst aid form	Notes
Total fresh-men	Percent receiving aid	Freshmen judged to have need	Percent offered aid	Need-based				Non-need-based							
				Acad	Music/ drama	Art	Athl	Acad	Music/ drama	Art	Athl	Priority	Closing		
1,195	39	416	100	X				X					2/1	X	
3,894	47			X	X	X	X	X	X	X	X	3/1	none		
734	64	402	90	X				X				3/15	none		
869	40			X				X				5/1	none	X	
1,053	40						X						5/1		
619	50	317	100										2/1	X	
536	62			X				X				3/1	none	X	
464	55	313	81	X								4/1	none	X	
824	50	311	100					X				4/1	none	X	
415	59	225	100										2/15	X	
177	78	125	100										3/1	X	
519	37	191	100										2/1	X	
610	80												3/1	X	
553	42	204	93					X				4/17	none	X	
291	93	240	99	X	X	X		X	X	X		3/15	none		
530	80							X	X	X		3/1	none		
413	95	321	100	X	X	X		X	X	X		2/15	5/1		
808	57	450	100	X				X			X	5/15	none		
368	90			X				X					1/31	X	
233	91			X	X	X	X	X	X	X	X	2/15	none		
211	70			X				X				2/15	none		
187	88			X				X					none	X	
1,373	63			X				X				2/15	none	X	
													none		
1,305	85			X				X				9/1	none	X	
								X				5/1	none	X	
220	50	98	100	X				X					none	X	
578	75							X				4/15	none		
808	88	512	100	X	X	X		X	X	X		2/15	none		
86	58			X	X					X		2/15	none	X	
2,539	55	1,250	99	X				X	X	X	X	3/1	none		
								X	X	X	X		5/31	X	
326	64	32	100	X				X				3/1	8/31	X	
121	85			X			X	X	X	X	X		5/31	X	
1,314	75							X				3/15	none		
								X					none	X	
1,585	37							X			X	2/15	none	X	
2,247	58	1,275	100	X	X	X	X	X	X	X	X	4/1	none	X	
2,486	65	1,590	96	X				X	X		X	4/1	none	X	
				X				X	X	X	X	5/15	none	X	
508	66	283	100	X				X				3/15	none	X	
300	75			X			X	X			X	3/15	none		
30	74							X	X			7/15	none	X	
170	73	147	100					X	X		X	3/1	9/1		
10,262	40	1,850	100	X				X	X	X	X	4/1	8/1		
1,627	66	908	100	X	X	X	X	X	X	X	X	2/15	none		
80	91	51	100					X	X			8/1	none		

Michigan: Great Lakes Junior College of Business

Institution	Tuition and fees	Add'l out-of-state/ district tuition	Books and supplies	Costs for campus residents Room and board	Trans- portation	Other costs	Costs for students at home Board only	Trans- portation	Other costs
Great Lakes Junior College of Business	† 4,695		450					818	490
Henry Ford Community College	‡ 1,450	—/690	500				2,160	890	520
Highland Park Community College	‡ 1,700	300/—	250				1,650	675	1,300
Hillsdale College	10,670		500	4,440	700	925	2,220	1,000	925
Hope College	11,542		450	4,156	290	825	1,500	465	550
Jackson Community College	‡ 1,371	598/346	386				2,430	890	634
Jordan College	5,760		1,050				2,500	915	
Kalamazoo College	15,135		450	4,839	180	450	598	600	450
Kalamazoo Valley Community College	‡ 868	1,488/744	384				1,575	840	2,415
Kellogg Community College	1,095	1,737/672	380				2,300	811	1,500
Kendall College of Art and Design	9,650		1,400				3,446	935	990
Kirtland Community College	1,380	1,200/495	415					915	915
Lake Michigan College	† 1,230	600/300	500				1,800	750	950
Lake Superior State University	† 2,880	2,730/—	500	4,080	375	600	1,800	375	600
Lansing Community College	† 1,260	1,590/780	650				2,500	1,000	1,000
Lawrence Technological University	6,975		1,300		1,000	800	2,000	1,200	800
Lewis College of Business	‡ 4,900		500						
Macomb Community College	‡ 1,380	1,200/750	440				2,200	840	700
Madonna University	4,770		396	3,700	500	638	1,210	899	638
Marygrove College	‡ 7,140		460	3,700	560	1,304		1,178	1,304
Michigan Christian College	‡ 4,812		300	2,800	455	640	1,500	1,000	640
Michigan State University	‡ 4,277	5,798/—	480	3,568	1,221	1,221	1,240		932
Michigan Technological University	‡ 3,249	4,077/—	600	3,604	450	550	1,200	450	550
Mid Michigan Community College	‡ 1,220	1,080/600	400				1,500	1,132	941
Monroe County Community College	‡ 900	—/420	700				2,200	1,100	650
Montcalm Community College	† 1,284	990/660	500				1,782	1,260	826
Muskegon Community College	1,130	915/495	400				1,600	1,000	800
Northern Michigan University	2,528	2,111/—	400	3,811	400	765	1,700	400	765
Northwestern Michigan College	† 1,620	1,296/996	450	3,344	475	750		850	825
Northwood University	9,065		575	4,266	565	582	1,500	620	582
Oakland Community College	† 1,425	1,815/885	700				2,300	1,900	360
Oakland University	‡ 2,499	4,718/—	400	3,890	500	650	1,800	900	650
Olivet College	10,500		500	3,500	460	490		460	490
Reformed Bible College	‡ 5,670		375	3,100	490	635		490	635
Sacred Heart Major Seminary	4,030		750	4,100	1,000	750	2,400	1,000	
Saginaw Valley State University	† 2,883	2,826/—	550	3,729	420	918	1,238	815	988
St. Clair County Community College	† 1,530	1,650/750	450				2,500	1,000	800
St. Mary's College	5,250		500	3,200					
Schoolcraft College	‡ 1,285	1,425/600	400				1,500	800	800
Siena Heights College	8,820		475	3,700	515	575		515	575
Southwestern Michigan College	‡ 1,200	600/300	500				1,500	900	2,400
Spring Arbor College	8,706		385	3,550	515	665	1,915	515	665
Suomi College	8,990		500	3,700	700	800	1,800	1,125	600
University of Detroit Mercy	8,550		510	3,192	530	1,370	1,850	862	1,400
University of Michigan									
Ann Arbor	‡ 4,365	9,704/—	460	4,285	212	1,207		212	1,207
Dearborn	‡ 2,954	6,348/—	440				1,500	850	1,040
Flint	‡ 2,700	6,100/—	470					1,000	900
Walsh College of Accountancy and Business Administration	‡ 4,500							800	900
Washtenaw Community College	† 1,416	1,140/600	500				2,000	600	600
Wayne County Community College	‡ 1,790	1,050/480	400				2,200	890	1,000

†Figures are projected for 1993-94. ‡Figures are for 1992-93.

Michigan: Wayne County Community College

Total freshmen	Percent receiving aid	Freshmen judged to have need	Percent offered aid	Acad	Music/drama	Art	Athl	Acad	Music/drama	Art	Athl	Priority	Closing	Inst aid form	Notes
466	72							X					none	X	
5,000	33			X	X	X	X	X		X	X	4/1	none	X	
950	95												none	X	
300	70			X	X	X	X	X		X	X	3/15	none		
687	73			X				X	X	X		2/15	none		
				X				X	X			4/1	none		
699	99							X			X				
353	94			X	X	X		X	X	X		2/15	5/1	X	
				X				X			X		none	X	
1,844	60			X	X	X	X	X	X	X	X	6/1	none		
88	73	73	100					X		X		2/15	none		
266	75			X				X				5/15	none	X	
783	30			X	X	X	X	X	X	X	X	6/1	none		
495	70	350	97	X				X			X	4/1	none		
4,313	35			X	X	X	X	X	X	X	X	7/1	none	X	
799	60	378	100	X				X				6/1	9/1		
195	98														
3,500	15			X	X		X	X	X		X	5/1	none	X	
258	24	40	100	X	X	X	X	X	X	X	X	2/15	none	X	
137	92			X	X	X		X	X	X		3/15	none	X	
								X	X		X	8/1	none		
6,219	50	2,970	100	X	X	X	X	X	X	X	X		none		
1,272	70	457	87	X				X			X		3/1	X	
976	55	343	100	X				X				5/1	none		
967	43			X		X		X	X	X		6/1	none		
422	64			X				X	X			4/1	none	X	
1,813	60			X				X	X	X	X	5/1	none	X	
1,432	70	720	100	X	X	X	X	X				2/1	none		
1,220	30	392	86	X	X	X		X	X	X		4/1	none		
342	89			X			X	X			X	3/15	none		
				X				X			X	7/1	none		
1,217	35	420	94	X				X	X		X	3/1	none	X	
158	98			X	X			X	X			4/15	8/1		
40	88			X									none		
9	100	4	75									4/1	none	X	
719	70	429	100					X	X		X	4/1	none		
1,069	45	375	100	X	X	X		X	X	X	X	6/1	none		
111	60			X				X			X		3/15		
1,525	25			X	X	X	X	X	X	X	X	3/31	none	X	
208	91	177	100					X	X	X		4/1	none		
2,049	45	900	100	X	X	X	X	X	X	X	X	6/1	none	X	
155	90							X	X	X	X	2/15	none		
285	94			X	X	X		X	X	X		5/1	none		
367	70			X				X			X	6/1	none	X	
4,870	35	1,850	100	X				X	X	X	X	2/1	9/30	X	
762	46	348	78	X				X			X	4/1	none	X	
582	38	203	100	X	X			X	X				4/15	X	
				X				X				8/1	none	X	
2,925	50							X		X		6/1	none	X	
2,277	42											8/1	none	X	

141

Michigan: Wayne State University

Institution	Tuition and fees	Add'l out-of-state/ district tuition	Books and supplies	Costs for campus residents			Costs for students at home		
				Room and board	Transportation	Other costs	Board only	Transportation	Other costs
Wayne State University	2,403	2,835/—	487	4,860	1,222	791	1,958	1,222	791
West Shore Community College	‡ 1,134	1,110/660	600				1,350	850	950
Western Michigan University	‡ 2,685	3,690/—	470	3,630	500	1,160	1,500	500	1,160
William Tyndale College	5,320		500		425	550		810	550
Minnesota									
Alexandria Technical College	‡ 1,677	1,618/—	400				1,800	1,350	900
Anoka-Ramsey Community College	‡ 1,687	1,688/—	500				1,500	990	650
Augsburg College	11,404		500	4,204	100	850	1,700	100	650
Austin Community College	† 1,893	1,890/—	600				1,740	900	675
Bemidji State University	† 2,545	2,000/—	660	2,800	525	1,191	1,600	716	1,000
Bethany Lutheran College	‡ 6,720		400	2,940	150	800	1,600		750
Brainerd Community College	† 2,021	1,920/—	510				1,500	720	1,230
Carleton College	18,405		500	3,750	500				
College of Associated Arts	7,600		1,600				2,200	300	1,200
College of St. Benedict	11,428		500	4,040	100	500	1,000	600	500
College of St. Catherine: St. Catherine Campus	11,530		450	4,210	200	800	345	400	630
College of St. Scholastica	11,280		450	3,588	420	648	1,735	420	648
Concordia College: Moorhead	9,700		450	3,050	200	600	2,710	200	600
Concordia College: St. Paul	‡ 9,000		450	3,180	100	750	1,800	100	750
Crown College	7,640		500	3,590	600	700	2,000	600	800
Dr. Martin Luther College	3,600		555	1,790	575	650	1,770	370	680
Fergus Falls Community College	‡ 1,850	1,750/—	550				1,773	500	622
Gustavus Adolphus College	13,400		400	3,500	500	750	1,850	500	750
Hamline University	13,022		425	4,100		675			675
Hibbing Community College	1,800	1,800/—	510				1,440	1,260	
Inver Hills Community College	‡ 1,687	1,688/—	500				2,000	550	590
Itasca Community College: Arrowhead Region	† 1,922	1,920/—	510				1,500	535	1,125
Lakewood Community College	‡ 1,687	1,688/—	550				1,440	400	750
Macalester College	15,107		500	4,502		700	2,160		700
Mankato State University	‡ 2,176	1,865/—	450	2,535	405	1,250	760	600	925
Mesabi Community College: Arrowhead Region	‡ 1,687	1,688/—	480				1,700	470	1,000
Metropolitan State University	‡ 1,959	1,865/—	500					960	1,800
Minneapolis College of Art and Design	12,014		1,200		300	500	1,500	300	500
Minneapolis Community College	‡ 1,687	1,586/—	525				1,695	970	450
Minnesota Bible College	‡ 4,286		300		250	1,650		500	1,650
Moorhead State University	‡ 2,172	1,865/—	600	2,535	200	1,514	850	600	1,111
NEI College of Technology	† 4,335		600				3,096	1,684	1,740
Normandale Community College	‡ 1,687	1,688/—	550				1,700	1,000	500
North Central Bible College	‡ 5,040		300	3,080	400	900	1,100	400	900
North Hennepin Community College	‡ 1,687	1,688/—	500				1,900	1,500	200
Northwest Technical Institute	7,465		300						
Northwestern College	10,659		400	2,895	760	1,186	1,650	760	500
Oak Hills Bible College	‡ 4,335		500	2,400					
Pillsbury Baptist Bible College	† 4,606		935	3,024	808	1,722	2,835	808	1,155
Rainy River Community College	† 1,922	1,920/—	510		650	1,200	1,500	400	900
Rochester Community College	‡ 1,699	1,688/—	500				2,000	750	950
St. Cloud State University	† 2,146	1,865/—	600	2,535	810	930	1,200	900	850
St. John's University	11,428		500	3,936	100	500	2,080	100	500

†Figures are projected for 1993-94. ‡Figures are for 1992-93.

Minnesota: St. John's University

All aid		Need-based aid		Grants and scholarships								Financial aid deadlines		Inst aid form	Notes
Total fresh-men	Percent receiving aid	Freshmen judged to have need	Percent offered aid	Need-based				Non-need-based							
				Acad	Music/drama	Art	Athl	Acad	Music/drama	Art	Athl	Priority	Closing		
2,236	50	650	100	X	X	X	X	X	X	X	X		5/1	X	
869	50	195	100	X				X	X			5/1	none	X	
2,819	68	1,230	100					X	X	X	X	3/1	none		
98	60			X	X			X	X			2/15	5/1		
1,082	95							X				5/1	none		
2,125	40			X				X				5/15	none		
250	90	204	100	X	X			X	X			4/15	none	X	
								X	X		X	3/15	none	X	
570	80	355	100					X	X	X	X	8/15	none		
184	88	138	76					X	X	X	X	5/1	none		
633	79			X	X	X	X	X	X	X	X	6/1	none	X	
494	72	263	100	X				X					3/1		
19	80	19	100					X	X				none		
443	85	279	100					X	X	X		8/16	none	X	
212	90	184	100	X	X			X	X			4/1	none	X	
459	93			X	X			X	X			3/1	none		
746	85			X	X			X	X				none	X	
150	90			X	X	X		X	X			5/1	none		
68	96							X	X			4/1	none	X	
167	96	85	100	X	X			X	X			5/15	none	X	
721	89			X	X	X	X	X	X	X	X	6/1	none		
619	82	457	100	X				X				3/1	5/1	X	
300	84			X	X	X		X				3/15	none		
511	64			X	X		X	X				7/1	none	X	
1,677	30							X	X	X	X	6/1	none		
604	65	320	100	X				X				5/1	none	X	
2,061	40	560	100	X				X					none	X	
476	70	299	100	X				X					3/1	X	
1,589	65	1,105	98	X				X	X	X	X	7/1	none		
401	82							X				4/22	none		
				X									none		
79	72	60	100			X		X		X		4/1	none		
2,836	50	600	83	X				X				6/1	none		
28	84							X	X			6/1	none		
1,519	78	1,036	100	X				X	X	X	X	3/15	none	X	
84	68	40	100					X					none	X	
2,584	33			X	X							5/1	none		
								X	X	X		4/30	none		
2,700	26	625	100	X	X	X			X	X			none		
													none	X	
340	87	261	100	X	X	X	X	X	X	X	X	3/1	8/1	X	
27	80											7/1	none		
101	77	69	100					X	X			7/15	none		
265	82			X	X	X	X	X	X	X	X	8/1	none	X	
1,407	50	950	95	X				X					none		
1,873	42	844	100	X	X	X	X	X	X	X	X		none	X	
435	70	325	100	X	X	X		X	X	X		3/1	none		

143

Minnesota: St. Mary's Campus of the College of St. Catherine

Institution		Tuition and fees	Add'l out-of-state/ district tuition	Books and supplies	Costs for campus residents			Costs for students at home		
					Room and board	Trans- portation	Other costs	Board only	Trans- portation	Other costs
St. Mary's Campus of the College of St. Catherine		8,550		500		500	900	900	750	600
St. Mary's College of Minnesota		10,380		350	3,470	300	520	1,575		
St. Olaf College		13,560		550	3,640		550		300	550
St. Paul Technical College	‡	1,663	1,618/—	700				4,300	450	900
Saint Cloud Technical College		1,737	1,681/—	435				1,800	500	500
Southwest State University	†	2,650	2,000/—	650	2,750	400	1,500	1,600	500	600
University of Minnesota										
Crookston	‡	2,678	5,418/—	450	3,355		1,250	1,150		1,250
Duluth	‡	3,061	5,418/—	693	3,213	663	1,401		663	1,401
Morris	†	3,666	6,189/—	654	3,927	500	1,200	1,200	350	1,200
Twin Cities	†	3,492	5,691/—	714	3,564	660	2,118	2,138	660	2,118
University of St. Thomas		11,200		500	4,000	400	900	1,560	500	800
Vermilion Community College	‡	1,687	1,688/—	480	2,980	365	1,160	1,400	200	1,865
Willmar Community College	†	1,901	1,803/—	600				2,100	425	275
Willmar Technical College	†	1,775	1,740/—	400				2,550	1,800	900
Winona State University	‡	2,214	1,865/—	600	2,535	300	600		300	600
Worthington Community College	†	1,687	1,688/—	500				1,500	1,500	1,000
Mississippi										
Alcorn State University	‡	2,376	1,960/—	400	2,098	500	900		900	900
Belhaven College		7,140		1,400	2,580	900	4,110		900	4,110
Copiah-Lincoln Community College		1,000	1,200/—	500	1,680					
Delta State University	‡	2,194	1,960/—	500	1,770	500	3,090	1,500	500	1,000
East Central Community College	†	1,000	1,200/—	350	1,830				500	
East Mississippi Community College	†	1,000	1,000/—	300	1,960	800	400			
Hinds Community College	†	1,120	1,186/—	400	1,648	431	1,309	1,531	1,497	1,052
Holmes Community College	‡	804	1,000/—	400	1,400					
Jackson State University	‡	2,223	1,960/—	500	2,413	600	1,018	1,774	500	500
Magnolia Bible College		2,560		400	1,441	500	3,549	1,000	750	800
Meridian Community College	‡	960	2,000/—	500	1,050				544	
Millsaps College		11,236		550	4,250	450	900	1,850	550	900
Mississippi College		5,618		600	2,730	700	1,500	1,500	1,500	1,500
Mississippi Delta Community College	‡	770	1,000/90	400	1,450		400	1,410	250	240
Mississippi Gulf Coast Community College										
Jackson County Campus		860	900/—	150				1,600	1,100	
Jefferson Davis Campus	‡	860	900/—	150				2,600	1,100	260
Perkinston		860	900/—		1,326					
Mississippi State University	‡	2,473	1,960/—	480	2,969		1,429	1,805		1,479
Mississippi University for Women	†	2,239	1,960/—	600	2,217	500	1,200	1,500	500	1,200
Mississippi Valley State University	‡	2,164	1,960/—	450	2,025	450	800	1,800	875	700
Northwest Mississippi Community College	†	1,000	1,000/90	200	1,690		375			375
Pearl River Community College	‡	910	1,000/—	200	1,648	300	1,085		550	1,085
Rust College	‡	4,152		225	1,948	225	150	1,050	300	
Southeastern Baptist College		2,220		250	1,700	175	325	475	200	300
Southwest Mississippi Community College	‡	850	1,050/—	400	1,650		1,300	1,100	1,300	
Tougaloo College		5,275		500	2,185	300	500	1,500	300	500
University of Mississippi										
Medical Center	†	2,101	1,959/—	660		450	4,950		900	2,250
University	‡	2,435	1,960/—	460	2,660	550	1,019	1,900	950	1,119
University of Southern Mississippi	†	2,404	1,960/—	500	2,335	250	1,380	900	970	1,380
William Carey College		4,450		500	2,110	1,200	1,200	1,200	1,200	500
Wood Junior College		2,750		400	2,560	100	1,000		1,100	1,000

†Figures are projected for 1993-94. ‡Figures are for 1992-93.

Mississippi: Wood Junior College

Total freshmen	Percent receiving aid	Freshmen judged to have need	Percent offered aid	Acad	Music/drama	Art	Athl	Acad	Music/drama	Art	Athl	Priority	Closing	Inst aid form	Notes
470	77			X				X				6/1	none	X	
373	70	223	100	X	X	X		X	X	X		3/15	none	X	
705	67	482	100	X								2/15	none	X	
													none	X	
													none		
781	82			X	X	X	X	X	X		X	4/14	none	X	
425	80							X				4/30	none		
1,568	79			X	X	X	X	X	X		X	3/31	none		
574	80	343	100	X	X			X	X			4/1	none		
3,260	41	1,185	97	X	X	X	X	X	X	X	X	4/1	none		
800	75	480	100	X				X	X			4/1	none		
370	93			X				X							
488	89			X				X	X	X		4/23	5/1		
775	80			X								5/1	none	X	
1,300	70	770	100	X	X	X	X	X	X	X	X	4/1	none		
386	40	200	100	X	X			X	X			5/1	none	X	
502	92			X	X		X	X	X		X	4/14	none	X	
157	92			X	X	X	X	X	X	X	X	4/1	none		
1,529	45	575	100	X				X	X	X	X	4/1	none	X	
443	68						X	X	X	X	X	6/1	none		
675	38	258	100					X	X	X	X	6/1	none		
996	76			X				X	X		X	4/30	6/30		
2,879	40							X	X	X	X	4/1	none	X	
				X	X	X	X	X	X	X	X		none		
1,658	76			X	X	X	X	X	X	X	X		4/1	X	
10	100	5	100	X				X				8/1	none		
1,125	45	260	99					X	X	X	X	3/1	none	X	
263	75	215	100	X	X	X		X	X	X		3/1	none	X	
293	75			X	X	X	X	X	X	X	X	4/1	none	X	
2,056	90							X	X	X	X		none	X	
2,355	50							X				6/1	none		
2,198	70			X				X	X		X	6/1	9/1	X	
494	58							X	X	X	X	6/1	none		
1,725	84	1,233	100					X	X		X	4/1	none		
334	89							X	X	X	X	6/1	none		
571	93	350	97	X	X		X	X	X		X	4/1	none	X	
1,368	80			X	X		X					3/15	4/15	X	
1,078	70	825	100	X				X	X		X	5/1	none		
288	98			X	X		X	X	X		X	5/1	7/15	X	
9	90			X	X							7/1	none		
506	45											8/5	none		
325	92			X				X	X			4/15	none		
				X				X				4/1	none	X	
1,692	56			X				X	X	X	X	4/1	none		
1,550	60			X				X	X	X	X	3/15	none	X	
229	90			X				X	X		X		4/1	X	
176	85			X	X	X		X	X			6/1	none		

145

Missouri

Institution	Tuition and fees	Add'l out-of-state/ district tuition	Books and supplies	Room and board	Transportation	Other costs	Board only	Transportation	Other costs
Missouri									
Avila College	8,530		600	3,600	600	1,600		1,200	1,450
Berean College	‡ 2,095		500						
Calvary Bible College	3,600		400	2,730		350	1,550	374	800
Central Christian College of the Bible	‡ 3,323		340	2,390	400	1,300	1,330	150	2,600
Central Methodist College	8,050		600	3,370	400	1,800	1,570	400	1,300
Central Missouri State University	‡ 2,040	1,950/—	250	2,986	315	630	525	1,050	157
College of the Ozarks	† 100		400	1,900		1,200	2,000	800	1,200
Conception Seminary College	5,542		350	2,974	550	800	1,750	550	800
Cottey College	5,700		425	2,800	1,000	755	1,500	400	6,000
Crowder College	† 990	1,080/330	500	2,400	900	1,000	960	900	1,000
Culver-Stockton College	7,650		400	3,500	500	1,200	1,500	500	1,200
Deaconess College of Nursing	6,020		600	2,184	300	300	1,600	400	300
DeVry Institute of Technology: Kansas City	5,609		525				2,125	1,928	
Drury College	8,760		700	3,380	1,000	750	2,000	1,000	750
East Central College	1,080	1,230/420	600				1,865	1,312	500
Evangel College	6,730		500	3,090	800	1,500	1,700	800	500
Fontbonne College	8,140		590	4,020	320	980	1,520	1,300	980
Hannibal-LaGrange College	6,000		500	2,400		1,300		300	1,300
Harris Stowe State College	‡ 1,635	1,572/—	500				2,100	1,500	1,200
Jefferson College	‡ 960	720/360	300				1,600	700	1,070
Kansas City Art Institute	12,810		1,470	4,090	915	735	3,740	915	735
Kemper Military School and College	‡ 8,300		1,800	2,600	900	1,080			
Lincoln University	‡ 1,498	1,478/—	480	2,728	926	1,496	2,057	1,466	1,496
Lindenwood College	8,950		1,000	4,600	1,050	2,625		1,840	2,635
Longview Community College	1,230	1,680/780	550				1,627	1,639	1,306
Maple Woods Community College	1,230	1,680/780	550				1,627	1,627	1,972
Maryville University	8,700		400	4,200	500	780	1,900	1,700	980
Mineral Area College	990	510/450	550				1,400		1,365
Missouri Baptist College	‡ 6,220		600	2,800	275	1,500	1,800	1,500	1,500
Missouri Southern State College	‡ 1,598	1,392/—	400	2,490	460	900	1,500	600	600
Missouri Valley College	8,650		1,000	4,950	1,400	1,880			9,030
Missouri Western State College	‡ 1,822	1,638/—	500	2,480	600	1,500	1,600	500	1,500
Moberly Area Community College	‡ 790	2,130/750	400					500	1,025
National College	‡ 6,363		600					500	
Northeast Missouri State University	2,456	1,880/—	400	3,080	640	1,690		640	2,475
Northwest Missouri Community College	‡ 7,680								
Northwest Missouri State University	2,010	1,560/—	250	3,000	630	1,000	1,710	630	1,000
Ozark Christian College	‡ 2,971		450	2,740	250			100	
Park College	3,540		800	3,780	350	3,620	1,700	350	1,120
Penn Valley Community College	1,230	1,680/780	550				1,627	1,627	1,972
Phillips Junior College	† 3,498		305		405	1,260	1,700	2,025	1,260
Ranken Technical College	4,650		1,648						
Research College of Nursing	9,430		675	4,440	770	850	2,600	1,155	850
Rockhurst College	9,090		525	4,020	600	1,373	1,630	1,635	1,373
St. Charles County Community College	1,177	1,620/600	550				1,900	800	1,000
St. Louis Christian College	‡ 3,400		300	2,420	400	600	1,500	405	1,200
St. Louis College of Pharmacy	7,390		350	4,150	400	1,400		1,100	2,100
St. Louis Community College									
Florissant Valley	1,148	588/280	500				1,200	700	1,500
Forest Park	‡ 1,170	630/300	500				1,200	770	1,440

†Figures are projected for 1993-94. ‡Figures are for 1992-93.

Missouri: St. Louis Community College at Forest Park

All aid		Need-based aid		Grants and scholarships								Financial aid deadlines		Inst aid form	Notes
Total freshmen	Percent receiving aid	Freshmen judged to have need	Percent offered aid	Need-based				Non-need-based				Priority	Closing		
				Acad	Music/drama	Art	Athl	Acad	Music/drama	Art	Athl				
95	95	74	100					X	X	X	X	7/1	none	X	
													none		
58	77			X				X				7/15	8/15	X	
40	82	18	100	X	X			X	X				4/1	X	
210	82			X	X		X	X	X		X	4/1	none		
1,943	55			X	X	X	X	X	X	X	X	3/1	5/1		
541	100			X				X			X		none		
19	100	15	100					X					5/1		
								X	X	X	X	4/15	none		
625	60	208	90					X	X	X	X	8/1	none	X	
288	85			X				X	X	X	X	3/15	none		
100	85			X				X				4/15	7/1	X	
425	77							X					none		
260	79			X	X	X	X	X	X	X	X	4/1	6/15	X	
570	50	483	100	X	X	X	X	X	X	X	X	7/1	none		
351	90							X	X	X			none	X	
143	82			X	X	X		X	X	X		4/1	none	X	
111	89							X	X	X	X	6/1	none	X	
				X				X			X		none		
2,013	37							X	X	X	X		none	X	
126	68	84	100							X		2/15	none		
94	99							X	X		X	7/1	none		
								X	X	X	X	3/1	none	X	
359	89			X	X	X	X	X	X	X	X	4/30	none		
1,980	17							X	X	X	X	5/31	none	X	
943	19							X	X	X	X	5/31	none	X	
131	69	80	100	X				X				4/15	none	X	
1,034	50	768	100	X	X	X	X	X	X	X	X	4/15	none		
99	77							X	X		X	4/1	none	X	
2,403	75	634	100					X	X	X	X	2/15	none	X	
376	97	280	100	X	X	X		X	X	X	X	4/15	9/1		
				X	X	X	X	X	X		X	4/1	none		
951	30	251	100	X	X		X	X	X		X		6/30		
79	100			X				X					none		
1,401	88	691	100	X	X	X	X	X	X	X	X	4/1	none		
146	90												5/1	X	
1,245	79			X				X				4/1	none	X	
137	68			X	X			X	X			5/1	none	X	
97	97							X	X	X	X	4/1	8/1		
1,090	29							X			X	5/31	none	X	
125	90												none		
				X				X					none		
				X				X				3/15	none	X	
202	87							X			X	4/1	none	X	
1,155	20							X	X			4/30	none		
28	85			X	X			X	X			7/1	none	X	
147	76			X				X				5/31	none	X	
6,618	18							X	X	X	X	8/1	none		
6,002	39	1,782	22					X	X	X	X	3/19	none		

147

Missouri: St. Louis Community College at Meramec

				Costs for campus residents			Costs for students at home		
Institution	Tuition and fees	Add'l out-of-state/ district tuition	Books and supplies	Room and board	Trans-portation	Other costs	Board only	Trans-portation	Other costs
Meramec	1,200	600/300	500				1,300	750	1,600
St. Louis University	10,820		750	4,610	4,360	3,470	3,970	4,360	
Southeast Missouri State University	‡ 2,158	1,664/—	210	3,085	460	1,350		1,800	1,150
Southwest Baptist University	6,660		500	2,380		600			
Southwest Missouri State University	2,386	2,250/—	600	3,024	790	2,000	1,710	790	2,000
State Fair Community College	‡ 795	1,619/441	300				1,550	950	500
Stephens College	13,410		450	5,040	700	1,450	2,250	700	1,450
Three Rivers Community College	‡ 840	960/300	256				1,300	1,200	900
University of Missouri									
Columbia	3,125	5,076/—	540	3,168		1,706	2,120		1,706
Kansas City	‡ 2,841	4,860/—	568	3,355	710	5,850	1,500	2,010	1,650
Rolla	3,254	5,016/—	600	3,498	550	862	1,749	550	862
St. Louis	3,171	5,439/—	500	3,964	515	855	1,000	930	859
Washington University	17,776		746	5,639	500	1,512		1,232	3,208
Webster University	8,560		800	4,004	1,500	1,500	2,500	500	1,500
Westminster College	9,950		600	3,800	350	1,200		350	1,200
William Jewell College	9,720		500	2,780	800	1,800	1,650	900	1,800
William Woods College	9,965		550	4,200	1,000	2,700		700	3,120
Montana									
Billings Vocational-Technical Center	1,946		500						
Blackfeet Community College	‡ 1,371		200				900	450	450
Butte Vocational-Technical Center	† 1,250	1,344/—	450		750		1,500	750	1,000
Carroll College	7,760		390	3,650	350	700	2,200	350	700
College of Great Falls	5,240		520		340	640	760	340	640
Dawson Community College	1,239	2,653/336	550		1,000	1,097	1,500	1,000	1,097
Dull Knife Memorial College	‡ 894								
Eastern Montana College	† 1,905	3,556/—	550	3,804	480	1,200	1,850	480	1,200
Flathead Valley Community College	‡ 1,080	1,080/432	500				1,170	900	600
Fort Belknap College	‡ 1,485		909				4,680	1,539	1,431
Fort Peck Community College	990		440						700
Helena Vocational-Technical Center	† 1,250	1,344/—	350		1,260			1,260	
Little Big Horn College	‡ 1,165		400					1,050	450
Miles Community College	1,288	2,604/658	600	2,300	550	630	1,000	550	630
Missoula Vocational-Technical Center	† 1,352	1,428/—	500						
Montana College of Mineral Science and									
Technology	† 1,767	3,892/—	500	3,250	700	1,100	1,900	500	
Montana State University	† 1,909	3,892/—	550	3,462	500	1,800	1,700	500	1,800
Northern Montana College	† 1,802	3,556/—	473	3,216	532	465	662	532	465
Rocky Mountain College	† 8,818		600	3,327		630	1,966	300	630
Salish Kootenai College	2,268		525				1,125	550	1,350
Stone Child College	‡ 1,630	300/—	150						
University of Montana	† 1,962	3,892/—	550	3,600		2,200	1,850		2,200
Western Montana College of the									
University of Montana	† 1,780	3,556/—	550	3,000	1,100	1,100			1,800
Nebraska									
Bellevue College	3,100		455				5,400	900	1,800
Central Community College	1,050	450/—	400	1,824	483	1,444		685	420
Chadron State College	† 1,708	1,170/—	600	2,591	500	450	750	250	352
Clarkson College	‡ 6,350		330		989	1,206	1,575	1,400	1,200
College of St. Mary	9,300		400	3,500	647	1,794	1,116	1,294	2,028
Concordia College	8,506		450	3,270	900	1,200	1,800	300	1,200
Creighton University	10,252		625	4,178	590	1,480	1,500	950	1,480

†Figures are projected for 1993-94. ‡Figures are for 1992-93.

Nebraska: Creighton University

All aid		Need-based aid		Grants and scholarships								Financial aid deadlines		Inst aid form	Notes
Total fresh-men	Percent receiving aid	Freshmen judged to have need	Percent offered aid	Need-based				Non-need-based				Priority	Closing		
				Acad	Music/drama	Art	Athl	Acad	Music/drama	Art	Athl				
2,480	25	1,952	100	X	X	X	X	X	X	X	X	5/1	none		
913	85			X	X	X	X	X	X	X	X	1/1	none	X	
1,474	45			X	X	X	X	X	X	X	X	3/31	none		
685	90							X	X		X	4/30	none	X	
3,313	50	1,440	93	X	X	X	X	X	X	X	X	3/31	none		
454	63			X				X	X	X	X	7/1	none		
187	65	117	100	X	X	X		X	X			3/15	none		
1,745	75			X				X					none		
2,951	62	1,115	98					X	X	X	X	3/1	none		
504	40			X	X	X		X	X	X	X	3/15	none	X	
821	62	545	92					X	X		X	3/31	none		
529	54	288	76	X				X			X	4/1	10/3		
1,104	61	521	100	X		X		X		X			2/15		
208	83	164	100	X	X	X		X	X	X		4/1	none	X	
205	75							X	X	X	X	3/31	none		
357	88							X	X	X	X	3/15	none		
267	80			X	X	X	X	X	X	X	X	4/30	6/1	X	
													none		
60	90														
75	65											4/1	none		
259	85			X				X	X		X	3/1	none		
202	95			X				X				4/1	none	X	
167	52	133	100					X	X	X	X	3/1	none	X	
64	65	17	100					X					none		
593	67							X	X	X	X	3/1	none	X	
				X			X	X			X	5/1	none	X	
													none	X	
128	67			X				X					none	X	
40	75			X				X				3/15	none	X	
				X									none		
150	93			X	X		X	X	X		X	3/1	none		
													none		
353	58	182	100					X			X	4/1	none		
1,613	83	790	100	X				X	X	X	X	3/1	none		
168	49			X	X		X	X	X		X	3/1	none		
178	80	109	100					X	X	X	X	4/1	Closing		
26	65											3/31	none		
				X				X				3/27	none		
1,330	60			X	X	X	X	X	X	X	X	3/1	none		
200	62	140	100	X		X	X	X	X	X	X	3/1	none		
85	61	85	100	X			X	X			X	4/15	6/15	X	
759	75			X	X	X	X	X	X	X	X	7/1	none	X	
473	90	290	100					X	X	X	X	7/1	none	X	
91	75							X				5/30	none	X	
145	96	87	100	X	X	X	X	X	X	X	X	4/15	none	X	
197	99							X	X	X	X	5/1	none	X	
845	80	517	100	X				X			X	4/1	none	X	

149

Nebraska: Dana College

Institution		Tuition and fees	Add'l out-of-state/ district tuition	Books and supplies	Costs for campus residents			Costs for students at home		
					Room and board	Trans- portation	Other costs	Board only	Trans- portation	Other costs
Dana College		8,780		450	3,130	300	1,000	1,500	300	1,000
Doane College		9,390		350	2,830	400	1,000	1,675	350	500
Grace College of the Bible		4,492	2,630/—	400	2,630	500	1,400		900	1,400
Lincoln School of Commerce		4,725		450		450	800	1,500	450	800
McCook Community College	‡	870	135/—	500	2,450	400	550	500	400	550
Metropolitan Community College		990	990/—	450				1,500	353	270
Mid Plains Community College	†	1,048	162/—	450		500	500	1,500	500	
Midland Lutheran College	‡	8,800		350	2,700	400	900	1,000	400	900
Nebraska Christian College		3,470		300	2,440	380	1,623	1,390	380	1,623
Nebraska College of Technical Agriculture	†	1,586	1,456/—	500	2,550	440	1,100	680	880	1,100
Nebraska Indian Community College	‡	2,000		420				1,860	710	800
Nebraska Methodist College of Nursing and Allied Health	‡	5,485		500		504	900	1,512	1,008	900
Nebraska Wesleyan University		9,186		450	3,200		1,800		300	1,800
Northeast Community College		966	258/—	500		450	700	1,260	250	600
Peru State College	†	1,704	1,140/—	520	2,600	630	951	1,500	630	891
Southeast Community College										
Beatrice Campus	†	1,064	270/—	450		500	500		750	500
Lincoln Campus	‡	1,049	315/—	450				1,500	450	900
Milford Campus		1,115	270/—	450	1,805	750	900	1,125	975	900
Union College	‡	8,100		500	2,510					
University of Nebraska										
Medical Center	†	2,077	3,339/—	450					457	1,500
Kearney	‡	1,721	1,050/—	450	2,400	500	1,200	1,800	500	1,200
Lincoln	‡	2,188	3,180/—	450	2,980		1,940	1,660		1,770
Omaha	‡	1,805	2,873/—	600				1,090	600	650
Wayne State College	‡	1,557	1,095/—	600		250	2,500	480	2,000	1,000
Western Nebraska Community College:										
Scottsbluff Campus		1,110	60/—	480	2,330	400	660	1,700	400	500
York College		4,760		600	2,850	800	1,600	1,500	350	
Nevada										
Deep Springs College		0			1,250	350				
Northern Nevada Community College	‡	840	3,000/—	500				1,350	960	1,195
Sierra Nevada College	‡	7,500		500		500	2,820	2,000	500	820
Truckee Meadows Community College	‡	840	3,000/—	440				1,575	525	470
University of Nevada										
Las Vegas		1,665	4,300/—	650	4,952	400	1,000	1,750	700	1,000
Reno		1,665	4,300/—	600	4,858	1,012	1,856		884	412
Western Nevada Community College		882	3,000/—	450				900	680	1,230
New Hampshire										
Castle College	†	4,550		400				2,400	1,161	1,541
Colby-Sawyer College		13,375		400	5,120	100	1,000			
Daniel Webster College	†	11,852		500	4,656	450	500	1,500	450	500
Dartmouth College		18,375		1,590	5,874					
Franklin Pierce College		13,105		500	4,450	400	800		500	800
Hesser College	‡	6,285		500	4,300	500	1,000	900	500	800
Keene State College	‡	2,856	4,480/—	500	3,772	350	800	1,500	600	525
McIntosh College	‡	3,480		363					400	100
New England College		12,690		400	5,180	150	1,000		400	1,000
New Hampshire College		10,608		500	4,634	300	900	1,980	700	900

†Figures are projected for 1993-94. ‡Figures are for 1992-93.

New Hampshire: New Hampshire College

All aid		Need-based aid		Grants and scholarships								Financial aid deadlines		Inst aid form	Notes
Total freshmen	Percent receiving aid	Freshmen judged to have need	Percent offered aid	Need-based				Non-need-based							
				Acad	Music/ drama	Art	Athl	Acad	Music/ drama	Art	Athl	Priority	Closing		
131	97				X	X		X			X	4/1	none	X	
243	99	195	100	X				X	X	X	X	3/15	none	X	
78	62	73	95	X	X			X	X			3/15	none	X	
325	95			X				X					none		
575	64	179	100	X		X	X	X	X	X	X	4/1	5/1		
2,927	31			X				X				3/30	none	X	
433	67			X				X	X	X	X	4/15	none		
325	93			X	X	X	X	X	X	X	X	5/1	8/1	X	
65	97	62	100	X				X				6/1	none	X	
133	85	85	100	X				X				4/1	none		
106	90	97	100	X								7/15	none		
								X				4/1	none	X	
367	93	250	100					X	X	X			none		
623	71			X	X	X	X	X	X	X	X	5/1	none	X	
253	89			X	X	X	X	X	X	X	X	4/1	none		
572	58	176	97	X	X	X	X	X	X	X	X	4/1	none	X	
847	50			X				X					none		
163	60			X				X				4/1	none	X	
106	71			X	X			X	X				none		
				X				X					none		
1,478	76	876	100					X	X	X	X	3/1	none	X	
3,480	48			X	X		X	X	X		X	3/1	none		
1,740	55	850	88	X	X	X	X	X	X	X	X	3/1	none		
646	70	500	100					X	X	X	X	5/1	none	X	
441	75	295	100	X	X		X	X	X	X	X	4/1	none	X	
207	91	117	100					X	X	X	X	7/15	none		
1,369	20			X		X		X				4/1	none		
90	53							X	X	X	X		none	X	
2,705	18											4/10	none	X	
1,383	43			X	X	X	X	X	X	X	X	2/15	none		
1,226	65							X	X		X	4/15	none	X	
4,356	32			X				X				6/1	none	X	
165	75	92	100					X				4/15	none		
203	43							X	X			2/15	none	X	
180	65	124	95					X				3/12	none	X	
1,075	37	553	100										2/1	X	
467	69			X		X					X	2/28	none		
475	70			X		X		X			X	3/1	none		
762	54	321	97					X	X	X	X	3/1	none		
102	30												none		
224	44			X	X	X		X				3/1	none	X	
331	73			X		X		X			X	3/15	none		

New Hampshire: New Hampshire Technical College: Berlin

Institution	Tuition and fees	Add'l out-of-state/ district tuition	Books and supplies	Room and board	Trans- portation	Other costs	Board only	Trans- portation	Other costs
New Hampshire Technical College									
Berlin	‡ 2,125	2,854/1,038	450				1,575	1,000	1,800
Claremont	‡ 2,135	2,854/—	550				1,800	1,600	1,100
Laconia	‡ 2,135	2,854/—	500				1,750	1,200	800
Manchester	‡ 2,145	2,854/—	500				1,700	1,000	1,770
Nashua	‡ 2,155	2,854/1,038	500				1,100	1,000	500
Stratham	‡ 2,135	2,854/—	750				1,300	1,100	2,000
New Hampshire Technical Institute	‡ 2,241	2,852/—	400	2,990	750	1,600	1,500	1,500	1,600
Notre Dame College	9,506		650	4,900	375	925	1,500	950	925
Plymouth State College of the University System of New Hampshire	† 3,281	4,840/—	600	3,884	300	850	1,500	1,000	700
Rivier College	9,870		600	4,600	200	900	3,585	900	900
St. Anselm College	11,840		450	5,200	200	1,000	1,500	1,400	1,000
School for Lifelong Learning	† 3,540		550						
University of New Hampshire									
Durham	‡ 3,941	7,060/—	500	3,728	300	1,100	1,200	600	1,100
Manchester	‡ 2,820	5,480/—	500				1,700	1,000	1,000
White Pines College	‡ 6,500		440	3,800	220	900		1,320	990
New Jersey									
Assumption College for Sisters	1,200		400	1,100					
Atlantic Community College	‡ 1,308	2,808/1,128	500				1,500	1,360	360
Bergen Community College	‡ 1,500	3,960/1,320	850						
Berkeley College of Business	9,255		763	1,530	1,335	1,044	1,530	1,335	1,044
Bloomfield College	8,050		400	4,100	300	1,415	2,780	1,100	1,250
Brookdale Community College	1,628	2,832/1,416	550				1,500	1,248	941
Burlington County College	‡ 1,325	2,170/250	762				1,386	1,016	1,350
Caldwell College	8,400		425	4,400	775	900	2,400	1,100	900
Camden County College	‡ 1,350	—/60	500				1,050	525	825
Centenary College	† 11,500		600	5,400	300	600	2,500	1,500	600
College of St. Elizabeth	10,900		380	5,000	350	650	1,700	850	650
County College of Morris	‡ 1,530	2,328/1,320	500				2,000	1,000	900
Cumberland County College	† 1,584	4,212/1,404	450				1,289	727	1,429
Drew University	18,058		520	5,348	230	370	1,500	600	500
Essex County College	‡ 1,848	3,300/1,650	600				1,500	900	1,061
Fairleigh Dickinson University									
Edward Williams College	10,295		473	5,336	557	1,050	1,040	2,100	1,050
Madison	10,988		570	5,336	509	1,273	2,257	1,773	1,748
Felician College	7,925		450					500	
Georgian Court College	8,750		500	3,850	800	800	1,800	1,600	800
Gloucester County College	‡ 1,590	4,320/30	400					1,000	800
Hudson County Community College	‡ 1,386	—/1,128	681					857	941
Jersey City State College	‡ 2,653	960/—	427	5,000	400	1,400	1,600	1,045	1,040
Katharine Gibbs School	7,545		500						
Kean College of New Jersey	‡ 2,613	780/—	500	3,690	650	800	900	875	700
Mercer County Community College	‡ 1,590	3,450/1,500	700				1,500	1,100	941
Monmouth College	11,820		520	5,160	360	1,330	2,330	650	1,330
Montclair State College	† 2,845	611/—	600	4,724	468	700	1,500	1,372	700
New Jersey Institute of Technology	† 4,714	4,323/—	700	5,119	450	750	1,504	850	780
Ocean County College	‡ 1,622	1,410/130	500				1,400	1,450	900
Passaic County Community College	† 2,017	1,708/—	735				2,250	850	945
Princeton University	18,940		665	5,710	350	1,500			
Ramapo College of New Jersey	‡ 3,024	1,887/—	600	4,626	800	855	1,700	1,800	602

†Figures are projected for 1993-94. ‡Figures are for 1992-93.

New Jersey: Ramapo College of New Jersey

All aid		Need-based aid		Grants and scholarships								Financial aid deadlines		Inst aid form	Notes
Total freshmen	Percent receiving aid	Freshmen judged to have need	Percent offered aid	Need-based				Non-need-based							
				Acad	Music/ drama	Art	Athl	Acad	Music/ drama	Art	Athl	Priority	Closing		
406	80	152	100									5/1	none		
216	76	128	100	X				X				5/1	none		
287	41	129	100	X				X				5/1	none	X	
380	32			X								5/1	none	X	
				X								5/1	none	X	
366	57	101	100	X								5/1	none	X	
898	45	187	100	X				X				5/1	none	X	
109	90			X				X				3/15	none	X	
778	60	426	99					X	X			3/1	none		
202	80	65	92	X				X				3/16	4/1	X	
513	54			X			X				X	3/1	4/15	X	
													none		
2,441	49	1,173	98	X			X	X	X	X	X	2/15	none		
89	26	21	100	X				X				5/1	none		
43	50	18	100	X				X				3/15	5/1	X	
												5/1	none		
													none		
1,880	25			X				X			X	6/15	none		
831	85	489	100	X				X					none	X	
354	82	278	100	X		X		X			X	6/1	none	X	
4,702	43	489	96	X				X			X	6/1	none		
1,409	50			X		X		X			X		none		
233	63			X		X	X	X		X	X	4/15	7/15		
2,298	10							X				7/1	12/2	X	
118	80	64	100	X		X		X			X	5/1	none	X	
138	87	97	100	X				X		X		4/1	none		
1,788	25	600	92	X	X	X		X			X	4/15	none		
544	33											6/1	none		
332	65	223	100	X				X					3/1	X	
2,278	65			X				X			X	6/30	none	X	
496	90			X	X	X	X	X				3/15	none		
566	85			X	X	X	X	X			X	3/15	none		
164	45			X				X				6/1	none	X	
137	64			X	X	X	X	X	X	X	X	3/1	10/1	X	
1,813	25			X				X				5/1	none		
987	48							X					none		
915	58	407	100	X				X	X			4/15	none		
													none		
1,222	55	627	100	X				X				4/1	none		
				X	X	X	X	X	X		X	5/1	none	X	
539	68	271	100	X				X			X	3/1	none		
1,120	60	550	100					X				2/15	none		
518	71	298	93	X				X				3/15	none	X	
								X				5/31	none		
1,102	50			X				X				8/1	none	X	
1,140	70	485	100										2/1	X	
457	45			X				X				3/15	5/1		

New Jersey: Raritan Valley Community College

Institution	Tuition and fees	Add'l out-of-state/ district tuition	Books and supplies	Room and board	Trans- portation	Other costs	Board only	Trans- portation	Other costs
				Costs for campus residents			*Costs for students at home*		
Raritan Valley Community College	1,513	3,951/1,317	600				1,500	1,080	900
Rider College	12,950		700	5,210		1,200			1,200
Rowan College of New Jersey	‡ 2,703	1,050/—	600	4,565	230	1,000	1,500	800	900
Rutgers—The State University of New Jersey									
Camden College of Arts and Sciences	4,082	3,538/—	650	4,604					
College of Engineering	4,638	3,924/—	650	4,454					
College of Nursing	4,068	3,538/—	650	4,624					
College of Pharmacy	4,638	3,924/—	650	4,454					
Cook College	4,625	3,924/—	650	4,596					
Douglass College	4,225	3,538/—	650	4,614					
Livingston College	4,307	3,538/—	650	4,610					
Mason Gross School of the Arts	4,263	3,538/—	650	4,454					
Newark College of Arts and Sciences	4,075	3,538/—	650	4,624					
Rutgers College	4,271	3,538/—	650	4,596					
St. Peter's College	8,835		600		500	600	1,500	650	600
Salem Community College	‡ 1,458	—/300	600					1,100	775
Seton Hall University	11,485		650	6,254	597	1,147	2,160	973	1,270
Stevens Institute of Technology	16,740		450	5,680	170	570		1,500	570
Stockton State College	† 2,648	600/—	725	4,288	800	1,125	1,500	1,050	1,025
Sussex County Community College	† 1,584	2,784/1,392	600				1,500	900	966
Trenton State College	† 3,810	1,650/—	700	5,325	100	1,000	1,600	900	600
Union County College	‡ 1,564	3,960/1,320	585				1,980	962	2,573
University of Medicine and Dentistry of New Jersey: School of Nursing	‡ 1,801	—/1,568							
Upsala College	12,500		600	5,260	375	6,072		670	2,375
Warren County Community College	‡ 1,680	3,120/1,560	500				1,080	864	900
Westminster Choir College School of Music of Rider College	12,750		500	5,515	150	700	2,280	1,000	700
William Paterson College of New Jersey	‡ 2,644	840/—	450	4,595	1,000	1,500	2,000	1,000	1,500
New Mexico									
Albuquerque Technical-Vocational Institute	† 924	1,548/—	497				2,023	1,208	1,691
Clovis Community College	† 536	992/24	500					800	850
College of Santa Fe	9,830		400	3,958	200	1,200	1,800	200	1,200
College of the Southwest	‡ 3,800		400	2,550	1,000	590	1,760	1,380	590
Dona Ana Branch Community College of New Mexico State University	‡ 696	1,224/120	300				1,360		
Eastern New Mexico University									
Portales	‡ 1,356	3,558/—	500	2,410	1,000	1,200		1,000	1,200
Roswell Campus	‡ 612	1,328/24	552	2,700	800	600		1,300	950
Institute of American Indian Arts	9,135		1,350	3,166	485	1,042	1,800	1,360	1,042
National College	‡ 6,288		800						
New Mexico Highlands University	† 1,480	3,754/—	600	2,780	1,100	800	2,000	2,000	800
New Mexico Institute of Mining and Technology	1,784	3,862/—	600	3,440	500	1,000	1,800	250	1,000
New Mexico Junior College	‡ 385	480/360	450	3,000	650	1,050	900	750	800
New Mexico Military Institute	‡ 1,495	1,425/—		2,300		1,000			
New Mexico State University									
Alamogordo	‡ 682	1,224/120	310						
Carlsbad	750	1,950/120	600					850	1,100
Las Cruces	1,872	4,200/—	550	3,998	886	1,066	1,500	886	1,066

†Figures are projected for 1993-94. ‡Figures are for 1992-93.

New Mexico: New Mexico State University

All aid		Need-based aid		Grants and scholarships								Financial aid deadlines		Inst aid form	Notes
Total freshmen	Percent receiving aid	Freshmen judged to have need	Percent offered aid	Need-based				Non-need-based							
				Acad	Music/drama	Art	Athl	Acad	Music/drama	Art	Athl	Priority	Closing		
1,200	20			X								7/15	none		
732	70			X			X	X	X		X	4/1	none		
793	69			X	X	X		X	X	X			4/15	X	
245	63			X	X		X	X				3/1	none		
594	62	329	83	X	X		X	X			X	3/1	none		
42	60	30	90	X	X		X	X				3/1	none		
181	73	180	93	X	X		X	X			X	3/1	none		
494	64	281	83	X	X		X	X			X	3/1	none		
658	61	389	83	X	X		X	X	X		X	3/1	none		
605	59	511	86	X	X		X	X	X		X	3/1	none		
97	56	54	80	X	X		X	X	X	X	X	3/1	none		
501	54	574	86	X	X		X	X				3/1	none		
1,585	69	846	85	X	X		X	X	X		X	3/1	none		
532	80	335	97					X			X	2/15	none		
				X				X			X	3/1	none	X	
1,000	75	740	99	X				X			X	4/1	none		
340	70	277	100	X				X				2/1	none		
741	76			X				X				3/1	none		
504	40							X				3/1	8/1	X	
891	50			X				X	X				5/1	X	
1,905	17							X		X	X	3/15	none	X	
												3/1	none		
383	98			X				X				3/1	none		
227	8	55	75	X				X				11/1	none	X	
47	87			X	X			X	X			3/15	none		
1,044	31			X	X			X	X			4/15	none		
				X								3/1	none		
583	30			X				X					none		
177	90	95	100	X	X	X		X	X	X		3/1	none	X	
32	83	10	100					X	X		X	4/1	6/1		
2,083	21	450	100	X								3/1	none		
572	80			X	X	X	X	X	X	X	X	3/1	none		
207	70			X				X				5/1	none	X	
68	85												4/15		
43	75			X				X					none	X	
374	73	313	95	X				X		X	X	3/1	none	X	
286	74	132	100	X				X				3/1	none	X	
1,059	37	353	100	X	X	X	X	X	X		X	4/1	none		
264	90	110	100	X				X			X	5/1	none	X	
				X									3/1	X	
				X				X				3/1	none		
				X				X	X		X	3/1	none	X	

155

New Mexico: Northern New Mexico Community College

Institution		Tuition and fees	Add'l out-of-state/ district tuition	Books and supplies	Room and board	Trans- portation	Other costs	Board only	Trans- portation	Other costs
					Costs for campus residents			*Costs for students at home*		
Northern New Mexico Community College	‡	528	900/—	460	2,768	1,200	1,300	2,128	935	1,025
Parks College	‡	4,320								
St. John's College		16,300		275	5,450	600	900	1,700	100	
San Juan College	‡	360	240/—	400					800	600
Santa Fe Community College		434	672/72	500				2,500	650	440
University of New Mexico		1,788	4,680/—	546	4,726	926	1,816	1,890	850	1,168
Western New Mexico University	‡	1,214	3,180/—	400	2,110	700	1,000	800	700	900

New York

Institution		Tuition and fees	Add'l out-of-state/ district tuition	Books and supplies	Room and board	Trans- portation	Other costs	Board only	Trans- portation	Other costs
Adelphi University		12,300		700	6,000	1,500	1,500		3,000	3,000
Adirondack Community College	†	1,873	1,750/—	530				925	700	1,697
Albany College of Pharmacy	‡	8,000		500		300	700	1,500	700	700
Alfred University		15,648		500	5,006	400	525	1,500	1,300	525
American Academy of Dramatic Arts		7,975		400				3,500	900	875
American Academy McAllister Institute of Funeral Service	‡	5,185		700						
Audrey Cohen College	‡	9,900		300				1,000	690	640
Bard College		19,164		550	6,030	400	450	2,225	600	600
Barnard College		17,756		520	7,736		850	660	630	830
Berkeley College	‡	8,625		630	4,225		1,010		660	660
Berkeley School: New York City	‡	9,195		700						
Boricua College	‡	5,229		450				6,515	560	844
Bramson ORT Technical Institute	‡	5,635		240					475	1,300
Broome Community College	†	1,938	1,830/—	500				750	600	750
Bryant & Stratton Business Institute										
Albany	‡	5,310		675				1,600	600	1,100
Rochester	‡	5,442		450						
Syracuse	‡	5,310		550					540	360
Canisius College		10,270		400	5,240	430	700	750	430	630
Catholic Medical Center of Brooklyn and Queens School of Nursing	‡	3,625		500		275	1,000	1,100	500	1,000
Cayuga County Community College	†	2,039	1,880/—	750				900	720	500
Cazenovia College		9,445		400	4,608	200	350	750	300	750
Central City Business Institute	‡	4,770		500	3,000	1,173	700	1,500	642	800
City University of New York										
Baruch College	†	2,552	2,600/—	500				1,802	675	2,100
Borough of Manhattan Community College	†	2,182	576/—	500				1,802	675	2,100
Bronx Community College	†	2,204	576/—	500				1,802	675	2,100
Brooklyn College	†	2,605	2,600/—	500				1,802	675	2,100
City College	†	2,547	2,600/—	500				1,802	675	2,100
College of Staten Island	†	2,556	2,600/—	500				1,802	675	2,100
Hostos Community College	†	2,174	576/—	500				1,802	675	2,100
Hunter College	†	2,553	2,600/—	500		675	2,188	1,802	675	2,100
John Jay College of Criminal Justice	†	2,554	2,600/—	500				1,802	675	2,100
Kingsborough Community College	†	2,190	576/—	500				1,802	675	2,100
La Guardia Community College	†	2,200	576/—	500				1,802	675	2,100
Lehman College	†	2,560	2,600/—	500				1,802	675	2,100
Medgar Evers College	†	2,150	576/—	500				1,802	675	2,100
New York City Technical College	†	2,499	2,600/—	500				1,802	675	2,100
Queens College	†	2,631	2,600/—	500				1,802	675	2,100
Queensborough Community College	†	2,200	576/—	500				1,802	675	2,100
York College	†	2,534	2,600/—	500				1,802	675	2,100
Clarkson University		15,383		700	5,326	400	691	2,828		691

†Figures are projected for 1993-94. ‡Figures are for 1992-93.

New York: Clarkson University

All aid		Need-based aid		Grants and scholarships								Financial aid deadlines		Inst aid form	Notes
Total freshmen	Percent receiving aid	Freshmen judged to have need	Percent offered aid	Need-based				Non-need-based							
				Acad	Music/drama	Art	Athl	Acad	Music/drama	Art	Athl	Priority	Closing		
239	85			X				X				3/1	none	X	
								X					5/31		
115	64	73	100	X								3/1	none	X	
512	60	275	100	X	X			X	X			5/1	none		
				X				X	X			3/1	none		
1,744	60	800	100	X				X	X		X	3/1	none	X	
541	43	175	95					X	X	X	X	4/1	none	X	
588	74	405	100	X				X	X	X	X	2/15	none		
967	60			X	X	X		X				4/15	none	X	
130	79	91	100									2/15	4/15		
487	90			X	X	X		X		X			none	X	
127	65			X	X							7/1	none	X	
50	65	35	100					X					none		
158	85			X									none	X	
313	65			X	X	X		X	X	X		2/15	none		
555	60	310	100										2/1	X	
256	80	170	100	X				X					none	X	
218	86	149	100	X				X					none	X	
150	87			X				X				5/2	7/15		
500	95	240	100	X				X					none	X	
2,126	60			X			X	X			X	4/1	none	X	
95	75	160	100	X									9/20		
													none		
													none		
753	90	464	100				X	X			X	2/1	none		
													none		
414	75			X				X				5/1	none	X	
558	87			X				X		X	X	3/1	none		
222	90			X				X				6/1	none	X	
1,423	70			X				X				4/15	5/30		
2,815	85												none		
4,000	90												none		
1,428	50	810	89	X	X	X	X	X	X	X		5/1	none		
1,160	86	1,050	100	X				X				5/1	none		
1,532	33											5/25	9/30		
865	95												none		
1,021	72			X				X				5/1	none		
1,367	70	900	100					X				6/1			
2,499	90											8/1	none		
2,207	83											7/1	none		
861	90							X				5/30	none	X	
686	90											6/1	8/31		
2,108	83											6/30	10/1		
1,647	60							X				5/31	8/1	X	
2,470	92											5/1	none		
742	70	390	90									4/1	8/1		
549	87	457	100	X	X	X	X	X	X	X	X	2/1	2/15		

New York: Clinton Community College

Institution	Tuition and fees	Add'l out-of-state/ district tuition	Books and supplies	Room and board	Trans-portation	Other costs	Board only	Trans-portation	Other costs
				Costs for campus residents			*Costs for students at home*		
Clinton Community College	† 1,810	1,700/—	500				1,200	900	739
Cochran School of Nursing-St. John's Riverside Hospital	‡ 7,970		650				2,200	1,541	2,050
Colgate University	18,620		500	5,400	80	750	1,580	80	750
College of Aeronautics	† 6,070		950				450	1,035	265
College of Insurance	10,500		500	6,888	400	1,016	3,000	440	1,016
College of Mount St. Vincent	11,330		500	5,600	150	850	1,500	600	850
College of New Rochelle									
New Rochelle	10,680		500	4,750	250	250	1,500	250	100
School of New Resources	4,960		500	4,760			1,500	250	100
College of St. Rose	9,592		750	5,428	325	1,600	1,886	1,000	1,199
Columbia University									
Columbia College	† 17,948		550	6,610		990			
School of Engineering and Applied Science	† 17,902		550	6,610		990	1,680	400	700
School of General Studies	‡ 14,972		900				2,529	414	400
School of Nursing	† 17,492		1,400		800	1,200	3,000	1,000	1,200
Columbia-Greene Community College	† 1,786	—/1,680	450				1,320	900	950
Concordia College	‡ 9,370		400	4,330	350	850	550	350	850
Cooper Union	300		1,255	8,415	150	1,260	1,350	500	1,260
Cornell University	18,226		500	6,044		1,030			
Cornell University: Statutory Divisions	7,426	6,680/—	500	6,044		1,030			
Corning Community College	† 2,146	2,000/—	520				1,880	805	400
Culinary Institute of America	‡ 11,615				600	1,300		600	1,300
Daemen College	8,730		700	4,350	700	800		700	800
Dominican College of Blauvelt	† 8,060		500	5,540	450	900	1,650	1,000	900
Dowling College	‡ 8,690		450		800	1,413	1,260	1,106	1,413
Dutchess Community College	† 1,845	1,750/—	560				1,785	850	750
D'Youville College	8,720		650	4,130	640	680	2,800	640	680
Eastman School of Music of the University of Rochester	15,779		600	6,286	650	850	2,450	650	850
Elmira College	13,900		450	4,550		550	1,500		550
Erie Community College									
City Campus	† 1,908	—/1,830	500				1,008	750	750
North Campus	† 1,908	—/1,830	500				1,380	750	750
South Campus	† 1,908	—/1,830	500				1,008	750	750
Eugene Lang College/New School for Social Research	‡ 12,940		680	8,426			2,886	600	975
Fashion Institute of Technology	† 2,210	2,650/—	1,200	4,655	600	1,050	1,600	800	900
Finger Lakes Community College	† 1,910	1,780/—	500				1,800	600	480
Five Towns College	6,750		600				2,425	1,800	2,000
Fordham University	13,400		600	6,825	580	875	1,800	750	800
Fulton-Montgomery Community College	† 2,014	1,900/—	500				1,800	600	500
Genesee Community College	† 1,950	1,800/—	520					680	550
Hamilton College	18,650		450	4,850	200	600			
Hartwick College	‡ 14,450		600	4,450	350	250	1,300	1,100	250
Helene Fuld School of Nursing	‡ 6,091		900				2,500	404	1,524
Herkimer County Community College	† 2,040	1,900/—	500				500	600	660
Hilbert College	7,200		500	4,250	400	660	1,500	500	660
Hobart College	18,309		650	5,616	200	600	1,500	300	
Hofstra University	† 11,240		660	6,100	675	1,000	1,800	1,675	1,000
Houghton College	9,720		500	3,400	250	600	800	550	600
Hudson Valley Community College	† 1,584	1,650/—	550				1,700	900	800

†Figures are projected for 1993-94. ‡Figures are for 1992-93.

New York: Hudson Valley Community College

All aid		Need-based aid		Grants and scholarships								Financial aid deadlines		Inst aid form	Notes
Total fresh-men	Percent receiving aid	Freshmen judged to have need	Percent offered aid	Need-based				Non-need-based							
				Acad	Music/drama	Art	Athl	Acad	Music/drama	Art	Athl	Priority	Closing		
679	80	275	100	X				X				4/15	none		
82	90	66	100	X									none	X	
691	61	292	100									2/1		X	
295	82	260	100	X				X				5/1	none	X	
155	88	12	100	X				X					none		
177	80	127	100					X					3/15	X	
181	95	100	100					X	X	X			none	X	
666	96												none	X	
244	85			X	X	X		X	X	X			3/1	X	
862	46	360	100										2/1	X	
261	59	136	100	X				X					2/1	X	
180	50			X									7/1	X	
				X				X				4/15	none		
471	75							X				5/1	none	X	
106	82							X	X		X		3/31		
213	42	93	100	X				X				2/15	5/1		
2,959	70	1,471	100	X									3/15	X	
													3/15	X	
1,034	85	800	100	X								7/1	none	X	
1,125	75			X				X					none		
312	93	223	100	X		X	X	X			X	2/15	none	X	
104	75	56	100	X			X	X			X	3/1	none	X	
357	70			X	X		X	X			X		8/1	X	
1,488	50			X				X				5/1	none		
181	95			X				X			X	4/15	none		
121	88	82	100		X			X	X			2/1	none	X	
360	80	250	100					X	X	X		3/1	none		
895	82											4/30	none	X	
				X								4/30	none		
1,069	53			X								4/30	none		
90	60			X				X				3/1	none	X	
1,517	51	730	92										3/15	X	
1,462	75							X	X	X	X	5/1	none	X	
307	67	192	96	X	X			X	X			5/15	8/21	X	
1,011	80			X	X		X	X	X		X		2/1	X	
674	75			X				X				4/1	none		
1,333	75	350	100	X	X	X	X	X	X	X			6/1		
463	57												2/1	X	
446	69	234	100	X	X	X	X	X	X		X		4/1	X	
19	84			X				X					none	X	
1,118	84	690	100	X			X	X			X		4/1		
170	76			X				X				2/28	none		
305	54	166	98	X	X	X							2/15	X	
1,485	80	1,393	75	X				X				3/1	none		
294	94			X	X	X	X	X	X	X	X	3/15	none		
4,063	60			X								5/30	none		

159

New York: Institute of Design and Construction

Institution	Tuition and fees	Add'l out-of-state/district tuition	Books and supplies	Room and board	Trans-portation	Other costs	Board only	Trans-portation	Other costs
				Costs for campus residents			*Costs for students at home*		
Institute of Design and Construction	3,650		600					200	400
Iona College	‡ 9,540		500	6,000	450	1,050	720	850	1,800
Ithaca College	13,642		500	5,842	240	910	2,604	1,240	910
Jamestown Business College	‡ 4,925		450				800	700	725
Jamestown Community College	† 2,000	1,800/—	500				2,000	500	400
Jefferson Community College	† 1,656	1,464/—	600				1,500	310	500
Jewish Theological Seminary of America	6,870		500		400	2,500		450	2,500
Juilliard School	‡ 11,250		2,400	5,900	500	6,500	2,300	1,300	
Katharine Gibbs School									
Melville	‡ 7,445		550				1,100	1,315	1,053
New York	‡ 7,350		600					1,300	
Keuka College	9,310		600	4,350	500	500	1,500	500	500
King's College	‡ 8,310		500	3,920	300	500	425	300	500
Le Moyne College	10,660		250	4,540	1,000		700	250	300
Long Island College Hospital School of Nursing	6,810		1,150				2,500	1,451	1,161
Long Island University									
Brooklyn Campus	† 10,805		700	5,790	450	800	2,000	450	800
C. W. Post Campus	† 11,450		500	5,370	500	1,150	1,800	900	800
Southampton Campus	† 11,520		525	5,680	400	550	2,674	500	550
Manhattan College	12,600		500	6,600	500	1,000	1,800	800	1,000
Manhattan School of Music	‡ 11,000		525		650	900	2,500	650	900
Manhattanville College	14,290		450	6,250	425	800	1,500	800	725
Mannes College of Music	12,000		1,200		600	1,000	2,850	600	1,000
Maria College	‡ 4,275		550					500	500
Marist College	† 10,545		500	5,817	305	548	1,956	607	548
Marymount College	11,150		500	6,200	420	600		1,000	600
Marymount Manhattan College	‡ 9,820		300	6,000	600	1,000	1,600	600	1,000
Mater Dei College	‡ 5,153		550	3,416	150	600	1,500	300	600
Medaille College	‡ 7,750		500	4,100	550	600		550	600
Mercy College	‡ 7,200		500	6,380			1,500	700	800
Mohawk Valley Community College	† 2,150	2,000/—	750	3,902	510	1,262	1,698	660	750
Molloy College	8,650		600				1,500	1,400	1,200
Monroe College	‡ 5,040		555				1,500	520	680
Monroe Community College	† 2,130	1,950/—	450				1,000	700	1,475
Mount St. Mary College	† 8,260		300	4,880	500	700	1,500	1,000	750
Nassau Community College	† 1,940	1,850/—	650					1,300	950
Nazareth College of Rochester	10,380		500	4,830	150	800	1,500	600	800
New York Institute of Technology	† 8,225		500	5,480	410	1,200	1,500	1,270	1,200
New York School of Interior Design	9,950		1,000				5,000	800	700
New York University	17,640		450	7,065		1,000	1,500	320	
Niagara County Community College	† 1,800	1,700/—	375				750	650	600
Niagara University	10,070		450	4,482	300	650	1,500	500	650
North Country Community College	† 1,905	1,800/—	500				700	800	700
Nyack College	‡ 7,860		500	3,610	300	600		600	900
Ohr Somayach Tanenbaum Education Center	‡ 3,600		300	3,600	150	725	1,800	1,000	725
Olean Business Institute	‡ 4,305		500				1,600		
Onondaga Community College	† 2,088	4,000/2,000	540				1,647	750	450
Orange County Community College	† 1,835	1,750/—	525				2,340	535	465
Pace University									
College of White Plains	10,780		550	4,760	150	925	1,600	500	875
New York	10,780		550	4,760	150	925	1,600	500	875

†Figures are projected for 1993-94. ‡Figures are for 1992-93.

New York: Pace University

All aid		Need-based aid		Grants and scholarships								Financial aid deadlines		Inst aid form	Notes
Total freshmen	Percent receiving aid	Freshmen judged to have need	Percent offered aid	Need-based				Non-need-based							
				Acad	Music/drama	Art	Athl	Acad	Music/drama	Art	Athl	Priority	Closing		
93	60												none		
1,123	89	960	100	X				X		X	X	4/1	none	X	
1,568	55			X	X				X				3/1		
123	89			X				X					none		
1,533	80			X	X		X	X	X		X	3/1	none		
850	86	700	100	X			X	X			X	4/1	none	X	
17	60	9	100					X				3/1		X	
110	87	76	100	X	X			X	X			2/15		X	
110	70			X									none		
				X									none	X	
174	96	142	100	X				X				3/1	none	X	
110	87	94	100	X	X		X	X	X		X	3/15	none	X	
376	75	330	98	X	X	X	X	X			X	2/15	4/15	X	
20	72			X				X				6/1	none		
863	90	680	100	X	X	X	X	X	X	X	X		none	X	
791	77	490	97	X	X	X	X	X	X	X	X	5/15	none		
387	85	210	74					X		X	X		none	X	
586	85	450	100	X				X			X	2/15	none	X	
81	69	57	100		X			X	X			3/1	4/15		
221	67			X	X	X		X	X	X		3/1	none		
18	81				X				X			5/15	none	X	
8	60											8/1	none		
833	75	581	100	X	X	X	X	X	X		X	3/15	none		
108	63	74	100	X		X	X	X	X	X		3/1	none		
290	93	250	100	X	X	X		X	X	X		3/1	4/1	X	
146	90			X			X	X			X	4/15	none		
				X				X				5/1	none		
2,102	80	470	92					X			X	3/1	none		
1,450	85			X				X				5/15	none	X	
171	70	122	100	X				X	X	X	X	4/15	none	X	
948	98	817	99										3/31		
2,540	70			X			X	X			X	5/1	none	X	
275	70	150	100	X				X				3/15	none		
				X	X	X		X	X	X	X	5/1	none	X	
212	79	156	100	X	X	X		X	X	X		3/30	none		
848	92							X			X	6/1	none		
21	36			X	X			X		X		7/1	none		
2,606	82			X	X			X	X				2/15		
1,585	70	880	82	X				X				4/1	none		
574	84	437	100	X	X		X	X	X		X	2/15	none		
394	85											4/30	none		
105	87			X	X		X	X				3/1	none	X	
				X									none	X	
												5/1			
6,143	80							X				3/1	none		
				X				X	X	X	X	5/1	none	X	
91	61			X				X				3/15	7/1		
392	76			X	X		X	X	X		X	3/15	7/1		

161

New York: Pace University: Pleasantville/Briarcliff

Institution	Tuition and fees	Add'l out-of-state/ district tuition	Books and supplies	Room and board	Trans-portation	Other costs	Board only	Trans-portation	Other costs
Pleasantville/Briarcliff	10,780		550	4,760	500	925	1,600	500	875
Parsons School of Design	14,060		1,200	7,560		1,080	1,800	800	1,080
Paul Smith's College	9,790		677	4,120	400	1,000	1,500	600	1,000
Phillips Beth Israel School of Nursing	6,710		910				3,770	860	1,180
Polytechnic University									
Brooklyn	‡ 15,620		436	4,400	1,200	1,225	1,205	705	1,186
Long Island Campus	‡ 15,620		436	4,400	1,200	1,225	1,205	705	1,186
Pratt Institute	13,298		1,400	6,456	500	630	1,785	500	630
Rensselaer Polytechnic Institute	17,325		525	5,742		658	1,500	1,072	658
Roberts Wesleyan College	9,931		520	3,366	450	950	1,156	1,000	950
Rochester Institute of Technology	13,515		500	5,511	300	575	1,500	300	575
Rockland Community College	† 2,036	1,950/—	600				1,800	800	600
Russell Sage College	11,930		500	4,860	200	650	1,500	300	700
Sage Junior College of Albany	‡ 6,620		500	4,500	300	650	3,300	300	700
St. Bonaventure University	10,026		450	4,736	400	650	1,500	600	650
St. Francis College	6,300		450				2,250	450	1,125
St. John Fisher College	10,040		400	5,340	200	600	1,500	600	600
St. John's University	9,100		500				2,700	750	1,350
St. Joseph's College									
Brooklyn	7,122		500				1,500	500	600
Suffolk Campus	7,332		500				1,500	1,000	600
St. Joseph's School of Nursing	‡ 4,316		600		100	780	1,500	300	780
St. Lawrence University	17,895		650	5,530		1,425		300	1,000
St. Thomas Aquinas College	8,150		500	5,400	750	1,000	3,100	1,000	1,000
Sarah Lawrence College	18,584		500	7,016	350	725	2,300	200	
Schenectady County Community College	† 1,853	1,750/—	550				1,750	900	900
School of Visual Arts	11,900		1,380		735	1,745	2,425	735	1,745
Siena College	10,505		575	4,905	350	565	850	575	575
Skidmore College	17,775		550	5,455	250	700	1,450	250	700
State University of New York									
Albany	† 2,877	3,900/—	500	3,666	260	900	1,600	525	900
Binghamton	† 2,987	3,900/—	600	4,634	400	704	1,468	740	1,054
Buffalo	† 3,020	3,900/—	683	4,578	861	924	1,904	861	924
Purchase	† 2,910	3,900/—	400	4,374	315	900	1,800	609	900
Stony Brook	† 2,942	3,900/—	750	4,698	600	1,120	1,500	1,928	1,120
College of Agriculture and Technology at Cobleskill	† 2,944	3,900/—	500	4,470	200	600	1,500	550	600
College of Agriculture and Technology at Morrisville	† 2,900	3,900/—	600	4,080	450	770	1,600	2,700	1,000
College at Brockport	† 2,940	3,900/—	500	4,360	440	730	1,700	735	730
College at Buffalo	† 3,074	3,900/—	708	4,731	892	957	2,112	892	957
College at Cortland	† 2,905	3,900/—	650	4,400	400	845	1,575	700	520
College of Environmental Science and Forestry	† 2,937	3,900/—	600	6,320	200	450	1,800	600	300
College at Fredonia	† 2,926	3,900/—	620	4,200	784	1,000	1,850	994	950
College at Geneseo	† 3,075	3,900/—	600	3,995	650	650	1,700	650	650
College at New Paltz	† 2,927	3,900/—	550	4,240	600	900	1,500	900	900
College at Old Westbury	† 2,898	3,900/—	660	4,120	715	1,210		1,595	990
College at Oneonta	† 2,916	3,900/—	450	4,620	350	1,000	575	1,000	950
College at Plattsburgh	† 2,925	3,900/—	600	3,812	466	857	900	1,512	857
College at Potsdam	† 2,890	3,900/—	500	4,560	300	700	985	600	700
College of Technology at Alfred	† 2,900	3,900/—	600	4,310	478	700	670	888	700

†Figures are projected for 1993-94. ‡Figures are for 1992-93.

New York: State University of New York College of Technology at Alfred

All aid		Need-based aid		Grants and scholarships								Financial aid deadlines		Inst aid form	Notes
Total freshmen	Percent receiving aid	Freshmen judged to have need	Percent offered aid	Need-based				Non-need-based				Priority	Closing		
				Acad	Music/drama	Art	Athl	Acad	Music/drama	Art	Athl				
397	58			X			X	X	X		X	3/15	7/1		
357	85			X	X							3/1	7/1	X	
469	82			X		X		X			X	2/28	none		
19	95			X				X					6/1	X	
212	93			X				X				3/1	none	X	
87	82			X				X				3/1	none	X	
326	85	240	100	X		X		X		X		3/1	none		
1,300	79	745	100					X			X	2/15	none	X	
277	97	151	100	X	X	X	X	X	X	X	X	5/15	none	X	
1,530	68	1,084	100	X		X		X		X		3/15	none		
1,807	58			X				X				6/15	none	X	
170	85			X				X				3/1	none		
420	77			X				X		X	X	3/15	none	X	
459	79			X				X	X		X		3/1		
470	80	237	100	X			X	X			X	2/15	none		
350	82	308	100	X				X				3/1	none		
				X				X	X	X	X	4/1	none		
78	90	35	100	X				X				2/25	none	X	
149	89	85	100	X				X				2/25	none		
4	85							X				5/29	none		
604	75	424	100	X				X				2/1	2/15	X	
227	65	180	100	X		X		X		X	X	3/1	none		
221	50	122	100	X	X								2/1	X	
1,236	70			X		X		X				5/1	none		
322	85	472	100	X		X		X		X		2/28	none	X	
578	78			X			X	X			X		2/1		
595	33	208	94					X					2/1	X	
1,925	76	1,280	92	X				X				4/25	none	X	
1,817	60	650	100	X	X	X		X	X	X		2/15	none		
2,399	65	1,200	100	X	X	X	X	X	X	X		3/16	none		
341	57	194	100	X	X	X		X	X	X		2/15	none	X	
								X				3/1	none	X	
1,274	65	830	100	X				X				4/1	none	X	
1,546	85	1,110	73					X				3/1	none		
877	75	657	100					X	X	X		5/1	Closing	X	
1,080	85			X	X	X	X	X	X	X	X	3/16	none		
1,018	79	797	99	X				X	X				5/1	X	
67	85	57	100	X				X				3/15	none	X	
862	71	634	95	X	X								none		
1,133	70	765	98	X				X	X			3/1	4/1	X	
664	60	384	100									3/15	4/1		
				X								5/1	none	X	
902	69	426	100	X				X				5/1	none		
996	57	411	100	X	X	X		X	X	X		4/15	none		
762	80	460	100	X	X			X	X			3/1	none		
1,730	75							X	X			5/1	5/31		

163

New York: State University of New York College of Technology at Canton

		Tuition and fees	Add'l out-of-state/district tuition	Books and supplies	Costs for campus residents			Costs for students at home		
Institution					Room and board	Transportation	Other costs	Board only	Transportation	Other costs
College of Technology at Canton		† 2,914	3,900/—	500	4,230	400	700	1,660	1,500	700
College of Technology at Delhi		† 2,945	3,900/—	500	4,544	500	1,000	1,000	860	1,000
College of Technology at Farmingdale		† 3,000	3,900/—	600	4,320	500	800	2,000	1,100	800
Empire State College		† 2,887	3,900/—	600				2,730	405	1,500
Health Science Center at Brooklyn		† 2,815	3,900/—	685		330	820	1,155	520	820
Health Science Center at Syracuse		† 2,865	3,900/—	515		615	700	1,540	835	700
Health Sciences Center at Stony Brook		† 2,928	3,900/—	1,000	4,528	1,770	1,730	1,500	1,770	1,730
Institute of Technology at Utica/Rome		† 2,809	3,900/—	480	4,660	300	800	750	870	1,340
Maritime College		† 2,933	3,900/—	500	4,344	400	1,200			
Oswego		† 2,975	3,900/—	450	4,425	600	900		600	900
Suffolk County Community College										
Eastern Campus		† 1,968	1,850/—	550				975	1,248	1,048
Selden		† 1,968	1,850/—	550				975	1,248	1,048
Western Campus		† 1,968	1,850/—	550				975	1,248	1,048
Sullivan County Community College		† 2,000	1,850/—	600				700	650	700
Syracuse University		14,705		580	6,600	265	575	3,031	605	575
Talmudical Institute of Upstate New York		‡ 4,250			3,300					
Talmudical Seminary Oholei Torah		‡ 5,700			5,400					
Taylor Business Institute		‡ 6,720						1,053	387	210
Technical Career Institutes		‡ 5,700		450				2,000	487	1,430
Tompkins-Cortland Community College		† 2,064	1,900/—	500				1,500	1,000	900
Touro College		7,130		600		450	1,400	2,300	450	1,400
Trocaire College		‡ 5,300		700				1,500	700	600
Ulster County Community College		† 1,964	1,850/—	500				1,491	700	600
Union College		17,877		450	5,940	250	783	1,550	250	573
United States Merchant Marine Academy		† 3,450								
United States Military Academy		0								
University of Rochester		17,355		500	6,286	200	859	1,590	631	859
University of the State of New York:										
Regents College		480								
Utica College of Syracuse University		11,980		500	4,734	450	625	1,197	550	625
Utica School of Commerce		4,325		650						
Vassar College		18,456		600	5,750	300	600	2,600	300	600
Villa Maria College of Buffalo		† 5,830		400				1,700	450	650
Wadhams Hall Seminary-College		3,800		1,000	3,800	300	700	2,700	1,500	1,000
Wagner College		12,500		580	5,250	440	1,080	1,200	490	1,080
Webb Institute of Naval Architecture		0		600	5,000	1,000	500			
Wells College		14,160		600	5,300		500			500
Westchester Business Institute		9,405		600					2,055	1,281
Westchester Community College		† 2,168	2,925/—	600				2,000	900	500
William Smith College		18,309		650	5,610	200	600		300	
Wood Tobe-Coburn School		‡ 9,635		700				2,490	1,200	2,800
Yeshiva Shaar Hatorah		6,000	(Comprehensive)							
Yeshiva University		‡ 11,877		445		600	600			2,900
North Carolina										
Alamance Community College		‡ 578	3,959/—	550				1,600	690	650
Anson Community College		‡ 578	3,959/—	650				1,500	1,300	900
Appalachian State University		‡ 1,405	5,672/—	250	2,620	1,000	1,000	1,500	1,000	1,000
Asheville Buncombe Technical Community College		‡ 578	3,959/—	800				950	188	1,750
Barber-Scotia College		4,494		736	2,795	1,000	1,000	1,500	800	1,000

†Figures are projected for 1993-94. ‡Figures are for 1992-93.

Note: Comprehensive fees include tuition, fees, room, and board.

164

North Carolina: Barber-Scotia College

All aid		Need–based aid		Grants and scholarships								Financial aid deadlines		Inst aid form	Notes
Total freshmen	Percent receiving aid	Freshmen judged to have need	Percent offered aid	Need-based				Non–need-based							
				Acad	Music/ drama	Art	Athl	Acad	Music/ drama	Art	Athl	Priority	Closing		
872	80			X				X				3/1	none		
1,137	79			X				X				4/1	none	X	
2,676	72	2,243	100	X				X				4/1	none		
				X									4/1	X	
												4/10	4/30		
19	79			X								4/1	none	X	
				X				X				3/15	none	X	
				X				X				5/1	none		
270	51			X				X				4/1	none	X	
1,449	80	637	91	X	X			X	X			3/1	none		
								X				6/1	none	X	
3,462	65							X				6/1	none	X	
1,486	65							X				6/1	none	X	
588	70			X				X		X		5/15	none	X	
2,595	72	1,500	100	X	X	X		X	X	X	X		1/31		
1	20												none		
													none		
175	100												none		
1,710	98												none		
624	75	510	100	X				X					none		
2,228	85			X				X				5/15	none		
134	86	383	100	X				X				3/15	none		
607	80			X				X				6/1	none	X	
538	50	246	100									2/1		X	
281	20	60										1/15	1/30		
1,270	76	882	100	X	X	X		X	X	X		2/1	none	X	
													7/1	X	
326	84	271	98	X				X				2/15	none		
268	85							X					none		
605	48	260	100										1/15	X	
121	65						X	X	X	X	X	5/1	none	X	
6	100	6	100					X				8/1	none	X	
315	70			X	X		X	X			X	4/1	5/1	X	
23	36	1	100					X					7/1	X	
89	90	83	100					X				2/15	none		
366	91							X					none		
				X				X	X	X			none	X	
263	67	130	96	X	X	X		X					2/15	X	
313	86	309	100					X					none	X	
577	75	251	100					X				4/15	none	X	
1,097	18	325	100	X				X				5/15	none	X	
254	30	85	100	X									none		
2,054	44	701	100	X				X	X	X	X	2/1	none		
2,161	32	295	100	X				X				3/1	none		
480	95	335	100					X			X	3/15	none	X	

North Carolina: Barton College

		Tuition and fees	Add'l out-of-state/ district tuition	Books and supplies	Costs for campus residents			Costs for students at home		
Institution					Room and board	Trans-portation	Other costs	Board only	Trans-portation	Other costs
Barton College		7,363		500	3,326	900	1,200	1,497	1,000	1,200
Beaufort County Community College	‡	575	3,959/—	600				1,400	1,500	400
Belmont Abbey College		9,084		500	4,506	1,100	1,280	2,500	1,400	960
Bennett College		6,011		600	2,909	1,500	1,000		400	1,000
Bladen Community College	‡	587	3,959/—	300				500	800	1,550
Blue Ridge Community College	‡	587	3,959/—	600				2,000	1,535	787
Brevard College		6,445		550	3,650	600	600	1,500	600	600
Brunswick Community College	‡	581	3,959/—	390				1,500	1,184	660
Caldwell Community College and Technical Institute	‡	578	3,959/—	450				1,700	900	1,350
Campbell University	‡	7,678		600	2,590	570	1,927	1,600	1,575	1,154
Cape Fear Community College	‡	576	3,959/—	460				1,000	1,200	770
Carteret Community College	‡	573	3,959/—	500				1,100	900	200
Catawba College		9,000		600	3,950	660	1,200	2,000	990	1,200
Catawba Valley Community College	‡	575	3,959/—	800					900	800
Central Carolina Community College	‡	578	3,959/—	450				1,550	1,400	850
Central Piedmont Community College	‡	572	3,959/—	600				1,800	1,800	1,125
Chowan College		6,730		450	3,250	470	1,000		1,250	1,000
Cleveland Community College	‡	585	3,959/—	490				2,000	750	1,175
Coastal Carolina Community College	‡	578	3,959/—	450				1,800	450	800
College of the Albemarle	‡	585	3,959/—	325				1,700	783	750
Craven Community College	‡	584	3,959/—	519				1,300	612	918
Davidson College		16,263		550	4,774		903	2,304		903
Davidson County Community College	‡	580	3,959/—	500				1,500	1,137	470
Duke University		17,163		592	5,550	455	1,045	2,730	600	1,045
Durham Technical Community College	‡	575	3,959/—	300				1,125	900	562
East Carolina University	‡	1,246	5,672/—	500	3,030	600	1,007	1,700	600	1,007
East Coast Bible College		3,950		550	2,400					
Edgecombe Community College	‡	575	3,959/—	500				2,550	925	1,800
Elizabeth City State University	‡	1,184	5,018/—	300	2,648	490	810	2,000	600	810
Elon College		8,630		425	3,660	625	1,150	2,020	625	1,150
Fayetteville State University	‡	1,246	5,672/—	350	2,250	190	750	1,500	185	750
Fayetteville Technical Community College	‡	569	3,959/—	600				1,600	495	525
Gardner-Webb University		7,680		500	4,070	570	900		650	450
Gaston College	‡	587	3,959/—	1,000					1,000	1,000
Greensboro College		7,816		550	3,680	650	970	1,500	650	820
Guilford College		12,610		475	5,070	450	665	2,424	450	665
Halifax Community College	‡	575	3,959/—	377				1,500	1,031	896
Haywood Community College	‡	577	3,959/—	400				1,000	1,200	870
High Point University		7,760		570	3,700	550	950	750	1,070	1,100
Isothermal Community College	‡	585	3,959/—	525				1,500	696	1,137
James Sprunt Community College	‡	581	3,959/—	500				1,268	1,237	600
John Wesley College		5,100		300	2,280	100	1,500	1,500	765	1,500
Johnson C. Smith University		6,338		638	2,438	938	1,608	1,500	618	773
Johnston Community College	‡	578	3,959/—	450				1,500	900	900
Lees-McRae College		8,200		450	3,050	400	750	1,300	800	750
Lenoir Community College	‡	584	3,959/—	450				1,500	680	540
Lenoir-Rhyne College		10,145		500	3,848	300	600	1,860	300	600
Livingstone College		5,200		600	3,400	850	1,000	1,904	800	800
Louisburg College		6,249		450	3,035	500	1,000	1,500	700	1,000
Mars Hill College		7,500		600	3,550	800	800	2,000	800	800

†Figures are projected for 1993-94. ‡Figures are for 1992-93.

North Carolina: Mars Hill College

All aid		Need-based aid		Grants and scholarships								Financial aid deadlines		Inst aid form	Notes
Total fresh-men	Percent receiving aid	Freshmen judged to have need	Percent offered aid	Need-based				Non-need-based							
				Acad	Music/drama	Art	Athl	Acad	Music/drama	Art	Athl	Priority	Closing		
318	80			X	X	X	X	X	X	X	X	4/15	none		
436	26			X				X				7/1	none		
180	75	120	100	X			X	X			X	4/1	none		
189	80			X				X	X				4/15	X	
269	37	258	100									8/15	none	X	
660	15			X				X				6/30	none		
414	72	194	100					X	X	X	X	3/15	none		
				X				X				8/1	none	X	
874	25	437	100	X				X				5/1	none		
536	86							X	X		X	3/15	none		
1,032	45			X				X				3/15	none		
275	60			X								8/1	none	X	
292	84	141	100					X	X		X	3/30	none	X	
1,304	12	400	69	X				X					none		
576	35	225	100	X								5/30	none		
1,386	15			X								4/1	none	X	
289	80			X	X	X		X	X	X	X	3/1	none		
944	10			X									none		
298	75			X								5/15	none	X	
927	35			X	X							6/1	none		
				X			X	X				4/1	none	X	
414	63	135	100	X				X	X	X	X		2/15	X	
378	35	225	100	X								5/30	none		
1,626	38	602	100	X				X	X	X	X	2/1	none		
1,793	50	483	100	X									none	X	
				X	X	X	X	X	X	X	X	4/15	none		
44	64			X	X	X							5/15		
222	40			X				X			X		7/15		
545	91							X	X		X	5/1	none	X	
820	43	289	100	X	X		X	X	X		X	4/1	none	X	
353	80			X	X		X	X	X		X		4/1	X	
598	69			X				X				6/1	8/1		
300	65	186	100	X	X		X	X	X		X	4/1	none		
580	42	76	100	X				X				3/15	none	X	
230	67	118	100	X	X	X		X	X	X		3/15	none		
340	79	215	100	X	X	X		X	X	X			3/1		
207	43			X				X				6/1	none		
432	27			X								4/1	none		
361	56	174	98	X				X			X	3/1	none	X	
185	33			X	X				X			7/1	none	X	
340	45	150	100	X				X				7/1	none	X	
9	67	9	100	X	X			X	X			5/1	none		
407	90	342	100	X				X	X		X	5/15	none		
1,080	45			X				X				6/1	none	X	
284	88	125	100	X	X		X	X	X		X	3/15	none	X	
												6/30	none	X	
259	60			X	X		X	X	X		X	3/1	none		
232	84			X	X		X	X	X		X	5/1	5/15		
401	83	216	100	X	X		X	X	X		X	4/1	none	X	
265	72	198	100					X	X		X	5/1	none	X	

North Carolina: Martin Community College

		Tuition and fees	Add'l out-of-state/ district tuition	Books and supplies	Costs for campus residents			Costs for students at home		
Institution					Room and board	Trans-portation	Other costs	Board only	Trans-portation	Other costs
Martin Community College	‡	572	3,959/—	400				3,024	990	400
Mayland Community College	‡	581	3,959/—	650				980	893	1,087
McDowell Technical Community College	‡	575	3,959/—	450				2,241	693	675
Meredith College		6,340		450	3,100	250	1,200	2,000	450	1,000
Methodist College		8,850		600	3,550	400	1,360	2,500	600	2,900
Mitchell Community College	‡	582	3,959/—	425				1,711	772	1,450
Montgomery Community College	‡	573	3,959/—	600				1,500	1,936	1,885
Montreat-Anderson College		7,600		500	3,372	600	2,358	2,850	1,000	2,014
Mount Olive College		7,100		500	2,550	600	900	1,500	600	900
Nash Community College	‡	578	3,959/—	750				1,200	1,050	450
North Carolina Agricultural and Technical State University	‡	1,270	5,672/—	600	2,960	464	1,147	1,500	774	1,083
North Carolina Central University	‡	1,211	5,672/—	450	2,894	386	1,250	1,726	680	1,256
North Carolina School of the Arts	‡	1,630	6,459/—	595	3,163		1,565	1,680		755
North Carolina State University	‡	1,302	6,584/—	600	3,350	250	1,050	2,220	550	1,050
North Carolina Wesleyan College	‡	8,350		500	4,130	432	863	2,500	757	938
Pamlico Community College	‡	572	3,959/—	340				3,165	1,356	1,623
Peace College		5,220		500	4,440	800	1,000	1,500	800	1,500
Pembroke State University	‡	948	5,018/—	450	2,530	600	900	1,800	900	675
Pfeiffer College		8,190		650	3,480	1,000	650	1,250	1,200	650
Piedmont Bible College		4,090		450	2,600	500	550	754	800	550
Piedmont Community College	‡	575	3,959/—	500				2,000	1,200	750
Pitt Community College	†	575	3,959/—	600				3,024	1,494	400
Queens College		10,400		550	4,550	1,000	900	1,800	500	900
Randolph Community College	‡	579	3,959/—	800				1,000	829	881
Richmond Community College	‡	584	3,959/—	450				1,500	900	700
Roanoke Bible College	‡	2,964		250	2,440	350	250	1,900	1,000	200
Roanoke-Chowan Community College	‡	581	3,959/—	360				1,500	1,620	150
Robeson Community College	‡	575	3,959/—	600				1,800	1,041	75
Rockingham Community College	‡	584	3,959/—	450				1,000	1,040	1,000
Rowan-Cabarrus Community College	‡	581	3,959/—	430				1,500	645	525
St. Andrews Presbyterian College		9,880		400	4,360	200	860			1,920
St. Augustine's College		5,700		450	3,600	1,166	1,300	2,088	980	1,300
St. Mary's College		6,780		600	5,835	575	1,400	1,300	575	1,000
Salem College		10,025		500	6,025	800	2,000	1,236	500	800
Sampson Community College	‡	587	3,969/—	600				1,800	800	900
Sandhills Community College	‡	578	3,959/—	514				1,800	1,260	578
Shaw University		5,362		600	3,374	500	500		600	500
Southeastern Baptist Theological Seminary	‡	1,050		300						
Southeastern Community College	‡	586	3,959/—	425				1,500	1,300	900
Southwestern Community College	‡	581	3,959/—	500				1,500	1,650	630
Stanly Community College	‡	578	3,959/—	450				2,000	795	1,200
Surry Community College	‡	575	3,959/—	500				1,500	1,238	495
Tri-County Community College	‡	570	3,959/—	300				600	2,000	450
University of North Carolina										
Asheville	‡	1,150	5,108/—	600	3,000	1,203	750	1,500	1,124	680
Chapel Hill	‡	1,261	6,584/—	500	3,950	100	1,050	1,500	100	800
Charlotte	‡	1,189	5,672/—	550	2,842	800	900	1,400	1,400	900
Greensboro	‡	1,540	6,584/—	450	3,552	300	840	800	750	840
Wilmington	‡	1,344	5,672/—	500	3,460	410	1,087	2,140	450	863
Vance-Granville Community College	‡	584	3,959/—	475				1,500	900	400

†Figures are projected for 1993-94. ‡Figures are for 1992-93.

North Carolina: Vance-Granville Community College

Total freshmen	Percent receiving aid	Freshmen judged to have need	Percent offered aid	Acad	Music/drama	Art	Athl	Acad	Music/drama	Art	Athl	Priority	Closing	Inst aid form	Notes
149	50			X				X				5/1	none		
303	52	226	91	X				X				4/30	none	X	
386	34			X				X				3/15	none		
383	61	154	100	X	X	X		X	X	X		2/15	none	X	
348	85	195	100	X				X	X			5/1	7/1		
372	24	60	93	X	X	X		X	X	X		4/1	none		
123	52											7/15	none	X	
79	85			X				X		X	X	3/1	none		
162	95	82	100					X	X	X	X	3/1	none	X	
565	9			X				X				3/15	none	X	
				X	X	X		X	X	X	X	5/15	none	X	
784	69							X					3/31		
122	66	93	88		X	X		X	X	X		3/15	none	X	
3,065	42	1,650	70	X				X			X	3/15	none	X	
211	70			X				X				4/15	none		
96	80			X									none		
253	69	90	100	X	X	X	X	X	X	X	X	4/1	none		
				X	X	X	X	X	X	X	X	4/15	none		
148	96							X	X		X	5/1	none		
55	100	55	100	X	X			X	X				none		
372	50	245	65	X								4/15	none		
				X		X		X				5/1	8/24	X	
171	90	102	100	X	X	X	X	X	X	X	X	3/1	none	X	
270	5			X				X					5/1	X	
162	65			X				X				8/1	none	X	
41	68	24	100	X				X	X			3/1	5/1	X	
111	68	101	100	X				X					none		
538	62			X								5/15	none		
568	25	130	100	X				X				4/15	none	X	
422	40	199	85	X				X				8/1	none		
186	99	128	100					X	X	X	X	4/1	7/1		
702	94	570	100					X	X		X	3/15	none	X	
207	33	30	100	X				X	X	X		4/1	none	X	
120	77			X				X	X			3/1	8/1	X	
316	27	255	100	X				X				7/1	none		
215	40			X				X	X			6/1	none	X	
753	85			X	X	X	X					6/1	7/31		
28	100												8/1		
292	32			X				X			X	4/1	none		
536	36	370	100	X								3/15	none		
				X				X				5/1	none	X	
240	50			X				X				6/1	none	X	
281	44			X								5/31	none		
361	57	64	100	X		X		X	X	X	X	3/1	none	X	
3,249	40	865	97	X				X	X		X	3/1	none		
1,641	44	890	100	X				X			X	4/1	none		
1,522	42	491	100	X	X	X	X	X	X		X	3/1	none		
1,237	38	520	87	X	X	X	X	X	X	X	X	3/15	none	X	
1,080	45			X				X					7/1		

North Carolina: Wake Forest University

| | | Tuition and fees | Add'l out-of-state/ district tuition | Books and supplies | Costs for campus residents ||| Costs for students at home |||
Institution					Room and board	Trans-portation	Other costs	Board only	Trans-portation	Other costs
Wake Forest University		13,000		500	4,280	500	1,000	1,500	500	500
Wake Technical Community College	‡	566	3,959/—	400				1,020	1,499	1,071
Warren Wilson College		10,015		500	2,852	560	738	1,500	900	738
Wayne Community College	‡	584	3,959/—	600				1,500	500	400
Western Carolina University	‡	1,375	5,672/—	200	2,310	525	756	1,500	840	756
Western Piedmont Community College	‡	575	3,959/—	500				1,500	800	1,200
Wilkes Community College	‡	577	3,958/—	600				1,800	450	1,125
Wilson Technical Community College	‡	572	3,959/—	800				2,200	800	2,500
Wingate College		7,240		500	3,200	680	800	650	680	800
Winston-Salem State University	‡	1,094	5,018/—	600	2,762	551	2,100	1,100	476	2,100
North Dakota										
Bismarck State College		1,665	2,508/—	600	2,160	400	1,600	1,380	635	1,365
Dickinson State University		1,782	2,680/—	400	2,010		1,200			1,200
Jamestown College		7,270		400	2,980	250	400	775	450	450
Little Hoop Community College	‡	1,130		175					650	875
Mayville State University		1,831	2,680/—	400	2,444	360	1,140		360	1,140
Medcenter One College of Nursing		5,510		1,040	2,640	585	900	1,934	585	900
Minot State University		1,836	2,764/—	600	1,948	500	1,369	1,714	500	1,369
North Dakota State College of Science		1,650	2,508/—	400	1,920	500	1,255	1,500	500	500
North Dakota State University										
Bottineau		1,692	2,508/—	600	2,186	600	1,200	1,000	600	1,200
Fargo		2,219	3,314/—	475	2,590	270	1,350		500	1,200
Standing Rock College		1,870		500				1,350	1,000	1,125
Trinity Bible College		4,734		450	2,994	807	900	1,800	400	800
Turtle Mountain Community College		1,152		360				1,200	900	1,320
United Tribes Technical College		2,740		400	2,400	450	1,880	700	600	1,880
University of Mary		6,190		500	2,550	300	700	1,000	900	700
University of North Dakota										
Grand Forks		2,298	3,314/—	450	2,654	460	1,200	1,500		1,660
Lake Region		1,698	2,508/—	600	2,260	600	1,300	1,050	600	1,300
Williston		1,758	2,508/—	600	1,080		400		550	300
Valley City State University		1,815	2,680/—	600	2,260	441	1,359		441	1,359
Ohio										
Antioch College		16,356		400	3,176	400	700		400	700
Antioch School for Adult and Experiential Learning	†	8,100		400					400	
Antonelli Institute of Art and Photography	‡	6,990		1,500	3,480					1,350
Art Academy of Cincinnati		8,450		1,000				2,000	1,140	590
Ashland University		10,933		500	4,520	150	900	2,065	518	900
Baldwin-Wallace College		10,980		500	4,230	250	250	1,700	250	250
Belmont Technical College	‡	1,800	630/—	450				1,668	1,230	4,507
Bliss College	‡	4,600		400						
Bluffton College		9,226		400	3,726		800		700	900
Bowling Green State University										
Bowling Green	‡	3,334	3,974/—	450	3,478	358	1,206		914	1,206
Firelands College	‡	2,604	3,974/—	400					720	1,511
Bradford School	†	7,970		800						
Capital University		12,500		480	3,910	120	670	450	540	1,430
Case Western Reserve University		15,320		510	4,590		1,140			1,140
Cedarville College		7,296		555	3,756		1,015	1,968		450
Central Ohio Technical College	‡	2,088	864/—	600				495	1,188	2,276

†Figures are projected for 1993-94. ‡Figures are for 1992-93.

Ohio: Central Ohio Technical College

All aid		Need-based aid		Grants and scholarships								Financial aid deadlines		Inst aid form	Notes
Total freshmen	Percent receiving aid	Freshmen judged to have need	Percent offered aid	\multicolumn{4}{c}{Need-based}	\multicolumn{4}{c}{Non-need-based}	Priority	Closing		
				Acad	Music/drama	Art	Athl	Acad	Music/drama	Art	Athl				
903	63	232	100	X				X	X	X	X	3/1	none	X	
596	16	543	79	X				X				8/31	none	X	
115	59	48	100	X				X				4/15	none		
687	16	410	83	X								4/15	none	X	
1,069	40	432	98	X	X	X	X	X	X	X	X	4/1	none	X	
608	40	450	98					X				4/15	none		
585	26			X	X	X		X	X	X			4/1	X	
259	30	250	80	X									none		
378	75							X	X		X	3/1	none		
408	86			X	X		X	X	X	X	X	6/1	none	X	
943	80	665	93					X	X		X	4/15	none	X	
355	82	234	100					X	X	X	X		none		
292	97	221	100	X	X			X	X		X		none		
				X									8/20	X	
183	81			X							X	4/15	none		
				X								5/1	none		
760	66	371	98	X	X	X	X	X	X		X	4/15	none		
815	81	564	100	X	X		X	X	X		X	4/15	none		
224	75			X	X		X	X			X	4/15	none		
1,710	62			X	X		X	X				3/15	4/15	X	
68	66	30	100	X				X				4/15	none	X	
158	90	90	100	X				X	X			3/1	none		
													5/1		
150	90			X				X				5/29	none	X	
364	94	286	100	X	X		X	X	X		X	3/15	none		
1,874	47							X	X	X	X	4/15	none		
196	87			X			X	X			X	3/15	none		
				X			X	X			X	4/15	none		
226	85			X	X	X	X	X	X	X	X	4/15	none		
162	78	130	100					X				3/1	none	X	
													none	X	
90	80												none		
33	84							X		X		4/1	none	X	
719	95	432	100	X	X	X	X	X	X	X	X	3/15	none	X	
589	95	330	100	X				X	X			3/1	none	X	
								X					none		
125	50												none	X	
179	90	160	100	X	X	X		X	X	X		5/15	none		
2,977	55	1,632	100	X				X	X	X	X	2/15	4/1		
								X				4/1	none		
157	85												none		
334	90	258	100	X				X	X			3/1	7/15		
767	76	584	100	X	X	X		X	X	X		2/1	none	X	
593	81	359	100	X				X	X		X	4/1	none	X	
483	50	258	100	X				X				4/15	none		

Ohio: Central State University

Institution	Tuition and fees	Add'l out-of-state/ district tuition	Books and supplies	Costs for campus residents			Costs for students at home		
				Room and board	Trans-portation	Other costs	Board only	Trans-portation	Other costs
Central State University	† 3,588	3,588/—	604	1,489	1,452	1,929		1,739	
Chatfield College	4,590		444				720	540	1,575
Cincinnati Bible College and Seminary	‡ 3,872		500	3,124	900	1,569	1,536	1,275	1,569
Cincinnati College of Mortuary Science	7,210		750		750	375		750	375
Circleville Bible College	‡ 4,020		400	2,992	450	910	500	910	2,000
Clark State Community College	‡ 2,183	2,003/—	600				1,500	330	750
Cleveland College of Jewish Studies	‡ 3,015		150						
Cleveland Institute of Art	11,200		1,000	4,600	520	800	1,900	1,560	800
Cleveland Institute of Music	† 13,965		650	5,200	650	650		650	650
Cleveland State University	† 3,090	3,090/—	555	3,975	525	865	1,500	525	865
College of Mount St. Joseph	9,180		400	4,242	400	600	1,830	650	600
College of Wooster	19,865	(Comprehensive)	450		150	450			
Columbus College of Art and Design	9,200		1,100	5,200	200	750		300	750
Columbus State Community College	‡ 1,764	2,052/—	600				1,827	770	731
Cuyahoga Community College									
Eastern Campus	‡ 1,440	2,340/450	675				1,503	525	1,053
Metropolitan Campus	‡ 1,440	2,340/450	675				1,503	525	1,053
Western Campus	‡ 1,440	2,340/450	675				1,503	525	1,053
Davis Junior College of Business	‡ 5,232		625				1,995	900	1,800
Defiance College	9,950		500	3,530	446	928	1,730	928	1,000
Denison University	16,730		500	4,450		600	1,500		600
DeVry Institute of Technology: Columbus	‡ 5,249		500				1,777	2,047	1,911
Dyke College	‡ 5,300		544				1,769	969	1,160
Edison State Community College	‡ 1,845	1,575/—	633				1,700	809	400
Franciscan University of Steubenville	9,180		600	4,200	1,400	1,000	2,000	1,400	1,000
Franklin University	‡ 4,110		450				4,300	630	510
God's Bible School and College	3,160		300	2,450	450	555	700	1,100	1,000
Heidelberg College	13,000		500	4,160	500	500		500	500
Hiram College	13,825		400	4,515		900	1,790	500	900
Hocking Technical College	‡ 1,773	1,758/—	600	3,504	312	1,189	970	1,760	489
ITT Technical Institute									
Dayton	‡ 7,402		1,400				2,050	575	1,500
Youngstown	‡ 7,402		1,000					750	
Jefferson Technical College	‡ 1,575	675/135	500				1,700	360	400
John Carroll University	11,060		600	5,450	800	450	2,500	1,600	450
Kent State University									
Ashtabula Regional Campus	2,885	3,740/—	560				1,745	940	1,370
East Liverpool Regional Campus	‡ 2,885	3,596/—	525				1,645	885	1,315
Kent	3,740	3,740/—	560	3,530	700	1,370		980	1,370
Salem Regional Campus	‡ 2,885	3,596/—	525				1,645	885	1,380
Stark Campus	2,885	3,740/—	560				1,745	940	1,370
Trumbull Regional Campus	‡ 2,885	3,596/—	525				1,645	885	1,380
Tuscarawas Campus	† 2,885	3,596/—	530					905	1,310
Kenyon College	18,730		750	3,700	100	320			
Kettering College of Medical Arts	4,850		550	3,408	296	130	1,000	888	130
Lake Erie College	9,000		500	4,400	1,360	1,740	1,500	1,360	1,740
Lakeland Community College	‡ 1,671	2,295/291	456				1,503	933	1,053
Lima Technical College	† 1,950	1,950/—	900				2,000	810	450
Lorain County Community College	‡ 2,003	3,150/450	580				1,500	500	950
Lourdes College	6,410		500				1,913	852	682
Malone College	9,172		450	3,400	400	800	400	400	640
Marietta College	13,170		430	3,770	430	350	430	350	

†Figures are projected for 1993-94. ‡Figures are for 1992-93.

Note: Comprehensive fees include tuition, fees, room, and board.

Ohio: Marietta College

All aid		Need-based aid		Grants and scholarships								Financial aid deadlines		Inst aid form	Notes
Total freshmen	Percent receiving aid	Freshmen judged to have need	Percent offered aid	Need-based				Non-need-based							
				Acad	Music/drama	Art	Athl	Acad	Music/drama	Art	Athl	Priority	Closing		
884	70			X	X	X		X	X	X		5/15	8/1		
44	65	22	100	X								7/15	none		
210	95	153	100	X	X			X	X			5/1	none	X	
10	50	8	100									7/1	none		
77	95			X	X								none	X	
				X			X						none	X	
													none		
80	60			X		X		X		X		4/20	none	X	
47	90	31	100	X	X			X	X			3/1	none	X	
1,208	33	525	90	X				X	X	X	X	4/15	none		
283	94							X		X	X	4/15	none		
459	68	255	100	X				X	X			2/15	none		
334	85	245	100							X		5/3	none	X	
4,963	35			X				X					3/31	X	
3,913	26			X	X	X	X	X				5/31	none		
													none		
				X	X	X	X	X	X	X	X		none	X	
393	80												none		
186	96	169	100	X	X			X	X				none		
570	60	262	100					X	X	X		4/1	none		
934	80							X					none		
194	80			X			X	X			X	8/15	none		
								X			X		4/1		
244	80	191	100	X				X				3/1	5/1		
				X				X				5/30	none	X	
54	79			X	X			X	X			6/1	none		
241	93	210	100					X	X			4/1	none		
269	85			X	X			X	X			3/1	8/1		
				X				X				4/30	none	X	
268	89											8/1	none		
226	91											9/29	none	X	
496	55			X				X				6/1	none	X	
740	80	550	100	X				X				3/1	none		
364	51											2/15	8/1		
326	65			X				X				4/1	none		
3,013	70			X				X	X	X	X	2/14	3/15		
								X				2/15	none		
								X				2/15	none		
615	70			X	X	X	X	X				4/1	none	X	
270	66	102	100	X				X				2/15	4/1		
412	40	201	79					X					2/15		
82	57			X								4/1	none	X	
				X	X	X	X	X	X	X	X	4/1	none	X	
				X	X	X	X	X	X	X	X	3/1	none	X	
1,767	50			X				X					3/15	X	
2,139	34	834	100		X			X					none	X	
602	29			X								3/1	none	X	
353	92			X	X		X	X	X		X	3/31	7/31	X	
370	89	163	100						X	X	X	5/1	none		

173

Ohio: Marion Technical College

Institution	Tuition and fees	Add'l out-of-state/ district tuition	Books and supplies	Costs for campus residents			Costs for students at home		
				Room and board	Trans- portation	Other costs	Board only	Trans- portation	Other costs
Marion Technical College	2,160	1,584/—	500					1,000	
Miami University									
Hamilton Campus	‡ 2,932	4,590/—	480				1,800	824	1,134
Middletown Campus	† 3,262	5,222/—	500				1,800	890	1,198
Oxford Campus	‡ 4,024	4,590/—	500	3,360	330	1,090	2,040	896	1,090
Miami-Jacobs College	‡ 3,750		850				2,000	1,000	2,500
Mount Union College	12,320		450	3,530	1,000	550	2,130	1,000	550
Muskingum College	13,010		500	3,740	400	700		400	700
North Central Technical College	† 2,115	1,845/—	600						
Northwest Technical College	† 2,358	1,674/—	660				750	1,230	450
Northwestern College	† 6,993		600	1,950	720	1,053		1,440	1,053
Notre Dame College of Ohio	7,200		500	3,690	450	650	1,700	800	650
Oberlin College	18,950		575	5,620		525	1,500		525
Ohio Dominican College	† 7,730		350	4,090	300	750	1,500	750	750
Ohio Institute of Photography and Technology	‡ 8,580		1,400						
Ohio Northern University	14,775		540	3,885	360	525	1,600	360	525
Ohio State University									
Agricultural Technical Institute	‡ 2,700	8,193/—	483		670	2,921	1,809	1,107	985
Columbus Campus	‡ 2,799	8,292/—	483	4,014	781	647	580	924	693
Lima Campus	‡ 2,700	8,193/—	650				1,991	810	400
Mansfield Campus	‡ 2,700	8,193/—	450				550	1,100	2,335
Marion Campus	‡ 2,700	8,193/—	483				1,000	1,092	2,500
Newark Campus	‡ 2,700	8,193/—	600				495	1,188	2,276
Ohio University									
Athens	3,234	3,453/—	425	4,353	425	1,200		1,800	
Chillicothe Campus	‡ 2,613	3,663/—	500					1,842	
Eastern Campus	‡ 2,613	3,663/—	390					1,995	
Lancaster Campus	‡ 2,613	3,663/—	500					400	
Southern Campus at Ironton	‡ 2,412	105/—	450				1,728	1,842	
Zanesville Campus	‡ 2,613	3,663/—	500					2,049	489
Ohio Valley Business College	3,315		425					225	
Ohio Wesleyan University	15,726		450	5,382	200	650	1,500	100	600
Otterbein College	12,192		400	4,314	210	720		1,250	550
Owens Technical College									
Findlay Campus	‡ 1,724	1,464/—	800				1,800	1,000	800
Toledo	‡ 1,724	1,464/—	800				1,800	1,000	
Pontifical College Josephinum	† 5,227		350	3,532		2,700			
Sinclair Community College	‡ 1,395	1,935/630	750				2,500	600	1,700
Southern Ohio College	‡ 5,860		500				1,250	600	
Southern State Community College	‡ 2,552	2,115/—	400				1,500	750	
Stark Technical College	‡ 2,700	960/—	735				1,500	1,120	1,475
Terra Technical College	‡ 1,905	2,730/—	600					750	400
Tiffin University	7,100		500	3,700	350	980	1,700	450	850
Union Institute	6,840		600						
University of Akron									
Akron	† 2,953	4,553/—	500	3,686	700		1,800	1,100	1,000
Wayne College	† 2,995	4,540/—	550				1,500	960	720
University of Cincinnati									
Access Colleges	‡ 3,372	4,677/—	500	4,431	537	1,195	2,053	930	1,067
Cincinnati	‡ 3,372	4,677/—	500	4,431	537	1,195	2,053	930	1,067
Clermont College	‡ 3,072	4,461/—	520				1,352		

†Figures are projected for 1993-94. ‡Figures are for 1992-93.

Ohio: University of Cincinnati: Clermont College

All aid		Need-based aid		Grants and scholarships								Financial aid deadlines		Inst aid form	Notes
Total freshmen	Percent receiving aid	Freshmen judged to have need	Percent offered aid	Need-based				Non-need-based							
				Acad	Music/drama	Art	Athl	Acad	Music/drama	Art	Athl	Priority	Closing		
1,225	65	350	86	X				X				7/1	none		
767	16	179	79	X				X				2/15	none		
1,000	25	280	59	X	X			X				3/1	none	X	
3,022	39	877	95	X				X	X	X	X	2/15	none		
99	85			X									none		
389	90	357	100					X	X	X		4/1	none		
308	88	257	100	X				X	X	X		3/1	8/1		
762	51	438	100					X				4/1	none	X	
								X					none		
415	63							X					none		
48	95			X			X	X				3/1	7/15	X	
618	50	328	100					X	X				2/1	X	
227	82							X			X	3/1	none		
50	58	29	100										none	X	
697	90							X	X	X		5/1	7/31	X	
				X				X					none		
5,411	65			X	X	X		X	X	X	X	2/15	none	X	
396	45	180	100	X	X	X		X	X	X		4/1	none	X	
316	40			X	X	X	X	X	X	X	X	4/1	none	X	
				X	X	X		X				4/1	none		
462	30			X				X				4/1	none		
3,271	52							X	X	X	X	2/15	3/15		
450	40												3/1	X	
													2/15		
												2/15	none		
													none		
								X				2/15	none		
120	80	83	100									4/15	8/30	X	
491	82	344	100					X	X	X		3/1	none		
427	90							X	X	X		3/1	4/15		
													none		
2,409	40						X	X				3/15	none	X	
14	95	3	100					X				6/30	none		
4,293	6			X								4/15	none		
150	85							X				3/15	none		
1,204	30							X	X	X		7/1	none		
				X				X				5/1	none	X	
2,167	60							X				8/20	none	X	
206	79			X			X	X			X	3/31	none		
													none		
3,278	50			X				X	X	X	X	4/1	5/1		
2,010	65	1,262	98	X				X	X	X	X	3/1	none		
2,105	65	1,169	98	X	X			X	X	X	X	3/1	none		
				X	X			X	X	X		3/1	none		

Ohio: University of Cincinnati: Raymond Walters College

		Tuition and fees	Add'l out-of-state/ district tuition	Books and supplies	Costs for campus residents			Costs for students at home		
Institution					Room and board	Trans-portation	Other costs	Board only	Trans-portation	Other costs
Raymond Walters College	‡	3,072	4,461/—	600				1,600	900	900
University of Dayton		11,090		500	4,270	300	900	1,700	300	600
University of Findlay		10,920		500	4,780	400	600	1,000	300	
University of Rio Grande		2,388	3,684/198	700	3,525	400	1,500	2,000	2,025	1,500
University of Toledo	‡	3,073	4,305/—	550	3,053	1,170	2,080	800	1,170	2,080
Urbana University		7,841		500	4,140	150	600	2,380	150	600
Ursuline College		9,180		450	4,000	850	750	2,000	850	900
Virginia Marti College of Fashion and Art	‡	6,120		600				2,700	368	1,512
Walsh University		8,404		500	3,950	500	500		900	1,500
Wilberforce University	†	6,984		550	3,562	970	1,490	1,760	890	1,800
Wilmington College		9,830		500	3,870	800	1,186	2,210	1,410	1,186
Wittenberg University		15,726		400	4,272		800			
Wright State University										
Dayton	‡	2,934	2,934/—	650	3,579	600	1,000		1,310	1,000
Lake Campus	‡	2,625	2,625/—	650					1,200	1,000
Xavier University		10,970		500	4,740	450	700	2,080	450	700
Youngstown State University	‡	2,589	1,800/—	500	3,555	375	950	1,800	900	950

Oklahoma

		Tuition and fees	Add'l out-of-state/ district tuition	Books and supplies	Room and board	Trans-portation	Other costs	Board only	Trans-portation	Other costs
Bacone College		3,450		600	2,900	500	500	3,500	1,000	1,000
Bartlesville Wesleyan College		6,350		600	3,050	800	1,000	2,500	500	1,000
Cameron University	‡	1,413	2,029/—	500	2,252		900	1,500	300	800
Carl Albert State College	‡	975	1,590/—	500		500	600		900	1,000
Connors State College	‡	960	1,590/—	500	1,836	900	1,000	1,500	900	1,000
East Central University	‡	1,614	2,394/—	400	2,274	653	1,148	1,548	930	1,148
Eastern Oklahoma State College	‡	960	1,590/—	500	2,124	250	500	1,250	900	500
Langston University	†	1,561	2,232/—	446	2,499					
Mid-America Bible College		4,712		400	3,672	1,250	1,530	1,350	660	2,100
Northeastern Oklahoma Agricultural and Mechanical College	‡	900	1,590/—	400	2,124	300	675			675
Northeastern State University	‡	1,426	2,028/—	350	2,400	540	625		440	625
Northwestern Oklahoma State University	‡	1,330	2,028/—	450	1,864	500	1,000	1,000	600	1,100
Oklahoma Baptist University		5,440		510	3,050	250	1,250	280	1,200	1,250
Oklahoma Christian University of Science and Arts	†	5,690		500	3,000	1,050	850	1,450	1,050	850
Oklahoma City Community College	‡	993	1,590/—	675					900	600
Oklahoma City University		6,185		350	3,420	106	947	625	775	947
Oklahoma Panhandle State University	‡	1,389	2,029/—		1,800	400	1,000	1,500	1,000	1,000
Oklahoma State University										
Oklahoma City		1,298	2,790/—	450				3,500	850	1,800
Stillwater	‡	1,802	3,191/—	720	3,070	200	1,200	1,700	1,100	1,200
Technical Branch: Okmulgee	‡	1,214	2,790/—	600	2,010	300	900	400	300	900
Oral Roberts University		7,369		600	4,044	1,175	1,400	1,700	1,175	1,400
Phillips University		9,310		600	2,904	640	960	1,500	480	640
Redlands Community College	‡	960	1,590/—	400					700	1,200
Rogers State College	‡	1,134	1,590/—	600	2,860	750	1,000		1,000	1,200
Rose State College	‡	923	1,590/—	625					225	125
St. Gregory's College		4,520		590	3,100	330	930	1,600	530	930
Seminole Junior College		975	1,590/—	315	1,880	90	175	1,290	510	855
Southeastern Oklahoma State University	‡	1,334	2,028/—	450	2,628	744	992	1,575	866	1,215
Southern Nazarene University		6,176		400	3,642	400	1,200	2,400	800	1,200

†Figures are projected for 1993-94. ‡Figures are for 1992-93.

Oklahoma: Southern Nazarene University

All aid		_Need–based aid_		_Grants and scholarships_								_Financial aid deadlines_		Inst aid form	Notes
Total freshmen	Percent receiving aid	Freshmen judged to have need	Percent offered aid	_Need-based_				_Non–need–based_				Priority	Closing		
				Acad	Music/drama	Art	Athl	Acad	Music/drama	Art	Athl				
410	25			X				X				3/1	none		
1,666	89							X	X	X	X	3/31	none	X	
432	85	350	94	X	X		X	X	X		X	4/1	8/1		
567	80			X	X	X	X	X	X		X	3/15	none	X	
3,716	52	1,937	87	X	X	X	X	X	X	X	X	4/1	none	X	
155	100			X				X	X		X	5/1	none		
				X		X		X				3/15	none	X	
75	34							X		X		5/30	none	X	
433	94	247	100	X			X	X			X	3/1	8/1	X	
195	95	190	100	X				X				4/30	6/1	X	
205	90	194	100					X	X			3/31	none	X	
575	50	321	100	X	X	X		X	X	X		3/1	none	X	
2,019	56	1,321	100	X				X	X	X	X	4/1	none	X	
176	70			X				X				3/1	none		
675	85							X	X	X	X	4/15	none		
2,106	60			X	X			X	X		X	4/1	none	X	
492	86			X		X	X				X	5/1	none	X	
111	85			X	X		X	X	X		X	3/1	none		
960	62	532	96	X	X	X	X	X	X	X	X	5/15	none		
													none		
673	68			X			X	X			X	3/31	none		
576	59			X	X	X	X	X	X	X	X	4/15	none	X	
1,766	70			X				X	X		X	3/1	none	X	
1,077	38	433	100					X	X		X	3/1	none	X	
45	75							X				6/1	none	X	
								X					3/1	X	
918	35			X	X	X	X	X	X	X	X	3/1	none		
346	65	260	100	X	X	X	X	X	X	X	X	8/1	none	X	
463	79	397	100	X	X	X	X	X	X	X	X	3/1	none	X	
361	82	208	100					X	X	X	X	4/15	7/31	X	
3,467	50							X				7/1	none	X	
325	49	158	100	X	X	X	X	X	X	X	X	3/1	none	
251	40	140	100	X	X		X	X	X		X	8/25	none	
2,529	30	750	100	X				X				7/1	none	
2,232	73	767	98	X	X	X	X	X	X	X	X	3/1	none	
750	60			X									none	
632	85			X				X	X	X	X	4/1	none	
176	85			X	X	X	X	X	X	X	X	5/1	8/15	
693	22	275	100	X			X	X			X	3/30	4/15	
1,990	46			X				X	X	X		4/15	none	
2,604	30			X	X	X	X	X	X	X	X	5/1	none	
162	78	67	100	X	X	X	X	X	X	X	X	6/1	none	X
410	60							X	X		X	5/1	none	
441	60	323	100	X	X		X	X	X		X	4/1	11/1	X
237	77	172	100					X	X	X	X	3/1	none	X

Oklahoma: Southwestern College of Christian Ministries

| | | | | Costs for campus residents ||| Costs for students at home |||
Institution	Tuition and fees	Add'l out-of-state/ district tuition	Books and supplies	Room and board	Trans-portation	Other costs	Board only	Trans-portation	Other costs
Southwestern College of Christian Ministries	3,584		400	2,450	600	1,000	800	600	1,000
Southwestern Oklahoma State University	† 1,500	2,250/—	500	2,330	800	900	1,650	800	900
Tulsa Junior College	‡ 945	1,590/—	405				1,688	768	678
University of Central Oklahoma	‡ 1,369	2,028/—	500	2,150	600	1,400		600	1,400
University of Oklahoma									
Health Sciences Center	‡ 1,545	3,191/—	850				1,625	850	1,521
Norman	‡ 1,783	3,191/—	590	3,358	1,197	1,752	1,978	1,197	1,752
University of Science and Arts of Oklahoma	† 1,380	2,100/—	600	1,920	250	1,200		350	1,200
University of Tulsa	9,995		1,200	3,948	1,000	1,350	1,800	1,420	850
Western Oklahoma State College	‡ 930	1,590/—	450					900	400
Oregon									
Bassist College	9,000		1,200		600	1,200	1,500	610	1,200
Blue Mountain Community College	‡ 900	1,440/—	450					600	900
Central Oregon Community College	1,152	3,906/558	650	3,360	900	700	1,800	900	700
Chemeketa Community College	1,080	3,024/—	600					840	840
Clackamas Community College	1,170	2,925/—	600				1,770	840	720
Clatsop Community College	† 1,350	4,185/—	660		1,200	1,000	2,000	1,000	1,000
Concordia College	9,300		500	3,000	400	900	1,500	400	900
Eastern Oregon State College	‡ 2,445		450	3,200	600	900	1,600	600	900
Eugene Bible College	† 4,020		600	2,610	1,000	500	1,800	750	1,000
George Fox College	11,740		400	3,890	350	800	1,935	350	800
Lane Community College	‡ 1,108	2,925/—	795				1,600	396	1,800
Lewis and Clark College	15,051		300	4,929		750	1,500	270	750
Linfield College	12,700		600	3,970	200	900	1,500	75	900
Linn-Benton Community College	1,260	3,915/—	600				1,620	990	810
Marylhurst College	‡ 7,644		500				1,760	600	1,688
Mount Hood Community College	† 1,302		621				1,038	816	540
Multnomah School of the Bible	5,790		400	3,200	600	900	1,600	900	810
Northwest Christian College	7,640		540	3,685		1,536	1,800		1,536
Oregon Health Sciences University	‡ 3,900	4,215/—	500		1,250	1,000	2,050	1,250	1,000
Oregon Institute of Technology	‡ 2,595	4,083/—	500	3,315	600	1,800	1,350	200	1,800
Oregon Polytechnic Institute	‡ 5,525		950				2,000	500	700
Oregon State University	‡ 2,691	4,281/—	513	3,177	470	1,717	1,759	300	1,746
Pacific Northwest College of Art	7,700		700					500	3,500
Pacific University	13,490		400	3,815	100	570	1,200	100	570
Portland Community College	† 1,305	2,835/—	675				1,680	780	720
Portland State University	‡ 2,658	4,281/—	750		657	1,098	1,800	657	846
Reed College	19,250		500	5,230	720	450	1,500		450
Rogue Community College	1,074	2,412/612	450				1,800	925	825
Southern Oregon State College	† 2,635	3,750/—	580	3,300	390	1,545	1,800	670	515
Treasure Valley Community College	‡ 966	864/—	350	3,111	700	750		700	750
Umpqua Community College	‡ 1,176	3,268/—	540				1,620	810	630
University of Oregon									
Eugene	‡ 2,721	5,130/—	425	3,212	250	1,145	1,575	250	1,145
Robert Donald Clark Honors College	‡ 2,721	5,130/—	450	3,212	275	1,150	1,600	275	1,150
University of Portland	11,040		600	3,940	500	600	1,800	500	600
Warner Pacific College	‡ 7,511		400	3,900	350	850	1,600	350	550
Western Baptist College	8,700		500	3,700	660	990	2,220	990	990
Western Oregon State College	2,640	4,170/—	630	3,540	650	1,090	1,830	630	1,090
Willamette University	13,665		400	4,420	400	720	1,500	1,200	720

†Figures are projected for 1993-94. ‡Figures are for 1992-93.

Oregon: Willamette University

All aid		Need-based aid		Grants and scholarships									Financial aid deadlines		Inst aid form	Notes
Total fresh-men	Percent receiving aid	Freshmen judged to have need	Percent offered aid	Need-based				Non-need-based								
				Acad	Music/drama	Art	Athl	Acad	Music/drama	Art	Athl	Priority	Closing		
39	80							X	X			5/15	7/15		
950	65	331	100					X	X	X	X		none	X	
												4/1	none		
1,376	30			X	X	X	X	X	X	X	X	6/1	none		
				X								3/1	none		
2,422	55	1,074	94					X	X	X	X	3/1	none		
227	79							X	X	X	X	3/15	none		
738	75	326	100	X				X	X	X	X	3/1	none	X	
767	60			X	X	X	X					3/30	none	X	
29	91	20	100					X				6/1	none	X	
					X		X		X		X	3/30	none		
896	33			X				X	X	X	X	3/1	none		
8,385	60			X							X	4/1	9/4	X	
1,273	45							X	X	X	X	3/1	none	X	
193	67			X				X				3/1	none	X	
100	90	93	100					X	X		X	5/1	none		
389	80	285	100	X	X			X	X				none		
74	80	28	100	X	X			X	X			4/15	9/1	X	
281	86	216	100					X	X		X	3/1	8/1		
3,621	22	1,672	100					X	X		X	3/15	none		
409	76			X	X		X	X	X			2/15	none		
501	91	286	100	X	X	X	X	X	X			3/1	none	X	
719	50			X				X		X	X	4/1	none	X	
				X	X	X				X	X	6/1	none		
				X	X	X	X	X	X	X	X	4/1	none	X	
119	80			X	X			X	X			3/1	none	X	
54	93			X				X				4/15	none		
													none		
375	60			X			X	X				3/1	none		
154	90											5/30	none	X	
1,722	60			X	X			X	X		X	3/1	none		
18	50							X		X		5/1	none	X	
243	80			X	X	X	X	X	X	X		3/15	none		
				X			X				X	3/1	none	X	
714	38	243	95	X				X	X	X	X	3/1	none	X	
310	45	140	92										3/1	X	
217	70							X				4/1	none		
745	60	649	100	X			X	X	X	X		3/1	none		
2,540	80			X				X	X	X	X	4/1	none		
1,335	60	525	100	X	X	X	X	X				3/1	none	X	
3,173	45			X				X	X	X	X	3/1	none		
				X				X	X	X	X	3/1	none		
461	76	249	100	X				X	X		X	3/15	none	X	
57	58							X	X			5/1	8/15		
120	92	67	100					X	X		X	2/15	none		
627	81	353	100	X	X		X	X	X	X		3/1	none		
395	70	300	100	X	X	X	X	X	X	X		2/15	6/1		

Pennsylvania

Institution	Tuition and fees	Add'l out-of-state/ district tuition	Books and supplies	Room and board	Trans-portation	Other costs	Board only	Trans-portation	Other costs
Pennsylvania									
Academy of the New Church	3,990			3,351		1,400			
Albright College	15,010		500	4,250	240	900	1,800	620	900
Allegheny College	16,700		400	4,320	200	400	750	600	400
Allentown College of St. Francis de Sales	9,320		500	4,620		800	2,210		800
Alvernia College	8,474		600	4,000	500	600	1,700	700	600
American Institute of Design	‡ 15,315		928						
Antonelli Institute of Art and Photography	‡ 8,470		1,320	3,850			1,500	1,225	1,320
Art Institute of Pittsburgh	‡ 8,050		1,073	5,340			2,315	623	1,212
Baptist Bible College of Pennsylvania	6,061		500	3,660	500	600	2,210	1,650	600
Beaver College	12,510		400	5,150	250	550	1,500	450	550
Bloomsburg University of Pennsylvania	‡ 3,068	3,394/—	400	2,754	385	1,400		935	1,400
Bryn Mawr College	17,660		530	6,450	300	750	2,700	400	750
Bucknell University	17,730		600	4,590	180	1,200	2,130	2,640	1,200
Bucks County Community College	† 1,855	3,640/1,820	500				750	2,100	1,350
Butler County Community College	† 1,182	2,280/1,140	558				1,500	1,060	900
Cabrini College	† 10,200		665	5,790	300	1,075	1,540	1,940	1,375
California University of Pennsylvania	‡ 3,384	3,394/—	400	3,460	225	1,275	900	1,005	1,275
Carlow College	9,650		500	4,264		1,200	1,500	240	760
Carnegie Mellon University	17,060		450	5,540	700	1,050	2,140	500	1,050
Cedar Crest College	13,720		500	5,210	500	500	1,500	500	500
Central Pennsylvania Business School	5,250		696		642	748	1,500	830	748
Chatham College	12,780		400	5,230		850	952	582	850
Chestnut Hill College	9,525		700	5,035	450	350	1,575	700	350
Cheyney University of Pennsylvania	‡ 2,938	3,394/—	400	3,540	675	1,000	1,500	675	700
CHI Institute	6,700								
Churchman Business School	‡ 4,285		675					650	
Clarion University of Pennsylvania	‡ 3,328	3,394/—	450	2,786	500	600	1,350	600	650
College Misericordia	10,460		500	5,360	500	400	1,200	500	400
Community College of Allegheny County									
Allegheny Campus	1,528	2,832/1,416	500				1,500	722	950
Boyce Campus	‡ 1,806	3,360/1,680	475			—	1,550	700	1,000
North Campus	1,528	2,832/1,416	500				1,500	722	950
South Campus	1,528	2,832/1,416	500				1,500	722	950
Community College of Beaver County	1,760	4,020/2,010	500				1,500	700	900
Community College of Philadelphia	‡ 1,810	3,540/1,770	455				1,560	480	575
Curtis Institute of Music	500		250				1,100	540	1,795
Dean Institute of Technology	‡ 4,900		500					1,000	
Delaware County Community College	‡ 1,240	2,400/1,200	400				875	650	1,580
Delaware Valley College	11,645		500	4,785	400	1,000	1,000	800	1,050
Dickinson College	17,775		445	4,930	200	900	1,620	200	900
Drexel University	12,326		500	6,500	350	1,500		780	1,500
DuBois Business College	4,825		450	4,300					
Duquesne University	11,320		400	5,114	586	450	1,500	500	450
East Stroudsburg University of Pennsylvania	‡ 3,352	3,394/—	450	3,040	250	750		900	1,350
Eastern College	10,590		400	4,530	200	970	1,400	900	800
Edinboro University of Pennsylvania	† 3,352	3,294/—	500	3,260	200	1,088		1,300	1,000

†Figures are projected for 1993-94. ‡Figures are for 1992-93.

Pennsylvania: Edinboro University of Pennsylvania

All aid		Need-based aid		Grants and scholarships								Financial aid deadlines		Inst aid form	Notes
Total fresh-men	Percent receiving aid	Freshmen judged to have need	Percent offered aid	Need-based				Non-need-based				Priority	Closing		
				Acad	Music/drama	Art	Athl	Acad	Music/drama	Art	Athl				
30	62	13	100									3/1	8/15		
310	67	250	100	X				X				3/1	4/1		
476	86	364	100	X	X	X		X	X	X		2/15	none		
239	90	175	87	X	X			X	X			2/15	none	X	
180	85			X			X	X			X		4/1		
300	90												none		
62	86			X		X						7/31	8/15		
871	80							X		X		3/1	none	X	
216	85			X	X			X	X				4/1	X	
173	76			X				X	X	X	X	3/15	4/15	X	
1,055	80			X	X		X	X				3/15	5/1		
275	48	143	97	X									1/15	X	
889	60	327	100	X	X	X							2/15		
				X	X	X		X	X	X		5/1	none	X	
1,009	55			X			X	X				4/16	5/1		
161	75	120	95	X				X				4/1	none	X	
1,028	74	670	94	X				X	X		X	4/1	none		
149	94			X			X	X		X	X	3/15	none		
1,144	70	686	100	X	X	X		X	X	X		2/15	none	X	
183	90	168	100					X				5/1	none		
339	47			X				X				5/1	none	X	
100	94	72	100	X	X			X	X			3/15		X	
134	65			X				X				3/15	none	X	
377	78			X				X	X		X	4/1	5/1		
325	88												9/20		
110	65	66	100										8/1		
1,190	76							X	X	X	X	3/15	5/1		
399	95			X				X				3/1	4/1	X	
3,364	45			X				X			X	5/1	none	X	
1,697	24	1,232	100					X	X	X	X	5/1	none		
1,230	24							X			X	5/1	none		
2,149	24	1,200	100					X	X	X	X		5/1	X	
745	61	625	88	X			X	X				5/1	none	X	
5,275	40							X					5/1	X	
20	100				X				X			5/1	6/1	X	
79	85	30	100										8/1	X	
2,627	30			X								5/1	none	X	
495	82	348	100	X				X				3/1	4/1	X	
575	62	302	100	X	X	X		X					2/15		
1,292	76	760	98					X	X	X	X	5/1	none	X	
170	90			X									8/1		
1,029	75	665	100	X				X	X		X		5/1	X	
641	77	468	100					X			X		3/15	X	
184	80			X				X				4/15	none		
1,546	80	1,200	100	X			X	X			X		5/1	X	

Pennsylvania: Electronic Institutes: Middletown

Institution	Tuition and fees	Add'l out-of-state/ district tuition	Books and supplies	Room and board	Trans-portation	Other costs	Board only	Trans-portation	Other costs
Electronic Institutes									
Middletown	4,950		170				2,064	2,984	1,350
Pittsburgh	7,350		500						
Elizabethtown College	13,600		500	4,250	150	600	1,500	350	600
Franklin and Marshall College	23,665	(Comprehensive)	590		200	880			2,680
Gannon University	9,838		508	4,040	470	911	1,634	795	1,029
Geneva College	8,810		500	4,220	750	1,100			1,100
Gettysburg College	18,870		300	4,090	200	500	1,900	500	300
Gratz College	‡ 4,200		600					370	
Grove City College	4,976		525	2,894	225	350	1,832	800	350
Gwynedd-Mercy College	10,200		500	5,250	250	600	900	600	600
Hahnemann University School of Health									
Sciences and Humanities	8,610		650	8,526	500	2,000	7,200	750	4,200
Harcum Junior College	‡ 7,070		400	4,300		1,500			1,500
Harrisburg Area Community College	‡ 1,500	2,880/1,440	500				1,500	650	600
Haverford College	18,000		650	5,950		925			
Holy Family College	8,300		500				1,500	600	850
Immaculata College	9,600		500	5,110	600	1,000		2,150	750
Indiana University of Pennsylvania	‡ 3,157	3,394/—	500	2,834			1,200		1,400
Johnson Technical Institute	† 5,296		400		100	1,305	2,322	952	1,305
Juniata College	14,150		450	4,240	250	420	1,650	600	420
Keystone Junior College	8,260		600	4,900	350	1,226	1,650	1,588	726
King's College	10,600		525	4,820	340	1,765	1,735	700	1,385
Kutztown University of Pennsylvania	† 3,690	3,810/—	550	2,970		1,750		900	1,750
La Roche College	8,682		600	4,555	100	1,000	1,500	300	1,000
La Salle University	11,590		500	5,980			1,015	1,500	
Lackawanna Junior College	5,920		516				2,750	402	2,400
Lafayette College	17,950		550	5,500	600	900		750	850
Lancaster Bible College	7,410		450	3,300	475	1,400	1,750	775	1,400
Lebanon Valley College of Pennsylvania	13,700		425	4,600	100	600	1,500	600	600
Lehigh County Community College	‡ 1,455	3,060/1,530	500				680	1,000	400
Lehigh University	17,750		650	5,500	150	1,100	2,520	450	1,080
Lincoln Technical Institute	‡ 5,472		750						
Lincoln University	3,140	1,510/—	350	3,000	500	915	950	650	1,016
Lock Haven University of Pennsylvania	‡ 3,260	3,394/—	450	3,524	200	1,000		400	1,000
Luzerne County Community College	‡ 1,470	2,640/1,320	375				725	500	625
Lycoming College	13,000		500	4,200	300	600	1,800	300	600
Manor Junior College	‡ 6,496		450	3,120	700	1,400	1,560	1,000	1,400
Mansfield University of Pennsylvania	† 3,304	4,824/—	650	2,988	800	800	1,700	800	800
Marywood College	10,590		500	4,300	300	700	750	600	700
Mercyhurst College	9,838		465	3,650	275	800		475	
Messiah College	9,804		450	4,890	400	800	750	400	800
Millersville University of Pennsylvania	‡ 3,488	3,394/—	450	3,620	300	958	1,056	600	989
Montgomery County Community College	‡ 1,890	4,500/3,000	550					1,020	975
Moore College of Art and Design	† 13,725		800	5,250	500	1,000	1,500	600	700
Moravian College	14,490		500	4,470	225	915	1,760	1,170	1,080
Mount Aloysius College	7,190		570	3,490		1,200			1,200
Muhlenberg College	16,385		550	4,410	150	800	2,060	1,100	800
National Education Center: Vale Tech									
Campus	† 5,706		761		406	938	1,673	406	938
Neumann College	‡ 9,406		650			500		800	500

†Figures are projected for 1993-94. ‡Figures are for 1992-93.

Note: Comprehensive fees include tuition, fees, room, and board.

Pennsylvania: Neumann College

All aid		Need-based aid		Grants and scholarships								Financial aid deadlines		Inst aid form	Notes
Total freshmen	Percent receiving aid	Freshmen judged to have need	Percent offered aid	Need-based				Non-need-based							
				Acad	Music/drama	Art	Athl	Acad	Music/drama	Art	Athl	Priority	Closing		
56	90											8/1	none		
614	81	337	100	X	X	X		X	X			8/1	none		
486	60	239	100	X				X				3/1	4/1	X	
630	86	544	100	X				X			X	3/1	3/1	X	
247	91			X			X	X	X			4/15	none	X	
572	42	290	100	X	X								2/15		
6	38			X	X							9/15	none	X	
618	53	252	94	X	X			X					5/1		
102	82			X				X				3/15	none	X	
				X				X				5/1	5/31	X	
221	77			X		X		X		X		5/1	none	X	
				X		X		X		X			6/1	X	
301	45	111	100										1/31	X	
592	88							X			X	2/15	5/1		
587	70			X	X		X	X	X		X	3/1	5/1		
1,425	83			X	X	X		X	X	X	X	5/1	none		
209	80			X				X				8/1	none		
259	80	201	100	X	X	X		X	X	X		3/1	none		
501	76	252	100	X		X		X				5/1	none	X	
472	81	313	100	X				X				3/1	none	X	
1,250	85	1,063	100	X	X	X	X	X		X	X		3/15		
128	82	96	100					X				5/1	none		
630	70			X				X			X		2/15		
223	80	194	77	X			X	X			X	5/1	none	X	
577	60	260	100	X	X	X	X					2/15	none	X	
83	94	56	100					X	X			6/1	none		
288	78			X	X							3/1	none	X	
1,224	30							X				3/31	none	X	
1,132	52	508	100	X	X		X	X					2/5	X	
366	91	301	100	X	X			X	X			3/1	none		
923	80	470	100	X	X		X	X	X		X	4/15	none	X	
2,354	80	860	92	X				X				4/15	none		
424	70			X	X	X		X	X	X		4/15	none		
218	90			X			X	X			X	3/15	8/15	X	
607	78	398	95	X				X	X	X	X		4/15		
260	90			X	X	X		X	X	X		2/15	none	X	
425	95	118	100	X				X	X	X	X	3/15	none	X	
571	86	386	100	X				X				4/1	none	X	
1,017	70	515	96					X	X	X	X		5/1	X	
2,400	16	1,300	61	X				X				5/1	none	X	
101	90	79	100			X				X		4/1	none	X	
294	73	226	95	X	X	X		X				2/15	3/15	X	
690	89			X				X			X	5/1	8/1		
467	63			X	X			X					3/15	X	
307	88												none		
95	79			X				X			X	3/15	4/30		

183

Pennsylvania: Northampton County Area Community College

Institution	Tuition and fees	Add'l out-of-state/ district tuition	Books and supplies	Room and board	Trans-portation	Other costs	Board only	Trans-portation	Other costs
Northampton County Area Community College	1,770	3,780/1,890	600	3,700	400	1,000		400	1,000
Penn State									
Erie Behrend College	‡ 4,618	5,026/—	440	3,790		2,124	750	970	1,794
Harrisburg Capital College	‡ 4,618	5,026/—	440	3,790		2,124	750	970	1,794
University Park Campus	‡ 4,618	5,026/—	440	3,790		2,124	750	970	1,794
Penn Technical Institute	‡ 6,420		600					350	1,000
Pennsylvania College of Technology	5,500	2,500/—	800				1,800	750	1,800
Pennsylvania Institute of Technology	† 6,903		700					600	
Philadelphia College of Bible	7,140		550	4,060	550	870	2,160	960	870
Philadelphia College of Pharmacy and Science	10,770		500	4,700	400	800	1,700	1,000	800
Philadelphia College of Textiles and Science	10,914		500	4,982	500	1,038		700	1,038
Pittsburgh Institute of Mortuary Science	7,660								
Pittsburgh Technical Institute	‡ 15,900		800		675	1,416	2,151	675	1,416
Point Park College	9,312		400	4,610	350	450		300	450
Reading Area Community College	† 1,680	3,240/1,620	450					600	1,200
Robert Morris College	6,300		500	4,106	400	600	1,800	400	600
Rosemont College	11,075		700	5,700	300	700		650	700
St. Charles Borromeo Seminary	5,500		800	3,500	800	2,200			
St. Francis College	11,124		475	4,720	409	800	1,500	409	800
St. Joseph's University	12,000		500	5,700	535	1,155	1,900	1,050	1,940
St. Vincent College	† 10,318		500	3,766		1,700	2,054		1,700
Seton Hill College	10,530		500	3,980	500	1,500	1,500	1,300	1,800
Shippensburg University of Pennsylvania	‡ 3,388	3,394/—	400	3,132	200	1,100		800	1,300
Slippery Rock University of Pennsylvania	† 3,510	4,730/—	500	3,364		1,276		400	876
Susquehanna University	15,580		400	4,370	200	600	1,500	200	600
Swarthmore College	18,482		700	6,300	420	738		1,200	738
Temple University	‡ 5,013	4,212/—	550	4,950		7,506	550	450	2,756
Thaddeus Stevens State School of Technology	‡ 7,000	(Comprehensive)			200		700	350	
Thiel College	‡ 9,953		600	4,505		1,280	1,700	600	680
Thomas Jefferson University: College of Allied Health Sciences	† 13,750		1,050	5,070	900	600	1,900	1,300	600
Triangle Tech									
Greensburg School	‡ 5,628		750					720	825
Pittsburgh Campus	† 5,850		1,450				1,500	1,364	1,305
University of the Arts	12,170		1,500	5,250	500	580	900	900	630
University of Pennsylvania	17,838		500	6,800		1,242	1,270		1,242
University of Pittsburgh									
Bradford	† 5,300	5,400/—	500	4,100	600	500		1,200	500
Greensburg	† 5,168	5,420/—	550	3,620	552	900	1,810	1,052	900
Johnstown	‡ 4,966	5,144/—	600	3,544		1,500			1,500
Pittsburgh	‡ 4,922	5,144/—	400	4,130	400	900	1,500	600	900
Titusville	† 5,010	5,200/—	500	3,970	400	500	1,500	900	500
University of Scranton	10,720		500	5,456	500	500	1,300	500	500
Ursinus College	14,265		500	4,900	135	800	900	450	800
Valley Forge Christian College	4,196		450	3,022	312	1,200	300	1,600	1,200
Valley Forge Military College	10,470		450	6,350		250			
Villanova University	14,460		800	6,060		1,200	2,000	500	800

†Figures are projected for 1993-94. ‡Figures are for 1992-93.

Note: Comprehensive fees include tuition, fees, room, and board.

Pennsylvania: Villanova University

All aid		Need-based aid		Grants and scholarships								Financial aid deadlines		Inst aid form	Notes
Total freshmen	Percent receiving aid	Freshmen judged to have need	Percent offered aid	Need-based				Non-need-based							
				Acad	Music/ drama	Art	Athl	Acad	Music/ drama	Art	Athl	Priority	Closing		
1,659	36			X		X	X	X			X	3/31	none	X	
655	65			X	X	X		X	X	X		3/15	none		
				X	X	X		X	X	X		2/15	none		
4,385	59			X	X	X	X	X	X	X	X	2/15	none		
													none	X	
1,496	70			X				X				3/1	none	X	
				X				X					8/1	X	
260	71	86	100	X	X			X	X			5/1	none		
374	75	280	100	X				X			X	3/15	4/15	X	
524	73							X			X		none	X	
				X				X					none		
				X				X					none	X	
194	79	146	100	X	X			X	X	X	X	5/1	none	X	
723	66			X				X				9/1	none	X	
461	70			X			X	X			X	5/1		X	
154	50	56	100	X		X		X		X		2/15	none		
11	80	8	100									4/1	8/1	X	
290	92	261	100	X			X	X			X		5/1	X	
558	85	401	100	X				X			X		3/1	X	
268	80							X	X		X	3/1	5/1		
160	83	148	100	X	X	X	X	X	X	X	X	5/1	8/1	X	
1,242	57	930	100	X			X	X			X	5/1	none	X	
1,183	80	760	90	X	X		X	X	X	X	X	5/1	none		
407	64							X	X			3/15	5/1		
354	44	155	100	X								2/1	4/1	X	
2,399	61	1,898	100	X				X	X		X		5/1	X	
327	90	119	100										none	X	
201	94			X				X				4/1	none		
				X				X					5/1	X	
40	80			X									none		
101	90							X					none	X	
252	91			X	X	X		X	X	X		2/15	none		
2,295	45											2/15	none	X	
230	58	155	100	X				X			X		3/1		
391	87	265	100	X				X					5/1	X	
710	83			X				X			X	4/1	none		
2,286	74			X				X			X	3/1	none	X	
186	87							X					5/1	X	
907	76			X				X				2/15	none		
410	77	370	100	X				X	X	X			2/15		
213	75	104	98					X	X			5/1	none		
101	80			X	X		X	X			X	5/1	none		
1,693	63	755	100	X				X			X	2/15	3/15	X	

Pennsylvania: Washington and Jefferson College

Institution	Tuition and fees	Add'l out-of-state/ district tuition	Books and supplies	Room and board	Trans- portation	Other costs	Board only	Trans- portation	Other costs
Washington and Jefferson College	15,620		200	3,740	140	500	1,780	1,100	500
Waynesburg College	8,580		500	3,380	350	751	1,864	1,000	1,101
West Chester University of Pennsylvania	‡ 3,158	3,394/—	450	3,630	514	1,000	1,200	870	1,000
Westminster College	11,770		425	3,270		675	1,590		675
Westmoreland County Community College	‡ 1,193	2,490/1,320	400				1,000	500	100
Widener University	11,740		500	5,100	450	900	1,500	900	900
Wilkes University	10,898		550	4,830	700	750	1,600	700	675
Williamson Free School of Mechanical Trades	185		60		450	400			
Wilson College	11,546		450	5,084	125	350	1,500	300	350
York College of Pennsylvania	4,995		500	3,350	400	850		750	500

Puerto Rico

Institution	Tuition and fees	Add'l	Books	Room/board	Trans	Other	Board	Trans	Other
American University of Puerto Rico	‡ 2,400		400					780	
Bayamon Central University	‡ 2,350		400				600	400	800
Caribbean University	‡ 2,550		640				1,200	955	1,950
Colegio Universitario del Este	‡ 2,750		300				1,080	720	1,045
Escuela de Artes Plasticas de Puerto Rico	† 906		2,000				1,250	500	1,260
Huertas Junior College	2,985		600				500	600	600
Inter American University of Puerto Rico									
Arecibo Campus	3,154		640				1,200	540	880
Guayama Campus	‡ 2,734		640					540	880
Metropolitan Campus	‡ 2,608		590	2,916			1,200	540	880
San German Campus	‡ 2,500		700	2,050	100	800	1,000	500	1,000
Pontifical Catholic University of Puerto Rico	‡ 2,413		350	2,452	408	1,050		552	1,050
Technological College of the Municipality of San Juan	655		540	1,800			900	490	800
Turabo University	‡ 2,750		300				1,080	720	1,045
Universidad Adventista de las Antillas	‡ 2,728		300	1,960	500	500	1,400	500	500
Universidad Metropolitana	2,940		300				1,080	720	1,045
Universidad Politecnica de Puerto Rico	† 3,300		1,016				2,208	596	952
University of Puerto Rico									
Aguadilla	970		800				1,000	700	600
Bayamon Technological University College	‡ 970		800				2,160	700	600
Carolina Regional College	970		800				2,160	700	600
Cayey University College	970		800				1,200	600	600
Humacao University College	‡ 970		800				2,160	700	600
La Montana Regional College	970		900				1,350	700	600
Mayaguez Campus	‡ 970		900				1,500	700	600
Medical Sciences Campus	‡ 970		350				2,700	700	600
Ponce Technological University College	970		800				1,500	700	600
Rio Piedras Campus	‡ 970		800	2,890	700	600	1,890	700	600
University of the Sacred Heart	‡ 2,690		500		700	640	750	465	536

Rhode Island

Institution	Tuition and fees	Add'l	Books	Room/board	Trans	Other	Board	Trans	Other
Brown University	19,006		680	5,612		1,200	1,780	315	1,200
Bryant College	12,120		500	6,225	200	700	1,500	950	700
Community College of Rhode Island	† 1,546	2,846/—	450				1,782	1,350	700
Johnson & Wales University	9,510		500	4,485	600	500	1,800	600	500
New England Institute of Technology	8,955		600				2,317	1,008	1,872

†Figures are projected for 1993-94. ‡Figures are for 1992-93.

Rhode Island: New England Institute of Technology

All aid		Need-based aid		Grants and scholarships								Financial aid deadlines		Inst aid form	Notes
Total fresh-men	Percent receiving aid	Freshmen judged to have need	Percent offered aid	Need-based				Non-need-based				Priority	Closing		
				Acad	Music/ drama	Art	Athl	Acad	Music/ drama	Art	Athl				
338	84	262	100	X				X				3/15	none		
442	93	404	100	X				X				3/15	none	X	
1,385	65	1,000	95					X	X		X	3/15	none		
366	70	269	100	X	X		X	X	X		X	5/1	6/30	X	
1,574	63	580	100	X								5/1	none		
574	87			X	X			X	X			3/1	4/1	X	
410	90	319	99	X	X	X	X	X	X	X	X	6/1	none	X	
94	100	94	100									4/15	5/1		
48	77	34	100	X				X					4/30	X	
746	65	283	100	X	X	X		X	X	X		4/15	none	X	
894	72			X			X					5/31	6/30	X	
597	94			X			X	X			X		8/1	X	
794	87			X								7/30	none		
1,136	90											3/30	5/30	X	
34	54	19	100	X									none	X	
1,141	95			X									none	X	
1,065	85							X				4/29	none	X	
458	98			X				X					4/29	X	
2,170	85												4/30		
993	80												4/30	X	
2,237	88			X					X	X	X	6/24	none	X	
313	98	945	21	X									9/30		
1,474	80												none	X	
230	89												none		
				X									6/30	X	
976	76											5/31	6/30	X	
882	60	354	67	X	X		X						6/30		
837	55			X				X			X		6/28		
600	60	420	100					X	X		X	5/14	5/28	X	
737	79			X	X	X	X					5/31	6/30		
867	84	710	100	X									6/30	X	
307	92	213	100	X			X		X		X	5/31	none	X	
2,163	73	1,414	100					X	X		X		6/29	X	
				X								4/30	none	X	
645	80	619	100	X				X	X		X		6/10	X	
				X	X	X	X	X	X	X	X		5/31	X	
													6/30	X	
1,464	40	556	100										1/1	X	
851	62			X				X			X		2/15	X	
2,809	40												none		
1,615	82							X				3/1	none	X	
900	80											6/1	none	X	

Rhode Island: Providence College

Institution	Tuition and fees	Add'l out-of-state/district tuition	Books and supplies	Room and board	Trans-portation	Other costs	Board only	Trans-portation	Other costs
Providence College	13,625		450	5,900		1,100	1,400	1,600	1,100
Rhode Island College	† 2,601	4,138/—	500	5,210	400	1,000	1,500	1,000	1,000
Rhode Island School of Design	15,900		1,300	6,415	470	1,100	2,950	2,485	1,100
Roger Williams University	12,070		500	5,910	500	300	2,475	800	300
Salve Regina University	13,800		500	6,300	600	900	2,250	800	1,100
University of Rhode Island	† 3,706	6,724/—	600	5,404	131	1,332	1,728	2,160	1,332
South Carolina									
Aiken Technical College	‡ 720	30/—	450				1,800	1,000	750
Allen University	‡ 4,750		300	2,900					
Anderson College	8,320		600	3,900	800	1,450	2,000	1,050	950
Benedict College	5,534		700	2,892	833	1,070		833	1,070
Central Carolina Technical College	726	554/194	750				1,500	500	1,000
Central Wesleyan College	8,100		800	3,080	750	500	2,100	800	600
Charleston Southern University	7,292		750	2,990	1,000	1,125	2,000	1,260	1,000
Chesterfield-Marlboro Technical College	‡ 675	330/50	600				2,000	1,694	1,884
The Citadel	‡ 2,949	3,710/—	630	2,369		850			
Claflin College	† 4,412		550	2,400	1,100	1,125	900		660
Clemson University	† 2,930	4,918/—	766	3,610	1,038	1,521	1,770	2,348	1,103
Coker College	† 9,510		750	4,280		900	750		750
College of Charleston	2,950	2,950/—	648	3,300	247	2,255	1,616	1,799	2,255
Columbia Bible College and Seminary	6,270		350	3,262	550	410	1,710	400	
Columbia College	9,750		650	3,770	800	1,500	2,000	1,000	1,400
Columbia Junior College of Business	‡ 3,045		375		150	300			
Converse College	12,050		500	3,700	300	700	750	400	750
Denmark Technical College	1,030	430/—	500	3,927	700	1,600	1,500	800	1,600
Erskine College	10,630		475	3,728	500	726	1,500	650	1,301
Florence-Darlington Technical College	‡ 910	376/150	700				1,200		700
Francis Marion University	‡ 2,460	2,460/—	400	3,078	1,550	860	1,500	1,550	860
Furman University	12,605		600	3,952	400	750		600	2,418
Greenville Technical College	‡ 906	540/72	500				3,000	1,700	1,250
Horry-Georgetown Technical College	‡ 900	900/—	300						
Lander University	‡ 2,920	1,248/—	485	2,930	465	1,150	1,500	800	550
Limestone College	7,200		690	3,500	345	837	3,042	1,035	
Medical University of South Carolina	‡ 2,330	4,030/—							
Midlands Technical College	990	990/248	300					900	600
Morris College	4,405		725	2,475	975	1,000	1,800	1,200	1,000
Newberry College	8,894		450	3,100	400	1,000		700	1,000
North Greenville College	‡ 5,900		500	3,400	350	500	1,600	300	1,000
Presbyterian College	11,984		554	3,416	499	916	1,598	796	1,004
South Carolina State University	‡ 2,200	2,180/—	400	2,736	400	700		300	700
Spartanburg Methodist College	5,850		500	3,660	700	500		700	500
Spartanburg Technical College	‡ 750	750/190	500					1,200	600
Technical College of the Lowcountry	‡ 916	314/110	410					1,050	1,600
Tri-County Technical College	‡ 762	690/—	480				2,000	1,361	1,295
Trident Technical College	‡ 830	708/160	650					1,584	1,000
University of South Carolina									
Aiken	‡ 2,145	3,180/—	440				1,665	1,176	910
Beaufort	‡ 1,425	2,200/—	440				1,665	1,176	910
Coastal Carolina College	2,195	3,254/—	440				1,665	1,176	910
Columbia	2,843	4,228/—	440	3,086	792	910	1,665	1,176	910
Salkehatchie Regional Campus	1,425	2,200/—	440				1,665	1,176	910
Spartanburg	‡ 2,145	3,180/—	440				1,665	1,176	910

†Figures are projected for 1993-94. ‡Figures are for 1992-93.

South Carolina: University of South Carolina at Spartanburg

All aid		Need-based aid		Grants and scholarships								Financial aid deadlines		Inst aid form	Notes
Total fresh-men	Percent receiving aid	Freshmen judged to have need	Percent offered aid	Need-based				Non-need-based							
				Acad	Music/drama	Art	Athl	Acad	Music/drama	Art	Athl	Priority	Closing		
941	58	428	100	X			X	X			X		2/15		
1,034	40			X				X	X	X			3/1		
374	57			X		X		X		X			2/15		
590	44			X				X				3/1	none	X	
403	63	235	100	X				X				3/1	none	X	
2,167	60			X	X	X	X	X	X		X	3/1	none	X	
531	39	193	75					X				5/1	none		
91	100											5/15	none		
318	82			X	X	X	X	X	X	X	X	4/1	none	X	
251	80			X	X		X	X			X	4/15	none	X	
535	50			X								8/1	none		
79	97	75	100				X	X	X		X	4/15	none	X	
601	90				X			X		X	X	3/1	none		
223	53												none		
629	60			X				X			X	3/15	none		
409	93	385	100	X	X	X	X						6/1		
2,469	59	684	96	X				X	X		X	4/1		X	
286	75			X	X	X	X	X	X	X	X		none		
1,129	63			X	X	X		X	X	X	X	4/15	none	X	
				X				X	X			3/10	none		
261	91	225	100					X	X	X	X	4/1	none	X	
140	76			X				X				5/30	none		
199	86	116	94					X	X		X	3/15	none		
460	95			X				X				5/1	8/15	X	
181	81	154	100	X	X		X	X	X		X	3/15	none	X	
642	52											5/1	none		
				X	X	X	X	X	X	X	X	3/1	none	X	
743	42	472	100	X				X	X	X	X		2/1	X	
				X				X		X		5/1	none	X	
								X				4/1	5/1		
416	45	220	79	X				X	X	X	X	4/15	none	X	
302	98			X	X	X	X	X	X	X	X	3/30	none	X	
													none		
1,523	45							X				6/1	none		
295	95			X	X		X	X				4/30	none	X	
178	90			X				X	X		X	5/1	8/1	X	
232	94			X	X	X	X	X	X	X	X	6/1	none	X	
348	80	173	100	X	X		X	X	X		X	3/1	6/1	X	
				X				X	X		X	6/1	none		
430	83	315	100	X	X		X	X	X		X	6/1	none	X	
738	38	202	100	X								2/28	5/1		
262	55	98	100										5/1		
				X				X				6/1	none	X	
				X				X				5/1	none	X	
737	40	175	86	X				X	X		X	3/15	none		
132	80			X				X				4/15	none		
635	45			X	X	X		X			X		4/1	X	
2,426	25	831	76	X				X	X	X	X	4/15	none		
250	52	194	100	X				X			X	4/15	none	X	
429	43			X			X	X	X		X	4/15	7/1	X	

189

South Carolina: University of South Carolina at Sumter

| | | | | Costs for campus residents ||| Costs for students at home |||
Institution	Tuition and fees	Add'l out-of-state/ district tuition	Books and supplies	Room and board	Trans- portation	Other costs	Board only	Trans- portation	Other costs
Sumter	1,425	2,200/—	440				1,665	1,176	910
Union	1,425	2,200/—	440				1,665	1,176	910
Voorhees College	4,250		500	2,522	1,200	1,500	1,700	1,200	1,500
Williamsburg Technical College	600		400						
Winthrop University	‡ 3,116	2,400/—	440	3,132	680	775	900	680	775
Wofford College	11,480		585	4,150	500	915	705	655	915
York Technical College	615	615/123	450					1,155	
South Dakota									
Augustana College	10,300		600	3,120	200	800		400	400
Black Hills State University	2,098	1,568/—	500	2,610	850	1,250	1,800	850	625
Dakota State University	2,139		600	2,480	500	750	1,500	500	750
Dakota Wesleyan University	7,110		550	2,600	480	920	1,500	450	850
Huron University	6,850		600	2,940	400		1,800	320	960
Kilian Community College	‡ 3,185		400				1,780	640	400
Lake Area Vocational Technical Institute	1,500								
Mitchell Vocational Technical Institute	2,100		750				3,000	300	750
Mount Marty College	7,470		500	2,980	540	900	1,800	540	900
National College	6,575		600	3,315	750	900	1,600	900	600
Northern State University	2,006	1,568/—	550	2,399	735	1,100	1,800	735	1,100
Oglala Lakota College	‡ 1,590		200					162	450
Presentation College	‡ 6,320		600	3,046	550	850	750	550	850
Sinte Gleska University	‡ 1,580		400					900	400
Sioux Falls College	‡ 7,996		600	3,084	700	900	1,750	650	650
Sisseton-Wahpeton Community College	‡ 2,475		375					500	
South Dakota School of Mines and Technology	2,169	1,839/—	500	2,420	555	1,152	1,140	642	1,152
South Dakota State University	2,130	1,839/—	560	2,514	666	1,170	950	568	926
University of South Dakota	2,171	1,839/—	650	2,538	620	1,050	870	570	1,045
Western Dakota Vocational Technical Institute	2,082		600				1,800	500	
Tennessee									
American Baptist College of ABT Seminary	‡ 2,000		400	1,984					
Aquinas Junior College	† 4,310		500				1,750	850	650
Austin Peay State University	1,800	3,782/—	465	2,860	1,382	1,500	1,500	1,382	1,500
Belmont University	7,300		580	3,490	820	900	1,880	820	900
Bethel College	‡ 5,250		500	2,650		1,000	650	700	
Bristol University	‡ 6,000								
Carson-Newman College	7,850		400	3,000	1,000	700	1,710	1,200	750
Chattanooga State Technical Community College	948	2,678/—	440				1,900	1,600	1,700
Christian Brothers University	‡ 8,090		600	3,080					
Cleveland State Community College	944	2,678/—	475				1,600	600	800
Columbia State Community College	† 938	2,678/—	420				1,200	820	610
Crichton College	4,750		500			2,000	1,500	300	2,000
Cumberland University	5,700		600	2,950					
David Lipscomb University	6,285		500	3,190	500	700	1,800	500	700
Draughons Junior College of Business: Nashville	† 4,010		500						
Dyersburg State Community College	944	2,678/—	400				1,500	1,225	480
East Tennessee State University	1,634	3,782/—	600		400	1,200		420	1,200

†Figures are projected for 1993-94. ‡Figures are for 1992-93.

Tennessee: East Tennessee State University

All aid		Need-based aid		Grants and scholarships								Financial aid deadlines		Inst aid form	Notes
Total fresh-men	Percent receiving aid	Freshmen judged to have need	Percent offered aid	Need-based				Non-need-based							
				Acad	Music/ drama	Art	Athl	Acad	Music/ drama	Art	Athl	Priority	Closing		
300	70	110	100					X				4/15	none	X	
264	96	204	100	X				X				5/15	8/15		
125	43			X				X					none	X	
805	68	326	96					X	X	X	X	5/1	5/1	X	
289	70	180	100	X	X		X	X	X		X	3/15	none		
701	38			X				X				3/31	none		
394	85	308	100	X			X	X	X	X	X	4/15	none		
566	76	314	97	X	X	X		X	X	X	X	4/1	none		
559	70			X			X	X	X		X	3/1	none		
135	95	95	100	X	X	X	X	X	X	X	X	3/15	none	X	
102	97	99	100	X			X	X			X		none		
62	80												none	X	
													none		
210	100												none		
129	97	124	100	X	X		X	X	X		X	3/1	none		
290	94			X				X				3/15	none	X	
623	75	399	94	X	X			X	X	X	X	3/1	none		
													none		
87	89							X				3/1	none		
														X	
163	94	148	100	X	X		X	X	X		X	4/1	none		
155	98	49	100	X									none		
408	48	178	100					X			X	4/1	none		
1,534	82							X	X	X	X	3/15	none	X	
1,282	81			X	X	X	X	X	X	X	X	2/15	none		
305	80	295	100									7/1	none		
													none		
280	5	16	100	X				X					none	X	
785	70							X	X	X	X	4/1	none		
895	70			X				X	X		X	3/15	none	X	
128	90							X	X		X	5/1	none		
113	60												none	X	
401	91			X	X	X	X	X	X	X	X	4/1	none	X	
1,345	39						X	X	X	X	X	4/1	none		
228	97			X	X			X	X		X	4/1	none		
615	30			X				X				5/15	none	X	
721	65	305	91					X			X	4/1	none	X	
52	89			X	X			X	X			7/15	none	X	
226	70			X				X			X	3/1	none	X	
								X	X	X	X	4/15	none		
117	82												none		
393	53			X			X	X	X		X	3/15	none		
1,623	40							X	X	X	X	4/15	none		

191

Tennessee: Fisk University

| | | | | Costs for campus residents ||| Costs for students at home |||
Institution	Tuition and fees	Add'l out-of-state/district tuition	Books and supplies	Room and board	Trans-portation	Other costs	Board only	Trans-portation	Other costs
Fisk University	6,305		600	3,690	1,050	1,750		950	1,600
Free Will Baptist Bible College	3,777		390	2,980	608	1,478	1,800	609	365
Freed-Hardeman University	5,940		575	3,020	650	850	1,500	850	850
Hiwassee College	‡ 4,200		350	2,700	300	800			
Johnson Bible College	‡ 3,650		600	2,800	500	700	1,800	1,100	1,200
King College	8,250		500	3,250	1,000	1,200	1,500	350	3,600
Knoxville Business College	‡ 4,800		550					1,200	1,000
Knoxville College	5,470		600	2,850	1,000	1,730	1,500	600	1,730
Lambuth University	‡ 4,834		400	3,160		1,200	1,872		1,000
Lane College	4,766		400	2,862	200	900	1,500	800	300
Lee College	4,692		500	3,160	840	840	1,020	980	410
LeMoyne-Owen College	‡ 3,750		400					500	900
Lincoln Memorial University	5,530		550	2,688	500	1,200	900	1,280	1,200
Maryville College	10,428		500	4,050	626	1,000	1,875	626	1,000
Memphis College of Art	8,990		1,000	4,150	700	470	2,000	700	470
Memphis State University	1,828	3,782/—	850	3,220	500	715	1,800	825	715
Middle Tennessee State University	1,668	3,782/—	600	2,600	750	1,046	1,500	2,350	1,046
Milligan College	† 7,590		550	3,100	1,240	940	975	820	1,900
Motlow State Community College	950	2,678/—	400						3,200
Nashville State Technical Institute	936	2,678/—	400						
Northeast State Technical Community College	938	2,678/—	500					750	890
Pellissippi State Technical Community College	974	2,678/—	400				1,800	1,900	1,300
Rhodes College	14,916		500	4,709	600	800	2,012	500	800
Roane State Community College	944	2,678/—	400				1,500	375	750
Shelby State Community College	934	2,678/—	400				1,500	540	675
Southern College of Seventh-day Adventists	7,988		480	3,360	525	525		400	525
State Technical Institute at Memphis	930	2,678/—	600				1,918	792	675
Tennessee State University	1,706	3,782/—	400	2,660	450	700	1,500	450	700
Tennessee Technological University	1,708	3,782/—	670	3,050	670	670		670	670
Tennessee Temple University	4,520		450	3,730	800	900		400	900
Tennessee Wesleyan College	6,520		400	3,340	1,000	1,200	2,066	1,200	900
Trevecca Nazarene College	6,656		500	3,272	744	800	2,700	594	630
Tusculum College	7,175		550	3,300	400	800	1,700	700	900
Union University	5,380		500	2,760		400		400	400
University of the South	14,910		450	3,920	300	810	1,990		810
University of Tennessee									
Chattanooga	1,770	3,780/—	525		500	850	1,457	1,187	850
Knoxville	1,982	3,780/—	760	3,200	494	1,432		1,760	1,432
Martin	1,810	3,780/—	640	2,870	466	1,591	580	577	1,591
Memphis	1,770	3,780/—	1,097	4,000	1,370	1,527		1,305	1,455
Vanderbilt University	17,202		550	6,220		550			550
Volunteer State Community College	938	2,678/—	500				1,370	1,444	400
Walters State Community College	938	2,678/—	500				1,500	1,200	900
William Jennings Bryan College	7,690		450	3,950	600	800	1,350	900	1,600
Texas									
Abilene Christian University	7,370		450	3,400	890	1,250	1,500	890	1,250
Alvin Community College	‡ 420	—/300	385				1,500	625	1,017
Amarillo College	‡ 470	1,081/222	525				1,160	1,136	851
Amber University	3,750		350						

†Figures are projected for 1993-94. ‡Figures are for 1992-93.

Texas: Amber University

All aid		Need-based aid		Grants and scholarships									Financial aid deadlines		Inst aid form	Notes
Total fresh-men	Percent receiving aid	Freshmen judged to have need	Percent offered aid	Need-based				Non-need-based				Priority	Closing			
				Acad	Music/drama	Art	Athl	Acad	Music/drama	Art	Athl				
238	80			X				X				4/20	none	X	
78	75	78	100						X	X		4/15	none	X	
286	84	236	100	X				X	X	X	X	4/1	none		
255	75			X	X		X	X	X		X	5/1	none	X	
99	80							X	X			7/1	none	X	
123	90	99	100	X	X		X	X	X		X	3/1	none	X	
89	95			X									none	X	
258	99	220	100	X	X			X	X			5/31	none	X	
254	75			X	X	X	X	X	X	X	X	3/15	none		
134	97											5/15	8/1	X	
384	90	227	99	X	X		X	X	X		X	4/15	none	X	
401	88											4/15	none		
515	70	135	100					X	X		X	4/1	none		
195	87	109	100					X	X	X		3/1	none	X	
55	84					X		X		X		4/1	none	X	
1,621	50							X	X	X	X	4/1	none	X	
2,154	60			X	X	X	X	X			X	3/15	5/15		
196	93			X	X	X	X	X	X	X	X	3/15	none	X	
672	62			X	X		X	X	X		X	5/1	none		
2,056	10			X				X				5/1	none	X	
702	36			X				X				8/1	none		
2,584	29	600	100					X	X	X		7/1			
366	76	196	100	X	X	X		X	X	X		3/1	none	X	
940	35							X	X	X	X	5/1	none		
967	42							X	X	X	X	5/1	none	X	
369	85	190	96	X	X			X	X			5/1	none	X	
1,053	25			X				X				3/15	none	X	
791	80	525	95	X	X		X	X	X		X	4/1	none	X	
1,622	65			X				X	X		X	3/15	none		
173	60	7	100					X	X		X	3/31	none	X	
80	95							X	X		X	4/1	7/31	X	
183	95			X	X		X					4/15	none		
138	95	107	100	X			X	X			X	4/1	none	X	
638	79	294	94					X	X	X	X	5/15	8/1	X	
334	62	158	100	X				X				3/1	none	X	
825	70							X	X	X	X	3/1	none		
3,219	50	1,536	84	X	X	X	X	X	X	X	X	4/1	none		
1,128	65			X				X	X		X	3/1	none		
				X				X				2/15	none	X	
1,408	49	516	100	X				X	X		X	2/15	none	X	
								X			X	4/15	none		
909	15	325	98	X				X	X		X	3/31	none		
108	88	95	100					X	X		X	5/1	none	X	
1,024	75	446	98					X	X	X	X	3/1	none	X	
689	23	322	100					X	X	X	X	6/15	none	X	
1,196	38							X				6/1	none		
													7/1		

Texas: Angelina College

| | | | | Costs for campus residents ||| Costs for students at home |||
Institution	Tuition and fees	Add'l out-of-state/district tuition	Books and supplies	Room and board	Trans-portation	Other costs	Board only	Trans-portation	Other costs
Angelina College	588	300/158	590	2,440	275	550	825	1,300	550
Angelo State University	1,489	4,080/—	450	3,592	590	1,320	1,286	1,320	1,320
Arlington Baptist College	‡ 2,050		700		600	720	1,100	600	800
Austin College	10,865		400	4,134	200	950	1,500	200	950
Austin Community College	794	2,688/392	440				1,746	940	1,236
Baptist Missionary Association Theological Seminary	1,260		450		600	1,200	4,000	600	1,200
Bauder Fashion College	‡ 5,990		800	2,980					
Baylor College of Dentistry	1,750		2,480						6,800
Baylor University	7,070		600	3,920	830	1,346	2,010	1,616	1,402
Bee County College	‡ 400	840/300	500	2,110	176	605	1,500	396	605
Blinn College	804	1,650/240	526	7,412	404	1,036		290	1,036
Brazosport College	460	1,650/150	540				2,090	720	880
Brookhaven College	‡ 450	1,470/570	390					1,560	1,245
Cedar Valley College	‡ 450	1,470/570	600				1,500	1,330	1,045
Central Texas College	696	1,400/—	800	2,995	529	1,531	3,351	621	1,531
Cisco Junior College	630	426/120	500	1,950	200	600	1,100	500	800
Clarendon College	‡ 620	4,482/60	350	1,550		1,000		400	800
College of the Mainland	341	960/290	427	1,880				1,190	1,005
Collin County Community College District	588	1,260/280	433				1,820	1,381	1,086
Commonwealth Institute of Funeral Service	6,075						150	250	100
Concordia Lutheran College	6,760		450	3,500	775	1,050	1,500	650	1,050
Cooke County College	‡ 600	300/—	450	2,300	800	1,075	1,620	950	1,075
Corpus Christi State University	1,427	4,080/—	425		630	1,100	1,500	1,100	1,100
Criswell College	† 2,650		200						
Dallas Baptist University	‡ 6,000		572	3,130	117	1,036	1,700	1,304	1,036
Dallas Christian College	2,790		650	2,790	160	625	2,500	650	
Dallas Institute of Funeral Service	5,225						3,650	1,200	1,190
Del Mar College	480	900/150	400				1,500	630	810
DeVry Institute of Technology: Irving	5,609		525				1,792	2,384	1,928
East Texas Baptist University	5,100		515	2,780	500	960	1,800	575	960
East Texas State University Commerce	1,381	4,080/—	600	3,500	850	950	1,500	850	950
Texarkana	1,350	4,080/—	650				1,590	875	970
Eastfield College	‡ 450	1,470/570	400				1,100	1,170	935
El Centro College	‡ 450	1,470/570	600					400	600
El Paso Community College	‡ 721	2,063/—	435						915
Frank Phillips College	‡ 630	120/60	475	1,800	600	900	1,500	1,150	865
Galveston College	538	336/—	566					1,176	1,390
Grayson County College	‡ 613	1,144/114	434	3,102	650	918	1,500	910	918
Hardin-Simmons University	6,480		700	2,980	795	1,284	1,162	795	1,284
Hill College	705	580/180	526	2,500	723	937		1,202	965
Houston Baptist University	6,837		525	2,160	1,260	1,370	1,700	1,260	1,370
Houston Community College	† 738	1,380/360	1,000				2,657	443	1,328
Howard College	780	400/50	350	2,100	800	1,175	750	800	1,175
Howard Payne University	5,070		450	2,820	620	1,250	1,500	745	1,085
Huston-Tillotson College	5,040		500	3,450	682	1,121	5,273	662	1,121
Incarnate Word College	8,325		750	4,060	900	1,875	1,825	1,365	1,875
Institute for Christian Studies	‡ 910		120	1,500					
Jacksonville College	2,520		400	2,496				500	

†Figures are projected for 1993-94. ‡Figures are for 1992-93.

Texas: Jacksonville College

All aid		Need-based aid		Grants and scholarships								Financial aid deadlines		Inst aid form	Notes
Total freshmen	Percent receiving aid	Freshmen judged to have need	Percent offered aid	Need-based				Non-need-based							
				Acad	Music/drama	Art	Athl	Acad	Music/drama	Art	Athl	Priority	Closing		
913	27	568	100	X	X	X	X	X	X	X	X	6/15	none	X	
				X				X				7/15	none		
37	95	24	100	X	X							8/15	none	X	
290	80	167	100	X				X	X	X		5/1	none	X	
								X				2/15	4/1	X	
												8/1	9/4		
147	40	125	100	X				X				7/1		X	
												6/1		X	
2,367	67	1,082	100	X	X	X	X	X	X	X	X	5/1	none	X	
652	50			X				X	X	X		4/1	none	X	
5,834	30			X			X	X	X		X	7/1	none	X	
2,090	21							X				8/1	none	X	
2,917	68			X		X		X				7/1	none		
				X	X	X		X	X	X			none		
1,043	21			X				X				7/1	8/1		
729	50							X	X		X	8/15	none		
192	80											8/1	none		
779	92	105	89					X	X	X			none		
1,798	10	790	100	X	X	X	X	X	X	X	X	6/1	none		
124	60	60	100									7/16	none		
155	80	79	100	X	X		X	X	X		X	4/15	7/1	X	
1,229	30							X	X		X		6/1		
								X	X	X			4/1		
50	20	25	100										7/15		
124	87							X	X	X		5/1	none	X	
14	71			X	X			X	X			7/1	8/1		
144	55			X				X					none		
2,357	40			X	X	X		X	X	X		5/1	none		
485	82							X					none		
289	77							X	X		X	6/1	none	X	
				X	X	X	X					3/1	10/1	X	
				X				X				5/1	11/1	X	
												6/1			
4,286	24			X	X	X		X	X	X		7/1	none	X	
3,679	65							X					6/1	X	
255	42	31	100					X	X		X	7/1	none	X	
424	18	203	74	X	X		X	X	X		X	6/1	none		
639	28							X	X	X	X		none		
446	72	220	100	X				X	X	X	X	3/15	none	X	
742	60	590	100	X	X	X	X	X	X		X	8/1	none	X	
188	70							X	X	X	X	5/1	none	X	
4,684	14	4,330	100	X								4/15	none	X	
1,652	60			X	X	X	X	X	X	X	X	4/1	none	X	
330	75			X				X	X	X		5/1	none	X	
77	95			X	X		X					5/1			
412	62	203	100					X	X	X	X	4/1	none	X	
				X				X					6/15		
111	94			X	X		X	X	X		X	6/10	none	X	

195

Texas: Jarvis Christian College

Institution	Tuition and fees	Add'l out-of-state/ district tuition	Books and supplies	Room and board	Trans-portation	Other costs	Board only	Trans-portation	Other costs
				Costs for campus residents			**Costs for students at home**		
Jarvis Christian College	‡ 4,015		300	2,999	750	900		750	900
Kilgore College	‡ 330	480/—	450	2,200		1,000			1,000
Lamar University—Beaumontt	1,404	4,080/—	698	2,878	1,896	1,794	1,750	1,846	1,200
Laredo Junior College	576	1,950/1,170	485	3,320				1,702	1,818
Laredo State University	1,110	4,080/—	549	3,302			6,628	3,076	1,569
Lee College	† 455	840/360	500				1,999	744	1,037
LeTourneau University	7,940		600	3,860	500	900	1,700	843	1,021
Lon Morris College	‡ 4,354		450	3,266	974	1,510	1,150	974	1,510
Lubbock Christian University	‡ 6,450		317	2,600	580	1,055	1,477	685	1,266
McMurry University	7,040		400	3,100	530	1,480	1,100	715	1,480
Midland College	‡ 642	366/48	400				1,500	990	1,210
Midwestern State University	1,636	4,080/—	630	3,144	900	938	1,024	670	526
Miss Wade's Fashion Merchandising College	4,985		575		1,160	936	1,440	1,160	936
Mountain View College	‡ 450	1,470/570	600				1,500	1,330	1,045
Navarro College	‡ 740	264/120	416	2,740	644	811	1,500	807	811
North Harris Montgomery Community College District	‡ 474	900/600	530				1,560	1,238	964
North Lake College	‡ 450	1,470/570	400						
Northeast Texas Community College	570	760/240	530	2,700	1,165	1,350	1,400	1,165	1,350
Northwood University: Texas Campus	9,126		525	4,334	500	4,335	1,500	750	650
Odessa College	500	240/80	400	2,875	525	3,705	1,500	710	810
Our Lady of the Lake University of San Antonio	8,180		750	3,756	720	1,532	1,544	894	1,360
Palo Alto College	‡ 510	750/—							
Panola College	‡ 440	400/150	400	1,990	100	300		900	300
Paris Junior College	‡ 2,130	5,400/1,440	400	2,584	600				
Paul Quinn College	‡ 3,635		400	2,975	600	700	1,500	600	700
Prairie View A&M University	1,568	4,080/—	581	3,500	2,185	1,473	1,500	2,586	1,624
Ranger Junior College	750	120/20	440	2,401	1,000	809	1,834	1,168	809
Rice University	9,650		425	5,460	300	1,300	1,500	700	825
Richland College	‡ 450	1,470/570	350						935
St. Edward's University	8,902		550	4,000	550	1,520		750	500
St. Mary's University	8,536		500	3,440	250	1,000	1,620	648	788
St. Philip's College	‡ 570	1,290/390	275				1,700	600	700
Sam Houston State University	1,536	4,080/—	498	3,380	1,176	1,282	1,370	2,482	1,214
San Antonio College	‡ 624	1,290/390	720				1,600	1,270	1,627
San Jacinto College: North	† 430	990/300	500				2,969	1,177	1,583
Schreiner College	8,650		500	5,900	372	1,116	1,500	478	1,066
South Plains College	936	480/—	400	2,300	700	1,100		700	1,100
Southern Methodist University	13,580		576	4,940	326	1,100	1,500	842	1,000
Southwest Texas Junior College	‡ 806	1,380/240	350	1,980	634	411	900	430	773
Southwest Texas State University	1,240	4,080/—	500	3,854	1,116	1,970	2,288	1,210	1,270
Southwestern Adventist College	7,064		430	3,466	769	1,088	1,700	903	1,088
Southwestern Assemblies of God College	2,900		481	2,762	938	1,272	1,600	763	1,272
Southwestern Christian College	4,386		460	2,793	600	400	850	700	400
Southwestern University	‡ 10,300		500	4,257	230	770	1,500	500	750
Stephen F. Austin State University	1,450	4,080/—	500	3,768	900	900	1,750	1,167	800
Sul Ross State University	1,461	4,080/—	650	2,990	600	1,150	1,600	875	1,150
Tarleton State University	1,478	4,080/—	425	3,100	404	1,266	1,500	506	1,094
Tarrant County Junior College	‡ 450	3,180/240	540					1,524	1,218
Temple Junior College	720	1,410/390	520	3,500	771	1,061	1,834	1,056	1,030

†Figures are projected for 1993-94. ‡Figures are for 1992-93.

Texas: Temple Junior College

All aid		Need-based aid		Grants and scholarships								Financial aid deadlines		Inst aid form	Notes
Total fresh-men	Percent receiving aid	Freshmen judged to have need	Percent offered aid	Need-based				Non-need-based							
				Acad	Music/drama	Art	Athl	Acad	Music/drama	Art	Athl	Priority	Closing		
128	95			X	X			X	X			7/30	none	X	
2,372	13							X				8/1	none		
1,276	31	743	100					X	X	X	X	4/1	none	X	
1,244	61			X	X		X	X	X		X	5/1	none	X	
				X				X				6/30	none		
3,706	19	110	98					X	X	X	X	7/1	none	X
184	78			X			X	X			X	2/15	none		
265	90	200	100	X	X	X	X	X	X	X	X	6/1	none	X
465	90			X	X		X					7/1	8/1	X	
250	79							X	X	X		3/15	none	X	
2,750	24							X	X	X	X	6/1	none		
1,693	44			X				X	X	X	X	4/1	none	X	
163	85	124	100										none	X	
4,889	12											6/1	none		
2,263	30							X	X	X	X	6/1	none		
3,664	15			X	X	X						4/15	none	X	
				X				X				7/1	none		
								X	X	X		5/1	none	X	
71	80			X			X	X			X	3/31	none		
1,101	31	372	100	X				X	X	X	X	6/1	none		
319	71							X	X			4/15	7/15		
													6/1		
1,081	40	174	98	X	X			X	X		X	6/1	none		
1,640	44											4/1	none		
245	75							X					none	X	
1,229	85							X	X	X	X	4/16	none	X	
332	75	168	100	X	X		X	X	X		X	8/1	7/31		
650	91			X				X	X		X	3/1	6/1	X	
9,594	10	500	60	X				X				6/1	none		
331	73							X			X	3/1	8/15	X	
549	73			X				X	X		X	4/1	none		
855	34			X				X	X				6/1	X	
1,603	31	963	100					X	X	X	X	3/31	5/31	X	
3,156	40			X	X	X		X	X	X		5/1	none	X	
2,459	15	327	100	X	X	X	X	X	X	X	X	6/1	none	X	
197	83	103	100					X	X		X	4/15	none		
2,402	30							X	X	X	X	6/10	none		
1,221	80	495	100	X	X	X	X	X	X	X	X	2/1	none	X	
715	37							X				6/15	none		
2,255	50	844	90	X	X			X	X		X	4/1	none		
189	75	135	100	X				X	X			3/15	none	X	
147	75	67	100					X	X			3/1	none		
104	90	8	100					X	X		X		7/15		
318	68	187	100	X				X	X	X		3/15	X		
2,169	45							X	X		X	4/1	6/1	X	
997	20			X				X	X			4/1	none		
								X	X			6/1	none		
4,976	10			X				X	X			4/15	none	X	
1,114	52			X	X	X	X	X	X		X	8/1	none		

197

Texas: Texarkana College

Institution	Tuition and fees	Add'l out-of-state/ district tuition	Books and supplies	Costs for campus residents			Costs for students at home		
				Room and board	Transportation	Other costs	Board only	Transportation	Other costs
Texarkana College	‡ 690	440/150	650					700	1,200
Texas A&I University	1,514	4,080/—	484	2,816	1,200	1,714		1,496	1,296
Texas A&M University									
College Station	1,526	4,080/—	560	4,062	728	1,224			
Galveston	1,300	4,080/—	680	3,384	700	800	1,000	700	800
Texas Christian University	8,970		596	3,210	522	1,850	1,800	522	1,286
Texas College	3,605		400	2,430	586	1,095	2,500	674	1,095
Texas Lutheran College	‡ 6,790		450	3,120	650	950	1,170	1,000	1,000
Texas Southern University	1,230	4,080/—	500	3,320	1,400	1,700	1,500	1,400	1,700
Texas State Technical College									
Amarillo	‡ 1,086	2,970/—	900	2,820	400	4,524	900	800	1,900
Harlingen	‡ 1,086	2,970/—	836	2,520	880	1,260	2,100	1,320	1,260
Sweetwater	‡ 1,086	2,970/—	800	2,760	1,380	585	1,605	1,380	585
Waco	‡ 1,086	2,970/—	650	2,895	300	1,200	1,820	1,500	1,200
Texas Tech University	1,411	4,080/—	600	4,000	1,200	1,480	1,830	1,300	900
Texas Wesleyan University	6,150		428	3,230	615	1,138	2,575	615	1,138
Texas Woman's University	1,498	4,080/—	450	3,049	404	1,156	1,560	988	1,216
Trinity University	11,720		500	4,950	540	490	2,050		
Trinity Valley Community College	420	1,560/300	400	2,420	780	850	1,000	870	850
Tyler Junior College	610	600/300	500	2,300	444	556		444	779
University of Dallas	10,180		500	4,650	700	600	1,500	500	600
University of Houston									
Clear Lake	1,451	4,080/—	600					1,779	1,669
Downtown	1,474	4,080/—	300					993	703
Houston	1,462	4,080/—	470	4,191	1,250	1,568	500	1,250	1,568
Victoria	1,452	4,080/—	431				1,722	1,022	1,468
University of Mary Hardin-Baylor	5,250		600	3,106	718	1,200	1,500	877	982
University of North Texas	1,500	4,100/—	450	3,508	3,600	1,100		1,000	1,600
University of St. Thomas	8,162		425	3,870	660	1,050	1,810	1,025	1,050
University of Texas									
Arlington	1,248	4,080/—	420	2,780	600	1,000	1,100	1,320	1,000
Austin	1,394	4,080/—	650	4,100	750	1,600	1,500	750	1,600
Brownsville	‡ 994	180/—							
Dallas	1,390	4,080/—	626		1,532	1,358	1,616	1,532	554
El Paso	1,408	4,080/—	374	3,550	1,350	1,142	1,750	1,350	1,142
Health Science Center at Houston	990	4,080/—	450		1,449	168	2,340	1,449	1,728
Health Science Center at San Antonio	905	4,080/—	792				4,137	997	1,022
Medical Branch at Galveston	951	4,080/—	800	4,586	2,112	3,190	5,489	2,299	3,630
Pan American	1,410	4,080/—	478	4,101	464	2,252	929	1,922	2,291
Permian Basin	1,432	4,080/—	555		1,452	1,375	1,000	1,452	1,375
San Antonio	1,579	4,080/—	500		1,763	1,439	1,560	1,763	1,439
Southwestern Medical Center at Dallas Southwestern Allied Health Sciences School	998	4,080/—	610				3,355	1,501	4,336
Tyler	1,616	4,080/—	400				1,620	580	934
Vernon Regional Junior College	‡ 680	150/20	600	1,860	2,500	3,000		2,500	3,000
Victoria College	668	2,010/—	405				2,500	465	1,105
Wayland Baptist University	4,766		482	3,121	654	1,000	1,721	668	899
Weatherford College	‡ 620	1,980/210	300	2,632	100	1,000	1,000	100	1,000
West Texas A & M University	1,466	4,080/—	500	2,588	580	1,040	1,560	1,100	770
Wharton County Junior College	720	1,740/570	575	2,050	1,200	1,090	1,340	1,200	1,090
Wiley College	3,946		210	2,672	314	556	1,500	590	700

†Figures are projected for 1993-94. ‡Figures are for 1992-93.

Texas: Wiley College

All aid		Need-based aid		Grants and scholarships								Financial aid deadlines		Inst aid form	Notes
Total freshmen	Percent receiving aid	Freshmen judged to have need	Percent offered aid	Need-based				Non-need-based							
				Acad	Music/ drama	Art	Athl	Acad	Music/ drama	Art	Athl	Priority	Closing		
2,212	85			X				X	X	X	X	6/1	7/15		
													4/15	X	
6,006	47	1,655	93	X				X				4/15	none		
282	48	152	100	X				X				4/1	none		
				X				X	X	X	X	5/1			
128	90	590	100	X	X	X	X	X	X	X	X		none	X	
246	85	113	100					X	X	X	X	5/1	none		
1,739	80											5/1	none		
138	51			X								7/1	none		
1,428	80			X								5/5	6/15		
441	60	274	100	X								7/15	none	X	
2,499	52			X				X				5/31	none	X	
2,746	30	1,284	75	X	X	X		X	X	X	X	4/1	none		
257	93	226	100	X				X	X	X	X	4/15	none	X	
445	58			X				X	X	X	X	4/1	none		
572	80			X	X	X		X	X	X			2/1		
1,469	65	940	100					X	X	X	X	7/1	none		
				X	X	X	X	X	X	X	X	7/1	none	X	
256	92	173	100					X	X	X		3/1	none	X	
								X				5/1	none	X	
1,432	70	790	100	X		X		X		X		6/1	none		
4,717	35			X	X	X		X	X	X	X	4/1	none		
				X				X				4/15	none		
259	80	175	100					X	X		X	5/1	none	X	
3,328	27			X	X	X	X	X	X	X	X	6/1	none		
178	50							X	X			3/1	none	X	
1,680	27							X	X	X	X	6/1	none	X	
5,157	46	1,350	100	X	X	X	X	X	X	X	X	4/1	none		
													none		
97	36	54	100	X				X				5/1	11/1	X	
2,341	55	866	86	X	X		X	X	X		X	3/15	none	X	
				X				X				3/1	12/3	X	
				X				X				3/12	none		
				X								3/15	none		
1,873	77	1,156	98	X	X	X	X	X	X	X	X		4/15		
				X				X				5/1	none	X	
2,213	76			X				X			X	3/31	none	X	
				X				X					none		
				X	X	X	X	X	X	X		6/1	7/1	X	
1,173	35	240	100	X	X		X	X	X	X	X	7/15	none		
2,018	25			X	X			X	X			7/31	none	X	
1,033	20	250	80	X	X	X	X	X	X		X		none		
													6/1		
884	55							X	X	X	X	7/15	none		
								X	X		X	6/1	none		
172	55			X	X		X	X	X		X	6/1	none	X	

Utah: Brigham Young University

Institution	Tuition and fees	Add'l out-of-state/ district tuition	Books and supplies	Costs for campus residents			Costs for students at home		
				Room and board	Trans-portation	Other costs	Board only	Trans-portation	Other costs
Utah									
Brigham Young University	2,200		630	3,450	910	1,110	1,700	910	1,110
College of Eastern Utah	1,128	2,390/—	562	2,625	986	1,106	1,746	845	1,187
Dixie College	1,282	2,913/—	525	2,460	600	900		225	300
LDS Business College	1,810		600		614	932	1,800	586	825
Phillips Junior College: Salt Lake City Campus	‡ 5,000						1,100	600	
Salt Lake Community College	1,359	2,679/—	630				1,575	450	1,020
Snow College	1,125	3,555/—	530	2,505	525	900	1,500	600	700
Southern Utah University	1,599	3,161/—	700						
Stevens-Henager College of Business	† 11,133		1,000						
University of Utah	† 2,244	4,497/—	700	5,175	486	2,178	1,575	486	2,087
Utah State University	1,878	3,645/—	660	3,990	975	1,380	1,996	465	725
Utah Valley Community College	1,366	2,643/—	670				1,500	650	650
Weber State University	1,638	3,228/—	504	3,345	849	1,059	1,890	849	1,059
Westminster College of Salt Lake City	8,220		600	3,880	950	1,650	1,500	675	1,070
Vermont									
Bennington College	24,850	(Comprehensive)	400			600	1,830	930	
Burlington College	7,630		600				1,900	1,150	2,160
Castleton State College	3,753	4,152/—	400	4,640	300	600	2,100	800	600
Champlain College	7,840		375	5,550		600	1,500	650	600
College of St. Joseph in Vermont	8,000		600	4,650	550	900	1,500	750	900
Community College of Vermont	2,560	2,490/—	350					600	
Goddard College	13,400		508	4,520	470	911	2,500	795	911
Green Mountain College	11,100		400	2,860	500	340	750	500	340
Johnson State College	3,753	4,152/—	500	4,640	312	624	750	312	624
Landmark College	22,550		500	5,200	1,200	1,500			
Lyndon State College	3,753	4,152/—	400	4,640	300	400		300	400
Marlboro College	17,615		400	5,680	200	320	2,020	50	320
Middlebury College	24,570	(Comprehensive)	530			1,000			
New England Culinary Institute	14,460		500	2,530	1,683	3,996		1,683	3,996
Norwich University	13,460		500	5,270		800			800
St. Michael's College	12,430		350	5,600	250	400	2,245	250	400
School for International Training	11,071		400	4,264	450	960	2,400	450	960
Southern Vermont College	8,620		500	4,304	600	550	1,000	600	550
Sterling College	17,317	(Comprehensive)	600		350	350			
Trinity College of Vermont	10,722		550	5,070	250	250	1,800	250	250
University of Vermont	‡ 6,150	8,600/—	475	4,266		972	1,500	910	972
Vermont Technical College	4,390	3,840/1,920	700	4,640	350	650	2,050	600	650
Virginia									
Averett College	9,710		400	3,900	500	600		400	500
Blue Ridge Community College	1,332	3,030/—	600				1,750	1,050	500
Bluefield College	6,500		400	4,100	800	800	2,600	1,250	1,250
Bridgewater College	10,770		525	4,530	200	875	2,400		875
Central Virginia Community College	1,340	3,030/—	450				600	500	3,000
Christendom College	† 8,350		416	3,400	520	312	1,456	624	312
Christopher Newport University	‡ 2,860	3,992/—	510				890	920	2,640
Clinch Valley College of the University of Virginia	‡ 2,650	3,374/—	600	3,200	600	750	1,500	1,000	750
College of Health Sciences	2,880		750		900	4,500	2,400	1,900	2,100
College of William and Mary	‡ 4,046	7,380/—	600	3,902	350	800	1,800	600	800

†Figures are projected for 1993-94. ‡Figures are for 1992-93.

Note: Comprehensive fees include tuition, fees, room, and board.

Virginia: College of William and Mary

All aid		Need-based aid		Grants and scholarships									Financial aid deadlines		Inst aid form	Notes
Total freshmen	Percent receiving aid	Freshmen judged to have need	Percent offered aid	Need-based				Non-need-based								
				Acad	Music/drama	Art	Athl	Acad	Music/drama	Art	Athl	Priority	Closing		
4,615	53							X	X	X	X	3/1	none	X	
				X	X	X		X	X	X	X	5/1	none	X	
890	45							X	X	X	X	6/1	none	X	
358	50							X					none	X	
250	90			X				X					none		
4,196	44			X				X		X	X	4/1	none	X	
1,754	42							X	X	X	X		7/15	X	
973	55	365	95					X	X				none	X	
240	95			X				X					none	X	
2,442	70	1,700	97	X	X	X	X	X	X	X	X	3/1	none	X	
								X	X	X	X	3/15	5/15	X	
2,475	65							X				7/1	none	X	
								X	X	X	X	5/1	none		
237	80			X				X	X	X		5/31	none	X	
147	73	109	100	X				X					3/1	X	
32	80			X								6/1	none	X	
338	80	224	100	X	X	X		X	X			3/15	none		
865	74	727	100								X	5/1	none		
61	75							X				3/1	5/1		
560	86							X					none	X	
27	55	23	100									4/1	6/15	X	
213	63	85	100	X				X		X	X	2/15	none		
265	65	209	100					X	X			3/1	none		
35	13	21	100	X									none	X	
242	59			X				X				3/15	none	X	
57	65			X								3/1	5/1	X	
467	38												1/31	X	
216	90												none	X	
470	84	374	98	X				X				3/1	none		
409	67	346	100	X	X	X	X	X			X	3/15	none	X	
				X				X				6/1	8/15		
108	92	73	100	X								5/1	none		
60	65	45	100									3/15	none		
102	77	84	100					X				3/1	none		
1,816	42	789	100	X	X	X	X	X	X	X	X	3/1	none		
404	70	274	100	X				X				3/1	none	X	
125	82			X	X			X				4/1	none	X	
736	15			X								5/15	none	X	
171	85	118	100	X	X	X	X	X	X	X	X	3/13	none	X	
255	97	184	100					X	X				3/15		
743	20			X				X				5/15	none	X	
25	64	15	100					X				4/15	6/1	X	
508	35	242	95	X				X	X			4/1	none	X	
340	62	239	80	X			X	X			X	4/1	none	X	
17	59			X				X				7/1	none	X	
1,194	23	290	100	X	X	X	X	X			X	2/15	none		

201

Virginia: Dabney S. Lancaster Community College

Institution	Tuition and fees	Add'l out-of-state/district tuition	Books and supplies	Room and board	Trans-portation	Other costs	Board only	Trans-portation	Other costs
				Costs for campus residents			**Costs for students at home**		
Dabney S. Lancaster Community College	1,342	3,030/—	500				1,500	840	1,500
Danville Community College	1,325	3,030/—	500				1,984	900	2,176
Eastern Mennonite College	9,100		600	3,600	200	400	2,500	200	400
Eastern Shore Community College	1,335	3,030/—	450						2,790
Emory and Henry College	8,546		700	4,230	600	1,000	1,500	1,100	800
Ferrum College	8,800		500	4,000	400	1,200	2,100	600	1,000
George Mason University	† 3,840	6,240/—	610	5,600	1,050	1,100	2,500	1,280	1,100
Hampden-Sydney College	12,974		600	4,398		600			
Hampton University	7,356		600	3,350	1,200	800	1,600	600	800
Hollins College	13,170		500	5,300	350	550		300	1,500
J. Sargeant Reynolds Community College	1,347	3,030/—	600				1,500	900	900
James Madison University	‡ 3,576	3,664/—	500	4,284	530	732	1,896	530	732
John Tyler Community College	‡ 1,244	3,030/—	500				1,500	900	800
Liberty University	6,600		550	4,380	825	825	1,600	1,050	825
Longwood College	4,106	5,084/—	550	3,842	1,000	1,200		1,000	2,000
Lord Fairfax Community College	‡ 1,250	3,030/—	450				1,500	1,152	990
Lynchburg College	11,600		450	5,400	430	440	1,500	390	
Mary Baldwin College	10,654		600	7,046	400	900	1,500	700	900
Mary Washington College	‡ 2,896	3,856/—	550	4,552	1,269	1,048	1,960	1,437	1,590
Marymount University	10,804		400	5,126	450	600	1,800	600	600
Mountain Empire Community College	1,338	3,030/—	500				500	1,000	
National Business College	‡ 4,710		495	4,653	960	500		1,060	500
New River Community College	1,344	3,030/—	250					1,200	950
Norfolk State University	2,745	3,280/—	500	3,600	700	1,200	1,700	1,300	1,200
Northern Virginia Community College	1,360	3,030/—	526				736	1,096	816
Old Dominion University	† 3,788	5,550/—	500	4,450	745	1,170	1,500	1,006	1,170
Patrick Henry Community College	1,330	3,030/—	425				1,500	1,040	840
Paul D. Camp Community College	‡ 1,230	3,030/—	450				1,500	900	900
Piedmont Virginia Community College	1,336	3,030/—	500				1,500	920	1,200
Radford University	‡ 2,746	3,524/—	500	3,922	300	750		600	750
Randolph-Macon College	12,230		350	4,480	250	550	2,535	650	550
Randolph-Macon Woman's College	13,440		350	5,780	265	570	1,500	225	570
Rappahannock Community College	‡ 1,242	3,030/—	500				1,100	1,000	600
Richard Bland College	‡ 1,720	3,230/—	500				1,600	750	1,700
Roanoke College	12,625		450	4,350	600	600	1,500	600	600
St. Paul's College	5,521		486	3,650	950	600	1,600	950	600
Shenandoah University	9,800		450	4,400	900	900	1,500	900	900
Southern Virginia College for Women	10,750		500	5,000	390	1,030	1,700	920	1,030
Southside Virginia Community College	1,330	3,030/—	523				1,500	1,440	1,602
Southwest Virginia Community College	1,330	3,030/—	500				1,500	1,200	1,258
Sweet Briar College	14,015		500	5,755	500	600		500	600
Tidewater Community College	‡ 1,305	3,030/—	400				1,500	750	810
University of Richmond	13,540		600	3,160		1,170	1,740		810
University of Virginia	4,350	7,904/—	600	3,800		1,000			
Virginia Commonwealth University	3,776	6,520/—	500	4,053	1,360	1,740	1,500	1,360	1,740
Virginia Intermont College	8,270		600	3,980	350	990	1,500	1,650	1,440
Virginia Military Institute	4,930	5,820/—	600	3,690	300	1,000			
Virginia Polytechnic Institute and State University	3,812	5,868/—	720	3,196	600	1,600	1,450	600	1,600
Virginia State University	‡ 2,913	3,402/—	500	4,127	500	500	1,350	600	525
Virginia Union University	7,061		500	3,494	450	1,000	1,866	450	1,000
Virginia Wesleyan College	10,275		600	4,800	1,100	1,100	600	1,100	1,100

†Figures are projected for 1993-94. ‡Figures are for 1992-93.

Virginia: Virginia Wesleyan College

All aid		Need-based aid		Grants and scholarships								Financial aid deadlines		Inst aid form	Notes
Total freshmen	Percent receiving aid	Freshmen judged to have need	Percent offered aid	Need-based				Non-need-based							
				Acad	Music/ drama	Art	Athl	Acad	Music/ drama	Art	Athl	Priority	Closing		
514	50	275	100	X				X				6/1	none	X	
													none	X	
236	90			X	X			X				5/1	none	X	
215	66							X				6/1	none		
188	94	130	100					X					4/1	X	
374	62			X				X				6/1	none	X	
2,650	38							X	X		X	3/1	none		
265	62			X				X				3/1	none		
1,139	70							X	X		X	3/31	6/1	X	
190	54			X	X			X	X	X		2/15	3/31		
205	40											6/30	none	X	
2,042	46	840	100	X	X	X		X	X	X	X	2/15	3/19		
				X				X				6/30	none	X	
769	85	539	100	X			X	X	X		X	4/15	none		
687	60	276	96	X				X	X	X	X	2/15	none	X	
800	44	331	91	X								5/1	none	X	
418	80	216	100	X				X	X			4/1	none	X	
199	74	123	100	X	X	X		X	X	X		3/15	4/15	X	
700	35	210	88					X					3/1		
220	48	136	100	X		X		X				3/1	none	X	
1,500	75	560	100	X				X				5/1	none	X	
				X				X					none	X	
434	42			X								4/15	none		
1,534	85							X				4/15	none	X	
5,653	14							X				3/1	none	X	
1,536	63			X	X	X	X	X	X	X	X	2/15	none		
				X				X				6/15	none	X	
782	48	300	100	X				X				7/30	8/16	X	
1,825	15											4/15	none	X	
1,821	47	547	97					X	X	X	X	3/1	none		
305	77	153	100					X				3/1	none	X	
198	62	119	100					X	X			3/1	none	X	
453	25	60	100	X				X				6/1	none		
431	48			X				X				4/1	6/1	X	
423	87	200	100	X	X	X		X	X	X		3/1	none		
196	80							X				6/1	8/11	X	
232	80	143	100	X	X			X	X			3/15	4/1	X	
120	100							X				4/1	8/1		
447	52							X				6/1	8/1	X	
								X				5/30	none	X	
193	56	99	100	X	X			X	X			3/1	none	X	
								X				8/1	none		
766	54	208	100					X	X		X	2/15	2/25		
2,802	40	950	82								X	3/1	none		
1,528	60	900	100					X	X	X	X	3/15	11/1		
130	62	89	100	X		X		X			X	3/1	none	X	
406	54	135	99	X				X			X	3/1	none	X	
3,857	55	2,366	79					X	X	X	X		3/15		
897	85			X		X		X				3/31	5/1	X	
453	87							X	X		X	5/15	none		
302	65			X	X	X		X				3/1	none		

Virginia: Virginia Western Community College

Institution	Tuition and fees	Add'l out-of-state/ district tuition	Books and supplies	Costs for campus residents			Costs for students at home		
				Room and board	Transportation	Other costs	Board only	Transportation	Other costs
Virginia Western Community College	1,324	3,030/—	550				1,600	800	1,200
Washington and Lee University	13,235		600	4,510	400	1,035	2,300	500	1,035
Wytheville Community College	1,335	3,130/—	525				1,600	1,000	800

Washington

Institution	Tuition and fees	Add'l	Books	Room/board	Transp.	Other	Board	Transp.	Other
Antioch University Seattle	‡ 7,845		350						
Art Institute of Seattle	† 8,215		937	4,686	1,767	1,305	2,322	1,017	1,305
Bastyr College	† 6,000		750				2,099	978	690
Bellevue Community College	1,170	3,300/—	700				1,800	900	700
Big Bend Community College	1,125	3,300/—	550	3,300	900	1,200	1,200	650	700
Central Washington University	1,971	4,977/—	650	3,673	780	1,368			
Centralia College	1,125	3,300/—	600					825	600
City University	‡ 6,575		800			1,200	1,050	850	1,200
Clark College	1,178	3,300/—	500				1,560	762	570
Cogswell College North	‡ 7,200		550						
Columbia Basin College	1,164	3,300/—	654				908	978	690
Cornish College of the Arts	‡ 8,730		1,333				1,825	840	600
Eastern Washington University	1,971	4,977/—	654	3,650	978	1,368	1,908	978	690
Edmonds Community College	1,155	3,300/—	654				1,908	978	690
Everett Community College	1,125	3,300/—	500					900	1,000
Evergreen State College	1,971	4,977/—	600		840	1,272	2,040	84	1,272
Gonzaga University	12,300		650	4,150	950	1,450	1,850	950	750
Grays Harbor College	1,125	3,300/—	500				1,570	800	570
Green River Community College	1,140	3,300/—	480				1,800	800	600
Heritage College	† 5,490		648				1,908	978	690
Highline Community College	1,125	3,300/—	560				1,740	880	630
Lower Columbia College	1,152	3,300/—	560				1,750	870	610
Lutheran Bible Institute of Seattle	2,840		500	3,600	760	950		1,000	600
North Seattle Community College	1,125	3,300/—	500				1,570	800	1,000
Northwest College of the Assemblies of God	6,646		660	3,250	200	1,370	1,908	980	690
Olympic College	1,125	3,300/—	653				1,908	978	690
Pacific Lutheran University	12,672		654	4,272	500	1,368	1,908	978	690
Peninsula College	1,125	3,300/—	600	3,600	945	1,350	1,020	945	1,000
Pierce College	1,156	3,300/—	600				1,920	1,000	660
Puget Sound Christian College	† 4,725		600	3,225	300	1,305	2,100	870	975
Renton Technical College	1,275								
St. Martin's College	10,870		654	4,060	880	1,230	1,810	880	614
Seattle Central Community College	1,125	3,300/—	594				1,844	933	668
Seattle Pacific University	11,979		600	4,524	300	1,250	1,500	300	600
Seattle University	12,150		654	4,680	978	1,368	1,908	978	690
Shoreline Community College	1,125	3,300/—	654				1,908	978	690
Skagit Valley College	1,125	3,300/—	690				1,890	975	690
South Puget Sound Community College	1,125	3,300/—	654				1,908	978	690
South Seattle Community College	1,125	3,300/—	600				1,860	960	675
Spokane Community College	1,125	3,300/—	654				1,650	840	510
Spokane Falls Community College	1,125	3,300/—	540				1,620	840	500
Tacoma Community College	1,145	3,300/—	594				1,650	943	600
University of Puget Sound	15,220		600	4,300	480	1,280	1,780	480	1,280
University of Washington	2,532	4,602/—	687	4,086	396	1,725	1,770	396	1,473
Walla Walla College	10,200		675	3,135	220	450	1,500	700	480
Walla Walla Community College	1,156	3,300/—	510				1,650	825	600

†Figures are projected for 1993-94. ‡Figures are for 1992-93.

Washington: Walla Walla Community College

All aid		Need–based aid		Grants and scholarships								Financial aid deadlines		Inst aid form	Notes
Total freshmen	Percent receiving aid	Freshmen judged to have need	Percent offered aid	Need-based				Non-need-based							
				Acad	Music/drama	Art	Athl	Acad	Music/drama	Art	Athl	Priority	Closing		
1,750	20			X				X					none		
435	32			X	X			X				2/1	none		
587	50	350	86	X				X				4/1	none	X	
													none		
300	86			X		X							none		
								X				4/15	none	X	
1,500	26	944	100					X			X	4/1	none	X	
799	50							X	X		X	7/1	none	X	
983	66	409	90	X				X	X			3/15	none		
1,300	50	350	100					X	X		X	4/15	none	X	
													none	X	
3,500	25							X	X		X	5/1	none	X	
				X									8/15	X	
1,005	41	603	95					X	X	X	X	4/1	none	X	
218	75	86	100	X	X	X		X	X	X		2/28	none	X	
803	50	449	93	X	X		X	X	X	X	X	2/15	none		
2,546	22	600	67	X	X		X	X	X	X	X	5/1	none	X	
1,320	20			X	X		X			X	X	5/1	none	X	
402	15							X	X	X	X	3/15	none		
638	83	414	100	X			X	X	X		X	2/10	none		
950	66							X	X	X	X	5/15	none		
2,372	17							X	X	X	X	5/1	none	X	
29	63			X				X				3/10	none	X	
800	28											4/1	none	X	
700	35			X	X	X	X	X	X		X	7/1	none	X	
38	73			X	X			X	X			5/1	none	X	
950	30			X	X	X		X	X	X		6/1	8/31	X	
145	96	110	100	X				X	X	X		3/1	none	X	
2,000	28	590	100	X			X	X	X	X	X	4/30	none	X	
508	79	375	93	X	X	X	X	X	X	X		3/1	5/1		
585	50	300	97	X				X	X	X		6/1	none	X	
3,360	18	515	100					X			X	4/1	none	X	
19	93	18	100	X				X	X			5/1	none	X	
													none		
89	66	31	100	X			X	X			X	3/1	none	X	
2,130	41							X				5/15	8/15	X	
				X	X	X		X	X	X	X	3/1	none		
454	72	290	100		X		X	X	X	X	X	3/1	none		
								X			X	4/1	none	X	
1,500	31	470	94	X	X	X	X	X	X	X	X	4/1	none	X	
1,980	45							X			X	5/15	none	X	
1,259	27							X	X			5/15	none	X	
2,130	70			X			X				X	3/15	none	X	
2,303	85	1,100	100	X			X				X	4/1	none	X	
300	20			X				X	X	X			4/1	X	
725	72	424	100	X	X	X	X	X	X	X		2/15	none		
3,626	30	1,302	89	X	X		X	X			X	2/28	none		
280	54	200	100	X				X	X	X		4/1	none	X	
				X				X	X		X	6/1	none	X	

205

Washington: Washington State University

Institution	Tuition and fees	Add'l out-of-state/district tuition	Books and supplies	Room and board	Trans-portation	Other costs	Board only	Trans-portation	Other costs
Washington State University	2,532	4,602/—	736	3,832	820	1,208	1,539	820	1,208
Wenatchee Valley College	1,125	3,300/—	654	4,236	978	1,368	1,908	978	690
Western Washington University	1,971	4,977/—	618	4,140	945	1,350	1,857	945	1,350
Whatcom Community College	1,125	3,300/—	594				1,845	933	669
Whitman College	15,805		750	4,790		500	2,650	700	1,290
Whitworth College	11,965		500	4,300	700	1,200	1,585	600	900
Yakima Valley Community College	1,156	3,300/—	550	3,570	850	1,150	1,650	850	600
West Virginia									
Alderson-Broaddus College	9,838		630	3,180	526	1,100	1,200	730	1,100
Appalachian Bible College	4,210		520	2,700	740	720	1,500	990	630
Bethany College	13,942		450	4,718	600	800	1,744	1,135	1,000
Bluefield State College	‡ 1,726	2,270/—	800				1,600	900	900
College of West Virginia	† 2,712		500				1,500	850	1,000
Concord College	‡ 1,736	2,130/—	400	3,018	350	1,008	790	697	1,008
Davis and Elkins College	‡ 8,180		400	3,930			2,100		
Fairmont State College	‡ 1,686	2,320/—	500	3,040		500		600	500
Glenville State College	‡ 1,606	2,214/—	350	2,928	200	1,000		900	1,000
Marshall University	‡ 1,792	2,886/1,344	600	3,780	500	1,000	1,500	468	202
Ohio Valley College	† 5,384		425	3,110	400	800	1,500	800	600
Potomac State College of West Virginia University	‡ 1,472	2,806/—	450	3,200		1,120	1,300		1,120
Salem-Teikyo University	9,233		400	3,952	320	300	1,600	320	300
Shepherd College	‡ 1,954	2,520/—	500	3,490	110	900	1,900	810	900
Southern West Virginia Community College	‡ 1,000	1,850/—	450				1,500		900
University of Charleston	9,250		400	3,540	250	500			1,800
West Liberty State College	‡ 1,590	2,670/—	500	2,650	200	900	500	800	650
West Virginia Institute of Technology	‡ 1,784	2,170/—	500	3,752	400	700	1,200	700	700
West Virginia Northern Community College	‡ 1,144	1,992/—	450				1,563	800	1,049
West Virginia State College	‡ 1,712	2,290/—	500	3,050	375	940	1,400	940	1,000
West Virginia University									
Morgantown	‡ 1,928	3,558/—	550	4,016	300	1,155	1,550	1,015	1,160
Parkersburg	‡ 864	2,016/—	470				1,730	1,100	1,270
West Virginia Wesleyan College	13,400		450	3,500	750	1,100	1,500	750	1,100
Wheeling Jesuit College	10,000		600	4,350	500	600		500	600
Wisconsin									
Alverno College	‡ 7,332		550	3,250	500	1,800	1,200	450	1,280
Bellin College of Nursing	† 6,700		470				963	711	666
Beloit College	15,430		350	3,520	400	700	1,500	600	700
Blackhawk Technical College	1,440	8,760/—	425				1,350	400	800
Cardinal Stritch College	7,704		500	3,480	350	1,200	1,700	800	1,200
Carroll College	11,790		400	3,740	200	900		900	
Carthage College	12,400		500	3,595	300	1,000	500	300	1,000
Chippewa Valley Technical College	1,440	8,760/—	400					450	800
Columbia College of Nursing	11,830		350	5,500	275	850		900	850
Concordia University Wisconsin	8,740		600	3,400	120	1,260	2,020	550	1,260
Edgewood College	8,100		575	3,600	265	1,250	950	400	1,250
Fox Valley Technical College	1,440	8,760/—	500					600	800
Gateway Technical College	1,440	8,760/—	538				1,545	562	937
Lakeland College	9,145		500	3,700	700	750	1,000	700	750
Lakeshore Technical College	1,440	8,760/—	625				1,800	650	1,100

†Figures are projected for 1993-94. ‡Figures are for 1992-93.

Wisconsin: Lakeshore Technical College

All aid		Need-based aid		Grants and scholarships								Financial aid deadlines		Inst aid form	Notes
Total freshmen	Percent receiving aid	Freshmen judged to have need	Percent offered aid	Need-based				Non-need-based				Priority	Closing		
				Acad	Music/drama	Art	Athl	Acad	Music/drama	Art	Athl				
2,354	35			X	X	X	X	X	X	X	X	3/1	none	X	
								X	X	X	X	4/1	none		
1,456	66			X	X	X		X	X	X	X	2/28	none		
		608	67					X				6/1	none	X	
344	79	210	100	X	X	X	X	X	X	X			2/15		
317	81	182	100	X	X	X	X	X	X	X		2/15	none	X	
1,925	51			X	X		X					5/1	none	X	
173	94	169	100	X	X		X	X	X		X	5/1	none		
73	91			X								6/1	none		
259	75			X				X				4/1	none		
454	60			X		X		X			X	3/1	none	X	
308	20			X				X				6/1	none		
957	64	392	100	X	X	X	X	X	X	X	X	4/15	none		
209	65			X	X	X	X	X	X	X	X	3/1	none		
1,537	60	1,031	100	X	X		X	X	X		X		3/1	X	
778	73	327	89	X	X	X	X	X	X	X	X		3/1		
2,028	44							X	X	X	X	3/1	none	X	
105	93			X	X	X	X	X	X	X	X	6/1	none		
				X	X		X	X				3/1	none	X	
		151	100	X			X	X			X	4/15	none		
522	22	117	100					X	X	X	X	3/1	none		
913	40			X	X	X		X					none	X	
257	70	143	99	X	X		X	X	X		X	3/1	none	X	
495	60	398	100	X	X	X	X	X	X	X	X	3/1	none		
675	40			X	X		X	X	X		X	1/31	4/1	X	
604	40			X				X				7/1	none	X	
807	55			X	X	X	X	X	X	X	X	3/1	8/10		
3,040	57			X				X	X	X	X	3/1	none	X	
				X				X				5/1	none		
475	94	411	100	X			X	X	X	X	X	3/1	none		
270	89	212	100					X	X		X	3/1	none		
231	75			X	X	X		X	X	X		3/15	none	X	
												3/1	none		
311	86			X	X			X	X			4/15	none	X	
838	30	294	83									4/1	6/15	X	
253	82	82	100	X				X	X	X	X	4/1	none	X	
460	90	258	100	X	X	X		X	X	X		4/15	none	X	
419	89	307	100					X	X	X		2/15	none		
2,500	76	1,470	93	X				X				3/15	none	X	
68	88			X				X				4/15	none		
295	90	240	100					X	X		X	5/1	6/1	X	
143	85	72	100	X	X	X		X	X	X		3/15	none	X	
1,902	75			X				X					none	X	
													5/1	X	
649	95			X	X		X	X				5/1	8/1	X	
874	70	605	78										none	X	

Wisconsin: Lawrence University

Institution	Tuition and fees	Add'l out-of-state/ district tuition	Books and supplies	Room and board	Trans-portation	Other costs	Board only	Trans-portation	Other costs
Lawrence University	16,431		500	3,555		700			700
Madison Area Technical College	1,440	8,760/—	600				1,600	600	950
Madison Junior College of Business	‡ 4,050						1,135	196	906
Maranatha Baptist Bible College	4,820		460	2,700	345	920	1,080	345	920
Marian College of Fond du Lac	8,700		500	4,790		1,100	1,505	1,100	1,100
Marquette University	10,850		600	4,450	1,000	1,350	1,790	1,000	1,350
Mid-State Technical College	1,440	8,760/—	643				1,797	1,280	464
Milwaukee College of Business	‡ 6,075								
Milwaukee Institute of Art & Design	‡ 8,410		1,000				2,250	630	1,080
Milwaukee School of Engineering	10,800		1,000	3,480	850	1,145	1,500	850	1,145
Moraine Park Technical College	1,440	8,760/—	643				1,797	653	1,091
Mount Mary College	8,100		500	2,868	400	1,125	1,485	650	1,125
Mount Senario College	7,720		600	3,250	580	1,350	1,825	970	1,800
Nicolet Area Technical College	1,440	8,760/—	660				1,770	654	1,092
Northcentral Technical College	1,440	8,760/—	600	3,500			1,750	700	1,200
Northeast Wisconsin Technical College	1,440	8,760/—	645				1,798	653	1,091
Northland College	9,800		450	3,750	600	1,000	2,190	500	1,000
Northwestern College	3,455		255	1,790	550	1,270		550	
Ripon College	14,520		350	3,810		650	2,000		650
St. Norbert College	11,465		425	4,245	350	750	900	450	750
Silver Lake College	8,280		500	3,414	1,000	972	1,704	1,000	972
Southwest Wisconsin Technical College	1,440	8,760/—	540				1,200	300	700
Stratton College	5,740		850				2,320	520	1,542
University of Wisconsin									
Eau Claire	† 2,189	4,454/—	175	3,300	750	1,235	1,010	880	750
Green Bay	† 2,120	4,478/—	470	2,807	387	1,332	963	711	666
La Crosse	† 2,200	4,450/—	150	2,300	320	1,630	750	170	1,430
Madison	† 2,550	5,960/—	535	4,000	265	1,200	1,500	285	1,200
Oshkosh	† 2,062	4,356/—	494	2,400	342	1,457		600	1,200
Parkside	† 2,100	4,500/—	500	3,650	650	1,100		650	950
Platteville	† 2,200	4,200/—	300	2,550	400	1,100	1,700	690	930
River Falls	‡ 1,958	4,185/—	175	2,240	456	1,100	1,700	676	1,100
Stevens Point	† 2,250	4,520/—	300	3,030	360	1,190	1,500	280	1,190
Stout	‡ 1,974	4,185/—	342	2,462	394	1,340		510	1,104
Superior	† 2,050	4,478/—	525	2,470	575	1,350		575	1,350
Whitewater	‡ 1,985	4,185/—	450	2,252	500	1,040	1,925	855	1,040
University of Wisconsin Center									
Baraboo/Sauk County	† 1,485	3,207/—	375				1,175	650	700
Barron County	† 1,784	3,482/—	450				1,240	665	2,645
Fox Valley	† 1,632	3,700/—	300				1,700	1,200	1,000
Manitowoc County	† 1,590	3,600/—	400				1,250	670	1,000
Marathon County	† 1,514	3,482/—	320	2,348	550	900	1,140	550	940
Marinette County	‡ 1,500	3,482/—	380				1,140	610	670
Marshfield/Wood County	† 1,514	3,482/—	250				1,100	600	800
Richland	† 1,630	3,482/—	450		670	1,170	1,250	670	770
Rock County	† 1,508	3,482/—	375				1,140	580	640
Sheboygan County	‡ 1,506	3,482/—	380				1,140	610	670
Washington County	† 1,560	3,482/—	450				1,250	670	770
Waukesha	‡ 1,500	3,482/—	375				1,140	580	640
Viterbo College	8,770		600	3,360	640	1,500	1,500	640	1,000
Waukesha County Technical College	1,440	8,760/—	643					653	1,091
Western Wisconsin Technical College	1,440	8,760/—	600		590	975	2,000	590	975

†Figures are projected for 1993-94. ‡Figures are for 1992-93.

Wisconsin: Western Wisconsin Technical College

All aid		Need-based aid		Grants and scholarships									Financial aid deadlines		Inst aid form	Notes
Total freshmen	Percent receiving aid	Freshmen judged to have need	Percent offered aid	Need-based					Non-need-based							
				Acad	Music/ drama	Art	Athl		Acad	Music/ drama	Art	Athl	Priority	Closing		
325	83	197	100	X	X				X	X			3/15	none	X	
									X				6/1	none		
78	48								X					none	X	
152	68	130	100	X					X				6/30	8/1	X	
350	90			X	X	X	X		X	X	X	X	3/1	none	X	
1,658	93	1,071	100	X					X	X		X	3/1	none	X	
2,117	65			X			X		X				5/1	none	X	
													6/1	none		
142	65	73	100								X		3/1	none	X	
530	85	375	100						X				4/1	none		
856	40	600	100						X				5/1	none	X	
124	93	72	100	X	X	X			X	X	X		3/15	none	X	
182	93	95	98	X					X				4/1	none		
666	75			X					X				4/15	none		
1,700	66												4/1	none		
									X					none		
215	80	160	100	X	X		X		X	X		X	5/1	none		
42	95	36	92	X					X				5/1	none	X	
191	85	158	100	X	X				X	X			3/1	none		
521	91	354	100	X	X	X			X	X	X		3/1	none	X	
40	95	31	100	X	X	X	X		X	X	X	X	3/15	none		
402	80			X									4/15	none		
255	76	185	100						X					none	X	
1,873	74	820	100	X	X				X	X			2/28	4/15	X	
802	60			X			X		X	X	X	X	4/15	none		
1,592	45	900	89	X					X	X			3/15	none	X	
4,416	39	1,772	100						X	X	X	X	3/1	none	X	
1,488	45	700	100	X					X	X	X		3/15	none		
746	35			X	X	X	X		X	X	X	X	4/1	6/15	X	
880	75	690	90	X					X				3/15	none	X	
1,026	72								X	X	X		3/18	none		
1,398	60								X	X	X		3/15	7/15		
999	59	543	93	X					X	X	X		4/15	none		
676	68	300	100	X	X	X			X				4/15	5/1	X	
				X	X				X	X			4/15	none		
313	48	150	100	X					X	X	X		4/15	none	X	
				X	X	X			X	X	X		3/1	none	X	
				X					X				4/15	none	X	
166	30			X					X				3/1	none	X	
371	73	221	100	X	X	X			X	X	X		4/15	none	X	
222	60			X					X				3/1	none	X	
289	46			X					X				4/15	none	X	
207	60			X	X	X			X	X	X		4/15	8/1	X	
365	50			X	X				X	X			4/15	none	X	
193	22			X					X				4/15	none	X	
269	23			X	X		X		X	X			4/15	none	X	
703	16			X					X	X			3/1	none	X	
247	88	190	100						X	X	X		3/1	none	X	
1,320	15			X					X					none	X	
973	60												3/1	none	X	

Wisconsin: Wisconsin Indianhead Technical College

				Costs for campus residents			Costs for students at home		
Institution	Tuition and fees	Add'l out-of-state/ district tuition	Books and supplies	Room and board	Trans-portation	Other costs	Board only	Trans-portation	Other costs
Wisconsin Indianhead Technical College	1,440	8,760/—	535					590	945
Wisconsin Lutheran College	8,680		500	3,500	300	1,125	1,500	600	990
Wyoming									
Casper College	820	1,400/—	500	2,330	450	900	1,500	450	450
Central Wyoming College	976	1,400/—	500	3,375	500	1,000	1,800	400	750
Eastern Wyoming College	880	1,400/—	500	2,400	525	1,300	1,750	325	1,300
Laramie County Community College	‡ 792	1,248/—	400	3,236	250	500		650	600
Northwest College	944	1,400/—	500	2,690	866	1,000	1,500	600	800
Sheridan College	844	1,400/—	450	2,450	540	800	1,500	540	800
University of Wyoming	1,698	3,534/—	560	3,344	548	1,500	1,660	302	780
Western Wyoming Community College	‡ 756	1,248/—	400	2,400	500	950	1,450	250	950
American Samoa, Caroline Islands, Guam, Marianas, Virgin Islands									
College of Micronesia-FSM	1,900		430	2,352	1,494	1,000	1,500	640	1,000
Guam Community College	325		504				1,500	825	1,447
Micronesian Occupational College	‡ 2,200		200	2,352	871	300	1,764		
University of the Virgin Islands	‡ 1,440	2,700/—	425	4,300	650	800	2,400	600	800
Arab Republic of Egypt									
American University in Cairo	8,045		600		1,400	1,200		100	
Canada									
McGill University	† 1,950	5,740/—	1,000	5,704		1,500		500	1,500
France									
American University of Paris	14,706		750				4,030	300	1,000
Mexico									
Sistema Instituto Tecnologico y de Estudios Superiores de Monterrey	‡ 4,967		500						
Switzerland									
American College of Switzerland	‡ 18,675		1,000	5,225		3,600			
Franklin College: Switzerland	‡ 16,430		400		1,000	3,600			

†Figures are projected for 1993-94. ‡Figures are for 1992-93.

Switzerland: Franklin College: Switzerland

All aid		Need–based aid		Grants and scholarships								Financial aid deadlines		Inst aid form	Notes
				Need–based				Non–need–based							
Total freshmen	Percent receiving aid	Freshmen judged to have need	Percent offered aid	Acad	Music/ drama	Art	Athl	Acad	Music/ drama	Art	Athl	Priority	Closing		
1,736	75			X				X					none		
75	90			X				X	X	X	X	4/1	none	X	
				X	X	X	X	X	X	X	X	4/1	none	X	
123	43			X	X	X	X	X	X	X	X	4/15	none	X	
520	76							X	X	X	X	3/15	none		
786	75			X	X	X	X	X	X	X	X	4/1	none		
672	78							X	X	X	X		none	X	
431	38							X	X	X	X	3/1	none		
1,309	54	590	98	X				X	X	X	X	3/1	none	X	
1,074	49							X	X	X	X	4/1	none		
443	100			X									none	X	
231	6			X				X				5/1	none	X	
166	98			X								6/1	none	X	
730	80							X					4/15		
772	80	166	100					X	X	X	X				
				X			X						none	X	
145	20	57	100	X				X				3/1	5/1	X	
				X				X					4/30	X	
				X								4/1	none	X	
		20	100	X									3/15	X	

211

Sources of information about state grant programs and the Federal Stafford Loan Program

State scholarships and grants

The major state scholarship and grant programs are described in the following list. Included in the description of each program are eligibility requirements, average awards, and the address of the administrative agency. Unless otherwise indicated, funds are available to state residents who are enrolled for full-time study at eligible postsecondary institutions in their state of residence.

Alabama

Alabama Student Assistance Program—Variable grants at in-state postsecondary institutions.

Alabama Student Grant Program—Non-need-based grants of up to $1,200 at private nonprofit colleges and universities.

National Guard Educational Assistance Program—Available to members of the Alabama National Guard for college study. Pays for tuition, fees, books, and supplies up to $500 per term or $1,000 per year.

Emergency Secondary Education Scholarship Loan Program—Available to mathematics and science education majors in accredited teacher education programs, up to $4,000 per year.

Teacher Re-Certification Scholarship Loan Program—Available to public school teachers working for their certification in critical-need fields, i.e. mathematics and science. Up to $4,000 per year.

For more information, contact the Alabama Commission on Higher Education, One Court Square, Suite 221, Montgomery, AL 36104-3584.

Alaska

Alaska State Educational Incentive Grant—Need-based grants of up to $1,500 for use by Alaska residents at eligible in-state and out-of-state postsecondary institutions.

For more information, contact the Alaska Commission on Postsecondary Education, P.O. Box 110505, Juneau, AK 99811-0505.

Arizona

Arizona State Student Incentive Grant Program—Need-based grants of up to $1,500 for use by Arizona residents at eligible in-state and out-of state postsecondary institutions.

For more information, contact the financial aid office at the institution you wish to attend.

Arkansas

Arkansas Student Assistance Grant Program—Need-based grants of $200 to $624 at colleges and universities.

Governor's Scholars Program—100 merit-based $2,000 scholarships for attendance at colleges and universities in Arkansas, renewable for four years, awarded to high school seniors.

Emergency Secondary Education Loan Program—Available to secondary school education majors in shortage areas. Must pursue secondary teacher certification in state. Loans up to $2,500.

Paul Douglas Teacher Scholarship Program—Loans up to $5,000 available to education majors. Must pursue teacher certification in state.

For more information, contact the Department of Higher Education, 114 East Capitol, Little Rock, AR 72201.

California

As of June 1993: Three state student aid programs: Cal Grant A—Grants of $700 to $5,250 at independent colleges, $700 to $1,854 at the University of California, and $700 to $1,025 at California State University. Cal Grant B—Subsistence grants of $700 to $1,410 and in some cases tuition. Cal Grant C—Grants of up to $2,360 for tuition plus $530 for training-related expenses at vocational and technical schools.

For more information, contact the California Student Aid Commission, P.O. Box 510845, Sacramento, CA 94245-0845.

Colorado

Student Grant—Need-based grants of up to $2,000 at eligible postsecondary institutions.

Scholarship Program for Undergraduate Students—Scholarships of up to the amount of resident tuition and mandatory student fees at in-state institutions.

For more information, contact the financial aid office at the institution you wish to attend.

Connecticut

State Scholastic Achievement Grant Program—Grants of up to $2,000 may be taken to Connecticut colleges. Grants of up to $500 may be taken to colleges located in reciprocal states. Based on academic performance and financial need. February 15 application deadline.

For more information, contact the Department of Higher Education, 61 Woodland Street, Hartford, CT 06105.

Delaware

Delaware Postsecondary Scholarship Fund—Need-based grants of $600 to $1,000 at approved Delaware or Pennsylvania colleges and at colleges in other states if the program of study is not offered at Delaware tax-supported colleges.

For more information, contact the Delaware Higher Education Commission, 820 North French Street, Fourth Floor, Wilmington, DE 19801.

District of Columbia

District of Columbia Student Incentive Grant Program—Grants of $400 to $1,000 for the 1993-94 academic year. Renewable.

Paul Douglas Teacher Scholarship—Scholarships of $5,000 per academic year for up to four years to outstanding high school graduates pursuing teaching careers. Students must rank in top 10 percent of graduating class.

For more information, contact the D.C. Office of Postsecondary Education, Research and Assistance, 2100 Martin Luther King, Jr. Ave., S.E., Suite 401, Washington, DC 20020.

Florida

Florida Student Assistance Grant Program—Grants of $200 to $1,500 at eligible Florida colleges. One-year state residency required.

State Tuition Voucher Fund—Non-need grants of up to $2,000 at eligible private Florida colleges and universities. One-year state residency required.

Florida Undergraduate Scholars' Fund—Scholarships of up to $2,500 at eligible Florida colleges and universities. One-year state residency required.

For more information, contact the Florida Department of Education, Office of Student Financial Assistance, 1344 Florida Education Center, Tallahassee, FL 32399-0400.

Georgia

Georgia Student Incentive Grant Program—Grants of $300 to $2,500 at nonprofit postsecondary institutions.

Georgia Tuition Equalization Grant Program—Grants of $1,000 at private colleges. Does not require financial need.

Law Enforcement Personnel Dependents Grant—$2,000 a year for dependents of Georgia Law Enforcement Personnel who have been killed or rendered disabled in the line of duty.

For more information, contact the Georgia Student Finance Authority, 2082 East Exchange Place, Suite 200, Tucker, GA 30084

Hawaii

Tuition Waivers and Pacific-Asian Scholarships—provide for tuition expenses at campuses of the University of Hawaii.

Hawaii Student Incentive Grant Program—Grants covering tuition expenses at nonprofit postsecondary institutions.

For more information, contact the financial aid office at the institution you wish to attend.

Idaho

State of Idaho Scholarship—Grants of up to $2,650 per year at public and private postsecondary institutions. Based on academic ability.

Paul Douglas Teacher Scholarship Program—Federally funded scholarships of $5,000 per year for students pursuing teacher certification.

Governor's Cup Scholarship Program—Grants of $3,000 based on academic ability.

Paul L. Fowler Scholarship Program—Memorial one-time grant of $2,830 to Idaho high school graduates. Based on academic ability.

For more information, contact the Office of the State Board of Education, 650 West State Street, Boise, ID 83720.

Illinois

General Assembly Scholarships—Waivers of tuition and fees at public postsecondary institutions. Selection by general assembly members from residents of their districts.

For more information on this program contact your district legislator directly.

Illinois Monetary Award Program—Need-based grants of up to $3,500 at approved postsecondary institutions for half-time (6 hours minimum) and full-time study.

Illinois Merit Recognition Scholarship—$1,000 scholarships to Illinois students who rank in the top 5 percent of their high school classes at the end of the seventh semester. Financial need is not a factor. Not renewable.

Paul Douglas Teacher Scholarship—A federally funded program administered by the Illinois Student Assistance Commission providing scholarships of up to $5,000 per year to outstanding Illinois students who plan to become teachers at the elementary or high school level. Students must rank in the top 10 percent of their high school classes and may receive the award for four years.

For more information, contact the Illinois Student Assistance Commission, 1755 Lake Cook Road, Deerfield, IL 60015.

Indiana

Higher Education Awards—Grants of $200 to $3,500 for full-time students at private, nonprofit in-state postsecondary institutions and of $200 to $1,500 at state-supported universities. Based on need. Awarded to Indiana residents working on their first undergraduate degree.

Hoosier Scholar Awards—One-time grants of $500 to residents in the top 20 percent of their graduating class who are nominated by their high schools. Financial need is not considered.

Paul Douglas Teacher Scholarship—Federally funded program providing renewable scholarships of up to $5,000 per year for students committed to a career in teaching who graduated in the top 10 percent of their high school class. Obligation to teach two years for every year scholarship is received.

Minority Teacher Scholarship—Grants of up to $1,000 for black or Hispanic students who want to be teachers. Renewable for up to four out of six years. Obligation to teach in Indiana for three out of five years following certification.

Services Special Education Scholarship—Grants of up to $1,000 for students who desire to teach in the field of Special Education. Renewable for up to four out of six years at eligible nonprofit or public postsecondary institutions. Obligation to teach in Indiana for three out of five years after certification.

Nursing Scholarship—Need-based grants for tuition of up to $5,000 for students who attend eligible nonprofit and public postsecondary institutions with nursing programs. Award is renewable.

State Work-Study Program—Summer work available to students who receive the Higher Education Grant or Lilly Grant during the preceding academic year. Funds awarded statewide to employers to reimburse 50 percent of student earnings.

For more information, contact the State Student Assistance Commission of Indiana, 150 W. Market Street, Suite 500, Indianapolis, IN 46204.

Iowa

Iowa Grants—Grants of $1,000 based on financial need for Iowa residents attending Iowa public, independent, and community colleges. Grants may be prorated for less than full-time study.

Iowa Tuition Grant program—Grants of up to $2,650 at private institutions (including nursing and business schools) for part-time and full-time study.

Iowa Vocational-Technical Tuition Grant Program—Grants of up to $600 at two-year public vocational and technical institutions for full-time study.

State of Iowa Scholarship Program—Grants of $400 to Iowa residents who rank in the top 15 percent of senior class. Based on academic ability. Award to freshmen only.

Paul Douglas Teacher Scholarship Program—Federally funded grants of up to $5,000 a year for Iowa students who plan to become teachers. Must rank in the top 10 percent of class and be a State of Iowa Scholarship applicant. Award is renewable for four years.

Robert C. Byrd Honors Scholarsh Program—Federally funded grants of $1,500 to promote student excellence and achievement and to recognize exceptionally able students who show promise of continued excellence. Applicants must be Iowa residents and accepted at an approved post-secondary school.

For more information, contact the Iowa College Student Aid Commission, 914 Grand Avenue, Suite 201, Des Moines, IA 50309-2824.

Kansas

Kansas Tuition Grant Program—Grants of up to $1,700 at private, nonprofit postsecondary institutions.

State Scholarship Program—Stipends of up to $1,000. Based on academic ability and financial need.

Kansas Minority Scholarship—Stipends of up to $1,500 a year for minority students attending in-state two- or four-year colleges. Based on academic ability and need.

Kansas Teacher Scholarship—Up to $5,000 a year for students who will teach in Kansas one year for each year of funding.

Paul T. Douglas Teacher Scholarship—Federally funded grants of up to $5,000 a year for Kansas students who plan to teach. Recipients must teach two years for every year of funding.

Kansas Nursing Scholarship—Up to $2,500 a year for students pursuing LPN degrees; $3,500 a year for those pursuing RPN degrees.

For more information, contact the Board of Regents, 700 SW Harrison, Suite 1410, Topeka, KS 66603-3760.

Kentucky

College Access Program Grant—Need-based grants of up to $840 per year for full-time undergraduates ($35 per semester hour for part-time) who attend public and private colleges and universities. All awards are based upon community college tuition rates.

Kentucky Tuition Grant Program—Need-based grants of up to $1,200 per year at eligible private, nonprofit postsecondary institutions.

Paul Douglas Teacher Scholarship Program—Federally funded awards of up to $5,000 per year to students who rank in the top 10 percent of class or on the GED and sign an intent to become a certified teacher and to render teaching service in any state.

Teacher Scholarship Program—Awards up to $5,000 per year to Kentucky residents who intend to become teachers or teachers who wish to pursue certification in a critical shortage area. One year of teaching in a Kentucky-accredited school required for each year of award or one semester of teaching in a critical shortage area required for every two semesters of award.

For more information, contact KHEAA Student Aid Program, 1050 U.S. 127 South, Suite 102, Frankfort, KY 40601.

Louisiana

State Student Incentive Grant Program—Grants of $200 to $2,000 at eligible postsecondary institutions.

Louisiana Honors Scholarship Program—Tuition waivers to students who graduate in top 5% of graduating class from Louisiana public or state-approved nonpublic high schools. Must be enrolled as full-time undergraduates.

Louisiana Tuition Assistance Plan—Tuition exemption for Louisiana residents who attend public colleges full-time and meet specific academic and financial need criteria.

T.H. Harris State Academic Scholarsh—Awards based on academic achievement for Louisiana high school graduates attending public colleges within the state. 3.0 GPA required. $400 per year with 5-year maximum of $2,000.

Rockefeller Scholarship for Wildlife Programs—Up to $1,000 per year for students in forestry, wildlife management, fisheries, and marine science programs. A 2.5 overall grade-point average is required. Does not require financial need.

Paul Douglas Teacher Scholarship Program—$5,000 per year for students with a high school average of 3.0 and ACT composite score of 23 and who rank in the top 10 percent of their high school graduating class or who have a college average of 3.0 with 24 or more hours of college credit and graduated in the top 10 percent of their high school class.

For more information, contact the Office of Student Financial Assistance for Louisiana, P.O. Box 91202, Baton Rouge, LA 70821-9202.

Maine

Maine Student Incentive Scholarship Program—Need-based grants of $500 to $1,000 for Maine Students attending eligible postsecondary institutions in New England, Pennsylvania, Maryland, District of Columbia, Alabama and Delaware.

For more information, contact the Finance Authority of Maine, Maine Education Assistance Division, State House Station 119, Augusta ME 04333.

Maryland

General State Scholarship Program—Grants of $200 to $2,500 at public or private postsecondary institutions. Undergraduate awards based on need.

House of Delegates Grant Program—Variable amounts, $200 minimum, to assist with tuition and fees at public and private postsecondary institutions for half-time and full-time study. Undergraduate and graduate students eligible.

Senatorial Scholarship Program—Grants of $200 to $2,000 at postsecondary institutions for half-time and full-time study. Undergraduate, graduate, and non-degree seeking students eligible.

Distinguished Scholar Program—$3,000 undergraduate annual awards based on merit or artistic talent for students nominated by their high schools or who are Merit/Achievement finalists.

For more information, contact the Maryland Higher Education Commission/State Scholarship Administration, 16 Francis Street, Annapolis, MD 21401-1781.

Massachusetts

General Scholarship Program—Grants of $200 to $2,500 for Massachusetts residents attending full-time eligible in-state (and reciprocal state) postsecondary institutions.

Tuition-Waiver Program—Up to the full cost of tuition waived for students attending a state-supported college or university. Amount of waiver determined by the financial aid office.

For more information, contact the Higher Education Coordinating Council, State Scholarship Office, 330 Stuart Street, Boston, MA 02116

Michigan

Tuition Grant Program—Need-based grants of up to $1,900 at independent nonprofit colleges and universities.

Competitive Scholarship Program—Awards based on ACT scores and financial need.

For more information, contact Michigan Department of Education, Office of Student Financial Assistance, P.O. Box 30008, Lansing, MI 48909.

Minnesota

Minnesota State Grant Program—Grants from $100 to $5,706.

Interstate Tuition Reciprocity Programs—Under these programs Minnesota residents pay a tuition rate that is less than the normal out-of-state charges at public collegiate and vocational institutions in Wisconsin, North Dakota, South Dakota, some Iowa institutions, and the Canadian province of Manitoba.

For more information, contact the Minnesota Higher Education Coordinating Board, 550 Cedar Street, Suite 400, St. Paul, MN 55101.

Mississippi

State Student Incentive Grant—Grants of $200 to $1,500.

For more information, contact your college financial aid office or the Mississippi Postsecondary Education Financial Assistance Board, 3825 Ridgewood Road, Jackson, MS 39211-6453.

Missouri

Student Grant Program—Grants of up to $1,500 (averaging $1,200) for study at undergraduate nonprofit Missouri postsecondary institutions. Divinity, theology, or religion majors are not eligible. Based on need; renewable.

Missouri Higher Education Academic Scholarship Program—Grants of up to $2,000 for full-time undergraduate students at eligible Missouri institutions. Students must have ACT composite scores or SAT combined scores in top 3 percent of all Missouri students taking those tests. Theology or divinity majors are not eligible. State residency required.

For more information, contact the Missouri Coordinating Board for Higher Education, P.O. Box 1438, Jefferson City, MO 65102.

Montana

Montana Student Incentive Grant Program—Grants of up to $900 at public postsecondary institutions and the three private colleges.

Honor Scholarships—Tuition and fee waivers at public postsecondary institutions.

For more information, contact the Montana University System, 2500 East Broadway, Helena, MT 59620-3101.

Nebraska

For more information about the Scholarship Assistance Program and State Scholarship Award Program, contact a Nebraska postsecondary education institution.

Nevada

Nevada Student Incentive Grant Program—Grants of up to $2,500 for half-time and full-time study.

For more information, contact Nevada Department of Education, Financial Aid, 400 West King Street, Carson City, NV 89710.

New Hampshire

New Hampshire Incentive Program—Need-based grants of $100 to $1,000 for undergraduate, full-time students. Grants portable by New Hampshire residents to five other New England states. Rank in upper three-fifths of high school graduating class required of first-time freshmen, 2.0 college average required of those with sophomore standing and above.

For more information, contact the New Hampshire Postsecondary Education Commission, 2 Industrial Park Drive, Concord, NH 03301.

New Jersey

Tuition Aid Grant Program—Grants of $400 to $4,580 at in-state colleges only.

Educational Opportunity Fund Grant Program—Grants of $200 to $1,950 at in-state colleges only.

Edward J. Bloustein Distinguished Scholars Program—Grants of $1,000 per year at in-state colleges only. Based on academic ability.

Garden State Scholar Program—Grants of $500 per year at in-state colleges only. Based on academic ability.

For more information, contact the Department of Higher Education, Office of Student Assistance, CN 540, Trenton, NJ 08625.

New Mexico

New Mexico Scholars Program—Scholarship provides tuition, required student fees, and books for an academic year for outstanding high school students attending eligible postsecondary institutions as full-time students. Renewable up to four times. Student must have combined family income below $30,000.

New Mexico Student Choice Grant Program—For undergraduates attending an eligible private postsecondary institution and who are enrolled at least half-time.

New Mexico Student Incentive Grant Program—Need-based grants of $200 to $2,500 per year at public and private postsecondary institutions.

New Mexico Vietnam Veterans' Scholarship Program—Tuition grants for undergraduate and graduate students attending postsecondary institutions.

For more information, contact New Mexico Educational Assistance Foundation, P.O. Box 27020, Albuquerque, NM 87125-7020.

New York

New York Tuition Assistance Program—Grants of $100 to $4,050 depending on type of institution and need. Annual; available to undergraduate or graduate students.

Vietnam Veterans Tuition Awards—Grants of $1,000 per semester for full-time study and $500 per semester for part-time study for eligible applicants who served in the U.S. Armed Forces between January 1, 1963, and May 7, 1975.

For more information, contact the Higher Education Services Corporation, Student Information, 99 Washington Avenue, 14th Floor, Albany, NY 12255.

North Carolina

North Carolina Legislative Tuition Grant Program—Grants of up to $1,150 annually at private colleges and universities. Does not require financial need.

North Carolina Student Incentive Grant Program—Grants of up to $1,500 or one-half of unmet need, whichever is less, at colleges, universities, and technical and vocational schools.

North Carolina Student Loan Program for Health, Science, and Mathematics—Scholarships/loans ranging from $2,500 to $7,500 annually depending on degree level, to be repaid through practice service in the state. Available to legal residents in accredited associate, baccalaureate, master's or doctoral programs.

North Carolina Teaching Fellows Program—Grants of up to $5,000 to encourage entry into the elementary and secondary teaching profession. May be used to attend 13 designated institutions of North Carolina (11 public, 2 private). Does not require financial need.

State Contractual Scholarship Fund—Grants at eligible North Carolina private colleges and universities, based on need.

For more information, contact the North Carolina State Education Assistance Authority, Box 2688, Chapel Hill, NC 27515-2688.

North Dakota

Student Financial Assistance Program—Grants of up to $600 for attendance at public and nonprofit postsecondary institutions.

North Dakota Scholars Program—Tuition Scholarships available to students who score at the 95th percentile or above on ACT, and who rank in the top 20 percent of their graduating class.

For more information, contact the Student Financial Assistance Program, State Capitol, Tenth Floor, 600 East Boulevard, Bismarck, ND 58505.

Ohio

Instructional Grant Program—Grants of up to $3,306 at Ohio and Pennsylvania approved private postsecondary institutions and up to $1,326 at Ohio and Pennsylvania approved public postsecondary institutions and up to $2,268 at Ohio and Pennsylvania approved proprietary institutions. For full-time undergraduates enrolled in eligible associate or bachelor's degree or nursing diploma programs.

Ohio Academic Scholarship Program—Scholarships of $1,000 per year at eligible public, private, and proprietary postsecondary Ohio institutions. Based on high school academic ability. For undergraduate students only.

Ohio Student Choice Grant Program—Grants in varying amounts at eligible private postsecondary Ohio institutions. For full-time undergraduates enrolled in a bachelor's degree program who did not attend any institution full-time before July 1, 1984.

For more information, contact the Student Assistance Office, Ohio Board of Regents, 3600 State Office Tower, 30 East Broad Street, Columbus OH 43266-0417.

Oklahoma

Tuition Aid Grant Program—Grants of up to $1,000 or 75 percent of tuition and fees, whichever is less, at eligible colleges, universities, and vocational-technical schools. Based on financial need. Available to undergraduate and graduate students, full-time and part-time.

For more information, contact the Oklahoma State Regents for Higher Education, Tuition Aid Grant Program, P.O. Box 3020, Oklahoma City, OK 73101-3020.

Oregon

Need Grant Program—Need-based grants of up to $1,920 at accredited non-profit postsecondary institutions.

For more information, contact the Oregon State Scholarship Commission, Valley River Office Park, 1500 Valley River Drive, Suite 100, Eugene, OR 97401.

Pennsylvania

State Higher Education Grant Program—Grants up to $2,400 or 80 percent of tuition and fees, whichever is less, at in-state postsecondary institutions; up to $600 at approved out-of-state postsecondary institutions.

POW/MIA Grant Program—Grants of $100 to $1,200 for dependents of U.S. Armed Forces veterans who were taken prisoner or declared missing-in-action; for use at in-state postsecondary institutions. Lower limits at eligible out-of-state institutions.

Veterans Grant Program—Grants up to $2,400 or 80 percent of tuition and fees, whichever is less, at in-state postsecondary institutions; up to $800 at approved out-of-state postsecondary institutions for applicants who served in the U.S. Armed Forces.

Paul Douglas Teacher Scholarship Program—Scholarships to outstanding high school graduates to enable and encourage them to pursue teaching careers at the preschool, elementary, or secondary levels. Grants of up to $5,000 for a maximum of four years.

For more information, contact the Pennsylvania Higher Education Assistance Agency, 660 Boas Street, Harrisburg, PA 17102.

Puerto Rico

Legislative Scholarship Program—Grants for attendance at the University of Puerto Rico.

Supplemental Aid Program—University of Puerto Rico institutional program for supplemental aid that provides additional aid to needy students.

Legislative Scholarship Program—Grants for attendance at private accredited institutions of higher education.

Educational Fund—Grants for attendance at private accredited institutions of higher education.

Paul Douglas Teacher Scholarship Program—Scholarship to outstanding high school graduates to enable and encourage them to pursue teaching careers at the preschool, elementary, or secondary levels. Grants of up to $5,000 for a maximum of four years.

Robert C. Byrd Honor Scholarship program—Scholarships to promote student excellence and to recognize exceptionally able students. Grants are $1,500 for one academic year.

Rosa A. Axtmayer Scholarship Program—Grants to needy students for attendance at the University of Puerto Rico.

For more information, contact the Council on Higher Education, Box 23305-UPR Station, Rio Piedras, PR 00931.

Rhode Island

State Grant or Scholarship Program—Scholarships and grants of up to $800 at eligible in-state and out-of-state postsecondary institutions. Scholarships based on SAT scores and financial need; grants based on financial need.

For more information, contact the Rhode Island Higher Education Assistance Authority, 560 Jefferson Boulevard, Warwick, RI 02886.

South Carolina

Tuition Grants Program—Need-based grants of up to $2,890 for 1993-94 at in-state private postsecondary institutions.

For more information, contact the Tuition Grants Commission, First Floor, Keenan Building, P.O. Box 12159, Columbia, SC 29211.

South Dakota

South Dakota Student Incentive Grant Program—Grants of up to $600 at participating postsecondary institutions.

South Dakota Tuition Equalization Grant—Grants of up to $300 at participating in-state private colleges.

South Dakota Superior Scholarship—South Dakota resident students identified as National Merit Scholarship semifinalists pursuant to the October 1982 Preliminary SATt/National Merit Scholarship Qualifying Test (PSAT/NMSQT) testing date through 1992, who were enrolled in 1992-93 at participating South Dakota colleges and universities are eligible for scholarships of up to $1,500.

National Guard Tuition—Members of the Army or Air National Guard of the state of South Dakota attending any undergraduate-level institution under the control of the Board of Regents or a state vocational institution are entitled to a 50 percent reduction of tuition charges. There is a four-year limit.

Paul Douglas Teacher Scholarship Program—Scholarships to outstanding high school graduates to enable and encourage them to pursue teaching careers at the preschool, elementary, or secondary levels. Grants of up to $5,000 for a maximum of four years.

Robert C. Byrd Honors Scholarship Program—Scholarships to promote student excellence and achievement and to recognize exceptionally able students who show promise of continued excellence. Grants are $1,500.

For more information, contact the Department of Education and Cultural Affairs, Office of the Secretary, 700 Governors Drive, Pierre, SD 57501-2291.

Tennessee

Tennessee Student Assistance Awards Program—Maximum grants of $1,482.

Dependent Children Scholarship—For dependent children of a law enforcement officer, firefighter, or emergency medical service technician in Tennessee who was killed or totally and permanently disabled while performing duties within the scope of his or her employment.

Paul Douglas Teacher Scholarship Program—Federally funded program for students entering the teaching field at the K-12 level. Grants of up to $5,000 for a maximum of four years.

Tennessee Academic Scholars Program—Awards up to $5,000 per academic year for academically superior high school graduates.

Tennessee Teacher Loan/Scholarship Program—For outstanding students who plan to become public school teachers in an academic shortage area designated by the State Board of Education (currently mathematics or science for grades 7-12, art or music for grades K-8, elementary education, and special education). Awards up to the maximum tuition at the highest-cost public institution. Awards may be received for four years.

Teacher Loan Program for Disadvantaged Areas of Tennessee—For students who plan to become public school teachers at the K-12 level in a geographic area designated by the State Board of Education as disadvantaged at the time the student completes the requirements for teacher certification. Awards of up to $1,500 per year, for a maximum of $6,000.

Robert C. Byrd Honors Scholarship - Federal scholarships to promote student excellence through awwards of $1,500 per academic year.

For more information, contact the Tennessee Student Assistance Corporation, Suite 1950, Parkway Towers, 404 James Robertson Parkway, Nashville, TN 37243-0820.

Texas

Texas Tuition Equalization Grant Program—Grants of up to $1,900 at private, nonprofit postsecondary institutions.

Texas Public Grant Program—Grants of up to $2,500 at public postsecondary institutions.

State Scholarship for Ethnic Recruitment—Scholarships of $500 to $1,000 for eligible minority students attending general academic teaching institutions.

Robert C. Byrd Honors Scholarship Program—Scholarships to promote student excellence and achievement and to recognize exceptionally able students who show promise of continued excellence. Grants are $1,500 for one academic year.

Paul Douglas Teacher Scholarship Program—Loans to outstanding high school graduates to enable and encourage them to pursue teaching careers at the preschool, elementary, or secondary levels. Loans of up to $5,000 per year for a maximum of four years.

For more information, contact the financial aid office at the institution you wish to attend.

Utah

State Student Incentive Grant Program—Grants of up to $2,500 based on need.

Utah Educational Career Teaching Scholarship—Available to students who plan a career teaching in the public educational institutions of Utah. Tuition and fees waived, with additional stipends in some instances awarded on merit. Recipient must teach in the public educational institutions of Utah one year for each year they received the scholarship, for a maximum of five years. This must begin no later than two years after certification.

National Guard State Tuition Assistance—Members of the National Guard may receive up to $1,000 per year, not to exceed a $4,000 maximum. Extended service period required.

For more information, contact the financial aid office at the institution you wish to attend.

Vermont

Vermont Incentive Grant Program—Grants of $400 to $5,050 at in-state postsecondary institutions, and grants of $400 to $3,850 at out-of-state postsecondary institutions.

Part-Time Student Grant Program—Grants of $200 to $3,780 for students going less than full time to in-state postsecondary institutions, and grants of $200 to $2,890 for study at out-of-state postsecondary institutions.

For more information, contact the Vermont Student Assistance Corporation, Champlain Mill, P.O. Box 2000, Winooski, VT 05404-2601.

Virginia

College Scholarship Assistance Program—Grants of $400 to $2,000 at public and private colleges.

Virginia Scholars Program—Merit-based scholarships of $3,000 for outstanding high school students enrolled full-time in a baccalaureate degree program at an accredited, degree-granting, public or private nonprofit institution. Renewable for up to three years. Also available to outstanding graduates of in-state two-year colleges who transfer to a senior in-state college to complete their baccalaureate degree; renewable for up to one year.

Virginia Tuition Assistance Grant—Non-need-based grants of up to $1,375 at private colleges for 1993-94.

Virginia Transfer Grant Program—Full tuition and mandatory fees or remaining need, whichever is lower, awarded to "other race" students who are enrolled in a traditionally white or black four-year public college or university in Virginia. Applicants must meet minimum merit criteria and be first-time transfer students.

Last Dollar Program—Need-based grants for black undergraduates enrolled for the first time in a state-supported college or university.

Paul Douglas Teacher Scholarship Program—Grants of up to $5,000 to undergraduate and graduate students matriculating full-time in a program leading to teacher certification and who ranked in the top 10 percent of their high school graduating class. Teaching service required upon completion of the program.

For more information, contact the Virginia Council of Higher Education, James Monroe Building, 101 North 14th Street, Richmond, VA 23219.

Washington

State Need Grant Program—Variable grants for low-income state residents attending in-state postsecondary institutions.

Educational Opportunity Grant—A $2,500 grant to needy students who choose to attend a college with existing unused capacity.

Future Teacher Conditional Scholarship Program—Renewable $3,000 conditional loans requiring a 10-year in-state public school teaching commitment to qualify for a 100 percent loan forgiveness.

Paul Douglas Teachers Scholarship Program—Renewable $5,000 conditional loans to those graduating in the top 10 percent of their high school class and intending to pursue a teaching career. Recipients must teach two years for each year of loan forgiveness.

Health Professional Scholarship Program—Renewable conditional loans of up to $15,000. Recipients agree to provide primary care services in state-defined shortage areas for a minimum of three years to qualify for a 100 percent loan forgiveness.

Scholars Tuition Waiver and Grant Program—Four-year tuition waivers at public institutions and grants for those attending private institutions. Recipients are high school seniors from the top 1 percent of their class, nominated for academic excellence, leadership, and community service by principals.

For more information, contact the Higher Education Coordinating Board, 917 Lakeridge Way, P.O. Box 43430, Olympia WA 98504-3430.

West Virginia

Higher Education Grant Program—Grants of up to $1,964 at approved in-state higher education institutions, and up to $600 at approved Pennsylvania institutions for full-time students.

Robert C. Byrd Honors Scholarship Program—Merit scholarships of $1,500 awarded for study at a degree-granting institution of higher education.

Paul Douglas Teacher Scholarship Program—Grants of up to $5,000 to state residents who graduated in the top 10 percent of their high school class; who are enrolled full-time at an in-state college or university in a course of study leading to teacher certification; and who agree to teach in any state for two years for each year of scholarship assistance.

Underwood-Smith Teacher Scholarship Program—Grants of up to $5,000 to state residents who graduated in the top 10 percent of their high school class or scored in the top 10 percent statewide of those students taking the ACT; who are enrolled in a West Virginia state college or university in a course of study leading to certification as a teacher; and who agree to teach in the state's public school system for two years for each year of scholarship assistance.

For more information, contact the State Colleges and University Systems of West Virginia Central Office, Higher Education Grant Program, P.O. Box 4007, Charleston, WV 25364.

Wisconsin

Wisconsin Higher Education Grants Program—Grants of up to $1,800 at eligible public postsecondary institutions for half-time and full-time study.

Tuition Grant Program—Grants of up to $2,172 at eligible private colleges, universities, and nursing schools for half-time and full-time study.

Interstate Program (Minnesota-Wisconsin)—A reciprocal arrangement paying for Wisconsin resident tuition at public collegiate and vocational institutions in Minnesota.

Minority Grant Program—Grants of up to $2,500 at public VTAE institutions and private nonprofit institutions for full-time study.

Wisconsin Indian Student Grant Program—Grants of up to $2,200 at any eligible public or private institution of higher education in Wisconsin for half-time or full-time students who are of at least 25 percent native American heritage.

For more information, contact the Wisconsin Higher Educational Aids Board, P.O. Box 7885, Madison WI 53707.

Wyoming

State Student Incentive Grants Program—Grants at public nonprofit postsecondary institutions averaging $300.

For more information, contact the Wyoming Community College Commission, 122 West 25th, Herschler Building, 1W, Cheyenne, WY 82002.

Guam

Government-sponsored scholarships for Teaching and Nursing programs for attendance at the University of Guam. Program covers tuition, fees, book allowance, and monthly stipends ranging from $100 to $450.

Government-sponsored loan programs for undergraduate and graduate students for attendance at the University of Guam and off-island U.S. accredited institutions, if the degree programs are not offered at the University of Guam. Programs range from $3,000 to $12,000 per academic year.

Government-sponsored Merit Program for graduating high school seniors for attendance at the University of Guam. Program covers tuition, fees, and monthly stipends of approximately $600.

For more information, contact the Financial Aid Office, UOG Station, Mangilao, GU 96923.

Virgin Islands

Student Incentive Grant Program—Grants of up to $2,500 at the College of the Virgin Islands and United States nonprofit postsecondary institutions.

Territorial Scholarship Program—Grants of $500 to $3,000 and loans of $1,000 to $4,000 for students at the College of the Virgin Islands and United States nonprofit postsecondary institutions.

For more information, contact the Financial Aid Office, Virgin Islands Board of Education, P.O. Box 11900, St. Thomas, VI 00801.

Sources of information about the Federal Stafford Loan Program

Alabama
Alabama Commission on
  Higher Education
One Court Square, Suite 221
Montgomery, AL 36104-3584
(205) 269-2700

Alaska
United Student Aid Funds, Inc.
Loan Information Services, M372
P.O. Box 6180
Indianapolis, IN 46206
(317) 849-6510
(800) LOAN USA (562-6872)

Arizona
Arizona Education Loan Program
25 S. Arizona Place, Suite 400
Chandler, AZ 85225
(800) 352-3083

Arkansas
Student Loan Guarantee
  Foundation of Arkansas
219 South Victory
Little Rock, AR 72201
(501) 372-1491
(800) 622-3446

California
California Student Aid Commission
P.O. Box 510845
Sacramento, CA 94245-0845
(916) 445-0880

Colorado
Colorado Student Loan Program
Denver Place
999 Eighteenth Street, Suite 425
Denver, CO 80202-2440
(303) 294-5050

Connecticut
Connecticut Student Loan
  Foundation
P.O. Box 1009
Rocky Hill, CT 06067
(203) 257-4001

Delaware
Higher Education Loan Program
Delaware Higher Education
  Commission
820 North French Street
Wilmington, DE 19801
(302) 577-6055

District of Columbia
Higher Education Loan Program of
  Washington, D.C.
1800 K Street NW, Suite 831
Washington, DC 20006

Florida
Office of Student Financial Assistance
Federal Programs
1344 Florida Education Center
Florida Department of Education
Tallahassee, FL 32399-0400
(904) 488-5160

Georgia
Georgia Higher Education Assistance
  Corporation
2082 East Exchange Place, Suite 200
Tucker, GA 30084
(404) 414-3000

Hawaii
Hawaii Education Loan Program
United Student Aid Funds, Inc.
P.O. Box 22187
Honolulu, HI 96823-2187
(808) 536-3731

Idaho
Student Loan Fund of Idaho, Inc.
6905 Highway 95
P.O. Box 730
Fruitland, ID 83619-0730
(208) 452-4058

Illinois
Illinois Student Assistance Commission
1755 Lake Cook Road
Deerfield, IL 60015
(708) 948-8550

Indiana
State Student Assistance Commission of
  Indiana
150 W. Market Street, Suite 500
Indianapolis, IN 46204
(317) 232-2366

Iowa
Iowa College Student Aid Commission
914 Grand Avenue, Suite 201
Des Moines, IA 50309-2824
(515) 281-4890

Kansas
Higher Education Loan Program of Kansas
6800 College Boulevard, Suite 600
Overland Park, KS 66211
(913) 345-1300

Kentucky
Kentucky Higher Education Assistance
  Authority
1050 U.S. 127 South, Suite 102
Frankfort, KY 40601
(502) 564-7990

Louisiana
Office of Student Financial Assistance
  for Louisiana Student Financial
  Assistance Commission
P.O. Box 91202
Baton Rouge, LA 70821-9202
(504) 922-1012

Maine
Maine Education Assistance Division
Finance Authority of Maine
State House Station 119
Augusta, ME 04333
(207) 287-2183

Maryland
Maryland Higher Education
  Loan Corporation
2100 Guilford Avenue
Baltimore, MD 21218
(410) 333-6555

Massachusetts
Massachusetts Higher Education
 Assistance Corporation
330 Stuart Street
Boston, MA 02116
(617) 426-9434

Michigan
Michigan Higher Education
 Assistance Authority
Michigan Guaranty Agency
P.O. Box 30047
Lansing, MI 48909
(517) 373-0760

Minnesota
Northstar Guarantee Inc.
444 Cedar Street, Suite 1910
St. Paul, MN 55101-2133
(612) 290-8795

Mississippi
Mississippi Guarantee Student Loan
 Agency
3825 Ridgewood Road
P.O. Box 342
Jackson, MS 39205-0342
(601) 982-6663

Missouri
Missouri Coordinating Board
 for Higher Education
P.O. Box 1438
Jefferson City, MO 65102
(314) 751-3940

Montana
Montana Guaranteed Student
 Loan Program
35 South Last Chance Gulch
Helena, MT 59620
(406) 444-6594

Nebraska
Nebraska Student Loan Program
1300 O Street
P.O. Box 82507
Lincoln, NE 68501-2507
(402) 475-8686

Nevada
United Student Aid Funds, Inc.
Western Regional Center
25 South Arizona Place, Suite 400
Chandler, AZ 85225
(800) 824-7044

New Hampshire
New Hampshire Higher Education
 Assistance Foundation
44 Warren Street
P.O. Box 877
Concord, NH 03302
(603) 225-6612
(800) 525-2577

New Jersey
New Jersey Higher Education
 Assistance Authority
4 Quaker Bridge Plaza
CN 543
Trenton, NJ 08625
(609) 588-3200
(800) 356-5562

New Mexico
New Mexico Student Loan Guarantee
 Corporation
P.O. Box 27020
Albuquerque, NM 87125-7020
(505) 345-8821

New York
New York State Higher Education
 Services Corporation
99 Washington Avenue
Albany, NY 12255
(518) 473-7087

North Carolina
North Carolina State Education
 Assistance Authority
P.O. Box 2688
Chapel Hill, NC 27515-2688
(919) 549-8614
 or
College Foundation
P.O. Box 12100
Raleigh, NC 27605
(919) 821-4771

North Dakota
Student Loans of North Dakota
 —Guarantor
Box 5524
Bismarck, ND 58502-5524
(701) 224-5753
(800) 472-2166

Ohio
Ohio Student Aid Commission
P.O. Box 16610
Columbus, OH 43266-0610
(614) 466-3091

Oklahoma
Oklahoma State Regents for
 Higher Education
P.O. Box 54054
Oklahoma City, OK 73154-2054
(405) 840-8300
(800) 442-8642

Oregon
Oregon State Scholarship
 Commission
Valley River Office Park
1500 Valley River Drive, Suite 100
Eugene, OR 97401
(503) 687-7400

Pennsylvania
Pennsylvania Higher Education
 Assistance Agency
660 Boas Street, Towne House Apts.
Harrisburg, PA 17102
(717) 257-2860
(800) 692-7392 (Pennsylvania)

Rhode Island
Rhode Island Higher Education
 Assistance Authority
560 Jefferson Boulevard
Warwick, RI 02886
(401) 277-2050

South Carolina
South Carolina Student Loan Corporation
Interstate Center, Suite 210
P.O. Box 21487
Columbia, SC 29221
(803) 798-0916

South Dakota
Education Assistance Corporation
115 First Avenue, S.W.
Aberdeen, SD 57401
(605) 225-6423

Tennessee
Tennessee Student Assistance Corporation
404 James Robertson Parkway
Parkway Towers, Suite 1950
Nashville, TN 37243-0820
(615) 741-1346

Texas
Texas Guaranteed Student Loan
    Corporation
P.O. Box 15996
Austin, TX 78761-5996
(800) 845-6267

Utah
EduServe
P.O. Box 30802
Salt Lake City, UT 84130
(801) 975-2200

Vermont
Vermont Student Assistance
    Corporation
Champlain Mill
P.O. Box 2000
Winooski, VT 05404-2601
(802) 655-9602
(800) 642-3177 (Vermont)

Virginia
Virginia Student Assistance Authorities
One Franklin Square
411 East Franklin Street
Richmond, VA 23219-2243
(804) 775-4000
(800) 792-LOAN

Washington
Northwest Education Loan Association
500 Colman Building
811 First Avenue
Seattle, WA 98104
(206) 461-5300

West Virginia
West Virginia Education Loan Services
P.O. Box 591
Charleston, WV 25322
(304) 345-7211

Wisconsin
Great Lakes Higher Education
    Corporation
2401 International Lane
Madison, WI 53704
(608) 246-1800

Wyoming
United Student Aid Funds
1912 Capitol Avenue, Suite 320
Cheyenne, WY 82001
(307) 635-3259

Puerto Rico
Puerto Rico Higher Education
    Assistance Corporation
P.O. Box 42001
Minillas Station
Santurce, PR 00940-2001
(809) 763-3535

Virgin Islands
Virgin Islands Board of Education
P.O. Box 11900
Charlotte Amalie
St. Thomas, VI 00801
(809) 774-4546

Guam, American Samoa, Northern Marianas, Palau
Hawaii Education Loan Program
United Student Aid Funds, Inc.
P.O. Box 22187
Honolulu, HI 96823-2187
(808) 536-3731

United Student Aid Funds, Inc.
United Student Aid Funds, Inc.
Loan Information Services, M372
P.O. Box 6180
Indianapolis, IN 46206
(800) LOAN USA (562-6872)
(317) 849-6510

Part III. College indexes

Colleges that offer academic, music or drama, and art scholarships

Academic scholarships

Alabama
Alabama Agricultural and Mechanical University
Alabama Aviation and Technical College
Alabama Southern Community College
Alabama State University
Athens State College
Auburn University
    Auburn
    Montgomery
Bessemer State Technical College
Bevill State Community College
Birmingham-Southern College
Bishop State Community College
Central Alabama Community College: Alexander City Campus
Chattahoochee Valley Community College
Douglas MacArthur State Technical College
Enterprise State Junior College
Faulkner University
Gadsden State Community College
George C. Wallace State Community College
    Dothan
    Selma
Huntingdon College
Jacksonville State University
James H. Faulkner State Community College
Jefferson Davis State Junior College
Jefferson State Community College
John C. Calhoun State Community College
John M. Patterson State Technical College
Judson College
Livingston University
Lurleen B. Wallace State Junior College
Marion Military Institute
Miles College
Northeast Alabama Community College
Samford University
Shelton State Community College
Shoals Community College
Snead State Community College
Southeastern Bible College
Southern Christian University
Spring Hill College
Stillman College
Talladega College
Troy State University at Dothan
Tuskegee University
University of Alabama
    Birmingham
    Huntsville
    Tuscaloosa
University of Mobile
University of Montevallo
University of North Alabama
University of South Alabama
Walker College
Wallace State Community College at Hanceville

Alaska
Alaska Bible College
Alaska Pacific University
Prince William Sound Community College
Sheldon Jackson College
University of Alaska
    Anchorage
    Southeast

Arizona
American Indian Bible College
Arizona College of the Bible
Arizona State University
Arizona Western College
Central Arizona College
Cochise College
DeVry Institute of Technology: Phoenix
Eastern Arizona College
Embry-Riddle Aeronautical University: Prescott Campus
Gateway Community College
Glendale Community College
Grand Canyon University
Mesa Community College
Mohave Community College
Navajo Community College
Northern Arizona University
Northland Pioneer College
Paradise Valley Community College
Phoenix College
Prescott College
South Mountain Community College
University of Arizona
Yavapai College

Arkansas
Arkansas Baptist College
Arkansas College
Arkansas State University
    Beebe Branch
    Jonesboro
Arkansas Tech University
Central Baptist College
Garland County Community College
Harding University
Henderson State University
Hendrix College
John Brown University
Mississippi County Community College
North Arkansas Community/Technical College
Ouachita Baptist University
Phillips County Community College
Rich Mountain Community College
South Arkansas Community College
Southern Arkansas University
    Magnolia
    Technical Branch
University of Arkansas
University of Arkansas
    Little Rock
    Monticello
University of the Ozarks
Westark Community College

California
Academy of Art College
Allan Hancock College
American Armenian International College
Antelope Valley College
Art Institute of Southern California
Azusa Pacific University
Bakersfield College
Barstow College
Bethany College
Biola University
Brooks College
Brooks Institute of Photography
California Baptist College
California College of Arts and Crafts
California Institute of Technology
California Lutheran University
California Maritime Academy
California Polytechnic State University: San Luis Obispo
California State Polytechnic University: Pomona
California State University
    Bakersfield
    Chico
    Dominguez Hills
    Fresno
    Fullerton
    Hayward
    Long Beach
    Los Angeles
    Northridge
    San Bernardino
    San Marcos
    Stanislaus
Cerritos Community College
Cerro Coso Community College
Chabot College
Chapman University
Charles R. Drew University: College of Allied Health
Christian Heritage College
Citrus College
City College of San Francisco
Claremont McKenna College
Cogswell Polytechnical College
Coleman College
College of the Canyons
College of Notre Dame
College of the Redwoods
College of the Sequoias
College of the Siskiyous
Columbia College
Compton Community College
Concordia University
Crafton Hills College
Cuesta College
DeVry Institute of Technology: City of Industry
Diablo Valley College
Dominican College of San Rafael
Evergreen Valley College
Feather River College
Foothill College
Fresno City College
Fresno Pacific College
Fullerton College
Golden Gate University
Golden West College
Grossmont Community College
Harvey Mudd College
Holy Names College
Humboldt State University
John F. Kennedy University
Kelsey-Jenney College
La Sierra University
Lake Tahoe Community College
LIFE Bible College
Long Beach City College
Los Angeles Harbor College
Los Angeles Mission College
Los Angeles Pierce College

Colleges that offer academic, music or drama, or art scholarships

Los Medanos College
Loyola Marymount University
Marymount College
Master's College
Menlo College
Merced College
Mills College
MiraCosta College
Mission College
Modesto Junior College
Monterey Institute of International Studies
Monterey Peninsula College
Mount St. Mary's College
Mount San Antonio College
Mount San Jacinto College
Napa Valley College
Occidental College
Pacific Christian College
Pacific Oaks College
Pacific Union College
Palomar College
Pasadena City College
Patten College
Pepperdine University
Point Loma Nazarene College
Porterville College
Rio Hondo College
Saddleback College
St. Mary's College of California
Samuel Merritt College
San Diego City College
San Diego Mesa College
San Diego State University
San Francisco State University
San Joaquin Delta College
San Jose Christian College
Santa Barbara City College
Santa Clara University
Santa Monica College
Santa Rosa Junior College
Scripps College
Shasta College
Sierra College
Simpson College
Sonoma State University
Southern California College
Southern California Institute of Architecture
Taft College
United States International University
University of California
    Berkeley
    Davis
    Irvine
    Los Angeles
    Riverside
    San Diego
    San Francisco
    Santa Barbara
    Santa Cruz
University of Judaism
University of Redlands
University of San Diego
University of San Francisco
University of Southern California
Victor Valley College
West Valley College
Westmont College
Whittier College
Woodbury University
Yuba College

Colorado

Adams State College
Aims Community College
Arapahoe Community College
Bel-Rea Institute of Animal Technology
Colorado Christian University
Colorado College
Colorado Institute of Art
Colorado Mountain College
    Alpine Campus
    Spring Valley Campus
    Timberline Campus
Colorado Northwestern Community College
Colorado School of Mines
Colorado State University
Colorado Technical College
Community College of Aurora
Community College of Denver
Fort Lewis College
Front Range Community College
Lamar Community College
Mesa State College
Metropolitan State College of Denver
Morgan Community College
Naropa Institute
National College
Nazarene Bible College
Northeastern Junior College
Pikes Peak Community College
Pueblo Community College
Red Rocks Community College
Regis University
Rocky Mountain College of Art & Design
Trinidad State Junior College
University of Colorado
    Boulder
    Colorado Springs
    Denver
    Health Sciences Center
University of Denver
University of Northern Colorado
University of Southern Colorado
Western State College of Colorado

Connecticut

Albertus Magnus College
Briarwood College
Capital Community-Technical College
Central Connecticut State University
Eastern Connecticut State University
Gateway Community-Technical College
Northwestern Connecticut Community-Technical College
Quinebaug Valley Community-Technical College
Quinnipiac College
Sacred Heart University
St. Joseph College
Southern Connecticut State University
Teikyo-Post University
Tunxis Community-Technical College
University of Bridgeport
University of Connecticut
University of Hartford
University of New Haven
Western Connecticut State University

Delaware

Delaware State College
Delaware Technical and Community College
    Southern Campus
    Stanton/Wilmington Campus
Goldey-Beacom College
University of Delaware
Wesley College
Wilmington College

District of Columbia

American University
Catholic University of America
Corcoran School of Art
George Washington University
Howard University
Mount Vernon College
Southeastern University
Strayer College
Trinity College
University of the District of Columbia

Florida

Barry University
Bethune-Cookman College
Brevard Community College
Broward Community College
Central Florida Community College
Chipola Junior College
Clearwater Christian College
Daytona Beach Community College
Eckerd College
Edison Community College
Embry-Riddle Aeronautical University
Flagler College
Florida Agricultural and Mechanical University
Florida Atlantic University
Florida Bible College
Florida Christian College
Florida College
Florida Community College at Jacksonville
Florida Institute of Technology
Florida International University
Florida Memorial College
Florida Southern College
Florida State University
Fort Lauderdale College
Gulf Coast Community College
Hillsborough Community College
Indian River Community College
Jacksonville University
Lake City Community College
Lake-Sumter Community College
Lynn University
Manatee Community College
Miami-Dade Community College
New College of the University of South Florida
New England Institute of Technology
North Florida Junior College
Nova University
Okaloosa-Walton Community College
Palm Beach Atlantic College
Palm Beach Community College
Pasco-Hernando Community College
Pensacola Junior College
Polk Community College
Rollins College
St. Johns River Community College
St. Leo College
St. Petersburg Junior College
Santa Fe Community College
Schiller International University
Seminole Community College
South Florida Community College
Southeastern College of the Assemblies of God
Stetson University
Tallahassee Community College
Trinity College at Miami
University of Central Florida
University of Florida
University of Miami
University of North Florida
University of South Florida
University of Tampa
University of West Florida
Valencia Community College
Warner Southern College
Webber College

Georgia

Abraham Baldwin Agricultural College
Agnes Scott College
Albany State College
American College for the Applied Arts
Andrew College
Armstrong State College
Atlanta Christian College
Augusta College
Brenau University
Brewton-Parker College
Brunswick College
Chattahoochee Technical Institute
Clark Atlanta University
Clayton State College
Columbus College
Covenant College
Dalton College
Darton College
DeKalb Technical Institute
DeVry Institute of Technology: Atlanta
East Georgia College
Emmanuel College
Emory University
Floyd College
Fort Valley State College
Gainesville College
Georgia College
Georgia Institute of Technology
Georgia Southern University
Georgia Southwestern College
Georgia State University
Gordon College
Kennesaw State College
LaGrange College
Macon College
Medical College of Georgia
Mercer University
    Atlanta
    Macon
Middle Georgia College
Morehouse College
Morris Brown College
North Georgia College
Oglethorpe University
Oxford College of Emory University
Piedmont College
Savannah College of Art and Design
Savannah State College
Savannah Technical Institute
Shorter College
South College
South Georgia College
Southern College of Technology
Spelman College
Thomas College
Toccoa Falls College
Truett-McConnell College
University of Georgia
Valdosta State College
Waycross College
Wesleyan College
West Georgia College
Young Harris College

Hawaii

Brigham Young University-Hawaii
Hawaii Pacific University

225

Colleges that offer academic, music or drama, or art scholarships

University of Hawaii
   Hawaii Community College
   Hilo
   Honolulu Community College
   Kapiolani Community College
   Kauai Community College
   Manoa
   West Oahu
   Windward Community College

Idaho

Albertson College
Boise Bible College
Boise State University
College of Southern Idaho
Idaho State University
Lewis Clark State College
North Idaho College
Northwest Nazarene College
Ricks College
University of Idaho

Illinois

Augustana College
Aurora University
Barat College
Belleville Area College
Black Hawk College
   East Campus
   Moline
Blackburn College
Blessing-Reiman College of Nursing
Bradley University
Carl Sandburg College
Chicago State University
City Colleges of Chicago: Olive-Harvey College
College of DuPage
College of Lake County
College of St. Francis
Columbia College
Concordia University
Danville Area Community College
De Paul University
DeVry Institute of Technology
   Addison
   Chicago
Eastern Illinois University
East-West University
Elgin Community College
Elmhurst College
Eureka College
Governors State University
Greenville College
Highland Community College
Illinois Benedictine College
Illinois Central College
Illinois College
Illinois Eastern Community Colleges
   Frontier Community College
   Lincoln Trail College
   Olney Central College
   Wabash Valley College
Illinois State University
Illinois Valley Community College
Illinois Wesleyan University
International Academy of Merchandising and Design
John A. Logan College
Joliet Junior College
Judson College
Kankakee Community College
Kaskaskia College
Kendall College
Kishwaukee College
Knox College
Lake Land College
Lewis and Clark Community College
Lewis University

Lexington Institute of Hospitality Careers
Lincoln Christian College and Seminary
Lincoln College
Lincoln Land Community College
Loyola University of Chicago
MacMurray College
McHenry County College
McKendree College
Mennonite College of Nursing
Millikin University
Monmouth College
Montay College
Moraine Valley Community College
Morrison Institute of Technology
Morton College
National College of Chiropractic
National-Louis University
North Central College
North Park College
Northeastern Illinois University
Oakton Community College
Olivet Nazarene University
Parks College of St. Louis University
Principia College
Quincy University
Ray College of Design
Richland Community College
Robert Morris College: Chicago
Rock Valley College
Rockford College
Roosevelt University
Rosary College
St. Augustine College
St. Francis Medical Center College of Nursing
St. Xavier University
Sangamon State University
Sauk Valley Community College
Shawnee Community College
Shimer College
Southeastern Illinois College
Southern Illinois University
   Carbondale
   Edwardsville
Spoon River College
Springfield College in Illinois
Trinity Christian College
Trinity College
Triton College
University of Chicago
University of Illinois
   Chicago
   Urbana-Champaign
Western Illinois University
Wheaton College
William Rainey Harper College

Indiana

Ancilla College
Anderson University
Ball State University
Bethel College
Butler University
Calumet College of St. Joseph
DePauw University
Earlham College
Franklin College
Goshen College
Grace College
Hanover College
Huntington College
Indiana State University
Indiana University
   Bloomington
   East
   Northwest
   South Bend

Indiana University—Purdue University
   Fort Wayne
   Indianapolis
Indiana Vocational Technical College
   Central Indiana
   Columbus
   Kokomo
   Lafayette
   Northcentral
   Northeast
   Southwest
Indiana Wesleyan University
Lutheran College of Health Professions
Manchester College
Marian College
Martin University
Oakland City College
Purdue University
   Calumet
   North Central Campus
   West Lafayette
Rose-Hulman Institute of Technology
St. Francis College
St. Joseph's College
St. Mary-of-the-Woods College
St. Meinrad College
Taylor University
Tri-State University
University of Evansville
University of Indianapolis
University of Southern Indiana
Valparaiso University
Vincennes University
Wabash College

Iowa

American Institute of Business
Briar Cliff College
Buena Vista College
Central College
Clarke College
Clinton Community College
Coe College
Cornell College
Des Moines Area Community College
Dordt College
Drake University
Ellsworth Community College
Emmaus Bible College
Faith Baptist Bible College and Theological Seminary
Graceland College
Grand View College
Grinnell College
Hawkeye Community College
Indian Hills Community College
Iowa Central Community College
Iowa Lakes Community College
Iowa State University
Iowa Wesleyan College
Iowa Western Community College
Loras College
Luther College
Marshalltown Community College
Morningside College
Mount Mercy College
Mount St. Clare College
Muscatine Community College
North Iowa Area Community College
Northeast Iowa Community College
Northwest Iowa Community College
Northwestern College
St. Ambrose University
Scott Community College
Simpson College

Southeastern Community College
   North Campus
   South Campus
Southwestern Community College
Teikyo Marycrest University
Teikyo Westmar University
University of Dubuque
University of Iowa
University of Northern Iowa
Upper Iowa University
Vennard College
Waldorf College
Wartburg College
William Penn College

Kansas

Allen County Community College
Baker University
Barclay College
Barton County Community College
Benedictine College
Bethany College
Bethel College
Brown Mackie College
Butler County Community College
Central College
Coffeyville Community College
Colby Community College
Dodge City Community College
Donnelly College
Emporia State University
Fort Hays State University
Friends University
Garden City Community College
Hesston College
Highland Community College
Hutchinson Community College
Independence Community College
Johnson County Community College
Kansas City Kansas Community College
Kansas State University
Kansas Wesleyan University
Manhattan Christian College
McPherson College
MidAmerica Nazarene College
Neosho County Community College
Pittsburg State University
Pratt Community College
St. Mary College
Southwestern College
Sterling College
Tabor College
University of Kansas
   Lawrence
   Medical Center
Washburn University of Topeka
Wichita State University

Kentucky

Alice Lloyd College
Asbury College
Ashland Community College
Bellarmine College
Brescia College
Campbellsville College
Centre College
Cumberland College
Eastern Kentucky University
Elizabethtown Community College
Georgetown College
Henderson Community College
Hopkinsville Community College
Jefferson Community College
Kentucky State University
Kentucky Wesleyan College
Lees College
Lexington Community College
Lindsey Wilson College
Louisville Technical Institute
Madisonville Community College

Colleges that offer academic, music or drama, or art scholarships

Maysville Community College
Midway College
Morehead State University
Murray State University
Northern Kentucky University
Owensboro Junior College of Business
Paducah Community College
Pikeville College
Prestonburg Community College
Southeast Community College
Spalding University
Thomas More College
Transylvania University
Union College
University of Kentucky
University of Louisville
Western Kentucky University

Louisiana

Bossier Parish Community College
Centenary College of Louisiana
Dillard University
Grambling State University
Louisiana College
Louisiana State University
   Agricultural and Mechanical College
   Alexandria
   Eunice
   Medical Center
   Shreveport
Louisiana Tech University
Loyola University
McNeese State University
Nicholls State University
Northeast Louisiana University
Northwestern State University
Our Lady of Holy Cross College
Southeastern Louisiana University
Southern University in Shreveport
Southern University and Agricultural and Mechanical College
Tulane University
University of New Orleans
University of Southwestern Louisiana
Xavier University of Louisiana

Maine

Andover College
Beal College
Husson College
Maine College of Art
Maine Maritime Academy
Northern Maine Technical College
St. Joseph's College
Thomas College
Unity College
University of Maine
   Augusta
   Farmington
   Fort Kent
   Orono
   Presque Isle
University of New England
University of Southern Maine

Maryland

Allegany Community College
Anne Arundel Community College
Baltimore City Community College
Baltimore International Culinary College
Bowie State University
Capitol College
Catonsville Community College
Cecil Community College
Charles County Community College
Chesapeake College

College of Notre Dame of Maryland
Columbia Union College
Dundalk Community College
Essex Community College
Frederick Community College
Frostburg State University
Goucher College
Hagerstown Business College
Hagerstown Junior College
Harford Community College
Hood College
Johns Hopkins University
Loyola College in Maryland
Maryland Institute College of Art
Morgan State University
Mount St. Mary's College
Ner Israel Rabbinical College
Prince George's Community College
St. Mary's College of Maryland
Salisbury State University
Sojourner-Douglass College
Towson State University
University of Baltimore
University of Maryland
   Baltimore County
   College Park
   Eastern Shore
   University College
Villa Julie College
Washington College
Western Maryland College
Wor-Wic Community College

Massachusetts

American International College
Anna Maria College for Men and Women
Aquinas College at Milton
Aquinas College at Newton
Atlantic Union College
Babson College
Bay Path College
Bay State College
Becker College: Worcester Campus
Bentley College
Berklee College of Music
Boston Architectural Center
Boston College
Boston University
Bradford College
Brandeis University
Bridgewater State College
Bristol Community College
Clark University
College of the Holy Cross
Eastern Nazarene College
Elms College
Emerson College
Emmanuel College
Fitchburg State College
Forsyth School for Dental Hygienists
Framingham State College
Gordon College
Hampshire College
Hellenic College
Holyoke Community College
Lasell College
Lesley College
Massachusetts Bay Community College
Massachusetts College of Pharmacy and Allied Health Sciences
Massachusetts Maritime Academy
Massasoit Community College
Newbury College
Nichols College
Northeastern University
Quinsigamond Community College
Regis College
St. Hyacinth College and Seminary

Salem State College
Simmons College
Springfield Technical Community College
Stonehill College
Suffolk University
Tufts University
University of Massachusetts
   Amherst
   Boston
   Dartmouth
Wentworth Institute of Technology
Westfield State College
Worcester State College

Michigan

Adrian College
Albion College
Alma College
Alpena Community College
Andrews University
Aquinas College
Baker College
   Auburn Hills
   Cadillac
   Flint
   Muskegon
   Owosso
   Port Huron
Bay de Noc Community College
Calvin College
Central Michigan University
Charles Stewart Mott Community College
Cleary College
Concordia College
Davenport College of Business
Delta College
Detroit College of Business
Eastern Michigan University
Ferris State University
Glen Oaks Community College
GMI Engineering & Management Institute
Gogebic Community College
Grace Bible College
Grand Rapids Baptist College and Seminary
Grand Rapids Community College
Grand Valley State University
Great Lakes Christian College
Great Lakes Junior College of Business
Henry Ford Community College
Hillsdale College
Hope College
Jackson Community College
Jordan College
Kalamazoo College
Kalamazoo Valley Community College
Kellogg Community College
Kendall College of Art and Design
Kirtland Community College
Lake Michigan College
Lake Superior State University
Lansing Community College
Lawrence Technological University
Macomb Community College
Madonna University
Marygrove College
Michigan Christian College
Michigan State University
Michigan Technological University
Mid Michigan Community College
Monroe County Community College
Montcalm Community College
Muskegon Community College
Northern Michigan University
Northwestern Michigan College
Northwood University

Oakland Community College
Oakland University
Olivet College
Saginaw Valley State University
St. Clair County Community College
St. Mary's College
Schoolcraft College
Siena Heights College
Southwestern Michigan College
Spring Arbor College
Suomi College
University of Detroit Mercy
University of Michigan
   Ann Arbor
   Dearborn
   Flint
Walsh College of Accountancy and Business Administration
Washtenaw Community College
Wayne State University
West Shore Community College
Western Michigan University
William Tyndale College

Minnesota

Alexandria Technical College
Anoka-Ramsey Community College
Augsburg College
Austin Community College
Bemidji State University
Bethany Lutheran College
Brainerd Community College
Carleton College
College of Associated Arts
College of St. Benedict
College of St. Catherine: St. Catherine Campus
College of St. Scholastica
Concordia College: Moorhead
Concordia College: St. Paul
Crown College
Dr. Martin Luther College
Fergus Falls Community College
Gustavus Adolphus College
Hamline University
Hibbing Community College
Inver Hills Community College
Itasca Community College: Arrowhead Region
Lakewood Community College
Macalester College
Mankato State University
Mesabi Community College: Arrowhead Region
Minneapolis College of Art and Design
Minneapolis Community College
Minnesota Bible College
Moorhead State University
NEI College of Technology
North Central Bible College
Northwestern College
Pillsbury Baptist Bible College
Rainy River Community College
Rochester Community College
St. Cloud State University
St. John's University
St. Mary's Campus of the College of St. Catherine
St. Mary's College of Minnesota
Southwest State University
University of Minnesota
   Crookston
   Duluth
   Morris
   Twin Cities
University of St. Thomas
Vermilion Community College
Willmar Community College
Winona State University
Worthington Community College

227

Colleges that offer academic, music or drama, or art scholarships

Mississippi
Alcorn State University
Belhaven College
Copiah-Lincoln Community College
Delta State University
East Central Community College
East Mississippi Community College
Hinds Community College
Holmes Community College
Jackson State University
Magnolia Bible College
Meridian Community College
Millsaps College
Mississippi College
Mississippi Delta Community College
Mississippi Gulf Coast Community College
    Jackson County Campus
    Jefferson Davis Campus
    Perkinston
Mississippi State University
Mississippi University for Women
Mississippi Valley State University
Pearl River Community College
Rust College
Tougaloo College
University of Mississippi
    Medical Center
    University
University of Southern Mississippi
William Carey College
Wood Junior College

Missouri
Avila College
Calvary Bible College
Central Christian College of the Bible
Central Methodist College
Central Missouri State University
College of the Ozarks
Conception Seminary College
Cottey College
Crowder College
Culver-Stockton College
Deaconess College of Nursing
DeVry Institute of Technology: Kansas City
Drury College
East Central College
Evangel College
Fontbonne College
Hannibal-LaGrange College
Harris Stowe State College
Jefferson College
Kemper Military School and College
Lincoln University
Lindenwood College
Longview Community College
Maple Woods Community College
Maryville University
Mineral Area College
Missouri Baptist College
Missouri Southern State College
Missouri Valley College
Missouri Western State College
Moberly Area Community College
National College
Northeast Missouri State University
Northwest Missouri State University
Ozark Christian College
Park College
Penn Valley Community College
Ranken Technical College
Research College of Nursing
Rockhurst College
St. Charles County Community College
St. Louis Christian College
St. Louis College of Pharmacy
St. Louis Community College
    Florissant Valley
    Forest Park
    Meramec
St. Louis University
Southeast Missouri State University
Southwest Baptist University
Southwest Missouri State University
State Fair Community College
Stephens College
Three Rivers Community College
University of Missouri
    Columbia
    Kansas City
    Rolla
    St. Louis
Washington University
Webster University
Westminster College
William Jewell College
William Woods College

Montana
Carroll College
College of Great Falls
Dawson Community College
Dull Knife Memorial College
Eastern Montana College
Flathead Valley Community College
Fort Peck Community College
Helena Vocational-Technical Center
Miles Community College
Montana College of Mineral Science and Technology
Montana State University
Northern Montana College
Rocky Mountain College
Stone Child College
University of Montana
Western Montana College of the University of Montana

Nebraska
Bellevue College
Central Community College
Chadron State College
Clarkson College
College of St. Mary
Concordia College
Creighton University
Dana College
Doane College
Grace College of the Bible
Lincoln School of Commerce
McCook Community College
Metropolitan Community College
Mid Plains Community College
Midland Lutheran College
Nebraska Christian College
Nebraska College of Technical Agriculture
Nebraska Methodist College of Nursing and Allied Health
Nebraska Wesleyan University
Northeast Community College
Peru State College
Southeast Community College
    Beatrice Campus
    Lincoln Campus
    Milford Campus
Union College
University of Nebraska
    Medical Center
    Kearney
    Lincoln
    Omaha
Wayne State College
Western Nebraska Community College: Scottsbluff Campus
York College

Nevada
Northern Nevada Community College
Sierra Nevada College
University of Nevada
    Las Vegas
    Reno
Western Nevada Community College

New Hampshire
Castle College
Colby-Sawyer College
Daniel Webster College
Franklin Pierce College
Hesser College
Keene State College
New England College
New Hampshire College
New Hampshire Technical College
    Claremont
    Laconia
New Hampshire Technical Institute
Notre Dame College
Plymouth State College of the University System of New Hampshire
Rivier College
University of New Hampshire
    Durham
    Manchester
White Pines College

New Jersey
Bergen Community College
Berkeley College of Business
Bloomfield College
Brookdale Community College
Burlington County College
Caldwell College
Camden County College
Centenary College
College of St. Elizabeth
County College of Morris
Drew University
Essex County College
Fairleigh Dickinson University
    Edward Williams College
    Madison
Felician College
Georgian Court College
Gloucester County College
Hudson County Community College
Jersey City State College
Kean College of New Jersey
Mercer County Community College
Monmouth College
Montclair State College
New Jersey Institute of Technology
Ocean County College
Passaic County Community College
Ramapo College of New Jersey
Rider College
Rowan College of New Jersey
Rutgers—The State University of New Jersey
    Camden College of Arts and Sciences
    College of Engineering
    College of Nursing
    College of Pharmacy
    Cook College
    Douglass College
    Livingston College
    Mason Gross School of the Arts
    Newark College of Arts and Sciences
    Rutgers College
St. Peter's College
Salem Community College
Seton Hall University
Stevens Institute of Technology
Stockton State College
Sussex County Community College
Trenton State College
Union County College
Upsala College
Warren County Community College
Westminster Choir College School of Music of Rider College
William Paterson College of New Jersey

New Mexico
Clovis Community College
College of Santa Fe
College of the Southwest
Eastern New Mexico University
    Portales
    Roswell Campus
National College
New Mexico Highlands University
New Mexico Institute of Mining and Technology
New Mexico Junior College
New Mexico Military Institute
New Mexico State University
    Carlsbad
    Las Cruces
Northern New Mexico Community College
Parks College
San Juan College
Santa Fe Community College
University of New Mexico
Western New Mexico University

New York
Adelphi University
Adirondack Community College
Alfred University
American Academy McAllister Institute of Funeral Service
Bard College
Berkeley College
Berkeley School: New York City
Boricua College
Bramson ORT Technical Institute
Broome Community College
Canisius College
Cayuga County Community College
Cazenovia College
Central City Business Institute
City University of New York
    Baruch College
    Brooklyn College
    City College
    Hunter College
    John Jay College of Criminal Justice
    Lehman College
    Queens College
Clarkson University
Clinton Community College
College of Aeronautics
College of Insurance
College of Mount St. Vincent
College of New Rochelle
College of St. Rose
Columbia University
    School of Engineering and Applied Science
    School of Nursing
Columbia-Greene Community College
Concordia College
Cooper Union
Culinary Institute of America
Daemen College
Dominican College of Blauvelt
Dowling College
Dutchess Community College
D'Youville College

Colleges that offer academic, music or drama, or art scholarships

Eastman School of Music of the University of Rochester
Elmira College
Eugene Lang College/New School for Social Research
Finger Lakes Community College
Five Towns College
Fordham University
Fulton-Montgomery Community College
Genesee Community College
Hartwick College
Helene Fuld School of Nursing
Herkimer County Community College
Hilbert College
Hofstra University
Houghton College
Iona College
Jamestown Business College
Jamestown Community College
Jefferson Community College
Jewish Theological Seminary of America
Juilliard School
Keuka College
King's College
Le Moyne College
Long Island College Hospital School of Nursing
Long Island University
   Brooklyn Campus
   C. W. Post Campus
   Southampton Campus
Manhattan College
Manhattan School of Music
Manhattanville College
Marist College
Marymount College
Marymount Manhattan College
Mater Dei College
Medaille College
Mercy College
Mohawk Valley Community College
Molloy College
Monroe Community College
Mount St. Mary College
Nassau Community College
Nazareth College of Rochester
New York Institute of Technology
New York School of Interior Design
New York University
Niagara County Community College
Niagara University
Nyack College
Onondaga Community College
Orange County Community College
Pace University
   College of White Plains
   New York
   Pleasantville/Briarcliff
Paul Smith's College
Phillips Beth Israel School of Nursing
Polytechnic University
   Brooklyn
   Long Island Campus
Pratt Institute
Rensselaer Polytechnic Institute
Roberts Wesleyan College
Rochester Institute of Technology
Rockland Community College
Russell Sage College
Sage Junior College of Albany
St. Bonaventure University
St. Francis College
St. John Fisher College
St. John's University
St. Joseph's College
   Brooklyn
   Suffolk Campus

St. Joseph's School of Nursing
St. Lawrence University
St. Thomas Aquinas College
Schenectady County Community College
School of Visual Arts
Siena College
State University of New York
   Albany
   Binghamton
   Buffalo
   Purchase
   Stony Brook
   College of Agriculture and Technology at Cobleskill
   College of Agriculture and Technology at Morrisville
   College at Brockport
   College at Buffalo
   College at Cortland
   College of Environmental Science and Forestry
   College at Geneseo
   College at Oneonta
   College at Plattsburgh
   College at Potsdam
   College of Technology at Alfred
   College of Technology at Canton
   College of Technology at Delhi
   College of Technology at Farmingdale
   Health Sciences Center at Stony Brook
   Institute of Technology at Utica/Rome
   Maritime College
   Oswego
Suffolk County Community College
   Eastern Campus
   Selden
   Western Campus
Sullivan County Community College
Syracuse University
Tompkins-Cortland Community College
Touro College
Trocaire College
Ulster County Community College
University of Rochester
Utica College of Syracuse University
Utica School of Commerce
Villa Maria College of Buffalo
Wadhams Hall Seminary-College
Wagner College
Webb Institute of Naval Architecture
Wells College
Westchester Business Institute
Westchester Community College
William Smith College
Wood Tobe-Coburn School
Yeshiva University

North Carolina
Alamance Community College
Appalachian State University
Asheville Buncombe Technical Community College
Barber-Scotia College
Barton College
Beaufort County Community College
Belmont Abbey College
Bennett College
Blue Ridge Community College
Brevard College
Brunswick Community College

Caldwell Community College and Technical Institute
Campbell University
Cape Fear Community College
Catawba College
Catawba Valley Community College
Chowan College
Craven Community College
Davidson College
Duke University
East Carolina University
Edgecombe Community College
Elizabeth City State University
Elon College
Fayetteville State University
Fayetteville Technical Community College
Gardner-Webb University
Gaston College
Greensboro College
Guilford College
Halifax Community College
High Point University
James Sprunt Community College
John Wesley College
Johnson C. Smith University
Johnston Community College
Lees-McRae College
Lenoir-Rhyne College
Livingstone College
Louisburg College
Mars Hill College
Martin Community College
Mayland Community College
McDowell Technical Community College
Meredith College
Methodist College
Mitchell Community College
Montreat-Anderson College
Mount Olive College
Nash Community College
North Carolina Agricultural and Technical State University
North Carolina Central University
North Carolina School of the Arts
North Carolina State University
North Carolina Wesleyan College
Peace College
Pembroke State University
Pfeiffer College
Piedmont Bible College
Pitt Community College
Queens College
Randolph Community College
Richmond Community College
Roanoke Bible College
Roanoke-Chowan Community College
Rockingham Community College
Rowan-Cabarrus Community College
St. Andrews Presbyterian College
St. Augustine's College
St. Mary's College
Salem College
Sampson Community College
Sandhills Community College
Southeastern Community College
Stanly Community College
Surry Community College
University of North Carolina
   Asheville
   Chapel Hill
   Charlotte
   Greensboro
   Wilmington
Vance-Granville Community College
Wake Forest University
Wake Technical Community College

Warren Wilson College
Western Carolina University
Western Piedmont Community College
Wilkes Community College
Wingate College
Winston-Salem State University

North Dakota
Bismarck State College
Dickinson State University
Jamestown College
Minot State University
North Dakota State College of Science
North Dakota State University
   Bottineau
   Fargo
Standing Rock College
Trinity Bible College
United Tribes Technical College
University of Mary
University of North Dakota
   Grand Forks
   Lake Region
   Williston
Valley City State University

Ohio
Antioch College
Art Academy of Cincinnati
Ashland University
Baldwin-Wallace College
Belmont Technical College
Bluffton College
Bowling Green State University
   Bowling Green
   Firelands College
Capital University
Case Western Reserve University
Cedarville College
Central Ohio Technical College
Central State University
Cincinnati Bible College and Seminary
Cleveland Institute of Art
Cleveland Institute of Music
Cleveland State University
College of Mount St. Joseph
College of Wooster
Columbus State Community College
Cuyahoga Community College
   Eastern Campus
   Western Campus
Defiance College
Denison University
DeVry Institute of Technology: Columbus
Dyke College
Edison State Community College
Franciscan University of Steubenville
Franklin University
God's Bible School and College
Heidelberg College
Hiram College
Hocking Technical College
Jefferson Technical College
John Carroll University
Kent State University
   East Liverpool Regional Campus
   Kent
   Salem Regional Campus
   Stark Campus
   Trumbull Regional Campus
   Tuscarawas Campus
Kenyon College
Lake Erie College
Lakeland Community College
Lima Technical College
Lorain County Community College

Colleges that offer academic, music or drama, or art scholarships

Malone College
Marietta College
Marion Technical College
Miami University
   Hamilton Campus
   Middletown Campus
   Oxford Campus
Mount Union College
Muskingum College
North Central Technical College
Northwest Technical College
Northwestern College
Notre Dame College of Ohio
Oberlin College
Ohio Dominican College
Ohio Northern University
Ohio State University
   Agricultural Technical Institute
   Columbus Campus
   Lima Campus
   Mansfield Campus
   Marion Campus
   Newark Campus
Ohio University
   Athens
   Zanesville Campus
Ohio Wesleyan University
Otterbein College
Owens Technical College: Toledo
Pontifical College Josephinum
Southern Ohio College
Southern State Community College
Stark Technical College
Terra Technical College
Tiffin University
University of Akron
University of Cincinnati
   Access Colleges
   Cincinnati
   Clermont College
   Raymond Walters College
University of Dayton
University of Findlay
University of Rio Grande
University of Toledo
Urbana University
Ursuline College
Virginia Marti College of Fashion and Art
Walsh University
Wilberforce University
Wilmington College
Wittenberg University
Wright State University
   Dayton
   Lake Campus
Xavier University
Youngstown State University

Oklahoma

Bartlesville Wesleyan College
Cameron University
Connors State College
East Central University
Eastern Oklahoma State College
Langston University
Mid-America Bible College
Northeastern Oklahoma Agricultural and Mechanical College
Northeastern State University
Northwestern Oklahoma State University
Oklahoma Baptist University
Oklahoma Christian University of Science and Arts
Oklahoma City Community College
Oklahoma City University
Oklahoma Panhandle State University
Oklahoma State University
   Oklahoma City
   Stillwater
Oral Roberts University
Phillips University
Redlands Community College
Rogers State College
Rose State College
St. Gregory's College
Seminole Junior College
Southeastern Oklahoma State University
Southern Nazarene University
Southwestern College of Christian Ministries
Southwestern Oklahoma State University
University of Central Oklahoma
University of Oklahoma
University of Science and Arts of Oklahoma
University of Tulsa

Oregon

Bassist College
Central Oregon Community College
Clackamas Community College
Clatsop Community College
Concordia College
Eastern Oregon State College
Eugene Bible College
George Fox College
Lane Community College
Lewis and Clark College
Linfield College
Linn-Benton Community College
Mount Hood Community College
Multnomah School of the Bible
Northwest Christian College
Oregon Institute of Technology
Oregon State University
Pacific Northwest College of Art
Pacific University
Portland State University
Rogue Community College
Southern Oregon State College
Treasure Valley Community College
Umpqua Community College
University of Oregon
   Eugene
   Robert Donald Clark Honors College
University of Portland
Warner Pacific College
Western Baptist College
Western Oregon State College
Willamette University

Pennsylvania

Albright College
Allegheny College
Allentown College of St. Francis de Sales
Alvernia College
Art Institute of Pittsburgh
Baptist Bible College of Pennsylvania
Beaver College
Bloomsburg University of Pennsylvania
Bucks County Community College
Butler County Community College
Cabrini College
California University of Pennsylvania
Carlow College
Carnegie Mellon University
Cedar Crest College
Central Pennsylvania Business School
Chatham College
Chestnut Hill College
Cheyney University of Pennsylvania
Clarion University of Pennsylvania
College Misericordia
Community College of Allegheny County
   Allegheny Campus
   Boyce Campus
   North Campus
   South Campus
Community College of Beaver County
Community College of Philadelphia
Delaware Valley College
Dickinson College
Drexel University
Duquesne University
East Stroudsburg University of Pennsylvania
Eastern College
Edinboro University of Pennsylvania
Elizabethtown College
Franklin and Marshall College
Gannon University
Geneva College
Grove City College
Gwynedd-Mercy College
Hahnemann University School of Health Sciences and Humanities
Harcum Junior College
Harrisburg Area Community College
Holy Family College
Immaculata College
Indiana University of Pennsylvania
Johnson Technical Institute
Juniata College
Keystone Junior College
King's College
Kutztown University of Pennsylvania
La Roche College
La Salle University
Lackawanna Junior College
Lancaster Bible College
Lebanon Valley College of Pennsylvania
Lehigh County Community College
Lehigh University
Lincoln University
Lock Haven University of Pennsylvania
Luzerne County Community College
Lycoming College
Manor Junior College
Mansfield University of Pennsylvania
Marywood College
Mercyhurst College
Messiah College
Millersville University of Pennsylvania
Montgomery County Community College
Moravian College
Mount Aloysius College
Muhlenberg College
Neumann College
Northampton County Area Community College
Penn State
   Erie Behrend College
   Harrisburg Capital College
   University Park Campus
Pennsylvania College of Technology
Pennsylvania Institute of Technology
Philadelphia College of Bible
Philadelphia College of Pharmacy and Science
Philadelphia College of Textiles and Science
Pittsburgh Institute of Mortuary Science
Pittsburgh Technical Institute
Point Park College
Reading Area Community College
Robert Morris College
Rosemont College
St. Francis College
St. Joseph's University
St. Vincent College
Seton Hill College
Shippensburg University of Pennsylvania
Slippery Rock University of Pennsylvania
Susquehanna University
Temple University
Thiel College
Thomas Jefferson University: College of Allied Health Sciences
Triangle Tech: Pittsburgh Campus
University of the Arts
University of Pittsburgh
   Bradford
   Johnstown
   Pittsburgh
   Titusville
University of Scranton
Ursinus College
Valley Forge Christian College
Villanova University
Washington and Jefferson College
Waynesburg College
West Chester University of Pennsylvania
Westminster College
Widener University
Wilkes University
Wilson College
York College of Pennsylvania

Puerto Rico

Bayamon Central University
University of Puerto Rico
   Bayamon Technological University College
   Carolina Regional College
   Mayaguez Campus
   Ponce Technological University College
   Rio Piedras Campus

Rhode Island

Bryant College
Johnson & Wales University
Providence College
Rhode Island College
Rhode Island School of Design
Roger Williams University
University of Rhode Island

South Carolina

Aiken Technical College
Anderson College
Benedict College
Central Wesleyan College
Charleston Southern University
The Citadel
Clemson University
Coker College
College of Charleston
Columbia Bible College and Seminary
Columbia College
Columbia Junior College of Business
Converse College
Denmark Technical College
Erskine College
Francis Marion University
Furman University

Colleges that offer academic, music or drama, or art scholarships

Greenville Technical College
Horry-Georgetown Technical College
Lander University
Limestone College
Midlands Technical College
Morris College
Newberry College
North Greenville College
Presbyterian College
South Carolina State University
Spartanburg Methodist College
Tri-County Technical College
Trident Technical College
University of South Carolina
    Aiken
    Beaufort
    Coastal Carolina College
    Columbia
    Salkehatchie Regional Campus
    Spartanburg
    Sumter
    Union
Voorhees College
Williamsburg Technical College
Winthrop University
Wofford College
York Technical College

South Dakota
Augustana College
Black Hills State University
Dakota State University
Dakota Wesleyan University
Huron University
Mount Marty College
National College
Northern State University
Presentation College
Sioux Falls College
South Dakota School of Mines and Technology
South Dakota State University
University of South Dakota

Tennessee
Aquinas Junior College
Austin Peay State University
Belmont University
Bethel College
Carson-Newman College
Chattanooga State Technical Community College
Christian Brothers University
Cleveland State Community College
Columbia State Community College
Crichton College
Cumberland University
David Lipscomb University
Dyersburg State Community College
East Tennessee State University
Fisk University
Freed-Hardeman University
Hiwassee College
Johnson Bible College
King College
Knoxville College
Lambuth University
Lee College
Lincoln Memorial University
Maryville College
Memphis College of Art
Memphis State University
Middle Tennessee State University
Milligan College
Motlow State Community College
Nashville State Technical Institute
Northeast State Technical Community College
Pellissippi State Technical Community College

Rhodes College
Roane State Community College
Shelby State Community College
Southern College of Seventh-day Adventists
State Technical Institute at Memphis
Tennessee State University
Tennessee Technological University
Tennessee Temple University
Tennessee Wesleyan College
Tusculum College
Union University
University of the South
University of Tennessee
    Chattanooga
    Knoxville
    Martin
    Memphis
Vanderbilt University
Volunteer State Community College
Walters State Community College
William Jennings Bryan College

Texas
Abilene Christian University
Alvin Community College
Amarillo College
Angelina College
Angelo State University
Austin College
Austin Community College
Bauder Fashion College
Baylor University
Bee County College
Blinn College
Brazosport College
Brookhaven College
Cedar Valley College
Central Texas College
Cisco Junior College
College of the Mainland
Collin County Community College District
Concordia Lutheran College
Cooke County College
Corpus Christi State University
Dallas Baptist University
Dallas Christian College
Dallas Institute of Funeral Service
Del Mar College
DeVry Institute of Technology: Irving
East Texas Baptist University
East Texas State University at Texarkana
El Centro College
El Paso Community College
Frank Phillips College
Galveston College
Grayson County College
Hardin-Simmons University
Hill College
Houston Baptist University
Howard College
Howard Payne University
Incarnate Word College
Institute for Christian Studies
Jacksonville College
Jarvis Christian College
Kilgore College
Lamar University—Beaumont
Laredo Junior College
Laredo State University
Lee College
LeTourneau University
Lon Morris College
McMurry University
Midland College
Midwestern State University
Navarro College
North Lake College

Northeast Texas Community College
Northwood University: Texas Campus
Odessa College
Our Lady of the Lake University of San Antonio
Panola College
Paul Quinn College
Prairie View A&M University
Ranger Junior College
Rice University
Richland College
St. Edward's University
St. Mary's University
St. Philip's College
Sam Houston State University
San Antonio College
San Jacinto College: North
Schreiner College
South Plains College
Southern Methodist University
Southwest Texas Junior College
Southwest Texas State University
Southwestern Adventist College
Southwestern Assemblies of God College
Southwestern Christian College
Southwestern University
Stephen F. Austin State University
Sul Ross State University
Tarleton State University
Tarrant County Junior College
Temple Junior College
Texas A&I University
Texas A&M University
    College Station
    Galveston
Texas Christian University
Texas College
Texas Lutheran College
Texas State Technical College: Waco
Texas Tech University
Texas Wesleyan University
Texas Woman's University
Trinity University
Trinity Valley Community College
Tyler Junior College
University of Dallas
University of Houston
    Clear Lake
    Downtown
    Houston
    Victoria
University of Mary Hardin-Baylor
University of North Texas
University of St. Thomas
University of Texas
    Arlington
    Austin
    Dallas
    El Paso
    Health Science Center at Houston
    Health Science Center at San Antonio
    Pan American
    Permian Basin
    San Antonio
    Southwestern Medical Center at Dallas Southwestern Allied Health Sciences School
    Tyler
Vernon Regional Junior College
Victoria College
Weatherford College
West Texas A & M University
Wharton County Junior College
Wiley College

Utah
Brigham Young University
College of Eastern Utah
Dixie College
LDS Business College
Phillips Junior College: Salt Lake City Campus
Salt Lake Community College
Snow College
Southern Utah University
Stevens-Henager College of Business
University of Utah
Utah State University
Utah Valley Community College
Weber State University
Westminster College of Salt Lake City

Vermont
Bennington College
Castleton State College
College of St. Joseph in Vermont
Community College of Vermont
Green Mountain College
Johnson State College
Lyndon State College
Norwich University
St. Michael's College
School for International Training
Trinity College of Vermont
University of Vermont
Vermont Technical College

Virginia
Averett College
Bluefield College
Bridgewater College
Central Virginia Community College
Christendom College
Christopher Newport University
Clinch Valley College of the University of Virginia
College of Health Sciences
College of William and Mary
Dabney S. Lancaster Community College
Eastern Mennonite College
Eastern Shore Community College
Emory and Henry College
Ferrum College
George Mason University
Hampden-Sydney College
Hampton University
Hollins College
James Madison University
John Tyler Community College
Liberty University
Longwood College
Lynchburg College
Mary Baldwin College
Mary Washington College
Marymount University
Mountain Empire Community College
National Business College
New River Community College
Norfolk State University
Northern Virginia Community College
Old Dominion University
Patrick Henry Community College
Paul D. Camp Community College
Radford University
Randolph-Macon College
Randolph-Macon Woman's College
Rappahannock Community College
Richard Bland College
Roanoke College
St. Paul's College
Shenandoah University

Colleges that offer academic, music or drama, or art scholarships

Southern Virginia College for Women
Southside Virginia Community College
Southwest Virginia Community College
Sweet Briar College
Tidewater Community College
University of Richmond
Virginia Commonwealth University
Virginia Intermont College
Virginia Military Institute
Virginia Polytechnic Institute and State University
Virginia State University
Virginia Union University
Virginia Wesleyan College
Virginia Western Community College
Washington and Lee University
Wytheville Community College

Washington

Bastyr College
Bellevue Community College
Big Bend Community College
Central Washington University
Centralia College
Clark College
Columbia Basin College
Cornish College of the Arts
Eastern Washington University
Edmonds Community College
Everett Community College
Evergreen State College
Gonzaga University
Grays Harbor College
Green River Community College
Heritage College
Lower Columbia College
Lutheran Bible Institute of Seattle
North Seattle Community College
Northwest College of the Assemblies of God
Olympic College
Pacific Lutheran University
Peninsula College
Pierce College
Puget Sound Christian College
St. Martin's College
Seattle Central Community College
Seattle Pacific University
Seattle University
Shoreline Community College
Skagit Valley College
South Puget Sound Community College
South Seattle Community College
Tacoma Community College
University of Puget Sound
University of Washington
Walla Walla College
Walla Walla Community College
Washington State University
Wenatchee Valley College
Western Washington University
Whatcom Community College
Whitman College
Whitworth College

West Virginia

Alderson-Broaddus College
Bethany College
Bluefield State College
College of West Virginia
Concord College
Davis and Elkins College
Fairmont State College
Glenville State College
Marshall University
Ohio Valley College

Potomac State College of West Virginia University
Salem-Teikyo University
Shepherd College
Southern West Virginia Community College
University of Charleston
West Liberty State College
West Virginia Institute of Technology
West Virginia Northern Community College
West Virginia State College
West Virginia University
  Morgantown
  Parkersburg
West Virginia Wesleyan College
Wheeling Jesuit College

Wisconsin

Alverno College
Beloit College
Cardinal Stritch College
Carroll College
Carthage College
Chippewa Valley Technical College
Columbia College of Nursing
Concordia University Wisconsin
Edgewood College
Fox Valley Technical College
Lakeland College
Lawrence University
Madison Area Technical College
Madison Junior College of Business
Maranatha Baptist Bible College
Marian College of Fond du Lac
Marquette University
Mid-State Technical College
Milwaukee School of Engineering
Moraine Park Technical College
Mount Mary College
Mount Senario College
Nicolet Area Technical College
Northeast Wisconsin Technical College
Northland College
Northwestern College
Ripon College
St. Norbert College
Silver Lake College
Stratton College
University of Wisconsin
  Eau Claire
  Green Bay
  La Crosse
  Madison
  Oshkosh
  Parkside
  Platteville
  River Falls
  Stevens Point
  Stout
  Superior
  Whitewater
University of Wisconsin Center
  Baraboo/Sauk County
  Barron County
  Fox Valley
  Manitowoc County
  Marathon County
  Marinette County
  Marshfield/Wood County
  Richland
  Rock County
  Sheboygan County
  Washington County
  Waukesha
Viterbo College
Waukesha County Technical College
Wisconsin Indianhead Technical College

Wisconsin Lutheran College

Wyoming

Casper College
Central Wyoming College
Eastern Wyoming College
Laramie County Community College
Northwest College
Sheridan College
University of Wyoming
Western Wyoming Community College

American Samoa, Caroline Islands, Guam, Marianas, Virgin Islands

Guam Community College
University of the Virgin Islands

Arab Republic of Egypt

American University in Cairo

France

American University of Paris

Mexico

Sistema Instituto Tecnologico y de Estudios Superiores de Monterrey

Music or drama scholarships

Alabama

Alabama Agricultural and Mechanical University
Alabama Southern Community College
Alabama State University
Athens State College
Auburn University
  Auburn
  Montgomery
Bevill State Community College
Birmingham-Southern College
Bishop State Community College
Central Alabama Community College: Alexander City Campus
Chattahoochee Valley Community College
Enterprise State Junior College
Gadsden State Community College
George C. Wallace State Community College
  Dothan
  Selma
Huntingdon College
Jacksonville State University
James H. Faulkner State Community College
Jefferson Davis State Junior College
Jefferson State Community College
John C. Calhoun State Community College
Judson College
Livingston University
Lurleen B. Wallace State Junior College
Marion Military Institute
Northeast Alabama Community College
Samford University
Shelton State Community College
Shoals Community College
Snead State Community College
Southeastern Bible College
Stillman College
Tuskegee University

University of Alabama
  Birmingham
  Huntsville
  Tuscaloosa
University of Mobile
University of Montevallo
University of North Alabama
University of South Alabama
Wallace State Community College at Hanceville

Alaska

Alaska Bible College
Sheldon Jackson College
University of Alaska
  Anchorage
  Fairbanks
  Southeast

Arizona

Arizona College of the Bible
Arizona State University
Arizona Western College
Central Arizona College
Eastern Arizona College
Glendale Community College
Grand Canyon University
Mohave Community College
Northern Arizona University
Northland Pioneer College
Phoenix College
South Mountain Community College
University of Arizona
Yavapai College

Arkansas

Arkansas College
Arkansas State University
  Beebe Branch
  Jonesboro
Arkansas Tech University
Central Baptist College
Garland County Community College
Harding University
Henderson State University
Hendrix College
John Brown University
Mississippi County Community College
North Arkansas Community/Technical College
Ouachita Baptist University
Phillips County Community College
South Arkansas Community College
Southern Arkansas University
  Magnolia
  Technical Branch
University of Arkansas
University of Arkansas
  Little Rock
  Monticello
University of Central Arkansas
University of the Ozarks

California

Allan Hancock College
Antelope Valley College
Azusa Pacific University
Biola University
California Baptist College
California Institute of the Arts
California Lutheran University

Colleges that offer academic, music or drama, or art scholarships

California State University
  Bakersfield
  Dominguez Hills
  Fresno
  Fullerton
  Long Beach
  Los Angeles
  Northridge
  Stanislaus
Cerro Coso Community College
Chapman University
Christian Heritage College
Citrus College
College of Notre Dame
Columbia College
Compton Community College
Concordia University
Cypress College
Dominican College of San Rafael
Evergreen Valley College
Foothill College
Fresno City College
Fresno Pacific College
Fullerton College
Grossmont Community College
Holy Names College
Humboldt State University
La Sierra University
Lake Tahoe Community College
Long Beach City College
Loyola Marymount University
Master's College
Mills College
MiraCosta College
Modesto Junior College
Monterey Peninsula College
Mount San Jacinto College
Napa Valley College
Occidental College
Pacific Christian College
Pacific Union College
Pasadena City College
Pepperdine University
Rio Hondo College
Saddleback College
San Diego City College
San Diego State University
San Francisco Conservatory of Music
San Francisco State University
San Joaquin Delta College
San Jose Christian College
Santa Clara University
Santa Monica College
Santa Rosa Junior College
Shasta College
Sierra College
Simpson College
Sonoma State University
University of California
  Irvine
  Los Angeles
  Riverside
  Santa Barbara
  Santa Cruz
University of the Pacific
University of Redlands
University of Southern California
Ventura College
Westmont College
Whittier College

Colorado
Adams State College
Colorado Christian University
Colorado Institute of Art
Colorado School of Mines
Colorado State University
Community College of Denver
Fort Lewis College
Mesa State College
Metropolitan State College of Denver
Northeastern Junior College
Trinidad State Junior College
University of Colorado
  Boulder
  Denver
University of Denver
University of Northern Colorado
University of Southern Colorado
Western State College of Colorado

Connecticut
Quinebaug Valley Community-Technical College
University of Connecticut
University of Hartford

Delaware
Delaware State College
University of Delaware
Wesley College

District of Columbia
Catholic University of America
George Washington University
Howard University
Mount Vernon College
University of the District of Columbia

Florida
Barry University
Bethune-Cookman College
Brevard Community College
Broward Community College
Central Florida Community College
Chipola Junior College
Daytona Beach Community College
Eckerd College
Edison Community College
Flagler College
Florida Agricultural and Mechanical University
Florida Atlantic University
Florida Bible College
Florida Christian College
Florida College
Florida Community College at Jacksonville
Florida International University
Florida Memorial College
Florida Southern College
Florida State University
Gulf Coast Community College
Hillsborough Community College
Indian River Community College
Jacksonville University
Lake-Sumter Community College
Manatee Community College
Miami-Dade Community College
North Florida Junior College
Okaloosa-Walton Community College
Palm Beach Atlantic College
Palm Beach Community College
Pensacola Junior College
Polk Community College
Rollins College
St. Johns River Community College
St. Leo College
St. Petersburg Junior College
Santa Fe Community College
Seminole Community College
South Florida Community College
Southeastern College of the Assemblies of God
Stetson University
Tallahassee Community College
University of Central Florida
University of Florida
University of Miami
University of North Florida
University of South Florida
University of Tampa
University of West Florida
Valencia Community College

Georgia
Abraham Baldwin Agricultural College
Agnes Scott College
Andrew College
Armstrong State College
Atlanta Christian College
Augusta College
Brenau University
Brewton-Parker College
Clark Atlanta University
Clayton State College
Columbus College
Covenant College
Darton College
Emmanuel College
Emory University
Floyd College
Fort Valley State College
Gainesville College
Georgia College
Georgia Southern University
Georgia Southwestern College
Georgia State University
Gordon College
Kennesaw State College
LaGrange College
Mercer University
Middle Georgia College
Morehouse College
Morris Brown College
North Georgia College
Oglethorpe University
Paine College
Piedmont College
Savannah State College
Shorter College
Spelman College
Toccoa Falls College
Truett-McConnell College
University of Georgia
Valdosta State College
Waycross College
Wesleyan College
West Georgia College
Young Harris College

Hawaii
Brigham Young University-Hawaii
Hawaii Pacific University
University of Hawaii
  Hilo
  Kauai Community College
  Manoa
  West Oahu

Idaho
Albertson College
Boise State University
College of Southern Idaho
Idaho State University
Lewis Clark State College
North Idaho College
Northwest Nazarene College
Ricks College
University of Idaho

Illinois
American Conservatory of Music
Augustana College
Barat College
Belleville Area College
Black Hawk College
Bradley University
Carl Sandburg College
Chicago State University
College of DuPage
College of Lake County
Concordia University
De Paul University
Eastern Illinois University
Elgin Community College
Elmhurst College
Eureka College
Governors State University
Highland Community College
Illinois Benedictine College
Illinois College
Illinois State University
Illinois Valley Community College
Illinois Wesleyan University
John A. Logan College
Joliet Junior College
Judson College
Kankakee Community College
Kaskaskia College
Knox College
Lake Land College
Lewis and Clark Community College
Lewis University
Lincoln College
Lincoln Land Community College
Loyola University of Chicago
MacMurray College
McKendree College
Millikin University
Monmouth College
Montay College
Morton College
North Central College
North Park College
Northeastern Illinois University
Northern Illinois University
Northwestern University
Oakton Community College
Olivet Nazarene University
Quincy University
Rock Valley College
Rockford College
Roosevelt University
St. Xavier University
Sauk Valley Community College
Shawnee Community College
Shimer College
Southeastern Illinois College
Southern Illinois University
  Carbondale
  Edwardsville
Spoon River College
Springfield College in Illinois
Trinity Christian College
Trinity College
University of Chicago
University of Illinois
  Chicago
  Urbana-Champaign
VanderCook College of Music
Western Illinois University
Wheaton College
William Rainey Harper College

Indiana
Anderson University
Ball State University
Bethel College
Butler University
DePauw University
Franklin College
Goshen College
Grace College
Huntington College
Indiana State University
Indiana University
  Bloomington
  South Bend
Indiana University—Purdue University at Fort Wayne

233

Colleges that offer academic, music or drama, or art scholarships

Indiana Wesleyan University
Marian College
Oakland City College
St. Joseph's College
St. Mary-of-the-Woods College
Taylor University
University of Evansville
University of Indianapolis
University of Southern Indiana
Valparaiso University
Vincennes University
Wabash College

Iowa
Briar Cliff College
Buena Vista College
Central College
Clarke College
Coe College
Cornell College
Dordt College
Drake University
Ellsworth Community College
Graceland College
Grand View College
Indian Hills Community College
Iowa Central Community College
Iowa Lakes Community College
Iowa State University
Iowa Wesleyan College
Loras College
Luther College
Morningside College
Mount Mercy College
Mount St. Clare College
Muscatine Community College
North Iowa Area Community
  College
Northwestern College
St. Ambrose University
Simpson College
Southwestern Community College
Teikyo Marycrest University
Teikyo Westmar University
University of Dubuque
University of Iowa
University of Northern Iowa
Vennard College
Waldorf College
Wartburg College
William Penn College

Kansas
Allen County Community College
Baker University
Barclay College
Barton County Community College
Benedictine College
Bethany College
Bethel College
Butler County Community College
Central College
Coffeyville Community College
Colby Community College
Dodge City Community College
Emporia State University
Fort Hays State University
Friends University
Garden City Community College
Hesston College
Highland Community College
Hutchinson Community College
Independence Community College
Johnson County Community
  College
Kansas City Kansas Community
  College
Kansas State University
Kansas Wesleyan University
McPherson College
MidAmerica Nazarene College
Neosho County Community College

Pittsburg State University
Pratt Community College
St. Mary College
Southwestern College
Sterling College
Tabor College
University of Kansas
Washburn University of Topeka
Wichita State University

Kentucky
Asbury College
Bellarmine College
Brescia College
Campbellsville College
Cumberland College
Eastern Kentucky University
Georgetown College
Kentucky State University
Kentucky Wesleyan College
Lindsey Wilson College
Midway College
Morehead State University
Murray State University
Northern Kentucky University
Spalding University
Thomas More College
Transylvania University
Union College
University of Kentucky
University of Louisville
Western Kentucky University

Louisiana
Centenary College of Louisiana
Grambling State University
Louisiana State University
  Agricultural and Mechanical
    College
  Alexandria
Louisiana Tech University
Loyola University
McNeese State University
Nicholls State University
Northeast Louisiana University
Northwestern State University
Southeastern Louisiana University
University of New Orleans
University of Southwestern
  Louisiana
Xavier University of Louisiana

Maine
University of Maine
  Augusta
  Orono
  Presque Isle
University of Southern Maine

Maryland
Bowie State University
Cecil Community College
Charles County Community College
College of Notre Dame of
  Maryland
Columbia Union College
Essex Community College
Frederick Community College
Frostburg State University
Goucher College
Harford Community College
Johns Hopkins University
Johns Hopkins University: Peabody
  Conservatory of Music
Prince George's Community College
St. Mary's College of Maryland
Towson State University
University of Maryland
  Baltimore County
  College Park
  Eastern Shore

Massachusetts
Anna Maria College for Men and
  Women
Atlantic Union College
Bay Path College
Berklee College of Music
Boston Conservatory
Boston University
Eastern Nazarene College
Emerson College
Fitchburg State College
Gordon College
Holyoke Community College
Massachusetts Bay Community
  College
New England Conservatory of
  Music
Quinsigamond Community College
Salem State College
Springfield Technical Community
  College
Stonehill College
University of Massachusetts at
  Amherst

Michigan
Adrian College
Albion College
Alma College
Aquinas College
Calvin College
Central Michigan University
Charles Stewart Mott Community
  College
Concordia College
Eastern Michigan University
Ferris State University
Glen Oaks Community College
Grace Bible College
Grand Rapids Baptist College and
  Seminary
Grand Rapids Community College
Grand Valley State University
Great Lakes Christian College
Henry Ford Community College
Hillsdale College
Hope College
Jackson Community College
Kalamazoo College
Kellogg Community College
Lake Michigan College
Lansing Community College
Macomb Community College
Madonna University
Marygrove College
Michigan Christian College
Michigan State University
Monroe County Community
  College
Montcalm Community College
Muskegon Community College
Northwestern Michigan College
Oakland University
Olivet College
Saginaw Valley State University
St. Clair County Community
  College
Schoolcraft College
Siena Heights College
Southwestern Michigan College
Spring Arbor College
Suomi College
University of Michigan
  Ann Arbor
  Flint
Wayne State University
West Shore Community College
Western Michigan University
William Tyndale College

Minnesota
Augsburg College

Austin Community College
Bemidji State University
Bethany Lutheran College
Brainerd Community College
College of St. Benedict
College of St. Catherine: St.
  Catherine Campus
College of St. Scholastica
Concordia College: Moorhead
Concordia College: St. Paul
Crown College
Dr. Martin Luther College
Fergus Falls Community College
Inver Hills Community College
Mankato State University
Minnesota Bible College
Moorhead State University
North Central Bible College
North Hennepin Community
  College
Northwestern College
Pillsbury Baptist Bible College
Rainy River Community College
St. Cloud State University
St. John's University
St. Mary's College of Minnesota
Southwest State University
University of Minnesota
  Duluth
  Morris
  Twin Cities
University of St. Thomas
Willmar Community College
Winona State University
Worthington Community College

Mississippi
Alcorn State University
Belhaven College
Copiah-Lincoln Community College
Delta State University
East Central Community College
East Mississippi Community College
Hinds Community College
Holmes Community College
Jackson State University
Meridian Community College
Millsaps College
Mississippi College
Mississippi Delta Community
  College
Mississippi Gulf Coast Community
  College
    Jefferson Davis Campus
    Perkinston
Mississippi State University
Mississippi University for Women
Mississippi Valley State University
Pearl River Community College
Rust College
Tougaloo College
University of Mississippi
University of Southern Mississippi
William Carey College
Wood Junior College

Missouri
Avila College
Central Christian College of the
  Bible
Central Methodist College
Central Missouri State University
Cottey College
Crowder College
Culver-Stockton College
Drury College
East Central College
Evangel College
Fontbonne College
Hannibal-LaGrange College
Jefferson College

Colleges that offer academic, music or drama, or art scholarships

Kemper Military School and
    College
Lincoln University
Lindenwood College
Longview Community College
Maple Woods Community College
Mineral Area College
Missouri Baptist College
Missouri Southern State College
Missouri Valley College
Missouri Western State College
Moberly Area Community College
Northeast Missouri State University
Ozark Christian College
Park College
St. Charles County Community
    College
St. Louis Christian College
St. Louis Community College
    Florissant Valley
    Forest Park
    Meramec
St. Louis University
Southeast Missouri State University
Southwest Baptist University
Southwest Missouri State University
State Fair Community College
Stephens College
University of Missouri
    Columbia
    Kansas City
    Rolla
Webster University
Westminster College
William Jewell College
William Woods College

Montana
Carroll College
Dawson Community College
Eastern Montana College
Miles Community College
Montana State University
Northern Montana College
Rocky Mountain College
University of Montana
Western Montana College of the
    University of Montana

Nebraska
Central Community College
Chadron State College
College of St. Mary
Concordia College
Doane College
Grace College of the Bible
McCook Community College
Mid Plains Community College
Midland Lutheran College
Nebraska Wesleyan University
Northeast Community College
Peru State College
Southeast Community College:
    Beatrice Campus
Union College
University of Nebraska
    Kearney
    Lincoln
    Omaha
Wayne State College
Western Nebraska Community
    College: Scottsbluff Campus
York College

Nevada
Sierra Nevada College
University of Nevada
    Las Vegas
    Reno

New Hampshire
Colby-Sawyer College

Keene State College
Plymouth State College of the
    University System of New
    Hampshire
University of New Hampshire

New Jersey
Georgian Court College
Jersey City State College
Mercer County Community College
Rider College
Rowan College of New Jersey
Rutgers—The State University of
    New Jersey
    Douglass College
    Livingston College
    Mason Gross School of the
        Arts
    Rutgers College
Trenton State College
Westminster Choir College School
    of Music of Rider College
William Paterson College of New
    Jersey

New Mexico
College of Santa Fe
College of the Southwest
Eastern New Mexico University
New Mexico Highlands University
New Mexico Junior College
New Mexico State University
San Juan College
Santa Fe Community College
University of New Mexico
Western New Mexico University

New York
Adelphi University
Bard College
City University of New York:
    Brooklyn College
Clarkson University
College of New Rochelle
College of St. Rose
Concordia College
Eastman School of Music of the
    University of Rochester
Elmira College
Finger Lakes Community College
Five Towns College
Fordham University
Genesee Community College
Hartwick College
Houghton College
Ithaca College
Jamestown Community College
Juilliard School
King's College
Long Island University
    Brooklyn Campus
    C. W. Post Campus
Manhattan School of Music
Manhattanville College
Mannes College of Music
Marist College
Marymount College
Marymount Manhattan College
Molloy College
Nassau Community College
Nazareth College of Rochester
New York University
Niagara University
Orange County Community College
Pace University
    New York
    Pleasantville/Briarcliff
Roberts Wesleyan College
St. Bonaventure University
St. John's University
Skidmore College

State University of New York
    Binghamton
    Buffalo
    Purchase
    College at Brockport
    College at Buffalo
    College at Cortland
    College at Geneseo
    College at Plattsburgh
    College at Potsdam
    College of Technology at
        Alfred
    Oswego
Syracuse University
University of Rochester
Villa Maria College of Buffalo
Wagner College
Westchester Community College

North Carolina
Appalachian State University
Barton College
Bennett College
Brevard College
Campbell University
Catawba College
Chowan College
Davidson College
Duke University
East Carolina University
Elizabeth City State University
Elon College
Fayetteville State University
Gardner-Webb University
Greensboro College
Guilford College
Isothermal Community College
John Wesley College
Johnson C. Smith University
Lees-McRae College
Lenoir-Rhyne College
Livingstone College
Louisburg College
Mars Hill College
Meredith College
Methodist College
Mitchell Community College
Mount Olive College
North Carolina Agricultural and
    Technical State University
North Carolina School of the Arts
Peace College
Pembroke State University
Pfeiffer College
Piedmont Bible College
Queens College
Roanoke Bible College
St. Andrews Presbyterian College
St. Augustine's College
St. Mary's College
Salem College
Sandhills Community College
University of North Carolina
    Asheville
    Chapel Hill
    Greensboro
    Wilmington
Wake Forest University
Western Carolina University
Wilkes Community College
Wingate College
Winston-Salem State University

North Dakota
Bismarck State College
Dickinson State University
Jamestown College
Minot State University
North Dakota State College of
    Science
Trinity Bible College
University of Mary

University of North Dakota
Valley City State University

Ohio
Ashland University
Baldwin-Wallace College
Bluffton College
Bowling Green State University
Capital University
Case Western Reserve University
Cedarville College
Central State University
Cincinnati Bible College and
    Seminary
Cleveland Institute of Music
Cleveland State University
College of Wooster
Cuyahoga Community College:
    Western Campus
Defiance College
Denison University
God's Bible School and College
Heidelberg College
Hiram College
Kent State University
Lake Erie College
Lakeland Community College
Malone College
Marietta College
Miami University: Oxford Campus
Mount Union College
Muskingum College
Oberlin College
Ohio Northern University
Ohio State University
    Columbus Campus
    Lima Campus
    Mansfield Campus
Ohio University
Ohio Wesleyan University
Otterbein College
Southern State Community College
University of Akron
University of Cincinnati
    Access Colleges
    Cincinnati
    Clermont College
University of Dayton
University of Findlay
University of Rio Grande
University of Toledo
Urbana University
Wilmington College
Wittenberg University
Wright State University
Xavier University
Youngstown State University

Oklahoma
Bartlesville Wesleyan College
Cameron University
East Central University
Eastern Oklahoma State College
Langston University
Northeastern State University
Northwestern Oklahoma State
    University
Oklahoma Baptist University
Oklahoma Christian University of
    Science and Arts
Oklahoma City University
Oklahoma Panhandle State
    University
Oklahoma State University
Oral Roberts University
Phillips University
Rogers State College
Rose State College
St. Gregory's College
Seminole Junior College
Southeastern Oklahoma State
    University

Colleges that offer academic, music or drama, or art scholarships

Southern Nazarene University
Southwestern College of Christian Ministries
Southwestern Oklahoma State University
University of Central Oklahoma
University of Oklahoma
University of Science and Arts of Oklahoma
University of Tulsa

Oregon

Blue Mountain Community College
Central Oregon Community College
Clackamas Community College
Concordia College
Eastern Oregon State College
Eugene Bible College
George Fox College
Lane Community College
Lewis and Clark College
Linfield College
Linn-Benton Community College
Marylhurst College
Mount Hood Community College
Multnomah School of the Bible
Oregon State University
Pacific University
Portland State University
Southern Oregon State College
Treasure Valley Community College
University of Oregon
  Eugene
  Robert Donald Clark Honors College
University of Portland
Warner Pacific College
Western Baptist College
Western Oregon State College
Willamette University

Pennsylvania

Allegheny College
Allentown College of St. Francis de Sales
Baptist Bible College of Pennsylvania
Beaver College
Bucks County Community College
California University of Pennsylvania
Carnegie Mellon University
Chatham College
Cheyney University of Pennsylvania
Clarion University of Pennsylvania
Community College of Allegheny County
  Boyce Campus
  South Campus
Curtis Institute of Music
Drexel University
Duquesne University
Elizabethtown College
Geneva College
Immaculata College
Indiana University of Pennsylvania
Juniata College
Lancaster Bible College
Lincoln University
Lock Haven University of Pennsylvania
Lycoming College
Mansfield University of Pennsylvania
Marywood College
Mercyhurst College
Millersville University of Pennsylvania
Penn State
  Erie Behrend College
  Harrisburg Capital College
  University Park Campus

Philadelphia College of Bible
Point Park College
St. Vincent College
Seton Hill College
Slippery Rock University of Pennsylvania
Susquehanna University
Temple University
University of the Arts
Ursinus College
Valley Forge Christian College
Valley Forge Military College
West Chester University of Pennsylvania
Westminster College
Widener University
Wilkes University
York College of Pennsylvania

Puerto Rico

Pontifical Catholic University of Puerto Rico
University of Puerto Rico
  Carolina Regional College
  La Montana Regional College
  Mayaguez Campus
  Ponce Technological University College
  Rio Piedras Campus

Rhode Island

Rhode Island College
University of Rhode Island

South Carolina

Anderson College
Central Wesleyan College
Clemson University
Coker College
College of Charleston
Columbia Bible College and Seminary
Columbia College
Converse College
Erskine College
Francis Marion University
Furman University
Lander University
Limestone College
Newberry College
North Greenville College
Presbyterian College
South Carolina State University
Spartanburg Methodist College
University of South Carolina
  Aiken
  Columbia
  Spartanburg
Winthrop University
Wofford College

South Dakota

Augustana College
Black Hills State University
Dakota State University
Dakota Wesleyan University
Mount Marty College
Northern State University
Sioux Falls College
South Dakota State University
University of South Dakota

Tennessee

Austin Peay State University
Belmont University
Bethel College
Carson-Newman College
Chattanooga State Technical Community College
Christian Brothers University
Crichton College
David Lipscomb University

Dyersburg State Community College
East Tennessee State University
Free Will Baptist Bible College
Freed-Hardeman University
Hiwassee College
Johnson Bible College
King College
Knoxville College
Lambuth University
Lee College
Lincoln Memorial University
Maryville College
Memphis State University
Milligan College
Motlow State Community College
Pellissippi State Technical Community College
Rhodes College
Roane State Community College
Shelby State Community College
Southern College of Seventh-day Adventists
Tennessee State University
Tennessee Technological University
Tennessee Temple University
Tennessee Wesleyan College
Union University
University of Tennessee
  Chattanooga
  Knoxville
  Martin
Vanderbilt University
Walters State Community College
William Jennings Bryan College

Texas

Abilene Christian University
Alvin Community College
Angelina College
Austin College
Baylor University
Bee County College
Blinn College
Cedar Valley College
Cisco Junior College
College of the Mainland
Collin County Community College District
Concordia Lutheran College
Cooke County College
Corpus Christi State University
Dallas Baptist University
Dallas Christian College
Del Mar College
East Texas Baptist University
El Centro College
Frank Phillips College
Galveston College
Grayson County College
Hardin-Simmons University
Hill College
Houston Baptist University
Howard College
Howard Payne University
Incarnate Word College
Jacksonville College
Jarvis Christian College
Lamar University—Beaumont
Laredo Junior College
Lee College
Lon Morris College
McMurry University
Midland College
Midwestern State University
Navarro College
Northeast Texas Community College
Odessa College
Our Lady of the Lake University of San Antonio
Panola College

Prairie View A&M University
Ranger Junior College
Rice University
St. Mary's University
St. Philip's College
Sam Houston State University
San Antonio College
San Jacinto College: North
Schreiner College
South Plains College
Southern Methodist University
Southwest Texas State University
Southwestern Adventist College
Southwestern Assemblies of God College
Southwestern Christian College
Southwestern University
Stephen F. Austin State University
Sul Ross State University
Tarleton State University
Tarrant County Junior College
Temple Junior College
Texas A&I University
Texas Christian University
Texas College
Texas Lutheran College
Texas Tech University
Texas Wesleyan University
Texas Woman's University
Trinity University
Trinity Valley Community College
Tyler Junior College
University of Dallas
University of Houston
University of Mary Hardin-Baylor
University of North Texas
University of St. Thomas
University of Texas
  Arlington
  Austin
  El Paso
  Pan American
  Tyler
Vernon Regional Junior College
Victoria College
Weatherford College
West Texas A & M University
Wharton County Junior College
Wiley College

Utah

Brigham Young University
College of Eastern Utah
Dixie College
Snow College
Southern Utah University
University of Utah
Utah State University
Weber State University
Westminster College of Salt Lake City

Vermont

Castleton State College
Johnson State College
University of Vermont

Virginia

Bluefield College
Bridgewater College
Christopher Newport University
George Mason University
Hampton University
Hollins College
James Madison University
Liberty University
Longwood College
Lynchburg College
Mary Baldwin College
Old Dominion University
Radford University
Randolph-Macon Woman's College

Colleges that offer academic, music or drama, or art scholarships

Roanoke College
Shenandoah University
Sweet Briar College
University of Richmond
Virginia Commonwealth University
Virginia Polytechnic Institute and
　State University
Virginia Union University

Washington
Big Bend Community College
Central Washington University
Centralia College
Clark College
Columbia Basin College
Cornish College of the Arts
Eastern Washington University
Edmonds Community College
Evergreen State College
Gonzaga University
Grays Harbor College
Green River Community College
Lower Columbia College
Lutheran Bible Institute of Seattle
North Seattle Community College
Northwest College of the
　Assemblies of God
Olympic College
Pacific Lutheran University
Peninsula College
Puget Sound Christian College
Seattle Pacific University
Seattle University
Skagit Valley College
South Seattle Community College
Tacoma Community College
University of Puget Sound
Walla Walla College
Walla Walla Community College
Washington State University
Wenatchee Valley College
Western Washington University
Whitman College
Whitworth College

West Virginia
Alderson-Broaddus College
Concord College
Davis and Elkins College
Fairmont State College
Glenville State College
Marshall University
Ohio Valley College
Shepherd College
University of Charleston
West Liberty State College
West Virginia Institute of
　Technology
West Virginia State College
West Virginia University
West Virginia Wesleyan College
Wheeling Jesuit College

Wisconsin
Alverno College
Beloit College
Cardinal Stritch College
Carroll College
Carthage College
Concordia University Wisconsin
Edgewood College
Lawrence University
Marian College of Fond du Lac
Marquette University
Mount Mary College
Northland College
Ripon College
St. Norbert College
Silver Lake College

University of Wisconsin
　Eau Claire
　Green Bay
　La Crosse
　Madison
　Oshkosh
　Parkside
　River Falls
　Stevens Point
　Stout
　Whitewater
University of Wisconsin Center
　Baraboo/Sauk County
　Barron County
　Marathon County
　Richland
　Rock County
　Washington County
　Waukesha
Viterbo College
Wisconsin Lutheran College

Wyoming
Casper College
Central Wyoming College
Eastern Wyoming College
Laramie County Community
　College
Northwest College
Sheridan College
University of Wyoming
Western Wyoming Community
　College

Arab Republic of Egypt
American University in Cairo

Art scholarships

Alabama
Alabama Southern Community
　College
Alabama State University
Athens State College
Auburn University
Birmingham-Southern College
Central Alabama Community
　College: Alexander City Campus
Chattahoochee Valley Community
　College
Enterprise State Junior College
Huntingdon College
Jacksonville State University
James H. Faulkner State
　Community College
Jefferson Davis State Junior College
John C. Calhoun State Community
　College
Judson College
Livingston University
Lurleen B. Wallace State Junior
　College
Northeast Alabama Community
　College
Samford University
Shelton State Community College
Snead State Community College
University of Alabama
　Birmingham
　Huntsville
　Tuscaloosa
University of Mobile
University of North Alabama
Walker College
Wallace State Community College
　at Hanceville

Alaska
University of Alaska
　Anchorage
　Fairbanks
　Southeast

Arizona
Arizona State University
Arizona Western College
Central Arizona College
Eastern Arizona College
Glendale Community College
Grand Canyon University
Northern Arizona University
Northland Pioneer College
Phoenix College
South Mountain Community
　College
University of Arizona
Yavapai College

Arkansas
Arkansas College
Arkansas State University
Garland County Community
　College
Harding University
Henderson State University
Hendrix College
John Brown University
Mississippi County Community
　College
North Arkansas Community/
　Technical College
Southern Arkansas University:
　Technical Branch
University of Arkansas
University of Arkansas at Little
　Rock
University of Central Arkansas

California
Academy of Art College
Allan Hancock College
Antelope Valley College
Art Institute of Southern California
Biola University
Brooks Institute of Photography
California College of Arts and
　Crafts
California Institute of the Arts
California Lutheran University
California Polytechnic State
　University: San Luis Obispo
California State University
　Bakersfield
　Dominguez Hills
　Fresno
　Fullerton
　Long Beach
　Los Angeles
　Northridge
　Stanislaus
Cerro Coso Community College
Chapman University
Citrus College
College of Notre Dame
College of the Redwoods
Columbia College
Compton Community College
Evergreen Valley College
Foothill College
Fresno City College
Fresno Pacific College
Fullerton College
Golden West College
Grossmont Community College
Holy Names College
Humboldt State University
La Sierra University
Lake Tahoe Community College
Long Beach City College

Mills College
MiraCosta College
Modesto Junior College
Monterey Peninsula College
Mount San Jacinto College
Napa Valley College
Pasadena City College
Pepperdine University
Rio Hondo College
Saddleback College
San Diego City College
San Diego State University
San Francisco Art Institute
San Joaquin Delta College
Santa Monica College
Santa Rosa Junior College
Shasta College
Sierra College
Southern California Institute of
　Architecture
University of California
　Irvine
　Los Angeles
　Riverside
　Santa Barbara
　Santa Cruz
University of Redlands
University of Southern California
Ventura College
Westmont College
Whittier College

Colorado
Adams State College
Colorado Institute of Art
Colorado State University
Community College of Denver
Fort Lewis College
Lamar Community College
Mesa State College
Northeastern Junior College
Rocky Mountain College of Art &
　Design
Trinidad State Junior College
University of Colorado
　Boulder
　Denver
University of Denver
University of Northern Colorado
University of Southern Colorado
Western State College of Colorado

Connecticut
Sacred Heart University
University of Connecticut
University of Hartford

District of Columbia
Corcoran School of Art
Howard University

Florida
Brevard Community College
Broward Community College
Chipola Junior College
Daytona Beach Community College
Eckerd College
Edison Community College
Flagler College
Florida Community College at
　Jacksonville
Florida International University
Florida Southern College
Florida State University
Gulf Coast Community College
Hillsborough Community College
Indian River Community College
Jacksonville University
Lake-Sumter Community College
Manatee Community College
Miami-Dade Community College
North Florida Junior College

237

Colleges that offer academic, music or drama, or art scholarships

Okaloosa-Walton Community College
Pensacola Junior College
Polk Community College
Ringling School of Art and Design
Rollins College
St. Johns River Community College
St. Leo College
St. Petersburg Junior College
Santa Fe Community College
Seminole Community College
University of Central Florida
University of South Florida
University of Tampa
Valencia Community College

Georgia

Abraham Baldwin Agricultural College
Andrew College
Armstrong State College
Augusta College
Brenau University
Brewton-Parker College
Clayton State College
Columbus College
Darton College
Floyd College
Gainesville College
Georgia Southwestern College
Georgia State University
Gordon College
Kennesaw State College
LaGrange College
Mercer University
Morris Brown College
North Georgia College
Piedmont College
Savannah College of Art and Design
Shorter College
Valdosta State College
Waycross College
Wesleyan College
West Georgia College
Young Harris College

Hawaii

Brigham Young University-Hawaii
University of Hawaii
    Hilo
    West Oahu

Idaho

Albertson College
Boise State University
College of Southern Idaho
Idaho State University
North Idaho College
Northwest Nazarene College
Ricks College
University of Idaho

Illinois

American Academy of Art
Augustana College
Barat College
Belleville Area College
Black Hawk College
Bradley University
Carl Sandburg College
Chicago State University
College of DuPage
College of Lake County
De Paul University
Eastern Illinois University
Elgin Community College
Eureka College
Governors State University
Highland Community College
Illinois Benedictine College
Illinois State University

Illinois Valley Community College
Illinois Wesleyan University
John A. Logan College
Joliet Junior College
Judson College
Kankakee Community College
Knox College
Lake Land College
Lewis University
Lincoln College
Lincoln Land Community College
Loyola University of Chicago
MacMurray College
McHenry County College
Millikin University
Monmouth College
Montay College
Morton College
North Central College
North Park College
Northeastern Illinois University
Northern Illinois University
Oakton Community College
Olivet Nazarene University
Quincy University
Ray College of Design
Rockford College
Roosevelt University
School of the Art Institute of Chicago
Shawnee Community College
Shimer College
Southeastern Illinois College
Southern Illinois University
    Carbondale
    Edwardsville
Spoon River College
Springfield College in Illinois
Trinity Christian College
University of Chicago
University of Illinois at Urbana-Champaign
Western Illinois University
William Rainey Harper College

Indiana

Anderson University
DePauw University
Franklin College
Grace College
Huntington College
Indiana State University
Indiana University
    Bloomington
    South Bend
Indiana University—Purdue University
    Fort Wayne
    Indianapolis
Indiana Wesleyan University
Marian College
Oakland City College
St. Francis College
St. Mary-of-the-Woods College
University of Evansville
University of Indianapolis
University of Southern Indiana
Vincennes University
Wabash College

Iowa

Briar Cliff College
Buena Vista College
Central College
Clarke College
Clinton Community College
Coe College
Cornell College
Dordt College
Drake University
Graceland College
Grand View College

Indian Hills Community College
Iowa Lakes Community College
Iowa State University
Iowa Wesleyan College
Loras College
Luther College
Morningside College
Mount Mercy College
Mount St. Clare College
North Iowa Area Community College
Northwestern College
St. Ambrose University
Simpson College
Teikyo Marycrest University
University of Iowa
University of Northern Iowa
Waldorf College
Wartburg College
William Penn College

Kansas

Baker University
Barton County Community College
Bethany College
Bethel College
Butler County Community College
Coffeyville Community College
Colby Community College
Emporia State University
Fort Hays State University
Friends University
Garden City Community College
Hesston College
Highland Community College
Hutchinson Community College
Independence Community College
Johnson County Community College
Kansas State University
Kansas Wesleyan University
Neosho County Community College
Pittsburg State University
Pratt Community College
St. Mary College
Southwestern College
Sterling College
University of Kansas
Washburn University of Topeka
Wichita State University

Kentucky

Asbury College
Bellarmine College
Brescia College
Campbellsville College
Cumberland College
Eastern Kentucky University
Georgetown College
Kentucky Wesleyan College
Lindsey Wilson College
Midway College
Morehead State University
Murray State University
Northern Kentucky University
Spalding University
Thomas More College
Transylvania University
University of Kentucky
University of Louisville
Western Kentucky University

Louisiana

Centenary College of Louisiana
Louisiana State University at Alexandria
Louisiana Tech University
Loyola University
McNeese State University
Northeast Louisiana University
Northwestern State University

University of Southwestern Louisiana
Xavier University of Louisiana

Maine

Maine College of Art
University of Maine
    Augusta
    Orono
    Presque Isle

Maryland

Cecil Community College
Charles County Community College
College of Notre Dame of Maryland
Frederick Community College
Frostburg State University
Goucher College
Maryland Institute College of Art
Towson State University
University of Maryland
    Baltimore County
    College Park
    Eastern Shore
Washington College

Massachusetts

Boston Architectural Center
Boston University
Bristol Community College
Fitchburg State College
Holyoke Community College
Massachusetts Bay Community College
Montserrat College of Art
Quinsigamond Community College
Salem State College
Springfield Technical Community College
University of Massachusetts at Amherst

Michigan

Adrian College
Albion College
Alma College
Aquinas College
Calvin College
Center for Creative Studies: College of Art and Design
Central Michigan University
Charles Stewart Mott Community College
Concordia College
Eastern Michigan University
Glen Oaks Community College
Grand Rapids Community College
Grand Valley State University
Henry Ford Community College
Hillsdale College
Hope College
Kalamazoo College
Kellogg Community College
Kendall College of Art and Design
Lake Michigan College
Lansing Community College
Madonna University
Marygrove College
Michigan State University
Monroe County Community College
Muskegon Community College
Northwestern Michigan College
St. Clair County Community College
Schoolcraft College
Siena Heights College
Southwestern Michigan College
Spring Arbor College
Suomi College
University of Michigan

238

Colleges that offer academic, music or drama, or art scholarships

Washtenaw Community College
Wayne State University
Western Michigan University

Minnesota
Bemidji State University
Bethany Lutheran College
Brainerd Community College
College of Associated Arts
College of St. Benedict
Fergus Falls Community College
Inver Hills Community College
Mankato State University
Minneapolis College of Art and Design
Moorhead State University
North Central Bible College
North Hennepin Community College
Northwestern College
Rainy River Community College
St. Cloud State University
St. John's University
St. Mary's College of Minnesota
University of Minnesota: Twin Cities
Willmar Community College
Winona State University

Mississippi
Belhaven College
Copiah-Lincoln Community College
Delta State University
East Central Community College
Hinds Community College
Holmes Community College
Jackson State University
Meridian Community College
Millsaps College
Mississippi College
Mississippi Delta Community College
Mississippi Gulf Coast Community College: Perkinston
Mississippi University for Women
University of Mississippi
University of Southern Mississippi

Missouri
Avila College
Central Missouri State University
Cottey College
Crowder College
Culver-Stockton College
Drury College
East Central College
Evangel College
Fontbonne College
Hannibal-LaGrange College
Jefferson College
Kansas City Art Institute
Lincoln University
Lindenwood College
Longview Community College
Maple Woods Community College
Mineral Area College
Missouri Southern State College
Missouri Valley College
Northeast Missouri State University
Park College
St. Louis Community College
    Florissant Valley
    Forest Park
    Meramec
St. Louis University
Southeast Missouri State University
Southwest Missouri State University
State Fair Community College
University of Missouri
    Columbia
    Kansas City
Washington University

Webster University
Westminster College
William Jewell College
William Woods College

Montana
Dawson Community College
Eastern Montana College
Montana State University
Rocky Mountain College
University of Montana
Western Montana College of the University of Montana

Nebraska
Central Community College
Chadron State College
College of St. Mary
Concordia College
Doane College
McCook Community College
Mid Plains Community College
Midland Lutheran College
Nebraska Wesleyan University
Northeast Community College
Peru State College
Southeast Community College: Beatrice Campus
University of Nebraska
    Kearney
    Omaha
Wayne State College
Western Nebraska Community College: Scottsbluff Campus
York College

Nevada
Sierra Nevada College
University of Nevada: Las Vegas

New Hampshire
Keene State College
University of New Hampshire

New Jersey
Caldwell College
College of St. Elizabeth
Georgian Court College
Rowan College of New Jersey
Rutgers—The State University of New Jersey: Mason Gross School of the Arts
Union County College

New Mexico
College of Santa Fe
Eastern New Mexico University
New Mexico Highlands University
Western New Mexico University

New York
Adelphi University
Alfred University
Bard College
Cazenovia College
City University of New York: Brooklyn College
Clarkson University
College of New Rochelle
College of St. Rose
Elmira College
Finger Lakes Community College
Genesee Community College
Houghton College
Iona College
Long Island University
    Brooklyn Campus
    C. W. Post Campus
    Southampton Campus
Manhattanville College
Marymount College
Marymount Manhattan College

Molloy College
Nassau Community College
Nazareth College of Rochester
New York School of Interior Design
Orange County Community College
Pratt Institute
Roberts Wesleyan College
Rochester Institute of Technology
Sage Junior College of Albany
St. John's University
St. Thomas Aquinas College
School of Visual Arts
State University of New York
    Binghamton
    Buffalo
    Purchase
    College at Brockport
    College at Buffalo
    College at Plattsburgh
Sullivan County Community College
Syracuse University
University of Rochester
Villa Maria College of Buffalo
Westchester Community College

North Carolina
Appalachian State University
Barton College
Brevard College
Chowan College
Davidson College
Duke University
East Carolina University
Greensboro College
Guilford College
Meredith College
Mitchell Community College
Montreat-Anderson College
Mount Olive College
North Carolina Agricultural and Technical State University
North Carolina School of the Arts
Peace College
Pembroke State University
Queens College
St. Andrews Presbyterian College
St. Mary's College
University of North Carolina
    Asheville
    Wilmington
Wake Forest University
Western Carolina University
Wilkes Community College
Winston-Salem State University

North Dakota
Dickinson State University
University of North Dakota
Valley City State University

Ohio
Art Academy of Cincinnati
Ashland University
Bluffton College
Bowling Green State University
Case Western Reserve University
Central State University
Cleveland Institute of Art
Cleveland State University
College of Mount St. Joseph
Columbus College of Art and Design
Cuyahoga Community College: Western Campus
Denison University
Kent State University
Lake Erie College
Lakeland Community College
Marietta College
Miami University: Oxford Campus

Mount Union College
Muskingum College
Ohio Northern University
Ohio State University
    Columbus Campus
    Lima Campus
    Mansfield Campus
Ohio University
Ohio Wesleyan University
Otterbein College
Southern State Community College
University of Akron
University of Cincinnati
    Access Colleges
    Cincinnati
    Clermont College
University of Dayton
University of Toledo
Virginia Marti College of Fashion and Art
Wittenberg University
Wright State University
Xavier University

Oklahoma
Cameron University
East Central University
Northeastern State University
Northwestern Oklahoma State University
Oklahoma Baptist University
Oklahoma Christian University of Science and Arts
Oklahoma City University
Oklahoma State University
Oral Roberts University
Phillips University
Rogers State College
Rose State College
St. Gregory's College
Southern Nazarene University
Southwestern Oklahoma State University
University of Central Oklahoma
University of Oklahoma
University of Science and Arts of Oklahoma
University of Tulsa

Oregon
Central Oregon Community College
Clackamas Community College
Linn-Benton Community College
Marylhurst College
Mount Hood Community College
Pacific Northwest College of Art
Pacific University
Portland State University
Southern Oregon State College
Treasure Valley Community College
University of Oregon
    Eugene
    Robert Donald Clark Honors College
Western Oregon State College
Willamette University

Pennsylvania
Allegheny College
Art Institute of Pittsburgh
Beaver College
Bucks County Community College
Carlow College
Carnegie Mellon University
Clarion University of Pennsylvania
Community College of Allegheny County
    Boyce Campus
    South Campus
Drexel University
Harcum Junior College

Colleges that offer academic, music or drama, or art scholarships

Harrisburg Area Community College
Indiana University of Pennsylvania
Juniata College
Kutztown University of Pennsylvania
Lycoming College
Mansfield University of Pennsylvania
Marywood College
Mercyhurst College
Millersville University of Pennsylvania
Moore College of Art and Design
Penn State
    Erie Behrend College
    Harrisburg Capital College
    University Park Campus
Point Park College
Rosemont College
Seton Hill College
Slippery Rock University of Pennsylvania
University of the Arts
Ursinus College
Wilkes University
York College of Pennsylvania

Puerto Rico

Pontifical Catholic University of Puerto Rico
University of Puerto Rico: Rio Piedras Campus

Rhode Island

Rhode Island College
Rhode Island School of Design

South Carolina

Anderson College
Charleston Southern University
Coker College
College of Charleston
Columbia College
Francis Marion University
Furman University
Greenville Technical College
Lander University
Limestone College
North Greenville College
University of South Carolina
Winthrop University

South Dakota

Augustana College
Black Hills State University
Dakota Wesleyan University
Northern State University
South Dakota State University
University of South Dakota

Tennessee

Austin Peay State University
Carson-Newman College
Chattanooga State Technical Community College
David Lipscomb University
East Tennessee State University
Free Will Baptist Bible College
Freed-Hardeman University
Lambuth University
Maryville College
Memphis College of Art
Memphis State University
Milligan College
Pellissippi State Technical Community College
Rhodes College
Roane State Community College
Shelby State Community College
Union University

University of Tennessee
    Chattanooga
    Knoxville

Texas

Abilene Christian University
Alvin Community College
Angelina College
Austin College
Baylor University
Bee County College
Cedar Valley College
College of the Mainland
Collin County Community College District
Corpus Christi State University
Dallas Baptist University
Del Mar College
El Centro College
Grayson County College
Hardin-Simmons University
Houston Baptist University
Howard College
Howard Payne University
Incarnate Word College
Lamar University—Beaumont
Lee College
Lon Morris College
McMurry University
Midland College
Midwestern State University
Navarro College
Northeast Texas Community College
Odessa College
Prairie View A&M University
Sam Houston State University
San Antonio College
San Jacinto College: North
South Plains College
Southern Methodist University
Southwestern University
Texas A&I University
Texas Christian University
Texas College
Texas Lutheran College
Texas Tech University
Texas Wesleyan University
Texas Woman's University
Trinity University
Trinity Valley Community College
Tyler Junior College
University of Dallas
University of Houston
    Downtown
    Houston
University of North Texas
University of Texas
    Arlington
    Austin
    Pan American
    Tyler
Vernon Regional Junior College
West Texas A & M University

Utah

Brigham Young University
College of Eastern Utah
Dixie College
Salt Lake Community College
Snow College
University of Utah
Utah State University
Weber State University
Westminster College of Salt Lake City

Vermont

Green Mountain College
University of Vermont

Virginia

Bluefield College
Hollins College
James Madison University
Longwood College
Mary Baldwin College
Old Dominion University
Radford University
Roanoke College
Virginia Commonwealth University
Virginia Polytechnic Institute and State University

Washington

Columbia Basin College
Cornish College of the Arts
Eastern Washington University
Edmonds Community College
Everett Community College
Evergreen State College
Grays Harbor College
Green River Community College
North Seattle Community College
Northwest College of the Assemblies of God
Olympic College
Pacific Lutheran University
Peninsula College
Seattle Pacific University
Seattle University
Skagit Valley College
Tacoma Community College
University of Puget Sound
Walla Walla College
Washington State University
Wenatchee Valley College
Western Washington University
Whitman College
Whitworth College

West Virginia

Concord College
Davis and Elkins College
Glenville State College
Marshall University
Ohio Valley College
Shepherd College
West Liberty State College
West Virginia State College
West Virginia University
West Virginia Wesleyan College

Wisconsin

Alverno College
Cardinal Stritch College
Carroll College
Carthage College
Edgewood College
Marian College of Fond du Lac
Milwaukee Institute of Art & Design
Mount Mary College
St. Norbert College
Silver Lake College
University of Wisconsin
    Green Bay
    Madison
    Oshkosh
    Parkside
    River Falls
    Stevens Point
    Stout
University of Wisconsin Center
    Baraboo/Sauk County
    Barron County
    Marathon County
    Richland
Viterbo College
Wisconsin Lutheran College

Wyoming

Casper College
Central Wyoming College
Eastern Wyoming College
Laramie County Community College
Northwest College
Sheridan College
University of Wyoming
Western Wyoming Community College

Arab Republic of Egypt

American University in Cairo

Colleges that offer athletic scholarships

Colleges that offer athletic scholarships

Archery

Arizona
Glendale Community College W
Navajo Community College M, W

Badminton

Missouri
Central Methodist College M

Wisconsin
Lakeland College M

Baseball

Alabama
Alabama Agricultural and Mechanical University M
Auburn University M
Bevill State Community College M
Chattahoochee Valley Community College M
Enterprise State Junior College M
Gadsden State Community College M
George C. Wallace State Community College at Selma M
Huntingdon College M
James H. Faulkner State Community College M
Jefferson Davis State Junior College M
Jefferson State Community College M
Lurleen B. Wallace State Junior College M
Miles College M
Selma University M
Snead State Community College M
Southern Union State Junior College M
Spring Hill College M
Troy State University M
Tuskegee University M
University of Alabama
   Birmingham M
   Tuscaloosa M
University of Mobile M
University of Montevallo M
University of North Alabama M
University of South Alabama M

Arizona
Arizona Western College M
Central Arizona College M
Cochise College M
Glendale Community College M
Grand Canyon University M
Pima Community College M
Scottsdale Community College M
University of Arizona M

Arkansas
University of Arkansas
   Little Rock M

California
Azusa Pacific University M
Biola University M
California Polytechnic State University: San Luis Obispo M
California State University
   Fresno M
   Fullerton M
   Northridge M
   San Bernardino M
Concordia University M
Master's College M
Pepperdine University M
Point Loma Nazarene College M
St. Mary's College of California M
Santa Clara University M
Southern California College M
Stanford University M
University of California
   Berkeley M
   Los Angeles M
   Riverside M
University of the Pacific M
University of San Diego M
University of San Francisco M
Westmont College M

Colorado
Colorado Northwestern Community College M
Colorado School of Mines M
Lamar Community College M
Mesa State College M
Metropolitan State College of Denver M
Otero Junior College M
Regis University M
Trinidad State Junior College M
University of Denver M
University of Northern Colorado M

Connecticut
Central Connecticut State University M
Fairfield University M
Quinnipiac College M
University of Connecticut M
University of Hartford M

Delaware
Delaware State College M
University of Delaware M

District of Columbia
George Washington University M
Howard University M

Florida
Brevard Community College M
Central Florida Community College M
Eckerd College M
Edward Waters College M
Flagler College M
Florida Atlantic University M
Florida Community College at Jacksonville M
Florida Institute of Technology M
Florida Memorial College M
Florida State University M
Hillsborough Community College M
Lake City Community College M
Lynn University M
Nova University M
Okaloosa-Walton Community College M
Palm Beach Atlantic College M
Palm Beach Community College M
Pasco-Hernando Community College M
Rollins College M
St. Johns River Community College M
St. Leo College M
St. Petersburg Junior College M
Stetson University M
Tallahassee Community College M
University of Miami M
University of North Florida M
University of West Florida M
Valencia Community College M
Warner Southern College M

Georgia
Abraham Baldwin Agricultural College M
Augusta College M
Brewton-Parker College M
Columbus College M
Emmanuel College M
Georgia College M
Georgia Institute of Technology M
Georgia Southern University M
Georgia Southwestern College M
Kennesaw State College M
Mercer University M
Middle Georgia College M
Paine College M
Piedmont College M
Savannah State College M
Shorter College M
Southern College of Technology M
Truett-McConnell College M
University of Georgia M
Valdosta State College M
West Georgia College M

Hawaii
Hawaii Pacific University M
University of Hawaii at Manoa M

Idaho
Albertson College M
College of Southern Idaho M
Lewis Clark State College M
North Idaho College M
Northwest Nazarene College M
Ricks College M

Illinois
Belleville Area College M
Bradley University M
Chicago State University M
College of St. Francis M
Eastern Illinois University M
Illinois Central College M
Illinois Eastern Community Colleges
   Lincoln Trail College M
   Olney Central College M
   Wabash Valley College M
Illinois Institute of Technology M
Illinois State University M
John A. Logan College M
Judson College M
Kankakee Community College M
Kaskaskia College M
Kishwaukee College M
Lake Land College M
Lewis University M
Lincoln College M
Lincoln Land Community College M
McKendree College M
Morton College M
Northwestern University M
Olivet Nazarene University M
Quincy University M
Rosary College M
St. Xavier University M
Sauk Valley Community College M
Southern Illinois University
   Carbondale M
   Edwardsville M
Trinity College M

242

Colleges that offer athletic scholarships

University of Illinois
   Chicago M
   Urbana-Champaign M
Western Illinois University M

Indiana

Ball State University M
Bethel College M
Butler University M
Goshen College M
Grace College M
Huntington College M
Indiana State University M
Indiana University Bloomington M
Indiana University—Purdue
   University at Indianapolis M
Indiana Wesleyan University M
Marian College M
Purdue University M
Tri-State University M
University of Evansville M
University of Indianapolis M
University of Notre Dame M
University of Southern Indiana M
Vincennes University M

Iowa

Briar Cliff College M
Ellsworth Community College M
Graceland College M
Grand View College M
Indian Hills Community College M
Iowa Central Community College M
Iowa Lakes Community College M
Iowa State University M
Iowa Wesleyan College M
Marshalltown Community College M
Morningside College M
Mount St. Clare College M
Muscatine Community College M
North Iowa Area Community College M
Northwestern College M
St. Ambrose University M
Teikyo Marycrest University M
Teikyo Westmar University M
University of Iowa M
University of Northern Iowa M
Waldorf College M

Kansas

Allen County Community College M
Baker University M
Benedictine College M
Brown Mackie College M
Butler County Community College M
Central College M
Coffeyville Community College M
Colby Community College M
Dodge City Community College M
Emporia State University M
Fort Scott Community College M
Friends University M
Johnson County Community College M
Kansas City Kansas Community College M
Kansas Newman College M
Kansas State University M
Neosho County Community College M
Ottawa University M
Sterling College M
University of Kansas M
Wichita State University M

Kentucky

Bellarmine College M

Campbellsville College M
Cumberland College M
Eastern Kentucky University M
Kentucky State University M
Lees College M
Lindsey Wilson College M
Morehead State University M
Murray State University M
Northern Kentucky University M
Union College M
University of Kentucky M
University of Louisville M
Western Kentucky University M

Louisiana

Bossier Parish Community College M
Grambling State University M
Louisiana State University and Agricultural and Mechanical College M
Louisiana Tech University M
Nicholls State University M
Northeast Louisiana University M
Southeastern Louisiana University M
Tulane University M
University of New Orleans M
University of Southwestern Louisiana M

Maine

University of Maine M

Maryland

Bowie State University M
Charles County Community College M
Dundalk Community College M
Mount St. Mary's College M
Towson State University M
University of Maryland
   College Park M
   Eastern Shore M

Massachusetts

American International College M
Becker College
   Leicester Campus M
   Worcester Campus M
Boston University M
Dean Junior College M
Northeastern University M
University of Massachusetts at Amherst M

Michigan

Aquinas College M
Eastern Michigan University M
Glen Oaks Community College M
Grand Rapids Baptist College and Seminary M
Henry Ford Community College M
Highland Park Community College M
Hillsdale College M
Kellogg Community College M
Lake Michigan College M
Macomb Community College M
Michigan Christian College M
Michigan State University M
Northwood University M
Oakland University M
Southwestern Michigan College M
University of Detroit Mercy M
University of Michigan M
Wayne State University M

Minnesota

Mankato State University M
St. Cloud State University M

University of Minnesota
   Duluth M
   Twin Cities M
Winona State University M

Mississippi

Belhaven College M
Copiah-Lincoln Community College M
Delta State University M
Hinds Community College M
Holmes Community College M
Mississippi College M
Mississippi State University M
University of Mississippi M
William Carey College M

Missouri

Avila College M
Central Methodist College M
Central Missouri State University M
College of the Ozarks M
Crowder College M
Culver-Stockton College M
Hannibal-LaGrange College M
Harris Stowe State College M
Kemper Military School and College M
Lincoln University M
Lindenwood College M
Longview Community College M
Maple Woods Community College M
Mineral Area College M
Missouri Southern State College M
Missouri Western State College M
Northeast Missouri State University M
Northwest Missouri Community College M
Research College of Nursing M
Rockhurst College M
St. Louis University M
Southwest Baptist University M
University of Missouri
   Columbia M
   Rolla M
William Jewell College M

Nebraska

Bellevue College M
Concordia College M
Creighton University M
Dana College M
Doane College M
Midland Lutheran College M
Peru State College M
University of Nebraska
   Kearney M
   Lincoln M
   Omaha M
Wayne State College M
York College M

New Hampshire

Franklin Pierce College M

New Jersey

Bloomfield College M
Burlington County College M
County College of Morris M
Fairleigh Dickinson University
   Edward Williams College M
   Madison M
Rider College M

Rutgers—The State University of New Jersey
   College of Engineering M
   College of Pharmacy M
   Cook College M
   Livingston College M
   Mason Gross School of the Arts M
   Rutgers College M
Seton Hall University M

New Mexico

Eastern New Mexico University M
New Mexico Junior College M
New Mexico State University M
University of New Mexico M

New York

Adelphi University M
Canisius College M
College of St. Rose M
Concordia College M
Dowling College M
Fordham University M
Hofstra University M
Iona College M
Jefferson Community College M
King's College M
Le Moyne College M
Long Island University
   Brooklyn Campus M
   C. W. Post Campus M
Manhattan College M
Marist College M
Mercy College M
New York Institute of Technology M
Niagara University M
Onondaga Community College M
Pace University
   College of White Plains M
   New York M
   Pleasantville/Briarcliff M
St. Bonaventure University M
St. Francis College M
St. John's University M
St. Thomas Aquinas College M
Siena College M
Wagner College M

North Carolina

Appalachian State University M
Barton College M
Belmont Abbey College M
Brevard College M
Campbell University M
Catawba College M
Duke University M
East Carolina University M
Elon College M
Gardner-Webb University M
High Point University M
Lees-McRae College M
Lenoir-Rhyne College M
Louisburg College M
Mars Hill College M
Montreat-Anderson College M
Mount Olive College M
North Carolina Agricultural and Technical State University M
North Carolina State University M
Pembroke State University M
Pfeiffer College M
St. Andrews Presbyterian College M
St. Augustine's College M
Southeastern Community College M
University of North Carolina
   Asheville M
   Chapel Hill M
   Charlotte M
   Greensboro M
   Wilmington M

Colleges that offer athletic scholarships

Wake Forest University M
Western Carolina University M
Wingate College M

North Dakota

Dickinson State University M
Mayville State University M
North Dakota State University
 Bottineau M
 Fargo M
University of North Dakota
 Grand Forks M
 Williston M

Ohio

Ashland University M
Bowling Green State University M
Cleveland State University M
Cuyahoga Community College:
 Western Campus M
Kent State University M
Malone College M
Miami University: Oxford Campus M
Ohio Dominican College M
Ohio State University: Columbus Campus M
Tiffin University M
University of Dayton M
University of Findlay M
University of Rio Grande M
University of Toledo M
Urbana University M
Walsh University M
Wright State University M
Xavier University M
Youngstown State University M

Oklahoma

Bacone College M
Cameron University M
Carl Albert State College M
Eastern Oklahoma State College M
Northwestern Oklahoma State University M
Oklahoma Baptist University M
Oklahoma Christian University of Science and Arts M
Oklahoma City University M
Oral Roberts University M
Redlands Community College M
Rose State College M
Southwestern Oklahoma State University M
University of Central Oklahoma M
University of Oklahoma M
Western Oklahoma State College M

Oregon

Clackamas Community College M
Concordia College M
George Fox College M
Mount Hood Community College M
Oregon State University M
Portland State University M
Treasure Valley Community College M
University of Portland M

Pennsylvania

California University of Pennsylvania M
Drexel University M
Duquesne University M
Eastern College M
Edinboro University of Pennsylvania M
Gannon University M
Geneva College M
Mercyhurst College M

Millersville University of Pennsylvania M
Philadelphia College of Pharmacy and Science M
Point Park College M
St. Joseph's University M
St. Vincent College M
Shippensburg University of Pennsylvania M
Temple University M
University of Pittsburgh M
Villanova University M
West Chester University of Pennsylvania M

Puerto Rico

University of Puerto Rico: Mayaguez Campus M

Rhode Island

Providence College M
University of Rhode Island M

South Carolina

Anderson College M
Charleston Southern University M
Clemson University M
Coker College M
College of Charleston M
Erskine College M
Francis Marion University M
Furman University M
Limestone College M
North Greenville College M
Presbyterian College M
Spartanburg Methodist College M
University of South Carolina
 Aiken M
 Columbia M
Voorhees College M
Winthrop University M
Wofford College M

South Dakota

Dakota Wesleyan University M
South Dakota State University M

Tennessee

Belmont University M
Bethel College M
Chattanooga State Technical Community College M
Christian Brothers University M
East Tennessee State University M
Freed-Hardeman University M
Lambuth University M
Lane College M
Lincoln Memorial University M
Middle Tennessee State University M
Milligan College M
Shelby State Community College M
Trevecca Nazarene College M
Tusculum College M
Union University M
University of Tennessee
 Knoxville M
 Martin M
Vanderbilt University M

Texas

Baylor University M
Blinn College M
Concordia Lutheran College M
Cooke County College M
Dallas Baptist University M
East Texas Baptist University M
Galveston College M
Houston Baptist University M
Lamar University—Beaumont M
Laredo Junior College M

LeTourneau University M
Ranger Junior College M
Rice University M
St. Edward's University M
St. Mary's University M
Schreiner College M
Southern Methodist University M
Southwest Texas State University M
Stephen F. Austin State University M
Texas Christian University M
Texas College M
Texas Lutheran College M
Texas Tech University M
Texas Wesleyan University M
University of Houston M
University of Mary Hardin-Baylor M
University of Texas at Austin M
Vernon Regional Junior College M
West Texas A & M University M

Utah

Brigham Young University M
College of Eastern Utah M
Dixie College M
University of Utah M
Utah Valley Community College M

Virginia

Bluefield College M
Clinch Valley College of the University of Virginia M
George Mason University M
James Madison University M
Liberty University M
Longwood College M
Norfolk State University M
Old Dominion University M
Radford University M
St. Paul's College M
University of Richmond M
University of Virginia M
Virginia Commonwealth University M
Virginia Intermont College M
Virginia Military Institute M
Virginia Polytechnic Institute and State University M

Washington

Big Bend Community College M
Centralia College M
Edmonds Community College M
Gonzaga University M
Green River Community College M
Lower Columbia College M
Olympic College M
Pacific Lutheran University M
Pierce College M
Shoreline Community College M
Spokane Community College M
Tacoma Community College M
University of Puget Sound M
University of Washington M
Walla Walla Community College M
Washington State University M
Yakima Valley Community College M

West Virginia

Bluefield State College M
Davis and Elkins College M
Ohio Valley College M
Potomac State College of West Virginia University M
University of Charleston M
West Liberty State College M
West Virginia Institute of Technology M

West Virginia State College M
West Virginia University M
West Virginia Wesleyan College M

Wisconsin

Cardinal Stritch College M
Lakeland College M

Wyoming

University of Wyoming M

Basketball

Alabama

Alabama Agricultural and Mechanical University M, W
Athens State College M
Auburn University M, W
Bevill State Community College M, W
Chattahoochee Valley Community College M, W
Concordia College M, W
Enterprise State Junior College M
Faulkner University M
Gadsden State Community College M, W
George C. Wallace State Community College
 Dothan M
 Selma M
James H. Faulkner State Community College M, W
Jefferson Davis State Junior College M
John C. Calhoun State Community College M, W
Judson College W
Lurleen B. Wallace State Junior College M, W
Miles College M, W
Northwest Alabama Community College M, W
Selma University M, W
Snead State Community College M, W
Southern Union State Junior College M, W
Spring Hill College M, W
Troy State University M, W
Tuskegee University M, W
University of Alabama
 Birmingham M, W
 Huntsville M, W
University of Mobile M, W
University of Montevallo M, W
University of North Alabama M, W
University of South Alabama M, W
Walker College M

Alaska

Sheldon Jackson College M, W
University of Alaska
 Anchorage M, W
 Fairbanks M, W

Arizona

Arizona Western College M
Central Arizona College M, W
Cochise College M, W
Eastern Arizona College M, W
Glendale Community College M, W
Grand Canyon University M, W
Northern Arizona University M, W
Pima Community College M, W
Scottsdale Community College M, W
University of Arizona M, W

Colleges that offer athletic scholarships

Arkansas
Arkansas College M, W
Henderson State University M, W
John Brown University M, W
Mississippi County Community College M, W
North Arkansas Community/Technical College M, W
Ouachita Baptist University M, W
Shorter College W
University of Arkansas
  Little Rock M
  Pine Bluff M, W
University of Central Arkansas M, W
Williams Baptist College M, W

California
Azusa Pacific University M, W
Biola University M, W
California Polytechnic State University: San Luis Obispo M, W
California State University
  Bakersfield M
  Fresno M, W
  Fullerton M, W
  Northridge M, W
  San Bernardino M, W
Concordia University M, W
Dominican College of San Rafael M, W
Master's College M, W
Pepperdine University M, W
Point Loma Nazarene College M, W
St. Mary's College of California M, W
Santa Clara University M, W
Southern California College M, W
Stanford University M, W
University of California
  Berkeley M, W
  Irvine M, W
  Los Angeles M, W
  Riverside M, W
  Santa Barbara M, W
University of the Pacific M, W
University of San Diego M, W
University of San Francisco M, W
Westmont College M

Colorado
Adams State College M, W
Colorado Christian University M, W
Colorado Northwestern Community College M, W
Colorado School of Mines M, W
Colorado State University M, W
Fort Lewis College M, W
Lamar Community College M
Mesa State College M, W
Metropolitan State College of Denver M, W
Northeastern Junior College M, W
Otero Junior College M, W
Regis University M, W
Trinidad State Junior College M
University of Colorado
  Boulder M, W
  Colorado Springs M, W
University of Denver M, W
University of Northern Colorado M, W
University of Southern Colorado M, W
Western State College of Colorado M, W

Connecticut
Central Connecticut State University M, W
Fairfield University M, W
Quinnipiac College M, W
University of Bridgeport M, W
University of Connecticut M, W
University of Hartford M, W

Delaware
Delaware State College M, W
University of Delaware M, W

District of Columbia
American University M, W
George Washington University M, W
Georgetown University M, W
Howard University M, W
University of the District of Columbia M, W

Florida
Bethune-Cookman College M, W
Brevard Community College M, W
Central Florida Community College M
Daytona Beach Community College M
Eckerd College M, W
Edward Waters College M, W
Embry-Riddle Aeronautical University M
Flagler College M, W
Florida Atlantic University M, W
Florida Community College at Jacksonville M, W
Florida Institute of Technology M, W
Florida Memorial College M, W
Florida State University M, W
Hillsborough Community College M, W
Lake City Community College M, W
Lynn University M, W
Nova University M
Okaloosa-Walton Community College M, W
Palm Beach Atlantic College M
Palm Beach Community College M, W
Pasco-Hernando Community College M
Rollins College M, W
St. Johns River Community College M
St. Leo College M, W
St. Petersburg Junior College M, W
St. Thomas University M
Stetson University M, W
Tallahassee Community College M
University of Central Florida M
University of Miami M, W
University of North Florida M, W
University of West Florida M, W
Valencia Community College M, W
Warner Southern College M, W
Webber College M, W

Georgia
Abraham Baldwin Agricultural College M
Augusta College M, W
Brewton-Parker College M, W
Clark Atlanta University M, W
Clayton State College M, W
Columbus College M, W
Covenant College M, W
Emmanuel College M, W
Fort Valley State College M, W
Georgia College M, W
Georgia Institute of Technology M, W
Georgia Southern University M, W
Georgia Southwestern College M, W
Kennesaw State College M, W
Macon College M
Mercer University M, W
Middle Georgia College M
Morehouse College W
Paine College M, W
Piedmont College M, W
Savannah State College M, W
Shorter College M, W
Southern College of Technology M
Truett-McConnell College M, W
University of Georgia M, W
Valdosta State College M, W
West Georgia College M, W

Hawaii
Hawaii Pacific University M
University of Hawaii
  Hilo M
  Manoa M, W

Idaho
Albertson College M
Boise State University M, W
College of Southern Idaho M, W
Idaho State University M, W
Lewis Clark State College M, W
North Idaho College M, W
Northwest Nazarene College M, W
Ricks College M, W
University of Idaho M, W

Illinois
Barat College M
Belleville Area College M, W
Bradley University M, W
Chicago State University M, W
City Colleges of Chicago: Kennedy-King College M, W
College of St. Francis M, W
Danville Area Community College M, W
De Paul University M, W
Eastern Illinois University M, W
Highland Community College M, W
Illinois Central College M, W
Illinois Eastern Community Colleges
  Lincoln Trail College M, W
  Olney Central College M, W
  Wabash Valley College M, W
Illinois Institute of Technology M, W
Illinois State University M, W
John A. Logan College M, W
Judson College M, W
Kankakee Community College M, W
Kaskaskia College M, W
Kishwaukee College M, W
Lake Land College M, W
Lewis University M, W
Lincoln College M, W
Lincoln Land Community College M, W
Loyola University of Chicago M, W
McKendree College M, W
Morton College M, W
Northwestern University M, W
Olivet Nazarene University M, W
Quincy University M, W
Rosary College M, W
St. Xavier University M, W
Sauk Valley Community College M, W
Southern Illinois University
  Carbondale M, W
  Edwardsville M, W
Springfield College in Illinois M
Trinity College M, W
University of Illinois
  Chicago M, W
  Urbana-Champaign M, W
Western Illinois University M, W

Indiana
Ball State University M, W
Bethel College M, W
Butler University M, W
Goshen College M, W
Grace College M, W
Huntington College M, W
Indiana State University M, W
Indiana University Bloomington M, W
Indiana University—Purdue University at Indianapolis M, W
Indiana Wesleyan University M, W
Marian College M, W
Purdue University M, W
Tri-State University M, W
University of Evansville M, W
University of Indianapolis M, W
University of Notre Dame M, W
University of Southern Indiana M, W
Valparaiso University M
Vincennes University M, W

Iowa
Briar Cliff College M, W
Clinton Community College M
Drake University M, W
Ellsworth Community College M, W
Graceland College M, W
Grand View College M, W
Indian Hills Community College M
Iowa Central Community College M, W
Iowa Lakes Community College M, W
Iowa State University M, W
Iowa Wesleyan College M, W
Marshalltown Community College M, W
Morningside College M, W
Mount St. Clare College M, W
North Iowa Area Community College M, W
Northwestern College M, W
St. Ambrose University M, W
Teikyo Marycrest University M, W
University of Iowa M, W
University of Northern Iowa M, W
Waldorf College M, W

Kansas
Allen County Community College M, W
Baker University M, W
Benedictine College M, W
Bethel College M, W
Brown Mackie College M, W
Butler County Community College M, W
Central College M, W
Coffeyville Community College M, W
Colby Community College M, W
Dodge City Community College M, W
Emporia State University M, W
Fort Hays State University M
Fort Scott Community College M, W
Friends University M, W

245

Colleges that offer athletic scholarships

Garden City Community College M, W
Johnson County Community College M, W
Kansas City Kansas Community College M, W
Kansas Newman College W
Kansas State University M, W
McPherson College M, W
Neosho County Community College M, W
Ottawa University M, W
Pratt Community College M, W
Seward County Community College M, W
Sterling College M, W
University of Kansas M, W
Wichita State University M, W

Kentucky
Bellarmine College M, W
Campbellsville College M, W
Cumberland College M, W
Eastern Kentucky University M, W
Georgetown College M, W
Kentucky State University M, W
Kentucky Wesleyan College M, W
Lees College M, W
Lindsey Wilson College M, W
Morehead State University M, W
Murray State University M, W
Northern Kentucky University M, W
Spalding University M, W
Transylvania University M, W
Union College M, W
University of Kentucky M, W
University of Louisville M, W
Western Kentucky University M, W

Louisiana
Bossier Parish Community College M
Grambling State University M, W
Louisiana State University and Agricultural and Mechanical College M, W
Louisiana Tech University M, W
Nicholls State University M, W
Northeast Louisiana University M, W
Southeastern Louisiana University M, W
Southern University and Agricultural and Mechanical College M
Tulane University M, W
University of Southwestern Louisiana M, W
Xavier University of Louisiana M, W

Maine
Unity College M
University of Maine M, W

Maryland
Bowie State University M, W
Charles County Community College M
Dundalk Community College M, W
Loyola College in Maryland M, W
Morgan State University M, W
Mount St. Mary's College M, W
Towson State University M, W
University of Maryland
Baltimore County M, W
College Park M, W
Eastern Shore M, W

Massachusetts
American International College M, W
Assumption College M, W
Becker College
Leicester Campus M
Worcester Campus M
Bentley College M, W
Boston College M, W
Boston University M, W
Dean Junior College M
Merrimack College M, W
Mount Ida College M
North Shore Community College M
Northeastern University M, W
Roxbury Community College M
Stonehill College M, W
University of Massachusetts
Amherst M, W
Lowell M, W

Michigan
Alpena Community College M, W
Aquinas College M, W
Delta College M, W
Eastern Michigan University M, W
Glen Oaks Community College M, W
Gogebic Community College M, W
Grand Rapids Baptist College and Seminary M, W
Henry Ford Community College M, W
Highland Park Community College M, W
Hillsdale College M, W
Kellogg Community College M, W
Lake Michigan College M, W
Lansing Community College M, W
Macomb Community College M, W
Michigan Christian College M, W
Michigan State University M, W
Michigan Technological University M, W
Northern Michigan University M, W
Northwood University M, W
Oakland University M, W
Southwestern Michigan College M, W
Spring Arbor College M, W
University of Detroit Mercy M
University of Michigan
Ann Arbor M, W
Dearborn M, W
Wayne State University M, W
Western Michigan University M, W

Minnesota
Bemidji State University M, W
Mankato State University M, W
Moorhead State University M, W
St. Cloud State University M, W
Southwest State University M, W
University of Minnesota
Duluth M, W
Twin Cities M, W
Winona State University M, W

Mississippi
Belhaven College M, W
Copiah-Lincoln Community College M, W
Delta State University M, W
East Central Community College M, W
Hinds Community College M, W
Holmes Community College M, W
Mississippi College M
Mississippi State University M, W
Mississippi University for Women W

University of Mississippi M, W
William Carey College M, W

Missouri
Avila College M, W
Central Missouri State University M, W
College of the Ozarks M, W
Crowder College W
Culver-Stockton College M, W
Hannibal-LaGrange College M, W
Harris Stowe State College M, W
Kemper Military School and College M
Lincoln University M, W
Lindenwood College M, W
Mineral Area College M, W
Missouri Southern State College M, W
Missouri Western State College M, W
Northeast Missouri State University M, W
Park College M, W
Penn Valley Community College M
Research College of Nursing M, W
Rockhurst College M, W
St. Louis Community College at Meramec M, W
St. Louis University M, W
Southeast Missouri State University M, W
Southwest Baptist University M, W
University of Missouri
Columbia M, W
Kansas City M, W
Rolla M, W
William Jewell College M, W
William Woods College W

Montana
Carroll College M, W
Dawson Community College M, W
Eastern Montana College M, W
Miles Community College M, W
Montana College of Mineral Science and Technology M, W
Montana State University M, W
Northern Montana College M, W
Rocky Mountain College M, W
University of Montana M, W
Western Montana College of the University of Montana M, W

Nebraska
Bellevue College M
Central Community College M, W
Chadron State College M, W
Concordia College M, W
Creighton University M, W
Dana College M, W
Doane College M, W
McCook Community College M, W
Midland Lutheran College M, W
Northeast Community College M, W
Peru State College M, W
Southeast Community College:
Beatrice Campus M, W
University of Nebraska
Kearney M, W
Lincoln M, W
Omaha M, W
Wayne State College M, W
Western Nebraska Community College: Scottsbluff Campus M, W
York College M, W

New Hampshire
Franklin Pierce College M, W
Hesser College M, W

New Hampshire College M, W
Notre Dame College M, W
St. Anselm College M, W
University of New Hampshire M, W

New Jersey
Bloomfield College M, W
Burlington County College M, W
Caldwell College M, W
Centenary College M
County College of Morris M, W
Fairleigh Dickinson University
Edward Williams College M, W
Madison M, W
Georgian Court College W
Rider College M, W
Rutgers—The State University of New Jersey
College of Engineering M, W
College of Pharmacy M, W
Cook College M, W
Douglass College W
Livingston College M, W
Mason Gross School of the Arts M, W
Rutgers College M, W
Seton Hall University M, W
Union County College W

New Mexico
Eastern New Mexico University M, W
New Mexico Junior College M, W
New Mexico State University M, W
University of New Mexico M, W

New York
Adelphi University M, W
Canisius College M, W
Cazenovia College M, W
City University of New York:
Queens College M, W
College of St. Rose M, W
Concordia College M, W
Daemen College M, W
Dowling College M
D'Youville College M, W
Hofstra University M, W
Houghton College M, W
Iona College M, W
Jefferson Community College M
King's College M, W
Le Moyne College M, W
Long Island University
Brooklyn Campus M, W
C. W. Post Campus M, W
Southampton Campus M, W
Manhattan College M, W
Marist College M, W
Mercy College M, W
Molloy College M, W
New York Institute of Technology M, W
Niagara University M, W
Nyack College M, W
Pace University
College of White Plains M, W
New York M, W
Pleasantville/Briarcliff M, W
Paul Smith's College M, W
Roberts Wesleyan College M, W
St. Bonaventure University M, W
St. Francis College M, W
St. John's University M, W
St. Thomas Aquinas College M, W
Siena College M, W
State University of New York at Buffalo M, W
Syracuse University M, W
Villa Maria College of Buffalo M

246

Colleges that offer athletic scholarships

Wagner College M, W

North Carolina
Appalachian State University M, W
Barber-Scotia College M, W
Barton College M, W
Belmont Abbey College M, W
Brevard College M, W
Campbell University M, W
Catawba College M, W
Craven Community College M
Davidson College M, W
Duke University M, W
East Carolina University M, W
Elizabeth City State University M, W
Elon College M, W
Fayetteville State University M, W
Gardner-Webb University M, W
High Point University M, W
Johnson C. Smith University M, W
Lees-McRae College M, W
Lenoir-Rhyne College M, W
Livingstone College M, W
Louisburg College M, W
Mars Hill College M, W
Montreat-Anderson College M, W
Mount Olive College M, W
North Carolina Agricultural and Technical State University M, W
North Carolina Central University M, W
North Carolina State University M, W
Pembroke State University M, W
Pfeiffer College M, W
Pitt Community College M
Queens College M, W
St. Andrews Presbyterian College M, W
St. Augustine's College M, W
University of North Carolina
　Asheville M, W
　Chapel Hill M, W
　Charlotte M, W
　Greensboro M, W
　Wilmington M, W
Wake Forest University M, W
Western Carolina University M, W
Wingate College M, W
Winston-Salem State University M, W

North Dakota
Dickinson State University M, W
Mayville State University M, W
North Dakota State College of Science M, W
North Dakota State University
　Bottineau M, W
　Fargo M, W
University of Mary M, W
University of North Dakota
　Grand Forks M, W
　Williston M, W

Ohio
Ashland University M
Bowling Green State University M, W
Cleveland State University M, W
Dyke College M
Kent State University M, W
Lake Erie College M, W
Malone College M, W
Miami University: Oxford Campus M, W
Notre Dame College of Ohio W
Ohio Dominican College M, W
Ohio State University: Columbus Campus M, W
Owens Technical College
　Findlay Campus M, W
　Toledo M, W
Southern State Community College M
Tiffin University M, W
University of Dayton M, W
University of Findlay M, W
University of Rio Grande M, W
University of Toledo M, W
Urbana University M, W
Walsh University M, W
Wright State University M, W
Xavier University M, W
Youngstown State University M, W

Oklahoma
Bacone College M, W
Bartlesville Wesleyan College M, W
Cameron University M, W
Carl Albert State College M
East Central University M, W
Eastern Oklahoma State College M, W
Northwestern Oklahoma State University M, W
Oklahoma Baptist University M, W
Oklahoma Christian University of Science and Arts M, W
Oklahoma City University M, W
Oklahoma Panhandle State University M, W
Oral Roberts University M, W
Phillips University M, W
Redlands Community College M, W
Rose State College M, W
St. Gregory's College M, W
Southwestern Oklahoma State University M, W
University of Central Oklahoma M, W
University of Oklahoma M, W
University of Tulsa M
Western Oklahoma State College M, W

Oregon
Clackamas Community College M, W
Concordia College M, W
George Fox College M, W
Mount Hood Community College M, W
Oregon State University M, W
Portland State University W
Treasure Valley Community College M, W
University of Portland M, W

Pennsylvania
California University of Pennsylvania M, W
Carlow College W
Cheyney University of Pennsylvania M, W
Community College of Beaver County M
Drexel University M, W
Duquesne University M, W
Eastern College M, W
Edinboro University of Pennsylvania M, W
Gannon University M, W
Geneva College M, W
Indiana University of Pennsylvania M, W
Kutztown University of Pennsylvania M, W
Lock Haven University of Pennsylvania M, W
Manor Junior College M, W
Mercyhurst College M, W
Millersville University of Pennsylvania M, W
Mount Aloysius College M, W
Philadelphia College of Pharmacy and Science M, W
Point Park College M, W
Robert Morris College M, W
St. Francis College M, W
St. Joseph's University M, W
St. Vincent College M, W
Seton Hill College W
Shippensburg University of Pennsylvania M, W
Temple University M, W
University of Pittsburgh
　Johnstown M, W
　Pittsburgh M, W
Villanova University M, W
West Chester University of Pennsylvania M, W
Westminster College M, W

Puerto Rico
University of Puerto Rico
　Bayamon Technological University College M, W
　La Montana Regional College M, W
　Mayaguez Campus M, W
University of the Sacred Heart M

Rhode Island
Bryant College M, W
Providence College M, W
University of Rhode Island M, W

South Carolina
Anderson College M, W
Charleston Southern University M, W
Claflin College M, W
Clemson University M, W
Coker College M, W
College of Charleston M, W
Converse College W
Erskine College M, W
Francis Marion University M, W
Furman University M, W
Lander University M, W
Limestone College M, W
North Greenville College M, W
Presbyterian College M, W
South Carolina State University M, W
Spartanburg Methodist College M, W
University of South Carolina
　Aiken M, W
　Columbia M, W
Voorhees College M, W
Winthrop University M, W
Wofford College M, W

South Dakota
Augustana College M, W
Black Hills State University M, W
Dakota State University M, W
Dakota Wesleyan University M, W
Huron University M, W
Northern State University M, W
Sioux Falls College M, W
South Dakota State University M, W

Tennessee
Belmont University M, W
Bethel College M, W
Chattanooga State Technical Community College M, W
Christian Brothers University M, W
East Tennessee State University M, W
Freed-Hardeman University M, W
Lambuth University M, W
Lane College M, W
Lee College M, W
LeMoyne-Owen College M, W
Lincoln Memorial University M, W
Middle Tennessee State University M, W
Milligan College M, W
Shelby State Community College M, W
Trevecca Nazarene College M
Tusculum College M, W
Union University M, W
University of Tennessee
　Chattanooga M, W
　Knoxville M, W
　Martin M, W
Vanderbilt University M, W
William Jennings Bryan College M, W

Texas
Baylor University M, W
Blinn College M, W
Clarendon College M, W
Concordia Lutheran College M, W
East Texas Baptist University M, W
East Texas State University M, W
Houston Baptist University M
Jacksonville College M
Kilgore College M, W
Lamar University—Beaumont M, W
LeTourneau University M
Ranger Junior College M, W
Rice University M, W
St. Edward's University M, W
St. Mary's University M, W
Schreiner College M, W
South Plains College M, W
Southern Methodist University M, W
Southwest Texas State University M, W
Stephen F. Austin State University M, W
Texas A&I University M, W
Texas Christian University M, W
Texas College M, W
Texas Lutheran College M, W
Texas Tech University M, W
Texas Wesleyan University M, W
Texas Woman's University W
University of Houston M, W
University of Mary Hardin-Baylor M, W
University of North Texas M, W
University of Texas
　Austin M, W
　San Antonio M, W
Wayland Baptist University M, W
Weatherford College M
West Texas A & M University M, W

Utah
Brigham Young University M, W
College of Eastern Utah M, W
Dixie College M, W
University of Utah M, W
Utah State University M
Utah Valley Community College M, W
Weber State University M, W

Vermont
Champlain College M
Green Mountain College M, W
St. Michael's College M, W

Virginia
Bluefield College M, W

247

Colleges that offer athletic scholarships

Clinch Valley College of the
  University of Virginia M, W
College of William and Mary M, W
George Mason University M, W
Hampton University M, W
James Madison University M, W
Liberty University M, W
Longwood College M, W
Norfolk State University M, W
Old Dominion University M, W
Radford University M, W
St. Paul's College M, W
University of Richmond M, W
University of Virginia M, W
Virginia Commonwealth University M, W
Virginia Intermont College M, W
Virginia Military Institute M
Virginia Polytechnic Institute and
  State University M, W
Virginia Union University M, W

Washington
Big Bend Community College M, W
Centralia College M, W
Eastern Washington University M, W
Edmonds Community College M, W
Gonzaga University M, W
Green River Community College M, W
Lower Columbia College M, W
Olympic College M, W
Pacific Lutheran University M, W
Pierce College M, W
St. Martin's College M, W
Seattle Pacific University M, W
Seattle University M, W
Shoreline Community College M, W
Spokane Community College M, W
Tacoma Community College M, W
University of Puget Sound M, W
University of Washington M, W
Walla Walla Community College M, W
Washington State University M, W
Wenatchee Valley College M, W
Western Washington University M, W
Yakima Valley Community College M, W

West Virginia
Bluefield State College M, W
Davis and Elkins College M, W
Ohio Valley College M, W
Potomac State College of West
  Virginia University M, W
Shepherd College M, W
University of Charleston M, W
West Liberty State College M, W
West Virginia Institute of
  Technology M, W
West Virginia State College M, W
West Virginia University M
West Virginia Wesleyan College M, W
Wheeling Jesuit College M, W

Wisconsin
Cardinal Stritch College M, W
Lakeland College M
Marquette University M, W
Northland College M, W
University of Wisconsin
  Green Bay M, W
  Madison M, W

Wyoming
Casper College M, W

Eastern Wyoming College M
Northwest College M, W
Sheridan College M, W
University of Wyoming M, W

Arab Republic of Egypt
American University in Cairo M, W

Bowling

Florida
University of Central Florida M, W

Indiana
Valparaiso University M, W
Vincennes University M, W

Kansas
Fort Hays State University M, W

Maryland
Dundalk Community College M, W

Michigan
Aquinas College M, W

Missouri
Avila College M

New Jersey
Seton Hall University M, W

North Carolina
North Carolina Central University M, W

Pennsylvania
Community College of Beaver County M

Utah
Weber State University W

Cross-country

Alabama
Alabama Agricultural and
  Mechanical University M, W
Auburn University M, W
Miles College M, W
Northwest Alabama Community College M
Southern Union State Junior College M, W
Spring Hill College W
Troy State University M, W
University of Alabama in Birmingham W
University of Mobile M, W
University of North Alabama M, W
University of South Alabama M, W

Alaska
University of Alaska
  Anchorage M
  Fairbanks M, W

Arizona
Central Arizona College M
Glendale Community College M, W
Grand Canyon University M, W
Navajo Community College M, W
Northern Arizona University M, W
Pima Community College M, W
Scottsdale Community College M, W
University of Arizona M, W

Arkansas
University of Arkansas at Little Rock M, W

California
Azusa Pacific University M, W
Biola University M, W
California Polytechnic State
  University: San Luis Obispo M, W
California State University
  Bakersfield M, W
  Fresno M
  Fullerton M, W
  Northridge M, W
Concordia University M, W
Dominican College of San Rafael M, W
MiraCosta College W
Mount St. Mary's College W
Point Loma Nazarene College M, W
St. Mary's College of California M, W
Southern California College M, W
University of California
  Berkeley M, W
  Irvine M, W
  Los Angeles M, W
  Riverside M, W
  Santa Barbara M, W
University of San Diego M, W
University of San Francisco M, W
Westmont College M, W

Colorado
Adams State College M, W
Colorado School of Mines M, W
Colorado State University M, W
Fort Lewis College M, W
Mesa State College W
Northeastern Junior College M, W
University of Colorado at Boulder M, W
Western State College of Colorado M, W

Connecticut
Central Connecticut State University M, W
Fairfield University M, W
Quinnipiac College M, W
University of Connecticut M, W
University of Hartford M, W

District of Columbia
American University M, W
George Washington University M, W
Howard University M, W

Florida
Brevard Community College M, W
Eckerd College M, W
Flagler College M, W
Florida Atlantic University M, W
Florida Community College at Jacksonville M, W
Florida Institute of Technology M, W
Florida State University M, W

Nova University M, W
Stetson University M, W
University of Central Florida M, W
University of Miami M, W
Webber College M, W

Georgia
Augusta College M, W
Georgia College M, W
Georgia Institute of Technology M, W
Kennesaw State College M, W
Mercer University M, W
Morehouse College M
Paine College M, W
Piedmont College M, W
Savannah State College W
Shorter College M, W
University of Georgia M, W
Valdosta State College M, W
West Georgia College M, W

Hawaii
Hawaii Pacific University M, W
University of Hawaii
  Hilo M, W
  Manoa W

Idaho
Boise State University M, W
College of Southern Idaho M, W
Idaho State University M, W
North Idaho College M, W
University of Idaho M, W

Illinois
Bradley University M, W
Chicago State University M, W
College of St. Francis W
Danville Area Community College M, W
De Paul University M, W
Eastern Illinois University M, W
Illinois Institute of Technology M, W
Illinois State University M, W
Judson College M, W
Lake Land College M, W
Lewis University M, W
Loyola University of Chicago M, W
Morton College M, W
Olivet Nazarene University M, W
Southern Illinois University
  Carbondale M, W
  Edwardsville M, W
Trinity College M, W
University of Illinois
  Chicago M, W
  Urbana-Champaign M, W
Western Illinois University M, W

Indiana
Ball State University M, W
Bethel College M, W
Butler University M, W
Goshen College M, W
Huntington College M, W
Indiana State University M, W
Indiana University Bloomington M, W
Indiana Wesleyan University M, W
Marian College M, W
Purdue University M, W
Tri-State University M, W
University of Evansville M, W
University of Indianapolis M, W
University of Notre Dame M, W
University of Southern Indiana M, W
Valparaiso University M, W
Vincennes University M, W

Colleges that offer athletic scholarships

Iowa
Drake University M, W
Graceland College M, W
Iowa State University M, W
Iowa Wesleyan College M, W
Morningside College M, W
Mount St. Clare College M, W
Northwestern College M, W
St. Ambrose University M, W
Teikyo Marycrest University M, W
University of Iowa M, W
University of Northern Iowa M, W

Kansas
Allen County Community College M, W
Baker University M, W
Butler County Community College M, W
Central College M, W
Coffeyville Community College M, W
Colby Community College M, W
Emporia State University M, W
Fort Hays State University M, W
Fort Scott Community College M, W
Friends University M, W
Garden City Community College M, W
Johnson County Community College M, W
Kansas City Kansas Community College M, W
Kansas State University M, W
McPherson College M, W
Neosho County Community College M, W
Ottawa University M, W
Pratt Community College M
Sterling College M, W
University of Kansas M, W
Wichita State University M, W

Kentucky
Bellarmine College M, W
Campbellsville College M, W
Cumberland College M, W
Eastern Kentucky University M, W
Georgetown College M, W
Kentucky State University M, W
Lindsey Wilson College M
Murray State University M, W
Northern Kentucky University M, W
Sue Bennett College M, W
Union College M, W
University of Kentucky M, W
University of Louisville M, W
Western Kentucky University M, W

Louisiana
Louisiana Tech University M, W
Nicholls State University M, W
Northeast Louisiana University M, W
Southeastern Louisiana University M
Tulane University M, W
University of Southwestern Louisiana M, W

Maine
Unity College M, W
University of Maine M, W

Maryland
Bowie State University M, W
Morgan State University M, W
Mount St. Mary's College M, W
Towson State University M, W
University of Maryland
  Baltimore County M, W
  College Park M, W
  Eastern Shore M, W

Massachusetts
Boston College W
Northeastern University M, W
University of Massachusetts
  Amherst M, W
  Lowell M, W

Michigan
Aquinas College M, W
Eastern Michigan University M, W
Grand Rapids Baptist College and Seminary M, W
Highland Park Community College M, W
Hillsdale College M, W
Lansing Community College M, W
Macomb Community College M, W
Michigan Christian College M, W
Michigan State University M, W
Northern Michigan University M, W
Oakland University M
Southwestern Michigan College M, W
Spring Arbor College M, W
University of Detroit Mercy M, W
University of Michigan M, W
Wayne State University M
Western Michigan University M, W

Minnesota
Mankato State University M, W
Moorhead State University M, W
St. Cloud State University M, W
University of Minnesota: Twin Cities M, W
Winona State University M, W

Mississippi
Delta State University W
Mississippi State University M, W

Missouri
Central Methodist College M, W
Central Missouri State University M, W
Lindenwood College M, W
Missouri Southern State College M, W
Northeast Missouri State University M, W
Northwest Missouri Community College M, W
Park College M, W
St. Louis University M, W
Southeast Missouri State University M, W
Southwest Baptist University M, W
University of Missouri
  Columbia M, W
  Kansas City M, W
  Rolla M, W
William Jewell College M, W

Montana
Eastern Montana College M, W
Montana State University M, W
University of Montana M, W

Nebraska
Concordia College M, W
Creighton University M, W
Doane College M, W
Midland Lutheran College M, W
University of Nebraska
  Kearney M, W
  Lincoln M, W
  Omaha W
Wayne State College M, W

New Jersey
Centenary College M
Fairleigh Dickinson University
  Edward Williams College M, W
  Madison M, W
Georgian Court College W
Rider College M, W
Rutgers—The State University of New Jersey
  College of Engineering M, W
  College of Pharmacy M, W
  Cook College M, W
  Douglass College W
  Livingston College M, W
  Mason Gross School of the Arts M, W
  Rutgers College M, W
Seton Hall University M, W

New Mexico
New Mexico State University M, W
University of New Mexico M, W

New York
Adelphi University M, W
Canisius College M, W
College of St. Rose M, W
Concordia College M, W
Fordham University M, W
Hofstra University M, W
Houghton College M, W
Iona College M
King's College M, W
Le Moyne College M, W
Long Island University: C. W. Post Campus M, W
Manhattan College M, W
Marist College M, W
Mercy College M, W
New York Institute of Technology M, W
Niagara University M, W
Pace University
  College of White Plains M, W
  New York M, W
  Pleasantville/Briarcliff M, W
Roberts Wesleyan College M, W
St. Francis College M, W
St. John's University M, W
St. Thomas Aquinas College M, W
Syracuse University M, W

North Carolina
Appalachian State University M, W
Brevard College M, W
Campbell University M, W
Davidson College W
East Carolina University M, W
Elon College M, W
Fayetteville State University M, W
High Point University M, W
Lees-McRae College M, W
Lenoir-Rhyne College M, W
Livingstone College M, W
Mars Hill College M, W
North Carolina Agricultural and Technical State University M, W
North Carolina Central University M, W
North Carolina State University M, W
Pembroke State University M, W
Pfeiffer College M, W
St. Andrews Presbyterian College M, W
St. Augustine's College M, W
University of North Carolina
  Asheville M, W
  Chapel Hill M, W
  Charlotte M, W
  Greensboro M
  Wilmington M, W
Wake Forest University M, W
Western Carolina University M, W
Winston-Salem State University M, W

North Dakota
Dickinson State University M, W
North Dakota State College of Science M, W
North Dakota State University M, W
University of Mary M, W

Ohio
Ashland University M, W
Bowling Green State University M, W
Kent State University M, W
Malone College M, W
Miami University: Oxford Campus M, W
Ohio State University: Columbus Campus M, W
Tiffin University M, W
University of Findlay M, W
University of Rio Grande M, W
University of Toledo M, W
Walsh University M, W
Wright State University M, W
Xavier University M, W
Youngstown State University M, W

Oklahoma
Oklahoma Baptist University M
Oklahoma Christian University of Science and Arts M, W
Oral Roberts University M, W
University of Central Oklahoma M, W
University of Oklahoma M, W
University of Tulsa M, W

Oregon
Central Oregon Community College M, W
Clackamas Community College M, W
George Fox College M, W
Mount Hood Community College M, W
Portland State University M, W
Treasure Valley Community College M, W
University of Portland M, W

Pennsylvania
Carlow College W
Cheyney University of Pennsylvania M, W
Drexel University M
Duquesne University M, W
Eastern College M, W
Edinboro University of Pennsylvania M, W
Gannon University M
Geneva College M, W
Indiana University of Pennsylvania M, W
Kutztown University of Pennsylvania M, W
Mercyhurst College M, W
Millersville University of Pennsylvania M, W
Robert Morris College M, W
St. Francis College M, W

Colleges that offer athletic scholarships

St. Joseph's University M, W
St. Vincent College M, W
Seton Hill College W
Shippensburg University of
 Pennsylvania M, W
University of Pittsburgh M, W
Villanova University M, W
Westminster College W

Puerto Rico
Inter American University of Puerto
 Rico: Guayama Campus M, W
University of Puerto Rico
    La Montana Regional College
     M, W
    Mayaguez Campus M, W
University of the Sacred Heart M,
 W

Rhode Island
Providence College M, W
University of Rhode Island M, W

South Carolina
Anderson College M, W
Charleston Southern University M,
 W
Clemson University M, W
College of Charleston M, W
Converse College W
Erskine College M
Francis Marion University M, W
Furman University M, W
Lander University M, W
University of South Carolina
    Aiken M, W
    Columbia M, W
Voorhees College M, W
Winthrop University M

South Dakota
Augustana College M, W
Black Hills State University M, W
Dakota State University M, W
Dakota Wesleyan University M, W
Sioux Falls College M, W
South Dakota State University M,
 W

Tennessee
Belmont University M, W
East Tennessee State University M,
 W
Lincoln Memorial University M, W
Middle Tennessee State University
 M, W
University of Tennessee
    Knoxville M, W
    Martin M, W
Vanderbilt University W
William Jennings Bryan College M,
 W

Texas
Baylor University M, W
Blinn College M
East Texas State University M, W
Lamar University—Beaumont M, W
Schreiner College W
South Plains College M
Southern Methodist University M,
 W
Stephen F. Austin State University
 M, W
Texas Christian University M, W
Texas Tech University M, W
University of Houston M, W
University of North Texas M, W
University of Texas
    Austin M, W
    San Antonio M, W
Wayland Baptist University M, W

Utah
Brigham Young University M, W
University of Utah M, W
Utah State University M, W
Weber State University M, W

Virginia
College of William and Mary M, W
George Mason University M, W
Hampton University M, W
James Madison University M, W
Liberty University M, W
Norfolk State University M, W
Old Dominion University M, W
Radford University M, W
St. Paul's College M, W
University of Virginia M, W
Virginia Commonwealth University
 M, W
Virginia Military Institute M
Virginia Polytechnic Institute and
 State University M, W

Washington
Eastern Washington University M,
 W
Gonzaga University M, W
Lower Columbia College M, W
Pacific Lutheran University M, W
Seattle Pacific University W
Seattle University M, W
Spokane Community College M, W
University of Puget Sound M, W
University of Washington M, W
Washington State University M, W
Western Washington University M,
 W

West Virginia
Bluefield State College M, W
Davis and Elkins College M, W
West Virginia University M, W
West Virginia Wesleyan College M,
 W
Wheeling Jesuit College M, W

Wisconsin
Lakeland College M
Marquette University M, W
University of Wisconsin
    Green Bay M, W
    Madison M, W

Wyoming
University of Wyoming M, W

Diving

Alabama
Auburn University M, W

Arizona
Northern Arizona University M, W
University of Arizona M, W

California
California State University:
    Northridge M, W
University of California
    Irvine M, W
    Los Angeles M
University of San Diego W

Colorado
University of Denver M, W

Connecticut
University of Connecticut M, W

District of Columbia
American University M, W
George Washington University M,
 W
Howard University M, W

Florida
Florida Atlantic University M, W
Florida State University M, W
University of Miami M, W

Georgia
University of Georgia M, W

Hawaii
University of Hawaii at Manoa M,
 W

Illinois
Bradley University M
Illinois Institute of Technology M,
 W
Illinois State University W
Lincoln College M, W
Northwestern University M, W
Southern Illinois University at
 Carbondale M, W
University of Illinois
    Chicago M, W
    Urbana-Champaign M, W
Western Illinois University M, W

Indiana
Butler University M, W
Indiana University Bloomington M,
 W
Purdue University M, W
University of Evansville M, W
University of Indianapolis M, W
University of Notre Dame M, W
Valparaiso University M, W

Iowa
University of Iowa M, W

Kansas
University of Kansas M, W

Kentucky
Campbellsville College M, W
Union College M, W
University of Kentucky M, W
University of Louisville M, W

Maine
University of Maine M, W

Maryland
Towson State University M, W
University of Maryland: Baltimore
 County M, W

Massachusetts
Boston College W
Boston University M, W
Northeastern University M, W
University of Massachusetts at
 Amherst M, W

Michigan
Eastern Michigan University M, W
Hillsdale College W
Northern Michigan University W
Oakland University M, W
Southwestern Michigan College M,
 W
University of Michigan M, W
Wayne State University M, W

Minnesota
Mankato State University M, W

University of Minnesota: Twin
 Cities M, W

Mississippi
Delta State University M, W

Missouri
Northeast Missouri State University
 W
St. Louis University M, W
University of Missouri
    Columbia M, W
    Rolla M
William Woods College W

Nebraska
University of Nebraska—Lincoln M,
 W

New Jersey
Rider College M, W
Rutgers—The State University of
 New Jersey
    College of Engineering M, W
    College of Pharmacy M, W
    Cook College M, W
    Douglass College W
    Livingston College M, W
    Mason Gross School of the
     Arts M, W
    Rutgers College M, W
Seton Hall University M, W

New Mexico
University of New Mexico M, W

New York
Canisius College M, W
Fordham University M, W
Marist College M, W
Niagara University M, W
St. Bonaventure University M, W
State University of New York at
 Buffalo M, W
Syracuse University M, W

North Carolina
Davidson College W
East Carolina University M, W
North Carolina State University M,
 W
University of North Carolina at
 Wilmington M, W

Ohio
Bowling Green State University M,
 W
Cleveland State University M, W
Miami University: Oxford Campus
 M, W
Ohio State University: Columbus
 Campus M, W
University of Toledo M, W
Wright State University M, W
Xavier University M, W

Oklahoma
Oral Roberts University M

Pennsylvania
Duquesne University M
Edinboro University of
 Pennsylvania M, W
Gannon University M, W
Indiana University of Pennsylvania
 M, W
Kutztown University of
 Pennsylvania M, W
University of Pittsburgh M, W
Villanova University M, W
Westminster College W

Rhode Island
University of Rhode Island M, W

South Carolina
Clemson University M, W
College of Charleston M, W

Tennessee
University of Tennessee: Knoxville M, W

Texas
Southern Methodist University M, W
Texas Christian University M, W
University of Houston W
University of Texas at Austin M, W

Utah
Brigham Young University M, W
University of Utah M, W

Virginia
James Madison University M, W
Old Dominion University M, W
University of Virginia M, W
Virginia Military Institute M

West Virginia
West Virginia Wesleyan College M, W

Wisconsin
University of Wisconsin
    Green Bay M, W
    Madison M, W

Fencing

California
California State University: Fullerton M, W

Florida
Florida Institute of Technology M, W

Illinois
University of Illinois at Urbana-Champaign M

Indiana
Tri-State University M, W
University of Notre Dame M, W

Michigan
University of Detroit Mercy M, W
Wayne State University M, W

Montana
Montana State University M

New Jersey
Fairleigh Dickinson University
    Edward Williams College W
    Madison W
Rutgers—The State University of New Jersey
    College of Engineering M, W
    College of Pharmacy M, W
    Cook College M, W
    Douglass College W
    Livingston College M, W
    Mason Gross School of the Arts M, W
    Rutgers College M, W

New York
St. John's University M, W

North Carolina
North Carolina State University M, W
University of North Carolina at Chapel Hill M, W

Ohio
Cleveland State University M, W
Ohio State University: Columbus Campus W
Urbana University W

Oklahoma
St. Gregory's College M, W

Pennsylvania
Temple University W

Virginia
Old Dominion University M

Arab Republic of Egypt
American University in Cairo M, W

Field hockey

California
University of the Pacific W

Connecticut
Fairfield University W
University of Connecticut W

Delaware
University of Delaware W

District of Columbia
American University W

Illinois
Northwestern University W

Iowa
University of Iowa W

Kentucky
Bellarmine College W
University of Louisville W

Maine
University of Maine W

Maryland
Towson State University W
University of Maryland: College Park W

Massachusetts
Becker College
    Leicester Campus W
    Worcester Campus W
Boston College W
Boston University W
Dean Junior College W
Northeastern University W
University of Massachusetts at Amherst W

Michigan
Michigan State University W
University of Michigan W

Minnesota
Winona State University W

Missouri
Central Methodist College W
St. Louis University W

New Hampshire
University of New Hampshire W

New Jersey
Rider College W
Rutgers—The State University of New Jersey
    College of Engineering W
    College of Pharmacy W
    Cook College W
    Douglass College W
    Livingston College W
    Mason Gross School of the Arts W
    Rutgers College W

New Mexico
New Mexico State University W

New York
Hofstra University W
Houghton College W
Long Island University: C. W. Post Campus W
Syracuse University W

North Carolina
Appalachian State University W
Catawba College W
Davidson College W
Duke University W
University of North Carolina at Chapel Hill W

Ohio
Kent State University W
Miami University: Oxford Campus W
Ohio State University: Columbus Campus W

Pennsylvania
Drexel University W
Eastern College W
Indiana University of Pennsylvania W
Kutztown University of Pennsylvania W
Lock Haven University of Pennsylvania W
Millersville University of Pennsylvania W
Shippensburg University of Pennsylvania W
Temple University W
Villanova University W
West Chester University of Pennsylvania W

Rhode Island
Providence College W
University of Rhode Island W

Virginia
College of William and Mary W
James Madison University W
Longwood College W
Radford University W
University of Richmond W
University of Virginia W
Virginia Commonwealth University W

West Virginia
Davis and Elkins College W

Football (tackle)

Alabama
Alabama Agricultural and Mechanical University M
Auburn University M
Miles College M
Troy State University M
Tuskegee University M
University of North Alabama M

Arizona
Arizona Western College M
Eastern Arizona College M
Glendale Community College M
Northern Arizona University M
Scottsdale Community College M
University of Arizona M

Arkansas
Henderson State University M
Ouachita Baptist University M
University of Arkansas at Pine Bluff M
University of Central Arkansas M

California
Azusa Pacific University M
California Polytechnic State University: San Luis Obispo M
California State University
    Fresno M
    Northridge M
St. Mary's College of California M
Santa Clara University M
Stanford University M
University of California
    Berkeley M
    Los Angeles M
University of the Pacific M

Colorado
Adams State College M
Colorado Christian University M
Colorado School of Mines M
Colorado State University M
Fort Lewis College M
Mesa State College M
University of Colorado at Boulder M
University of Northern Colorado M
Western State College of Colorado M

Connecticut
Central Connecticut State University M
University of Connecticut M

Delaware
Delaware State College M
University of Delaware M

District of Columbia
Howard University M

Florida
Bethune-Cookman College M
Florida State University M
University of Central Florida M
University of Miami M

Georgia
Clark Atlanta University M
Fort Valley State College M
Georgia Institute of Technology M
Georgia Military College M
Georgia Southern University M
Morehouse College M
Savannah State College M

Colleges that offer athletic scholarships

University of Georgia M
Valdosta State College M
West Georgia College M

Hawaii
University of Hawaii at Manoa M

Idaho
Boise State University M
Idaho State University M
Ricks College M
University of Idaho M

Illinois
College of St. Francis M
Eastern Illinois University M
Illinois State University M
Northwestern University M
Olivet Nazarene University M
St. Xavier University M
Southern Illinois University at Carbondale M
Trinity College M
University of Illinois at Urbana-Champaign M
Western Illinois University M

Indiana
Ball State University M
Butler University M
Indiana State University M
Indiana University Bloomington M
Purdue University M
University of Indianapolis M
University of Notre Dame M
Valparaiso University M

Iowa
Ellsworth Community College M
Graceland College M
Iowa Central Community College M
Iowa Lakes Community College M
Iowa State University M
Iowa Wesleyan College M
Morningside College M
North Iowa Area Community College M
Northwestern College M
Teikyo Westmar University M
University of Iowa M
University of Northern Iowa M
Waldorf College M

Kansas
Baker University M
Benedictine College M
Bethel College M
Butler County Community College M
Coffeyville Community College M
Dodge City Community College M
Emporia State University M
Fort Hays State University M
Fort Scott Community College M
Friends University M
Garden City Community College M
Kansas State University M
McPherson College M
Ottawa University M
Sterling College M
University of Kansas M

Kentucky
Eastern Kentucky University M
Kentucky State University M
Morehead State University M
Murray State University M
Union College M
University of Kentucky M
University of Louisville M
Western Kentucky University M

Louisiana
Grambling State University M
Louisiana State University and Agricultural and Mechanical College M
Louisiana Tech University M
Nicholls State University M
Northeast Louisiana University M
Southern University and Agricultural and Mechanical College M
Tulane University M
University of Southwestern Louisiana M

Maine
University of Maine M

Maryland
Bowie State University M
Morgan State University M
Towson State University M
University of Maryland: College Park M

Massachusetts
American International College M
Boston College M
Boston University M
Dean Junior College M
Northeastern University M

Michigan
Eastern Michigan University M
Hillsdale College M
Michigan State University M
Michigan Technological University M
Northern Michigan University M
Northwood University M
University of Michigan M
Wayne State University M
Western Michigan University M

Minnesota
Bemidji State University M
Mankato State University M
Moorhead State University M
St. Cloud State University M
Southwest State University M
University of Minnesota
  Duluth M
  Twin Cities M
Winona State University M

Mississippi
Copiah-Lincoln Community College M
Delta State University M
East Central Community College M
Hinds Community College M
Holmes Community College M
Mississippi College M
Mississippi State University M
University of Mississippi M

Missouri
Central Methodist College M
Central Missouri State University M
Culver-Stockton College M
Kemper Military School and College M
Lindenwood College M
Missouri Southern State College M
Missouri Western State College M
Northeast Missouri State University M
Southeast Missouri State University M
Southwest Baptist University M

University of Missouri
  Columbia M
  Rolla M
William Jewell College M

Montana
Carroll College M
Montana College of Mineral Science and Technology M
Montana State University M
Rocky Mountain College M
University of Montana M
Western Montana College of the University of Montana M

Nebraska
Chadron State College M
Concordia College M
Dana College M
Doane College M
McCook Community College M
Midland Lutheran College M
Peru State College M
University of Nebraska
  Kearney M
  Lincoln M
  Omaha M
Wayne State College M

New Hampshire
University of New Hampshire M

New Jersey
Rutgers—The State University of New Jersey
  College of Engineering M
  College of Pharmacy M
  Cook College M
  Livingston College M
  Mason Gross School of the Arts M
  Rutgers College M

New Mexico
Eastern New Mexico University M
New Mexico State University M
University of New Mexico M

New York
Fordham University M
Syracuse University M

North Carolina
Appalachian State University M
Catawba College M
Duke University M
East Carolina University M
Elizabeth City State University M
Elon College M
Fayetteville State University M
Gardner-Webb University M
Johnson C. Smith University M
Lees-McRae College M
Lenoir-Rhyne College M
Livingstone College M
Mars Hill College M
North Carolina Agricultural and Technical State University M
North Carolina Central University M
North Carolina State University M
University of North Carolina at Chapel Hill M
Wake Forest University M
Western Carolina University M
Wingate College M
Winston-Salem State University M

North Dakota
Dickinson State University M
Mayville State University M

North Dakota State College of Science M
North Dakota State University M
University of Mary M
University of North Dakota M

Ohio
Ashland University M
Bowling Green State University M
Kent State University M
Miami University: Oxford Campus M
Ohio State University: Columbus Campus M
Tiffin University M
University of Findlay M
University of Toledo M
Urbana University M
Youngstown State University M

Oklahoma
East Central University M
Northwestern Oklahoma State University M
Oklahoma Panhandle State University M
Southwestern Oklahoma State University M
University of Central Oklahoma M
University of Oklahoma M
University of Tulsa M

Oregon
Oregon State University M
Portland State University M

Pennsylvania
California University of Pennsylvania M
Cheyney University of Pennsylvania M
Duquesne University M
Edinboro University of Pennsylvania M
Geneva College M
Indiana University of Pennsylvania M
Kutztown University of Pennsylvania M
Lock Haven University of Pennsylvania M
Millersville University of Pennsylvania M
Shippensburg University of Pennsylvania M
Temple University M
University of Pittsburgh M
Villanova University M
West Chester University of Pennsylvania M
Westminster College M

Rhode Island
University of Rhode Island M

South Carolina
Clemson University M
Francis Marion University M
Furman University M
North Greenville College M
Presbyterian College M
South Carolina State University M
University of South Carolina M
Wofford College M

South Dakota
Augustana College M
Black Hills State University M
Dakota State University M
Dakota Wesleyan University M
Huron University M
Northern State University M

Colleges that offer athletic scholarships

Sioux Falls College M
South Dakota State University M

Tennessee
East Tennessee State University M
Lane College M
Middle Tennessee State University M
University of Tennessee
  Knoxville M
  Martin M
Vanderbilt University M

Texas
Baylor University M
Blinn College M
East Texas State University M
Kilgore College M
Ranger Junior College M
Rice University M
Southern Methodist University M
Southwest Texas State University M
Stephen F. Austin State University M
Texas A&I University M
Texas Christian University M
Texas Tech University M
University of Houston M
University of North Texas M
University of Texas at Austin M

Utah
Brigham Young University M
Dixie College M
University of Utah M
Utah State University M
Weber State University M

Virginia
College of William and Mary M
Hampton University M
James Madison University M
Liberty University M
Norfolk State University M
University of Richmond M
University of Virginia M
Virginia Military Institute M
Virginia Polytechnic Institute and State University M
Virginia Union University M

Washington
Eastern Washington University M
Pacific Lutheran University M
University of Puget Sound M
University of Washington M
Walla Walla Community College M
Washington State University M
Western Washington University M

West Virginia
Potomac State College of West Virginia University M
Shepherd College M
West Liberty State College M
West Virginia Institute of Technology M
West Virginia State College M
West Virginia University M
West Virginia Wesleyan College M

Wisconsin
University of Wisconsin: Madison M

Wyoming
University of Wyoming M

Golf

Alabama
Auburn University M, W
Huntingdon College M
James H. Faulkner State Community College M, W
Judson College W
Snead State Community College M
Spring Hill College M, W
University of Alabama in Birmingham M, W
University of Mobile M
University of North Alabama M
University of South Alabama M, W

Arizona
Glendale Community College M
Grand Canyon University M
Pima Community College M
Scottsdale Community College M
University of Arizona M, W

California
California State University
  Fresno M
  Northridge M
  San Bernardino M
Pepperdine University M, W
Point Loma Nazarene College M
St. Mary's College of California M
University of California
  Berkeley M
  Irvine M
  Los Angeles M, W
University of the Pacific M
University of San Diego M
University of San Francisco M, W

Colorado
Colorado Christian University M, W
Colorado School of Mines M
Colorado State University M, W
Fort Lewis College M
Regis University M
University of Colorado
  Boulder M
  Colorado Springs M
University of Northern Colorado M
University of Southern Colorado M, W

Connecticut
Central Connecticut State University M
Fairfield University M
Quinnipiac College M
University of Connecticut M
University of Hartford M, W

District of Columbia
American University M
George Washington University M
Georgetown University M

Florida
Brevard Community College M
Eckerd College M
Flagler College M
Florida Atlantic University M, W
Florida Community College at Jacksonville M
Florida State University M, W
Lynn University M, W
Nova University M
Palm Beach Community College M, W
Rollins College M, W
St. Petersburg Junior College M, W
Stetson University M, W
University of Central Florida M, W
University of Miami W
University of North Florida M
University of West Florida M, W
Webber College M

Georgia
Abraham Baldwin Agricultural College M
Augusta College M
Brewton-Parker College M
Clayton State College M, W
Columbus College M
Georgia College M, W
Georgia Southern University M
Georgia Southwestern College M
Kennesaw State College M
Mercer University M
Piedmont College M, W
Shorter College M
University of Georgia M, W
Valdosta State College M
West Georgia College M

Hawaii
University of Hawaii
  Hilo M
  Manoa M, W

Idaho
Boise State University M, W
University of Idaho M

Illinois
Bradley University M, W
College of St. Francis M
Danville Area Community College M, W
De Paul University M
Highland Community College M, W
Illinois Eastern Community Colleges: Lincoln Trail College M
Illinois State University M, W
John A. Logan College M
Kishwaukee College M, W
Lewis University M, W
Lincoln College M, W
Loyola University of Chicago M
McKendree College M, W
Morton College M, W
Northwestern University M, W
Sauk Valley Community College M
Southern Illinois University
  Carbondale M, W
  Edwardsville M
Trinity College M
University of Illinois at Urbana-Champaign M, W
Western Illinois University M

Indiana
Bethel College M
Butler University M
Goshen College M
Grace College M
Huntington College M, W
Indiana University Bloomington M, W
Indiana Wesleyan University M
Marian College M, W
Purdue University M, W
Tri-State University M
University of Evansville M
University of Indianapolis M, W
University of Notre Dame M, W
University of Southern Indiana M
Vincennes University M, W

Iowa
Briar Cliff College M, W
Drake University M
Graceland College M, W
Grand View College M, W
Indian Hills Community College M
Iowa Central Community College M, W
Iowa Lakes Community College M, W
Iowa State University M, W
Iowa Wesleyan College M, W
Marshalltown Community College M, W
Mount St. Clare College M, W
North Iowa Area Community College M
Northwestern College M, W
Teikyo Westmar University M, W
University of Iowa M, W
University of Northern Iowa W
Waldorf College M, W

Kansas
Allen County Community College M
Baker University M
Benedictine College M
Butler County Community College M
Coffeyville Community College M
Dodge City Community College M, W
Emporia State University M
Garden City Community College M
Johnson County Community College M
Kansas Newman College M
Kansas State University M, W
McPherson College M, W
Ottawa University M
University of Kansas M, W
Wichita State University M, W

Kentucky
Bellarmine College M
Campbellsville College M
Cumberland College M, W
Eastern Kentucky University M
Georgetown College M
Kentucky State University M
Kentucky Wesleyan College M, W
Lindsey Wilson College M
Morehead State University M
Murray State University M
Northern Kentucky University M
Transylvania University M
Union College M
University of Kentucky M, W
University of Louisville M
Western Kentucky University M, W

Louisiana
Bossier Parish Community College M
Grambling State University M
Louisiana State University and Agricultural and Mechanical College M, W
Louisiana Tech University M
Nicholls State University M
Northeast Louisiana University M
Southeastern Louisiana University M
Southern University and Agricultural and Mechanical College M
Tulane University M, W
University of Southwestern Louisiana M

Maryland
Charles County Community College M, W

253

Colleges that offer athletic scholarships

University of Maryland
   Baltimore County M
   College Park M

Michigan
Aquinas College M
Detroit College of Business M
Eastern Michigan University M
Glen Oaks Community College M
Grand Rapids Baptist College and
   Seminary M
Hillsdale College M
Kellogg Community College M, W
Lake Michigan College M
Lansing Community College M
Macomb Community College M
Michigan State University M, W
Northern Michigan University M
Northwood University M
Oakland University M, W
Spring Arbor College M
University of Michigan M, W
Wayne State University M

Minnesota
Mankato State University M, W
Moorhead State University M, W
University of Minnesota: Twin
   Cities M, W
Winona State University M, W

Mississippi
Belhaven College M
Delta State University M
Mississippi State University M, W
University of Mississippi M, W

Missouri
Central Missouri State University M
Culver-Stockton College M
Lincoln University M
Lindenwood College M, W
Missouri Southern State College M
Missouri Western State College M
Northeast Missouri State University
   M
Penn Valley Community College M
St. Louis University M
Southwest Baptist University M
University of Missouri
   Columbia M, W
   Kansas City M, W
   Rolla M
William Jewell College M

Nebraska
Central Community College M, W
Chadron State College W
Concordia College M, W
Creighton University M, W
McCook Community College M, W
Midland Lutheran College M, W
Northeast Community College M,
   W
Southeast Community College:
   Beatrice Campus M
University of Nebraska
   Kearney M
   Lincoln M, W
Wayne State College M, W
Western Nebraska Community
   College: Scottsbluff Campus M

New Jersey
Fairleigh Dickinson University
   Edward Williams College M
   Madison M
Rider College M

Rutgers—The State University of
   New Jersey
   College of Engineering M, W
   College of Pharmacy M, W
   Cook College M, W
   Douglass College W
   Livingston College M, W
   Mason Gross School of the
      Arts M, W
   Rutgers College M, W
Seton Hall University M

New Mexico
New Mexico Junior College M
University of New Mexico M, W

New York
Adelphi University M
Canisius College M
Cazenovia College M
Fordham University M
Iona College M
Le Moyne College M
Long Island University: Brooklyn
   Campus M
Manhattan College M
Mercy College M, W
Niagara University M
St. John's University M
St. Thomas Aquinas College M
Wagner College M

North Carolina
Appalachian State University M, W
Barton College M
Belmont Abbey College M
Brevard College M
Campbell University M, W
Duke University M, W
East Carolina University M
Edgecombe Community College M
Elon College M
Fayetteville State University M
Gardner-Webb University M
High Point University M
Johnson C. Smith University M
Lenoir-Rhyne College M
Livingstone College M
Louisburg College M
Mars Hill College M
Mount Olive College M
North Carolina State University M,
   W
Pembroke State University M
Pfeiffer College M
Queens College M
St. Andrews Presbyterian College
   M, W
St. Augustine's College M, W
University of North Carolina
   Asheville M
   Chapel Hill M, W
   Charlotte M
   Greensboro M, W
   Wilmington M, W
Wake Forest University M, W
Western Carolina University M
Wingate College M

North Dakota
Dickinson State University M, W

Ohio
Bowling Green State University M,
   W
Cleveland State University M
Kent State University M
Malone College M
Miami University: Oxford Campus
   M
Ohio State University: Columbus
   Campus M, W

Tiffin University M
University of Findlay M
University of Toledo M
Urbana University M, W
Walsh University M
Wright State University M
Xavier University M, W
Youngstown State University M

Oklahoma
Cameron University M
Oklahoma City University M
Oral Roberts University M
Phillips University M
St. Gregory's College M, W
Southwestern Oklahoma State
   University M
University of Central Oklahoma M
University of Oklahoma M, W
University of Tulsa M, W

Oregon
Oregon State University M, W
Portland State University M
Treasure Valley Community College
   M
University of Portland M

Pennsylvania
Duquesne University M
Edinboro University of
   Pennsylvania M
Gannon University M
Indiana University of Pennsylvania
   M
Mercyhurst College M, W
Millersville University of
   Pennsylvania M
Robert Morris College M, W
St. Francis College M, W
St. Joseph's University M
Temple University M
Villanova University M
West Chester University of
   Pennsylvania M

South Carolina
Anderson College M
Charleston Southern University M,
   W
Clemson University M
Coker College M
College of Charleston M, W
Francis Marion University M
Furman University M, W
Limestone College M
North Greenville College M
Presbyterian College M, W
Spartanburg Methodist College M
University of South Carolina at
   Aiken M
Winthrop University M, W
Wofford College M

South Dakota
Northern State University W

Tennessee
Bethel College M
East Tennessee State University M
Freed-Hardeman University M
Lambuth University M
Lee College M
Lincoln Memorial University M
Middle Tennessee State University
   M
Milligan College M
Shelby State Community College M
Tusculum College M
Union University M

University of Tennessee
   Knoxville M, W
   Martin W
Vanderbilt University M, W

Texas
Baylor University M, W
Concordia Lutheran College M
East Texas State University M
Lamar University—Beaumont M, W
St. Edward's University M
St. Mary's University M
Southern Methodist University M,
   W
Southwest Texas State University M
Stephen F. Austin State University
   M
Texas Christian University M, W
Texas Lutheran College M
Texas Tech University M, W
Texas Wesleyan University M
University of Houston M
University of Mary Hardin-Baylor
   M
University of North Texas M, W
University of Texas
   Austin M
   San Antonio M
West Texas A & M University M

Utah
Brigham Young University M, W
University of Utah M
Utah State University M
Weber State University M, W

Virginia
Bluefield College M
College of William and Mary M, W
George Mason University M
Hampton University M
James Madison University M, W
Liberty University M
Longwood College M, W
Old Dominion University M
Radford University M, W
St. Paul's College M
University of Richmond M
University of Virginia M
Virginia Commonwealth University
   M, W
Virginia Military Institute M
Virginia Polytechnic Institute and
   State University M
Virginia Union University M, W

Washington
Eastern Washington University M,
   W
Edmonds Community College M,
   W
Green River Community College
   M, W
St. Martin's College M, W
Spokane Community College M
Tacoma Community College M, W
University of Puget Sound M
University of Washington M, W
Walla Walla Community College M,
   W
Washington State University M, W
Western Washington University M

West Virginia
Bluefield State College M
Davis and Elkins College M
University of Charleston M
West Liberty State College M
West Virginia Wesleyan College M

Colleges that offer athletic scholarships

Wisconsin
University of Wisconsin
 Green Bay M
 Madison M, W

Wyoming
University of Wyoming M, W

Gymnastics

Alabama
Auburn University W
University of Alabama W

Alaska
University of Alaska Anchorage W

Arizona
University of Arizona W

California
California Polytechnic State
 University: San Luis Obispo W
California State University:
 Fullerton W
University of California
 Berkeley M, W
 Los Angeles M, W
 Santa Barbara M, W

Colorado
University of Denver W

Connecticut
University of Bridgeport W

District of Columbia
George Washington University W
Howard University M, W

Georgia
University of Georgia W

Idaho
Boise State University W

Illinois
Illinois State University W
University of Illinois
 Chicago M, W
 Urbana-Champaign M, W

Indiana
Ball State University W

Iowa
Iowa State University M, W
University of Iowa M, W

Kansas
Fort Hays State University M

Louisiana
Louisiana State University and
 Agricultural and Mechanical
 College W

Maryland
Towson State University W
University of Maryland: College
 Park W

Massachusetts
Northeastern University W
University of Massachusetts at
 Amherst M, W

Michigan
Eastern Michigan University W
Michigan State University M, W
Northwood University M
University of Michigan M, W
Western Michigan University M, W

Minnesota
University of Minnesota: Twin
 Cities M, W
Winona State University W

Missouri
Southeast Missouri State University
 W
University of Missouri: Columbia W

Nebraska
University of Nebraska—Lincoln M,
 W

New Hampshire
University of New Hampshire W

New Jersey
Rutgers—The State University of
 New Jersey
 College of Engineering W
 College of Pharmacy W
 Cook College W
 Douglass College W
 Livingston College W
 Mason Gross School of the
  Arts W
 Rutgers College W
Seton Hall University W

New Mexico
University of New Mexico M, W

New York
Syracuse University M

North Carolina
North Carolina State University M,
 W
University of North Carolina at
 Chapel Hill W

Ohio
Bowling Green State University W
Kent State University M, W
Ohio State University: Columbus
 Campus M, W

Oklahoma
University of Oklahoma M, W

Oregon
Oregon State University W

Pennsylvania
Indiana University of Pennsylvania
 W
Temple University M, W
University of Pittsburgh M, W
West Chester University of
 Pennsylvania W

Puerto Rico
University of Puerto Rico: La
 Montana Regional College M

Rhode Island
University of Rhode Island W

Texas
Texas Woman's University W

Utah
Brigham Young University M, W
University of Utah W
Utah State University W

Virginia
College of William and Mary M, W
James Madison University M, W
Radford University M, W

Washington
Seattle Pacific University W

West Virginia
West Virginia University W

Arab Republic of Egypt
American University in Cairo M, W

Horseback riding

Kentucky
Murray State University M, W

Michigan
Hillsdale College M

Missouri
Park College M, W

New York
Cazenovia College M, W

North Carolina
St. Andrews Presbyterian College
 M, W

Ohio
Lake Erie College M, W

Virginia
Southern Virginia College for
 Women W

Ice hockey

Alabama
University of Alabama in Huntsville
 M

Alaska
University of Alaska
 Anchorage M
 Fairbanks M

Colorado
Colorado College M
University of Denver M

Connecticut
Fairfield University M
University of Connecticut M

Illinois
University of Illinois at Chicago M

Indiana
University of Notre Dame M

Maine
University of Maine M

Massachusetts
Boston College M
Boston University M
Merrimack College M
Northeastern University M
University of Massachusetts
 Amherst M
 Lowell M

Michigan
Michigan State University M
Michigan Technological University
 M
Northern Michigan University M
University of Michigan M

Minnesota
Mankato State University M
St. Cloud State University M
University of Minnesota
 Duluth M
 Twin Cities M

New Hampshire
University of New Hampshire M

New Jersey
County College of Morris M

New York
Canisius College M
Clarkson University M
Rensselaer Polytechnic Institute M

North Dakota
North Dakota State University:
 Bottineau *M*
University of North Dakota M

Ohio
Bowling Green State University M
Kent State University M
Ohio State University: Columbus
 Campus M

Pennsylvania
Villanova University M

Rhode Island
Providence College M, W

Wisconsin
University of Wisconsin: Madison
 M

Lacrosse

Colorado
Colorado School of Mines M
University of Denver M

Connecticut
Fairfield University M
University of Hartford M

Delaware
University of Delaware M, W

District of Columbia
American University W
Georgetown University M

Indiana
Butler University M

Louisiana
Bossier Parish Community College
 W

Maryland
Johns Hopkins University M
Loyola College in Maryland M, W
Mount St. Mary's College M
Towson State University M, W
University of Maryland
 Baltimore County M, W
 College Park M, W

Colleges that offer athletic scholarships

Massachusetts
Boston College W
Dean Junior College M
Mount Ida College M
University of Massachusetts
  Amherst M, W
  Lowell M

Michigan
Michigan State University M

New Jersey
Rutgers—The State University of
  New Jersey
  College of Engineering M, W
  College of Pharmacy M, W
  Cook College M, W
  Douglass College W
  Livingston College M, W
  Mason Gross School of the
    Arts M, W
  Rutgers College M, W

New York
Adelphi University M
Canisius College M
Hofstra University M, W
Long Island University: C. W. Post
  Campus M
Manhattan College M
Marist College M
New York Institute of Technology
  M
St. John's University M

North Carolina
Duke University M
University of North Carolina at
  Chapel Hill M

Ohio
Ohio State University: Columbus
  Campus M

Pennsylvania
Drexel University M
Eastern College W
Lock Haven University of
  Pennsylvania W
Millersville University of
  Pennsylvania W
St. Joseph's University M, W
St. Vincent College M
Shippensburg University of
  Pennsylvania W
Temple University W
Villanova University M, W
West Chester University of
  Pennsylvania M, W

South Carolina
Limestone College M

Virginia
College of William and Mary W
James Madison University W
Old Dominion University W
Radford University M
University of Richmond W
University of Virginia M, W
Virginia Military Institute M

Rifle

Alabama
University of North Alabama M

Alaska
University of Alaska Fairbanks M,
W

Illinois
De Paul University M, W

Kentucky
Murray State University M, W

Missouri
Northeast Missouri State University
  M, W
St. Louis University M, W
University of Missouri: Kansas City
  M, W

New Mexico
Eastern New Mexico University M,
W

New York
Canisius College M, W
St. John's University M, W

Ohio
Xavier University M, W

Pennsylvania
Duquesne University M, W

Virginia
George Mason University M, W

West Virginia
West Virginia University M, W

Wyoming
University of Wyoming M, W

Rowing (crew)

District of Columbia
George Washington University M,
W

Florida
Florida Institute of Technology M,
W

Massachusetts
Boston University M, W
Northeastern University M, W

New Jersey
Rutgers—The State University of
  New Jersey
  College of Engineering M, W
  College of Pharmacy M, W
  Cook College M, W
  Douglass College W
  Livingston College M, W
  Mason Gross School of the
    Arts M, W
  Rutgers College M, W

New York
Syracuse University M, W

Pennsylvania
Drexel University M
Mercyhurst College M, W
Temple University M, W

Washington
Washington State University W

West Virginia
University of Charleston M, W

Wisconsin
University of Wisconsin: Madison
  M, W

Arab Republic of Egypt
American University in Cairo M, W

Sailing

Virginia
Old Dominion University M, W

Skiing

Alaska
University of Alaska
  Anchorage M, W
  Fairbanks M, W

Colorado
Colorado School of Mines M, W
University of Colorado at Boulder
  M, W
University of Denver M, W
Western State College of Colorado
  M, W

Idaho
Albertson College M, W

Michigan
Northern Michigan University M,
W

Minnesota
University of Minnesota: Twin
  Cities M, W

Montana
Rocky Mountain College M, W

New Mexico
University of New Mexico M, W

New York
Paul Smith's College M, W

North Carolina
Lees-McRae College M, W

Oregon
Central Oregon Community College
  M, W

Utah
Brigham Young University M, W
University of Utah M, W

Vermont
Green Mountain College M, W

Washington
Seattle University M, W

Soccer

Alabama
Alabama Agricultural and
  Mechanical University M
Huntingdon College M, W
Spring Hill College M

University of Alabama
  Birmingham M
  Huntsville M
University of Mobile M, W
University of South Alabama M

Arizona
Arizona Western College M
Glendale Community College M
Grand Canyon University M
Pima Community College M
Scottsdale Community College M

Arkansas
John Brown University M
University of Arkansas at Little
  Rock M, W

California
Azusa Pacific University M, W
Biola University M
California Polytechnic State
  University: San Luis Obispo M
California State University
  Bakersfield M
  Fresno M
  Fullerton M, W
  Northridge M
  San Bernardino M, W
Concordia University M
Master's College M, W
Pepperdine University W
Point Loma Nazarene College M
St. Mary's College of California M,
  W
Santa Clara University M, W
Southern California College M
University of California
  Berkeley M, W
  Los Angeles M
  Santa Barbara M, W
University of San Diego M, W
University of San Francisco M, W
Westmont College M, W

Colorado
Colorado Christian University M,
W
Colorado College W
Colorado School of Mines M
Fort Lewis College M
Metropolitan State College of
  Denver M, W
Regis University M, W
University of Colorado at Colorado
  Springs M
University of Denver M, W
University of Northern Colorado W
University of Southern Colorado M

Connecticut
Central Connecticut State
  University M
Fairfield University M, W
Quinnipiac College M, W
University of Bridgeport M, W
University of Connecticut M, W
University of Hartford M, W

Delaware
Goldey-Beacom College M
University of Delaware M, W

District of Columbia
American University M, W
George Washington University M,
W
Howard University M
University of the District of
  Columbia M

256

Colleges that offer athletic scholarships

Florida
Eckerd College M, W
Flagler College M
Florida Atlantic University M, W
Florida Institute of Technology M, W
Lynn University M, W
Nova University M
Palm Beach Atlantic College M
Rollins College M
St. Leo College M
St. Thomas University M, W
Stetson University M, W
University of Central Florida M, W
University of North Florida M
University of West Florida M
Warner Southern College M
Webber College M

Georgia
Augusta College M
Brewton-Parker College M
Clayton State College M
Columbus College M
Covenant College M
Georgia Southern University M
Mercer University M, W
Piedmont College M, W
Truett-McConnell College M
Valdosta State College W

Hawaii
Hawaii Pacific University M

Idaho
Albertson College M, W
Northwest Nazarene College M

Illinois
Belleville Area College M
Bradley University M
College of St. Francis M
De Paul University M
Eastern Illinois University M
Illinois State University M
Judson College M, W
Kishwaukee College M
Lewis University M, W
Lincoln College M, W
Lincoln Land Community College M
Loyola University of Chicago M, W
McKendree College M, W
Olivet Nazarene University M
Quincy University M, W
Rosary College M
St. Xavier University M
Southern Illinois University at Edwardsville M, W
Springfield College in Illinois M
Trinity College M, W
University of Illinois at Chicago M
Western Illinois University M

Indiana
Bethel College M
Butler University M
Goshen College M, W
Grace College M
Huntington College M
Indiana University Bloomington M
Indiana University—Purdue University at Indianapolis M
Indiana Wesleyan University M, W
Tri-State University M, W
University of Evansville M, W
University of Indianapolis M
University of Notre Dame M, W
University of Southern Indiana M
Valparaiso University M, W

Iowa
Briar Cliff College M
Drake University M
Graceland College M
Grand View College M
Mount St. Clare College M
St. Ambrose University M
Teikyo Marycrest University M
Teikyo Westmar University M, W
Waldorf College M

Kansas
Allen County Community College M
Baker University M, W
Benedictine College M, W
Bethany College M
Bethel College M, W
Central College M, W
Coffeyville Community College M
Friends University M, W
Garden City Community College M
Johnson County Community College M
Kansas Newman College M, W
McPherson College M, W
Ottawa University W
Sterling College M, W

Kentucky
Bellarmine College M, W
Campbellsville College M
Cumberland College W
Georgetown College M
Kentucky Wesleyan College M, W
Lindsey Wilson College M, W
Northern Kentucky University M
Sue Bennett College M
Transylvania University M
Union College M, W
University of Kentucky M, W
University of Louisville M, W

Maine
Unity College M
University of Maine M, W

Maryland
Charles County Community College M
Dundalk Community College M, W
Loyola College in Maryland M, W
Mount St. Mary's College M, W
Towson State University M, W
University of Maryland
 Baltimore County M, W
 College Park M, W
 Eastern Shore M

Massachusetts
Becker College
 Leicester Campus M, W
 Worcester Campus M, W
Boston College M, W
Boston University M
Dean Junior College M, W
Mount Ida College M, W
Northeastern University M
University of Massachusetts
 Amherst M, W
 Lowell M, W

Michigan
Aquinas College M, W
Detroit College of Business M
Eastern Michigan University M
Macomb Community College M
Michigan Christian College M
Michigan State University M, W
Oakland University M
Spring Arbor College M, W
University of Detroit Mercy M
Western Michigan University M

Mississippi
Belhaven College M
Mississippi College M
William Carey College M, W

Missouri
Avila College M
Central Methodist College M, W
Culver-Stockton College M
Harris Stowe State College M
Lincoln University M
Lindenwood College M, W
Missouri Southern State College M
Northeast Missouri State University M, W
Northwest Missouri Community College M
Park College M, W
Research College of Nursing M, W
Rockhurst College M, W
St. Louis Community College at Meramec M, W
St. Louis University M
University of Missouri
 Kansas City M
 Rolla M
William Jewell College M, W
William Woods College W

Nebraska
Central Community College M
Concordia College M
Creighton University M, W
York College M, W

New Hampshire
Franklin Pierce College M, W
Hesser College M, W
New Hampshire College M, W
Notre Dame College M, W
University of New Hampshire W

New Jersey
Bloomfield College M
Burlington County College M, W
Caldwell College M
Centenary College M
County College of Morris M
Fairleigh Dickinson University
 Edward Williams College M
 Madison M
Georgian Court College W
Rider College M
Rutgers—The State University of New Jersey
 College of Engineering M, W
 College of Pharmacy M, W
 Cook College M, W
 Douglass College W
 Livingston College M, W
 Mason Gross School of the Arts M, W
 Rutgers College M, W
Seton Hall University M

New Mexico
University of New Mexico M, W

New York
Adelphi University M, W
Canisius College M, W
City University of New York:
 Queens College M
College of St. Rose M, W
Concordia College M, W
Dowling College M
Fordham University M, W
Hartwick College M
Hofstra University M
Houghton College M, W
Iona College M
King's College M, W
Le Moyne College M, W
Long Island University
 Brooklyn Campus M
 C. W. Post Campus M
 Southampton Campus M, W
Manhattan College M, W
Marist College M
Mercy College M
New York Institute of Technology M, W
Niagara University M, W
Paul Smith's College M, W
Roberts Wesleyan College M, W
St. Bonaventure University M
St. Francis College M
St. John's University M, W
Siena College M, W
Syracuse University M
Wagner College W

North Carolina
Appalachian State University M
Barton College M
Belmont Abbey College M
Brevard College M, W
Campbell University M, W
Catawba College M, W
Davidson College W
Duke University M, W
East Carolina University M
Elon College M, W
Gardner-Webb University M
High Point University M, W
Lees-McRae College M, W
Lenoir-Rhyne College M, W
Mars Hill College M, W
Montreat-Anderson College M, W
Mount Olive College M
North Carolina State University M, W
Pembroke State University M
Pfeiffer College M, W
Queens College M, W
St. Andrews Presbyterian College M, W
University of North Carolina
 Asheville M
 Chapel Hill M, W
 Charlotte M
 Greensboro M, W
 Wilmington M
Wake Forest University M
Wingate College M, W

Ohio
Bowling Green State University M
Cleveland State University M
Malone College M
Ohio Dominican College M
Ohio State University: Columbus Campus M
Southern State Community College M
Tiffin University M, W
University of Dayton M, W
University of Findlay M, W
University of Rio Grande M
Walsh University M, W
Wright State University M, W
Xavier University M, W

Oklahoma
Bartlesville Wesleyan College M, W
Oklahoma Christian University of Science and Arts M, W
Oklahoma City University M
Oral Roberts University M
University of Tulsa M, W

Colleges that offer athletic scholarships

Oregon
Concordia College M
George Fox College M, W
Oregon State University M, W
University of Portland M, W

Pennsylvania
California University of Pennsylvania M, W
Cheyney University of Pennsylvania M
Drexel University M
Eastern College M, W
Gannon University M, W
Geneva College M, W
Kutztown University of Pennsylvania M, W
Lock Haven University of Pennsylvania M
Manor Junior College M
Mercyhurst College M, W
Millersville University of Pennsylvania M
Point Park College M
Robert Morris College M, W
St. Francis College M, W
St. Joseph's University M
St. Vincent College M
Seton Hill College W
Shippensburg University of Pennsylvania M
Temple University M, W
University of Pittsburgh M, W
Villanova University M, W
West Chester University of Pennsylvania M, W

Puerto Rico
University of Puerto Rico: Mayaguez Campus M

Rhode Island
Providence College M, W
University of Rhode Island M, W

South Carolina
Anderson College M, W
Charleston Southern University M, W
Clemson University M
Coker College M, W
College of Charleston M, W
Erskine College M
Francis Marion University M
Furman University M
Lander University M
Limestone College M, W
Presbyterian College M, W
Spartanburg Methodist College M, W
University of South Carolina at Aiken M
Winthrop University M
Wofford College M

Tennessee
Belmont University M
Christian Brothers University M
Lambuth University M, W
Lee College M, W
Lincoln Memorial University M
Middle Tennessee State University W
Milligan College M
Tusculum College M, W
Vanderbilt University M, W
William Jennings Bryan College M

Texas
LeTourneau University M
St. Edward's University M, W
St. Mary's University M, W
Schreiner College M, W
Southern Methodist University M, W
Texas Lutheran College M
Texas Wesleyan University M
University of Mary Hardin-Baylor M
University of North Texas M

Vermont
Champlain College M, W
Green Mountain College M, W

Virginia
Bluefield College M
College of William and Mary M, W
George Mason University M, W
James Madison University M, W
Liberty University M, W
Longwood College M
Old Dominion University M
Radford University M, W
University of Richmond M
University of Virginia M, W
Virginia Commonwealth University M
Virginia Polytechnic Institute and State University M, W

Washington
Edmonds Community College M
Evergreen State College M, W
Gonzaga University M, W
Green River Community College M
Lower Columbia College M
Pacific Lutheran University M, W
Pierce College M
Seattle Pacific University M
Seattle University M, W
Shoreline Community College M
Spokane Community College M, W
Tacoma Community College M
University of Puget Sound M, W
University of Washington M, W
Washington State University W
Western Washington University M, W

West Virginia
Davis and Elkins College M
University of Charleston M, W
West Virginia University M
West Virginia Wesleyan College M, W
Wheeling Jesuit College M, W

Wisconsin
Cardinal Stritch College M
Lakeland College M
Marquette University M, W
Northland College M
University of Wisconsin
  Green Bay M, W
  Madison M, W

Arab Republic of Egypt
American University in Cairo M

Softball

Alabama
Athens State College W
Bevill State Community College W
Chattahoochee Valley Community College W
Enterprise State Junior College W
Faulkner University W
Gadsden State Community College W
George C. Wallace State Community College at Selma W
Huntingdon College W
James H. Faulkner State Community College W
John C. Calhoun State Community College W
Lurleen B. Wallace State Junior College W
Miles College W
Northwest Alabama Community College W
Snead State Community College W
Southern Union State Junior College W
Troy State University W
University of Mobile W

Arizona
Arizona Western College W
Central Arizona College W
Eastern Arizona College W
Glendale Community College W
Pima Community College W
Scottsdale Community College W
University of Arizona W

California
Azusa Pacific University W
California Polytechnic State University: San Luis Obispo W
California State University
  Bakersfield W
  Fresno W
  Fullerton W
  Northridge W
  San Bernardino W
Concordia University W
Point Loma Nazarene College W
St. Mary's College of California W
Southern California College W
University of California
  Berkeley W
  Los Angeles W
  Riverside W
University of the Pacific W
University of San Diego W

Colorado
Adams State College W
Colorado Northwestern Community College W
Colorado School of Mines W
Fort Lewis College W
Mesa State College W
Northeastern Junior College W
Regis University W
University of Colorado at Colorado Springs W

Connecticut
Central Connecticut State University W
Fairfield University W
Quinnipiac College W
University of Bridgeport W
University of Connecticut W

Delaware
Goldey-Beacom College W

Florida
Brevard Community College W
Central Florida Community College W
Daytona Beach Community College W
Eckerd College W
Florida Community College at Jacksonville W
Florida Institute of Technology W
Florida State University W
Hillsborough Community College W
Lake City Community College W
Okaloosa-Walton Community College W
Palm Beach Community College W
Pasco-Hernando Community College W
St. Johns River Community College W
St. Leo College W
St. Petersburg Junior College W
St. Thomas University W
Tallahassee Community College W
University of North Florida W
Valencia Community College W
Webber College W

Georgia
Abraham Baldwin Agricultural College W
Augusta College W
Brewton-Parker College W
Georgia College W
Georgia Southern University W
Kennesaw State College W
Macon College W
Mercer University W
Middle Georgia College W
Paine College W
Piedmont College W
Shorter College W
Truett-McConnell College W
Valdosta State College W
West Georgia College W

Hawaii
University of Hawaii
  Hilo W
  Manoa W

Illinois
Belleville Area College W
Bradley University W
College of St. Francis W
De Paul University W
Eastern Illinois University W
Illinois Central College W
Illinois Eastern Community Colleges
  Lincoln Trail College W
  Olney Central College W
  Wabash Valley College W
Illinois Institute of Technology W
Illinois State University W
John A. Logan College W
Judson College W
Kankakee Community College W
Kaskaskia College W
Kishwaukee College W
Lake Land College W
Lewis University W
Lincoln College M, W
Lincoln Land Community College W
Loyola University of Chicago M, W
McKendree College W
Morton College W
Northwestern University W
Olivet Nazarene University W
Quincy University W
St. Xavier University W
Southern Illinois University
  Carbondale W
  Edwardsville W
Trinity College W
Western Illinois University W

Indiana
Ball State University W
Bethel College W
Butler University W
Goshen College W

258

Colleges that offer athletic scholarships

Grace College W
Huntington College W
Indiana State University W
Indiana University—Purdue
 University at Indianapolis W
Indiana Wesleyan University W
Marian College W
Purdue University W
Tri-State University W
University of Evansville W
University of Indianapolis W
University of Notre Dame W
University of Southern Indiana W
Valparaiso University W

Iowa
Briar Cliff College W
Drake University W
Ellsworth Community College W
Graceland College W
Grand View College W
Indian Hills Community College W
Iowa Central Community College W
Iowa Lakes Community College W
Iowa State University W
Iowa Wesleyan College W
Marshalltown Community College W
Morningside College W
Mount St. Clare College W
Muscatine Community College W
North Iowa Area Community College W
Northwestern College W
St. Ambrose University W
Teikyo Marycrest University W
Teikyo Westmar University W
University of Iowa W
University of Northern Iowa W
Waldorf College W

Kansas
Allen County Community College W
Baker University W
Benedictine College W
Brown Mackie College W
Butler County Community College W
Central College W
Coffeyville Community College W
Colby Community College W
Dodge City Community College W
Emporia State University W
Fort Scott Community College W
Friends University W
Johnson County Community College W
Kansas City Kansas Community College W
Kansas Newman College W
Neosho County Community College W
Sterling College W
University of Kansas W
Wichita State University W

Kentucky
Bellarmine College W
Campbellsville College W
Cumberland College W
Eastern Kentucky University W
Georgetown College W
Kentucky State University W
Kentucky Wesleyan College W
Lees College W
Murray State University W
Northern Kentucky University W
Union College W

Louisiana
Louisiana Tech University W
Nicholls State University W
Northeast Louisiana University W
University of Southwestern Louisiana W

Maine
University of Maine W

Maryland
Bowie State University W
Charles County Community College W
Dundalk Community College W
Mount St. Mary's College W
Towson State University W
University of Maryland
 Baltimore County W
 Eastern Shore W

Massachusetts
American International College W
Becker College
 Leicester Campus W
 Worcester Campus W
Boston College W
Boston University W
Dean Junior College W
Mount Ida College W
University of Massachusetts at Amherst W

Michigan
Aquinas College W
Eastern Michigan University W
Grand Rapids Baptist College and Seminary W
Henry Ford Community College W
Hillsdale College W
Kellogg Community College W
Lake Michigan College W
Macomb Community College W
Michigan Christian College W
Michigan State University W
Northwood University W
Southwestern Michigan College W
Spring Arbor College W
University of Detroit Mercy W
University of Michigan W
Wayne State University W
Western Michigan University W

Minnesota
Mankato State University W
Moorhead State University W
St. Cloud State University W
Southwest State University W
University of Minnesota
 Duluth W
 Twin Cities W
Winona State University W

Mississippi
Delta State University W
East Central Community College W
Mississippi State University W
Mississippi University for Women W

Missouri
Avila College W
Central Methodist College W
Central Missouri State University W
Culver-Stockton College W
Hannibal-LaGrange College W
Lincoln University W
Lindenwood College W
Missouri Southern State College W
Missouri Western State College W
Northeast Missouri State University W
Northwest Missouri Community College W
St. Louis Community College at Meramec W
St. Louis University W
Southwest Baptist University W
University of Missouri
 Columbia W
 Kansas City W
 Rolla W
William Jewell College W
William Woods College W

Nebraska
College of St. Mary W
Concordia College W
Creighton University W
Dana College W
Doane College W
Midland Lutheran College W
Peru State College W
University of Nebraska
 Kearney W
 Lincoln W
 Omaha W
Wayne State College W

New Hampshire
Franklin Pierce College W
Hesser College M

New Jersey
Bloomfield College W
Burlington County College W
Caldwell College W
County College of Morris W
Georgian Court College W
Rider College W
Rutgers—The State University of New Jersey
 College of Engineering W
 College of Pharmacy W
 Cook College W
 Douglass College W
 Livingston College W
 Mason Gross School of the Arts W
 Rutgers College W
Seton Hall University W

New Mexico
New Mexico State University W
University of New Mexico W

New York
Adelphi University W
Canisius College W
City University of New York:
 Queens College W
College of St. Rose W
Concordia College W
Fordham University W
Hofstra University W
Iona College W
Jefferson Community College W
King's College W
Le Moyne College W
Long Island University
 Brooklyn Campus W
 C. W. Post Campus W
 Southampton Campus W
Manhattan College W
Marist College W
Mercy College W
New York Institute of Technology W
Niagara University W
Pace University
 College of White Plains W
 New York W
 Pleasantville/Briarcliff W
St. Bonaventure University W

St. Francis College W
St. John's University W
St. Thomas Aquinas College W
Siena College W
Wagner College W

North Carolina
Barber-Scotia College W
Barton College W
Campbell University W
East Carolina University W
Elon College W
Fayetteville State University W
Gardner-Webb University W
Johnson C. Smith University W
Lenoir-Rhyne College W
Livingstone College W
Louisburg College W
Mars Hill College W
Montreat-Anderson College W
Mount Olive College W
North Carolina Central University W
Pembroke State University W
Pfeiffer College W
St. Andrews Presbyterian College W
St. Augustine's College W
Southeastern Community College W
University of North Carolina
 Asheville W
 Chapel Hill W
 Charlotte W
 Greensboro W
 Wilmington W
Wingate College W
Winston-Salem State University W

North Dakota
Mayville State University W
North Dakota State University W
University of Mary W
University of North Dakota W

Ohio
Ashland University W
Bowling Green State University W
Cleveland State University W
Kent State University W
Lake Erie College W
Malone College W
Miami University: Oxford Campus W
Notre Dame College of Ohio W
Ohio Dominican College W
Ohio State University: Columbus Campus W
Tiffin University W
University of Findlay W
University of Rio Grande W
University of Toledo W
Urbana University W
Walsh University W
Wright State University W
Youngstown State University W

Oklahoma
Bacone College W
Cameron University W
Eastern Oklahoma State College W
Oklahoma Baptist University W
Oklahoma City University W
University of Central Oklahoma W
University of Oklahoma W
University of Tulsa W

Oregon
Clackamas Community College W
Concordia College W
George Fox College W
Oregon State University W
Portland State University W

Colleges that offer athletic scholarships

Pennsylvania
California University of Pennsylvania W
Community College of Beaver County W
Drexel University W
Eastern College W
Edinboro University of Pennsylvania W
Gannon University W
Geneva College W
Indiana University of Pennsylvania W
Kutztown University of Pennsylvania W
Lock Haven University of Pennsylvania W
Mercyhurst College W
Millersville University of Pennsylvania W
Philadelphia College of Pharmacy and Science W
Point Park College W
Robert Morris College W
St. Francis College W
St. Joseph's University W
St. Vincent College W
Seton Hill College W
Shippensburg University of Pennsylvania W
Temple University W
Villanova University W
West Chester University of Pennsylvania W
Westminster College W

Puerto Rico
University of Puerto Rico: Mayaguez Campus W

Rhode Island
Providence College W
University of Rhode Island W

South Carolina
Anderson College W
Charleston Southern University W
Claflin College W
Coker College W
College of Charleston W
Erskine College W
Francis Marion University W
Furman University W
Lander University W
Limestone College W
North Greenville College W
Spartanburg Methodist College W
University of South Carolina at Aiken W
Voorhees College W
Winthrop University W

South Dakota
Augustana College W
Northern State University W

Tennessee
Belmont University W
Bethel College W
Freed-Hardeman University W
Lambuth University W
Lincoln Memorial University W
Milligan College W
Trevecca Nazarene College W
Tusculum College W
University of Tennessee: Martin W

Texas
Houston Baptist University W
Ranger Junior College W
St. Edward's University W
St. Mary's University W
Southwest Texas State University W
Stephen F. Austin State University W
Texas Lutheran College W
Texas Wesleyan University W
University of Mary Hardin-Baylor W

Utah
College of Eastern Utah W
Dixie College W
University of Utah W
Utah State University W
Utah Valley Community College W

Vermont
Champlain College W
Green Mountain College W

Virginia
Bluefield College W
George Mason University W
Hampton University W
Longwood College W
Norfolk State University W
Radford University W
St. Paul's College W
University of Virginia W
Virginia Union University W

Washington
Edmonds Community College W
Green River Community College W
Lower Columbia College W
Olympic College W
Pacific Lutheran University W
Pierce College W
St. Martin's College W
Shoreline Community College W
Spokane Community College W
University of Puget Sound W
University of Washington W
Wenatchee Valley College W
Western Washington University W
Yakima Valley Community College W

West Virginia
Bluefield State College W
Davis and Elkins College W
Shepherd College W
University of Charleston W
West Liberty State College W
West Virginia Institute of Technology W
West Virginia State College W
West Virginia Wesleyan College W

Wisconsin
Cardinal Stritch College W
Lakeland College W
University of Wisconsin: Green Bay W

Squash

Arab Republic of Egypt
American University in Cairo M, W

Swimming

Alabama
Auburn University M, W

Alaska
University of Alaska Anchorage M

Arizona
Northern Arizona University M, W
University of Arizona M, W

Arkansas
John Brown University M, W
University of Arkansas at Little Rock M, W

California
California State University
  Bakersfield M, W
  Fresno M
  Northridge M, W
  San Bernardino M, W
Pepperdine University W
Stanford University M, W
University of California
  Berkeley M, W
  Irvine M, W
  Los Angeles W
  Santa Barbara M, W
University of the Pacific M, W
University of San Diego W

Colorado
Colorado School of Mines M, W
Metropolitan State College of Denver M, W
University of Denver M, W
University of Northern Colorado W

Connecticut
Central Connecticut State University M, W
Fairfield University M, W
University of Connecticut M, W

District of Columbia
American University M, W
George Washington University M, W
Howard University M, W

Florida
Brevard Community College M, W
Florida Atlantic University M, W
Florida State University M, W
St. Petersburg Junior College M, W
University of Miami M, W

Georgia
Georgia Institute of Technology M, W
Georgia Southern University M, W
Morehouse College M
University of Georgia M, W

Illinois
Bradley University M, W
Illinois Institute of Technology M, W
Lincoln College M, W
Loyola University of Chicago M
Northwestern University M, W
Southern Illinois University at Carbondale M, W
University of Illinois
  Chicago M, W
  Urbana-Champaign M, W
Western Illinois University M, W

Indiana
Ball State University M, W
Butler University M, W
Indiana University Bloomington M, W
Purdue University M, W
University of Evansville M, W
University of Indianapolis M, W
University of Notre Dame M, W
Valparaiso University M, W

Vincennes University M, W

Iowa
Iowa State University M, W
University of Iowa M, W
University of Northern Iowa W

Kansas
University of Kansas M, W

Kentucky
Campbellsville College M, W
Transylvania University M, W
Union College M, W
University of Kentucky M, W
University of Louisville M, W
Western Kentucky University M

Louisiana
Louisiana State University and Agricultural and Mechanical College M, W
Northeast Louisiana University M, W

Maine
University of Maine M, W

Maryland
Towson State University M, W
University of Maryland
  Baltimore County M, W
  College Park M, W

Massachusetts
Boston College W
Boston University M, W
Northeastern University M, W
University of Massachusetts
  Amherst M, W
  Lowell M

Michigan
Eastern Michigan University M, W
Hillsdale College W
Michigan State University M, W
Northern Michigan University W
Oakland University M, W
University of Michigan M, W
Wayne State University M, W

Minnesota
Mankato State University M, W
St. Cloud State University M, W
University of Minnesota: Twin Cities M, W

Mississippi
Mississippi University for Women W

Missouri
Lindenwood College M, W
Northeast Missouri State University W
St. Louis University M, W
University of Missouri
  Columbia M, W
  Rolla M
William Jewell College M, W
William Woods College W

Nebraska
University of Nebraska
  Kearney W
  Lincoln M, W

New Jersey
Rider College M, W

Colleges that offer athletic scholarships

Rutgers—The State University of New Jersey
　College of Engineering M, W
　College of Pharmacy M, W
　Cook College M, W
　Douglass College W
　Livingston College M, W
　Mason Gross School of the Arts M, W
　Rutgers College M, W
Seton Hall University M, W

New Mexico
New Mexico State University M, W
University of New Mexico M, W

New York
Adelphi University M, W
Canisius College M, W
City University of New York:
　Queens College M, W
College of St. Rose M, W
Fordham University M, W
Manhattan College W
Marist College M, W
Niagara University M, W
St. Bonaventure University M, W
St. Francis College W
St. John's University M, W
State University of New York at Buffalo M, W
Syracuse University M, W

North Carolina
Davidson College W
East Carolina University M, W
North Carolina State University M, W
Pfeiffer College W
University of North Carolina
　Chapel Hill M, W
　Charlotte M, W
　Wilmington M, W

North Dakota
University of North Dakota M, W

Ohio
Ashland University M, W
Bowling Green State University M, W
Cleveland State University M, W
Miami University: Oxford Campus M, W
Ohio State University: Columbus Campus M, W
University of Findlay M, W
University of Toledo M, W
Walsh University W
Wright State University M, W
Xavier University M, W

Oklahoma
Oral Roberts University M

Oregon
Oregon State University W

Pennsylvania
Drexel University M, W
Duquesne University M, W
Edinboro University of Pennsylvania M, W
Gannon University M, W
Indiana University of Pennsylvania M, W
Kutztown University of Pennsylvania M, W
Lock Haven University of Pennsylvania W
Millersville University of Pennsylvania W

Shippensburg University of Pennsylvania M, W
University of Pittsburgh M, W
Villanova University M, W
West Chester University of Pennsylvania M, W
Westminster College W

Puerto Rico
University of Puerto Rico
　La Montana Regional College M, W
　Mayaguez Campus M, W
University of the Sacred Heart M, W

Rhode Island
Providence College M, W
University of Rhode Island M, W

South Carolina
Clemson University M, W
College of Charleston M, W

South Dakota
South Dakota State University M, W

Tennessee
University of Tennessee: Knoxville M, W

Texas
Rice University W
Southern Methodist University M, W
Texas Christian University M, W
University of Houston W
University of Texas at Austin M, W

Utah
Brigham Young University M, W
University of Utah M, W

Virginia
College of William and Mary W
James Madison University M, W
Old Dominion University M, W
University of Richmond W
University of Virginia M, W
Virginia Military Institute M

Washington
Evergreen State College M, W
University of Puget Sound M, W
University of Washington M, W
Washington State University M, W

West Virginia
West Virginia University M, W
West Virginia Wesleyan College M, W

Wisconsin
University of Wisconsin
　Green Bay M, W
　Madison M, W

Wyoming
University of Wyoming M, W

Arab Republic of Egypt
American University in Cairo M, W

Table tennis

Alabama
Snead State Community College M, W

Ohio
Ohio State University: Columbus Campus M, W

Puerto Rico
University of Puerto Rico:
　Mayaguez Campus M, W

South Carolina
Anderson College M, W
South Carolina State University M

Texas
Rice University M, W

Arab Republic of Egypt
American University in Cairo M, W

Tennis

Alabama
Alabama Agricultural and Mechanical University M
Auburn University M, W
Enterprise State Junior College M, W
George C. Wallace State Community College at Selma M, W
Huntingdon College M, W
Jefferson Davis State Junior College M, W
Jefferson State Community College M, W
Judson College W
Lurleen B. Wallace State Junior College M
Miles College M, W
Spring Hill College M, W
Troy State University M, W
University of Alabama
　Birmingham M, W
　Huntsville M, W
University of Mobile M, W
University of North Alabama M, W
University of South Alabama M, W

Arizona
Glendale Community College M, W
Grand Canyon University W
Northern Arizona University M, W
Pima Community College M, W
Scottsdale Community College M, W
University of Arizona M, W

Arkansas
John Brown University M, W
University of Arkansas at Little Rock M, W

California
Azusa Pacific University M
Biola University W
California Polytechnic State University: San Luis Obispo M, W
California State University
　Bakersfield M, W
　Fresno M
　Fullerton W
　Northridge W
Dominican College of San Rafael M, W
Mount St. Mary's College W
Pepperdine University M, W
Point Loma Nazarene College M, W

St. Mary's College of California M, W
Southern California College M, W
Stanford University M, W
University of California
　Berkeley M, W
　Irvine M, W
　Los Angeles M, W
　Riverside M, W
　Santa Barbara M, W
University of the Pacific M, W
University of San Diego M, W
University of San Francisco M, W
Westmont College M, W

Colorado
Colorado Christian University M, W
Colorado School of Mines M
Colorado State University M, W
Mesa State College M, W
Metropolitan State College of Denver M, W
Northeastern Junior College M, W
Regis University M, W
University of Colorado
　Boulder M, W
　Colorado Springs M, W
University of Denver M, W
University of Northern Colorado M, W
University of Southern Colorado M, W

Connecticut
Central Connecticut State University M, W
Fairfield University M, W
Quinnipiac College M, W
University of Connecticut M, W
University of Hartford M, W

Delaware
Delaware State College M, W

District of Columbia
American University M, W
George Washington University M, W
Georgetown University W
Howard University M, W
University of the District of Columbia M, W

Florida
Eckerd College M, W
Flagler College M, W
Florida Atlantic University M, W
Florida Community College at Jacksonville M, W
Florida Institute of Technology M
Florida State University M, W
Hillsborough Community College W
Lynn University M, W
Nova University W
Palm Beach Community College M, W
Rollins College M, W
St. Leo College M, W
St. Thomas University W
Stetson University M, W
University of Central Florida M, W
University of Miami M, W
University of North Florida M, W
University of West Florida M, W
Webber College M, W

Georgia
Abraham Baldwin Agricultural College M
Augusta College M, W
Brewton-Parker College M, W

261

Colleges that offer athletic scholarships

Clark Atlanta University M, W
Columbus College M, W
Fort Valley State College M, W
Georgia College M, W
Georgia Southern University M, W
Kennesaw State College W
Mercer University M, W
Morehouse College M
Piedmont College M, W
Savannah State College W
Shorter College M, W
Southern College of Technology M
Truett-McConnell College M, W
University of Georgia M, W
Valdosta State College M, W
West Georgia College M, W

Hawaii
Hawaii Pacific University M, W
University of Hawaii
  Hilo M, W
  Manoa M, W

Idaho
Albertson College W
Boise State University M, W
Idaho State University M, W
Lewis Clark State College M, W
Northwest Nazarene College W
University of Idaho M, W

Illinois
Belleville Area College M, W
Bradley University M, W
Chicago State University M, W
College of St. Francis M, W
De Paul University M, W
Eastern Illinois University W
Illinois Eastern Community
  Colleges: Olney Central College
  M
Illinois Institute of Technology M, W
Illinois State University M, W
John A. Logan College M, W
Judson College M, W
Lake Land College M
Lewis University M, W
Northwestern University M, W
Olivet Nazarene University M, W
Quincy University W
Rosary College M, W
Sauk Valley Community College M, W
Southern Illinois University
  Carbondale M, W
  Edwardsville M, W
Springfield College in Illinois W
Trinity College M, W
University of Illinois
  Chicago M, W
  Urbana-Champaign M, W
Western Illinois University M, W

Indiana
Ball State University M, W
Bethel College M, W
Butler University M, W
Goshen College M, W
Grace College M
Huntington College M, W
Indiana State University M, W
Indiana University Bloomington M, W
Indiana University—Purdue
  University at Indianapolis M
Indiana Wesleyan University M, W
Marian College M, W
Purdue University M, W
Tri-State University M, W
University of Evansville M, W
University of Indianapolis M, W

University of Notre Dame M, W
University of Southern Indiana M, W
Valparaiso University M, W
Vincennes University M, W

Iowa
Drake University M, W
Graceland College M, W
Grand View College M, W
Iowa State University M, W
Mount St. Clare College M, W
Northwestern College M, W
St. Ambrose University M, W
University of Iowa M, W
University of Northern Iowa W

Kansas
Baker University M, W
Bethel College M, W
Butler County Community College M, W
Central College M, W
Coffeyville Community College M, W
Fort Hays State University W
Friends University M, W
Johnson County Community College M, W
Kansas City Kansas Community College M, W
McPherson College M, W
Ottawa University M, W
Pratt Community College M, W
Seward County Community College M, W
University of Kansas M, W
Wichita State University M, W

Kentucky
Bellarmine College M, W
Campbellsville College M, W
Cumberland College M, W
Eastern Kentucky University M, W
Georgetown College M, W
Kentucky State University M, W
Kentucky Wesleyan College M, W
Morehead State University M, W
Murray State University M, W
Northern Kentucky University M, W
Union College M, W
University of Kentucky M, W
University of Louisville M, W
Western Kentucky University M, W

Louisiana
Bossier Parish Community College M, W
Grambling State University M, W
Louisiana State University and Agricultural and Mechanical College M, W
Louisiana Tech University W
Nicholls State University W
Northeast Louisiana University M, W
Southeastern Louisiana University M, W
Southern University and Agricultural and Mechanical College M
Tulane University M, W
University of Southwestern Louisiana M, W

Maryland
Charles County Community College M, W
Dundalk Community College M, W
Morgan State University M, W
Mount St. Mary's College M, W

Towson State University M, W
University of Maryland
  Baltimore County M, W
  College Park M, W
  Eastern Shore M, W

Massachusetts
Becker College
  Leicester Campus M
  Worcester Campus M
Boston College W
Boston University M, W
Dean Junior College M
University of Massachusetts
  Amherst W
  Lowell M, W

Michigan
Aquinas College M, W
Eastern Michigan University M, W
Henry Ford Community College M, W
Hillsdale College M, W
Macomb Community College M, W
Michigan State University M, W
Northern Michigan University W
Northwood University M, W
Oakland University M, W
Spring Arbor College M, W
University of Detroit Mercy M
University of Michigan M, W
Wayne State University M, W
Western Michigan University M, W

Minnesota
Bemidji State University W
Mankato State University M, W
Moorhead State University M, W
St. Cloud State University M, W
Southwest State University W
University of Minnesota: Twin Cities M, W
Winona State University M, W

Mississippi
Belhaven College M, W
Delta State University M, W
Holmes Community College M, W
Mississippi State University M, W
Mississippi University for Women W
University of Mississippi M, W
William Carey College M, W

Missouri
Central Methodist College M, W
Central Missouri State University M, W
Culver-Stockton College M, W
Lincoln University W
Missouri Southern State College W
Missouri Western State College W
Northeast Missouri State University M, W
Research College of Nursing M, W
St. Louis University M, W
Southwest Baptist University M, W
University of Missouri
  Columbia M, W
  Kansas City M, W
William Jewell College M, W
William Woods College W

Montana
Eastern Montana College M, W
Montana State University M, W
University of Montana M, W

Nebraska
College of St. Mary W
Concordia College M
Creighton University M, W

Midland Lutheran College M, W
University of Nebraska
  Kearney M, W
  Lincoln M, W
York College M, W

New Hampshire
Franklin Pierce College M, W

New Jersey
Burlington County College M, W
Fairleigh Dickinson University
  Edward Williams College M, W
  Madison M, W
Rider College M, W
Rutgers—The State University of New Jersey
  College of Engineering M, W
  College of Pharmacy M, W
  Cook College M, W
  Douglass College W
  Livingston College M, W
  Mason Gross School of the Arts M, W
  Rutgers College M, W
Seton Hall University M, W

New Mexico
Eastern New Mexico University W
New Mexico State University M, W
University of New Mexico M, W

New York
Adelphi University M, W
Canisius College M, W
City University of New York:
  Queens College M, W
College of St. Rose M, W
Concordia College M, W
Dowling College M, W
Fordham University M, W
Hofstra University M, W
Iona College M, W
Le Moyne College M, W
Manhattan College M, W
Marist College M, W
Mercy College M
Molloy College W
New York Institute of Technology M
Niagara University M, W
Pace University
  College of White Plains W
  New York W
  Pleasantville/Briarcliff W
St. Bonaventure University M, W
St. Francis College M, W
St. John's University M, W
Syracuse University W
Wagner College M, W

North Carolina
Appalachian State University M, W
Barber-Scotia College M, W
Barton College M, W
Belmont Abbey College M, W
Campbell University M, W
Catawba College M, W
Davidson College W
Duke University M, W
East Carolina University M, W
Elon College M, W
Fayetteville State University W
Gardner-Webb University M, W
High Point University M, W
Johnson C. Smith University M
Lees-McRae College M, W
Lenoir-Rhyne College M, W
Livingstone College M
Mars Hill College M, W
Mount Olive College M, W

262

Colleges that offer athletic scholarships

North Carolina Central University M, W
North Carolina State University M, W
Peace College W
Pfeiffer College M, W
Queens College M, W
St. Augustine's College M
University of North Carolina
  Asheville M, W
  Chapel Hill M, W
  Charlotte M, W
  Greensboro M, W
  Wilmington M, W
Wake Forest University M, W
Western Carolina University M, W
Wingate College M, W
Winston-Salem State University M, W

North Dakota
Dickinson State University M, W
University of Mary M, W

Ohio
Bowling Green State University M, W
Cleveland State University W
Malone College M, W
Miami University: Oxford Campus M, W
Ohio State University: Columbus Campus M, W
Tiffin University M, W
University of Findlay M, W
University of Toledo M, W
Walsh University M, W
Wright State University M, W
Xavier University M, W
Youngstown State University M, W

Oklahoma
Cameron University M
East Central University W
Oklahoma Baptist University M
Oklahoma Christian University of Science and Arts M
Oklahoma City University M, W
Oral Roberts University M, W
St. Gregory's College M, W
Southwestern Oklahoma State University M, W
University of Central Oklahoma M, W
University of Oklahoma M, W
University of Tulsa M, W

Oregon
Portland State University W
University of Portland M, W

Pennsylvania
California University of Pennsylvania W
Cheyney University of Pennsylvania M, W
Drexel University M
Duquesne University M, W
Eastern College M, W
Edinboro University of Pennsylvania M, W
Gannon University M, W
Geneva College M, W
Indiana University of Pennsylvania W
Kutztown University of Pennsylvania M, W
Mercyhurst College M, W
Millersville University of Pennsylvania M, W
Robert Morris College M, W
St. Francis College M, W
St. Joseph's University M, W
St. Vincent College M
Shippensburg University of Pennsylvania W
Temple University M, W
University of Pittsburgh M, W
Villanova University M, W
West Chester University of Pennsylvania M, W
Westminster College W

Puerto Rico
University of Puerto Rico
  Bayamon Technological University College M, W
  Mayaguez Campus M, W
University of the Sacred Heart M, W

Rhode Island
Providence College M, W

South Carolina
Anderson College M, W
Charleston Southern University M, W
Claflin College M, W
Clemson University M, W
Coker College M, W
College of Charleston M, W
Converse College W
Erskine College M, W
Francis Marion University M, W
Furman University M, W
Lander University M, W
Limestone College M, W
Presbyterian College M, W
Spartanburg Methodist College W
University of South Carolina M, W
Winthrop University M, W
Wofford College M, W

South Dakota
Augustana College M, W
Huron University M, W
Northern State University W
Sioux Falls College M, W

Tennessee
Belmont University M, W
Bethel College W
Christian Brothers University M, W
East Tennessee State University M, W
Freed-Hardeman University M, W
Lambuth University M, W
Lee College M, W
Lincoln Memorial University M, W
Middle Tennessee State University M, W
Milligan College M
Union University M, W
University of Tennessee
  Chattanooga M, W
  Knoxville M, W
  Martin M, W
Vanderbilt University M, W

Texas
Baylor University M, W
Collin County Community College District M
Concordia Lutheran College M, W
Cooke County College W
Lamar University—Beaumont M, W
Laredo Junior College M, W
Rice University M, W
St. Edward's University M, W
St. Mary's University M, W
Schreiner College M, W
Southern Methodist University M, W
Southwest Texas State University M, W
Texas A&I University M, W
Texas Christian University M, W
Texas Tech University M, W
Texas Wesleyan University M, W
Texas Woman's University W
University of Houston W
University of Mary Hardin-Baylor M, W
University of North Texas M, W
University of Texas
  Austin M, W
  San Antonio M, W
Weatherford College M
West Texas A & M University M, W

Utah
Brigham Young University M, W
University of Utah M, W
Utah State University M, W
Weber State University M, W

Virginia
Bluefield College M
Clinch Valley College of the University of Virginia M, W
College of William and Mary M, W
George Mason University M, W
Hampton University M
James Madison University M, W
Liberty University M
Longwood College W
Old Dominion University M, W
Radford University M, W
St. Paul's College M, W
University of Richmond M, W
University of Virginia M, W
Virginia Commonwealth University M, W
Virginia Intermont College M, W
Virginia Military Institute M
Virginia Polytechnic Institute and State University M, W
Virginia Union University M, W

Washington
Eastern Washington University M, W
Green River Community College M, W
Lower Columbia College W
Shoreline Community College M, W
Spokane Community College M, W
Tacoma Community College W
University of Puget Sound M, W
University of Washington M, W
Walla Walla Community College M, W
Washington State University M, W
Western Washington University M, W
Yakima Valley Community College M, W

West Virginia
Bluefield State College M, W
Davis and Elkins College M, W
University of Charleston M, W
West Liberty State College M, W
West Virginia University M, W
West Virginia Wesleyan College M, W

Wisconsin
Lakeland College M
Marquette University M, W
University of Wisconsin
  Green Bay M, W
  Madison M, W

Arab Republic of Egypt
American University in Cairo M, W

Track and field

Alabama
Alabama Agricultural and Mechanical University M, W
Auburn University M, W
Miles College M, W
Northwest Alabama Community College M
Troy State University M, W
University of Alabama in Birmingham M, W
University of South Alabama M, W

Arizona
Central Arizona College M
Glendale Community College M, W
Northern Arizona University M, W
Pima Community College M, W
Scottsdale Community College M, W
University of Arizona M, W

Arkansas
University of Arkansas at Pine Bluff M, W

California
Azusa Pacific University M, W
Biola University M, W
California Polytechnic State University: San Luis Obispo M, W
California State University
  Bakersfield M, W
  Fresno M
  Fullerton M, W
  Northridge M, W
Point Loma Nazarene College M, W
Southern California College M, W
University of California
  Irvine M, W
  Los Angeles M, W
  Riverside M, W
  Santa Barbara M, W
Westmont College M, W

Colorado
Adams State College M, W
Colorado School of Mines M, W
Colorado State University M, W
Northeastern Junior College M, W
University of Colorado at Boulder M, W
University of Northern Colorado M, W
Western State College of Colorado M, W

Connecticut
University of Connecticut M, W

Delaware
Delaware State College M, W

District of Columbia
Georgetown University M, W
Howard University M, W
University of the District of Columbia M, W

Florida
Brevard Community College M, W
Edward Waters College M

Colleges that offer athletic scholarships

Florida Community College at
   Jacksonville M, W
Florida Memorial College M
Florida State University M, W
University of Central Florida M, W
University of Miami M, W

Georgia
Fort Valley State College M, W
Georgia Institute of Technology M, W
Morehouse College M
Paine College M, W
Savannah State College M, W
Shorter College M

Idaho
Boise State University M, W
College of Southern Idaho M, W
Idaho State University M, W
North Idaho College M, W
Northwest Nazarene College M, W
Ricks College M, W
University of Idaho M, W

Illinois
Chicago State University M, W
De Paul University M, W
Eastern Illinois University M, W
Illinois State University M, W
Lewis University M, W
Loyola University of Chicago M, W
Olivet Nazarene University M, W
Southern Illinois University
   Carbondale M, W
   Edwardsville M, W
University of Illinois at Urbana-
   Champaign M, W
Western Illinois University W

Indiana
Ball State University M, W
Butler University M
Goshen College M, W
Grace College M, W
Huntington College M, W
Indiana State University M, W
Indiana University Bloomington M, W
Indiana Wesleyan University M, W
Marian College M, W
Purdue University M, W
Tri-State University M, W
University of Indianapolis M, W
University of Notre Dame M, W
Vincennes University M, W

Iowa
Drake University M, W
Graceland College M, W
Iowa State University M, W
Iowa Wesleyan College M, W
Morningside College M, W
Northwestern College M, W
St. Ambrose University M, W
Teikyo Westmar University M, W
University of Iowa M, W
University of Northern Iowa M, W

Kansas
Allen County Community College M, W
Baker University M, W
Benedictine College M, W
Bethel College M, W
Butler County Community College M, W
Coffeyville Community College M, W
Colby Community College M, W
Emporia State University M, W
Fort Hays State University M, W

Fort Scott Community College M, W
Garden City Community College M, W
Johnson County Community
   College M, W
Kansas City Kansas Community
   College W
Kansas State University M, W
McPherson College M, W
Neosho County Community College M, W
Ottawa University M, W
Pratt Community College M, W
Sterling College M, W
University of Kansas M, W
Wichita State University M, W

Kentucky
Eastern Kentucky University M, W
Kentucky State University M, W
Murray State University M, W
Union College M, W
University of Louisville M, W
Western Kentucky University M, W

Louisiana
Grambling State University M, W
Louisiana State University and
   Agricultural and Mechanical
   College M, W
Louisiana Tech University M, W
Nicholls State University M, W
Northeast Louisiana University M, W
Southeastern Louisiana University M, W
Tulane University M, W
University of Southwestern
   Louisiana M, W

Maine
University of Maine M, W

Maryland
Bowie State University M, W
Morgan State University M, W
Mount St. Mary's College M, W
Towson State University M, W
University of Maryland
   Baltimore County M, W
   College Park M, W
   Eastern Shore M, W

Massachusetts
Boston College M, W
Boston University M, W
Northeastern University M, W
University of Massachusetts
   Amherst M, W
   Lowell M, W

Michigan
Aquinas College M, W
Eastern Michigan University M, W
Hillsdale College M, W
Kellogg Community College W
Macomb Community College M, W
Michigan Christian College M, W
Michigan State University M, W
Southwestern Michigan College M, W
University of Michigan M, W
Western Michigan University M, W

Minnesota
Bemidji State University M, W
Mankato State University M, W
Moorhead State University M, W
St. Cloud State University M, W
University of Minnesota: Twin
   Cities M, W

Winona State University M, W

Mississippi
Mississippi State University M, W
University of Mississippi M, W

Missouri
Central Methodist College M, W
Central Missouri State University M, W
Harris Stowe State College W
Lincoln University M, W
Lindenwood College M, W
Missouri Southern State College M, W
Northeast Missouri State University M, W
Northwest Missouri Community
   College M, W
Park College M, W
Southeast Missouri State University M, W
Southwest Baptist University M, W
University of Missouri
   Columbia M, W
   Kansas City M, W
   Rolla M, W
William Jewell College M, W

Montana
Montana State University M, W
University of Montana M, W

Nebraska
Chadron State College M, W
Concordia College M, W
Dana College W
Doane College M, W
Midland Lutheran College M, W
University of Nebraska
   Kearney M, W
   Lincoln M, W
Wayne State College M, W

New Jersey
Fairleigh Dickinson University
   Edward Williams College M, W
   Madison M, W
Rider College M, W
Rutgers—The State University of
   New Jersey
   College of Engineering M, W
   College of Pharmacy M, W
   Cook College M, W
   Douglass College W
   Livingston College M, W
   Mason Gross School of the
      Arts M, W
   Rutgers College M, W
Seton Hall University W

New Mexico
New Mexico State University M, W
University of New Mexico M, W

New York
Canisius College M, W
City University of New York:
   Queens College M, W
College of St. Rose M
Fordham University M, W
Houghton College M, W
Iona College M, W
Long Island University
   Brooklyn Campus M, W
   C. W. Post Campus M, W
Manhattan College M, W
Marist College M, W
Mercy College W
New York Institute of Technology M, W

Roberts Wesleyan College M, W
St. Francis College M, W
St. John's University M, W
Syracuse University M, W
Wagner College M, W

North Carolina
Appalachian State University M, W
Barber-Scotia College M, W
Brevard College M, W
Campbell University M, W
Davidson College W
East Carolina University M, W
Elon College M
Fayetteville State University W
High Point University M
Johnson C. Smith University M, W
Lees-McRae College W
Lenoir-Rhyne College M
Livingstone College M, W
North Carolina Agricultural and
   Technical State University M, W
North Carolina Central University M, W
North Carolina State University M, W
Pembroke State University M
St. Augustine's College M, W
University of North Carolina
   Chapel Hill M, W
   Wilmington M, W
Wake Forest University M, W
Western Carolina University M, W
Winston-Salem State University M, W

North Dakota
Dickinson State University M, W
North Dakota State College of
   Science M, W
North Dakota State University M, W
University of Mary M, W
University of North Dakota M, W

Ohio
Ashland University M, W
Bowling Green State University M, W
Cleveland State University W
Kent State University M, W
Malone College M, W
Miami University: Oxford Campus M, W
Ohio State University: Columbus
   Campus M, W
University of Findlay M, W
University of Rio Grande M, W
University of Toledo M, W
Urbana University M, W
Walsh University M, W
Youngstown State University M, W

Oklahoma
Oklahoma Baptist University M
Oklahoma Christian University of
   Science and Arts M, W
Oral Roberts University M, W
Southwestern Oklahoma State
   University M, W
University of Central Oklahoma M, W
University of Oklahoma M, W
University of Tulsa M, W

Oregon
Clackamas Community College M, W
George Fox College M, W
Mount Hood Community College M, W
Portland State University M, W

Treasure Valley Community College M, W
University of Portland M, W

Pennsylvania
Cheyney University of Pennsylvania M, W
Drexel University M
Duquesne University M, W
Edinboro University of Pennsylvania M, W
Geneva College M, W
Indiana University of Pennsylvania M, W
Kutztown University of Pennsylvania M, W
Lock Haven University of Pennsylvania M, W
Millersville University of Pennsylvania M, W
Robert Morris College M, W
St. Francis College M, W
St. Joseph's University M, W
Shippensburg University of Pennsylvania M, W
Temple University M, W
University of Pittsburgh M, W
Villanova University M, W
West Chester University of Pennsylvania M, W

Puerto Rico
Inter American University of Puerto Rico: Metropolitan Campus M, W
University of Puerto Rico
 Bayamon Technological University College M, W
 La Montana Regional College M, W
 Mayaguez Campus M, W
University of the Sacred Heart M, W

Rhode Island
Providence College M, W
University of Rhode Island M, W

South Carolina
Anderson College M, W
Charleston Southern University M, W
Claflin College M, W
Clemson University M, W
Francis Marion University M
Furman University M, W
Voorhees College M, W

South Dakota
Black Hills State University M, W
Dakota State University M, W
Dakota Wesleyan University M, W
Huron University M, W
Northern State University M, W
Sioux Falls College M, W
South Dakota State University M, W

Tennessee
Belmont University M, W
East Tennessee State University M, W
Middle Tennessee State University M, W
University of Tennessee
 Chattanooga M, W
 Knoxville M, W
 Martin M, W

Texas
Baylor University M, W
Blinn College M

East Texas State University M, W
Lamar University—Beaumont M, W
Ranger Junior College M, W
Rice University M, W
South Plains College M
Southern Methodist University M, W
Southwest Texas State University M, W
Stephen F. Austin State University M, W
Texas Christian University M, W
Texas Tech University M, W
University of Houston M, W
University of North Texas M, W
University of Texas
 Austin M, W
 San Antonio M, W
Wayland Baptist University M, W

Utah
Brigham Young University M, W
University of Utah M, W
Utah State University M, W
Weber State University M, W

Virginia
College of William and Mary M, W
George Mason University M, W
Hampton University M, W
James Madison University M, W
Liberty University M, W
Norfolk State University M, W
St. Paul's College M, W
University of Virginia M, W
Virginia Commonwealth University M, W
Virginia Military Institute M
Virginia Polytechnic Institute and State University M, W
Virginia Union University M, W

Washington
Eastern Washington University M, W
Pacific Lutheran University M, W
Seattle Pacific University M, W
Spokane Community College M, W
University of Puget Sound M, W
University of Washington M, W
Washington State University M, W
Western Washington University M, W
Yakima Valley Community College M, W

West Virginia
West Virginia State College M, W
West Virginia University M, W
West Virginia Wesleyan College M, W

Wisconsin
Lakeland College M
Marquette University M, W
University of Wisconsin: Madison M, W

Wyoming
University of Wyoming M, W

Arab Republic of Egypt
American University in Cairo M, W

Volleyball

Alabama
Alabama Agricultural and Mechanical University W

Auburn University W
Bevill State Community College W
Gadsden State Community College W
Huntingdon College W
James H. Faulkner State Community College W
Miles College W
Northwest Alabama Community College W
Snead State Community College W
Southern Union State Junior College W
Tuskegee University W
University of Alabama in Birmingham W
University of Montevallo W
University of North Alabama W
University of South Alabama W

Alaska
University of Alaska
 Anchorage W
 Fairbanks W

Arizona
Arizona Western College W
Central Arizona College W
Eastern Arizona College W
Glendale Community College W
Grand Canyon University W
Northern Arizona University W
Pima Community College W
Scottsdale Community College W
University of Arizona W

Arkansas
Henderson State University W
John Brown University W
Ouachita Baptist University W
University of Central Arkansas W

California
Azusa Pacific University W
California Polytechnic State University: San Luis Obispo W
California State University
 Bakersfield W
 Fresno W
 Fullerton W
 Northridge M, W
 San Bernardino W
Concordia University W
Dominican College of San Rafael W
Master's College W
Mount St. Mary's College W
Pepperdine University M, W
Point Loma Nazarene College W
St. Mary's College of California W
Santa Clara University W
Southern California College W
University of California
 Berkeley W
 Irvine W
 Los Angeles M, W
 Riverside W
 Santa Barbara M, W
University of the Pacific M, W
University of San Diego W
University of San Francisco W
Westmont College W

Colorado
Adams State College W
Colorado Christian University W
Colorado Northwestern Community College W
Colorado School of Mines W
Colorado State University W
Fort Lewis College W
Lamar Community College W
Mesa State College W

Metropolitan State College of Denver W
Northeastern Junior College W
Otero Junior College W
Regis University W
Trinidad State Junior College W
University of Colorado
 Boulder W
 Colorado Springs W
University of Denver W
University of Northern Colorado W
University of Southern Colorado W
Western State College of Colorado W

Connecticut
Central Connecticut State University W
Fairfield University M, W
Quinnipiac College W
University of Bridgeport M
University of Connecticut W
University of Hartford W

Delaware
Delaware State College W
University of Delaware W

District of Columbia
American University W
George Washington University W
Georgetown University W
Howard University W
University of the District of Columbia W

Florida
Brevard Community College W
Eckerd College M, W
Flagler College W
Florida Atlantic University W
Florida Community College at Jacksonville W
Florida Institute of Technology W
Florida Memorial College W
Florida State University W
Hillsborough Community College W
Nova University W
Palm Beach Atlantic College W
Pasco-Hernando Community College W
Rollins College W
St. Leo College W
Stetson University W
University of North Florida W
Warner Southern College W
Webber College M, W

Georgia
Augusta College W
Fort Valley State College W
Georgia Institute of Technology W
Georgia Southern University W
Mercer University W
Paine College W
University of Georgia M
West Georgia College W

Hawaii
Hawaii Pacific University W
University of Hawaii
 Hilo W
 Manoa M, W

Idaho
Albertson College W
Boise State University W
College of Southern Idaho W
Idaho State University W
Lewis Clark State College W
North Idaho College W
Northwest Nazarene College W

Colleges that offer athletic scholarships

Ricks College W
University of Idaho W

Illinois
Barat College W
Belleville Area College W
Bradley University W
Chicago State University W
College of St. Francis W
De Paul University W
Eastern Illinois University W
Highland Community College W
Illinois Central College W
Illinois Eastern Community
  Colleges
    Lincoln Trail College W
    Olney Central College W
    Wabash Valley College W
Illinois Institute of Technology M,
  W
Illinois State University W
John A. Logan College W
Judson College W
Kankakee Community College W
Kaskaskia College W
Kishwaukee College W
Lake Land College W
Lewis University M, W
Lincoln College W
Loyola University of Chicago W
McKendree College W
Morton College W
Northwestern University W
Olivet Nazarene University W
Quincy University M, W
Rosary College W
St. Xavier University W
Sauk Valley Community College W
Southern Illinois University at
  Carbondale W
Trinity College M, W
University of Illinois
  Chicago W
  Urbana-Champaign W
Western Illinois University W

Indiana
Ball State University M, W
Bethel College W
Butler University W
Goshen College W
Grace College M
Huntington College W
Indiana State University W
Indiana University Bloomington W
Indiana University—Purdue
  University at Indianapolis W
Indiana Wesleyan University M, W
Marian College W
Purdue University W
Tri-State University M, W
University of Evansville W
University of Indianapolis W
University of Notre Dame W
University of Southern Indiana W
Valparaiso University W
Vincennes University M, W

Iowa
Briar Cliff College W
Clinton Community College W
Drake University W
Ellsworth Community College W
Graceland College M, W
Grand View College W
Iowa Central Community College
  W
Iowa Lakes Community College M,
  W
Iowa State University W
Iowa Wesleyan College W
Morningside College W

North Iowa Area Community
  College W
Northwestern College W
St. Ambrose University W
Teikyo Marycrest University W
Teikyo Westmar University W
University of Iowa W
University of Northern Iowa W
Waldorf College W

Kansas
Allen County Community College
  W
Baker University W
Benedictine College W
Bethel College W
Brown Mackie College W
Butler County Community College
  W
Central College W
Coffeyville Community College W
Colby Community College W
Dodge City Community College W
Emporia State University W
Fort Scott Community College W
Friends University W
Garden City Community College W
Johnson County Community
  College W
Kansas City Kansas Community
  College W
Kansas Newman College W
Kansas State University W
McPherson College W
Neosho County Community College
  W
Ottawa University W
Pratt Community College W
Seward County Community College
  W
Sterling College W
University of Kansas W
Wichita State University W

Kentucky
Bellarmine College W
Campbellsville College W
Eastern Kentucky University W
Georgetown College W
Kentucky State University W
Morehead State University W
Murray State University W
Northern Kentucky University W
Sue Bennett College W
Union College W
University of Kentucky W
University of Louisville W
Western Kentucky University W

Louisiana
Louisiana State University and
  Agricultural and Mechanical
  College W
Louisiana Tech University W
Nicholls State University W
Northeast Louisiana University W
Southeastern Louisiana University
  W
Southern University and
  Agricultural and Mechanical
  College W
Tulane University W

Maine
Unity College W

Maryland
Bowie State University W
Charles County Community College
  W
Dundalk Community College W
Loyola College in Maryland W

Morgan State University W
Towson State University W
University of Maryland
  Baltimore County W
  College Park W
  Eastern Shore W

Massachusetts
American International College W
Becker College
  Leicester Campus W
  Worcester Campus M
Boston College W
Dean Junior College W
Mount Ida College M
Northeastern University W
University of Massachusetts
  Amherst W
  Lowell W

Michigan
Aquinas College W
Eastern Michigan University W
Glen Oaks Community College W
Grand Rapids Baptist College and
  Seminary W
Hillsdale College W
Kellogg Community College W
Lake Michigan College W
Lansing Community College W
Macomb Community College W
Michigan Christian College W
Michigan State University W
Michigan Technological University
  W
Northwood University W
Oakland University W
Southwestern Michigan College W
Spring Arbor College W
University of Michigan
  Ann Arbor W
  Dearborn W
Wayne State University W
Western Michigan University W

Minnesota
Bemidji State University W
Mankato State University W
Moorhead State University W
St. Cloud State University W
Southwest State University W
University of Minnesota
  Duluth W
  Twin Cities W
Winona State University W

Mississippi
Mississippi State University W
Mississippi University for Women
  W
University of Mississippi W

Missouri
Avila College W
Central Methodist College W
Central Missouri State University W
College of the Ozarks W
Culver-Stockton College W
Harris Stowe State College W
Lindenwood College M, W
Longview Community College W
Mineral Area College W
Missouri Southern State College W
Missouri Western State College W
Northeast Missouri State University
  W
Northwest Missouri Community
  College M, W
Park College M, W
Research College of Nursing W
Rockhurst College M, W
St. Louis University W

Southeast Missouri State University
  W
Southwest Baptist University W
University of Missouri
  Columbia W
  Kansas City W
William Jewell College W
William Woods College W

Montana
Carroll College W
Eastern Montana College W
Miles Community College W
Montana College of Mineral
  Science and Technology W
Montana State University W
Northern Montana College W
Rocky Mountain College W
University of Montana W
Western Montana College of the
  University of Montana W

Nebraska
Bellevue College W
Central Community College W
Chadron State College W
College of St. Mary W
Concordia College W
Creighton University W
Dana College W
Doane College M, W
McCook Community College W
Midland Lutheran College W
Northeast Community College W
Peru State College W
Southeast Community College:
  Beatrice Campus W
University of Nebraska
  Kearney M, W
  Lincoln W
  Omaha W
Wayne State College W
Western Nebraska Community
  College: Scottsbluff Campus W
York College W

New Hampshire
Franklin Pierce College W
Hesser College M, W

New Jersey
Bloomfield College W
Fairleigh Dickinson University
  Edward Williams College W
  Madison W
Rider College W
Rutgers—The State University of
  New Jersey
  College of Engineering W
  College of Nursing M
  College of Pharmacy W
  Cook College W
  Douglass College W
  Livingston College W
  Mason Gross School of the
    Arts W
  Newark College of Arts and
    Sciences M
  Rutgers College W

New Mexico
Eastern New Mexico University W
New Mexico State University W
University of New Mexico W

New York
Adelphi University W
Canisius College W
City University of New York:
  Queens College W
College of St. Rose W
Concordia College M, W

266

Colleges that offer athletic scholarships

D'Youville College M
Fordham University W
Hofstra University W
Houghton College W
Iona College W
Jefferson Community College W
King's College W
Le Moyne College W
Long Island University
   Brooklyn Campus W
   C. W. Post Campus W
   Southampton Campus M, W
Manhattan College W
Marist College M, W
Mercy College W
Molloy College W
New York Institute of Technology W
Niagara University W
Pace University
   College of White Plains W
   New York W
   Pleasantville/Briarcliff W
St. Bonaventure University W
St. Francis College W
St. Thomas Aquinas College W
Siena College W
State University of New York at Buffalo W
Syracuse University W
Villa Maria College of Buffalo W
Wagner College W

North Carolina

Appalachian State University W
Barber-Scotia College W
Barton College M, W
Belmont Abbey College W
Campbell University W
Catawba College W
Davidson College W
Duke University W
East Carolina University W
Elon College W
Fayetteville State University W
Gardner-Webb University W
High Point University W
Johnson C. Smith University W
Lees-McRae College W
Lenoir-Rhyne College W
Livingstone College W
Mars Hill College W
Montreat-Anderson College W
Mount Olive College W
North Carolina Agricultural and Technical State University W
North Carolina Central University W
North Carolina State University W
Pembroke State University W
Pfeiffer College W
Queens College W
St. Andrews Presbyterian College W
St. Augustine's College W
University of North Carolina
   Asheville W
   Chapel Hill W
   Charlotte W
   Greensboro W
   Wilmington W
Western Carolina University W
Wingate College W
Winston-Salem State University W

North Dakota

Dickinson State University W
North Dakota State College of Science W
North Dakota State University
   Bottineau W
   Fargo W
University of Mary W

University of North Dakota
   Grand Forks W
   Williston W

Ohio

Ashland University W
Bowling Green State University W
Cleveland State University W
Kent State University W
Lake Erie College W
Malone College W
Miami University: Oxford Campus W
Notre Dame College of Ohio W
Ohio Dominican College W
Ohio State University: Columbus Campus M, W
Southern State Community College W
Tiffin University W
University of Dayton W
University of Findlay W
University of Rio Grande W
University of Toledo W
Urbana University W
Walsh University W
Wright State University W
Xavier University W
Youngstown State University W

Oklahoma

Bartlesville Wesleyan College W
Cameron University M
Oral Roberts University W
University of Central Oklahoma W
University of Oklahoma W
University of Tulsa W

Oregon

Clackamas Community College W
Concordia College W
George Fox College W
Mount Hood Community College W
Oregon State University W
Portland State University W
Treasure Valley Community College W
University of Portland W

Pennsylvania

California University of Pennsylvania W
Carlow College W
Cheyney University of Pennsylvania W
Community College of Beaver County W
Duquesne University W
Eastern College M, W
Edinboro University of Pennsylvania W
Gannon University W
Geneva College W
Indiana University of Pennsylvania W
Kutztown University of Pennsylvania W
Lock Haven University of Pennsylvania W
Manor Junior College W
Mercyhurst College W
Millersville University of Pennsylvania W
Point Park College W
Robert Morris College W
St. Francis College M, W
St. Vincent College W
Seton Hill College W
Shippensburg University of Pennsylvania W
University of Pittsburgh W

Villanova University W
West Chester University of Pennsylvania W
Westminster College W

Puerto Rico

University of Puerto Rico
   Bayamon Technological University College M, W
   La Montana Regional College M, W
   Mayaguez Campus M, W
University of the Sacred Heart M, W

Rhode Island

Providence College W
University of Rhode Island W

South Carolina

Anderson College W
Charleston Southern University W
Claflin College M, W
Clemson University W
Coker College W
College of Charleston W
Converse College W
Erskine College W
Francis Marion University W
Furman University W
Limestone College W
Presbyterian College W
South Carolina State University W
Spartanburg Methodist College W
University of South Carolina at Aiken W
Voorhees College W
Winthrop University W
Wofford College W

South Dakota

Augustana College W
Black Hills State University W
Dakota State University W
Dakota Wesleyan University W
Huron University W
Sioux Falls College W
South Dakota State University W

Tennessee

Belmont University W
Christian Brothers University W
East Tennessee State University W
Freed-Hardeman University W
Lambuth University M, W
Lane College W
Lee College W
Lincoln Memorial University W
Middle Tennessee State University W
Milligan College W
Trevecca Nazarene College W
Tusculum College W
University of Tennessee
   Chattanooga W
   Knoxville W
   Martin W
William Jennings Bryan College W

Texas

Baylor University W
Concordia Lutheran College W
Cooke County College W
East Texas State University W
Houston Baptist University W
Lamar University—Beaumont W
Laredo Junior College W
LeTourneau University W
Rice University W
St. Edward's University W
St. Mary's University W
Schreiner College W

Southwest Texas State University M
Stephen F. Austin State University W
Texas A&I University W
Texas College W
Texas Lutheran College W
Texas Tech University W
Texas Wesleyan University W
Texas Woman's University W
University of Houston W
University of Mary Hardin-Baylor W
University of North Texas W
University of Texas
   Austin W
   San Antonio W
Vernon Regional Junior College W
Weatherford College M
West Texas A & M University W

Utah

Brigham Young University M, W
College of Eastern Utah W
Dixie College W
University of Utah W
Utah State University W
Utah Valley Community College W
Weber State University W

Virginia

Bluefield College W
Clinch Valley College of the University of Virginia W
College of William and Mary W
George Mason University M, W
Hampton University W
James Madison University W
Liberty University W
Norfolk State University W
Radford University W
St. Paul's College W
University of Virginia W
Virginia Commonwealth University W
Virginia Polytechnic Institute and State University W
Virginia Union University W

Washington

Big Bend Community College W
Centralia College W
Eastern Washington University W
Edmonds Community College W
Gonzaga University W
Green River Community College W
Lower Columbia College W
Olympic College W
Pierce College W
St. Martin's College W
Seattle Pacific University W
Shoreline Community College W
Spokane Community College W
Tacoma Community College W
University of Puget Sound W
University of Washington W
Walla Walla Community College W
Washington State University W
Western Washington University W
Yakima Valley Community College W

West Virginia

Ohio Valley College W
Potomac State College of West Virginia University W
University of Charleston W
West Virginia Institute of Technology W
West Virginia University W
West Virginia Wesleyan College W
Wheeling Jesuit College W

267

Colleges that offer athletic scholarships

Wisconsin
Cardinal Stritch College W
Marquette University W
Northland College W
University of Wisconsin: Green Bay W

Wyoming
Casper College W
Eastern Wyoming College W
Northwest College W
Sheridan College W
University of Wyoming W

Arab Republic of Egypt
American University in Cairo M, W

Water polo

Arkansas
University of Arkansas at Little Rock M

California
California State University: Fresno M
Pepperdine University M
Stanford University M
University of California
    Berkeley M
    Irvine M
    Los Angeles M
    Riverside M
    Santa Barbara M
University of the Pacific M

District of Columbia
George Washington University M

Kansas
Wichita State University W

Massachusetts
University of Massachusetts at Amherst M

Nebraska
University of Nebraska—Kearney W

New York
City University of New York: Queens College M
Fordham University M
Manhattan College M
St. Francis College M

Ohio
Bowling Green State University W

Pennsylvania
Villanova University M

Puerto Rico
University of Puerto Rico: Mayaguez Campus M

Arab Republic of Egypt
American University in Cairo M

Wrestling

California
California Polytechnic State University: San Luis Obispo M

California State University
    Bakersfield M
    Fresno M
    Fullerton M

Colorado
Adams State College M
Colorado Northwestern Community College M
Colorado School of Mines M
Fort Lewis College M
University of Northern Colorado M
University of Southern Colorado M
Western State College of Colorado M

Connecticut
Central Connecticut State University M

Delaware
Delaware State College M

District of Columbia
American University M
Howard University M

Georgia
Georgia Institute of Technology M

Idaho
Boise State University M
North Idaho College M
Ricks College M

Illinois
Belleville Area College M
Chicago State University M
Eastern Illinois University M
Illinois State University M
Lincoln College M
Northwestern University M
Olivet Nazarene University M
Southern Illinois University at Edwardsville M
Trinity College M
University of Illinois at Urbana-Champaign M

Indiana
Indiana University Bloomington M
Purdue University M
University of Indianapolis M
Valparaiso University M

Iowa
Drake University M
Ellsworth Community College M
Iowa Central Community College M
Iowa State University M
Northwestern College M
Teikyo Westmar University M
University of Iowa M
University of Northern Iowa M
Waldorf College M

Kansas
Colby Community College M
Fort Hays State University M
Garden City Community College M

Maryland
Morgan State University M
University of Maryland: College Park M

Massachusetts
Boston University M
University of Massachusetts at Lowell M

Michigan
Eastern Michigan University M
Michigan State University M
University of Michigan M

Minnesota
Mankato State University M
Moorhead State University M
St. Cloud State University M
Southwest State University M
University of Minnesota
    Duluth M
    Twin Cities M

Missouri
Central Missouri State University M
Lindenwood College M
Northeast Missouri State University M
St. Louis Community College at Meramec M
University of Missouri: Columbia M
William Jewell College M

Montana
Montana College of Mineral Science and Technology M
Northern Montana College M
Western Montana College of the University of Montana M

Nebraska
Chadron State College M
Dana College M
University of Nebraska
    Kearney M
    Lincoln M
    Omaha M

New Jersey
Rider College M
Rutgers—The State University of New Jersey
    College of Engineering M
    College of Pharmacy M
    Cook College M
    Livingston College M
    Mason Gross School of the Arts M
    Rutgers College M
Seton Hall University M

New Mexico
University of New Mexico M

New York
Hofstra University M
Manhattan College M
State University of New York at Buffalo M
Syracuse University M
Wagner College M

North Carolina
Appalachian State University M
Campbell University M
Duke University M
Gardner-Webb University M
North Carolina State University M
Pembroke State University M
University of North Carolina at Chapel Hill M

North Dakota
Dickinson State University M
Mayville State University M
North Dakota State College of Science M
North Dakota State University M
University of Mary M
University of North Dakota M

Ohio
Ashland University M
Cleveland State University M
Cuyahoga Community College: Western Campus M
Kent State University M
Miami University: Oxford Campus M
Ohio State University: Columbus Campus M
University of Findlay M
University of Toledo M

Oklahoma
University of Central Oklahoma M
University of Oklahoma M

Oregon
Clackamas Community College M

Oregon State University M
Portland State University M

Pennsylvania
California University of Pennsylvania M
Cheyney University of Pennsylvania M
Drexel University M
Duquesne University M
Edinboro University of Pennsylvania M
Gannon University M
Kutztown University of Pennsylvania M
Lehigh University M
Lock Haven University of Pennsylvania M
Millersville University of Pennsylvania M
Shippensburg University of Pennsylvania M
University of Pittsburgh
    Johnstown M
    Pittsburgh M
Wilkes University M

Puerto Rico
University of Puerto Rico
    Bayamon Technological University College M
    Mayaguez Campus M

South Carolina
Anderson College M
Clemson University M

South Dakota
Augustana College M
Northern State University M
South Dakota State University M

Tennessee
University of Tennessee: Chattanooga M

Utah
Brigham Young University M

Virginia
College of William and Mary M
George Mason University M
James Madison University M
Liberty University M
Longwood College M
Norfolk State University M
Old Dominion University M
University of Virginia M
Virginia Military Institute M
Virginia Polytechnic Institute and State University M

Colleges that offer athletic scholarships

Washington
Big Bend Community College M
Lower Columbia College M
Yakima Valley Community College M

West Virginia
West Virginia University M

Wisconsin
Marquette University M
University of Wisconsin: Madison M

Wyoming
Northwest College M
University of Wyoming M

Arab Republic of Egypt
American University in Cairo M

Colleges that offer tuition and/or fee waivers and special tuition payment plans

Tuition and/or fee waiver for adult students

Alabama
Birmingham-Southern College
Central Alabama Community College: Childersburg Campus
Community College of the Air Force
Faulkner University

Arizona
Western International University

Arkansas
John Brown University
Southern Arkansas University: Technical Branch

California
Barstow College
California State University: Dominguez Hills
Cerritos Community College
City College of San Francisco
Compton Community College
Contra Costa College
Cosumnes River College
D-Q University
Feather River College
Fresno City College
Fullerton College
Napa Valley College
Porterville College
Saddleback College

Colorado
Aims Community College
Northeastern Junior College
Regis University

Connecticut
Teikyo-Post University
Trinity College

District of Columbia
Mount Vernon College

Florida
Webber College

Georgia
Andrew College
Wesleyan College

Hawaii
University of Hawaii at Manoa

Idaho
Albertson College

Illinois
Northeastern Illinois University
Shimer College
Springfield College in Illinois

Indiana
Anderson University
Calumet College of St. Joseph
Indiana Vocational Technical College: Columbus
St. Francis College

Iowa
Coe College
Northwestern College
Simpson College

Kansas
Fort Hays State University
Kansas Newman College
Kansas Wesleyan University
St. Mary College
Sterling College
Tabor College

Kentucky
Brescia College
Campbellsville College
Kentucky State University
University of Kentucky

Louisiana
University of New Orleans

Maryland
Harford Community College
Ner Israel Rabbinical College
Western Maryland College

Massachusetts
Atlantic Union College
Bay Path College
Massasoit Community College
Middlesex Community College
Pine Manor College
Simmons College

Michigan
Aquinas College
Baker College of Auburn Hills
Lake Michigan College
Mid Michigan Community College

Minnesota
Fergus Falls Community College
St. Olaf College
University of Minnesota: Crookston
Willmar Community College
Worthington Community College

Mississippi
Millsaps College

Missouri
St. Louis University
William Jewell College

Montana
Fort Peck Community College
Northern Montana College

Nebraska
Chadron State College
College of St. Mary
Metropolitan Community College

New Jersey
Felician College

New York
Long Island University: Southampton Campus
Medaille College
Nyack College

North Carolina
Campbell University
Guilford College
Salem College

North Dakota
United Tribes Technical College
University of North Dakota: Lake Region

Ohio
Cleveland College of Jewish Studies
Cleveland Institute of Electronics
Defiance College
Denison University
Urbana University

Oklahoma
Oklahoma State University: Oklahoma City
Phillips University
Redlands Community College
Southeastern Oklahoma State University
University of Central Oklahoma

Oregon
Central Oregon Community College
Concordia College
Pacific Northwest College of Art

Pennsylvania
Chatham College
Immaculata College
Juniata College
Keystone Junior College
Mercyhurst College
Messiah College
Muhlenberg College
Rosemont College
St. Charles Borromeo Seminary
St. Francis College
Seton Hill College
Thiel College

South Carolina
Anderson College
Coker College
Spartanburg Methodist College

Tennessee
Carson-Newman College
Freed-Hardeman University
Lambuth University
William Jennings Bryan College

Texas
Concordia Lutheran College

Virginia
Bluefield College
Randolph-Macon Woman's College

Washington
Lower Columbia College

West Virginia
Fairmont State College

Wisconsin
Beloit College
Blackhawk Technical College
Mount Senario College
Viterbo College

Wyoming
Eastern Wyoming College

Tuition and/or fee waiver for children of alumni

Alaska
University of Alaska Fairbanks

Arizona
Arizona College of the Bible

Tuition and/or fee waivers: senior citizens

Arkansas
Arkansas State University

California
Brooks Institute of Photography
California Baptist College
Compton Community College
D-Q University
LIFE Bible College
Mount St. Mary's College
Patten College
Porterville College
Saddleback College

Colorado
Colorado Christian University

Connecticut
Teikyo-Post University

Florida
Florida Bible College
Webber College

Georgia
Shorter College
Wesleyan College

Idaho
Albertson College

Illinois
Augustana College
Chicago State University
Illinois Benedictine College
Lewis University
MacCormac Junior College
MacMurray College

Indiana
Indiana State University
Indiana Vocational Technical
   College: Columbus
Manchester College
Marian College
St. Joseph's College
University of Evansville
Valparaiso University

Iowa
Clarke College
Loras College
Morningside College
Northwestern College
St. Ambrose University
Teikyo Marycrest University
Upper Iowa University

Kansas
Kansas Newman College
Kansas Wesleyan University

Kentucky
Brescia College
Cumberland College
Sue Bennett College
Thomas More College
Union College
Western Kentucky University

Louisiana
Grambling State University
Louisiana State University
   Agricultural and Mechanical
      College
   Medical Center
      Shreveport
Louisiana Tech University
McNeese State University
University of New Orleans

Maine
University of New England

Maryland
Dundalk Community College
Ner Israel Rabbinical College

Massachusetts
Anna Maria College for Men and
   Women
Curry College
Eastern Nazarene College
Hellenic College
Pine Manor College
Wheelock College

Michigan
Aquinas College
Concordia College
Detroit College of Business
Lake Superior State University
Michigan Christian College
Michigan Technological University
Northwood University
University of Detroit Mercy
Wayne State University

Mississippi
Delta State University
Millsaps College
Mississippi State University
Mississippi University for Women
University of Mississippi
University of Southern Mississippi

Missouri
Avila College
Calvary Bible College
Kemper Military School and
   College
Missouri Baptist College
Missouri Valley College
Northwest Missouri State
   University
University of Missouri: Rolla
Westminster College
William Jewell College

Nebraska
College of St. Mary
Concordia College
Grace College of the Bible

Nevada
University of Nevada: Reno

New Hampshire
Notre Dame College
Rivier College
White Pines College

New Jersey
Bloomfield College

New Mexico
College of the Southwest

New York
Adelphi University
Boricua College
Daemen College
Dowling College
Iona College
Long Island University: Brooklyn
   Campus
St. Joseph's College

North Carolina
Greensboro College
Montreat-Anderson College

North Dakota
United Tribes Technical College

Ohio
Ashland University
Cedarville College
College of Mount St. Joseph
Defiance College
Kent State University
Malone College
Mount Union College
Muskingum College
University of Findlay
Walsh University
Wilmington College

Oklahoma
Oklahoma Baptist University
Oklahoma Christian University of
   Science and Arts
Southeastern Oklahoma State
   University
University of Central Oklahoma
University of Oklahoma
   Health Sciences Center
      Norman

Oregon
Bassist College
Warner Pacific College

Pennsylvania
Chatham College
Eastern College
Keystone Junior College
Lancaster Bible College
Mercyhurst College
Philadelphia College of Bible
Point Park College
University of the Arts
Wilkes University
Wilson College

Rhode Island
Salve Regina University

South Carolina
Anderson College
North Greenville College
Spartanburg Methodist College
University of South Carolina

South Dakota
Augustana College
Black Hills State University
Northern State University
South Dakota School of Mines and
   Technology
South Dakota State University

Tennessee
Christian Brothers University
Crichton College
Johnson Bible College
William Jennings Bryan College

Texas
Dallas Baptist University
Southwestern Christian College
University of Mary Hardin-Baylor
University of St. Thomas

Virginia
Marymount University
Southern Virginia College for
   Women

Washington
Pacific Lutheran University

West Virginia
Appalachian Bible College
Fairmont State College

Wisconsin
Blackhawk Technical College
Carroll College
Concordia University Wisconsin
Viterbo College

Wyoming
Eastern Wyoming College
University of Wyoming

Arab Republic of Egypt
American University in Cairo

Tuition and/or fee waiver for senior citizens

Alabama
Alabama Agricultural and
   Mechanical University
Alabama Aviation and Technical
   College
Alabama Southern Community
   College
Athens State College
Bessemer State Technical College
Bevill State Community College
Bishop State Community College
Central Alabama Community
   College
      Alexander City Campus
      Childersburg Campus
Chattahoochee Valley Community
   College
Douglas MacArthur State Technical
   College
Enterprise State Junior College
Faulkner University
Gadsden State Community College
George C. Wallace State
   Community College
      Dothan
      Selma
Harry M. Ayers State Technical
   College
J. F. Drake State Technical College
James H. Faulkner State
   Community College
Jefferson Davis State Junior College
Jefferson State Community College
John C. Calhoun State Community
   College
John M. Patterson State Technical
   College
Lawson State Community College
Lurleen B. Wallace State Junior
   College
Northeast Alabama Community
   College
Northwest Alabama Community
   College
Reid State Technical College
Shelton State Community College
Shoals Community College
Snead State Community College
Southern Union State Junior
   College
Trenholm State Technical College
Wallace State Community College
   at Hanceville

Alaska
Alaska Pacific University
Prince William Sound Community
   College

Tuition and/or fee waivers: senior citizens

Sheldon Jackson College
University of Alaska
   Anchorage
   Fairbanks
   Southeast

Arizona

Arizona Western College
Central Arizona College
Cochise College
Gateway Community College
Mohave Community College
Southwestern College
Yavapai College

Arkansas

Arkansas Baptist College
Arkansas State University
   Beebe Branch
   Jonesboro
Arkansas Tech University
East Arkansas Community College
Garland County Community
   College
Harding University
Henderson State University
John Brown University
Mississippi County Community
   College
North Arkansas Community/
   Technical College
Phillips County Community College
Rich Mountain Community College
South Arkansas Community College
Southern Arkansas University
   Magnolia
   Technical Branch
University of Arkansas
University of Arkansas
   Little Rock
   Medical Sciences
   Monticello
   Pine Bluff
University of Central Arkansas
Westark Community College
Williams Baptist College

California

Azusa Pacific University
California Polytechnic State
   University: San Luis Obispo
California State Polytechnic
   University: Pomona
California State University
   Bakersfield
   Chico
   Dominguez Hills
   Fresno
   Fullerton
   Hayward
   Los Angeles
   Northridge
   Sacramento
   San Bernardino
   San Marcos
   Stanislaus
Cerritos Community College
Citrus College
City College of San Francisco
College of Notre Dame
Compton Community College
D-Q University
Foothill College
Fullerton College
Humboldt State University
Los Angeles Harbor College
Pacific Christian College
Point Loma Nazarene College
Porterville College
Saddleback College
San Diego State University
San Francisco State University

San Jose State University
Sonoma State University
West Valley College
Whittier College

Colorado

Adams State College
Aims Community College
Arapahoe Community College
Colorado Mountain College
   Alpine Campus
   Spring Valley Campus
   Timberline Campus
Colorado Northwestern Community
   College
Community College of Aurora
Community College of Denver
Front Range Community College
Lamar Community College
Mesa State College
Metropolitan State College of
   Denver
Morgan Community College
Naropa Institute
Northeastern Junior College
Pikes Peak Community College
Pueblo Community College
Red Rocks Community College
University of Colorado at Boulder
University of Northern Colorado
University of Southern Colorado
Western State College of Colorado

Connecticut

Asnuntuck Community-Technical
   College
Capital Community-Technical
   College
Central Connecticut State
   University
Eastern Connecticut State
   University
Gateway Community-Technical
   College
Housatonic Community-Technical
   College
Middlesex Community-Technical
   College
Northwestern Connecticut
   Community-Technical College
Norwalk Community-Technical
   College
Quinebaug Valley Community-
   Technical College
Quinnipiac College
Southern Connecticut State
   University
Teikyo-Post University
Three Rivers Community-Technical
   College
Tunxis Community-Technical
   College
University of Connecticut
University of New Haven
Western Connecticut State
   University

Delaware

Delaware State College
Delaware Technical and
   Community College
   Southern Campus
   Stanton/Wilmington Campus
   Terry Campus

Florida

Brevard Community College
Broward Community College
Daytona Beach Community College
Edison Community College
Florida Agricultural and Mechanical
   University

Florida Atlantic University
Florida Institute of Technology
Florida International University
Florida State University
Hillsborough Community College
Lake City Community College
Lake-Sumter Community College
North Florida Junior College
Palm Beach Atlantic College
Palm Beach Community College
Pensacola Junior College
St. Petersburg Junior College
Santa Fe Community College
Seminole Community College
Tallahassee Community College
University of Central Florida
University of North Florida
University of South Florida
Valencia Community College
Webber College

Georgia

Abraham Baldwin Agricultural
   College
Albany State College
Armstrong State College
Atlanta Metropolitan College
Augusta College
Bainbridge College
Brunswick College
Chattahoochee Technical Institute
Clayton State College
Columbus College
Darton College
DeKalb College
DeKalb Technical Institute
Floyd College
Fort Valley State College
Georgia College
Georgia Southwestern College
Georgia State University
Gordon College
Kennesaw State College
Macon College
Middle Georgia College
North Georgia College
Savannah State College
Savannah Technical Institute
Shorter College
South Georgia College
Southern College of Technology
Thomas College
Toccoa Falls College
University of Georgia
Valdosta State College
Waycross College
Wesleyan College
West Georgia College

Hawaii

University of Hawaii
   Hawaii Community College
   Hilo
   Honolulu Community College
   Kapiolani Community College
   Kauai Community College
   Manoa
   West Oahu
   Windward Community College

Idaho

Albertson College
Boise Bible College
Boise State University
College of Southern Idaho
Idaho State University
Lewis Clark State College
North Idaho College
Northwest Nazarene College

Illinois

American Academy of Art
Aurora University
Belleville Area College
Black Hawk College
   East Campus
   Moline
Bradley University
Carl Sandburg College
Chicago State University
City Colleges of Chicago
   Harold Washington College
   Kennedy-King College
   Malcolm X College
   Olive-Harvey College
College of DuPage
College of Lake County
Danville Area Community College
Eastern Illinois University
Elgin Community College
Elmhurst College
Governors State University
Greenville College
Highland Community College
Illinois Central College
Illinois College
Illinois Eastern Community
   Colleges
   Frontier Community College
   Lincoln Trail College
   Olney Central College
   Wabash Valley College
Illinois State University
Illinois Valley Community College
John A. Logan College
Joliet Junior College
Judson College
Kankakee Community College
Kaskaskia College
Kendall College
Kishwaukee College
Lake Land College
Lewis and Clark Community
   College
Lincoln Land Community College
Loyola University of Chicago
MacMurray College
McHenry County College
Montay College
Moraine Valley Community College
Morton College
Northeastern Illinois University
Northern Illinois University
Oakton Community College
Quincy University
Richland Community College
Rock Valley College
Roosevelt University
St. Xavier University
Sangamon State University
Sauk Valley Community College
Shawnee Community College
Southeastern Illinois College
Southern Illinois University
   Carbondale
   Edwardsville
Spoon River College
Springfield College in Illinois
State Community College
Trinity Christian College
Triton College
University of Illinois at Urbana-
   Champaign
Western Illinois University
William Rainey Harper College

Indiana

Anderson University
Ball State University
Calumet College of St. Joseph
Franklin College
Huntington College

Indiana State University
Indiana University Bloomington
Indiana University—Purdue University at Fort Wayne
Indiana Vocational Technical College
    Columbus
    Lafayette
    Northwest
Indiana Wesleyan University
Marian College
Oakland City College
Purdue University: North Central Campus
St. Francis College
Taylor University
University of Evansville
University of Indianapolis
University of Southern Indiana
Vincennes University

Iowa

Briar Cliff College
Clarke College
Clinton Community College
Des Moines Area Community College
Drake University
Emmaus Bible College
Graceland College
Indian Hills Community College
Iowa Wesleyan College
Iowa Western Community College
Kirkwood Community College
Maharishi International University
Morningside College
Mount St. Clare College
Muscatine Community College
St. Ambrose University
Scott Community College
Simpson College
Southeastern Community College: South Campus
Teikyo Westmar University

Kansas

Barton County Community College
Brown Mackie College
Butler County Community College
Coffeyville Community College
Dodge City Community College
Donnelly College
Emporia State University
Friends University
Garden City Community College
Hesston College
Hutchinson Community College
Independence Community College
Johnson County Community College
Kansas Newman College
Kansas Wesleyan University
Labette Community College
Manhattan Christian College
MidAmerica Nazarene College
Neosho County Community College
St. Mary College
Southwestern College
Sterling College
Tabor College
Washburn University of Topeka
Wichita State University

Kentucky

Asbury College
Ashland Community College
Bellarmine College
Brescia College
Campbellsville College
Cumberland College
Eastern Kentucky University
Elizabethtown Community College
Hopkinsville Community College
Jefferson Community College
Kentucky State University
Kentucky Wesleyan College
Lees College
Lexington Community College
Madisonville Community College
Maysville Community College
Mid-Continent Baptist Bible College
Midway College
Morehead State University
Murray State University
Northern Kentucky University
Paducah Community College
Pikeville College
Prestonburg Community College
Southeast Community College
Spalding University
Sue Bennett College
Union College
University of Kentucky
University of Louisville
Western Kentucky University

Louisiana

Bossier Parish Community College
Grambling State University
Louisiana College
Louisiana State University
    Agricultural and Mechanical College
    Alexandria
    Eunice
    Medical Center
    Shreveport
Louisiana Tech University
McNeese State University
Nicholls State University
Northeast Louisiana University
Northwestern State University
Nunez Community College
Our Lady of Holy Cross College
Southeastern Louisiana University
Southern University in Shreveport
Southern University and Agricultural and Mechanical College
University of New Orleans
University of Southwestern Louisiana
Xavier University of Louisiana

Maine

Colby College
Eastern Maine Technical College
Husson College
Unity College
University of Maine
    Augusta
    Farmington
    Fort Kent
    Machias
    Orono
    Presque Isle
University of Southern Maine

Maryland

Allegany Community College
Anne Arundel Community College
Baltimore City Community College
Baltimore Hebrew University
Bowie State University
Catonsville Community College
Cecil Community College
Charles County Community College
Chesapeake College
Coppin State College
Dundalk Community College
Essex Community College
Frederick Community College
Frostburg State University
Hagerstown Junior College
Harford Community College
Hood College
Howard Community College
Maryland Institute College of Art
Montgomery College
    Germantown Campus
    Rockville Campus
    Takoma Park Campus
Morgan State University
Mount St. Mary's College
Prince George's Community College
St. Mary's College of Maryland
Salisbury State University
Towson State University
University of Baltimore
University of Maryland
    Baltimore County
    College Park
    Eastern Shore
    University College
Wor-Wic Community College

Massachusetts

American International College
Anna Maria College for Men and Women
Atlantic Union College
Becker College
    Leicester Campus
    Worcester Campus
Bentley College
Boston University
Bridgewater State College
Bristol Community College
Bunker Hill Community College
Cape Cod Community College
Eastern Nazarene College
Elms College
Fitchburg State College
Framingham State College
Greenfield Community College
Holyoke Community College
Marian Court Junior College
Massachusetts Bay Community College
Massachusetts College of Art
Massasoit Community College
Merrimack College
Middlesex Community College
Mount Wachusett Community College
Nichols College
North Adams State College
North Shore Community College
Northeastern University
Northern Essex Community College
Quincy College
Quinsigamond Community College
Roxbury Community College
Salem State College
Springfield Technical Community College
Stonehill College
Suffolk University
University of Massachusetts
    Amherst
    Boston
    Lowell
Western New England College
Westfield State College
Worcester State College

Michigan

Alpena Community College
Aquinas College
Bay de Noc Community College
Charles Stewart Mott Community College
Delta College
Glen Oaks Community College
Gogebic Community College
Great Lakes Junior College of Business
Henry Ford Community College
Highland Park Community College
Jackson Community College
Jordan College
Kalamazoo Valley Community College
Kellogg Community College
Kirtland Community College
Lake Michigan College
Lake Superior State University
Madonna University
Marygrove College
Michigan Christian College
Michigan Technological University
Mid Michigan Community College
Monroe County Community College
Montcalm Community College
Muskegon Community College
Northern Michigan University
Reformed Bible College
Saginaw Valley State University
St. Clair County Community College
Schoolcraft College
Southwestern Michigan College
University of Michigan
    Dearborn
    Flint
Washtenaw Community College
Wayne County Community College
Wayne State University
West Shore Community College
Western Michigan University
William Tyndale College

Minnesota

Alexandria Technical College
Anoka-Ramsey Community College
Augsburg College
Austin Community College
Bemidji State University
Brainerd Community College
College of St. Catherine: St. Catherine Campus
College of St. Scholastica
Concordia College: St. Paul
Fergus Falls Community College
Itasca Community College: Arrowhead Region
Lakewood Community College
Mankato State University
Mesabi Community College: Arrowhead Region
Metropolitan State University
Minneapolis Community College
Minnesota Bible College
Moorhead State University
Normandale Community College
North Central Bible College
North Hennepin Community College
Northwestern College
Rainy River Community College
Rochester Community College
St. Cloud State University
St. Olaf College
St. Paul Technical College
Southwest State University
University of Minnesota
    Crookston
    Duluth
    Twin Cities
University of St. Thomas
Willmar Community College
Winona State University
Worthington Community College

Tuition and/or fee waivers: senior citizens

Mississippi
Belhaven College
Copiah-Lincoln Community College
Delta State University
East Central Community College
East Mississippi Community College
Hinds Community College
Holmes Community College
Meridian Community College
Millsaps College
Mississippi Gulf Coast Community College
    Jackson County Campus
    Jefferson Davis Campus
    Perkinston
Northwest Mississippi Community College
Pearl River Community College
Southeastern Baptist College
Southwest Mississippi Community College
University of Mississippi
Wood Junior College

Missouri
Avila College
Calvary Bible College
Central Methodist College
Crowder College
Culver-Stockton College
East Central College
Fontbonne College
Hannibal-LaGrange College
Lincoln University
Lindenwood College
Longview Community College
Maple Woods Community College
Maryville University
Missouri Baptist College
Missouri Southern State College
Missouri Western State College
Moberly Area Community College
Northeast Missouri State University
Northwest Missouri State University
Ozark Christian College
Park College
Penn Valley Community College
St. Louis Community College
    Forest Park
    Meramec
Southeast Missouri State University
Southwest Missouri State University
State Fair Community College
Three Rivers Community College
William Jewell College

Montana
Carroll College
College of Great Falls
Dawson Community College
Dull Knife Memorial College
Eastern Montana College
Flathead Valley Community College
Fort Peck Community College
Miles Community College
Montana College of Mineral Science and Technology
Montana State University
Northern Montana College
Stone Child College
University of Montana
Western Montana College of the University of Montana

Nebraska
Chadron State College
Doane College
Grace College of the Bible
McCook Community College
Metropolitan Community College
Mid Plains Community College
Midland Lutheran College
Nebraska Indian Community College
Nebraska Wesleyan University
Southeast Community College
    Beatrice Campus
    Lincoln Campus
Western Nebraska Community College: Scottsbluff Campus

Nevada
Northern Nevada Community College
Truckee Meadows Community College
University of Nevada
    Las Vegas
    Reno
Western Nevada Community College

New Hampshire
Franklin Pierce College
Hesser College
Keene State College
New England College
New Hampshire Technical College
    Berlin
    Claremont
    Laconia
    Manchester
    Nashua
    Stratham
New Hampshire Technical Institute
Notre Dame College
Plymouth State College of the University System of New Hampshire
Rivier College
St. Anselm College
University of New Hampshire
    Durham
    Manchester
White Pines College

New Jersey
Atlantic Community College
Bergen Community College
Bloomfield College
Brookdale Community College
Burlington County College
Caldwell College
Camden County College
Centenary College
College of St. Elizabeth
County College of Morris
Cumberland County College
Drew University
Essex County College
Fairleigh Dickinson University
    Edward Williams College
    Madison
Felician College
Georgian Court College
Gloucester County College
Hudson County Community College
Jersey City State College
Kean College of New Jersey
Monmouth College
Montclair State College
Ocean County College
Passaic County Community College
Ramapo College of New Jersey
Raritan Valley Community College
Rutgers—The State University of New Jersey
    Camden College of Arts and Sciences
    College of Engineering
    College of Nursing
    College of Pharmacy
    Cook College
    Douglass College
    Livingston College
    Mason Gross School of the Arts
    Newark College of Arts and Sciences
    Rutgers College
    University College Camden
    University College New Brunswick
    University College Newark
Salem Community College
Seton Hall University
Stockton State College
Sussex County Community College
Thomas Edison State College
Trenton State College
Union County College
Upsala College
Warren County Community College
William Paterson College of New Jersey

New Mexico
Clovis Community College
College of Santa Fe
Dona Ana Branch Community College of New Mexico State University
Eastern New Mexico University: Roswell Campus
National College
New Mexico Institute of Mining and Technology
New Mexico State University
    Alamogordo
    Carlsbad
    Las Cruces
San Juan College
Santa Fe Community College
Western New Mexico University

New York
Adelphi University
Adirondack Community College
Broome Community College
Cayuga County Community College
City University of New York
    Baruch College
    Borough of Manhattan Community College
    Bronx Community College
    Brooklyn College
    City College
    College of Staten Island
    Hostos Community College
    Hunter College
    John Jay College of Criminal Justice
    Lehman College
    Medgar Evers College
    New York City Technical College
    Queens College
    York College
Clinton Community College
College of Mount St. Vincent
College of New Rochelle
College of St. Rose
Columbia-Greene Community College
Concordia College
Daemen College
Dominican College of Blauvelt
Dowling College
Dutchess Community College
D'Youville College
Erie Community College
    North Campus
    South Campus
Finger Lakes Community College
Five Towns College
Fordham University
Fulton-Montgomery Community College
Hofstra University
Houghton College
Iona College
Jamestown Community College
Jefferson Community College
Jewish Theological Seminary of America
Long Island University: Southampton Campus
Maria College
Mercy College
Mohawk Valley Community College
Nassau Community College
New York Institute of Technology
Niagara County Community College
North Country Community College
Nyack College
Orange County Community College
Pace University
    College of White Plains
    New York
    Pleasantville/Briarcliff
Roberts Wesleyan College
Rockland Community College
Russell Sage College
Sage Junior College of Albany
St. Bonaventure University
St. John Fisher College
St. John's University
St. Joseph's College: Suffolk Campus
St. Thomas Aquinas College
Schenectady County Community College
State University of New York
    Albany
    Purchase
    College of Agriculture and Technology at Cobleskill
    College at Cortland
    College at Old Westbury
    Institute of Technology at Utica/Rome
Suffolk County Community College
    Eastern Campus
    Selden
    Western Campus
Sullivan County Community College
Tompkins-Cortland Community College
Trocaire College
Ulster County Community College
Utica College of Syracuse University
Villa Maria College of Buffalo
Wagner College
Westchester Business Institute

North Carolina
Alamance Community College
Anson Community College
Appalachian State University
Asheville Buncombe Technical Community College
Beaufort County Community College
Belmont Abbey College
Bladen Community College
Blue Ridge Community College
Brunswick Community College

Tuition and/or fee waivers: senior citizens

Caldwell Community College and
  Technical Institute
Cape Fear Community College
Carteret Community College
Catawba Valley Community College
Central Carolina Community
  College
Central Piedmont Community
  College
Cleveland Community College
Coastal Carolina Community
  College
College of the Albemarle
Craven Community College
Davidson County Community
  College
Durham Technical Community
  College
East Carolina University
Edgecombe Community College
Fayetteville State University
Fayetteville Technical Community
  College
Gaston College
Halifax Community College
Haywood Community College
Isothermal Community College
James Sprunt Community College
Johnston Community College
Lenoir Community College
Lenoir-Rhyne College
Martin Community College
Mayland Community College
McDowell Technical Community
  College
Methodist College
Mitchell Community College
Montgomery Community College
Montreat-Anderson College
Nash Community College
North Carolina Agricultural and
  Technical State University
North Carolina State University
Pamlico Community College
Pembroke State University
Piedmont Community College
Pitt Community College
Richmond Community College
Roanoke Bible College
Roanoke-Chowan Community
  College
Robeson Community College
Rockingham Community College
Rowan-Cabarrus Community
  College
Sampson Community College
Sandhills Community College
Southeastern Community College
Southwestern Community College
Stanly Community College
Surry Community College
Tri-County Community College
University of North Carolina
  Asheville
  Chapel Hill
  Charlotte
  Greensboro
  Wilmington
Vance-Granville Community
  College
Wake Technical Community
  College
Wayne Community College
Western Carolina University
Western Piedmont Community
  College
Wilkes Community College
Wilson Technical Community
  College
Winston-Salem State University

North Dakota
Bismarck State College
Mayville State University
North Dakota State University:
  Bottineau
Standing Rock College
University of Mary
University of North Dakota
  Grand Forks
  Lake Region
  Williston
Valley City State University

Ohio
Belmont Technical College
Bowling Green State University
  Bowling Green
  Firelands College
Cedarville College
Central Ohio Technical College
Central State University
Chatfield College
Cincinnati Bible College and
  Seminary
Clark State Community College
Cleveland College of Jewish Studies
Cleveland State University
Columbus College of Art and
  Design
Columbus State Community College
Cuyahoga Community College
  Eastern Campus
  Western Campus
Defiance College
Denison University
Edison State Community College
Hiram College
Jefferson Technical College
Kent State University
  East Liverpool Regional
    Campus
  Trumbull Regional Campus
  Tuscarawas Campus
Lake Erie College
Lakeland Community College
Lima Technical College
Lourdes College
Malone College
Marion Technical College
Miami University: Hamilton
  Campus
Mount Union College
North Central Technical College
Northwest Technical College
Ohio Dominican College
Ohio Northern University
Ohio State University
  Mansfield Campus
  Marion Campus
  Newark Campus
Ohio University
  Chillicothe Campus
  Zanesville Campus
Owens Technical College
  Findlay Campus
  Toledo
Sinclair Community College
Southern Ohio College
Stark Technical College
Terra Technical College
University of Akron
University of Cincinnati: Raymond
  Walters College
University of Dayton
University of Findlay
University of Rio Grande
University of Toledo
Urbana University
Walsh University
Wittenberg University
Wright State University
  Dayton
  Lake Campus
Xavier University
Youngstown State University

Oklahoma
Bartlesville Wesleyan College
Cameron University
Connors State College
East Central University
Northeastern State University
Northwestern Oklahoma State
  University
Oklahoma Baptist University
Oklahoma City Community College
Oklahoma City University
Oklahoma Panhandle State
  University
Oklahoma State University
  Oklahoma City
  Stillwater
Phillips University
Redlands Community College
Rogers State College
Rose State College
Southeastern Oklahoma State
  University
Southern Nazarene University
Southwestern Oklahoma State
  University
Tulsa Junior College
University of Central Oklahoma
University of Oklahoma
  Health Sciences Center
  Norman
University of Science and Arts of
  Oklahoma
Western Oklahoma State College

Oregon
Central Oregon Community College
Chemeketa Community College
Clackamas Community College
Clatsop Community College
Concordia College
George Fox College
Lane Community College
Linfield College
Linn-Benton Community College
Portland Community College
Portland State University
Rogue Community College
Treasure Valley Community College
Umpqua Community College
Warner Pacific College
Western Oregon State College

Pennsylvania
Academy of the New Church
Albright College
Alvernia College
Beaver College
Bucks County Community College
Butler County Community College
California University of
  Pennsylvania
Chestnut Hill College
Clarion University of Pennsylvania
College Misericordia
Community College of Beaver
  County
Community College of Philadelphia
Delaware County Community
  College
Delaware Valley College
Duquesne University
East Stroudsburg University of
  Pennsylvania
Edinboro University of
  Pennsylvania
Gannon University
Gratz College
Gwynedd-Mercy College
Harcum Junior College
Holy Family College
Immaculata College
Indiana University of Pennsylvania
Juniata College
Keystone Junior College
King's College
Lackawanna Junior College
Lancaster Bible College
Lehigh County Community College
Lock Haven University of
  Pennsylvania
Luzerne County Community
  College
Manor Junior College
Marywood College
Messiah College
Millersville University of
  Pennsylvania
Montgomery County Community
  College
Northampton County Area
  Community College
Point Park College
Reading Area Community College
Robert Morris College
Rosemont College
Seton Hill College
Shippensburg University of
  Pennsylvania
Temple University
University of Pittsburgh at Bradford
University of Scranton
Ursinus College
Villanova University
West Chester University of
  Pennsylvania
Westmoreland County Community
  College
Wilkes University

Rhode Island
Community College of Rhode
  Island
Rhode Island College
Salve Regina University
University of Rhode Island

South Carolina
Aiken Technical College
Anderson College
Benedict College
Central Carolina Technical College
Central Wesleyan College
Chesterfield-Marlboro Technical
  College
The Citadel
Clemson University
College of Charleston
Denmark Technical College
Florence-Darlington Technical
  College
Francis Marion University
Furman University
Greenville Technical College
Horry-Georgetown Technical
  College
Lander University
Limestone College
Midlands Technical College
South Carolina State University
Spartanburg Methodist College
Spartanburg Technical College
Technical College of the
  Lowcountry
Tri-County Technical College
Trident Technical College

Tuition and/or fee waivers: senior citizens

University of South Carolina
  Aiken
  Beaufort
  Coastal Carolina College
  Columbia
  Salkehatchie Regional Campus
  Spartanburg
  Sumter
  Union
Williamsburg Technical College
Winthrop University
York Technical College

South Dakota

Augustana College
Black Hills State University
Dakota State University
Kilian Community College
Mount Marty College
National College
Northern State University
Presentation College
Sioux Falls College
Sisseton-Wahpeton Community College
South Dakota School of Mines and Technology
South Dakota State University

Tennessee

Austin Peay State University
Belmont University
Bethel College
Carson-Newman College
Chattanooga State Technical Community College
Cleveland State Community College
Columbia State Community College
Dyersburg State Community College
East Tennessee State University
Freed-Hardeman University
King College
Lambuth University
Lee College
Lincoln Memorial University
Memphis College of Art
Memphis State University
Middle Tennessee State University
Motlow State Community College
Nashville State Technical Institute
Pellissippi State Technical Community College
Roane State Community College
Shelby State Community College
Southern College of Seventh-day Adventists
State Technical Institute at Memphis
Tennessee Technological University
University of Tennessee
  Chattanooga
  Knoxville
  Martin
Volunteer State Community College
Walters State Community College

Texas

Alvin Community College
Angelina College
Bee County College
College of the Mainland
Corpus Christi State University
Del Mar College
East Texas State University
El Paso Community College
Frank Phillips College
Galveston College
Hardin-Simmons University
Hill College
Houston Baptist University
Houston Community College

Howard College
Howard Payne University
Incarnate Word College
Laredo Junior College
Lee College
McMurry University
Northeast Texas Community College
Paris Junior College
St. Philip's College
Southwest Texas Junior College
Southwestern Adventist College
Tarleton State University
Temple Junior College
Texarkana College
Texas A&M University
Texas Christian University
Trinity Valley Community College
Vernon Regional Junior College
Wayland Baptist University
Weatherford College

Utah

College of Eastern Utah
Dixie College
Salt Lake Community College
Snow College
University of Utah
Utah Valley Community College
Weber State University

Vermont

Burlington College
Castleton State College
Champlain College
College of St. Joseph in Vermont
Community College of Vermont
Johnson State College
Lyndon State College
Southern Vermont College
University of Vermont

Virginia

Averett College
Blue Ridge Community College
Bluefield College
Bridgewater College
Central Virginia Community College
Christopher Newport University
Clinch Valley College of the University of Virginia
College of William and Mary
Dabney S. Lancaster Community College
Danville Community College
Eastern Mennonite College
Eastern Shore Community College
Ferrum College
George Mason University
J. Sargeant Reynolds Community College
John Tyler Community College
Longwood College
Lord Fairfax Community College
Mary Washington College
Marymount University
Mountain Empire Community College
New River Community College
Norfolk State University
Northern Virginia Community College
Old Dominion University
Patrick Henry Community College
Paul D. Camp Community College
Piedmont Virginia Community College
Radford University
Rappahannock Community College
Richard Bland College
Roanoke College

Southside Virginia Community College
Southwest Virginia Community College
Tidewater Community College
University of Virginia
Virginia Commonwealth University
Virginia Western Community College
Wytheville Community College

Washington

Big Bend Community College
Central Washington University
Centralia College
Clark College
Columbia Basin College
Edmonds Community College
Everett Community College
Gonzaga University
Grays Harbor College
Green River Community College
Heritage College
Lower Columbia College
North Seattle Community College
Northwest College of the Assemblies of God
Olympic College
Peninsula College
Pierce College
Puget Sound Christian College
Seattle Central Community College
Seattle Pacific University
Shoreline Community College
South Seattle Community College
Spokane Falls Community College
Tacoma Community College
University of Washington
Walla Walla College
Walla Walla Community College
Whatcom Community College
Whitworth College
Yakima Valley Community College

West Virginia

Appalachian Bible College
Fairmont State College
University of Charleston
Wheeling Jesuit College

Wisconsin

Blackhawk Technical College
Lakeland College
Marian College of Fond du Lac
Mount Mary College
Northland College
Silver Lake College
University of Wisconsin
  Eau Claire
  Green Bay
  La Crosse
  Oshkosh
  River Falls
  Stout
  Whitewater
University of Wisconsin Center
  Fox Valley
  Richland
  Washington County
  Waukesha
Viterbo College

Wyoming

Casper College
Central Wyoming College
Eastern Wyoming College
Laramie County Community College
Northwest College
Sheridan College
University of Wyoming

Western Wyoming Community College

American Samoa, Caroline Islands, Guam, Marianas, Virgin Islands

Guam Community College
University of the Virgin Islands

Tuition and/or fee waiver for minority students

Alabama

Faulkner University

Alaska

Prince William Sound Community College
University of Alaska Southeast

Arizona

Arizona State University
Northern Arizona University
University of Arizona

California

Antioch Southern California at Los Angeles
California Baptist College
Cerritos Community College
City College of San Francisco
Compton Community College
Fresno City College
Fullerton College
Napa Valley College
Porterville College
Saddleback College
Westmont College

Colorado

Aims Community College
Colorado State University
Colorado Technical College
Fort Lewis College
Northeastern Junior College
Red Rocks Community College

Connecticut

Albertus Magnus College
Fairfield University
Sacred Heart University
Teikyo-Post University
University of Hartford

Florida

Brevard Community College
Broward Community College
Central Florida Community College
Florida Atlantic University
Florida International University
Lake City Community College
Rollins College
Santa Fe Community College
University of Florida

Hawaii

University of Hawaii at Manoa

Idaho

University of Idaho

Illinois

Governors State University
Illinois Benedictine College
Loyola University of Chicago
Northern Illinois University

Tuition and/or fee waivers: family members enrolled simultaneously

Indiana
Indiana Vocational Technical College: Columbus
Indiana Wesleyan University
Purdue University: North Central Campus
St. Joseph's College
St. Mary's College

Iowa
Hawkeye Community College
St. Ambrose University

Kansas
Labette Community College

Kentucky
Bellarmine College
Murray State University
Transylvania University
University of Kentucky

Louisiana
Bossier Parish Community College
Grambling State University
Louisiana State University and Agricultural and Mechanical College

Maine
Central Maine Technical College
Eastern Maine Technical College
University of Maine
  Augusta
  Farmington
  Machias
  Orono
  Presque Isle

Maryland
Morgan State University
University of Maryland
  College Park
  Eastern Shore

Massachusetts
Eastern Nazarene College
Greenfield Community College
Hellenic College
Merrimack College
St. John's Seminary College
Stonehill College
University of Massachusetts at Boston

Michigan
Concordia College
Northern Michigan University
Northwestern Michigan College

Minnesota
University of Minnesota
  Crookston
  Morris
  Twin Cities

Mississippi
Mississippi University for Women
University of Mississippi

Missouri
Northwest Missouri State University
St. Louis University
University of Missouri: Rolla
William Woods College

Montana
Eastern Montana College
Montana State University
Northern Montana College
Salish Kootenai College
University of Montana
Western Montana College of the University of Montana

Nebraska
Chadron State College
College of St. Mary
Concordia College

Nevada
University of Nevada: Reno

New Mexico
Institute of American Indian Arts

New York
Canisius College
Iona College
St. Bonaventure University
State University of New York
  Buffalo
  College at Buffalo

North Carolina
Lenoir-Rhyne College
Western Carolina University

North Dakota
United Tribes Technical College
University of North Dakota: Lake Region

Ohio
Bluffton College
Cleveland Institute of Electronics
Hiram College
Northwestern College
Walsh University
Wilmington College

Oklahoma
Oklahoma State University
  Oklahoma City
  Stillwater
Southeastern Oklahoma State University
University of Central Oklahoma
University of Oklahoma Health Sciences Center

Oregon
Eastern Oregon State College
George Fox College
Oregon Health Sciences University
Oregon Institute of Technology
Portland State University
Southern Oregon State College
University of Oregon
  Eugene
  Robert Donald Clark Honors College
Warner Pacific College
Western Oregon State College

Pennsylvania
Bloomsburg University of Pennsylvania
California University of Pennsylvania
Cheyney University of Pennsylvania
Clarion University of Pennsylvania
Edinboro University of Pennsylvania
Immaculata College
Kutztown University of Pennsylvania
Lock Haven University of Pennsylvania
Lycoming College
Manor Junior College
Mansfield University of Pennsylvania
Millersville University of Pennsylvania
St. Charles Borromeo Seminary
West Chester University of Pennsylvania

Puerto Rico
American University of Puerto Rico
Caribbean University

Rhode Island
Providence College
Salve Regina University

South Carolina
Furman University
Greenville Technical College
Spartanburg Methodist College

Tennessee
Carson-Newman College
Johnson Bible College
Northeast State Technical Community College
University of Tennessee: Memphis
Volunteer State Community College
Walters State Community College

Texas
Dallas Baptist University
El Centro College
Hardin-Simmons University
Lon Morris College
Texas Southern University
University of Mary Hardin-Baylor

Vermont
Lyndon State College

Virginia
Blue Ridge Community College
Norfolk State University
Randolph-Macon Woman's College
St. Paul's College
Virginia State University

Washington
Edmonds Community College
Grays Harbor College
Skagit Valley College
Western Washington University

West Virginia
Fairmont State College

Wisconsin
Blackhawk Technical College
University of Wisconsin
  La Crosse
  Superior

Tuition and/or fee waiver for family members enrolled simultaneously

Alabama
International Bible College
Marion Military Institute
Phillips Junior College: Birmingham
Spring Hill College
Tuskegee University
Virginia College

Arizona
Arizona College of the Bible
Western International University

Arkansas
East Arkansas Community College
Philander Smith College

California
Azusa Pacific University
Bethany College
California Baptist College
California Lutheran University
Cerritos Community College
City College of San Francisco
Compton Community College
LIFE Bible College
Monterey Institute of International Studies
Pacific Christian College
Patten College
Porterville College
St. Mary's College of California
San Jose Christian College
Santa Clara University
Solano Community College
University of San Francisco

Colorado
Colorado Christian University
Denver Institute of Technology

Connecticut
Albertus Magnus College
Briarwood College
Fairfield University
Sacred Heart University
Teikyo-Post University
University of Bridgeport
University of Hartford
University of New Haven

Delaware
Goldey-Beacom College

District of Columbia
George Washington University
Trinity College

Florida
Barry University
Florida Christian College
Florida Southern College
Jacksonville University
St. Leo College
Santa Fe Community College
Schiller International University
Trinity College at Miami

Georgia
Oglethorpe University
Paine College
Shorter College
Toccoa Falls College
Truett-McConnell College
Wesleyan College

Idaho
Northwest Nazarene College

Illinois
Augustana College
College of St. Francis
Illinois Benedictine College
Judson College
Kendall College
Lewis University
Lincoln Christian College and Seminary
MacCormac Junior College
Olivet Nazarene University
Quincy University
Rockford College
Rosary College

Tuition and/or fee waivers: family members enrolled simultaneously

Indiana
Bethel College
Huntington College
Indiana State University
Indiana Vocational Technical College: Columbus
Indiana Wesleyan University
Manchester College
Marian College
St. Joseph's College
St. Mary's College
Vincennes University

Iowa
American Institute of Business
Clarke College
Ellsworth Community College
Faith Baptist Bible College and Theological Seminary
Loras College
Mount St. Clare College
Northwestern College
Simpson College
Teikyo Marycrest University
Teikyo Westmar University
University of Dubuque
Upper Iowa University

Kansas
Benedictine College
Colby Community College
Kansas Newman College
Kansas Wesleyan University
Ottawa University
St. Mary College
Southwestern College

Kentucky
Asbury College
Spalding University
Sue Bennett College

Maine
St. Joseph's College
University of New England

Maryland
College of Notre Dame of Maryland
Coppin State College
Hood College
Loyola College in Maryland
Mount St. Mary's College
Ner Israel Rabbinical College
Western Maryland College

Massachusetts
American International College
Anna Maria College for Men and Women
Atlantic Union College
Bay Path College
Becker College
    Leicester Campus
    Worcester Campus
Eastern Nazarene College
Elms College
Lasell College
Merrimack College
Nichols College
Pine Manor College
Stonehill College
Suffolk University
Western New England College
Wheelock College

Michigan
Andrews University
Great Lakes Christian College
Marygrove College
Michigan Christian College
Northwood University

Reformed Bible College
Saginaw Valley State University
Siena Heights College
West Shore Community College

Minnesota
College of St. Scholastica
North Central Bible College
Northwestern College
University of St. Thomas
Willmar Community College

Mississippi
Holmes Community College
Magnolia Bible College
Rust College

Missouri
Avila College
Calvary Bible College
Central Methodist College
Fontbonne College
Kemper Military School and College
Maryville University
National College
Research College of Nursing
Rockhurst College
Stephens College
William Woods College

Montana
Carroll College
College of Great Falls

Nebraska
College of St. Mary
Creighton University
Grace College of the Bible
Midland Lutheran College
Nebraska Christian College
York College

Nevada
Sierra Nevada College
Western Nevada Community College

New Hampshire
Hesser College
Notre Dame College
Rivier College
St. Anselm College

New Jersey
Bloomfield College
Caldwell College
Centenary College
College of St. Elizabeth
Fairleigh Dickinson University
    Edward Williams College
    Madison
Felician College
Georgian Court College
Monmouth College
Seton Hall University

New Mexico
National College

New York
Canisius College
College of Mount St. Vincent
College of New Rochelle
    New Rochelle
    School of New Resources
Daemen College
D'Youville College
Elmira College
Hartwick College
Houghton College
Iona College

King's College
Long Island University: Brooklyn Campus
Marymount College
Molloy College
Nazareth College of Rochester
Nyack College
Russell Sage College
Sage Junior College of Albany
St. Bonaventure University
St. John's University
St. Joseph's College
    Brooklyn
    Suffolk Campus
St. Thomas Aquinas College
Villa Maria College of Buffalo
Wagner College

North Carolina
Alamance Community College
Belmont Abbey College
East Coast Bible College
Greensboro College
John Wesley College
Lenoir-Rhyne College
Livingstone College
Peace College
Pfeiffer College
Piedmont Bible College
Queens College
Roanoke Bible College

North Dakota
Trinity Bible College
United Tribes Technical College
University of Mary

Ohio
Antioch College
Ashland University
Capital University
Central State University
Cincinnati Bible College and Seminary
Defiance College
Franciscan University of Steubenville
Hiram College
Malone College
Mount Union College
Muskingum College
Notre Dame College of Ohio
Ohio Northern University
Otterbein College
Terra Technical College
University of Dayton
University of Findlay
Ursuline College
Walsh University
Wilmington College
Xavier University

Oklahoma
Northeastern Oklahoma Agricultural and Mechanical College
Oklahoma Christian University of Science and Arts
Oral Roberts University
Southeastern Oklahoma State University
University of Central Oklahoma

Oregon
Bassist College
Clatsop Community College
Eugene Bible College
George Fox College
Lewis and Clark College
Linfield College
Linn-Benton Community College
Multnomah School of the Bible

Pennsylvania
Allentown College of St. Francis de Sales
Art Institute of Pittsburgh
Baptist Bible College of Pennsylvania
Carlow College
Cedar Crest College
Eastern College
Elizabethtown College
Gannon University
Gratz College
Immaculata College
La Roche College
Lackawanna Junior College
Lancaster Bible College
Lycoming College
Marywood College
Mercyhurst College
Messiah College
Moore College of Art and Design
Mount Aloysius College
Philadelphia College of Bible
Point Park College
Robert Morris College
Rosemont College
St. Francis College
Seton Hill College
Thiel College
University of the Arts
University of Scranton
Ursinus College
Valley Forge Christian College
Valley Forge Military College
Waynesburg College
Wilkes University

Puerto Rico
Caribbean University
Universidad Adventista de las Antillas

Rhode Island
Bryant College
Johnson & Wales University
Providence College
Salve Regina University

South Carolina
Central Wesleyan College
Erskine College
Limestone College
North Greenville College
Spartanburg Methodist College

South Dakota
Augustana College
Mount Marty College
National College

Tennessee
Belmont University
Carson-Newman College
Free Will Baptist Bible College
Johnson Bible College
Knoxville College
Lee College
Southern College of Seventh-day Adventists
Tennessee Temple University
Tennessee Wesleyan College
Union University

Texas
Arlington Baptist College
Dallas Baptist University
Lon Morris College
Lubbock Christian University
Northwood University: Texas Campus
Paul Quinn College
Southwestern Adventist College

Southwestern Assemblies of God College
Southwestern Christian College
University of Dallas

Utah
Westminster College of Salt Lake City

Vermont
Champlain College
Green Mountain College
Johnson State College
Lyndon State College
St. Michael's College

Virginia
Averett College
Christendom College
Ferrum College
Mary Baldwin College
Marymount University
Randolph-Macon College
Southern Virginia College for Women
Virginia Intermont College

Washington
Gonzaga University
Northwest College of the Assemblies of God
Puget Sound Christian College
St. Martin's College
Seattle University
Walla Walla College

West Virginia
Appalachian Bible College

Wisconsin
Alverno College
Beloit College
Blackhawk Technical College
Cardinal Stritch College
Marian College of Fond du Lac
Marquette University
Mount Mary College
St. Norbert College
Viterbo College
Wisconsin Lutheran College

Wyoming
Northwest College

Mexico
Sistema Instituto Tecnologico y de Estudios Superiores de Monterrey

Tuition and/or fee waiver for unemployed or children of unemployed workers

Alabama
Bessemer State Technical College
Faulkner University

Arizona
Mohave Community College

Arkansas
Southern Arkansas University: Technical Branch
Williams Baptist College

California
Barstow College
Cerritos Community College
City College of San Francisco
Coastline Community College
Compton Community College
Contra Costa College
D-Q University
Feather River College
Fresno City College
Fullerton College
Moorpark College
Pasadena City College
Porterville College
Queen of the Holy Rosary College
Saddleback College
San Diego City College
Santa Barbara City College
Santa Monica College
Sierra College
West Hills Community College
West Valley College

Connecticut
Teikyo-Post University

Georgia
South Georgia College

Hawaii
University of Hawaii: Kauai Community College

Idaho
Northwest Nazarene College

Iowa
Drake University

Kansas
Labette Community College
Neosho County Community College

Louisiana
Northeast Louisiana University

Maryland
Ner Israel Rabbinical College

Massachusetts
Atlantic Union College
Bridgewater State College
Bristol Community College
Bunker Hill Community College
Massachusetts Bay Community College
Massachusetts College of Art
Massasoit Community College
Mount Wachusett Community College
North Adams State College
Salem State College

Michigan
St. Mary's College
Wayne State University

Minnesota
Gustavus Adolphus College
Rainy River Community College

Missouri
Calvary Bible College

Nebraska
Metropolitan Community College
York College

Nevada
Western Nevada Community College

New Jersey
Brookdale Community College
Camden County College
County College of Morris
Cumberland County College
Essex County College
Mercer County Community College
Ocean County College
Passaic County Community College
Raritan Valley Community College
Sussex County Community College
Warren County Community College
William Paterson College of New Jersey

New York
Bramson ORT Technical Institute
Bryant & Stratton Business Institute: Albany
Herkimer County Community College
Mannes College of Music
New York Institute of Technology
Villa Maria College of Buffalo
William Smith College

North Carolina
Chowan College

Ohio
Belmont Technical College
Cleveland Institute of Electronics
Hiram College

Oregon
Linn-Benton Community College
Marylhurst College
Rogue Community College
Warner Pacific College

Pennsylvania
Bucks County Community College
Gratz College
King's College
Manor Junior College
Mercyhurst College
Point Park College
St. Charles Borromeo Seminary
Thaddeus Stevens State School of Technology
University of the Arts

Rhode Island
Salve Regina University
University of Rhode Island

South Carolina
Greenville Technical College
Spartanburg Methodist College

Texas
El Centro College
North Harris Montgomery Community College District

Washington
Big Bend Community College
Centralia College
Columbia Basin College
Edmonds Community College
Everett Community College
Lower Columbia College
North Seattle Community College
Peninsula College
Pierce College
Seattle Central Community College
Skagit Valley College
South Puget Sound Community College
South Seattle Community College
Tacoma Community College
Walla Walla Community College
Whatcom Community College
Yakima Valley Community College

West Virginia
Alderson-Broaddus College

Wisconsin
Blackhawk Technical College

Tuition payment by credit card

Alabama
Alabama Agricultural and Mechanical University
Alabama Southern Community College
Alabama State University
Bessemer State Technical College
Bevill State Community College
Birmingham-Southern College
Bishop State Community College
Central Alabama Community College: Alexander City Campus
Enterprise State Junior College
Faulkner University
Gadsden State Community College
George C. Wallace State Community College at Dothan
Huntingdon College
J. F. Drake State Technical College
Jacksonville State University
Jefferson Davis State Junior College
Jefferson State Community College
John C. Calhoun State Community College
John M. Patterson State Technical College
Judson College
Lurleen B. Wallace State Junior College
Northwest Alabama Community College
Reid State Technical College
Samford University
Shelton State Community College
Southeastern Bible College
Talladega College
Trenholm State Technical College
Troy State University
  Dothan
  Montgomery
University of Alabama
  Birmingham
  Tuscaloosa
University of Mobile
University of South Alabama
Walker College

Alaska
Alaska Pacific University
Prince William Sound Community College
Sheldon Jackson College
University of Alaska
  Anchorage
  Fairbanks
  Southeast

Arizona
Arizona College of the Bible
Arizona State University
Arizona Western College
Central Arizona College
Cochise College
DeVry Institute of Technology: Phoenix
Eastern Arizona College

Tuition payment plans: credit card payment

Embry-Riddle Aeronautical
　University: Prescott Campus
Gateway Community College
Glendale Community College
Grand Canyon University
ITT Technical Institute: Tucson
Mesa Community College
Mohave Community College
Northern Arizona University
Paradise Valley Community College
Phoenix College
Prescott College
Rio Salado Community College
Scottsdale Community College
University of Arizona
University of Phoenix
Western International University
Yavapai College

Arkansas

East Arkansas Community College
Garland County Community
　College
Henderson State University
Mississippi County Community
　College
North Arkansas Community/
　Technical College
South Arkansas Community College
Southern Arkansas University
　Magnolia
　Technical Branch
University of Arkansas
University of Arkansas
　Little Rock
　Medical Sciences
　Monticello
　Pine Bluff
University of Central Arkansas
Westark Community College

California

Academy of Art College
Allan Hancock College
American Armenian International
　College
American College for the Applied
　Arts: Los Angeles
Antioch Southern California at Los
　Angeles
Armstrong University
Art Center College of Design
Art Institute of Southern California
Azusa Pacific University
Bethany College
Biola University
Brooks College
Brooks Institute of Photography
California Baptist College
California College of Arts and
　Crafts
California College for Health
　Sciences
California Lutheran University
California State University
　Bakersfield
　Dominguez Hills
　Fresno
　Hayward
　Los Angeles
　San Bernardino
　San Marcos
　Stanislaus
Canada College
Chaffey Community College
Chapman University
Christian Heritage College
Citrus College
Coastline Community College
Cogswell Polytechnical College
Coleman College
College of Marin: Kentfield

College of Notre Dame
College of Oceaneering
College of San Mateo
College of the Sequoias
Columbia College: Hollywood
Compton Community College
Contra Costa College
Cosumnes River College
Crafton Hills College
DeVry Institute of Technology: City
　of Industry
Diablo Valley College
Dominican College of San Rafael
Evergreen Valley College
Fashion Institute of Design and
　Merchandising
Foothill College
Fresno Pacific College
Golden Gate University
Heald Business College
　Concord
　San Jose
Holy Names College
Humboldt State University
Humphreys College
ITT Technical Institute: Sacramento
John F. Kennedy University
La Sierra University
Lake Tahoe Community College
Lincoln University
Long Beach City College
Los Medanos College
Marymount College
Master's College
MiraCosta College
Mission College
Modesto Junior College
Monterey Institute of International
　Studies
Moorpark College
Mount St. Mary's College
National University
Otis School of Art and Design
Pacific Christian College
Pacific Oaks College
Palomar College
Patten College
Pepperdine University
Phillips Junior College: Condie
　Campus
Point Loma Nazarene College
Sacramento City College
Saddleback College
St. Mary's College of California
Samuel Merritt College
San Diego City College
San Diego Mesa College
San Diego Miramar College
San Francisco Conservatory of
　Music
San Francisco State University
San Jose City College
Santa Clara University
Santa Monica College
Scripps College
Simpson College
Skyline College
Solano Community College
Sonoma State University
Southern California College
Southern California Institute of
　Architecture
Southwestern College
University of California: Los
　Angeles
University of Judaism
University of the Pacific
University of Redlands
University of San Francisco
University of Southern California
University of West Los Angeles
West Valley College

Whittier College
Woodbury University

Colorado

Adams State College
Aims Community College
Arapahoe Community College
Colorado Christian University
Colorado Institute of Art
Colorado Mountain College
　Alpine Campus
　Spring Valley Campus
　Timberline Campus
Colorado Northwestern Community
　College
Colorado School of Mines
Colorado State University
Colorado Technical College
Community College of Aurora
Denver Institute of Technology
Denver Technical College
Fort Lewis College
Front Range Community College
ITT Technical Institute: Aurora
Lamar Community College
Mesa State College
Metropolitan State College of
　Denver
Morgan Community College
Naropa Institute
Northeastern Junior College
Pikes Peak Community College
Pueblo Community College
Red Rocks Community College
Regis University
Rocky Mountain College of Art &
　Design
Trinidad State Junior College
University of Colorado
　Colorado Springs
　Denver
University of Denver
University of Northern Colorado
University of Southern Colorado
Western State College of Colorado

Connecticut

Albertus Magnus College
Asnuntuck Community-Technical
　College
Briarwood College
Bridgeport Engineering Institute
Capital Community-Technical
　College
Central Connecticut State
　University
Eastern Connecticut State
　University
Gateway Community-Technical
　College
Housatonic Community-Technical
　College
Middlesex Community-Technical
　College
Mitchell College
Norwalk Community-Technical
　College
Quinebaug Valley Community-
　Technical College
Quinnipiac College
Sacred Heart University
St. Joseph College
Teikyo-Post University
Three Rivers Community-Technical
　College
Tunxis Community-Technical
　College
University of Bridgeport
University of Hartford
University of New Haven
Yale University

Delaware

Delaware State College
Delaware Technical and
　Community College
　Southern Campus
　Stanton/Wilmington Campus
　Terry Campus
Goldey-Beacom College
Wesley College
Wilmington College

District of Columbia

American University
Corcoran School of Art
Howard University
Mount Vernon College
Southeastern University
Strayer College
Trinity College
University of the District of
　Columbia

Florida

Art Institute of Fort Lauderdale
Barry University
Bethune-Cookman College
Brevard Community College
Central Florida Community College
Clearwater Christian College
Daytona Beach Community College
Edison Community College
Embry-Riddle Aeronautical
　University
Florida Agricultural and Mechanical
　University
Florida Community College at
　Jacksonville
Florida Institute of Technology
Florida Memorial College
Florida State University
Fort Lauderdale College
Gulf Coast Community College
Hillsborough Community College
Hobe Sound Bible College
Indian River Community College
Jacksonville University
Jones College
Keiser College of Technology
Lake-Sumter Community College
Lynn University
Manatee Community College
Miami-Dade Community College
New England Institute of
　Technology
Nova University
Okaloosa-Walton Community
　College
Palm Beach Atlantic College
Pensacola Junior College
Phillips Junior College: Melbourne
Polk Community College
Ringling School of Art and Design
Rollins College
St. Johns River Community College
St. Leo College
St. Petersburg Junior College
St. Thomas University
Santa Fe Community College
Seminole Community College
South College: Palm Beach Campus
South Florida Community College
Southeastern College of the
　Assemblies of God
Southern College
Tallahassee Community College
Tampa College
Trinity College at Miami
University of Central Florida
University of Florida
University of Miami
University of North Florida
University of South Florida

University of Tampa
University of West Florida
Valencia Community College
Warner Southern College
Webber College

Georgia

Abraham Baldwin Agricultural College
Albany State College
Atlanta Christian College
Augusta College
Brenau University
Brunswick College
Clark Atlanta University
Columbus College
Covenant College
Darton College
DeKalb Technical Institute
DeVry Institute of Technology: Atlanta
Emmanuel College
Fort Valley State College
Gainesville College
Georgia College
Georgia Southern University
Georgia Southwestern College
Gordon College
LaGrange College
Macon College
Meadows College of Business
Mercer University
  Atlanta
  Macon
Morris Brown College
North Georgia College
Oglethorpe University
Savannah College of Art and Design
Savannah Technical Institute
Shorter College
South College
South Georgia College
Southern College of Technology
Thomas College
Waycross College
Wesleyan College
West Georgia College

Hawaii

Hawaii Pacific University
University of Hawaii
  Hawaii Community College
  Hilo
  Honolulu Community College
  Kapiolani Community College
  Kauai Community College
  Manoa
  West Oahu
  Windward Community College

Idaho

Albertson College
Boise State University
College of Southern Idaho
Lewis Clark State College
North Idaho College
Ricks College

Illinois

American Academy of Art
American Conservatory of Music
Aurora University
Barat College
Belleville Area College
Black Hawk College
  East Campus
  Moline
Blackburn College
Bradley University
Carl Sandburg College
Chicago State University
City Colleges of Chicago
  Harold Washington College
  Kennedy-King College
  Malcolm X College
  Olive-Harvey College
College of DuPage
College of Lake County
College of St. Francis
Columbia College
Concordia University
Danville Area Community College
De Paul University
DeVry Institute of Technology
  Addison
  Chicago
Elgin Community College
Elmhurst College
Eureka College
Gem City College
Governors State University
Highland Community College
Illinois Benedictine College
Illinois Central College
Illinois Institute of Technology
International Academy of Merchandising and Design
ITT Technical Institute: Hoffman Estates
Joliet Junior College
Judson College
Kankakee Community College
Kendall College
Kishwaukee College
Lake Land College
Lewis and Clark Community College
Lewis University
Lincoln Land Community College
Loyola University of Chicago
MacMurray College
McHenry County College
McKendree College
Millikin University
Montay College
Moraine Valley Community College
Morrison Institute of Technology
Morton College
National-Louis University
North Central College
Northeastern Illinois University
Oakton Community College
Olivet Nazarene University
Quincy University
Ray College of Design
Richland Community College
Rock Valley College
Rockford College
Roosevelt University
Rosary College
St. Augustine College
St. Xavier University
Sangamon State University
Sauk Valley Community College
School of the Art Institute of Chicago
Shimer College
Southern Illinois University at Edwardsville
Spoon River College
Springfield College in Illinois
Triton College
University of Chicago
VanderCook College of Music
William Rainey Harper College

Indiana

Butler University
Calumet College of St. Joseph
DePauw University
Goshen College
Huntington College
Indiana State University
Indiana University
  Bloomington
  East
  Northwest
  South Bend
Indiana University—Purdue University
  Fort Wayne
  Indianapolis
Indiana Vocational Technical College
  Central Indiana
  Columbus
  Kokomo
  Lafayette
  Northcentral
  Northeast
  Northwest
  Southcentral
  Southwest
  Wabash Valley
  Whitewater
Indiana Wesleyan University
Lutheran College of Health Professions
Marian College
Martin University
Purdue University
  Calumet
  North Central Campus
Rose-Hulman Institute of Technology
St. Francis College
St. Mary-of-the-Woods College
Tri-State University
University of Evansville
University of Indianapolis
University of Southern Indiana
Valparaiso University
Vincennes University

Iowa

American Institute of Business
American Institute of Commerce
Briar Cliff College
Central College
Clarke College
Clinton Community College
Coe College
Des Moines Area Community College
Drake University
Hamilton Technical College
Hawkeye Community College
Indian Hills Community College
Iowa Lakes Community College
Iowa Wesleyan College
Iowa Western Community College
Kirkwood Community College
Luther College
Maharishi International University
Marshalltown Community College
Morningside College
Mount St. Clare College
Muscatine Community College
North Iowa Area Community College
Northeast Iowa Community College
St. Ambrose University
Scott Community College
Simpson College
Teikyo Marycrest University
Teikyo Westmar University
University of Dubuque
Western Iowa Tech Community College
William Penn College

Kansas

Baker University
Barton County Community College
Benedictine College
Bethany College
Brown Mackie College
Butler County Community College
Central College
Coffeyville Community College
Colby Community College
Dodge City Community College
Emporia State University
Fort Hays State University
Fort Scott Community College
Friends University
Highland Community College
Hutchinson Community College
Johnson County Community College
Kansas Newman College
Kansas State University
Labette Community College
MidAmerica Nazarene College
Neosho County Community College
Pittsburg State University
St. Mary College
Seward County Community College
Southwestern College
Tabor College
University of Kansas
  Lawrence
  Medical Center
Washburn University of Topeka
Wichita State University

Kentucky

Ashland Community College
Bellarmine College
Campbellsville College
Eastern Kentucky University
Elizabethtown Community College
Georgetown College
Hopkinsville Community College
Jefferson Community College
Kentucky State University
Lexington Community College
Louisville Technical Institute
Maysville Community College
Midway College
Morehead State University
Murray State University
Northern Kentucky University
Pikeville College
Prestonburg Community College
Spalding University
Sullivan College
Thomas More College
University of Louisville
Western Kentucky University

Louisiana

Dillard University
Grambling State University
Louisiana Tech University
Loyola University
McNeese State University
Nicholls State University
Northeast Louisiana University
Our Lady of Holy Cross College
Southeastern Louisiana University
Southern University in Shreveport
Southern University and Agricultural and Mechanical College
University of New Orleans
University of Southwestern Louisiana

Maine

Andover College
Beal College
Casco Bay College
Central Maine Technical College
Husson College
Maine College of Art
St. Joseph's College

Southern Maine Technical College
Thomas College
Unity College
University of Maine
    Augusta
    Fort Kent
    Machias
    Orono
    Presque Isle
University of New England
University of Southern Maine
Westbrook College

Maryland

Allegany Community College
Anne Arundel Community College
Baltimore City Community College
Baltimore Hebrew University
Baltimore International Culinary College
Bowie State University
Capitol College
Catonsville Community College
Cecil Community College
Charles County Community College
Chesapeake College
College of Notre Dame of Maryland
Coppin State College
Dundalk Community College
Essex Community College
Frederick Community College
Frostburg State University
Hagerstown Business College
Hagerstown Junior College
Harford Community College
Hood College
Howard Community College
Johns Hopkins University: Peabody Conservatory of Music
Loyola College in Maryland
Montgomery College
    Germantown Campus
    Rockville Campus
    Takoma Park Campus
Morgan State University
Mount St. Mary's College
Prince George's Community College
St. Mary's College of Maryland
Towson State University
University of Baltimore
University of Maryland
    Baltimore
    Baltimore County
    College Park
    Eastern Shore
    University College
Villa Julie College
Washington College
Western Maryland College
Wor-Wic Community College

Massachusetts

American International College
Anna Maria College for Men and Women
Atlantic Union College
Babson College
Bentley College
Berklee College of Music
Boston Architectural Center
Boston University
Bradford College
Bridgewater State College
Bristol Community College
Cape Cod Community College
Clark University
Eastern Nazarene College
Elms College
Emerson College
Emmanuel College
Endicott College
Fisher College
Framingham State College
Franklin Institute of Boston
Greenfield Community College
Hebrew College
Holyoke Community College
Lasell College
Marian Court Junior College
Massachusetts Bay Community College
Massasoit Community College
Merrimack College
Middlesex Community College
Montserrat College of Art
Mount Holyoke College
Mount Ida College
Mount Wachusett Community College
New England Conservatory of Music
Newbury College
Nichols College
North Shore Community College
Northeastern University
Northern Essex Community College
Pine Manor College
Quincy College
Quinsigamond Community College
Roxbury Community College
School of the Museum of Fine Arts
Springfield Technical Community College
Suffolk University
Tufts University
University of Massachusetts at Dartmouth
Wentworth Institute of Technology
Western New England College
Westfield State College
Wheelock College
Worcester State College

Michigan

Alma College
Alpena Community College
Andrews University
Aquinas College
Baker College
    Auburn Hills
    Cadillac
    Flint
    Muskegon
    Owosso
    Port Huron
Center for Creative Studies: College of Art and Design
Charles Stewart Mott Community College
Cleary College
Concordia College
Davenport College of Business
Delta College
Detroit College of Business
Eastern Michigan University
Glen Oaks Community College
GMI Engineering & Management Institute
Grace Bible College
Grand Rapids Baptist College and Seminary
Grand Rapids Community College
Grand Valley State University
Great Lakes Junior College of Business
Henry Ford Community College
Highland Park Community College
Jackson Community College
Jordan College
Kalamazoo Valley Community College
Kellogg Community College
Kendall College of Art and Design
Kirtland Community College
Lake Michigan College
Macomb Community College
Madonna University
Marygrove College
Michigan Christian College
Mid Michigan Community College
Monroe County Community College
Montcalm Community College
Muskegon Community College
Northwestern Michigan College
Oakland Community College
Olivet College
Sacred Heart Major Seminary
Saginaw Valley State University
St. Clair County Community College
St. Mary's College
Schoolcraft College
Southwestern Michigan College
Spring Arbor College
Suomi College
University of Detroit Mercy
University of Michigan
    Dearborn
    Flint
Walsh College of Accountancy and Business Administration
Washtenaw Community College
Wayne County Community College
Wayne State University
West Shore Community College
Western Michigan University

Minnesota

Augsburg College
Austin Community College
Bethany Lutheran College
College of St. Benedict
College of St. Catherine: St. Catherine Campus
College of St. Scholastica
Concordia College: St. Paul
Lakewood Community College
Minneapolis Community College
Normandale Community College
North Central Bible College
North Hennepin Community College
Northwestern College
Pillsbury Baptist Bible College
Rochester Community College
St. Paul Technical College
Willmar Technical College

Mississippi

Alcorn State University
Belhaven College
Hinds Community College
Jackson State University
Magnolia Bible College
Millsaps College
Mississippi Gulf Coast Community College
    Jackson County Campus
    Jefferson Davis Campus
    Perkinston
Mississippi State University
Mississippi University for Women
Northwest Mississippi Community College
Pearl River Community College
Rust College
Tougaloo College
University of Mississippi
University of Southern Mississippi
William Carey College

Missouri

Avila College
Calvary Bible College
Central Methodist College
Central Missouri State University
Crowder College
DeVry Institute of Technology: Kansas City
East Central College
Evangel College
Fontbonne College
Hannibal-LaGrange College
Harris Stowe State College
ITT Technical Institute: St. Louis
Jefferson College
Kemper Military School and College
Lincoln University
Lindenwood College
Longview Community College
Maple Woods Community College
Maryville University
Missouri Baptist College
Missouri Southern State College
Missouri Valley College
Missouri Western State College
Moberly Area Community College
Northeast Missouri State University
Northwest Missouri State University
Park College
Penn Valley Community College
Phillips Junior College
Ranken Technical College
Research College of Nursing
Rockhurst College
St. Charles County Community College
St. Louis Community College
    Florissant Valley
    Forest Park
    Meramec
Southeast Missouri State University
Southwest Baptist University
Southwest Missouri State University
State Fair Community College
Stephens College
Three Rivers Community College
University of Missouri
    Columbia
    Kansas City
    Rolla
    St. Louis
Webster University
William Jewell College
William Woods College

Montana

College of Great Falls
Flathead Valley Community College
Montana State University
University of Montana

Nebraska

Bellevue College
Central Community College
Chadron State College
Clarkson College
College of St. Mary
Concordia College
Creighton University
Dana College
Doane College
Lincoln School of Commerce
Metropolitan Community College
Midland Lutheran College
Nebraska Christian College
Nebraska Methodist College of Nursing and Allied Health
Nebraska Wesleyan University
Northeast Community College
Peru State College

Tuition payment plans: credit card payment

Southeast Community College
  Beatrice Campus
  Lincoln Campus
  Milford Campus
Union College
University of Nebraska Medical Center
Wayne State College
Western Nebraska Community College: Scottsbluff Campus
York College

Nevada
Northern Nevada Community College
Sierra Nevada College
Truckee Meadows Community College
University of Nevada
  Las Vegas
  Reno
Western Nevada Community College

New Hampshire
Colby-Sawyer College
Daniel Webster College
Franklin Pierce College
Hesser College
Keene State College
New England College
New Hampshire Technical College
  Berlin
  Claremont
  Laconia
  Manchester
  Nashua
  Stratham
New Hampshire Technical Institute
Notre Dame College
Rivier College
University of New Hampshire at Manchester

New Jersey
Atlantic Community College
Bergen Community College
Berkeley College of Business
Bloomfield College
Brookdale Community College
Burlington County College
Caldwell College
Camden County College
Centenary College
Cumberland County College
Drew University
Essex County College
Fairleigh Dickinson University
  Edward Williams College
  Madison
Felician College
Gloucester County College
Hudson County Community College
Katharine Gibbs School
Kean College of New Jersey
Mercer County Community College
Monmouth College
Montclair State College
New Jersey Institute of Technology
Passaic County Community College
Ramapo College of New Jersey
Raritan Valley Community College
Rider College
Rowan College of New Jersey
St. Peter's College
Salem Community College
Seton Hall University
Stockton State College
Thomas Edison State College
Union County College
Upsala College

Westminster Choir College School of Music of Rider College
William Paterson College of New Jersey

New Mexico
Albuquerque Technical-Vocational Institute
Clovis Community College
College of Santa Fe
College of the Southwest
Dona Ana Branch Community College of New Mexico State University
Eastern New Mexico University
  Portales
  Roswell Campus
New Mexico Highlands University
New Mexico Institute of Mining and Technology
New Mexico Junior College
New Mexico Military Institute
New Mexico State University
Northern New Mexico Community College
Parks College
San Juan College
Santa Fe Community College
University of New Mexico
Western New Mexico University

New York
Adelphi University
Adirondack Community College
American Academy of Dramatic Arts
Audrey Cohen College
Barnard College
Berkeley College
Bramson ORT Technical Institute
Broome Community College
Bryant & Stratton Business Institute: Albany
Canisius College
Cayuga County Community College
Cazenovia College
Central City Business Institute
City University of New York
  City College
  John Jay College of Criminal Justice
  Queens College
  Queensborough Community College
Clinton Community College
Cochran School of Nursing-St. John's Riverside Hospital
College of Aeronautics
College of Insurance
College of Mount St. Vincent
College of New Rochelle
  New Rochelle
  School of New Resources
College of St. Rose
Columbia University
  Columbia College
  School of Engineering and Applied Science
  School of General Studies
  School of Nursing
Columbia-Greene Community College
Corning Community College
Daemen College
Dominican College of Blauvelt
Dowling College
Dutchess Community College
D'Youville College
Eastman School of Music of the University of Rochester

Erie Community College
  North Campus
  South Campus
Eugene Lang College/New School for Social Research
Fashion Institute of Technology
Finger Lakes Community College
Fordham University
Fulton-Montgomery Community College
Genesee Community College
Herkimer County Community College
Hilbert College
Hofstra University
Hudson Valley Community College
Iona College
Ithaca College
Jamestown Community College
Jefferson Community College
Keuka College
King's College
Long Island College Hospital School of Nursing
Long Island University
  Brooklyn Campus
  C. W. Post Campus
  Southampton Campus
Manhattan College
Manhattanville College
Marist College
Marymount College
Marymount Manhattan College
Mater Dei College
Medaille College
Mercy College
Mohawk Valley Community College
Molloy College
Monroe Community College
Mount St. Mary College
Nazareth College of Rochester
New York Institute of Technology
New York School of Interior Design
New York University
Niagara County Community College
Niagara University
North Country Community College
Nyack College
Onondaga Community College
Orange County Community College
Pace University
  College of White Plains
  New York
  Pleasantville/Briarcliff
Paul Smith's College
Phillips Beth Israel School of Nursing
Polytechnic University
  Brooklyn
  Long Island Campus
Pratt Institute
Rensselaer Polytechnic Institute
Roberts Wesleyan College
Rochester Institute of Technology
Rockland Community College
Russell Sage College
Sage Junior College of Albany
St. Francis College
St. John Fisher College
St. John's University
St. Joseph's College
  Brooklyn
  Suffolk Campus
St. Thomas Aquinas College
Schenectady County Community College
School of Visual Arts
Siena College

State University of New York
  Albany
  Binghamton
  Buffalo
  Purchase
  Stony Brook
  College of Agriculture and Technology at Cobleskill
  College of Agriculture and Technology at Morrisville
  College at Brockport
  College at Buffalo
  College at Cortland
  College at Fredonia
  College at Geneseo
  College at New Paltz
  College at Old Westbury
  College at Oneonta
  College at Plattsburgh
  College at Potsdam
  College of Technology at Alfred
  College of Technology at Canton
  College of Technology at Delhi
  College of Technology at Farmingdale
  Institute of Technology at Utica/Rome
  Oswego
Suffolk County Community College
  Selden
  Western Campus
Sullivan County Community College
Taylor Business Institute
Tompkins-Cortland Community College
Touro College
Trocaire College
Ulster County Community College
University of Rochester
University of the State of New York: Regents College
Utica College of Syracuse University
Utica School of Commerce
Villa Maria College of Buffalo
Wagner College
Wells College
Westchester Business Institute
Westchester Community College
William Smith College

North Carolina
Alamance Community College
Anson Community College
Appalachian State University
Belmont Abbey College
Bennett College
Brevard College
Brunswick Community College
Campbell University
Catawba College
Catawba Valley Community College
Central Piedmont Community College
Davidson County Community College
East Carolina University
East Coast Bible College
Elon College
Fayetteville State University
Fayetteville Technical Community College
Gardner-Webb University
Gaston College
Greensboro College
John Wesley College
Johnson C. Smith University
Lenoir-Rhyne College
Louisburg College

283

Tuition payment plans: credit card payment

Methodist College
Mount Olive College
Nash Community College
North Carolina Agricultural and Technical State University
North Carolina Central University
Pfeiffer College
Piedmont Bible College
Queens College
Roanoke-Chowan Community College
Sandhills Community College
University of North Carolina
    Chapel Hill
    Charlotte
    Greensboro
    Wilmington
Warren Wilson College

North Dakota

Trinity Bible College
University of North Dakota

Ohio

Antioch School for Adult and Experiential Learning
Antonelli Institute of Art and Photography
Art Academy of Cincinnati
Ashland University
Baldwin-Wallace College
Bliss College
Bluffton College
Bowling Green State University
    Bowling Green
    Firelands College
Bradford School
Capital University
Central Ohio Technical College
Central State University
Chatfield College
Cincinnati Bible College and Seminary
Circleville Bible College
Clark State Community College
Cleveland Institute of Art
Cleveland Institute of Electronics
Cleveland Institute of Music
College of Mount St. Joseph
Columbus College of Art and Design
Columbus State Community College
Cuyahoga Community College
    Eastern Campus
    Metropolitan Campus
    Western Campus
Davis Junior College of Business
Defiance College
DeVry Institute of Technology:
    Columbus
Dyke College
Edison State Community College
Franciscan University of Steubenville
Franklin University
God's Bible School and College
Heidelberg College
Hiram College
Hocking Technical College
ITT Technical Institute
    Dayton
    Youngstown
John Carroll University
Kent State University
    Ashtabula Regional Campus
    East Liverpool Regional Campus
    Kent
    Salem Regional Campus
    Stark Campus
    Trumbull Regional Campus
    Tuscarawas Campus

Kenyon College
Kettering College of Medical Arts
Lake Erie College
Lakeland Community College
Lima Technical College
Lorain County Community College
Lourdes College
Malone College
Marietta College
Marion Technical College
Miami University
    Hamilton Campus
    Middletown Campus
Miami-Jacobs College
Mount Union College
Muskingum College
North Central Technical College
Northwest Technical College
Northwestern College
Ohio Dominican College
Ohio Northern University
Ohio State University
    Agricultural Technical Institute
    Columbus Campus
    Lima Campus
    Mansfield Campus
    Marion Campus
    Newark Campus
Ohio University
    Athens
    Chillicothe Campus
    Eastern Campus
    Southern Campus at Ironton
    Zanesville Campus
Ohio Valley Business College
Ohio Wesleyan University
Otterbein College
Owens Technical College
    Findlay Campus
    Toledo
Sinclair Community College
Southern State Community College
Stark Technical College
Terra Technical College
Tiffin University
Union Institute
University of Akron
University of Cincinnati
    Access Colleges
    Cincinnati
    Clermont College
    Raymond Walters College
University of Dayton
University of Toledo
Urbana University
Ursuline College
Virginia Marti College of Fashion and Art
Wilberforce University
Wilmington College
Wright State University
    Dayton
    Lake Campus
Xavier University
Youngstown State University

Oklahoma

Bacone College
Bartlesville Wesleyan College
Cameron University
Connors State College
East Central University
Langston University
Northeastern Oklahoma Agricultural and Mechanical College
Northeastern State University
Oklahoma Baptist University
Oklahoma Panhandle State University

Oklahoma State University
    Oklahoma City
    Stillwater
Oral Roberts University
Phillips University
Redlands Community College
Rogers State College
Rose State College
Southeastern Oklahoma State University
Southern Nazarene University
Southwestern Oklahoma State University
Tulsa Junior College
University of Oklahoma
University of Science and Arts of Oklahoma
University of Tulsa
Western Oklahoma State College

Oregon

Bassist College
Central Oregon Community College
Chemeketa Community College
Clackamas Community College
Clatsop Community College
Concordia College
Eastern Oregon State College
ITT Technical Institute: Portland
Lane Community College
Lewis and Clark College
Linfield College
Linn-Benton Community College
Marylhurst College
Oregon Health Sciences University
Oregon Institute of Technology
Portland Community College
Portland State University
Rogue Community College
Southern Oregon State College
Treasure Valley Community College
University of Portland
Warner Pacific College
Western Baptist College
Western Oregon State College
Willamette University

Pennsylvania

Albright College
Allentown College of St. Francis de Sales
Alvernia College
American Institute of Design
Art Institute of Pittsburgh
Baptist Bible College of Pennsylvania
Beaver College
Bucks County Community College
Butler County Community College
Cabrini College
Carlow College
Cedar Crest College
Chatham College
Chestnut Hill College
Cheyney University of Pennsylvania
Clarion University of Pennsylvania
Community College of Allegheny County
    Allegheny Campus
    North Campus
    South Campus
Community College of Beaver County
Community College of Philadelphia
Delaware County Community College
Delaware Valley College
Duquesne University
East Stroudsburg University of Pennsylvania
Eastern College
Elizabethtown College

Gannon University
Gratz College
Gwynedd-Mercy College
Holy Family College
ICS Center for Degree Studies
Johnson Technical Institute
King's College
Kutztown University of Pennsylvania
La Roche College
La Salle University
Lackawanna Junior College
Lebanon Valley College of Pennsylvania
Lehigh County Community College
Lincoln University
Luzerne County Community College
Manor Junior College
Mansfield University of Pennsylvania
Marywood College
Mercyhurst College
Millersville University of Pennsylvania
Montgomery County Community College
Moore College of Art and Design
Mount Aloysius College
National Education Center: Vale Tech Campus
Neumann College
Northampton County Area Community College
Pennsylvania Institute of Technology
Philadelphia College of Textiles and Science
Pittsburgh Institute of Mortuary Science
Pittsburgh Technical Institute
Point Park College
Reading Area Community College
Robert Morris College
Rosemont College
St. Joseph's University
Seton Hill College
Slippery Rock University of Pennsylvania
Temple University
Thomas Jefferson University: College of Allied Health Sciences
Triangle Tech
    Erie School
    Greensburg School
    Pittsburgh Campus
University of the Arts
University of Pittsburgh
    Bradford
    Greensburg
University of Scranton
Valley Forge Christian College
Villanova University
West Chester University of Pennsylvania
Widener University
Wilkes University
Wilson College

Puerto Rico

American University of Puerto Rico
Caribbean University
Colegio Universitario del Este
Inter American University of Puerto Rico
    Arecibo Campus
    Guayama Campus
    San German Campus
Pontifical Catholic University of Puerto Rico
Turabo University
Universidad Metropolitana

Tuition payment plans: credit card payment

Universidad Politecnica de Puerto Rico
University of Puerto Rico: Ponce Technological University College
University of the Sacred Heart

Rhode Island

Bryant College
Community College of Rhode Island
Johnson & Wales University
New England Institute of Technology
Rhode Island College
Roger Williams University
Salve Regina University

South Carolina

Central Carolina Technical College
Central Wesleyan College
Chesterfield-Marlboro Technical College
The Citadel
Claflin College
Clemson University
Coker College
College of Charleston
Columbia Junior College of Business
Converse College
Florence-Darlington Technical College
Francis Marion University
Greenville Technical College
Horry-Georgetown Technical College
Lander University
Limestone College
Midlands Technical College
Newberry College
North Greenville College
Spartanburg Technical College
Technical College of the Lowcountry
Tri-County Technical College
Trident Technical College
University of South Carolina
  Aiken
  Beaufort
  Coastal Carolina College
  Columbia
  Salkehatchie Regional Campus
  Spartanburg
  Sumter
  Union
Winthrop University
York Technical College

South Dakota

Augustana College
Black Hills State University
Dakota State University
Dakota Wesleyan University
Kilian Community College
National College
Northern State University
Sioux Falls College
South Dakota State University
University of South Dakota

Tennessee

Aquinas Junior College
Austin Peay State University
Belmont University
Carson-Newman College
Chattanooga State Technical Community College
Christian Brothers University
Cleveland State Community College
Crichton College
Draughons Junior College of Business: Nashville

Dyersburg State Community College
East Tennessee State University
Fisk University
Freed-Hardeman University
King College
Knoxville College
Lee College
LeMoyne-Owen College
Lincoln Memorial University
Maryville College
Memphis College of Art
Memphis State University
Middle Tennessee State University
Milligan College
Nashville State Technical Institute
Northeast State Technical Community College
Pellissippi State Technical Community College
Roane State Community College
Shelby State Community College
Southern College of Seventh-day Adventists
State Technical Institute at Memphis
Tennessee State University
Tennessee Technological University
Tennessee Wesleyan College
Tusculum College
University of the South
University of Tennessee
  Chattanooga
  Knoxville
  Martin
  Memphis
Volunteer State Community College
Walters State Community College

Texas

Amarillo College
Angelina College
Arlington Baptist College
Brazosport College
Brookhaven College
Cedar Valley College
Central Texas College
Cisco Junior College
Collin County Community College District
Concordia Lutheran College
Cooke County College
Corpus Christi State University
Dallas Baptist University
Dallas Christian College
Del Mar College
DeVry Institute of Technology: Irving
East Texas Baptist University
Eastfield College
El Centro College
El Paso Community College
Galveston College
Grayson County College
Hardin-Simmons University
Houston Baptist University
Houston Community College
Howard College
Howard Payne University
Huston-Tillotson College
Incarnate Word College
ITT Technical Institute: Houston
Jarvis Christian College
Lamar University—Beaumont
Laredo State University
Lee College
Lubbock Christian University
McMurry University
Midwestern State University
Mountain View College
Navarro College
North Lake College

Northeast Texas Community College
Odessa College
Our Lady of the Lake University of San Antonio
Prairie View A&M University
Richland College
St. Edward's University
St. Mary's University
St. Philip's College
Sam Houston State University
San Antonio College
San Jacinto College: North
South Plains College
Southwest Texas State University
Southwestern Assemblies of God College
Southwestern Christian College
Tarleton State University
Temple Junior College
Texas A&I University
Texas College
Texas Southern University
Texas Tech University
Texas Wesleyan University
Texas Woman's University
Tyler Junior College
University of Dallas
University of Houston: Downtown
University of Mary Hardin-Baylor
University of St. Thomas
University of Texas
  Arlington
  Dallas
  El Paso
  Permian Basin
  San Antonio
  Tyler
Wayland Baptist University
Weatherford College

Utah

LDS Business College
Phillips Junior College: Salt Lake City Campus
Salt Lake Community College
Stevens-Henager College of Business
University of Utah
Utah Valley Community College
Weber State University

Vermont

Burlington College
Castleton State College
Champlain College
College of St. Joseph in Vermont
Community College of Vermont
Goddard College
Johnson State College
Lyndon State College
Marlboro College
New England Culinary Institute
Norwich University
St. Michael's College
School for International Training
Southern Vermont College
Trinity College of Vermont
University of Vermont

Virginia

Blue Ridge Community College
Central Virginia Community College
Christopher Newport University
College of Health Sciences
College of William and Mary
Dabney S. Lancaster Community College
Danville Community College
Eastern Shore Community College
Ferrum College
George Mason University

Hampton University
J. Sargeant Reynolds Community College
James Madison University
John Tyler Community College
Liberty University
Longwood College
Lord Fairfax Community College
Mary Baldwin College
Mary Washington College
Marymount University
Mountain Empire Community College
New River Community College
Norfolk State University
Northern Virginia Community College
Old Dominion University
Patrick Henry Community College
Paul D. Camp Community College
Piedmont Virginia Community College
Rappahannock Community College
Richard Bland College
St. Paul's College
Shenandoah University
Southern Virginia College for Women
Southside Virginia Community College
Southwest Virginia Community College
Tidewater Community College
Virginia Commonwealth University
Virginia Intermont College
Virginia Polytechnic Institute and State University
Virginia State University
Virginia Union University
Virginia Wesleyan College
Virginia Western Community College
Wytheville Community College

Washington

Art Institute of Seattle
Bellevue Community College
Big Bend Community College
Central Washington University
Centralia College
City University
Clark College
Cogswell College North
Columbia Basin College
Cornish College of the Arts
Eastern Washington University
Edmonds Community College
Everett Community College
Evergreen State College
Gonzaga University
Green River Community College
Heritage College
Highline Community College
Lower Columbia College
North Seattle Community College
Northwest College of the Assemblies of God
Olympic College
Pacific Lutheran University
Peninsula College
Pierce College
Puget Sound Christian College
St. Martin's College
Seattle Central Community College
Seattle Pacific University
Seattle University
Shoreline Community College
Skagit Valley College
South Puget Sound Community College
South Seattle Community College
Spokane Community College

Tuition payment plans: credit card payment

Spokane Falls Community College
Tacoma Community College
Walla Walla College
Walla Walla Community College
Wenatchee Valley College
Western Washington University
Whatcom Community College
Whitworth College

West Virginia
Alderson-Broaddus College
Bluefield State College
College of West Virginia
Davis and Elkins College
University of Charleston

Wisconsin
Alverno College
Carroll College
Fox Valley Technical College
Lakeland College
Lakeshore Technical College
Madison Area Technical College
Madison Junior College of Business
Marquette University
Moraine Park Technical College
Mount Senario College
Northeast Wisconsin Technical College
Northland College
St. Norbert College
Stratton College
University of Wisconsin: Stout
Viterbo College
Waukesha County Technical College

Wyoming
Casper College
Central Wyoming College
Northwest College

American Samoa, Caroline Islands, Guam, Marianas, Virgin Islands
Guam Community College

France
American University of Paris

Mexico
Sistema Instituto Tecnologico y de Estudios Superiores de Monterrey

Tuition payment by installments

Alabama
Alabama State University
Auburn University at Montgomery
Birmingham-Southern College
Concordia College
Faulkner University
Huntingdon College
International Bible College
Judson College
Livingston University
Marion Military Institute
Miles College
Selma University
Southeastern Bible College
Stillman College
Talladega College
Trenholm State Technical College
Tuskegee University
University of Alabama
University of Montevallo

Virginia College
Walker College

Alaska
Alaska Bible College
University of Alaska
 Fairbanks
 Southeast

Arizona
American Indian Bible College
Arizona College of the Bible
DeVry Institute of Technology: Phoenix
Gateway Community College
Grand Canyon University
ITT Technical Institute
 Phoenix
 Tucson
Navajo Community College
Prescott College
South Mountain Community College
Southwestern College
Western International University

Arkansas
Arkansas Baptist College
Arkansas College
Arkansas State University
Arkansas Tech University
Central Baptist College
Harding University
Hendrix College
John Brown University
Mississippi County Community College
North Arkansas Community/Technical College
Ouachita Baptist University
Philander Smith College
Phillips County Community College
Rich Mountain Community College
Shorter College
South Arkansas Community College
Southern Arkansas University
 Magnolia
 Technical Branch
University of Arkansas
University of Arkansas
 Little Rock
 Pine Bluff
University of the Ozarks
Westark Community College
Williams Baptist College

California
Academy of Art College
American Armenian International College
American College for the Applied Arts: Los Angeles
Antelope Valley College
Antioch Southern California at Los Angeles
Armstrong University
Art Center College of Design
Art Institute of Southern California
Azusa Pacific University
Barstow College
Bethany College
Biola University
Brooks College
Brooks Institute of Photography
California Baptist College
California College of Arts and Crafts
California College for Health Sciences
California Institute of Technology
California Lutheran University

California State Polytechnic University: Pomona
California State University
 Bakersfield
 Chico
 Hayward
 Stanislaus
Canada College
Central California Commercial College
Cerro Coso Community College
Chabot College
Chapman University
Charles R. Drew University: College of Allied Health
Christian Heritage College
Claremont McKenna College
Cogswell Polytechnical College
College of Notre Dame
College of Oceaneering
College of San Mateo
College of the Sequoias
Columbia College: Hollywood
Compton Community College
Cosumnes River College
DeVry Institute of Technology: City of Industry
Dominican College of San Rafael
Dominican School of Philosophy and Theology
Fashion Institute of Design and Merchandising
Feather River College
Fresno Pacific College
Golden Gate University
Harvey Mudd College
Heald Business College
 Concord
 San Jose
Hebrew Union College: Jewish Institute of Religion
Holy Names College
Humphreys College
ITT Technical Institute: Sacramento
John F. Kennedy University
Kelsey-Jenney College
La Sierra University
Lassen College
LIFE Bible College
Loyola Marymount University
Marymount College
Master's College
Menlo College
Mills College
Mission College
Monterey Institute of International Studies
Monterey Peninsula College
Mount St. Mary's College
Mount San Jacinto College
Napa Valley College
New College of California
Occidental College
Otis School of Art and Design
Pacific Christian College
Pacific Oaks College
Pacific Union College
Patten College
Pepperdine University
Phillips Junior College
 Condie Campus
 Fresno Campus
Pitzer College
Point Loma Nazarene College
Pomona College
Porterville College
Sacramento City College
St. Mary's College of California
Samuel Merritt College
San Diego State University
San Francisco Art Institute

San Francisco Conservatory of Music
San Francisco State University
San Jose Christian College
Santa Clara University
Scripps College
Sierra College
Simpson College
Southern California College
Stanford University
Taft College
Thomas Aquinas College
United States International University
University of California
 Berkeley
 Santa Cruz
University of Judaism
University of the Pacific
University of Redlands
University of San Diego
University of San Francisco
University of Southern California
University of West Los Angeles
Victor Valley College
Westmont College
Whittier College
Woodbury University
Yuba College

Colorado
Adams State College
Arapahoe Community College
Bel-Rea Institute of Animal Technology
Colorado Christian University
Colorado College
Colorado Institute of Art
Colorado Northwestern Community College
Colorado School of Mines
Colorado State University
Colorado Technical College
Denver Institute of Technology
Denver Technical College
Fort Lewis College
ITT Technical Institute: Aurora
Lamar Community College
National College
Northeastern Junior College
Otero Junior College
Parks Junior College
Red Rocks Community College
Regis University
Rocky Mountain College of Art & Design
Trinidad State Junior College
University of Colorado
 Colorado Springs
 Denver
University of Denver
University of Northern Colorado
Western State College of Colorado

Connecticut
Albertus Magnus College
Briarwood College
Bridgeport Engineering Institute
Connecticut College
Eastern Connecticut State University
Mitchell College
Norwalk Community-Technical College
Paier College of Art
Quinnipiac College
Sacred Heart University
St. Joseph College
Teikyo-Post University
Trinity College
University of Bridgeport
University of Hartford

Tuition payment plans: installment payment

University of New Haven
Wesleyan University
Yale University

Delaware

Delaware State College
Delaware Technical and
 Community College: Southern
 Campus
Goldey-Beacom College
University of Delaware
Wesley College
Wilmington College

District of Columbia

American University
Catholic University of America
Corcoran School of Art
Gallaudet University
George Washington University
Georgetown University
Mount Vernon College
Oblate College
Strayer College
Trinity College
University of the District of
 Columbia

Florida

Art Institute of Fort Lauderdale
Barry University
Brevard Community College
Clearwater Christian College
Flagler Career Institute
Florida Atlantic University
Florida Baptist Theological College
Florida Bible College
Florida Christian College
Florida College
Florida Memorial College
Florida Southern College
Florida State University
Fort Lauderdale College
Hobe Sound Bible College
Jacksonville University
Keiser College of Technology
National Education Center: Bauder
 Campus
New England Institute of
 Technology
North Florida Junior College
Nova University
Okaloosa-Walton Community
 College
Palm Beach Atlantic College
Phillips Junior College: Melbourne
Rollins College
St. John Vianney College Seminary
South College: Palm Beach Campus
Southeastern College of the
 Assemblies of God
Southern College
Stetson University
Tampa College
Trinity College at Miami
University of Miami
University of South Florida
University of Tampa
University of West Florida
Warner Southern College
Webber College

Georgia

Agnes Scott College
Atlanta Christian College
Bauder College
Brenau University
Clark Atlanta University
Covenant College
DeVry Institute of Technology:
 Atlanta
Emory University

Georgia Institute of Technology
LaGrange College
Meadows College of Business
Morris Brown College
Oglethorpe University
Paine College
Reinhardt College
Savannah College of Art and
 Design
Shorter College
South College
Thomas College
Toccoa Falls College
Truett-McConnell College
Wesleyan College
Young Harris College

Hawaii

Hawaii Pacific University

Idaho

Albertson College
Boise Bible College

Illinois

American Conservatory of Music
Augustana College
Aurora University
Barat College
Belleville Area College
Black Hawk College
Blackburn College
Blessing-Reiman College of Nursing
Bradley University
Carl Sandburg College
City Colleges of Chicago
 Harold Washington College
 Kennedy-King College
 Malcolm X College
College of Lake County
College of St. Francis
Columbia College
Concordia University
Danville Area Community College
De Paul University
DeVry Institute of Technology
 Addison
 Chicago
Eastern Illinois University
East-West University
Elgin Community College
Elmhurst College
Governors State University
Greenville College
Harrington Institute of Interior
 Design
Illinois Benedictine College
Illinois College
Illinois Institute of Technology
Illinois State University
Illinois Wesleyan University
International Academy of
 Merchandising and Design
ITT Technical Institute: Hoffman
 Estates
Kaskaskia College
Kendall College
Kishwaukee College
Knox College
Lake Forest College
Lakeview College of Nursing
Lewis and Clark Community
 College
Lewis University
Lexington Institute of Hospitality
 Careers
Lincoln Christian College and
 Seminary
Lincoln College
Loyola University of Chicago
MacCormac Junior College
MacMurray College

McHenry County College
Millikin University
Monmouth College
Montay College
Moraine Valley Community College
Morrison Institute of Technology
National College of Chiropractic
National-Louis University
North Central College
North Park College
Northeastern Illinois University
Northern Illinois University
Northwestern University
Olivet Nazarene University
Parks College of St. Louis
 University
Principia College
Quincy University
Ray College of Design
Richland Community College
Robert Morris College: Chicago
Rockford College
Roosevelt University
Rosary College
St. Augustine College
St. Francis Medical Center College
 of Nursing
St. Joseph College of Nursing
St. Xavier University
School of the Art Institute of
 Chicago
Shawnee Community College
Shimer College
Southeastern Illinois College
Southern Illinois University
 Carbondale
 Edwardsville
Spoon River College
Springfield College in Illinois
State Community College
Trinity Christian College
Trinity College
University of Chicago
University of Illinois
 Chicago
 Urbana-Champaign
VanderCook College of Music
West Suburban College of Nursing
Western Illinois University
Wheaton College
William Rainey Harper College

Indiana

Anderson University
Ball State University
Bethel College
Butler University
Calumet College of St. Joseph
Earlham College
Franklin College
Goshen College
Grace College
Hanover College
Huntington College
Indiana Vocational Technical
 College
 Columbus
 Kokomo
 Wabash Valley
 Whitewater
Indiana Wesleyan University
ITT Technical Institute:
 Indianapolis
Lutheran College of Health
 Professions
Manchester College
Marian College
Martin University
Mid-America College of Funeral
 Service

Purdue University
 Calumet
 West Lafayette
St. Francis College
St. Mary-of-the-Woods College
St. Meinrad College
Taylor University
University of Evansville
University of Indianapolis
University of Notre Dame
University of Southern Indiana
Vincennes University
Wabash College

Iowa

American Institute of Commerce
Briar Cliff College
Buena Vista College
Central College
Clarke College
Coe College
Cornell College
Des Moines Area Community
 College
Divine Word College
Drake University
Ellsworth Community College
Emmaus Bible College
Faith Baptist Bible College and
 Theological Seminary
Graceland College
Grinnell College
Hamilton Technical College
Hawkeye Community College
Indian Hills Community College
Iowa Central Community College
Iowa Lakes Community College
Iowa State University
Iowa Western Community College
Kirkwood Community College
Loras College
Luther College
Maharishi International University
Marshalltown Community College
Morningside College
Mount Mercy College
Mount St. Clare College
North Iowa Area Community
 College
Northwest Iowa Community
 College
Northwestern College
St. Ambrose University
Simpson College
Southeastern Community College:
 South Campus
Teikyo Marycrest University
Teikyo Westmar University
University of Dubuque
University of Iowa
University of Northern Iowa
Upper Iowa University
Vennard College
Waldorf College
Wartburg College
William Penn College

Kansas

Baker University
Benedictine College
Bethany College
Bethel College
Brown Mackie College
Central College
Coffeyville Community College
Dodge City Community College
Donnelly College
Emporia State University
Fort Scott Community College
Friends University
Hesston College
Independence Community College

287

Tuition payment plans: installment payment

Kansas Newman College
Kansas Wesleyan University
Manhattan Christian College
MidAmerica Nazarene College
Neosho County Community College
Ottawa University
Pratt Community College
St. Mary College
Seward County Community College
Southwestern College
Sterling College
Tabor College
Washburn University of Topeka
Wichita State University

Kentucky
Alice Lloyd College
Asbury College
Bellarmine College
Brescia College
Campbellsville College
Centre College
Cumberland College
Eastern Kentucky University
Georgetown College
Institute of Electronic Technology
Kentucky State University
Kentucky Wesleyan College
Lees College
Lindsey Wilson College
Louisville Technical Institute
Mid-Continent Baptist Bible College
Midway College
Morehead State University
Murray State University
Owensboro Junior College of Business
Pikeville College
RETS Electronic Institute
Southeast Community College
Spalding University
Sue Bennett College
Sullivan College
Transylvania University
Union College
University of Louisville

Louisiana
Centenary College of Louisiana
Dillard University
Louisiana College
Northwestern State University
Nunez Community College
St. Joseph Seminary College
Southeastern Louisiana University
Southern University in Shreveport
Xavier University of Louisiana

Maine
Beal College
Bowdoin College
Casco Bay College
Central Maine Technical College
Colby College
College of the Atlantic
Eastern Maine Technical College
Husson College
Maine College of Art
Maine Maritime Academy
Southern Maine Technical College
Thomas College
Unity College
University of Maine
  Augusta
  Farmington
  Fort Kent
  Machias
  Orono
  Presque Isle
University of New England
University of Southern Maine

Maryland
Baltimore City Community College
Baltimore International Culinary College
Bowie State University
Capitol College
Cecil Community College
Columbia Union College
Dundalk Community College
Goucher College
Hagerstown Business College
Harford Community College
Hood College
Johns Hopkins University
Montgomery College
  Germantown Campus
  Rockville Campus
  Takoma Park Campus
Mount St. Mary's College
Ner Israel Rabbinical College
St. John's College
Sojourner-Douglass College
University of Maryland
  Baltimore
  College Park
Villa Julie College
Washington College
Western Maryland College

Massachusetts
American International College
Anna Maria College for Men and Women
Aquinas College at Newton
Assumption College
Atlantic Union College
Babson College
Bay Path College
Bay State College
Bentley College
Boston Architectural Center
Boston College
Boston Conservatory
Boston University
Brandeis University
Bridgewater State College
Clark University
Dean Junior College
Elms College
Emerson College
Emmanuel College
Endicott College
Essex Agricultural and Technical Institute
Fisher College
Fitchburg State College
Framingham State College
Franklin Institute of Boston
Gordon College
Hampshire College
Harvard and Radcliffe Colleges
Hebrew College
Hellenic College
Katharine Gibbs School
Marian Court Junior College
Massachusetts Institute of Technology
Massasoit Community College
Merrimack College
Middlesex Community College
Montserrat College of Art
Mount Holyoke College
Mount Ida College
Newbury College
Nichols College
North Adams State College
Northeastern University
Pine Manor College
Regis College
St. Hyacinth College and Seminary
Salem State College
School of the Museum of Fine Arts

Simon's Rock College of Bard
Smith College
Springfield College
Suffolk University
Tufts University
University of Massachusetts
  Amherst
  Dartmouth
  Lowell
Wellesley College
Western New England College
Westfield State College
Wheaton College
Williams College
Worcester Polytechnic Institute

Michigan
Adrian College
Albion College
Alma College
Andrews University
Aquinas College
Baker College
  Auburn Hills
  Cadillac
  Flint
  Muskegon
  Owosso
  Port Huron
Calvin College
Center for Creative Studies: College of Art and Design
Cleary College
Concordia College
Davenport College of Business
Eastern Michigan University
GMI Engineering & Management Institute
Grace Bible College
Grand Rapids Baptist College and Seminary
Grand Rapids Community College
Grand Valley State University
Great Lakes Christian College
Great Lakes Junior College of Business
Highland Park Community College
Hillsdale College
Hope College
Jordan College
Kalamazoo College
Kellogg Community College
Kendall College of Art and Design
Lake Michigan College
Lake Superior State University
Lawrence Technological University
Madonna University
Marygrove College
Michigan Christian College
Mid Michigan Community College
Montcalm Community College
Northern Michigan University
Olivet College
Reformed Bible College
Sacred Heart Major Seminary
Saginaw Valley State University
St. Mary's College
Siena Heights College
Southwestern Michigan College
Spring Arbor College
Suomi College
University of Detroit Mercy
University of Michigan
  Ann Arbor
  Dearborn
  Flint
Walsh College of Accountancy and Business Administration
Wayne County Community College
William Tyndale College

Minnesota
Augsburg College
Bemidji State University
Bethany Lutheran College
Carleton College
College of St. Benedict
College of St. Catherine: St. Catherine Campus
College of St. Scholastica
Concordia College: Moorhead
Concordia College: St. Paul
Dr. Martin Luther College
Hamline University
Macalester College
Minneapolis College of Art and Design
Minnesota Bible College
NEI College of Technology
North Central Bible College
Northwest Technical Institute
Northwestern College
Oak Hills Bible College
Pillsbury Baptist Bible College
St. John's University
St. Mary's Campus of the College of St. Catherine
St. Mary's College of Minnesota
St. Olaf College
Southwest State University
University of Minnesota
  Crookston
  Duluth
  Morris
  Twin Cities
University of St. Thomas

Mississippi
Alcorn State University
Delta State University
East Mississippi Community College
Jackson State University
Magnolia Bible College
Millsaps College
Mississippi College
Mississippi Gulf Coast Community College: Perkinston
Mississippi University for Women
Mississippi Valley State University
Northwest Mississippi Community College
Pearl River Community College
Rust College
Southeastern Baptist College
Tougaloo College
University of Mississippi Medical Center University
University of Southern Mississippi

Missouri
Avila College
Calvary Bible College
Central Christian College of the Bible
Central Methodist College
Central Missouri State University
Conception Seminary College
Crowder College
Culver-Stockton College
DeVry Institute of Technology: Kansas City
Drury College
East Central College
Evangel College
Fontbonne College
Hannibal-LaGrange College
Harris Stowe State College
ITT Technical Institute: St. Louis
Jefferson College
Kansas City Art Institute
Kemper Military School and College

Lincoln University
Lindenwood College
Maryville University
Missouri Baptist College
Missouri Southern State College
Missouri Valley College
Missouri Western State College
Moberly Area Community College
National College
Northeast Missouri State University
Northwest Missouri Community College
Northwest Missouri State University
Ozark Christian College
Park College
Phillips Junior College
Ranken Technical College
Research College of Nursing
Rockhurst College
St. Louis Christian College
St. Louis College of Pharmacy
St. Louis University
Southeast Missouri State University
Stephens College
University of Missouri
    Columbia
    Rolla
    St. Louis
Washington University
Webster University
Westminster College
William Jewell College
William Woods College

Montana
Carroll College
College of Great Falls
Dawson Community College
Dull Knife Memorial College
Eastern Montana College
Flathead Valley Community College
Fort Peck Community College
Little Big Horn College
Miles Community College
Montana State University
Rocky Mountain College
Salish Kootenai College
Stone Child College
University of Montana
Western Montana College of the University of Montana

Nebraska
Bellevue College
Central Community College
Chadron State College
Clarkson College
College of St. Mary
Concordia College
Creighton University
Dana College
Doane College
Lincoln School of Commerce
McCook Community College
Mid Plains Community College
Midland Lutheran College
Nebraska Christian College
Nebraska Indian Community College
Nebraska Methodist College of Nursing and Allied Health
Nebraska Wesleyan University
Southeast Community College: Beatrice Campus
Union College
Wayne State College
Western Nebraska Community College: Scottsbluff Campus
York College

Nevada
University of Nevada: Las Vegas

New Hampshire
Castle College
Daniel Webster College
Dartmouth College
Franklin Pierce College
Hesser College
New England College
New Hampshire College
New Hampshire Technical College
    Berlin
    Laconia
    Manchester
    Nashua
    Stratham
New Hampshire Technical Institute
Notre Dame College
White Pines College

New Jersey
Assumption College for Sisters
Berkeley College of Business
Bloomfield College
Burlington County College
Caldwell College
College of St. Elizabeth
Drew University
Essex County College
Fairleigh Dickinson University
    Edward Williams College
    Madison
Felician College
Georgian Court College
Jersey City State College
Katharine Gibbs School
Monmouth College
Montclair State College
New Jersey Institute of Technology
Passaic County Community College
Princeton University
Ramapo College of New Jersey
Rider College
Rowan College of New Jersey
Rutgers—The State University of New Jersey
    Camden College of Arts and Sciences
    College of Engineering
    College of Nursing
    College of Pharmacy
    Cook College
    Douglass College
    Livingston College
    Mason Gross School of the Arts
    Newark College of Arts and Sciences
    Rutgers College
    University College Camden
    University College New Brunswick
    University College Newark
St. Peter's College
Salem Community College
Seton Hall University
Stockton State College
Trenton State College
Upsala College
Westminster Choir College School of Music of Rider College
William Paterson College of New Jersey

New Mexico
College of Santa Fe
College of the Southwest
Dona Ana Branch Community College of New Mexico State University
Eastern New Mexico University
Institute of American Indian Arts
National College
New Mexico Highlands University
New Mexico State University
    Alamogordo
    Las Cruces
St. John's College

New York
Adelphi University
Adirondack Community College
Albany College of Pharmacy
Alfred University
American Academy of Dramatic Arts
Audrey Cohen College
Bard College
Barnard College
Berkeley College
Berkeley School: New York City
Boricua College
Bramson ORT Technical Institute
Bryant & Stratton Business Institute: Albany
Canisius College
Catholic Medical Center of Brooklyn and Queens School of Nursing
Cazenovia College
Central City Business Institute
City University of New York
    Borough of Manhattan Community College
    John Jay College of Criminal Justice
Clarkson University
Cochran School of Nursing-St. John's Riverside Hospital
Colgate University
College of Aeronautics
College of Insurance
College of Mount St. Vincent
College of New Rochelle
    New Rochelle
    School of New Resources
College of St. Rose
Columbia University
    Columbia College
    School of Engineering and Applied Science
Columbia-Greene Community College
Concordia College
Cornell University
Daemen College
Dowling College
D'Youville College
Eastman School of Music of the University of Rochester
Elmira College
Eugene Lang College/New School for Social Research
Fashion Institute of Technology
Fordham University
Hamilton College
Hartwick College
Herkimer County Community College
Hilbert College
Hobart College
Houghton College
Hudson Valley Community College
Iona College
Ithaca College
Jamestown Community College
Jewish Theological Seminary of America
Juilliard School
Katharine Gibbs School
    Melville
    New York
Keuka College
King's College
Le Moyne College
Long Island College Hospital School of Nursing
Long Island University
    Brooklyn Campus
    C. W. Post Campus
    Southampton Campus
Manhattan School of Music
Manhattanville College
Mannes College of Music
Maria College
Marist College
Marymount College
Marymount Manhattan College
Mater Dei College
Medaille College
Mercy College
Molloy College
Monroe College
Monroe Community College
Nazareth College of Rochester
New York Institute of Technology
New York School of Interior Design
New York University
Niagara University
Ohr Somayach Tanenbaum Education Center
Pace University
    College of White Plains
    New York
    Pleasantville/Briarcliff
Parsons School of Design
Paul Smith's College
Phillips Beth Israel School of Nursing
Pratt Institute
Rensselaer Polytechnic Institute
Roberts Wesleyan College
Rochester Institute of Technology
Sage Junior College of Albany
St. John Fisher College
St. Joseph's College
    Brooklyn
    Suffolk Campus
St. Joseph's School of Nursing
St. Lawrence University
St. Thomas Aquinas College
Sarah Lawrence College
School of Visual Arts
Skidmore College
State University of New York
    Albany
    Binghamton
    Buffalo
    Purchase
    Stony Brook
    College at Brockport
    College at Buffalo
    College at Cortland
    College at Fredonia
    College at New Paltz
    College at Oneonta
    College at Plattsburgh
    College at Potsdam
    College of Technology at Alfred
    College of Technology at Delhi
    Institute of Technology at Utica/Rome
Sullivan County Community College
Syracuse University
Talmudical Institute of Upstate New York
Talmudical Seminary Oholei Torah
Taylor Business Institute
Tompkins-Cortland Community College
Touro College
Trocaire College

Tuition payment plans: installment payment

Ulster County Community College
University of Rochester
University of the State of New York: Regents College
Utica College of Syracuse University
Utica School of Commerce
Vassar College
Villa Maria College of Buffalo
Wadhams Hall Seminary-College
Wagner College
Wells College
Westchester Business Institute
William Smith College
Wood Tobe-Coburn School
Yeshiva University

North Carolina
Barber-Scotia College
Barton College
Belmont Abbey College
Bennett College
Campbell University
Catawba College
Chowan College
Davidson College
Duke University
Elon College
Fayetteville State University
Gardner-Webb University
Greensboro College
Guilford College
High Point University
John Wesley College
Johnson C. Smith University
Lees-McRae College
Lenoir-Rhyne College
Livingstone College
Louisburg College
Mars Hill College
McDowell Technical Community College
Meredith College
Methodist College
Montreat-Anderson College
Mount Olive College
North Carolina Agricultural and Technical State University
North Carolina Wesleyan College
Peace College
Pfeiffer College
Piedmont Bible College
Roanoke Bible College
St. Andrews Presbyterian College
St. Augustine's College
St. Mary's College
Salem College
Shaw University
University of North Carolina at Wilmington
Wake Forest University
Warren Wilson College
Wingate College
Winston-Salem State University

North Dakota
Bismarck State College
Jamestown College
Little Hoop Community College
Mayville State University
Turtle Mountain Community College
University of Mary

Ohio
Antioch School for Adult and Experiential Learning
Antonelli Institute of Art and Photography
Art Academy of Cincinnati
Ashland University
Baldwin-Wallace College
Bliss College
Bluffton College
Bowling Green State University
    Bowling Green
    Firelands College
Bradford School
Capital University
Case Western Reserve University
Cedarville College
Chatfield College
Cincinnati Bible College and Seminary
Circleville Bible College
Cleveland College of Jewish Studies
Cleveland Institute of Art
Cleveland Institute of Electronics
Cleveland State University
College of Mount St. Joseph
College of Wooster
Columbus College of Art and Design
Davis Junior College of Business
Defiance College
Denison University
DeVry Institute of Technology: Columbus
Dyke College
Franciscan University of Steubenville
Franklin University
God's Bible School and College
Heidelberg College
Hiram College
Hocking Technical College
ITT Technical Institute
    Dayton
    Youngstown
Jefferson Technical College
John Carroll University
Kent State University
    Ashtabula Regional Campus
    East Liverpool Regional Campus
    Kent
    Salem Regional Campus
    Stark Campus
    Trumbull Regional Campus
    Tuscarawas Campus
Kettering College of Medical Arts
Lake Erie College
Lakeland Community College
Lourdes College
Malone College
Marietta College
Miami University
    Hamilton Campus
    Middletown Campus
    Oxford Campus
Miami-Jacobs College
Mount Union College
Muskingum College
North Central Technical College
Northwestern College
Notre Dame College of Ohio
Oberlin College
Ohio Dominican College
Ohio Institute of Photography and Technology
Ohio Northern University
Ohio University
    Athens
    Eastern Campus
Ohio Valley Business College
Ohio Wesleyan University
Otterbein College
Owens Technical College
    Findlay Campus
    Toledo
Pontifical College Josephinum
Southern Ohio College
Stark Technical College
Terra Technical College
Tiffin University
Union Institute
University of Akron
University of Findlay
University of Rio Grande
Urbana University
Ursuline College
Virginia Marti College of Fashion and Art
Walsh University
Wilmington College
Wittenberg University
Wright State University
    Dayton
    Lake Campus
Xavier University

Oklahoma
Bacone College
Bartlesville Wesleyan College
Connors State College
Mid-America Bible College
Northeastern Oklahoma Agricultural and Mechanical College
Oklahoma Baptist University
Oklahoma Christian University of Science and Arts
Oklahoma City University
Oral Roberts University
Phillips University
Redlands Community College
Rogers State College
St. Gregory's College
Southern Nazarene University
Southwestern College of Christian Ministries
Southwestern Oklahoma State University
University of Tulsa

Oregon
Bassist College
Central Oregon Community College
Clackamas Community College
Clatsop Community College
Concordia College
Eugene Bible College
George Fox College
ITT Technical Institute: Portland
Lane Community College
Lewis and Clark College
Linfield College
Linn-Benton Community College
Northwest Christian College
Oregon Institute of Technology
Oregon Polytechnic Institute
Oregon State University
Pacific Northwest College of Art
Pacific University
Portland Community College
Portland State University
Reed College
Southern Oregon State College
University of Oregon
    Eugene
    Robert Donald Clark Honors College
University of Portland
Warner Pacific College
Western Baptist College
Western Oregon State College
Willamette University

Pennsylvania
Academy of the New Church
Albright College
Allegheny College
Allentown College of St. Francis de Sales
Alvernia College
American Institute of Design
Antonelli Institute of Art and Photography
Art Institute of Pittsburgh
Baptist Bible College of Pennsylvania
Beaver College
Bryn Mawr College
Bucknell University
Bucks County Community College
Cabrini College
Carlow College
Carnegie Mellon University
Cedar Crest College
Central Pennsylvania Business School
Chatham College
CHI Institute
Churchman Business School
Clarion University of Pennsylvania
College Misericordia
Community College of Allegheny County
    North Campus
    South Campus
Community College of Beaver County
Dean Institute of Technology
Delaware Valley College
Dickinson College
Drexel University
DuBois Business College
East Stroudsburg University of Pennsylvania
Eastern College
Elizabethtown College
Franklin and Marshall College
Gannon University
Geneva College
Gettysburg College
Gratz College
Gwynedd-Mercy College
Hahnemann University School of Health Sciences and Humanities
Harcum Junior College
Harrisburg Area Community College
Haverford College
Holy Family College
ICS Center for Degree Studies
Immaculata College
Indiana University of Pennsylvania
Johnson Technical Institute
Juniata College
Keystone Junior College
King's College
Kutztown University of Pennsylvania
La Roche College
La Salle University
Lackawanna Junior College
Lafayette College
Lebanon Valley College of Pennsylvania
Lehigh University
Lincoln University
Lock Haven University of Pennsylvania
Manor Junior College
Marywood College
McCarrie Schools of Health Sciences and Technology
Mercyhurst College
Messiah College
Millersville University of Pennsylvania
Montgomery County Community College
Moore College of Art and Design
National Education Center: Vale Tech Campus
Neumann College

Pennsylvania Institute of Technology
Philadelphia College of Bible
Philadelphia College of Pharmacy and Science
Philadelphia College of Textiles and Science
Pittsburgh Institute of Mortuary Science
Pittsburgh Technical Institute
Point Park College
Reading Area Community College
Robert Morris College
St. Charles Borromeo Seminary
St. Francis College
St. Joseph's University
Seton Hill College
Shippensburg University of Pennsylvania
Slippery Rock University of Pennsylvania
Swarthmore College
Thaddeus Stevens State School of Technology
Thiel College
Thomas Jefferson University: College of Allied Health Sciences
Triangle Tech
 Erie School
 Greensburg School
 Pittsburgh Campus
University of the Arts
University of Pennsylvania
University of Pittsburgh
 Bradford
 Greensburg
 Titusville
Ursinus College
Valley Forge Christian College
Valley Forge Military College
Villanova University
Waynesburg College
West Chester University of Pennsylvania
Widener University
Wilkes University
Wilson College

Puerto Rico

American University of Puerto Rico
Colegio Universitario del Este
Huertas Junior College
Inter American University of Puerto Rico: San German Campus
Pontifical Catholic University of Puerto Rico
Turabo University
Universidad Adventista de las Antillas
Universidad Politecnica de Puerto Rico
University of Puerto Rico
 Cayey University College
 Mayaguez Campus
 Ponce Technological University College
 Rio Piedras Campus

Rhode Island

Brown University
Bryant College
Johnson & Wales University
New England Institute of Technology
Providence College
Rhode Island College
Rhode Island School of Design

South Carolina

Anderson College
Benedict College
Central Wesleyan College

Charleston Southern University
Claflin College
Coker College
College of Charleston
Columbia College
Columbia Junior College of Business
Erskine College
Francis Marion University
Furman University
Greenville Technical College
Lander University
Limestone College
Morris College
Newberry College
North Greenville College
Presbyterian College
Spartanburg Methodist College
University of South Carolina
 Spartanburg
 Union
Voorhees College

South Dakota

Augustana College
Black Hills State University
Dakota Wesleyan University
Huron University
Kilian Community College
Mount Marty College
National College
Oglala Lakota College
Presentation College
Sioux Falls College
Sisseton-Wahpeton Community College
South Dakota School of Mines and Technology
University of South Dakota

Tennessee

Aquinas Junior College
Belmont University
Bethel College
Carson-Newman College
Christian Brothers University
David Lipscomb University
Draughons Junior College of Business: Nashville
Free Will Baptist Bible College
Freed-Hardeman University
Hiwassee College
King College
Knoxville Business College
Knoxville College
Lambuth University
Lee College
LeMoyne-Owen College
Lincoln Memorial University
Maryville College
Memphis College of Art
Milligan College
Rhodes College
Tennessee Temple University
Tennessee Wesleyan College
Trevecca Nazarene College
Union University
University of the South
University of Tennessee
 Chattanooga
 Knoxville
 Memphis
Vanderbilt University
William Jennings Bryan College

Texas

Angelo State University
Arlington Baptist College
Austin College
Baptist Missionary Association Theological Seminary
Bauder Fashion College
Central Texas College

Cisco Junior College
Commonwealth Institute of Funeral Service
Concordia Lutheran College
Corpus Christi State University
Criswell College
Dallas Baptist University
Dallas Christian College
Dallas Institute of Funeral Service
DeVry Institute of Technology: Irving
East Texas Baptist University
East Texas State University
 Commerce
 Texarkana
Hardin-Simmons University
Houston Baptist University
Howard Payne University
Huston-Tillotson College
Incarnate Word College
Institute for Christian Studies
ITT Technical Institute: Houston
Jacksonville College
Jarvis Christian College
Lamar University—Beaumont
Laredo State University
LeTourneau University
Lon Morris College
Lubbock Christian University
McMurry University
Midwestern State University
Miss Wade's Fashion Merchandising College
Our Lady of the Lake University of San Antonio
Paul Quinn College
Prairie View A&M University
Ranger Junior College
Rice University
St. Edward's University
St. Mary's University
Sam Houston State University
Schreiner College
Southern Methodist University
Southwest Texas State University
Southwestern Adventist College
Southwestern Assemblies of God College
Southwestern Christian College
Southwestern University
Stephen F. Austin State University
Sul Ross State University
Tarleton State University
Texas A&I University
Texas A&M University
 College Station
 Galveston
Texas Christian University
Texas College
Texas Lutheran College
Texas State Technical College
 Harlingen
 Sweetwater
 Waco
Texas Tech University
Texas Wesleyan University
Texas Woman's University
University of Dallas
University of Houston
 Clear Lake
 Downtown
 Houston
 Victoria
University of North Texas

University of Texas
 Arlington
 Austin
 Dallas
 El Paso
 Health Science Center at Houston
 Health Science Center at San Antonio
 Medical Branch at Galveston
 Pan American
 Permian Basin
 San Antonio
 Southwestern Medical Center at Dallas Southwestern Allied Health Sciences School
 Tyler
Wayland Baptist University
Wiley College

Utah

LDS Business College
Phillips Junior College: Salt Lake City Campus
Salt Lake Community College
Stevens-Henager College of Business
Westminster College of Salt Lake City

Vermont

Bennington College
Burlington College
Castleton State College
Champlain College
College of St. Joseph in Vermont
Community College of Vermont
New England Culinary Institute
Norwich University
Southern Vermont College
Sterling College
Trinity College of Vermont
University of Vermont
Vermont Technical College

Virginia

Averett College
Bluefield College
Christendom College
Christopher Newport University
Clinch Valley College of the University of Virginia
College of William and Mary
Emory and Henry College
Ferrum College
George Mason University
Hampden-Sydney College
Hollins College
James Madison University
Liberty University
Longwood College
Lord Fairfax Community College
Lynchburg College
Mary Baldwin College
Norfolk State University
Radford University
Randolph-Macon College
Randolph-Macon Woman's College
Roanoke College
St. Paul's College
Shenandoah University
Southern Virginia College for Women
Sweet Briar College
Virginia Commonwealth University
Virginia Intermont College
Virginia Military Institute
Virginia Polytechnic Institute and State University
Virginia State University
Virginia Union University

Tuition payment plans: installment payment

Virginia Wesleyan College

Washington
Antioch University Seattle
Art Institute of Seattle
Cornish College of the Arts
Evergreen State College
Gonzaga University
Heritage College
ITT Technical Institute: Seattle
Lutheran Bible Institute of Seattle
Northwest College of the
　Assemblies of God
Pacific Lutheran University
Puget Sound Christian College
St. Martin's College
Seattle Pacific University
Seattle University
University of Puget Sound
Walla Walla College
Whitman College
Whitworth College

West Virginia
Appalachian Bible College
Bethany College
College of West Virginia
Davis and Elkins College
Fairmont State College
Ohio Valley College
Shepherd College
University of Charleston
West Virginia Institute of
　Technology
West Virginia University
West Virginia Wesleyan College
Wheeling Jesuit College

Wisconsin
Alverno College
Bellin College of Nursing
Beloit College
Cardinal Stritch College
Carroll College
Carthage College
Concordia University Wisconsin
Edgewood College
Lakeland College
Lawrence University
Maranatha Baptist Bible College
Marian College of Fond du Lac
Marquette University
Milwaukee College of Business
Milwaukee Institute of Art &
　Design
Milwaukee School of Engineering
Mount Mary College
Mount Senario College
Northland College
Northwestern College
Ripon College
St. Norbert College
Silver Lake College
Stratton College
University of Wisconsin
　Eau Claire
　Green Bay
　La Crosse
　Oshkosh
　Parkside
　Platteville
　River Falls
　Stevens Point
　Stout
　Superior
　Whitewater

University of Wisconsin Center
　Baraboo/Sauk County
　Fox Valley
　Manitowoc County
　Marathon County
　Marinette County
　Marshfield/Wood County
　Richland
　Rock County
　Sheboygan County
　Washington County
　Waukesha
Viterbo College
Wisconsin Lutheran College

Wyoming
Casper College
Central Wyoming College
Eastern Wyoming College
Sheridan College

American Samoa, Caroline Islands, Guam, Marianas, Virgin Islands
College of Micronesia-FSM
Micronesian Occupational College

Canada
McGill University

France
American University of Paris

Switzerland
Franklin College: Switzerland

Tuition discount for prepayment

Alabama
Faulkner University

California
American College for the Applied
　Arts: Los Angeles
Azusa Pacific University
Biola University
California Maritime Academy
Christian Heritage College
College of Oceaneering
Compton Community College
Fashion Institute of Design and
　Merchandising
LIFE Bible College
Pacific Christian College
Pacific Union College
St. Mary's College of California
Southern California College
Thomas Aquinas College
University of Redlands
University of San Diego
University of San Francisco
University of Southern California
Westmont College

Colorado
Colorado Technical College

District of Columbia
Catholic University of America
Mount Vernon College
Southeastern University

Florida
Hobe Sound Bible College
Lynn University
New College of the University of
　South Florida

University of Miami

Georgia
Meadows College of Business
Morris Brown College
Oglethorpe University
Shorter College

Idaho
Albertson College

Illinois
Barat College
Columbia College
National-Louis University
State Community College
Trinity College

Indiana
Anderson University
Butler University
Goshen College
Huntington College

Iowa
Coe College
Emmaus Bible College
Luther College
Teikyo Westmar University
Vennard College

Kansas
Barclay College
Brown Mackie College
Hesston College
Ottawa University
Seward County Community College

Kentucky
Centre College

Maine
Unity College
University of New England

Maryland
Johns Hopkins University
Mount St. Mary's College

Massachusetts
American International College
Atlantic Union College
Boston College
Boston University
Gordon College
Marian Court Junior College
Pine Manor College

Michigan
Alma College
Andrews University
Cleary College
Ferris State University
Great Lakes Junior College of
　Business
Kendall College of Art and Design
Kirtland Community College
Marygrove College

Minnesota
College of St. Benedict
Concordia College: Moorhead
Hamline University
North Central Bible College
Northwest Technical Institute
St. John's University
St. Olaf College
University of St. Thomas

Mississippi
Tougaloo College
Wood Junior College

Missouri
Evangel College
Kemper Military School and
　College
Lindenwood College
Research College of Nursing

Nebraska
Union College

New Hampshire
Colby-Sawyer College
Franklin Pierce College
New England College
Notre Dame College

New Jersey
Berkeley College of Business

New Mexico
St. John's College

New York
Alfred University
American Academy of Dramatic
　Arts
Barnard College
Berkeley College
Berkeley School: New York City
Colgate University
Columbia University: Columbia
　College
Hobart College
Medaille College
New York Institute of Technology
New York University
Nyack College
Touro College
Wells College
William Smith College

North Carolina
Duke University
Pfeiffer College
Piedmont Bible College

North Dakota
Trinity Bible College

Ohio
Cedarville College
Cincinnati Bible College and
　Seminary
Circleville Bible College
Cleveland Institute of Electronics
God's Bible School and College
Hiram College
Lake Erie College
Malone College
Marietta College
Ohio Northern University
Ohio Wesleyan University
Union Institute
Wittenberg University

Oklahoma
Oklahoma Christian University of
　Science and Arts

Oregon
Bassist College
Clatsop Community College
Linfield College
Pacific University

Pennsylvania
Academy of the New Church
Allegheny College
Baptist Bible College of
　Pennsylvania
Duquesne University
Eastern College

Gettysburg College
Lafayette College
Mercyhurst College
Philadelphia College of Bible
Thomas Jefferson University:
  College of Allied Health Sciences
University of Pennsylvania

Rhode Island

Brown University

South Dakota

Dakota Wesleyan University
Sioux Falls College

Tennessee

Milligan College
Southern College of Seventh-day
  Adventists

Texas

Huston-Tillotson College
Lon Morris College
St. Mary's University
Schreiner College
Southwestern Adventist College
Southwestern Assemblies of God
  College

Vermont

Champlain College
Lyndon State College
Middlebury College
Norwich University
Southern Vermont College

Virginia

Liberty University
Lynchburg College
Marymount University
Southern Virginia College for
  Women

Washington

City University
Lutheran Bible Institute of Seattle
Pacific Lutheran University
Walla Walla College

Wisconsin

Carthage College
Lakeland College
Lawrence University
Marquette University

France

American University of Paris

Tuition payment by deferred payments

Alabama

Alabama Agricultural and
  Mechanical University
Alabama State University
Auburn University at Montgomery
Birmingham-Southern College
Bishop State Community College
Huntingdon College
Livingston University
Marion Military Institute
Southern Union State Junior
  College
Spring Hill College
Trenholm State Technical College
Troy State University in
  Montgomery
University of Alabama

University of Mobile

Alaska

Prince William Sound Community
  College
Sheldon Jackson College
University of Alaska
  Fairbanks
  Southeast

Arizona

Cochise College
DeVry Institute of Technology:
  Phoenix
Embry-Riddle Aeronautical
  University: Prescott Campus
Gateway Community College
Grand Canyon University
Mohave Community College
Navajo Community College
Northern Arizona University
Paradise Valley Community College
Phoenix College
Prescott College
Southwestern College
University of Arizona
Western International University
Yavapai College

Arkansas

Arkansas Baptist College
Mississippi County Community
  College
Shorter College
University of Arkansas
University of the Ozarks
Westark Community College
Williams Baptist College

California

Academy of Art College
Allan Hancock College
American Academy of Dramatic
  Arts: West
American Armenian International
  College
Antelope Valley College
Antioch Southern California at Los
  Angeles
Armstrong University
Bakersfield College
Biola University
California College of Arts and
  Crafts
California Lutheran University
California State University:
  Northridge
Canada College
Cerritos Community College
Charles R. Drew University: College
  of Allied Health
Christian Heritage College
Cogswell Polytechnical College
College of Notre Dame
College of San Mateo
Columbia College: Hollywood
Compton Community College
Cosumnes River College
DeVry Institute of Technology: City
  of Industry
Dominican College of San Rafael
Evergreen Valley College
Fashion Institute of Design and
  Merchandising
Feather River College
Glendale Community College
Golden Gate University
Golden West College
Heald Business College: Concord
Holy Names College
Kelsey-Jenney College
Long Beach City College

Los Angeles City College
Los Angeles Harbor College
Los Angeles Mission College
Los Angeles Pierce College
Los Angeles Trade and Technical
  College
Los Medanos College
Loyola Marymount University
Master's College
Merced College
Mills College
MiraCosta College
Mission College
Modesto Junior College
Monterey Institute of International
  Studies
Monterey Peninsula College
Mount St. Mary's College
Mount San Antonio College
Napa Valley College
New College of California
Otis School of Art and Design
Pacific Christian College
Pacific Union College
Pasadena City College
Patten College
Pepperdine University
Pomona College
Sacramento City College
Samuel Merritt College
San Jose City College
Santa Barbara City College
Santa Clara University
Santa Monica College
Santa Rosa Junior College
Scripps College
Shasta College
Sierra College
Skyline College
Sonoma State University
Stanford University
Taft College
United States International
  University
University of California
  San Diego
  Santa Barbara
University of Judaism
University of the Pacific
University of San Francisco
University of Southern California
University of West Los Angeles
Ventura College
Victor Valley College
West Hills Community College
West Valley College
Woodbury University

Colorado

Adams State College
Aims Community College
Arapahoe Community College
Colorado Christian University
Colorado Institute of Art
Colorado Mountain College
  Alpine Campus
  Spring Valley Campus
  Timberline Campus
Colorado School of Mines
Community College of Denver
Denver Technical College
Fort Lewis College
ITT Technical Institute: Aurora
Mesa State College
Metropolitan State College of
  Denver
Morgan Community College
Naropa Institute
National College
Northeastern Junior College
Pikes Peak Community College
Pueblo Community College

Red Rocks Community College
Regis University
Trinidad State Junior College
University of Colorado at Boulder
University of Denver
University of Southern Colorado
Western State College of Colorado

Connecticut

Briarwood College
Capital Community-Technical
  College
Central Connecticut State
  University
Connecticut College
Middlesex Community-Technical
  College
Norwalk Community-Technical
  College
Quinebaug Valley Community-
  Technical College
Quinnipiac College
Sacred Heart University
Tunxis Community-Technical
  College
University of Bridgeport
Wesleyan University

Delaware

Delaware State College
Delaware Technical and
  Community College
    Stanton/Wilmington Campus
    Terry Campus
Goldey-Beacom College

District of Columbia

American University
George Washington University
Georgetown University
Howard University
Strayer College
Trinity College
University of the District of
  Columbia

Florida

Art Institute of Fort Lauderdale
Barry University
Bethune-Cookman College
Brevard Community College
Broward Community College
Central Florida Community College
Chipola Junior College
Embry-Riddle Aeronautical
  University
Florida Atlantic University
Florida Christian College
Florida Community College at
  Jacksonville
Florida International University
Jacksonville University
Lake City Community College
Lake-Sumter Community College
Nova University
Okaloosa-Walton Community
  College
Phillips Junior College: Melbourne
St. John Vianney College Seminary
St. Thomas University
Schiller International University
Tampa College
University of Florida
University of Miami
University of North Florida
Warner Southern College

Georgia

Atlanta Christian College
Clark Atlanta University
Covenant College
DeKalb Technical Institute

Tuition payment plans: deferred payment

DeVry Institute of Technology:
　Atlanta
Emmanuel College
Fort Valley State College
Georgia Southern University
LaGrange College
Meadows College of Business
Morris Brown College
Oglethorpe University
Reinhardt College
South College
Spelman College
Thomas College
Toccoa Falls College

Idaho

Boise State University
College of Southern Idaho
Idaho State University
Lewis Clark State College
University of Idaho

Illinois

Aurora University
Barat College
Belleville Area College
Black Hawk College
　East Campus
　Moline
Blackburn College
Bradley University
Carl Sandburg College
Chicago State University
City Colleges of Chicago
　Malcolm X College
　Olive-Harvey College
College of DuPage
College of Lake County
Danville Area Community College
De Paul University
DeVry Institute of Technology
　Addison
　Chicago
East-West University
Elgin Community College
Governors State University
Greenville College
Illinois Central College
International Academy of
　Merchandising and Design
Joliet Junior College
Judson College
Kankakee Community College
Kaskaskia College
Kishwaukee College
Knox College
Lake Land College
Lakeview College of Nursing
Lewis and Clark Community
　College
Lewis University
Lincoln Christian College and
　Seminary
Lincoln College
Lincoln Land Community College
MacMurray College
Moody Bible Institute
Morton College
National College of Chiropractic
National-Louis University
Parks College of St. Louis
　University
Quincy University
Richland Community College
Rockford College
Roosevelt University
Rush University
St. Xavier University
Sangamon State University
Sauk Valley Community College
Southeastern Illinois College

Southern Illinois University at
　Edwardsville
State Community College
Trinity Christian College
Trinity College
Triton College
VanderCook College of Music
Western Illinois University
Wheaton College

Indiana

Ancilla College
Anderson University
Bethel College
DePauw University
Earlham College
Goshen College
Indiana State University
Indiana University
　Bloomington
　East
　Northwest
　South Bend
Indiana University—Purdue
　University at Indianapolis
Indiana Vocational Technical
　College
　Columbus
　Eastcentral
　Kokomo
　Lafayette
　Northcentral
　Northwest
　Southcentral
　Southeast
　Southwest
　Wabash Valley
Indiana Wesleyan University
Manchester College
Oakland City College
Purdue University
　Calumet
　West Lafayette
St. Mary-of-the-Woods College
St. Meinrad College
University of Indianapolis

Iowa

Briar Cliff College
Cornell College
Drake University
Ellsworth Community College
Emmaus Bible College
Grand View College
Indian Hills Community College
Iowa Wesleyan College
Iowa Western Community College
Marshalltown Community College
Morningside College
North Iowa Area Community
　College
St. Ambrose University
Southeastern Community College
　North Campus
　South Campus
Teikyo Marycrest University
University of Dubuque
University of Northern Iowa
Vennard College
Wartburg College

Kansas

Allen County Community College
Barclay College
Bethel College
Brown Mackie College
Coffeyville Community College
Colby Community College
Dodge City Community College
Emporia State University
Fort Hays State University
Fort Scott Community College

Garden City Community College
Highland Community College
Independence Community College
Kansas City Kansas Community
　College
Manhattan Christian College
Neosho County Community College
Pittsburg State University
Pratt Community College
St. Mary College
Seward County Community College
Southwestern College
University of Kansas
Washburn University of Topeka
Wichita State University

Kentucky

Asbury College
Brescia College
Campbellsville College
Cumberland College
Eastern Kentucky University
Georgetown College
Jefferson Community College
Kentucky State University
Kentucky Wesleyan College
Lindsey Wilson College
Louisville Technical Institute
Maysville Community College
Midway College
Morehead State University
Murray State University
Northern Kentucky University
Sullivan College
Transylvania University

Louisiana

Bossier Parish Community College
Dillard University
Grambling State University
Grantham College of Engineering
Louisiana State University
　Agricultural and Mechanical
　　College
　Alexandria
　Eunice
　Medical Center
McNeese State University
Northwestern State University
Nunez Community College
Southeastern Louisiana University
Southern University in Shreveport
Southern University and
　Agricultural and Mechanical
　College
University of New Orleans

Maine

Beal College
Bowdoin College
Casco Bay College
Central Maine Medical Center
　School of Nursing
Unity College
University of Maine
　Augusta
　Fort Kent
University of Southern Maine

Maryland

Allegany Community College
Anne Arundel Community College
Baltimore City Community College
Bowie State University
Capitol College
Catonsville Community College
Cecil Community College
Coppin State College
Dundalk Community College
Essex Community College
Frostburg State University
Hagerstown Junior College

Hood College
Johns Hopkins University
Loyola College in Maryland
Montgomery College
　Germantown Campus
　Rockville Campus
　Takoma Park Campus
Morgan State University
Mount St. Mary's College
Ner Israel Rabbinical College
University of Baltimore
University of Maryland: College
　Park
Wor-Wic Community College

Massachusetts

Anna Maria College for Men and
　Women
Atlantic Union College
Boston Conservatory
Boston University
Bristol Community College
Elms College
Emerson College
Forsyth School for Dental
　Hygienists
Hampshire College
Massachusetts Bay Community
　College
Merrimack College
Middlesex Community College
Mount Holyoke College
Quincy College
Quinsigamond Community College
School of the Museum of Fine Arts
Smith College
Springfield Technical Community
　College
Suffolk University
Wellesley College
Western New England College

Michigan

Albion College
Alma College
Aquinas College
Baker College of Port Huron
Center for Creative Studies: College
　of Art and Design
Charles Stewart Mott Community
　College
Concordia College
Eastern Michigan University
Ferris State University
Glen Oaks Community College
Grand Rapids Community College
Grand Valley State University
Great Lakes Junior College of
　Business
Highland Park Community College
Jackson Community College
Kalamazoo College
Kalamazoo Valley Community
　College
Kellogg Community College
Kendall College of Art and Design
Kirtland Community College
Lawrence Technological University
Marygrove College
Michigan Christian College
Michigan State University
Mid Michigan Community College
Monroe County Community
　College
Northwestern Michigan College
Sacred Heart Major Seminary
St. Clair County Community
　College
St. Mary's College
Siena Heights College
Spring Arbor College
Suomi College

Tuition payment plans: deferred payment

University of Detroit Mercy
University of Michigan: Dearborn
Walsh College of Accountancy and Business Administration
Washtenaw Community College
Wayne County Community College
Wayne State University
West Shore Community College
William Tyndale College

Minnesota
Anoka-Ramsey Community College
Bemidji State University
Brainerd Community College
College of St. Catherine: St. Catherine Campus
Lakewood Community College
Mankato State University
NEI College of Technology
Rainy River Community College
Southwest State University
University of Minnesota: Morris
University of St. Thomas
Vermilion Community College
Willmar Technical College

Mississippi
Alcorn State University
Belhaven College
Copiah-Lincoln Community College
East Central Community College
Hinds Community College
Jackson State University
Magnolia Bible College
Meridian Community College
Millsaps College
Mississippi College
Mississippi Gulf Coast Community College
    Jackson County Campus
    Jefferson Davis Campus
Mississippi State University
Mississippi Valley State University
Northwest Mississippi Community College
Pearl River Community College
Tougaloo College
University of Mississippi
    Medical Center
    University
University of Southern Mississippi
William Carey College
Wood Junior College

Missouri
Avila College
Central Christian College of the Bible
Conception Seminary College
Deaconess College of Nursing
DeVry Institute of Technology: Kansas City
Drury College
East Central College
Fontbonne College
Hannibal-LaGrange College
Harris Stowe State College
Jefferson College
Kemper Military School and College
Lincoln University
Lindenwood College
Maryville University
Missouri Baptist College
Missouri Western State College
Northwest Missouri Community College
Park College
Research College of Nursing
Rockhurst College
St. Louis University
Southeast Missouri State University

Southwest Baptist University
Three Rivers Community College
University of Missouri
    Columbia
    Rolla
Washington University
Webster University
William Jewell College

Montana
College of Great Falls
Dawson Community College
Eastern Montana College
Flathead Valley Community College
Miles Community College
Montana College of Mineral Science and Technology
Montana State University
Northern Montana College
Salish Kootenai College
Western Montana College of the University of Montana

Nebraska
Bellevue College
Central Community College
Chadron State College
College of St. Mary
Dana College
Grace College of the Bible
Metropolitan Community College
Midland Lutheran College
Nebraska Christian College
Nebraska College of Technical Agriculture
Nebraska Indian Community College
Nebraska Methodist College of Nursing and Allied Health
Nebraska Wesleyan University
University of Nebraska—Omaha
Western Nebraska Community College: Scottsbluff Campus

Nevada
Northern Nevada Community College
Truckee Meadows Community College
University of Nevada
    Las Vegas
    Reno
Western Nevada Community College

New Hampshire
Dartmouth College
Franklin Pierce College
New Hampshire Technical College
    Berlin
    Laconia
    Manchester
    Nashua
Rivier College

New Jersey
Bloomfield College
Burlington County College
Camden County College
Essex County College
Fairleigh Dickinson University
    Edward Williams College
    Madison
Hudson County Community College
Jersey City State College
Kean College of New Jersey
Monmouth College
New Jersey Institute of Technology
Ocean County College
Passaic County Community College
Princeton University
Raritan Valley Community College

Rutgers—The State University of New Jersey
    Camden College of Arts and Sciences
    College of Engineering
    College of Nursing
    College of Pharmacy
    Cook College
    Douglass College
    Livingston College
    Mason Gross School of the Arts
    Newark College of Arts and Sciences
    Rutgers College
    University College Camden
    University College New Brunswick
    University College Newark
Salem Community College
Seton Hall University
Stevens Institute of Technology
Stockton State College
Trenton State College
Union County College
University of Medicine and Dentistry of New Jersey: School of Health Related Professions
William Paterson College of New Jersey

New Mexico
Albuquerque Technical-Vocational Institute
Clovis Community College
College of the Southwest
Dona Ana Branch Community College of New Mexico State University
Eastern New Mexico University: Roswell Campus
National University
New Mexico Highlands University
New Mexico Institute of Mining and Technology
New Mexico Military Institute
New Mexico State University
    Alamogordo
    Carlsbad
    Las Cruces
Northern New Mexico Community College
Santa Fe Community College
Western New Mexico University

New York
Adelphi University
Adirondack Community College
Albany College of Pharmacy
American Academy of Dramatic Arts
Berkeley School: New York City
Boricua College
Bramson ORT Technical Institute
Broome Community College
Bryant & Stratton Business Institute: Albany
Catholic Medical Center of Brooklyn and Queens School of Nursing
Cayuga County Community College
Cazenovia College
Central City Business Institute

City University of New York
    Baruch College
    Bronx Community College
    City College
    College of Staten Island
    Hostos Community College
    Hunter College
    John Jay College of Criminal Justice
    Lehman College
    Medgar Evers College
    New York City Technical College
    Queensborough Community College
    York College
Clinton Community College
College of Insurance
College of Mount St. Vincent
College of New Rochelle
    New Rochelle
    School of New Resources
Columbia University: School of Engineering and Applied Science
Columbia-Greene Community College
Concordia College
Dowling College
Dutchess Community College
D'Youville College
Elmira College
Erie Community College: North Campus
Eugene Lang College/New School for Social Research
Finger Lakes Community College
Five Towns College
Fordham University
Fulton-Montgomery Community College
Genesee Community College
Hilbert College
Hofstra University
Hudson Valley Community College
Ithaca College
Long Island College Hospital School of Nursing
Long Island University
    Brooklyn Campus
    C. W. Post Campus
    Southampton Campus
Manhattan College
Mannes College of Music
Marymount Manhattan College
Mater Dei College
Medaille College
Mercy College
Mohawk Valley Community College
Molloy College
Monroe College
Mount St. Mary College
New York Institute of Technology
New York School of Interior Design
New York University
Niagara County Community College
Niagara University
Onondaga Community College
Pace University
    College of White Plains
    New York
    Pleasantville/Briarcliff
Paul Smith's College
Polytechnic University
    Brooklyn
    Long Island Campus
Pratt Institute
Rochester Institute of Technology
Sage Junior College of Albany
St. Bonaventure University
St. John Fisher College
School of Visual Arts

Tuition payment plans: deferred payment

State University of New York
  Albany
  Binghamton
  Stony Brook
  College at Brockport
  College of Environmental
    Science and Forestry
  College at New Paltz
  College at Potsdam
  College of Technology at
    Alfred
  College of Technology at Delhi
Tompkins-Cortland Community
  College
Trocaire College
Ulster County Community College
Utica College of Syracuse
  University
Vassar College
Wadhams Hall Seminary-College
Westchester Business Institute
Westchester Community College
Yeshiva University

North Carolina

Alamance Community College
Anson Community College
Asheville Buncombe Technical
  Community College
Bladen Community College
Chowan College
East Coast Bible College
Guilford College
Halifax Community College
Mayland Community College
McDowell Technical Community
  College
Methodist College
Montgomery Community College
North Carolina Agricultural and
  Technical State University
Peace College
Pfeiffer College
Pitt Community College
Richmond Community College
St. Andrews Presbyterian College
Southwestern Community College
University of North Carolina at
  Asheville
Wayne Community College
Western Piedmont Community
  College
Wilson Technical Community
  College

North Dakota

North Dakota State University
Trinity Bible College

Ohio

Antioch School for Adult and
  Experiential Learning
Art Academy of Cincinnati
Bluffton College
Cedarville College
Central Ohio Technical College
Chatfield College
Circleville Bible College
Clark State Community College
Cleveland Institute of Electronics
Cleveland State University
Cuyahoga Community College
  Eastern Campus
  Metropolitan Campus
  Western Campus
Davis Junior College of Business
Denison University
DeVry Institute of Technology:
  Columbus
Edison State Community College
Franklin University
God's Bible School and College

Hiram College
Kent State University
  Ashtabula Regional Campus
  East Liverpool Regional
    Campus
  Salem Regional Campus
  Stark Campus
  Trumbull Regional Campus
Lorain County Community College
Malone College
Marietta College
Marion Technical College
Miami-Jacobs College
Muskingum College
North Central Technical College
Oberlin College
Ohio Dominican College
Southern Ohio College
Southern State Community College
Terra Technical College
Tiffin University
University of Cincinnati
  Cincinnati
  Clermont College
  Raymond Walters College
University of Dayton
University of Toledo
Urbana University
Walsh University
Wilberforce University
Wilmington College
Xavier University

Oklahoma

Bartlesville Wesleyan College
Northeastern State University
Oklahoma Christian University of
  Science and Arts
Oklahoma City Community College
Oklahoma City University
Rogers State College
Southeastern Oklahoma State
  University
University of Central Oklahoma

Oregon

Bassist College
Central Oregon Community College
Chemeketa Community College
Clackamas Community College
Clatsop Community College
Concordia College
Eastern Oregon State College
George Fox College
Lane Community College
Lewis and Clark College
Linfield College
Marylhurst College
Multnomah School of the Bible
Northwest Christian College
Oregon Health Sciences University
Oregon Institute of Technology
Pacific Northwest College of Art
Pacific University
Portland Community College
Treasure Valley Community College
University of Portland
Western Baptist College
Western Oregon State College
Willamette University

Pennsylvania

Academy of the New Church
Albright College
Allentown College of St. Francis de
  Sales
Art Institute of Pittsburgh
Baptist Bible College of
  Pennsylvania
Bryn Mawr College
Bucks County Community College

California University of
  Pennsylvania
Carnegie Mellon University
Central Pennsylvania Business
  School
Chestnut Hill College
Churchman Business School
Clarion University of Pennsylvania
College Misericordia
Community College of Allegheny
  County
  Allegheny Campus
  South Campus
Community College of Beaver
  County
Delaware County Community
  College
Delaware Valley College
Drexel University
Duquesne University
East Stroudsburg University of
  Pennsylvania
Eastern College
Elizabethtown College
Gannon University
Gettysburg College
Gratz College
Harcum Junior College
Haverford College
Holy Family College
ICS Center for Degree Studies
Immaculata College
Kutztown University of
  Pennsylvania
La Roche College
La Salle University
Lackawanna Junior College
Lafayette College
Lancaster Bible College
Manor Junior College
Mansfield University of
  Pennsylvania
Marywood College
Moravian College
Neumann College
Penn State
  Erie Behrend College
  Harrisburg Capital College
  University Park Campus
Pennsylvania College of Technology
Point Park College
Reading Area Community College
Robert Morris College
St. Charles Borromeo Seminary
St. Vincent College
Temple University
University of the Arts
University of Pennsylvania
Ursinus College
Valley Forge Military College
Wilkes University
York College of Pennsylvania

Puerto Rico

Bayamon Central University
Caribbean University
Colegio Universitario del Este
Escuela de Artes Plasticas de
  Puerto Rico
Inter American University of Puerto
  Rico
  Arecibo Campus
  Guayama Campus
  San German Campus
Pontifical Catholic University of
  Puerto Rico
Technological College of the
  Municipality of San Juan
Turabo University
Universidad Metropolitana
Universidad Politecnica de Puerto
  Rico

University of Puerto Rico
  Aguadilla
  Bayamon Technological
    University College
  Humacao University College
  La Montana Regional College
  Mayaguez Campus
  Ponce Technological
    University College
  Rio Piedras Campus
University of the Sacred Heart

Rhode Island

Brown University
Rhode Island School of Design
Salve Regina University

South Carolina

Central Wesleyan College
The Citadel
Columbia Bible College and
  Seminary
Columbia College
Columbia Junior College of Business
Technical College of the
  Lowcountry
University of South Carolina
  Aiken
  Coastal Carolina College
  Columbia
  Spartanburg
  Sumter
  Union
Winthrop University

South Dakota

Black Hills State University
Dakota State University
Dakota Wesleyan University
Huron University
Kilian Community College
Northern State University
Presentation College
Western Dakota Vocational
  Technical Institute

Tennessee

Carson-Newman College
Christian Brothers University
Free Will Baptist Bible College
Johnson Bible College
Lee College
Lincoln Memorial University
Memphis College of Art
Tennessee Temple University
Tennessee Wesleyan College
Trevecca Nazarene College
Union University
University of Tennessee
  Chattanooga
  Knoxville
  Martin
Vanderbilt University

Texas

Abilene Christian University
Amber University
Arlington Baptist College
Concordia Lutheran College
Corpus Christi State University
Dallas Christian College
DeVry Institute of Technology:
  Irving
East Texas State University
  Commerce
  Texarkana
Huston-Tillotson College
Jarvis Christian College
LeTourneau University
Midwestern State University
North Lake College
Odessa College

Prairie View A&M University
St. Edward's University
St. Mary's University
San Jacinto College: North
Southern Methodist University
Southwestern University
Texas College
Texas State Technical College: Sweetwater
Texas Wesleyan University
University of Houston: Downtown
University of Mary Hardin-Baylor
University of Texas
   El Paso
   Health Science Center at Houston
   Medical Branch at Galveston
   Tyler

Utah
Stevens-Henager College of Business
University of Utah
Utah State University
Utah Valley Community College

Vermont
Champlain College
Community College of Vermont
Goddard College
Southern Vermont College
Trinity College of Vermont
University of Vermont
Vermont Technical College

Virginia
George Mason University
Hampton University
Lord Fairfax Community College
Norfolk State University
Old Dominion University
Randolph-Macon Woman's College
Southern Virginia College for Women
Tidewater Community College
Virginia State University
Virginia Union University

Washington
Antioch University Seattle
Art Institute of Seattle
Cornish College of the Arts
Eastern Washington University
Gonzaga University
Grays Harbor College
Heritage College
Lower Columbia College
Northwest College of the Assemblies of God
Peninsula College
Pierce College
St. Martin's College
Skagit Valley College
Tacoma Community College
University of Puget Sound
Western Washington University
Whitman College
Yakima Valley Community College

West Virginia
West Virginia State College

Wisconsin
Blackhawk Technical College
Carroll College
Fox Valley Technical College
Gateway Technical College
Lakeshore Technical College
Madison Area Technical College
Marquette University
Mid-State Technical College
Milwaukee Institute of Art & Design
Moraine Park Technical College
Northcentral Technical College
St. Norbert College
Silver Lake College
University of Wisconsin Center
   Baraboo/Sauk County
   Barron County
   Fox Valley
   Manitowoc County
   Marathon County
   Marinette County
   Marshfield/Wood County
   Rock County
   Washington County
   Waukesha
Waukesha County Technical College
Western Wisconsin Technical College

Wyoming
Central Wyoming College
Sheridan College
Western Wyoming Community College

American Samoa, Caroline Islands, Guam, Marianas, Virgin Islands
Guam Community College
Micronesian Occupational College

Arab Republic of Egypt
American University in Cairo

Canada
McGill University

Mexico
Sistema Instituto Tecnologico y de Estudios Superiores de Monterrey

Alphabetical list of colleges

Abilene Christian University, Abilene, TX 79699
Abraham Baldwin Agricultural College, Tifton, GA 31794-2693
Academy of Art College, San Francisco, CA 94115
Academy of the New Church, Bryn Athyn, PA 19009
Adams State College, Alamosa, CO 81102
Adelphi University, Garden City, NY 11530
Adirondack Community College, Queensbury, NY 12804-1498
Adrian College, Adrian, MI 49221-2575
Agnes Scott College, Decatur, GA 30030
Aiken Technical College, Aiken, SC 29802-0696
Aims Community College, Greeley, CO 80632
Alabama Agricultural and Mechanical University, Normal, AL 35762
Alabama Aviation and Technical College, Ozark, AL 36361-1209
Alabama Southern Community College, Monroeville, AL 36461-2000
Alabama State University, Montgomery, AL 36101-0271
Alamance Community College, Goraham, NC 27253
Alaska Bible College, Glennallen, AK 99588
Alaska Pacific University, Anchorage, AK 99508-4672
Albany College of Pharmacy, Albany, NY 12208
Albany State College, Albany, GA 31705-2796
Albertson College, Caldwell, ID 83605
Albertus Magnus College, New Haven, CT 06511-1189
Albion College, Albion, MI 49224
Albright College, Reading, PA 19612-5234
Albuquerque Technical-Vocational Institute, Albuquerque, NM 87106
Alcorn State University, Lorman, MS 39096
Alderson-Broaddus College, Philippi, WV 26416
Alexandria Technical College, Alexandria, MN 56308-3799
Alfred University, Alfred, NY 14802-9987
Alice Lloyd College, Pippa Passes, KY 41844
Allan Hancock College, Santa Maria, CA 93454
Allegany Community College, Cumberland, MD 21502
Allegheny College, Meadville, PA 16335
Allen County Community College, Iola, KS 66749
Allen University, Columbia, SC 29204
Allentown College of St. Francis de Sales, Center Valley, PA 18034-9568
Alma College, Alma, MI 48801-1599
Alpena Community College, Alpena, MI 49707
Alvernia College, Reading, PA 19607-1799
Alverno College, Milwaukee, WI 53234-3922
Alvin Community College, Alvin, TX 77511-4898
Amarillo College, Amarillo, TX 79178
Amber University, Garland, TX 75041-5595
American Academy of Art, Chicago, IL 60603-6191
American Academy of Dramatic Arts
   New York, New York, NY 10016
   West, Pasadena, CA 91107
American Academy McAllister Institute of Funeral Service, New York, NY 10019
American Armenian International College, LaVerne, CA 91750
American Baptist College of ABT Seminary, Nashville, TN 37207
American College for the Applied Arts
   Atlanta, Atlanta, GA 30326
   Los Angeles, Los Angeles, CA 90024-5603
American College of Switzerland, Leysin, Switzerland 34698-4964
American Conservatory of Music, Chicago, IL 60602-4792
American Indian Bible College, Phoenix, AZ 85021-2199
American Institute of Business, Des Moines, IA 50321
American Institute of Commerce, Davenport, IA 52807-2095
American Institute of Design, Philadelphia, PA 19124

American International College, Springfield, MA 01109-3184
American University, Washington, DC 20016-8001
American University in Cairo, Cairo, Arab Republic of 9959 10017-1889
American University of Paris, Paris, France
American University of Puerto Rico, Bayamon, PR 00960-2037
Amherst College, Amherst, MA 01002
Ancilla College, Donaldson, IN 46513
Anderson College, Anderson, SC 29621
Anderson University, Anderson, IN 46012-3462
Andover College, Portland, ME 04103
Andrew College, Cuthbert, GA 31740-1395
Andrews University, Berrien Springs, MI 49104
Angelina College, Lufkin, TX 75902-1768
Angelo State University, San Angelo, TX 76909
Anna Maria College for Men and Women, Paxton, MA 01612-1198
Anne Arundel Community College, Arnold, MD 21012
Anoka-Ramsey Community College, Coon Rapids, MN 55433
Anson Community College, Polkton, NC 28135
Antelope Valley College, Lancaster, CA 93536-5426
Antioch College, Yellow Springs, OH 45387
Antioch School for Adult and Experiential Learning, Yellow Springs, OH 45387
Antioch Southern California at Los Angeles, Marina Del Rey, CA 90292-7090
Antioch University Seattle, Seattle, WA 98121
Antonelli Institute of Art and Photography, Plymouth Meeting, PA 19462
Antonelli Institute of Art and Photography, Cincinnati, OH 45202
Appalachian Bible College, Bradley, WV 25818-1353
Appalachian State University, Boone, NC 28608
Aquinas College, Grand Rapids, MI 49506-1799
Aquinas College at Milton, Milton, MA 02186
Aquinas College at Newton, Newton, MA 02158-9990
Aquinas Junior College, Nashville, TN 37205
Arapahoe Community College, Littleton, CO 80160-9002
Arizona College of the Bible, Phoenix, AZ 85021-5197
Arizona State University, Tempe, AZ 85287-0112
Arizona Western College, Yuma, AZ 85366-0929
Arkansas Baptist College, Little Rock, AR 72202
Arkansas College, Batesville, AR 72503-2317
Arkansas State University
   Beebe Branch, Beebe, AR 72012-1008
   Jonesboro, Jonesboro, AR 72467-1630
Arkansas Tech University, Russellville, AR 72801-2222
Arlington Baptist College, Arlington, TX 76012-3425
Armstrong State College, Savannah, GA 31419-1997
Armstrong University, Berkeley, CA 94704
Art Academy of Cincinnati, Cincinnati, OH 45202-1597
Art Center College of Design, Pasadena, CA 91103
Art Institute of Atlanta, Atlanta, GA 30326
Art Institute of Fort Lauderdale, Fort Lauderdale, FL 33316-3000
Art Institute of Pittsburgh, Pittsburgh, PA 15222
Art Institute of Seattle, Seattle, WA 98121
Art Institute of Southern California, Laguna Beach, CA 92651
Asbury College, Wilmore, KY 40390-1198
Asheville Buncombe Technical Community College, Asheville, NC 28801
Ashland Community College, Ashland, KY 41101-3683
Ashland University, Ashland, OH 44805-9981
Asnuntuck Community-Technical College, Enfield, CT 06082
Assumption College, Worcester, MA 01615-0005
Assumption College for Sisters, Mendham, NJ 07945-0800

Athens Area Technical Institute, Athens, GA 30610-0399
Athens State College, Athens, AL 35611
Atlanta Christian College, East Point, GA 30344
Atlanta Metropolitan College, Atlanta, GA 30310
Atlantic Community College, Mays Landing, NJ 08330-2699
Atlantic Union College, South Lancaster, MA 01561
Auburn University
    Auburn, Auburn, AL 36849-5145
    Montgomery, Montgomery, AL 36117-3596
Audrey Cohen College, New York, NY 10014-9931
Augsburg College, Minneapolis, MN 55454
Augusta College, Augusta, GA 30904-2200
Augustana College, Rock Island, IL 61201-2296
Augustana College, Sioux Falls, SD 57197-9990
Aurora University, Aurora, IL 60506-4892
Austin College, Sherman, TX 75091-1177
Austin Community College, Austin, MN 55912
Austin Community College, Austin, TX 78752-4390
Austin Peay State University, Clarksville, TN 37044
Averett College, Danville, VA 24541
Avila College, Kansas City, MO 64145-1698
Azusa Pacific University, Azusa, CA 91702-7000
Babson College, Babson Park, MA 02157-0310
Bacone College, Muskogee, OK 74403-1597
Bainbridge College, Bainbridge, GA 31717-0953
Baker College
    Auburn Hills, Auburn Hills, MI 48326
    Cadillac, Cadillac, MI 49601
    Flint, Flint, MI 48507-5508
    Mount Clemens, Clinton Township, MI 48043
    Muskegon, Muskegon, MI 49442
    Owosso, Owosso, MI 48867
    Port Huron, Port Huron, MI 48060
Baker University, Baldwin City, KS 66006
Bakersfield College, Bakersfield, CA 93305
Baldwin-Wallace College, Berea, OH 44017-2088
Ball State University, Muncie, IN 47306-0855
Baltimore City Community College, Baltimore, MD 21215
Baltimore Hebrew University, Baltimore, MD 21215-3996
Baltimore International Culinary College, Baltimore, MD 21202-1503
Baptist Bible College of Pennsylvania, Clarks Summit, PA 18411
Baptist Missionary Association Theological Seminary, Jacksonville, TX 75766-5414
Barat College, Lake Forest, IL 60045
Barber-Scotia College, Concord, NC 28025
Barclay College, Haviland, KS 67059
Bard College, Annandale-on-Hudson, NY 12504
Barnard College, New York, NY 10027-6598
Barry University, Miami Shores, FL 33161
Barstow College, Barstow, CA 92311-9984
Bartlesville Wesleyan College, Bartlesville, OK 74006
Barton College, Wilson, NC 27893
Barton County Community College, Great Bend, KS 67530-9283
Bassist College, Portland, OR 97201
Bastyr College, Seattle, WA 98105
Bates College, Lewiston, ME 04240-9917
Bauder College, Atlanta, GA 30326-9975
Bauder Fashion College, Arlington, TX 76010
Bay de Noc Community College, Escanaba, MI 49829
Bay Path College, Longmeadow, MA 01106
Bay State College, Boston, MA 02116
Bayamon Central University, Bayamon, PR 00960-1725
Baylor College of Dentistry, Dallas, TX 75246-2098
Baylor University, Waco, TX 76798-7056
Beal College, Bangor, ME 04401
Beaufort County Community College, Washington, NC 27889
Beaver College, Glenside, PA 19038-3295
Becker College
    Leicester Campus, Leicester, MA 01524
    Worcester Campus, Worcester, MA 01615-0071
Bee County College, Beeville, TX 78102
Belhaven College, Jackson, MS 39202-1789
Bellarmine College, Louisville, KY 40205-0671
Belleville Area College, Belleville, IL 62221-9989
Bellevue College, Bellevue, NE 68005-3098
Bellevue Community College, Bellevue, WA 98007-6484
Bellin College of Nursing, Green Bay, WI 54305-3400
Belmont Abbey College, Belmont, NC 28012-2795
Belmont Technical College, St. Clairsville, OH 43950
Belmont University, Nashville, TN 37212-3757
Beloit College, Beloit, WI 53511-5595
Bel-Rea Institute of Animal Technology, Denver, CO 80231

Bemidji State University, Bemidji, MN 56601
Benedict College, Columbia, SC 29204
Benedictine College, Atchison, KS 66002-1499
Bennett College, Greensboro, NC 27401-3239
Bennington College, Bennington, VT 05201
Bentley College, Waltham, MA 02154-4705
Berea College, Berea, KY 40404
Berean College, Springfield, MO 65802
Bergen Community College, Paramus, NJ 07652-1595
Berkeley College, White Plains, NY 10604-9990
Berkeley College of Business, West Paterson, NJ 07424-0440
Berkeley School: New York City, New York, NY 10017
Berklee College of Music, Boston, MA 02215
Bessemer State Technical College, Bessemer, AL 35021
Bethany College, Scotts Valley, CA 95066-2898
Bethany College, Bethany, WV 26032
Bethany College, Lindsborg, KS 67456-1897
Bethany Lutheran College, Mankato, MN 56001-4490
Bethel College, McKenzie, TN 38201
Bethel College, Mishawaka, IN 46545
Bethel College, North Newton, KS 67117-9899
Beth-El College of Nursing, Colorado Springs, CO 80909
Bethune-Cookman College, Daytona Beach, FL 32115
Bevill State Community College, Sumiton, AL 35148
Big Bend Community College, Moses Lake, WA 98837-3299
Billings Vocational-Technical Center, Billings, MT 59102
Biola University, La Mirada, CA 90639-0001
Birmingham-Southern College, Birmingham, AL 35254
Bishop State Community College, Mobile, AL 36603-5898
Bismarck State College, Bismarck, ND 58501
Black Hawk College
    East Campus, Kewanee, IL 61443-0489
    Moline, Moline, IL 61265
Black Hills State University, Spearfish, SD 57799-9502
Blackburn College, Carlinville, IL 62626
Blackfeet Community College, Browning, MT 59417
Blackhawk Technical College, Janesville, WI 53547
Bladen Community College, Dublin, NC 28332
Blessing-Reiman College of Nursing, Quincy, IL 62301
Blinn College, Brenham, TX 77833
Bliss College, Columbus, OH 43214
Bloomfield College, Bloomfield, NJ 07003
Bloomsburg University of Pennsylvania, Bloomsburg, PA 17815
Blue Mountain Community College, Pendleton, OR 97801
Blue Ridge Community College, Flat Rock, NC 28731-9624
Blue Ridge Community College, Weyers Cave, VA 24486-9989
Bluefield College, Bluefield, VA 24605-1799
Bluefield State College, Bluefield, WV 24701
Bluffton College, Bluffton, OH 45817-1196
Boise Bible College, Boise, ID 83714-1220
Boise State University, Boise, ID 83725
Boricua College, New York, NY 10032
Bossier Parish Community College, Bossier City, LA 71111
Boston Architectural Center, Boston, MA 02115-2795
Boston College, Chestnut Hill, MA 02167-3804
Boston Conservatory, Boston, MA 02215
Boston University, Boston, MA 02215
Bowdoin College, Brunswick, ME 04011-2595
Bowie State University, Bowie, MD 20715
Bowling Green State University
    Bowling Green, Bowling Green, OH 43403-0080
    Firelands College, Huron, OH 44839
Bradford College, Bradford, MA 01835-7393
Bradford School, Columbus, OH 43229
Bradley University, Peoria, IL 61625
Brainerd Community College, Brainerd, MN 56401
Bramson ORT Technical Institute, Forest Hills, NY 11375
Brandeis University, Waltham, MA 02254-9110
Brazosport College, Lake Jackson, TX 77566
Brenau University, Gainesville, GA 30501-3697
Brescia College, Owensboro, KY 42301-3023
Brevard College, Brevard, NC 28712
Brevard Community College, Cocoa, FL 32922-9987
Brewton-Parker College, Mount Vernon, GA 30445
Briar Cliff College, Sioux City, IA 51104-2100
Briarwood College, Southington, CT 06489
Bridgeport Engineering Institute, Fairfield, CT 06430
Bridgewater College, Bridgewater, VA 22812-1599
Bridgewater State College, Bridgewater, MA 02325
Brigham Young University
    Provo, Provo, UT 84602
    Hawaii, Laie, HI 96762-1294

Bristol Community College, Fall River, MA 02720
Bristol University, Bristol, TN 37625
Brookdale Community College, Lincroft, NJ 07738
Brookhaven College, Farmers Branch, TX 75244
Brooks College, Long Beach, CA 90804
Brooks Institute of Photography, Santa Barbara, CA 93108
Broome Community College, Binghamton, NY 13902
Broward Community College, Fort Lauderdale, FL 33301
Brown Mackie College, Salina, KS 67402-1787
Brown University, Providence, RI 02912
Brunswick College, Brunswick, GA 31523
Brunswick Community College, Supply, NC 28462
Bryant College, Smithfield, RI 02917-1285
Bryant & Stratton Business Institute
    Albany, Albany, NY 12205
    Rochester, Rochester, NY 14604-1381
    Syracuse, Syracuse, NY 13202
Bryn Mawr College, Bryn Mawr, PA 19010
Bucknell University, Lewisburg, PA 17837-9988
Bucks County Community College, Newtown, PA 18940
Buena Vista College, Storm Lake, IA 50588-1798
Bunker Hill Community College, Boston, MA 02129
Burlington College, Burlington, VT 05401
Burlington County College, Pemberton, NJ 08068-1599
Butler County Community College, Butler, PA 16003-1203
Butler County Community College, Eldorado, KS 67042-3280
Butler University, Indianapolis, IN 46208
Butte Vocational-Technical Center, Butte, MT 59701
Cabrini College, Radnor, PA 19087-3699
Caldwell College, Caldwell, NJ 07006-6195
Caldwell Community College and Technical Institute, Hudson, NC 28638-2397
California Baptist College, Riverside, CA 92504-3297
California College of Arts and Crafts, Oakland, CA 94618-1487
California Institute of the Arts, Valencia, CA 91355
California Institute of Technology, Pasadena, CA 91125
California Lutheran University, Thousand Oaks, CA 91360-2787
California Maritime Academy, Vallejo, CA 94590-0644
California Polytechnic State University: San Luis Obispo, San Luis Obispo, CA 93407
California State Polytechnic University: Pomona, Pomona, CA 91768-4019
California State University
    Bakersfield, Bakersfield, CA 93311-1099
    Chico, Chico, CA 95929-0720
    Dominguez Hills, Carson, CA 90747-9960
    Fresno, Fresno, CA 93740-0057
    Fullerton, Fullerton, CA 92634
    Hayward, Hayward, CA 94542-3035
    Long Beach, Long Beach, CA 90840-0108
    Los Angeles, Los Angeles, CA 90032-8530
    Northridge, Northridge, CA 91328-1286
    Sacramento, Sacramento, CA 95819-6048
    San Bernardino, San Bernardino, CA 92407-2397
    San Marcos, San Marcos, CA 92096-0001
    Stanislaus, Turlock, CA 95380-0283
California University of Pennsylvania, California, PA 15419-1394
Calumet College of St. Joseph, Hammond, IN 46394-2195
Calvary Bible College, Kansas City, MO 64147-1341
Calvin College, Grand Rapids, MI 49546
Camden County College, Blackwood, NJ 08012
Cameron University, Lawton, OK 73505-6377
Campbell University, Buies Creek, NC 27506
Campbellsville College, Campbellsville, KY 42718-2799
Canada College, Redwood City, CA 94061
Canisius College, Buffalo, NY 14208-9989
Cape Cod Community College, West Barnstable, MA 02668-1599
Cape Fear Community College, Wilmington, NC 28401
Capital City Junior College, Little Rock, AR 72204
Capital Community-Technical College, Hartford, CT 06105-2354
Capital University, Columbus, OH 43209-2394
Capitol College, Laurel, MD 20708
Cardinal Stritch College, Milwaukee, WI 53217-3985
Caribbean Center for Advanced Studies: Miami Institute of Psychology, Miami, FL 33166
Caribbean University, Bayamon, PR 00960-0493
Carl Albert State College, Poteau, OK 74953-5208
Carl Sandburg College, Galesburg, IL 61401
Carleton College, Northfield, MN 55057
Carlow College, Pittsburgh, PA 15213-3165
Carnegie Mellon University, Pittsburgh, PA 15213-3890
Carroll College, Waukesha, WI 53186
Carroll College, Helena, MT 59625

Carson-Newman College, Jefferson City, TN 37760
Carteret Community College, Morehead City, NC 28557-2989
Carthage College, Kenosha, WI 53140
Casco Bay College, Portland, ME 04101-3483
Case Western Reserve University, Cleveland, OH 44106-7055
Casper College, Casper, WY 82601
Castle College, Windham, NH 03087-1297
Castleton State College, Castleton, VT 05735-9987
Catawba College, Salisbury, NC 28144-2488
Catawba Valley Community College, Hickory, NC 28602
Catholic Medical Center of Brooklyn and Queens School of Nursing, Woodhaven, NY 11421
Catholic University of America, Washington, DC 20064
Catonsville Community College, Catonsville, MD 21228
Cayuga County Community College, Auburn, NY 13021
Cazenovia College, Cazenovia, NY 13035-9989
Cecil Community College, North East, MD 21901-1999
Cedar Crest College, Allentown, PA 18104-6196
Cedar Valley College, Lancaster, TX 75134
Cedarville College, Cedarville, OH 45314-0601
Centenary College, Hackettstown, NJ 07840-9989
Centenary College of Louisiana, Shreveport, LA 71134-1188
Center for Creative Studies: College of Art and Design, Detroit, MI 48202-4034
Central Alabama Community College
    Alexander City Campus, Alexander City, AL 35010
    Childersburg Campus, Childersburg, AL 35044
Central Arizona College, Coolidge, AZ 85228
Central Baptist College, Conway, AR 72032
Central California Commercial College, Fresno, CA 93704-1706
Central Carolina Community College, Sanford, NC 27330
Central Carolina Technical College, Sumter, SC 29150
Central Christian College of the Bible, Moberly, MO 65270-1997
Central City Business Institute, Syracuse, NY 13202
Central College, Pella, IA 50219-9989
Central College, McPherson, KS 67460-5740
Central Community College, Grand Island, NE 68802-4903
Central Connecticut State University, New Britain, CT 06050
Central Florida Community College, Ocala, FL 34478
Central Maine Medical Center School of Nursing, Lewiston, ME 04240-9986
Central Maine Technical College, Auburn, ME 04210-6498
Central Methodist College, Fayette, MO 65248-1198
Central Michigan University, Mount Pleasant, MI 48859
Central Missouri State University, Warrensburg, MO 64093
Central Ohio Technical College, Newark, OH 43055
Central Oregon Community College, Bend, OR 97701-5998
Central Pennsylvania Business School, Summerdale, PA 17093-0309
Central Piedmont Community College, Charlotte, NC 28235-5009
Central State University, Wilberforce, OH 45384-3002
Central Texas College, Killeen, TX 76540-9990
Central Virginia Community College, Lynchburg, VA 24502
Central Washington University, Ellensburg, WA 98926
Central Wesleyan College, Central, SC 29630-1020
Central Wyoming College, Riverton, WY 82501
Centralia College, Centralia, WA 98531
Centre College, Danville, KY 40422
Cerritos Community College, Norwalk, CA 90650
Cerro Coso Community College, Ridgecrest, CA 93555-7777
Chabot College, Hayward, CA 94545
Chadron State College, Chadron, NE 69337
Chaffey Community College, Rancho Cucamonga, CA 91701-3002
Champlain College, Burlington, VT 05402
Chapman University, Orange, CA 92666
Charles County Community College, La Plata, MD 20646
Charles R. Drew University: College of Allied Health, Los Angeles, CA 90059
Charles Stewart Mott Community College, Flint, MI 48503
Charleston Southern University, Charleston, SC 29411
Chatfield College, St. Martin, OH 45118-9705
Chatham College, Pittsburgh, PA 15232-9987
Chattahoochee Technical Institute, Marietta, GA 30060
Chattahoochee Valley Community College, Phenix City, AL 36869
Chattanooga State Technical Community College, Chattanooga, TN 37406
Chemeketa Community College, Salem, OR 97309-7070
Chesapeake College, Wye Mills, MD 21679-0008
Chesterfield-Marlboro Technical College, Cheraw, SC 29520
Chestnut Hill College, Philadelphia, PA 19118-2695
Cheyney University of Pennsylvania, Cheyney, PA 19319-0019
CHI Institute, Southampton, PA 18966
Chicago State University, Chicago, IL 60628
Chipola Junior College, Marianna, FL 32446

Chippewa Valley Technical College, Eau Claire, WI 54701
Chowan College, Murfreesboro, NC 27855-9901
Christendom College, Front Royal, VA 22630
Christian Brothers University, Memphis, TN 38104-5581
Christian Heritage College, El Cajon, CA 92019
Christopher Newport University, Newport News, VA 23606-2998
Churchman Business School, Easton, PA 18042
Cincinnati Bible College and Seminary, Cincinnati, OH 45204-3200
Cincinnati College of Mortuary Science, Cincinnati, OH 45207-1033
Circleville Bible College, Circleville, OH 43113
Cisco Junior College, Cisco, TX 76437
The Citadel, Charleston, SC 29409
Citrus College, Glendora, CA 91740-1899
City College of San Francisco, San Francisco, CA 94112
City Colleges of Chicago
    Harold Washington College, Chicago, IL 60601
    Kennedy-King College, Chicago, IL 60621
    Malcolm X College, Chicago, IL 60612
    Olive-Harvey College, Chicago, IL 60628
City University, Bellevue, WA 98007-3713
City University of New York
    Baruch College, New York, NY 10010
    Borough of Manhattan Community College, New York, NY 10007-1097
    Bronx Community College, New York, NY 10453
    Brooklyn College, Brooklyn, NY 11210
    City College, New York, NY 10031
    College of Staten Island, Staten Island, NY 10314
    Hostos Community College, Bronx, NY 10451
    Hunter College, New York, NY 10021
    John Jay College of Criminal Justice, New York, NY 10019
    Kingsborough Community College, Brooklyn, NY 11235
    La Guardia Community College, Long Island City, NY 11101
    Lehman College, Bronx, NY 10468
    Medgar Evers College, Brooklyn, NY 11225-2201
    New York City Technical College, Brooklyn, NY 11201-2983
    Queens College, Flushing, NY 11367
    Queensborough Community College, Bayside, NY 11364-1497
    York College, Jamaica, NY 11451-9989
Clackamas Community College, Oregon City, OR 97045
Claflin College, Orangeburg, SC 29115
Claremont McKenna College, Claremont, CA 91711-6420
Clarendon College, Clarendon, TX 79226
Clarion University of Pennsylvania, Clarion, PA 16214
Clark Atlanta University, Atlanta, GA 30314
Clark College, Vancouver, WA 98663
Clark State Community College, Springfield, OH 45501
Clark University, Worcester, MA 01610-1477
Clarke College, Dubuque, IA 52001-3198
Clarkson College, Omaha, NE 68131-2739
Clarkson University, Potsdam, NY 13699
Clatsop Community College, Astoria, OR 97103
Clayton State College, Morrow, GA 30260-1221
Clearwater Christian College, Clearwater, FL 34619-9997
Cleary College, Ypsilanti, MI 48197
Clemson University, Clemson, SC 29634-5124
Cleveland College of Jewish Studies, Beachwood, OH 44122
Cleveland Community College, Shelby, NC 28150
Cleveland Institute of Art, Cleveland, OH 44106
Cleveland Institute of Music, Cleveland, OH 44106
Cleveland State Community College, Cleveland, TN 37320-3570
Cleveland State University, Cleveland, OH 44115-2403
Clinch Valley College of the University of Virginia, Wise, VA 24293
Clinton Community College, Plattsburgh, NY 12901-4297
Clinton Community College, Clinton, IA 52732-6299
Clovis Community College, Clovis, NM 88101-8345
Coastal Carolina Community College, Jacksonville, NC 28540-6877
Coastline Community College, Fountain Valley, CA 92708
Cochise College, Douglas, AZ 85607
Cochran School of Nursing-St. John's Riverside Hospital, Yonkers, NY 10701
Coe College, Cedar Rapids, IA 52402-9983
Coffeyville Community College, Coffeyville, KS 67337
Cogswell College North, Kirkland, WA 98033
Cogswell Polytechnical College, Cupertino, CA 95014
Coker College, Hartsville, SC 29550
Colby College, Waterville, ME 04901-4799
Colby Community College, Colby, KS 67701
Colby-Sawyer College, New London, NH 03257
Colegio Universitario del Este, Carolina, PR 00983-2010
Coleman College, La Mesa, CA 92042-1532
Colgate University, Hamilton, NY 13346-1383

College of Aeronautics, Flushing, NY 11371
College of the Albemarle, Elizabeth City, NC 27906-2327
College of Associated Arts, St. Paul, MN 55102-2199
College of the Atlantic, Bar Harbor, ME 04609
College of the Canyons, Valencia, CA 91355
College of Charleston, Charleston, SC 29424
College of DuPage, Glen Ellyn, IL 60137-6599
College of Eastern Utah, Price, UT 84501
College of Great Falls, Great Falls, MT 59405
College of Health Sciences, Roanoke, VA 24031-3186
College of the Holy Cross, Worcester, MA 01610-2395
College of Insurance, New York, NY 10007-2132
College of Lake County, Grayslake, IL 60030-1198
College of the Mainland, Texas City, TX 77591
College of Marin: Kentfield, Kentfield, CA 94904
College of Micronesia-FSM, Ponape, TT 96941
College Misericordia, Dallas, PA 18612-9984
College of Mount St. Joseph, Cincinnati, OH 45233-1672
College of Mount St. Vincent, Riverdale, NY 10471
College of New Rochelle
    New Rochelle, New Rochelle, NY 10805-2308
    School of New Resources, New Rochelle, NY 10805-2308
College of Notre Dame, Belmont, CA 94002-1997
College of Notre Dame of Maryland, Baltimore, MD 21210-2476
College of Oceaneering, Wilmington, CA 90744
College of the Ozarks, Point Lookout, MO 65726-0017
College of the Redwoods, Eureka, CA 95501-9302
College of St. Benedict, St. Joseph, MN 56374-2099
College of St. Catherine: St. Catherine Campus, St. Paul, MN 55105
College of St. Elizabeth, Morristown, NJ 07960-6989
College of St. Francis, Joliet, IL 60435-6188
College of St. Joseph in Vermont, Rutland, VT 05701-9945
College of St. Mary, Omaha, NE 68124
College of St. Rose, Albany, NY 12203
College of St. Scholastica, Duluth, MN 55811-4199
College of San Mateo, San Mateo, CA 94402
College of Santa Fe, Santa Fe, NM 87501-5634
College of the Sequoias, Visalia, CA 93277
College of the Siskiyous, Weed, CA 96094
College of Southern Idaho, Twin Falls, ID 83303-1238
College of the Southwest, Hobbs, NM 88240-9987
College of West Virginia, Beckley, WV 25802-2830
College of William and Mary, Williamsburg, VA 23187-8795
College of Wooster, Wooster, OH 44691-2363
Collin County Community College District, McKinney, TX 75070-2906
Colorado Christian University, Denver, CO 80226
Colorado College, Colorado Springs, CO 80903
Colorado Institute of Art, Denver, CO 80203
Colorado Mountain College
    Alpine Campus, Steamboat Springs, CO 80477
    Spring Valley Campus, Glenwood Springs, CO 81601
    Timberline Campus, Leadville, CO 80461
Colorado Northwestern Community College, Rangely, CO 81648-9988
Colorado School of Mines, Golden, CO 80401-1873
Colorado State University, Fort Collins, CO 80523-0015
Colorado Technical College, Colorado Springs, CO 80907-3896
Columbia Basin College, Pasco, WA 99301
Columbia Bible College and Seminary, Columbia, SC 29230-3122
Columbia College, Chicago, IL 60605-1996
Columbia College, Columbia, CA 95310
Columbia College, Columbia, SC 29203-5998
Columbia College: Hollywood, Los Angeles, CA 90038
Columbia College of Nursing, Milwaukee, WI 53186
Columbia Junior College of Business, Columbia, SC 29203
Columbia State Community College, Columbia, TN 38401
Columbia Union College, Takoma Park, MD 20912
Columbia University
    Columbia College, New York, NY 10027
    School of Engineering and Applied Science, New York, NY 10027
    School of General Studies, New York, NY 10027
    School of Nursing, New York, NY 10032
Columbia-Greene Community College, Hudson, NY 12534
Columbus College, Columbus, GA 31907-2079
Columbus College of Art and Design, Columbus, OH 43215-3875
Columbus State Community College, Columbus, OH 43216-1609
Commonwealth Institute of Funeral Service, Houston, TX 77090-5913
Community College of Allegheny County
    Allegheny Campus, Pittsburgh, PA 15212
    Boyce Campus, Monroeville, PA 15146
    North Campus, Pittsburgh, PA 15237
    South Campus, West Mifflin, PA 15122
Community College of Aurora, Aurora, CO 80011

Community College of Beaver County, Monaca, PA 15061
Community College of Denver, Denver, CO 80217-3363
Community College of Philadelphia, Philadelphia, PA 19130-3991
Community College of Rhode Island, Warwick, RI 02886-1807
Community College of Vermont, Waterbury, VT 05676
Compton Community College, Compton, CA 90221
Conception Seminary College, Conception, MO 64433
Concord College, Athens, WV 24712
Concordia College, Ann Arbor, MI 48105
Concordia College, Selma, AL 36701
Concordia College, Bronxville, NY 10708
Concordia College, Portland, OR 97211-6099
Concordia College, Seward, NE 68434-9989
Concordia College: Moorhead, Moorhead, MN 56562-9981
Concordia College: St. Paul, St. Paul, MN 55104-5494
Concordia Lutheran College, Austin, TX 78705-2799
Concordia University, River Forest, IL 60305-1499
Concordia University, Irvine, CA 92715-3299
Concordia University Wisconsin, Mequon, WI 53092-9650
Connecticut College, New London, CT 06320
Connors State College, Warner, OK 74469-9700
Contra Costa College, San Pablo, CA 94806
Converse College, Spartanburg, SC 29302-0006
Cooke County College, Gainesville, TX 76240
Cooper Union, New York, NY 10003-7183
Copiah-Lincoln Community College, Wesson, MS 39191
Coppin State College, Baltimore, MD 21216
Corcoran School of Art, Washington, DC 20006
Cornell College, Mount Vernon, IA 52314-1098
Cornell University, Ithaca, NY 14850
Cornell University: Statutory Divisions, Ithaca, NY 14850
Corning Community College, Corning, NY 14830
Cornish College of the Arts, Seattle, WA 98102
Corpus Christi State University, Corpus Christi, TX 78412
Cosumnes River College, Sacramento, CA 95823-5799
Cottey College, Nevada, MO 64772
County College of Morris, Randolph, NJ 07869-2086
Covenant College, Lookout Mountain, GA 30750
Crafton Hills College, Yucaipa, CA 92399-1799
Craven Community College, New Bern, NC 28560
Creighton University, Omaha, NE 68178
Crichton College, Memphis, TN 38175-7830
Criswell College, Dallas, TX 75246
Crowder College, Neosho, MO 64850
Crown College, St. Bonifacius, MN 55375-9001
Cuesta College, San Luis Obispo, CA 93403-8106
Culinary Institute of America, Hyde Park, NY 12538-1499
Culver-Stockton College, Canton, MO 63435-1299
Cumberland College, Williamsburg, KY 40769-6178
Cumberland County College, Vineland, NJ 08360
Cumberland University, Lebanon, TN 37087
Curry College, Milton, MA 02186-9984
Curtis Institute of Music, Philadelphia, PA 19103
Cuyahoga Community College
    Eastern Campus, Highland Hills, OH 44122
    Metropolitan Campus, Cleveland, OH 44115-2878
    Western Campus, Parma, OH 44130
Cuyamaca College, El Cajon, CA 92019-4304
Cypress College, Cypress, CA 90630
Dabney S. Lancaster Community College, Clifton Forge, VA 24422-1000
Daemen College, Amherst, NY 14226-3592
Dakota State University, Madison, SD 57042
Dakota Wesleyan University, Mitchell, SD 57301-4398
Dallas Baptist University, Dallas, TX 75211-9800
Dallas Christian College, Dallas, TX 75234-7299
Dallas Institute of Funeral Service, Dallas, TX 75227
Dalton College, Dalton, GA 30720
Dana College, Blair, NE 68008-1099
Daniel Webster College, Nashua, NH 03063-1300
Danville Area Community College, Danville, IL 61832
Danville Community College, Danville, VA 24541
Dartmouth College, Hanover, NH 03755
Darton College, Albany, GA 31707-3098
Davenport College of Business, Grand Rapids, MI 49503
David Lipscomb University, Nashville, TN 37204-3951
Davidson College, Davidson, NC 28036
Davidson County Community College, Lexington, NC 27293-1287
Davis and Elkins College, Elkins, WV 26241
Davis Junior College of Business, Toledo, OH 43623
Dawson Community College, Glendive, MT 59330
Daytona Beach Community College, Daytona Beach, FL 32120-2811
De Paul University, Chicago, IL 60604

Deaconess College of Nursing, St. Louis, MO 63139
Dean Institute of Technology, Pittsburgh, PA 15226
Dean Junior College, Franklin, MA 02038-1994
Defiance College, Defiance, OH 43512-1695
DeKalb College, Decatur, GA 30021-2396
DeKalb Technical Institute, Clarkston, GA 30021
Del Mar College, Corpus Christi, TX 78404-3897
Delaware County Community College, Media, PA 19063-1094
Delaware State College, Dover, DE 19901
Delaware Technical and Community College
    Southern Campus, Georgetown, DE 19947
    Stanton/Wilmington Campus, Wilmington, DE 19850
    Terry Campus, Dover, DE 19903
Delaware Valley College, Doylestown, PA 18901-2697
Delta College, University Center, MI 48710
Delta State University, Cleveland, MS 38733
Denison University, Granville, OH 43023
Denmark Technical College, Denmark, SC 29042-0327
Denver Technical College, Denver, CO 80222-1658
DePauw University, Greencastle, IN 46135-0037
Des Moines Area Community College, Ankeny, IA 50021
Detroit College of Business, Dearborn, MI 48126-3799
DeVry Institute of Technology
    Addison, Addison, IL 60101-6106
    Atlanta, Decatur, GA 30030-2198
    Chicago, Chicago, IL 60618-5994
    City of Industry, City of Industry, CA 91746-3495
    Columbus, Columbus, OH 43209-2764
    Irving, Irving, TX 75038-4299
    Kansas City, Kansas City, MO 64131-3626
    Phoenix, Phoenix, AZ 85021-2995
Diablo Valley College, Pleasant Hill, CA 94523
Dickinson College, Carlisle, PA 17013-2896
Dickinson State University, Dickinson, ND 58601-4896
Dillard University, New Orleans, LA 70122-3097
Divine Word College, Epworth, IA 52045
Dixie College, St. George, UT 84770
Doane College, Crete, NE 68333
Dodge City Community College, Dodge City, KS 67801-2399
Dominican College of Blauvelt, Orangeburg, NY 10962
Dominican College of San Rafael, San Rafael, CA 94901-8008
Dominican School of Philosophy and Theology, Berkeley, CA 94709
Dona Ana Branch Community College of New Mexico State University, Las Cruces, NM 88003-0001
Donnelly College, Kansas City, KS 66102
Dordt College, Sioux Center, IA 51250
Douglas MacArthur State Technical College, Opp, AL 36467
Dowling College, Oakdale, NY 11769-1999
D-Q University, Davis, CA 95617
Dr. Martin Luther College, New Ulm, MN 56073-3300
Drake University, Des Moines, IA 50311-4505
Draughons Junior College, Montgomery, AL 36104
Draughons Junior College of Business: Nashville, Nashville, TN 37217
Drew University, Madison, NJ 07940
Drexel University, Philadelphia, PA 19104
Drury College, Springfield, MO 65802-9977
DuBois Business College, DuBois, PA 15801
Duke University, Durham, NC 27706
Dull Knife Memorial College, Lame Deer, MT 59043
Dundalk Community College, Baltimore, MD 21222-4692
Duquesne University, Pittsburgh, PA 15282-0201
Durham Technical Community College, Durham, NC 27703
Dutchess Community College, Poughkeepsie, NY 12601-1595
Dyersburg State Community College, Dyersburg, TN 38025-0648
Dyke College, Cleveland, OH 44115
D'Youville College, Buffalo, NY 14201-1084
Earlham College, Richmond, IN 47374
East Arkansas Community College, Forrest City, AR 72335-9598
East Carolina University, Greenville, NC 27858-4353
East Central College, Union, MO 63084
East Central Community College, Decatur, MS 39327
East Central University, Ada, OK 74820-6899
East Coast Bible College, Charlotte, NC 28214
East Georgia College, Swainsboro, GA 30401-2699
East Mississippi Community College, Scooba, MS 39358
East Stroudsburg University of Pennsylvania, East Stroudsburg, PA 18301
East Tennessee State University, Johnson City, TN 37614-0002
East Texas Baptist University, Marshall, TX 75670-1498
East Texas State University
    Commerce, Commerce, TX 75429-3011
    Texarkana, Texarkana, TX 75505-0518
Eastern Arizona College, Thatcher, AZ 85552-0769

Eastern College, St. Davids, PA 19087-3696
Eastern Connecticut State University, Willimantic, CT 06226-2295
Eastern Illinois University, Charleston, IL 61920-3099
Eastern Kentucky University, Richmond, KY 40475-3101
Eastern Maine Technical College, Bangor, ME 04401
Eastern Mennonite College, Harrisonburg, VA 22801-9980
Eastern Michigan University, Ypsilanti, MI 48197-2260
Eastern Montana College, Billings, MT 59101-0298
Eastern Nazarene College, Quincy, MA 02170
Eastern New Mexico University
    Portales, Portales, NM 88130
    Roswell Campus, Roswell, NM 88202-6000
Eastern Oklahoma State College, Wilburton, OK 74578-4999
Eastern Oregon State College, LaGrande, OR 97850-2899
Eastern Shore Community College, Melfa, VA 23410-9755
Eastern Washington University, Cheney, WA 99004-2496
Eastern Wyoming College, Torrington, WY 82240
Eastfield College, Mesquite, TX 75150-1212
Eastman School of Music of the University of Rochester, Rochester, NY 14604-2599
East-West University, Chicago, IL 60605
Eckerd College, St. Petersburg, FL 33711
Edgecombe Community College, Tarboro, NC 27886
Edgewood College, Madison, WI 53711
Edinboro University of Pennsylvania, Edinboro, PA 16444
Edison Community College, Fort Myers, FL 33906-6210
Edison State Community College, Piqua, OH 45356
Edmonds Community College, Lynnwood, WA 98036
Edward Waters College, Jacksonville, FL 32209
El Centro College, Dallas, TX 75202
El Paso Community College, El Paso, TX 79998
Electronic Institutes
    Middletown, Middletown, PA 17057-4851
    Pittsburgh, Pittsburgh, PA 15217
Elgin Community College, Elgin, IL 60123
Elizabeth City State University, Elizabeth City, NC 27909
Elizabethtown College, Elizabethtown, PA 17022-2298
Elizabethtown Community College, Elizabethtown, KY 42701
Ellsworth Community College, Iowa Falls, IA 50126
Elmhurst College, Elmhurst, IL 60126-3296
Elmira College, Elmira, NY 14901-2345
Elms College, Chicopee, MA 01013-2839
Elon College, Elon College, NC 27244-2010
Embry-Riddle Aeronautical University
    Daytona Beach, Daytona Beach, FL 32114-9970
    Prescott Campus, Prescott, AZ 32114-3900
Emerson College, Boston, MA 02116-1596
Emmanuel College, Boston, MA 02115
Emmanuel College, Franklin Springs, GA 30639-0129
Emmaus Bible College, Dubuque, IA 52001
Emory and Henry College, Emory, VA 24327
Emory University, Atlanta, GA 30322
Emporia State University, Emporia, KS 66801-5087
Endicott College, Beverly, MA 01915-9985
Enterprise State Junior College, Enterprise, AL 36331
Erie Community College
    City Campus, Buffalo, NY 14203-2601
    North Campus, Williamsville, NY 14221
    South Campus, Orchard Park, NY 14127-2199
Erskine College, Due West, SC 29639-0176
Escuela de Artes Plasticas de Puerto Rico, San Juan, PR 00902-1112
Essex Agricultural and Technical Institute, Hathorne, MA 01937
Essex Community College, Baltimore, MD 21237-3899
Essex County College, Newark, NJ 07102
Eugene Bible College, Eugene, OR 97405
Eugene Lang College/New School for Social Research, New York, NY 10114-0059
Eureka College, Eureka, IL 61530
Evangel College, Springfield, MO 65802
Everett Community College, Everett, WA 98201
Evergreen State College, Olympia, WA 98505
Evergreen Valley College, San Jose, CA 95135
Fairfield University, Fairfield, CT 06430-7524
Fairleigh Dickinson University
    Edward Williams College, Hackensack, NJ 07601
    Madison, Madison, NJ 07070
Fairmont State College, Fairmont, WV 26554
Faith Baptist Bible College and Theological Seminary, Ankeny, IA 50021
Fashion Institute of Design and Merchandising
    Los Angeles, Los Angeles, CA 90015
    San Francisco, San Francisco, CA 94108-5805
Fashion Institute of Technology, New York, NY 10001-5992

Faulkner University, Montgomery, AL 36109-3398
Fayetteville State University, Fayetteville, NC 28301-4298
Fayetteville Technical Community College, Fayetteville, NC 28303-0236
Feather River College, Quincy, CA 95971
Felician College, Lodi, NJ 07644-2198
Fergus Falls Community College, Fergus Falls, MN 56537-1000
Ferris State University, Big Rapids, MI 49307-2295
Ferrum College, Ferrum, VA 24088
Finger Lakes Community College, Canandaigua, NY 14424-8399
Fisher College, Boston, MA 02116
Fisk University, Nashville, TN 37208
Fitchburg State College, Fitchburg, MA 01420
Five Towns College, Dix Hills, NY 11746-6055
Flagler College, St. Augustine, FL 32084
Flathead Valley Community College, Kalispell, MT 59901
Florence-Darlington Technical College, Florence, SC 29501-0548
Florida Agricultural and Mechanical University, Tallahassee, FL 32307
Florida Atlantic University, Boca Raton, FL 33431-0991
Florida Baptist Theological College, Graceville, FL 32440-1830
Florida Bible College, Kissimmee, FL 34758
Florida Christian College, Kissimmee, FL 34744-4402
Florida College, Temple Terrace, FL 33617
Florida Community College at Jacksonville, Jacksonville, FL 32202-4030
Florida Institute of Technology, Melbourne, FL 32901-6988
Florida International University, Miami, FL 33199
Florida Memorial College, Miami, FL 33054
Florida Southern College, Lakeland, FL 33801-5698
Florida State University, Tallahassee, FL 32306-1009
Floyd College, Rome, GA 30162-1864
Fontbonne College, St. Louis, MO 63105
Foothill College, Los Altos Hills, CA 94022-4599
Fordham University, Bronx, NY 10458
Forsyth School for Dental Hygienists, Boston, MA 02115
Fort Belknap College, Harlem, MT 59526-0159
Fort Hays State University, Hays, KS 67601-4099
Fort Lauderdale College, Fort Lauderdale, FL 33304
Fort Lewis College, Durango, CO 81301
Fort Peck Community College, Poplar, MT 59255-0398
Fort Scott Community College, Fort Scott, KS 66701
Fort Valley State College, Fort Valley, GA 31030
Fox Valley Technical College, Appleton, WI 54913-2277
Framingham State College, Framingham, MA 01701
Francis Marion University, Florence, SC 29501-0547
Franciscan University of Steubenville, Steubenville, OH 43952-6701
Frank Phillips College, Borger, TX 79008-5118
Franklin College, Franklin, IN 46131-2598
Franklin College: Switzerland, Lugano, Switzerland 10021
Franklin Institute of Boston, Boston, MA 02116
Franklin and Marshall College, Lancaster, PA 17604-3003
Franklin Pierce College, Rindge, NH 03461-0060
Franklin University, Columbus, OH 43215-5399
Frederick Community College, Frederick, MD 21702
Free Will Baptist Bible College, Nashville, TN 37205-0117
Freed-Hardeman University, Henderson, TN 38340
Fresno City College, Fresno, CA 93741
Fresno Pacific College, Fresno, CA 93702
Friends University, Wichita, KS 67213
Front Range Community College, Westminster, CO 80030
Frostburg State University, Frostburg, MD 21532-1099
Fullerton College, Fullerton, CA 92634
Fulton-Montgomery Community College, Johnstown, NY 12095-9609
Furman University, Greenville, SC 29613-0645
Gadsden State Community College, Gadsden, AL 35902-0227
Gainesville College, Gainesville, GA 30503
Gallaudet University, Washington, DC 20002
Galveston College, Galveston, TX 77550
Gannon University, Erie, PA 16541-0001
Garden City Community College, Garden City, KS 67846
Gardner-Webb University, Boiling Springs, NC 28017-9980
Garland County Community College, Hot Springs, AR 71913-9120
Gaston College, Dallas, NC 28034-1499
Gateway Community College, Phoenix, AZ 85034
Gateway Community-Technical College, New Haven, CT 06511-5970
Gateway Technical College, Kenosha, WI 53141-1582
Gem City College, Quincy, IL 62306
Genesee Community College, Batavia, NY 14020
Geneva College, Beaver Falls, PA 15010-3599
George C. Wallace State Community College
    Dothan, Dothan, AL 36303-9234
    Selma, Selma, AL 36701-1049
George Fox College, Newberg, OR 97132-9987
George Mason University, Fairfax, VA 22030-4444

George Washington University, Washington, DC 20052
Georgetown College, Georgetown, KY 40324-1696
Georgetown University, Washington, DC 20057
Georgia College, Milledgeville, GA 31061
Georgia Institute of Technology, Atlanta, GA 30332-0320
Georgia Military College, Milledgeville, GA 31061
Georgia Southern University, Statesboro, GA 30460-8024
Georgia Southwestern College, Americus, GA 31709-4693
Georgia State University, Atlanta, GA 30303-3083
Georgian Court College, Lakewood, NJ 08701-2697
Gettysburg College, Gettysburg, PA 17325-1484
Glen Oaks Community College, Centreville, MI 49032
Glendale Community College, Glendale, CA 91208
Glendale Community College, Glendale, AZ 85302-3090
Glenville State College, Glenville, WV 26351-1292
Gloucester County College, Sewell, NJ 08080
GMI Engineering & Management Institute, Flint, MI 48504-4898
Goddard College, Plainfield, VT 05667
God's Bible School and College, Cincinnati, OH 45210
Gogebic Community College, Ironwood, MI 49938
Golden Gate University, San Francisco, CA 94105-2968
Golden West College, Huntington Beach, CA 92647-0592
Goldey-Beacom College, Wilmington, DE 19808
Gonzaga University, Spokane, WA 99258-0001
Gordon College, Wenham, MA 01984-1899
Gordon College, Barnesville, GA 30204
Goshen College, Goshen, IN 46526-9988
Goucher College, Baltimore, MD 21204
Governors State University, University Park, IL 60466
Grace Bible College, Grand Rapids, MI 49509-0910
Grace College, Winona Lake, IN 46590
Grace College of the Bible, Omaha, NE 68108
Graceland College, Lamoni, IA 50140
Grambling State University, Grambling, LA 71245
Grand Canyon University, Phoenix, AZ 85061-1097
Grand Rapids Baptist College and Seminary, Grand Rapids, MI 49505
Grand Rapids Community College, Grand Rapids, MI 49503
Grand Valley State University, Allendale, MI 49401-9403
Grand View College, Des Moines, IA 50316
Grantham College of Engineering, Slidell, LA 70469-5700
Gratz College, Melrose Park, PA 19126
Grays Harbor College, Aberdeen, WA 98520-7599
Grayson County College, Denison, TX 75020
Great Lakes Christian College, Lansing, MI 48917
Great Lakes Junior College of Business, Saginaw, MI 48607
Green Mountain College, Poultney, VT 05764
Green River Community College, Auburn, WA 98002-3699
Greenfield Community College, Greenfield, MA 01301
Greensboro College, Greensboro, NC 27401-1875
Greenville College, Greenville, IL 62246
Greenville Technical College, Greenville, SC 29606-5616
Grinnell College, Grinnell, IA 50112-0807
Grossmont Community College, El Cajon, CA 92020
Grove City College, Grove City, PA 16127-2104
Guam Community College, Barrigada, GU 96921
Guilford College, Greensboro, NC 27410
Gulf Coast Community College, Panama City, FL 32401-1041
Gustavus Adolphus College, St. Peter, MN 56082-1498
Gwinnett Technical Institute, Lawrenceville, GA 30246-1505
Gwynedd-Mercy College, Gwynedd Valley, PA 19437
Hagerstown Business College, Hagerstown, MD 21742
Hagerstown Junior College, Hagerstown, MD 21742-6590
Hahnemann University School of Health Sciences and Humanities, Philadelphia, PA 19102-1192
Halifax Community College, Weldon, NC 27890
Hamilton College, Clinton, NY 13323-1293
Hamilton Technical College, Davenport, IA 52807
Hamline University, St. Paul, MN 55104-1284
Hampden-Sydney College, Hampden-Sydney, VA 23943
Hampshire College, Amherst, MA 01002
Hampton University, Hampton, VA 23668
Hannibal-LaGrange College, Hannibal, MO 63401
Hanover College, Hanover, IN 47243-0108
Harcum Junior College, Bryn Mawr, PA 19010-3476
Harding University, Searcy, AR 72143
Hardin-Simmons University, Abilene, TX 79698
Harford Community College, Bel Air, MD 21015
Harrington Institute of Interior Design, Chicago, IL 60605
Harris Stowe State College, St. Louis, MO 63103
Harrisburg Area Community College, Harrisburg, PA 17110-2999
Harry M. Ayers State Technical College, Anniston, AL 36202
Hartwick College, Oneonta, NY 13820-9989

Harvard and Radcliffe Colleges, Cambridge, MA 02138
Harvey Mudd College, Claremont, CA 91711-5990
Haskell Indian Junior College, Lawrence, KS 66046-4800
Haverford College, Haverford, PA 19041-1392
Hawaii Pacific University, Honolulu, HI 96813
Hawkeye Community College, Waterloo, IA 50704
Haywood Community College, Clyde, NC 28721
Heald Business College
    Concord, Concord, CA 94520
    San Jose, San Jose, CA 95130
Hebrew Union College: Jewish Institute of Religion, Los Angeles, CA 90007
Heidelberg College, Tiffin, OH 44883-2462
Helena Vocational-Technical Center, Helena, MT 59601
Helene Fuld School of Nursing, New York, NY 10035
Hellenic College, Brookline, MA 02146
Henderson Community College, Henderson, KY 42420
Henderson State University, Arkadelphia, AR 71923
Hendrix College, Conway, AR 72032-3080
Henry Ford Community College, Dearborn, MI 48128
Heritage College, Toppenish, WA 98948-9599
Herkimer County Community College, Herkimer, NY 13350-1598
Hesser College, Manchester, NH 03103-9969
Hesston College, Hesston, KS 67062-2093
Hibbing Community College, Hibbing, MN 55746
High Point University, High Point, NC 27262-3598
Highland Community College, Freeport, IL 61032-9341
Highland Community College, Highland, KS 66035-0068
Highland Park Community College, Highland Park, MI 48203
Highline Community College, Des Moines, WA 98198-9800
Hilbert College, Hamburg, NY 14075
Hill College, Hillsboro, TX 76645
Hillsborough Community College, Tampa, FL 33631-3127
Hillsdale College, Hillsdale, MI 49242
Hinds Community College, Raymond, MS 39154-9799
Hiram College, Hiram, OH 44234
Hiwassee College, Madisonville, TN 37354
Hobart College, Geneva, NY 14456-3385
Hobe Sound Bible College, Hobe Sound, FL 33475-1065
Hocking Technical College, Nelsonville, OH 45764-9704
Hofstra University, Hempstead, NY 11550-1090
Hollins College, Roanoke, VA 24020-1707
Holmes Community College, Goodman, MS 39079
Holy Cross College, Notre Dame, IN 46556-0308
Holy Family College, Philadelphia, PA 19114-2094
Holy Names College, Oakland, CA 94619-1699
Holyoke Community College, Holyoke, MA 01040
Hood College, Frederick, MD 21701-8575
Hope College, Holland, MI 49423-3698
Hopkinsville Community College, Hopkinsville, KY 42241-2100
Horry-Georgetown Technical College, Conway, SC 29526-1966
Houghton College, Houghton, NY 14744-9989
Housatonic Community-Technical College, Bridgeport, CT 06608
Houston Baptist University, Houston, TX 77074
Houston Community College, Houston, TX 77270
Howard College, Big Spring, TX 79720
Howard Community College, Columbia, MD 21044
Howard Payne University, Brownwood, TX 76801-2794
Howard University, Washington, DC 20059
Hudson County Community College, Jersey City, NJ 07306
Hudson Valley Community College, Troy, NY 12180
Huertas Junior College, Caguas, PR 00726
Humboldt State University, Arcata, CA 95521
Humphreys College, Stockton, CA 95207-3896
Huntingdon College, Montgomery, AL 36106-2148
Huntington College, Huntington, IN 46750
Huron University, Huron, SD 57350
Husson College, Bangor, ME 04401
Huston-Tillotson College, Austin, TX 78702
Hutchinson Community College, Hutchinson, KS 67501
Idaho State University, Pocatello, ID 83209
Illinois Benedictine College, Lisle, IL 60532-0900
Illinois Central College, East Peoria, IL 61635
Illinois College, Jacksonville, IL 62650-9990
Illinois Eastern Community Colleges
    Frontier Community College, Fairfield, IL 62837-9801
    Lincoln Trail College, Robinson, IL 62454-9803
    Olney Central College, Olney, IL 62450
    Wabash Valley College, Mount Carmel, IL 62863-2657
Illinois Institute of Technology, Chicago, IL 60616
Illinois State University, Normal, IL 61761-6901
Illinois Valley Community College, Oglesby, IL 61348-1099
Illinois Wesleyan University, Bloomington, IL 61702-9965

Immaculata College, Immaculata, PA 19345
Incarnate Word College, San Antonio, TX 78209-6397
Independence Community College, Independence, KS 67301
Indian Hills Community College, Ottumwa, IA 52501
Indian River Community College, Fort Pierce, FL 34981-5599
Indiana State University, Terre Haute, IN 47809
Indiana University
    Bloomington, Bloomington, IN 47405-7700
    East, Richmond, IN 47374-1289
    Northwest, Gary, IN 46408
    South Bend, South Bend, IN 46634-7111
Indiana University of Pennsylvania, Indiana, PA 15705-1088
Indiana University—Purdue University
    Fort Wayne, Fort Wayne, IN 46805
    Indianapolis, Indianapolis, IN 46202-5143
Indiana Vocational Technical College
    Central Indiana, Indianapolis, IN 46206-1763
    Columbus, Columbus, IN 47203
    Eastcentral, Muncie, IN 47307
    Kokomo, Kokomo, IN 46903-1373
    Lafayette, Lafayette, IN 47903
    Northcentral, South Bend, IN 46619
    Northeast, Fort Wayne, IN 46805
    Northwest, Gary, IN 46409-1499
    Southcentral, Sellersburg, IN 47172
    Southeast, Madison, IN 47250
    Southwest, Evansville, IN 47710
    Wabash Valley, Terre Haute, IN 47802
    Whitewater, Richmond, IN 47374
Indiana Wesleyan University, Marion, IN 46953-9980
Institute of American Indian Arts, Santa Fe, NM 87504
Institute for Christian Studies, Austin, TX 78705
Institute of Design and Construction, Brooklyn, NY 11201-5380
Institute of Electronic Technology, Paducah, KY 42001
Inter American University of Puerto Rico
    Arecibo Campus, Arecibo, PR 00613
    Guayama Campus, Guayama, PR 00784
    Metropolitan Campus, San Juan, PR 00919
    San German Campus, San German, PR 00683
International Academy of Merchandising and Design, Chicago, IL 60654-1596
International Bible College, Florence, AL 35630
Inver Hills Community College, Inver Grove Heights, MN 55076-3209
Iona College, New Rochelle, NY 10801-1890
Iowa Central Community College, Fort Dodge, IA 50501
Iowa Lakes Community College, Estherville, IA 51334
Iowa State University, Ames, IA 50011-2010
Iowa Wesleyan College, Mount Pleasant, IA 52641
Iowa Western Community College, Council Bluffs, IA 51502
Isothermal Community College, Spindale, NC 28160
Itasca Community College: Arrowhead Region, Grand Rapids, MN 55744
Ithaca College, Ithaca, NY 14850
ITT Technical Institute
    Dayton, Dayton, OH 45414
    Hoffman Estates, Hoffman Estates, IL 60195
    Phoenix, Phoenix, AZ 85008
    Sacramento, Sacramento, CA 95827
    Youngstown, Youngstown, OH 44501-0779
J. F. Drake State Technical College, Huntsville, AL 35811-3421
J. Sargeant Reynolds Community College, Richmond, VA 23285-5622
Jackson Community College, Jackson, MI 49201
Jackson State University, Jackson, MS 39217
Jacksonville College, Jacksonville, TX 75766
Jacksonville State University, Jacksonville, AL 36265-9982
Jacksonville University, Jacksonville, FL 32211
James H. Faulkner State Community College, Bay Minette, AL 36507
James Madison University, Harrisonburg, VA 22807
James Sprunt Community College, Kenansville, NC 28349-0398
Jamestown Business College, Jamestown, NY 14701
Jamestown College, Jamestown, ND 58401-9989
Jamestown Community College, Jamestown, NY 14701
Jarvis Christian College, Hawkins, TX 75765
Jefferson College, Hillsboro, MO 63050-2441
Jefferson Community College, Louisville, KY 40202
Jefferson Community College, Watertown, NY 13601
Jefferson Davis State Junior College, Brewton, AL 36426
Jefferson State Community College, Birmingham, AL 35215-3098
Jefferson Technical College, Steubenville, OH 43952
Jersey City State College, Jersey City, NJ 07305-1597
Jewish Theological Seminary of America, New York, NY 10027
John A. Logan College, Carterville, IL 62918
John Brown University, Siloam Springs, AR 72761

John C. Calhoun State Community College, Decatur, AL 35609-2216
John Carroll University, University Heights, OH 44118-4581
John F. Kennedy University, Orinda, CA 94563
John M. Patterson State Technical College, Montgomery, AL 36116
John Tyler Community College, Chester, VA 23831-5399
John Wesley College, High Point, NC 27265-3197
Johns Hopkins University, Baltimore, MD 21218
Johns Hopkins University: Peabody Conservatory of Music, Baltimore, MD 21202
Johnson Bible College, Knoxville, TN 37998
Johnson C. Smith University, Charlotte, NC 28216-5398
Johnson County Community College, Overland Park, KS 66210-1299
Johnson State College, Johnson, VT 05656
Johnson Technical Institute, Scranton, PA 18508
Johnson & Wales University, Providence, RI 02903-3703
Johnston Community College, Smithfield, NC 27577-2350
Joliet Junior College, Joliet, IL 60436-9985
Jones College, Jacksonville, FL 32211
Jordan College, Cedar Springs, MI 49319
Judson College, Marion, AL 36756
Judson College, Elgin, IL 60123
Juilliard School, New York, NY 10023-6590
Juniata College, Huntingdon, PA 16652-2119
Kalamazoo College, Kalamazoo, MI 49006-3295
Kalamazoo Valley Community College, Kalamazoo, MI 49009
Kankakee Community College, Kankakee, IL 60901
Kansas City Art Institute, Kansas City, MO 64111
Kansas City Kansas Community College, Kansas City, KS 66112
Kansas Newman College, Wichita, KS 67213-2097
Kansas State University, Manhattan, KS 66506
Kansas Wesleyan University, Salina, KS 67401-6196
Kaskaskia College, Centralia, IL 62801
Katharine Gibbs School
    Boston, Boston, MA 02116
    Melville, Melville, NY 11747
    Montclair, Montclair, NJ 07042
    New York, New York, NY 10166
Kean College of New Jersey, Union, NJ 07083-7131
Keene State College, Keene, NH 03431
Kellogg Community College, Battle Creek, MI 49016-3397
Kelsey-Jenney College, San Diego, CA 92101
Kemper Military School and College, Boonville, MO 65233
Kendall College, Evanston, IL 60201
Kendall College of Art and Design, Grand Rapids, MI 49503-3194
Kennesaw State College, Marietta, GA 30061
Kent State University
    Ashtabula Regional Campus, Ashtabula, OH 44004
    East Liverpool Regional Campus, East Liverpool, OH 43920
    Kent, Kent, OH 44242-0001
    Salem Regional Campus, Salem, OH 44460
    Stark Campus, Canton, OH 44720
    Trumbull Regional Campus, Warren, OH 44483
    Tuscarawas Campus, New Philadelphia, OH 44663-9447
Kentucky State University, Frankfort, KY 40601
Kentucky Wesleyan College, Owensboro, KY 42302-1039
Kenyon College, Gambier, OH 43022-9623
Kettering College of Medical Arts, Kettering, OH 45429
Keuka College, Keuka Park, NY 14478-0098
Keystone Junior College, La Plume, PA 18440-0200
Kilgore College, Kilgore, TX 75662-3299
Kilian Community College, Sioux Falls, SD 57105-1698
King College, Bristol, TN 37620-2699
King's College, Briarcliff Manor, NY 10510-9985
King's College, Wilkes-Barre, PA 18711-0801
Kirkwood Community College, Cedar Rapids, IA 52406
Kirtland Community College, Roscommon, MI 48653
Kishwaukee College, Malta, IL 60150-9699
Knox College, Galesburg, IL 61401-4999
Knoxville Business College, Knoxville, TN 37917
Knoxville College, Knoxville, TN 37921
Kutztown University of Pennsylvania, Kutztown, PA 19530
La Roche College, Pittsburgh, PA 15237
La Salle University, Philadelphia, PA 19141
La Sierra University, Riverside, CA 92515-8247
Labette Community College, Parsons, KS 67357
Lackawanna Junior College, Scranton, PA 18505
Lafayette College, Easton, PA 18042-1770
LaGrange College, LaGrange, GA 30240
Lake Area Vocational Technical Institute, Watertown, SD 57201-0730
Lake City Community College, Lake City, FL 32055
Lake Erie College, Painesville, OH 44077-3389
Lake Forest College, Lake Forest, IL 60045-2399

Lake Land College, Mattoon, IL 61938
Lake Michigan College, Benton Harbor, MI 49022-1899
Lake Superior State University, Sault Ste. Marie, MI 49783
Lake Tahoe Community College, South Lake Tahoe, CA 96151
Lakeland College, Sheboygan, WI 53082-0359
Lakeland Community College, Mentor, OH 44060-7594
Lakeshore Technical College, Cleveland, WI 53015-9761
Lake-Sumter Community College, Leesburg, FL 34788
Lakeview College of Nursing, Danville, IL 61832
Lakewood Community College, White Bear Lake, MN 55110
Lamar Community College, Lamar, CO 81052
Lamar University—Beaumont, Beaumont, TX 77710
Lambuth University, Jackson, TN 38301-5296
Lancaster Bible College, Lancaster, PA 17601
Lander University, Greenwood, SC 29649
Landmark College, Putney, VT 05346
Lane College, Jackson, TN 38301
Lane Community College, Eugene, OR 97405
Laney College, Oakland, CA 94607
Langston University, Langston, OK 73050
Lansing Community College, Lansing, MI 48901
Laramie County Community College, Cheyenne, WY 82007
Laredo Junior College, Laredo, TX 78040-4395
Laredo State University, Laredo, TX 78040-9960
Lasell College, Newton, MA 02166
Lassen College, Susanville, CA 96130
Lawrence Technological University, Southfield, MI 48075-1058
Lawrence University, Appleton, WI 54912-0599
Lawson State Community College, Birmingham, AL 35221-1717
LDS Business College, Salt Lake City, UT 84111-1392
Le Moyne College, Syracuse, NY 13214-1399
Lebanon Valley College of Pennsylvania, Annville, PA 17003-0501
Lee College, Cleveland, TN 37311
Lee College, Baytown, TX 77522-0818
Lees College, Jackson, KY 41339
Lees-McRae College, Banner Elk, NC 28604
Lehigh County Community College, Schnecksville, PA 18078-2598
Lehigh University, Bethlehem, PA 18015-3094
LeMoyne-Owen College, Memphis, TN 38126
Lenoir Community College, Kinston, NC 28501
Lenoir-Rhyne College, Hickory, NC 28603
Lesley College, Cambridge, MA 02138-2790
LeTourneau University, Longview, TX 75607-7001
Lewis and Clark College, Portland, OR 97219-7899
Lewis and Clark Community College, Godfrey, IL 62035-2466
Lewis Clark State College, Lewiston, ID 83501-2698
Lewis College of Business, Detroit, MI 48235
Lewis University, Romeoville, IL 60441-2298
Lexington Community College, Lexington, KY 40506-0235
Lexington Institute of Hospitality Careers, Chicago, IL 60643-3294
Liberty University, Lynchburg, VA 24506-8001
LIFE Bible College, San Dimas, CA 91773-3298
Lima Technical College, Lima, OH 45804
Limestone College, Gaffney, SC 29340
Lincoln Christian College and Seminary, Lincoln, IL 62656-2111
Lincoln College, Lincoln, IL 62656
Lincoln Land Community College, Springfield, IL 62794-9256
Lincoln Memorial University, Harrogate, TN 37752
Lincoln School of Commerce, Lincoln, NE 68501-2826
Lincoln Technical Institute, Allentown, PA 18104
Lincoln University, Lincoln University, PA 19352-0999
Lincoln University, San Francisco, CA 94118
Lincoln University, Jefferson City, MO 65102-0029
Lindenwood College, St. Charles, MO 63301-1695
Lindsey Wilson College, Columbia, KY 42728
Linfield College, McMinnville, OR 97128-6894
Linn-Benton Community College, Albany, OR 97321-3779
Little Big Horn College, Crow Agency, MT 59022
Little Hoop Community College, Fort Totten, ND 58335
Livingston University, Livingston, AL 35470
Livingstone College, Salisbury, NC 28144-5213
Lock Haven University of Pennsylvania, Lock Haven, PA 17745
Lon Morris College, Jacksonville, TX 75766
Long Beach City College, Long Beach, CA 90808
Long Island College Hospital School of Nursing, Brooklyn, NY 11201
Long Island University
    Brooklyn Campus, Brooklyn, NY 11201
    C. W. Post Campus, Brookville, NY 11548
    Southampton Campus, Southampton, NY 11968
Longview Community College, Lee's Summit, MO 64081
Longwood College, Farmville, VA 23909-1898
Lorain County Community College, Elyria, OH 44035-1697

Loras College, Dubuque, IA 52001
Lord Fairfax Community College, Middletown, VA 22645
Los Angeles City College, Los Angeles, CA 90029-3589
Los Angeles Harbor College, Wilmington, CA 90744
Los Angeles Mission College, Sylmar, CA 91342
Los Angeles Pierce College, Woodland Hills, CA 91371
Los Angeles Trade and Technical College, Los Angeles, CA 90015-4181
Los Angeles Valley College, Van Nuys, CA 91401-4096
Los Medanos College, Pittsburg, CA 94565
Louisburg College, Louisburg, NC 27549
Louise Salinger Academy of Fashion, San Francisco, CA 94105
Louisiana College, Pineville, LA 71359-0560
Louisiana State University
    Agricultural and Mechanical College, Baton Rouge, LA 70803-2750
    Alexandria, Alexandria, LA 71302-9633
    Eunice, Eunice, LA 70535
    Medical Center, New Orleans, LA 70112-2223
    Shreveport, Shreveport, LA 71115
Louisiana Tech University, Ruston, LA 71272
Louisville Technical Institute, Louisville, KY 40218-4524
Lourdes College, Sylvania, OH 43560-2898
Lower Columbia College, Longview, WA 98632
Loyola College in Maryland, Baltimore, MD 21210-2699
Loyola Marymount University, Los Angeles, CA 90045-2699
Loyola University, New Orleans, LA 70118-6143
Loyola University of Chicago, Chicago, IL 60611
Lubbock Christian University, Lubbock, TX 79407
Lurleen B. Wallace State Junior College, Andalusia, AL 36420-1418
Luther College, Decorah, IA 52101-1042
Lutheran Bible Institute of Seattle, Issaquah, WA 98027
Lutheran College of Health Professions, Fort Wayne, IN 46807
Luzerne County Community College, Nanticoke, PA 18634-9804
Lycoming College, Williamsport, PA 17701
Lynchburg College, Lynchburg, VA 24501-9986
Lyndon State College, Lyndonville, VT 05851
Lynn University, Boca Raton, FL 33431-5598
Macalester College, St. Paul, MN 55105-1899
MacCormac Junior College, Chicago, IL 60605
MacMurray College, Jacksonville, IL 62650-2590
Macomb Community College, Warren, MI 48093-3896
Macon College, Macon, GA 31297
Madison Area Technical College, Madison, WI 53704-2599
Madison Junior College of Business, Madison, WI 53705-1399
Madisonville Community College, Madisonville, KY 42431
Madonna University, Livonia, MI 48150-1173
Magnolia Bible College, Kosciusko, MS 39090
Maharishi International University, Fairfield, IA 52557-1155
Maine College of Art, Portland, ME 04101-3987
Maine Maritime Academy, Castine, ME 04420-5000
Malone College, Canton, OH 44709-3897
Manatee Community College, Bradenton, FL 34206-1849
Manchester College, North Manchester, IN 46962-0365
Manhattan Christian College, Manhattan, KS 66502
Manhattan College, Riverdale, NY 10471
Manhattan School of Music, New York, NY 10027-4698
Manhattanville College, Purchase, NY 10577
Mankato State University, Mankato, MN 56002-8400
Mannes College of Music, New York, NY 10024
Manor Junior College, Jenkintown, PA 19046-3399
Mansfield University of Pennsylvania, Mansfield, PA 16933
Maple Woods Community College, Kansas City, MO 64156-1299
Maranatha Baptist Bible College, Watertown, WI 53094
Maria College, Albany, NY 12208
Marian College, Indianapolis, IN 46222
Marian College of Fond du Lac, Fond du Lac, WI 54935-4699
Marian Court Junior College, Swampscott, MA 01907-2896
Marietta College, Marietta, OH 45750-4005
Marion Military Institute, Marion, AL 36756-0420
Marion Technical College, Marion, OH 43302-5694
Marist College, Poughkeepsie, NY 12601-1387
Marlboro College, Marlboro, VT 05344-0300
Marquette University, Milwaukee, WI 53233-9988
Mars Hill College, Mars Hill, NC 28754
Marshall University, Huntington, WV 25755-2020
Marshalltown Community College, Marshalltown, IA 50158
Martin Community College, Williamston, NC 27892-9988
Martin University, Indianapolis, IN 46218
Mary Baldwin College, Staunton, VA 24401
Mary Washington College, Fredericksburg, VA 22401-5358
Marygrove College, Detroit, MI 48221
Maryland Institute College of Art, Baltimore, MD 21217
Marylhurst College, Marylhurst, OR 97036

Marymount College, Tarrytown, NY 10591-3796
Marymount College, Rancho Palos Verdes, CA 90274-6299
Marymount Manhattan College, New York, NY 10021-4597
Marymount University, Arlington, VA 22207-4299
Maryville College, Maryville, TN 37801
Maryville University, St. Louis, MO 63141
Marywood College, Scranton, PA 18509-9989
Massachusetts Bay Community College, Wellesley Hills, MA 02181
Massachusetts College of Art, Boston, MA 02115-5882
Massachusetts College of Pharmacy and Allied Health Sciences, Boston, MA 02115
Massachusetts Institute of Technology, Cambridge, MA 02139
Massachusetts Maritime Academy, Buzzards Bay, MA 02532-1803
Massasoit Community College, Brockton, MA 02402
Master's College, Santa Clarita, CA 91322-0878
Mater Dei College, Ogdensburg, NY 13669
Mayland Community College, Spruce Pine, NC 28777
Maysville Community College, Maysville, KY 41056
Mayville State University, Mayville, ND 58257
McCook Community College, McCook, NE 69001
McDowell Technical Community College, Marion, NC 28752
McGill University, Montreal, Quebec, Canada H3A 2T5
McHenry County College, Crystal Lake, IL 60012
McIntosh College, Dover, NH 03820
McKendree College, Lebanon, IL 62254
McMurry University, Abilene, TX 79697-0001
McNeese State University, Lake Charles, LA 70609-2495
McPherson College, McPherson, KS 67460
Meadows College of Business, Columbus, GA 31906
Medaille College, Buffalo, NY 14214
Medcenter One College of Nursing, Bismarck, ND 58501
Medical College of Georgia, Augusta, GA 30912
Medical University of South Carolina, Charleston, SC 29425-2970
Memphis College of Art, Memphis, TN 38112
Memphis State University, Memphis, TN 38152
Mendocino College, Ukiah, CA 95482
Menlo College, Atherton, CA 94027-4301
Mennonite College of Nursing, Bloomington, IL 61701
Merced College, Merced, CA 95348-2898
Mercer County Community College, Trenton, NJ 08690-1099
Mercer University
    Atlanta, Atlanta, GA 30341-4115
    Macon, Macon, GA 31207-0001
Mercy College, Dobbs Ferry, NY 10522
Mercyhurst College, Erie, PA 16546
Meredith College, Raleigh, NC 27607-5298
Meridian Community College, Meridian, MS 39307
Merrimack College, North Andover, MA 01845
Merritt College, Oakland, CA 94619
Mesa Community College, Mesa, AZ 85202
Mesa State College, Grand Junction, CO 81502
Mesabi Community College: Arrowhead Region, Virginia, MN 55792
Messiah College, Grantham, PA 17027-0800
Methodist College, Fayetteville, NC 28311-1420
Metropolitan Community College, Omaha, NE 68103-3777
Metropolitan State College of Denver, Denver, CO 80217-3362
Metropolitan State University, St. Paul, MN 55106-5000
Miami University
    Hamilton Campus, Hamilton, OH 45011
    Middletown Campus, Middletown, OH 45042
    Oxford Campus, Oxford, OH 45056
Miami-Dade Community College, Miami, FL 33132-2297
Miami-Jacobs College, Dayton, OH 45401
Michigan Christian College, Rochester Hills, MI 48307-2764
Michigan State University, East Lansing, MI 48824-1046
Michigan Technological University, Houghton, MI 49931-1295
Micronesian Occupational College, Koror, TT 96940-9999
Mid Michigan Community College, Harrison, MI 48625
Mid Plains Community College, North Platte, NE 69101-0001
Mid-America Bible College, Oklahoma City, OK 73170
MidAmerica Nazarene College, Olathe, KS 66062-1899
Mid-Continent Baptist Bible College, Mayfield, KY 42066-0357
Middle Georgia College, Cochran, GA 31014-1599
Middle Tennessee State University, Murfreesboro, TN 37132
Middlebury College, Middlebury, VT 05753-6002
Middlesex Community College, Bedford, MA 01730
Middlesex Community-Technical College, Middletown, CT 06457
Midland College, Midland, TX 79705
Midland Lutheran College, Fremont, NE 68025
Midlands Technical College, Columbia, SC 29202
Mid-State Technical College, Wisconsin Rapids, WI 54494
Midway College, Midway, KY 40347-1120

Midwestern State University, Wichita Falls, TX 76308
Miles College, Fairfield, AL 35064
Miles Community College, Miles City, MT 59301
Millersville University of Pennsylvania, Millersville, PA 17551-0302
Milligan College, Milligan College, TN 37682
Millikin University, Decatur, IL 62522-9982
Mills College, Oakland, CA 94613
Millsaps College, Jackson, MS 39210
Milwaukee College of Business, Milwaukee, WI 53203
Milwaukee Institute of Art & Design, Milwaukee, WI 53202
Milwaukee School of Engineering, Milwaukee, WI 53201-0644
Mineral Area College, Flat River, MO 63601
Minneapolis College of Art and Design, Minneapolis, MN 55404
Minneapolis Community College, Minneapolis, MN 55403-1779
Minnesota Bible College, Rochester, MN 55902
Minot State University, Minot, ND 58702-5002
MiraCosta College, Oceanside, CA 92056-3899
Miss Wade's Fashion Merchandising College, Dallas, TX 75258
Mission College, Santa Clara, CA 95054-1897
Mississippi College, Clinton, MS 39058
Mississippi County Community College, Blytheville, AR 72316-1109
Mississippi Delta Community College, Moorhead, MS 38761
Mississippi Gulf Coast Community College
    Jackson County Campus, Gautier, MS 39553
    Jefferson Davis Campus, Gulfport, MS 39507-3894
    Perkinston, Perkinston, MS 39573
Mississippi State University, Mississippi State, MS 39762
Mississippi University for Women, Columbus, MS 39701
Mississippi Valley State University, Itta Bena, MS 38941
Missoula Vocational-Technical Center, Missoula, MT 59801
Missouri Baptist College, St. Louis, MO 63141
Missouri Southern State College, Joplin, MO 64801-1595
Missouri Valley College, Marshall, MO 65340
Missouri Western State College, St. Joseph, MO 64507-2294
Mitchell College, New London, CT 06320
Mitchell Community College, Statesville, NC 28677
Mitchell Vocational Technical Institute, Mitchell, SD 57301
Moberly Area Community College, Moberly, MO 65270
Modesto Junior College, Modesto, CA 95350
Mohave Community College, Kingman, AZ 86401
Mohawk Valley Community College, Utica, NY 13501-9979
Molloy College, Rockville Centre, NY 11570
Monmouth College, Monmouth, IL 61462-9989
Monmouth College, West Long Branch, NJ 07764-1898
Monroe College, Bronx, NY 10468
Monroe Community College, Rochester, NY 14623
Monroe County Community College, Monroe, MI 48161
Montana College of Mineral Science and Technology, Butte, MT 59701
Montana State University, Bozeman, MT 59717-0016
Montay College, Chicago, IL 60659-3115
Montcalm Community College, Sidney, MI 48885-0300
Montclair State College, Upper Montclair, NJ 07043-1624
Monterey Institute of International Studies, Monterey, CA 93940
Monterey Peninsula College, Monterey, CA 93940
Montgomery College
    Germantown Campus, Germantown, MD 20876
    Rockville Campus, Rockville, MD 20850
    Takoma Park Campus, Takoma Park, MD 20912
Montgomery Community College, Troy, NC 27371-0787
Montgomery County Community College, Blue Bell, PA 19422-0758
Montreat-Anderson College, Montreat, NC 28757-9987
Montserrat College of Art, Beverly, MA 01915
Moody Bible Institute, Chicago, IL 60610-3284
Moore College of Art and Design, Philadelphia, PA 19103-1179
Moorhead State University, Moorhead, MN 56563
Moorpark College, Moorpark, CA 93021
Moraine Park Technical College, Fond du Lac, WI 54935
Moraine Valley Community College, Palos Hills, IL 60465-0937
Moravian College, Bethlehem, PA 18018
Morehead State University, Morehead, KY 40351
Morehouse College, Atlanta, GA 30314
Morgan Community College, Fort Morgan, CO 80701
Morgan State University, Baltimore, MD 21239
Morningside College, Sioux City, IA 51106-1751
Morris Brown College, Atlanta, GA 30314
Morris College, Sumter, SC 29150-3599
Morrison Institute of Technology, Morrison, IL 61270-0410
Morton College, Cicero, IL 60650
Motlow State Community College, Tullahoma, TN 37388-8100
Mount Aloysius College, Cresson, PA 16630
Mount Holyoke College, South Hadley, MA 01075-1488
Mount Hood Community College, Gresham, OR 97030

Mount Ida College, Newton Centre, MA 02159
Mount Marty College, Yankton, SD 57078-3724
Mount Mary College, Milwaukee, WI 53222-4597
Mount Mercy College, Cedar Rapids, IA 52402
Mount Olive College, Mount Olive, NC 28365
Mount St. Clare College, Clinton, IA 52732
Mount St. Mary College, Newburgh, NY 12550
Mount St. Mary's College, Los Angeles, CA 90049-1597
Mount St. Mary's College, Emmitsburg, MD 21727-7796
Mount San Antonio College, Walnut, CA 91789
Mount San Jacinto College, San Jacinto, CA 92583-2399
Mount Senario College, Ladysmith, WI 54848
Mount Union College, Alliance, OH 44601-3993
Mount Vernon College, Washington, DC 20007
Mount Wachusett Community College, Gardner, MA 01440
Mountain Empire Community College, Big Stone Gap, VA 24219
Mountain View College, Dallas, TX 75211-6599
Muhlenberg College, Allentown, PA 18104
Multnomah School of the Bible, Portland, OR 97220-5898
Murray State University, Murray, KY 42071
Muscatine Community College, Muscatine, IA 52761-5396
Muskegon Community College, Muskegon, MI 49442
Muskingum College, New Concord, OH 43762
Napa Valley College, Napa, CA 94558
Naropa Institute, Boulder, CO 80302
Nash Community College, Rocky Mount, NC 27804-7488
Nashville State Technical Institute, Nashville, TN 37209
Nassau Community College, Garden City, NY 11530-6793
National Business College, Roanoke, VA 24017-0400
National College, Denver, CO 80222
National College, Kansas City, MO 64111
National College, Albuquerque, NM 87110-3156
National College, Rapid City, SD 57709-1780
National College of Chiropractic, Lombard, IL 60148
National Education Center
    Bauder Campus, Fort Lauderdale, FL 33334-3971
    Vale Tech Campus, Blairsville, PA 15717
National University, San Diego, CA 92108-4107
National-Louis University, Evanston, IL 60201-1796
Navajo Community College, Tsaile, AZ 86556
Navarro College, Corsicana, TX 75110
Nazarene Bible College, Colorado Springs, CO 80935
Nazareth College of Rochester, Rochester, NY 14618-3790
Nebraska Christian College, Norfolk, NE 68701
Nebraska College of Technical Agriculture, Curtis, NE 69025-0069
Nebraska Indian Community College, Winnebago, NE 68071
Nebraska Methodist College of Nursing and Allied Health, Omaha, NE 68114
Nebraska Wesleyan University, Lincoln, NE 68504
NEI College of Technology, Minneapolis, MN 55421-9990
Neosho County Community College, Chanute, KS 66720
Ner Israel Rabbinical College, Baltimore, MD 21208-9964
Neumann College, Aston, PA 19014-1297
New College of California, San Francisco, CA 94110
New College of the University of South Florida, Sarasota, FL 34243-2197
New England Banking Institute, Boston, MA 02111
New England College, Henniker, NH 03242-0792
New England Conservatory of Music, Boston, MA 02115
New England Culinary Institute, Montpelier, VT 05602
New England Institute of Technology
    Warwick, Warwick, RI 02886
    West Palm Beach, West Palm Beach, FL 33407
New Hampshire College, Manchester, NH 03106-1045
New Hampshire Technical College
    Berlin, Berlin, NH 03570
    Claremont, Claremont, NH 03743-9707
    Laconia, Laconia, NH 03246
    Manchester, Manchester, NH 03102-8518
    Nashua, Nashua, NH 03061-2052
    Stratham, Stratham, NH 03885-2297
New Hampshire Technical Institute, Concord, NH 03301
New Jersey Institute of Technology, Newark, NJ 07102-9938
New Mexico Highlands University, Las Vegas, NM 87701
New Mexico Institute of Mining and Technology, Socorro, NM 87801
New Mexico Junior College, Hobbs, NM 88240
New Mexico Military Institute, Roswell, NM 88201-5173
New Mexico State University
    Alamogordo, Alamogordo, NM 88310
    Carlsbad, Carlsbad, NM 88220
    Las Cruces, Las Cruces, NM 88003-0001
New River Community College, Dublin, VA 24084
New York Institute of Technology, Old Westbury, NY 11568-0170

New York School of Interior Design, New York, NY 10022
New York University, New York, NY 10011-9108
Newberry College, Newberry, SC 29108
Newbury College, Brookline, MA 02146
Niagara County Community College, Sanborn, NY 14132
Niagara University, Niagara Falls, NY 14109
Nicholls State University, Thibodaux, LA 70310
Nichols College, Dudley, MA 01570-5000
Nicolet Area Technical College, Rhinelander, WI 54501
Norfolk State University, Norfolk, VA 23504
Normandale Community College, Bloomington, MN 55431
North Adams State College, North Adams, MA 01247
North Arkansas Community/Technical College, Harrison, AR 72601
North Carolina Agricultural and Technical State University, Greensboro, NC 27411
North Carolina Central University, Durham, NC 27707
North Carolina School of the Arts, Winston-Salem, NC 27117-2189
North Carolina State University, Raleigh, NC 27695-7103
North Carolina Wesleyan College, Rocky Mount, NC 27804
North Central Bible College, Minneapolis, MN 55404
North Central College, Naperville, IL 60566-7065
North Central Technical College, Mansfield, OH 44901
North Country Community College, Saranac Lake, NY 12983
North Dakota State College of Science, Wahpeton, ND 58076
North Dakota State University
    Bottineau, Bottineau, ND 58318-1198
    Fargo, Fargo, ND 58105
North Florida Junior College, Madison, FL 32340
North Georgia College, Dahlonega, GA 30597
North Greenville College, Tigerville, SC 29688-1892
North Harris Montgomery Community College District, Houston, TX 77060-2000
North Hennepin Community College, Minneapolis, MN 55445
North Idaho College, Coeur d'Alene, ID 83814
North Iowa Area Community College, Mason City, IA 50401
North Lake College, Irving, TX 75038-3899
North Park College, Chicago, IL 60625-4987
North Seattle Community College, Seattle, WA 98103-3599
North Shore Community College, Danvers, MA 01923
Northampton County Area Community College, Bethlehem, PA 18017
Northcentral Technical College, Wausau, WI 54401
Northeast Alabama Community College, Rainsville, AL 35986
Northeast Community College, Norfolk, NE 68702-0469
Northeast Iowa Community College, Calmar, IA 52132
Northeast Louisiana University, Monroe, LA 71209-0730
Northeast Missouri State University, Kirksville, MO 63501-9980
Northeast State Technical Community College, Blountville, TN 37617
Northeast Texas Community College, Mount Pleasant, TX 75455-1307
Northeast Wisconsin Technical College, Green Bay, WI 54307-9042
Northeastern Illinois University, Chicago, IL 60625
Northeastern Junior College, Sterling, CO 80751
Northeastern Oklahoma Agricultural and Mechanical College, Miami, OK 74354-6497
Northeastern State University, Tahlequah, OK 74464
Northeastern University, Boston, MA 02115-9959
Northern Arizona University, Flagstaff, AZ 86011-4084
Northern Essex Community College, Haverhill, MA 01830-2399
Northern Illinois University, DeKalb, IL 60115-2854
Northern Kentucky University, Highland Heights, KY 41099-7010
Northern Maine Technical College, Presque Isle, ME 04769
Northern Michigan University, Marquette, MI 49855
Northern Montana College, Havre, MT 59501
Northern Nevada Community College, Elko, NV 89801
Northern New Mexico Community College, Espanola, NM 87532
Northern State University, Aberdeen, SD 57401
Northern Virginia Community College, Annandale, VA 22003
Northland College, Ashland, WI 54806
Northland Pioneer College, Holbrook, AZ 86025
Northwest Alabama Community College, Phil Campbell, AL 35581
Northwest Christian College, Eugene, OR 97401-9983
Northwest College, Powell, WY 82435
Northwest College of the Assemblies of God, Kirkland, WA 98083-0579
Northwest Iowa Community College, Sheldon, IA 51201
Northwest Mississippi Community College, Senatobia, MS 38668
Northwest Missouri Community College, St. Joseph, MO 64503-2911
Northwest Missouri State University, Maryville, MO 64468-6001
Northwest Nazarene College, Nampa, ID 83686
Northwest Technical College, Archbold, OH 43502
Northwest Technical Institute, Eden Prairie, MN 55344-5351
Northwestern College, Watertown, WI 53094-4899
Northwestern College, Lima, OH 45805
Northwestern College, Roseville, MN 55113

Northwestern College, Orange City, IA 51041
Northwestern Connecticut Community-Technical College, Winsted, CT 06098
Northwestern Michigan College, Traverse City, MI 49684
Northwestern Oklahoma State University, Alva, OK 73717
Northwestern State University, Natchitoches, LA 71497
Northwestern University, Evanston, IL 60204-3060
Northwood University, Midland, MI 48640
Northwood University: Texas Campus, Cedar Hill, TX 75104-0058
Norwalk Community-Technical College, Norwalk, CT 06854
Norwich University, Northfield, VT 05663
Notre Dame College, Manchester, NH 03104-2299
Notre Dame College of Ohio, South Euclid, OH 44121
Nova University, Fort Lauderdale, FL 33314
Nunez Community College, Chalmette, LA 70043
Nyack College, Nyack, NY 10960
Oak Hills Bible College, Bemidji, MN 56601
Oakland City College, Oakland City, IN 47660
Oakland Community College, Bloomfield Hills, MI 48304-2266
Oakland University, Rochester, MI 48309-4401
Oakton Community College, Des Plaines, IL 60016
Oakwood College, Huntsville, AL 35896
Oberlin College, Oberlin, OH 44074
Oblate College, Washington, DC 20017-1587
Occidental College, Los Angeles, CA 90041-3393
Ocean County College, Toms River, NJ 08753-2001
Odessa College, Odessa, TX 79764-7127
Oglala Lakota College, Kyle, SD 57752
Oglethorpe University, Atlanta, GA 30319-2797
Ohio Dominican College, Columbus, OH 43219-2099
Ohio Institute of Photography and Technology, Dayton, OH 45439
Ohio Northern University, Ada, OH 45810-1599
Ohio State University
    Agricultural Technical Institute, Wooster, OH 44691-4099
    Columbus Campus, Columbus, OH 43210-1200
    Lima Campus, Lima, OH 45804-3596
    Mansfield Campus, Mansfield, OH 44906
    Marion Campus, Marion, OH 43302
    Newark Campus, Newark, OH 43055
Ohio University
    Athens, Athens, OH 45701-2979
    Chillicothe Campus, Chillicothe, OH 45601
    Eastern Campus, St. Clairsville, OH 43950
    Lancaster Campus, Lancaster, OH 43130
    Southern Campus at Ironton, Ironton, OH 45638
    Zanesville Campus, Zanesville, OH 43701
Ohio Valley Business College, East Liverpool, OH 43920
Ohio Valley College, Parkersburg, WV 26101-9975
Ohio Wesleyan University, Delaware, OH 43015
Ohr Somayach Tanenbaum Education Center, Monsey, NY 10952
Okaloosa-Walton Community College, Niceville, FL 32578
Oklahoma Baptist University, Shawnee, OK 74801
Oklahoma Christian University of Science and Arts, Oklahoma City, OK 73136-1100
Oklahoma City Community College, Oklahoma City, OK 73159
Oklahoma City University, Oklahoma City, OK 73106
Oklahoma Panhandle State University, Goodwell, OK 73939-0430
Oklahoma State University
    Oklahoma City, Oklahoma City, OK 73107
    Stillwater, Stillwater, OK 74078
    Technical Branch: Okmulgee, Okmulgee, OK 74447-3901
Old Dominion University, Norfolk, VA 23529-0050
Olean Business Institute, Olean, NY 14760-2691
Olivet College, Olivet, MI 49076
Olivet Nazarene University, Kankakee, IL 60901-0592
Olympic College, Bremerton, WA 98310-1699
Onondaga Community College, Syracuse, NY 13215
Oral Roberts University, Tulsa, OK 74171
Orange County Community College, Middletown, NY 10940
Oregon Health Sciences University, Portland, OR 97201
Oregon Institute of Technology, Klamath Falls, OR 97601-8801
Oregon Polytechnic Institute, Portland, OR 97214
Oregon State University, Corvallis, OR 97331-2130
Otero Junior College, La Junta, CO 81050
Otis School of Art and Design, Los Angeles, CA 90057
Ottawa University, Ottawa, KS 66067-3399
Otterbein College, Westerville, OH 43081
Ouachita Baptist University, Arkadelphia, AR 71998-0001
Our Lady of Holy Cross College, New Orleans, LA 70131-7399
Our Lady of the Lake University of San Antonio, San Antonio, TX 78207-4689

Owens Technical College
    Findlay Campus, Findlay, OH 45840
    Toledo, Toledo, OH 43699-1947
Owensboro Junior College of Business, Owensboro, KY 42303
Oxford College of Emory University, Oxford, GA 30267-1328
Ozark Christian College, Joplin, MO 64801
Pace University
    College of White Plains, White Plains, NY 10603-3796
    New York, New York, NY 10038
    Pleasantville/Briarcliff, Pleasantville, NY 10570
Pacific Christian College, Fullerton, CA 92631
Pacific Lutheran University, Tacoma, WA 98447-0003
Pacific Northwest College of Art, Portland, OR 97205-2486
Pacific Oaks College, Pasadena, CA 91103
Pacific Union College, Angwin, CA 94508
Pacific University, Forest Grove, OR 97116-1797
Paducah Community College, Paducah, KY 42002-7380
Paier College of Art, Hamden, CT 06517-4025
Paine College, Augusta, GA 30901-3182
Palm Beach Atlantic College, West Palm Beach, FL 33416-4708
Palm Beach Community College, Lake Worth, FL 33461
Palo Alto College, San Antonio, TX 78224
Palomar College, San Marcos, CA 92069
Pamlico Community College, Grantsboro, NC 28529
Panola College, Carthage, TX 75633
Paradise Valley Community College, Phoenix, AZ 85032
Paris Junior College, Paris, TX 75460
Park College, Parkville, MO 64152-9970
Parks College, Albuquerque, NM 87102
Parks College of St. Louis University, Cahokia, IL 62206
Parsons School of Design, New York, NY 10011
Pasadena City College, Pasadena, CA 91106
Pasco-Hernando Community College, Dade City, FL 34654-5199
Passaic County Community College, Paterson, NJ 07509
Patrick Henry Community College, Martinsville, VA 24115-5311
Patten College, Oakland, CA 94601-2699
Paul D. Camp Community College, Franklin, VA 23851-0737
Paul Quinn College, Dallas, TX 75241
Paul Smith's College, Paul Smiths, NY 12970-0265
Peace College, Raleigh, NC 27604-1194
Pearl River Community College, Poplarville, MS 39470
Pellissippi State Technical Community College, Knoxville, TN 37933-0990
Pembroke State University, Pembroke, NC 28372
Peninsula College, Port Angeles, WA 98362
Penn State
    Erie Behrend College, Erie, PA 16563
    Harrisburg Capital College, Middletown, PA 17057-4898
    University Park Campus, University Park, PA 16802
Penn Technical Institute, Pittsburgh, PA 15222
Penn Valley Community College, Kansas City, MO 64111
Pennsylvania College of Technology, Williamsport, PA 17701-5799
Pennsylvania Institute of Technology, Media, PA 19063-4098
Pensacola Junior College, Pensacola, FL 32504
Pepperdine University, Malibu, CA 90263-4392
Peru State College, Peru, NE 68421
Pfeiffer College, Misenheimer, NC 28109
Philadelphia College of Bible, Langhorne, PA 19047-2992
Philadelphia College of Pharmacy and Science, Philadelphia, PA 19104-4495
Philadelphia College of Textiles and Science, Philadelphia, PA 19144-5497
Philander Smith College, Little Rock, AR 72202
Phillips Beth Israel School of Nursing, New York, NY 10010
Phillips County Community College, Helena, AR 72342
Phillips Junior College
    Fresno Campus, Fresno, CA 93727
    Melbourne, Melbourne, FL 32935
    New Orleans, New Orleans, LA 70121
    Salt Lake City Campus, Salt Lake City, UT 84106
    Springfield, Springfield, MO 65807
Phillips Junior College: Birmingham, Birmingham, AL 35223
Phillips University, Enid, OK 73701-6439
Phoenix College, Phoenix, AZ 85013
Piedmont Bible College, Winston-Salem, NC 27101-5197
Piedmont College, Demorest, GA 30535
Piedmont Community College, Roxboro, NC 27573-1197
Piedmont Virginia Community College, Charlottesville, VA 22901-8714
Pierce College, Tacoma, WA 98498-1999
Pikes Peak Community College, Colorado Springs, CO 80906-5498
Pikeville College, Pikeville, KY 41501-1194
Pillsbury Baptist Bible College, Owatonna, MN 55060
Pima Community College, Tucson, AZ 85709-3010
Pine Manor College, Chestnut Hill, MA 02167
Pitt Community College, Greenville, NC 27835-7007

Pittsburg State University, Pittsburg, KS 66762
Pittsburgh Institute of Mortuary Science, Pittsburgh, PA 15206-3706
Pittsburgh Technical Institute, Pittsburgh, PA 15222
Pitzer College, Claremont, CA 91711-6114
Plymouth State College of the University System of New Hampshire, Plymouth, NH 03264
Point Loma Nazarene College, San Diego, CA 92106-2899
Point Park College, Pittsburgh, PA 15222
Polk Community College, Winter Haven, FL 33881-4299
Polytechnic University
    Brooklyn, Brooklyn, NY 11201-2999
    Long Island Campus, Farmingdale, NY 11735-3995
Pomona College, Claremont, CA 91711-6312
Pontifical Catholic University of Puerto Rico, Ponce, PR 00732
Pontifical College Josephinum, Columbus, OH 43085
Porterville College, Porterville, CA 93257
Portland Community College, Portland, OR 97219-0990
Portland State University, Portland, OR 97207-0751
Potomac State College of West Virginia University, Keyser, WV 26726
Prairie View A&M University, Prairie View, TX 77446
Pratt Community College, Pratt, KS 67124
Pratt Institute, Brooklyn, NY 11205
Presbyterian College, Clinton, SC 29325-9989
Prescott College, Prescott, AZ 86301
Presentation College, Aberdeen, SD 57401
Prestonburg Community College, Prestonburg, KY 41653
Prince George's Community College, Largo, MD 20772-2199
Prince William Sound Community College, Valdez, AK 99686
Princeton University, Princeton, NJ 08544-0430
Principia College, Elsah, IL 62028-9799
Providence College, Providence, RI 02918-0001
Pueblo Community College, Pueblo, CO 81004
Puget Sound Christian College, Edmonds, WA 98020-3171
Purdue University
    Calumet, Hammond, IN 46323-2094
    North Central Campus, Westville, IN 46391-9528
    West Lafayette, West Lafayette, IN 47907-1080
Queen of the Holy Rosary College, Fremont, CA 94539
Queens College, Charlotte, NC 28274
Quincy College, Quincy, MA 02169
Quincy University, Quincy, IL 62301-2699
Quinebaug Valley Community-Technical College, Danielson, CT 06239-1440
Quinnipiac College, Hamden, CT 06518-1908
Quinsigamond Community College, Worcester, MA 01606
Radford University, Radford, VA 24142-6903
Rainy River Community College, International Falls, MN 56649
Ramapo College of New Jersey, Mahwah, NJ 07430-1680
Randolph Community College, Asheboro, NC 27204-1009
Randolph-Macon College, Ashland, VA 23005-1697
Randolph-Macon Woman's College, Lynchburg, VA 24503
Ranger Junior College, Ranger, TX 76470
Ranken Technical College, St. Louis, MO 63113
Rappahannock Community College, Glenns, VA 23149
Raritan Valley Community College, Somerville, NJ 08876-1265
Ray College of Design, Chicago, IL 60611
Reading Area Community College, Reading, PA 19603-1706
Red Rocks Community College, Lakewood, CO 80401
Redlands Community College, El Reno, OK 73036
Reed College, Portland, OR 97202-8199
Reformed Bible College, Grand Rapids, MI 49505-9749
Regis College, Weston, MA 02193
Regis University, Denver, CO 80221-1099
Reid State Technical College, Evergreen, AL 36401
Reinhardt College, Waleska, GA 30183
Rensselaer Polytechnic Institute, Troy, NY 12180-3590
Renton Technical College, Renton, WA 98056-4195
Research College of Nursing, Kansas City, MO 64110-2508
RETS Electronic Institute, Louisville, KY 40219
Rhode Island College, Providence, RI 02908
Rhode Island School of Design, Providence, RI 02903
Rhodes College, Memphis, TN 38112-1690
Rice University, Houston, TX 77251
Rich Mountain Community College, Mena, AR 71953
Richard Bland College, Petersburg, VA 23805
Richland College, Dallas, TX 75243-2199
Richland Community College, Decatur, IL 62521
Richmond Community College, Hamlet, NC 28345
Ricks College, Rexburg, ID 83460-4104
Rider College, Lawrenceville, NJ 08648-3099
Ringling School of Art and Design, Sarasota, FL 34234
Rio Hondo College, Whittier, CA 90608
Rio Salado Community College, Phoenix, AZ 85003

Ripon College, Ripon, WI 54971
Rivier College, Nashua, NH 03060-5086
Roane State Community College, Harriman, TN 37748
Roanoke Bible College, Elizabeth City, NC 27909
Roanoke College, Salem, VA 24153-3794
Roanoke-Chowan Community College, Ahoskie, NC 27910-9522
Robert Morris College, Coraopolis, PA 15108-1189
Robert Morris College: Chicago, Chicago, IL 60601
Roberts Wesleyan College, Rochester, NY 14624-1997
Robeson Community College, Lumberton, NC 28359
Rochester Community College, Rochester, MN 55904-4999
Rochester Institute of Technology, Rochester, NY 14623-0887
Rock Valley College, Rockford, IL 61114
Rockford College, Rockford, IL 61108-2393
Rockhurst College, Kansas City, MO 64110-2508
Rockingham Community College, Wentworth, NC 27375-0038
Rockland Community College, Suffern, NY 10901
Rocky Mountain College, Billings, MT 59102-1796
Rocky Mountain College of Art & Design, Denver, CO 80224-2359
Roger Williams University, Bristol, RI 02809-2923
Rogers State College, Claremore, OK 74017-2099
Rogue Community College, Grants Pass, OR 97527
Rollins College, Winter Park, FL 32789-4499
Roosevelt University, Chicago, IL 60605-1394
Rosary College, River Forest, IL 60305-1099
Rose State College, Midwest City, OK 73110-2799
Rose-Hulman Institute of Technology, Terre Haute, IN 47803-9989
Rosemont College, Rosemont, PA 19010
Rowan College of New Jersey, Glassboro, NJ 08028
Rowan-Cabarrus Community College, Salisbury, NC 28145-1595
Roxbury Community College, Boston, MA 02120-3400
Rush University, Chicago, IL 60612
Russell Sage College, Troy, NY 12180
Rust College, Holly Springs, MS 38635-2328
Rutgers—The State University of New Jersey
    Camden College of Arts and Sciences, Camden, NJ 08102
    College of Engineering, New Brunswick, NJ 08903-2101
    College of Nursing, Newark, NJ 07102-1896
    College of Pharmacy, New Brunswick, NJ 08903-2101
    Cook College, New Brunswick, NJ 08903-2101
    Douglass College, New Brunswick, NJ 08903-2101
    Livingston College, New Brunswick, NJ 08903-2101
    Mason Gross School of the Arts, New Brunswick, NJ 08903-2101
    Newark College of Arts and Sciences, Newark, NJ 07102-1896
    Rutgers College, New Brunswick, NJ 08903-2101
Sacramento City College, Sacramento, CA 95822
Sacred Heart Major Seminary, Detroit, MI 48206
Sacred Heart University, Fairfield, CT 06432-1000
Saddleback College, Mission Viejo, CA 92692
Sage Junior College of Albany, Albany, NY 12208
Saginaw Valley State University, University Center, MI 48710-0001
St. Ambrose University, Davenport, IA 52803
St. Andrews Presbyterian College, Laurinburg, NC 28352-9151
St. Anselm College, Manchester, NH 03102-1310
St. Augustine College, Chicago, IL 60640-3501
St. Augustine's College, Raleigh, NC 27610-2298
St. Bonaventure University, St. Bonaventure, NY 14778-2284
St. Charles Borromeo Seminary, Overbrook, PA 19096-3099
St. Charles County Community College, St. Peters, MO 63376
St. Clair County Community College, Port Huron, MI 48061-5015
St. Cloud State University, St. Cloud, MN 56301-4498
St. Edward's University, Austin, TX 78704-6489
St. Francis College, Fort Wayne, IN 46808
St. Francis College, Brooklyn Heights, NY 11201
St. Francis College, Loretto, PA 15940-0600
St. Francis Medical Center College of Nursing, Peoria, IL 61603
St. Gregory's College, Shawnee, OK 74801
St. Hyacinth College and Seminary, Granby, MA 01033-9742
St. John Fisher College, Rochester, NY 14618-3597
St. John Vianney College Seminary, Miami, FL 33165
St. John's College, Santa Fe, NM 87501-4599
St. John's College, Annapolis, MD 21404-2800
St. Johns River Community College, Palatka, FL 32177-3897
St. John's Seminary College, Brighton, MA 02135
St. John's University, Jamaica, NY 11439
St. John's University, Collegeville, MN 56321
St. Joseph College, West Hartford, CT 06117-2700
St. Joseph College of Nursing, Joliet, IL 60435
St. Joseph Seminary College, St. Benedict, LA 70457-9990
St. Joseph's College, Rensselaer, IN 47978
St. Joseph's College, Windham, ME 04062-1198

St. Joseph's College
    Brooklyn, Brooklyn, NY 11205-3688
    Suffolk Campus, Patchogue, NY 11772-2603
St. Joseph's School of Nursing, Syracuse, NY 13203
St. Joseph's University, Philadelphia, PA 19131
St. Lawrence University, Canton, NY 13617-1447
St. Leo College, St. Leo, FL 33574-2008
St. Louis Christian College, Florissant, MO 63033
St. Louis College of Pharmacy, St. Louis, MO 63110
St. Louis Community College
    Florissant Valley, St. Louis, MO 63135
    Forest Park, St. Louis, MO 63110
    Meramec, St. Louis, MO 63122-5799
St. Louis University, St. Louis, MO 63103-2097
St. Martin's College, Lacey, WA 98503-1297
St. Mary College, Leavenworth, KS 66048-5082
St. Mary-of-the-Woods College, St. Mary-of-the-Woods, IN 47876-0068
St. Mary's Campus of the College of St. Catherine, Minneapolis, MN 55454
St. Mary's College, Notre Dame, IN 46556
St. Mary's College, Orchard Lake, MI 48324
St. Mary's College, Raleigh, NC 27603-1689
St. Mary's College of California, Moraga, CA 94575-9988
St. Mary's College of Maryland, St. Mary's City, MD 20686-9998
St. Mary's College of Minnesota, Winona, MN 55987-1399
St. Mary's University, San Antonio, TX 78228-8503
St. Meinrad College, St. Meinrad, IN 47577-1030
St. Michael's College, Colchester, VT 05439
St. Norbert College, De Pere, WI 54115-2099
St. Olaf College, Northfield, MN 55057-1098
St. Paul Technical College, St. Paul, MN 55102-9913
St. Paul's College, Lawrenceville, VA 23868
St. Peter's College, Jersey City, NJ 07306-5944
St. Petersburg Junior College, St. Petersburg, FL 33733
St. Philip's College, San Antonio, TX 78203-2098
St. Thomas Aquinas College, Sparkill, NY 10976
St. Thomas University, Miami, FL 33054
St. Vincent College, Latrobe, PA 15650-2690
St. Xavier University, Chicago, IL 60655
Saint Cloud Technical College, St. Cloud, MN 56303
Salem College, Winston-Salem, NC 27108
Salem Community College, Carneys Point, NJ 08069-2799
Salem State College, Salem, MA 01970
Salem-Teikyo University, Salem, WV 26426
Salisbury State University, Salisbury, MD 21801-6862
Salish Kootenai College, Pablo, MT 59855
Salt Lake Community College, Salt Lake City, UT 84130-0808
Salve Regina University, Newport, RI 02840-4192
Sam Houston State University, Huntsville, TX 77341-2418
Samford University, Birmingham, AL 35229-0000
Sampson Community College, Clinton, NC 28328
Samuel Merritt College, Oakland, CA 94609-9954
San Antonio College, San Antonio, TX 78212-4299
San Diego City College, San Diego, CA 92101
San Diego Mesa College, San Diego, CA 92111
San Diego Miramar College, San Diego, CA 92126-2999
San Diego State University, San Diego, CA 92182-0771
San Francisco Art Institute, San Francisco, CA 94133-2299
San Francisco College of Mortuary Science, San Francisco, CA 94115-3912
San Francisco Conservatory of Music, San Francisco, CA 94122
San Francisco State University, San Francisco, CA 94132
San Jacinto College: North, Houston, TX 77049
San Joaquin Delta College, Stockton, CA 95207
San Jose Christian College, San Jose, CA 95108-1090
San Jose City College, San Jose, CA 95128-2798
San Jose State University, San Jose, CA 95192-0009
San Juan College, Farmington, NM 87402
Sandhills Community College, Pinehurst, NC 28374
Sangamon State University, Springfield, IL 62794-9243
Santa Barbara City College, Santa Barbara, CA 93109-2394
Santa Clara University, Santa Clara, CA 95053
Santa Fe Community College, Santa Fe, NM 87502-4187
Santa Fe Community College, Gainesville, FL 32602
Santa Monica College, Santa Monica, CA 90405-1628
Santa Rosa Junior College, Santa Rosa, CA 95401
Sarah Lawrence College, Bronxville, NY 10708
Sauk Valley Community College, Dixon, IL 61021-9110
Savannah College of Art and Design, Savannah, GA 31402-3146
Savannah State College, Savannah, GA 31404
Savannah Technical Institute, Savannah, GA 31499
Schenectady County Community College, Schenectady, NY 12305
Schiller International University, Dunedin, FL 34698-4964
School of the Art Institute of Chicago, Chicago, IL 60603

School for International Training, Brattleboro, VT 05301
School for Lifelong Learning, Durham, NH 03824-3545
School of the Museum of Fine Arts, Boston, MA 02115
School of Visual Arts, New York, NY 10010-3994
Schoolcraft College, Livonia, MI 48152-2696
Schreiner College, Kerrville, TX 78028
Scott Community College, Bettendorf, IA 52722-6804
Scottsdale Community College, Scottsdale, AZ 85250-2699
Scripps College, Claremont, CA 91711-3948
Seattle Central Community College, Seattle, WA 98122
Seattle Pacific University, Seattle, WA 98119-1997
Seattle University, Seattle, WA 98122
Selma University, Selma, AL 36701
Seminole Community College, Sanford, FL 32773-6199
Seminole Junior College, Seminole, OK 74818-0351
Seton Hall University, South Orange, NJ 07079-2689
Seton Hill College, Greensburg, PA 15601-1599
Seward County Community College, Liberal, KS 67905-1137
Shasta College, Redding, CA 96099
Shaw University, Raleigh, NC 27601
Shawnee Community College, Ullin, IL 62992
Shelby State Community College, Memphis, TN 38174-0568
Sheldon Jackson College, Sitka, AK 99835
Shelton State Community College, Tuscaloosa, AL 35405
Shenandoah University, Winchester, VA 22601-5195
Shepherd College, Shepherdstown, WV 25443-1569
Sheridan College, Sheridan, WY 82801-1500
Shimer College, Waukegan, IL 60079-0500
Shippensburg University of Pennsylvania, Shippensburg, PA 17257
Shoals Community College, Muscle Shoals, AL 35662
Shoreline Community College, Seattle, WA 98133
Shorter College, Rome, GA 30165-4298
Shorter College, North Little Rock, AR 72114
Siena College, Loudonville, NY 11211-1462
Siena Heights College, Adrian, MI 49221-9937
Sierra College, Rocklin, CA 95677
Sierra Nevada College, Incline Village, NV 89450-4269
Silver Lake College, Manitowoc, WI 54220-9391
Simmons College, Boston, MA 02115-5898
Simon's Rock College of Bard, Great Barrington, MA 01230
Simpson College, Redding, CA 96003-8606
Simpson College, Indianola, IA 50125-1299
Sinclair Community College, Dayton, OH 45402
Sinte Gleska University, Rosebud, SD 57570
Sioux Falls College, Sioux Falls, SD 57105
Sisseton-Wahpeton Community College, Sisseton, SD 57262-0689
Sistema Instituto Tecnologico y de Estudios Superiores de Monterrey, Monterrey, Nuevo Leon, Mexico 64849
Skagit Valley College, Mount Vernon, WA 98273
Skidmore College, Saratoga Springs, NY 12866
Skyline College, San Bruno, CA 94066-1698
Slippery Rock University of Pennsylvania, Slippery Rock, PA 16057
Smith College, Northampton, MA 01063
Snead State Community College, Boaz, AL 35957
Snow College, Ephraim, UT 84627
Sojourner-Douglass College, Baltimore, MD 21205
Solano Community College, Suisun City, CA 94585
Sonoma State University, Rohnert Park, CA 94928
South Arkansas Community College, El Dorado, AR 71731-7010
South Carolina State University, Orangeburg, SC 29117-0001
South College
    Palm Beach Campus, West Palm Beach, FL 33409
    Savannah, Savannah, GA 31406
South Dakota School of Mines and Technology, Rapid City, SD 57701-3995
South Dakota State University, Brookings, SD 57007-0649
South Florida Community College, Avon Park, FL 33825
South Georgia College, Douglas, GA 31533-5098
South Mountain Community College, Phoenix, AZ 85040
South Plains College, Levelland, TX 79336
South Puget Sound Community College, Olympia, WA 98512-6218
South Seattle Community College, Seattle, WA 98106
Southeast Community College, Cumberland, KY 40823
Southeast Community College
    Beatrice Campus, Beatrice, NE 68310
    Lincoln Campus, Lincoln, NE 68520
    Milford Campus, Milford, NE 68405
Southeast Missouri State University, Cape Girardeau, MO 63701
Southeastern Baptist College, Laurel, MS 39440
Southeastern Baptist Theological Seminary, Wake Forest, NC 27587-1889
Southeastern Bible College, Birmingham, AL 35243-4181
Southeastern College of the Assemblies of God, Lakeland, FL 33801
Southeastern Community College, Whiteville, NC 28472

Southeastern Community College
    North Campus, West Burlington, IA 52655-0605
    South Campus, Keokuk, IA 52632-1088
Southeastern Illinois College, Harrisburg, IL 62946
Southeastern Louisiana University, Hammond, LA 70402-0752
Southeastern Oklahoma State University, Durant, OK 74701
Southeastern University, Washington, DC 20024
Southern Arkansas University
    Magnolia, Magnolia, AR 71753-5000
    Technical Branch, Camden, AR 71701
Southern California College, Costa Mesa, CA 92626-9601
Southern California Institute of Architecture, Los Angeles, CA 90066
Southern Christian University, Montgomery, AL 36117-3553
Southern College, Orlando, FL 32807
Southern College of Seventh-day Adventists, Collegedale, TN 37315
Southern College of Technology, Marietta, GA 30060-2896
Southern Connecticut State University, New Haven, CT 06515
Southern Illinois University
    Carbondale, Carbondale, IL 62901-4710
    Edwardsville, Edwardsville, IL 62026-1600
Southern Maine Technical College, South Portland, ME 04106
Southern Methodist University, Dallas, TX 75275-0296
Southern Nazarene University, Bethany, OK 73008-2694
Southern Ohio College, Cincinnati, OH 45237
Southern Oregon State College, Ashland, OR 97520-5032
Southern State Community College, Hillsboro, OH 45133
Southern Union State Junior College, Wadley, AL 36276
Southern University
    New Orleans, New Orleans, LA 70126
    Shreveport, Shreveport, LA 71107
Southern University and Agricultural and Mechanical College, Baton Rouge, LA 70813
Southern Utah University, Cedar City, UT 84720
Southern Vermont College, Bennington, VT 05201
Southern Virginia College for Women, Buena Vista, VA 24416-3097
Southern West Virginia Community College, Logan, WV 25601
Southside Virginia Community College, Alberta, VA 23821
Southwest Baptist University, Bolivar, MO 65613-2496
Southwest Mississippi Community College, Summit, MS 39666
Southwest Missouri State University, Springfield, MO 65804-0094
Southwest State University, Marshall, MN 56258-1598
Southwest Texas Junior College, Uvalde, TX 78801
Southwest Texas State University, San Marcos, TX 78666
Southwest Virginia Community College, Richlands, VA 24641-1510
Southwest Wisconsin Technical College, Fennimore, WI 53809
Southwestern Adventist College, Keene, TX 76059
Southwestern Assemblies of God College, Waxahachie, TX 75165
Southwestern Christian College, Terrell, TX 75160
Southwestern College, Chula Vista, CA 92010
Southwestern College, Phoenix, AZ 85032-7042
Southwestern College, Winfield, KS 67156-9988
Southwestern College of Christian Ministries, Bethany, OK 73008
Southwestern Community College, Sylva, NC 28779
Southwestern Community College, Creston, IA 50801
Southwestern Michigan College, Dowagiac, MI 49047
Southwestern Oklahoma State University, Weatherford, OK 73096
Southwestern University, Georgetown, TX 78626
Spalding University, Louisville, KY 40203
Sparks State Technical College, Eufaula, AL 36072-0580
Spartanburg Methodist College, Spartanburg, SC 29301
Spartanburg Technical College, Spartanburg, SC 29305
Spelman College, Atlanta, GA 30314-4399
Spokane Community College, Spokane, WA 99207-5399
Spokane Falls Community College, Spokane, WA 99204-5288
Spoon River College, Canton, IL 61520
Spring Arbor College, Spring Arbor, MI 49283
Spring Hill College, Mobile, AL 36608
Springfield College, Springfield, MA 01109
Springfield College in Illinois, Springfield, IL 62702-2694
Springfield Technical Community College, Springfield, MA 01105-1296
Standing Rock College, Fort Yates, ND 58538
Stanford University, Stanford, CA 94305
Stanly Community College, Albemarle, NC 28001
Stark Technical College, Canton, OH 44720
State Community College, East St. Louis, IL 62201
State Fair Community College, Sedalia, MO 65301-2199
State Technical Institute at Memphis, Memphis, TN 38134

State University of New York
    Albany, Albany, NY 12222
    Binghamton, Binghamton, NY 13902-6001
    Buffalo, Buffalo, NY 14214
    Purchase, Purchase, NY 10577-1400
    Stony Brook, Stony Brook, NY 11794-1901
    College of Agriculture and Technology at Cobleskill, Cobleskill, NY 12043
    College of Agriculture and Technology at Morrisville, Morrisville, NY 13408
    College at Brockport, Brockport, NY 14420-2915
    College at Buffalo, Buffalo, NY 14222-1095
    College at Cortland, Cortland, NY 13045
    College of Environmental Science and Forestry, Syracuse, NY 13210-2779
    College at Fredonia, Fredonia, NY 14063
    College at Geneseo, Geneseo, NY 14454-1471
    College at New Paltz, New Paltz, NY 12561-2499
    College at Old Westbury, Old Westbury, NY 11568-0307
    College at Oneonta, Oneonta, NY 13820-4016
    College at Plattsburgh, Plattsburgh, NY 12901
    College at Potsdam, Potsdam, NY 13676-2294
    College of Technology at Alfred, Alfred, NY 14802-1196
    College of Technology at Canton, Canton, NY 13617-1098
    College of Technology at Delhi, Delhi, NY 13753-1190
    College of Technology at Farmingdale, Farmingdale, NY 11735
    Empire State College, Saratoga Springs, NY 12866-4390
    Health Science Center at Brooklyn, Brooklyn, NY 11203-2098
    Health Science Center at Syracuse, Syracuse, NY 13210
    Health Sciences Center at Stony Brook, Stony Brook, NY 11794-8276
    Institute of Technology at Utica/Rome, Utica, NY 13504-3050
    Maritime College, Throggs Neck, NY 10465-4198
    Oswego, Oswego, NY 13126-3599
Stephen F. Austin State University, Nacogdoches, TX
Stephens College, Columbia, MO 65215-9986
Sterling College, Craftsbury Common, VT 05827-0072
Sterling College, Sterling, KS 67579-9989
Stetson University, DeLand, FL 32720
Stevens Institute of Technology, Hoboken, NJ 07030
Stevens-Henager College of Business, Provo, UT 84606-6157
Stillman College, Tuscaloosa, AL 35403
Stockton State College, Pomona, NJ 08240-9988
Stone Child College, Box Elder, MT 59521-9796
Stonehill College, North Easton, MA 02357-5610
Stratton College, Milwaukee, WI 53202-2608
Strayer College, Washington, DC 20005
Sue Bennett College, London, KY 40741
Suffolk County Community College
    Eastern Campus, Riverhead, NY 11901
    Selden, Selden, NY 11784
    Western Campus, Brentwood, NY 11717
Suffolk University, Boston, MA 02108-2772
Sul Ross State University, Alpine, TX 79832
Sullivan County Community College, Loch Sheldrake, NY 12759
Suomi College, Hancock, MI 49930
Surry Community College, Dobson, NC 27017
Susquehanna University, Selinsgrove, PA 17870-1001
Sussex County Community College, Newton, NJ 07860
Swarthmore College, Swarthmore, PA 19081-1397
Sweet Briar College, Sweet Briar, VA 24595
Syracuse University, Syracuse, NY 13244-1120
Tabor College, Hillsboro, KS 67063
Tacoma Community College, Tacoma, WA 98465-9971
Taft College, Taft, CA 93268
Talladega College, Talladega, AL 35160
Tallahassee Community College, Tallahassee, FL 32304-2895
Talmudical Institute of Upstate New York, Rochester, NY 14607
Talmudical Seminary Oholei Torah, Brooklyn, NY 11213-3397
Tampa College, Tampa, FL 33614
Tarleton State University, Stephenville, TX 76402
Tarrant County Junior College, Fort Worth, TX 76102-6599
Taylor Business Institute, New York, NY 10119-0118
Taylor University, Upland, IN 46989-1001
Technical Career Institutes, New York, NY 10001
Technical College of the Lowcountry, Beaufort, SC 29902-1288
Technological College of the Municipality of San Juan, Hato Rey, PR 00936
Teikyo Marycrest University, Davenport, IA 52804-4096
Teikyo Westmar University, Le Mars, IA 51031
Teikyo-Post University, Waterbury, CT 06723-2540
Temple Junior College, Temple, TX 76504-7435
Temple University, Philadelphia, PA 19122-1803
Tennessee State University, Nashville, TN 37203

Tennessee Technological University, Cookeville, TN 38505
Tennessee Temple University, Chattanooga, TN 37404
Tennessee Wesleyan College, Athens, TN 37371-0040
Terra Technical College, Fremont, OH 43420
Texarkana College, Texarkana, TX 75599
Texas A&I University, Kingsville, TX 78363-8201
Texas A&M University
    College Station, College Station, TX 77843-0100
    Galveston, Galveston, TX 77553-1675
Texas Christian University, Fort Worth, TX 76129
Texas College, Tyler, TX 75702-2404
Texas Lutheran College, Seguin, TX 78155
Texas Southern University, Houston, TX 77004
Texas State Technical College
    Amarillo, Amarillo, TX 79111
    Harlingen, Harlingen, TX 78550-3697
    Sweetwater, Sweetwater, TX 79556
    Waco, Waco, TX 76705
Texas Tech University, Lubbock, TX 79409-5005
Texas Wesleyan University, Fort Worth, TX 76105-1536
Texas Woman's University, Denton, TX 76204-0909
Thaddeus Stevens State School of Technology, Lancaster, PA 17602
Thiel College, Greenville, PA 16125
Thomas Aquinas College, Santa Paula, CA 93060
Thomas College, Waterville, ME 04901-9986
Thomas College, Thomasville, GA 31792-7499
Thomas Jefferson University: College of Allied Health Sciences, Philadelphia, PA 19107
Thomas More College, Crestview Hills, KY 41017
Three Rivers Community College, Poplar Bluff, MO 63901-1308
Three Rivers Community-Technical College, Norwich, CT 06360-2479
Tidewater Community College, Portsmouth, VA 23703
Tiffin University, Tiffin, OH 44883
Toccoa Falls College, Toccoa Falls, GA 30598-0368
Tompkins-Cortland Community College, Dryden, NY 13053-0139
Tougaloo College, Tougaloo, MS 39174
Touro College, New York, NY 10010
Towson State University, Towson, MD 21204-7097
Transylvania University, Lexington, KY 40508-1797
Treasure Valley Community College, Ontario, OR 97914
Trenholm State Technical College, Montgomery, AL 36108
Trenton State College, Trenton, NJ 08650-4700
Trevecca Nazarene College, Nashville, TN 37210
Triangle Tech
    Greensburg School, Greensburg, PA 15601
    Pittsburgh Campus, Pittsburgh, PA 15214-3897
Tri-County Community College, Murphy, NC 28906
Tri-County Technical College, Pendleton, SC 29670
Trident Technical College, Charleston, SC 29411
Trinidad State Junior College, Trinidad, CO 81082
Trinity Bible College, Ellendale, ND 58436-7150
Trinity Christian College, Palos Heights, IL 60463
Trinity College, Deerfield, IL 60015
Trinity College, Hartford, CT 06106
Trinity College, Washington, DC 20017-1094
Trinity College at Miami, Miami, FL 33101-9674
Trinity College of Vermont, Burlington, VT 05401
Trinity University, San Antonio, TX 78212-7200
Trinity Valley Community College, Athens, TX 75751
Tri-State University, Angola, IN 46703-0307
Triton College, River Grove, IL 60171
Trocaire College, Buffalo, NY 14220
Troy State University
    Dothan, Dothan, AL 36304-0368
    Montgomery, Montgomery, AL 36103-4419
    Troy, Troy, AL 36082
Truckee Meadows Community College, Reno, NV 89512
Truett-McConnell College, Cleveland, GA 30528
Tufts University, Medford, MA 02155-5555
Tulane University, New Orleans, LA 70118-5680
Tulsa Junior College, Tulsa, OK 74135-6198
Tunxis Community-Technical College, Farmington, CT 06032-9980
Turabo University, Gurabo, PR 00778
Turtle Mountain Community College, Belcourt, ND 58316-0340
Tusculum College, Greeneville, TN 37743
Tuskegee University, Tuskegee, AL 36088
Tyler Junior College, Tyler, TX 75711-9020
Ulster County Community College, Stone Ridge, NY 12484
Umpqua Community College, Roseburg, OR 97470
Union College, Barbourville, KY 40906
Union College, Schenectady, NY 12308-2311
Union College, Lincoln, NE 68506-4300

Union County College, Cranford, NJ 07016-1599
Union Institute, Cincinnati, OH 45206-1947
Union University, Jackson, TN 38305
United States International University, San Diego, CA 92131-1799
United States Merchant Marine Academy, Kings Point, NY 11024
United Tribes Technical College, Bismarck, ND 58504
Unity College, Unity, ME 04988
Universidad Adventista de las Antillas, Mayaguez, PR 00681
Universidad Metropolitana, Rio Piedras, PR 00928
Universidad Politecnica de Puerto Rico, Hato Rey, PR 00918
University of Akron
    Akron, Akron, OH 44325-2001
    Wayne College, Orrville, OH 44667
University of Alabama
    Birmingham, Birmingham, AL 35294-1150
    Huntsville, Huntsville, AL 35899
    Tuscaloosa, Tuscaloosa, AL 35487-0132
University of Alaska
    Anchorage, Anchorage, AK 99508-4675
    Fairbanks, Fairbanks, AK 99775-0060
    Southeast, Juneau, AK 99801
University of Arizona, Tucson, AZ 85721
University of Arkansas, Fayetteville, AR 72701
University of Arkansas
    Little Rock, Little Rock, AR 72204
    Medical Sciences, Little Rock, AR 72205-7199
    Monticello, Monticello, AR 71655
    Pine Bluff, Pine Bluff, AR 71601
University of the Arts, Philadelphia, PA 19102
University of Baltimore, Baltimore, MD 21201-5779
University of Bridgeport, Bridgeport, CT 06601
University of California
    Berkeley, Berkeley, CA 94720
    Davis, Davis, CA 95616
    Irvine, Irvine, CA 92717
    Los Angeles, Los Angeles, CA 90024
    Riverside, Riverside, CA 92521
    San Diego, La Jolla, CA 92093-0337
    San Francisco, San Francisco, CA 94143-0244
    Santa Barbara, Santa Barbara, CA 93106
    Santa Cruz, Santa Cruz, CA 95064
University of Central Arkansas, Conway, AR 72035-0001
University of Central Florida, Orlando, FL 32816
University of Central Oklahoma, Edmond, OK 73034-0151
University of Charleston, Charleston, WV 25304-1099
University of Chicago, Chicago, IL 60637
University of Cincinnati
    Access Colleges, Cincinnati, OH 45221
    Cincinnati, Cincinnati, OH 45221-0091
    Clermont College, Batavia, OH 45103
    Raymond Walters College, Cincinnati, OH 45236
University of Colorado
    Boulder, Boulder, CO 80309-0030
    Colorado Springs, Colorado Springs, CO 80933-7150
    Denver, Denver, CO 80217-3364
    Health Sciences Center, Denver, CO 80262
University of Connecticut, Storrs, CT 06269-3088
University of Dallas, Irving, TX 75062-4799
University of Dayton, Dayton, OH 45469-1611
University of Delaware, Newark, DE 19716
University of Denver, Denver, CO 80208-0132
University of Detroit Mercy, Detroit, MI 48221
University of the District of Columbia, Washington, DC 20008
University of Dubuque, Dubuque, IA 52001
University of Evansville, Evansville, IN 47722
University of Findlay, Findlay, OH 45840-3695
University of Florida, Gainesville, FL 32611
University of Georgia, Athens, GA 30602
University of Hartford, West Hartford, CT 06117-0395
University of Hawaii
    Hawaii Community College, Hilo, HI 96720-4091
    Hilo, Hilo, HI 96720-4091
    Honolulu Community College, Honolulu, HI 96817
    Kapiolani Community College, Honolulu, HI 96816-4421
    Kauai Community College, Lihue, HI 96766
    Manoa, Honolulu, HI 96822
    West Oahu, Pearl City, HI 96782
    Windward Community College, Kaneohe, HI 96817

University of Houston
    Clear Lake, Houston, TX 77058-1080
    Downtown, Houston, TX 77002
    Houston, Houston, TX 77204-2161
    Victoria, Victoria, TX 77901-4450
University of Idaho, Moscow, ID 83844-3133
University of Illinois
    Chicago, Chicago, IL 60680
    Urbana-Champaign, Urbana, IL 61801
University of Indianapolis, Indianapolis, IN 46227-3697
University of Iowa, Iowa City, IA 52242-1396
University of Judaism, Los Angeles, CA 90077
University of Kansas
    Lawrence, Lawrence, KS 66045
    Medical Center, Kansas City, KS 66160
University of Kentucky, Lexington, KY 40506-0054
University of La Verne, La Verne, CA 91750-4443
University of Louisville, Louisville, KY 40292
University of Maine
    Augusta, Augusta, ME 04330
    Farmington, Farmington, ME 04938-1994
    Fort Kent, Fort Kent, ME 04743-1292
    Machias, Machias, ME 04654
    Orono, Orono, ME 04469-5713
    Presque Isle, Presque Isle, ME 04769-2888
University of Mary, Bismarck, ND 58504-9652
University of Mary Hardin-Baylor, Belton, TX 76513
University of Maryland
    Baltimore, Baltimore, MD 21201
    Baltimore County, Baltimore, MD 21228-5398
    College Park, College Park, MD 20742-5235
    Eastern Shore, Princess Anne, MD 21853-1299
    University College, College Park, MD 20742-1672
University of Massachusetts
    Amherst, Amherst, MA 01003
    Boston, Boston, MA 02125-3393
    Dartmouth, North Dartmouth, MA 02747-2300
    Lowell, Lowell, MA 01854
University of Medicine and Dentistry of New Jersey: School of Nursing, Newark, NJ 07107-3006
University of Miami, Coral Gables, FL 33124
University of Michigan
    Ann Arbor, Ann Arbor, MI 48109-1316
    Dearborn, Dearborn, MI 48128-1491
    Flint, Flint, MI 48502-2186
University of Minnesota
    Crookston, Crookston, MN 56716
    Duluth, Duluth, MN 55812-2496
    Morris, Morris, MN 56267-2199
    Twin Cities, Minneapolis-St. Paul, MN 55455-0213
University of Mississippi
    Medical Center, Jackson, MS 39216
    University, University, MS 38677
University of Missouri
    Columbia, Columbia, MO 65211
    Kansas City, Kansas City, MO 64110-2944
    Rolla, Rolla, MO 65401
    St. Louis, St. Louis, MO 63121
University of Mobile, Mobile, AL 36663-0220
University of Montana, Missoula, MT 59812
University of Montevallo, Montevallo, AL 35115-6030
University of Nebraska
    Medical Center, Omaha, NE 68198-4230
    Kearney, Kearney, NE 68849
    Lincoln, Lincoln, NE 68588-0417
    Omaha, Omaha, NE 68182-0005
University of Nevada
    Las Vegas, Las Vegas, NV 89154-1021
    Reno, Reno, NV 89557-0002
University of New England, Biddeford, ME 04005
University of New Hampshire
    Durham, Durham, NH 03824
    Manchester, Manchester, NH 03102
University of New Haven, West Haven, CT 06516
University of New Mexico, Albuquerque, NM 87131
University of New Orleans, New Orleans, LA 70148
University of North Alabama, Florence, AL 35632-0001

University of North Carolina
    Asheville, Asheville, NC 28804-3299
    Chapel Hill, Chapel Hill, NC 27599-2200
    Charlotte, Charlotte, NC 28223
    Greensboro, Greensboro, NC 27412-5001
    Wilmington, Wilmington, NC 28403-3297
University of North Dakota
    Grand Forks, Grand Forks, ND 58202-8357
    Lake Region, Devils Lake, ND 58301-1598
    Williston, Williston, ND 58802-1326
University of North Florida, Jacksonville, FL 32224-2645
University of North Texas, Denton, TX 76203-3797
University of Northern Colorado, Greeley, CO 80639
University of Northern Iowa, Cedar Falls, IA 50614-0018
University of Notre Dame, Notre Dame, IN 46556-5602
University of Oklahoma
    Health Sciences Center, Oklahoma City, OK 73190
    Norman, Norman, OK 73069-0520
University of Oregon
    Eugene, Eugene, OR 97403-1217
    Robert Donald Clark Honors College, Eugene, OR 97403-1293
University of Osteopathic Medicine and Health Sciences, Des Moines, IA 50312
University of the Ozarks, Clarksville, AR 72830
University of the Pacific, Stockton, CA 95211-0197
University of Pennsylvania, Philadelphia, PA 19104-6376
University of Phoenix, Phoenix, AZ 85072-2069
University of Pittsburgh
    Bradford, Bradford, PA 16701-2898
    Greensburg, Greensburg, PA 15601-5898
    Johnstown, Johnstown, PA 15904
    Pittsburgh, Pittsburgh, PA 15260
    Titusville, Titusville, PA 16354
University of Portland, Portland, OR 97203-5798
University of Puerto Rico
    Aguadilla, Aguadilla, PR 00604
    Bayamon Technological University College, Bayamon, PR 00619-1919
    Carolina Regional College, Carolina, PR 00984-4800
    Cayey University College, Cayey, PR 00633
    Humacao University College, Humacao, PR 00791
    La Montana Regional College, Utuado, PR 00641-2500
    Mayaguez Campus, Mayaguez, PR 00681-5000
    Medical Sciences Campus, Rio Piedras, PR 00936-5067
    Ponce Technological University College, Ponce, PR 00732
    Rio Piedras Campus, Rio Piedras, PR 00931-1907
University of Puget Sound, Tacoma, WA 98416-0003
University of Redlands, Redlands, CA 92373-0999
University of Rhode Island, Kingston, RI 02881-0806
University of Richmond, Richmond, VA 23173
University of Rio Grande, Rio Grande, OH 45674
University of Rochester, Rochester, NY 14627-0251
University of the Sacred Heart, Santurce, PR 00914
University of St. Thomas, St. Paul, MN 55105-1096
University of St. Thomas, Houston, TX 77006-4696
University of San Diego, San Diego, CA 92110
University of San Francisco, San Francisco, CA 94117-1080
University of Science and Arts of Oklahoma, Chickasha, OK 73018
University of Scranton, Scranton, PA 18510-4699
University of the South, Sewanee, TN 37375-1000
University of South Alabama, Mobile, AL 36688
University of South Carolina
    Aiken, Aiken, SC 29801
    Beaufort, Beaufort, SC 29902
    Coastal Carolina College, Conway, SC 29526
    Columbia, Columbia, SC 29208
    Salkehatchie Regional Campus, Allendale, SC 29810
    Spartanburg, Spartanburg, SC 29303
    Sumter, Sumter, SC 29150
    Union, Union, SC 29379
University of South Dakota, Vermillion, SD 57069-2390
University of South Florida, Tampa, FL 33620-6900
University of Southern California, Los Angeles, CA 90089-0911
University of Southern Colorado, Pueblo, CO 81001-4901
University of Southern Indiana, Evansville, IN 47712
University of Southern Maine, Portland, ME 04103
University of Southern Mississippi, Hattiesburg, MS 39406-5167
University of Southwestern Louisiana, Lafayette, LA 70504
University of the State of New York: Regents College, Albany, NY 12203
University of Tampa, Tampa, FL 33606

University of Tennessee
    Chattanooga, Chattanooga, TN 37403
    Knoxville, Knoxville, TN 37996-0230
    Martin, Martin, TN 38238
    Memphis, Memphis, TN 38163
University of Texas
    Arlington, Arlington, TX 76019-0088
    Austin, Austin, TX 78712-1159
    Brownsville, Brownsville, TX 78520
    Dallas, Richardson, TX 75083-0688
    El Paso, El Paso, TX 79968
    Health Science Center at Houston, Houston, TX 77030
    Health Science Center at San Antonio, San Antonio, TX 78284-7702
    Medical Branch at Galveston, Galveston, TX 77555-1305
    Pan American, Edinburg, TX 78539
    Permian Basin, Odessa, TX 79762
    San Antonio, San Antonio, TX 78285
    Southwestern Medical Center at Dallas Southwestern Allied Health Sciences School, Dallas, TX 75235-9096
    Tyler, Tyler, TX 75701-6699
University of Toledo, Toledo, OH 43606-3398
University of Tulsa, Tulsa, OK 74104-3189
University of Utah, Salt Lake City, UT 84112
University of Vermont, Burlington, VT 05401-3596
University of the Virgin Islands, Charlotte Amalie, VI 00802
University of Virginia, Charlottesville, VA 22903
University of Washington, Seattle, WA 98195
University of West Florida, Pensacola, FL 32514-5750
University of West Los Angeles, Inglewood, CA 90301
University of Wisconsin
    Eau Claire, Eau Claire, WI 54701
    Green Bay, Green Bay, WI 54311-7001
    La Crosse, La Crosse, WI 54601
    Madison, Madison, WI 53706-1490
    Oshkosh, Oshkosh, WI 54901
    Parkside, Kenosha, WI 53141-2000
    Platteville, Platteville, WI 53818
    River Falls, River Falls, WI 54022
    Stevens Point, Stevens Point, WI 54481
    Stout, Menomonie, WI 54751
    Superior, Superior, WI 54880
    Whitewater, Whitewater, WI 53190-1791
University of Wisconsin Center
    Baraboo/Sauk County, Baraboo, WI 53913-1098
    Barron County, Rice Lake, WI 54868
    Fox Valley, Menasha, WI 54952-8002
    Manitowoc County, Manitowoc, WI 54220-6699
    Marathon County, Wausau, WI 54401-5396
    Marinette County, Marinette, WI 54143
    Marshfield/Wood County, Marshfield, WI 54449
    Richland, Richland Center, WI 53581
    Rock County, Janesville, WI 53546-5699
    Sheboygan County, Sheboygan, WI 53081-4789
    Washington County, West Bend, WI 53095
    Waukesha, Waukesha, WI 53188-2799
University of Wyoming, Laramie, WY 82071-3435
Upper Iowa University, Fayette, IA 52142-1859
Upsala College, East Orange, NJ 07019
Urbana University, Urbana, OH 43078-2091
Ursinus College, Collegeville, PA 19426
Ursuline College, Pepper Pike, OH 44124-4398
Utah State University, Logan, UT 84322-1600
Utah Valley Community College, Orem, UT 84058
Utica College of Syracuse University, Utica, NY 13502-4892
Utica School of Commerce, Utica, NY 13501
Valdosta State College, Valdosta, GA 31698
Valencia Community College, Orlando, FL 32802-3028
Valley City State University, Valley City, ND 58072
Valley Forge Christian College, Phoenixville, PA 19460
Valley Forge Military College, Wayne, PA 19087-3695
Valparaiso University, Valparaiso, IN 46383-6493
Vance-Granville Community College, Henderson, NC 27536
Vanderbilt University, Nashville, TN 37203-1700
VanderCook College of Music, Chicago, IL 60616-3886
Vassar College, Poughkeepsie, NY 12601
Vennard College, University Park, IA 52595
Ventura College, Ventura, CA 93003
Vermilion Community College, Ely, MN 55731-9989
Vermont Technical College, Randolph Center, VT 05061
Vernon Regional Junior College, Vernon, TX 76384-4092
Victor Valley College, Victorville, CA 92392-9699
Victoria College, Victoria, TX 77901

Villa Julie College, Stevenson, MD 21153
Villa Maria College of Buffalo, Buffalo, NY 14225-3999
Villanova University, Villanova, PA 19085-1672
Vincennes University, Vincennes, IN 47591
Virginia College, Birmingham, AL 35234
Virginia Commonwealth University, Richmond, VA 23284-2526
Virginia Intermont College, Bristol, VA 24201-4298
Virginia Marti College of Fashion and Art, Lakewood, OH 44107
Virginia Military Institute, Lexington, VA 24450-9967
Virginia Polytechnic Institute and State University, Blacksburg, VA 24061-0202
Virginia State University, Petersburg, VA 23806
Virginia Union University, Richmond, VA 23220
Virginia Wesleyan College, Norfolk, VA 23502-5599
Virginia Western Community College, Roanoke, VA 24038
Viterbo College, La Crosse, WI 54601
Volunteer State Community College, Gallatin, TN 37066
Voorhees College, Denmark, SC 29042
Wabash College, Crawfordsville, IN 47933-0352
Wadhams Hall Seminary-College, Ogdensburg, NY 13669-9308
Wagner College, Staten Island, NY 10301-4495
Wake Forest University, Winston-Salem, NC 27109
Wake Technical Community College, Raleigh, NC 27603
Waldorf College, Forest City, IA 50436
Walker College, Jasper, AL 35501
Walla Walla College, College Place, WA 99324-1198
Walla Walla Community College, Walla Walla, WA 99362-9267
Wallace State Community College at Hanceville, Hanceville, AL 35077-2000
Walsh College of Accountancy and Business Administration, Troy, MI 48007-7006
Walsh University, North Canton, OH 44720-3396
Walters State Community College, Morristown, TN 37813-6899
Warner Pacific College, Portland, OR 97215
Warner Southern College, Lake Wales, FL 33853-8725
Warren County Community College, Washington, NJ 07882-9605
Warren Wilson College, Swannanoa, NC 28778-2099
Wartburg College, Waverly, IA 50677
Washburn University of Topeka, Topeka, KS 66621
Washington College, Chestertown, MD 21620-1197
Washington and Jefferson College, Washington, PA 15301
Washington and Lee University, Lexington, VA 24450
Washington State University, Pullman, WA 99164-1036
Washington University, St. Louis, MO 63130-4899
Washtenaw Community College, Ann Arbor, MI 48106-0978
Waukesha County Technical College, Pewaukee, WI 53072
Waycross College, Waycross, GA 31501
Wayland Baptist University, Plainview, TX 79072-6998
Wayne Community College, Goldsboro, NC 27533-8002
Wayne County Community College, Detroit, MI 48226
Wayne State College, Wayne, NE 68787
Wayne State University, Detroit, MI 48202
Waynesburg College, Waynesburg, PA 15370
Weatherford College, Weatherford, TX 76086
Webber College, Babson Park, FL 33827-0096
Weber State University, Ogden, UT 84408-1015
Webster University, Webster Groves, MO 63119-3194
Wellesley College, Wellesley, MA 02181-8292
Wells College, Aurora, NY 13026
Wenatchee Valley College, Wenatchee, WA 98801
Wentworth Institute of Technology, Boston, MA 02115
Wesley College, Dover, DE 19901-3875
Wesleyan College, Macon, GA 31297-4299
Wesleyan University, Middletown, CT 06457
West Chester University of Pennsylvania, West Chester, PA 19383
West Coast University, Los Angeles, CA 90020-1765
West Georgia College, Carrollton, GA 30118-0001
West Hills Community College, Coalinga, CA 93210
West Liberty State College, West Liberty, WV 26074
West Shore Community College, Scottville, MI 49454-0277
West Suburban College of Nursing, Oak Park, IL 60302
West Texas A & M University, Canyon, TX 79016
West Valley College, Saratoga, CA 95070-5698
West Virginia Institute of Technology, Montgomery, WV 25136-2436
West Virginia Northern Community College, Wheeling, WV 26003
West Virginia State College, Institute, WV 25112-0335
West Virginia University
    Morgantown, Morgantown, WV 26506-6009
    Parkersburg, Parkersburg, WV 26101-9577
West Virginia Wesleyan College, Buckhannon, WV 26201-2998
Westark Community College, Fort Smith, AR 72913-3649
Westbrook College, Portland, ME 04103
Westchester Business Institute, White Plains, NY 10602

Westchester Community College, Valhalla, NY 10595-1698
Western Baptist College, Salem, OR 97301-9392
Western Carolina University, Cullowhee, NC 28723
Western Connecticut State University, Danbury, CT 06810
Western Dakota Vocational Technical Institute, Rapid City, SD 57701
Western Illinois University, Macomb, IL 61455
Western International University, Phoenix, AZ 85021
Western Iowa Tech Community College, Sioux City, IA 51102
Western Kentucky University, Bowling Green, KY 42101
Western Maryland College, Westminster, MD 21157-4390
Western Michigan University, Kalamazoo, MI 49008
Western Montana College of the University of Montana, Dillon, MT 59725
Western Nebraska Community College: Scottsbluff Campus, Scottsbluff, NE 69361
Western Nevada Community College, Carson City, NV 89703
Western New England College, Springfield, MA 01119-2688
Western New Mexico University, Silver City, NM 88062
Western Oklahoma State College, Altus, OK 73521
Western Oregon State College, Monmouth, OR 97361-1394
Western Piedmont Community College, Morganton, NC 28655
Western State College of Colorado, Gunnison, CO 81231
Western Washington University, Bellingham, WA 98225-9009
Western Wisconsin Technical College, La Crosse, WI 54602-0908
Western Wyoming Community College, Rock Springs, WY 82901
Westfield State College, Westfield, MA 01086
Westminster Choir College School of Music of Rider College, Princeton, NJ 08540-3899
Westminster College, New Wilmington, PA 16172-0001
Westminster College, Fulton, MO 65251-1299
Westminster College of Salt Lake City, Salt Lake City, UT 84105
Westmont College, Santa Barbara, CA 93108-1099
Westmoreland County Community College, Youngwood, PA 15697
Wharton County Junior College, Wharton, TX 77488-0080
Whatcom Community College, Bellingham, WA 98226
Wheaton College, Wheaton, IL 60187-5593
Wheaton College, Norton, MA 02766
Wheeling Jesuit College, Wheeling, WV 26003
Wheelock College, Boston, MA 02215-4176
White Pines College, Chester, NH 03036
Whitman College, Walla Walla, WA 99362-2085
Whittier College, Whittier, CA 90608-0634
Whitworth College, Spokane, WA 99251-0002
Wichita State University, Wichita, KS 67208-1595
Widener University, Chester, PA 19013
Wilberforce University, Wilberforce, OH 45384-1091
Wiley College, Marshall, TX 75670
Wilkes Community College, Wilkesboro, NC 28697-0120
Wilkes University, Wilkes-Barre, PA 18766-0001
Willamette University, Salem, OR 97301-3922
William Carey College, Hattiesburg, MS 39401-5499
William Jennings Bryan College, Dayton, TN 37321-7000
William Jewell College, Liberty, MO 64068
William Paterson College of New Jersey, Wayne, NJ 07470
William Penn College, Oskaloosa, IA 52577
William Rainey Harper College, Palatine, IL 60067-7398
William Smith College, Geneva, NY 14456-3381
William Tyndale College, Farmington Hills, MI 48331-9985
William Woods College, Fulton, MO 65251-1098
Williams Baptist College, Walnut Ridge, AR 72476
Williams College, Williamstown, MA 01267
Williamsburg Technical College, Kingstree, SC 29556-4197
Williamson Free School of Mechanical Trades, Media, PA 19063-5299
Willmar Community College, Willmar, MN 56201
Willmar Technical College, Willmar, MN 56201
Wilmington College, Wilmington, OH 45177
Wilmington College, New Castle, DE 19720
Wilson College, Chambersburg, PA 17201-1285
Wilson Technical Community College, Wilson, NC 27893
Wingate College, Wingate, NC 28174-0157
Winona State University, Winona, MN 55987
Winston-Salem State University, Winston-Salem, NC 27110
Winthrop University, Rock Hill, SC 29733
Wisconsin Indianhead Technical College, Shell Lake, WI 54871
Wisconsin Lutheran College, Milwaukee, WI 53226
Wittenberg University, Springfield, OH 45501
Wofford College, Spartanburg, SC 29303-3663
Wood Junior College, Mathiston, MS 39752
Wood Tobe-Coburn School, New York, NY 10016-0190
Woodbury University, Burbank, CA 91510-7846
Worcester Polytechnic Institute, Worcester, MA 01609-2280
Worcester State College, Worcester, MA 01602-2597
Worthington Community College, Worthington, MN 56187

Wor-Wic Community College, Salisbury, MD 21801-7164
Wright State University
    Dayton, Dayton, OH 45435
    Lake Campus, Celina, OH 45822
Wytheville Community College, Wytheville, VA 24382
Xavier University, Cincinnati, OH 45207-5311
Xavier University of Louisiana, New Orleans, LA 70125-1098
Yakima Valley Community College, Yakima, WA 98907
Yale University, New Haven, CT 06520
Yavapai College, Prescott, AZ 86301
Yeshiva Shaar Hatorah, Kew Gardens, NY 11418
Yeshiva Toras Chaim Talmudical Seminary, Denver, CO 80204
Yeshiva University, New York, NY 10033-3299
York College, York, NE 68467-2699
York College of Pennsylvania, York, PA 17403-3426
York Technical College, Rock Hill, SC 29730
Young Harris College, Young Harris, GA 30582-0116
Youngstown State University, Youngstown, OH 44555-0001
Yuba College, Marysville, CA 95901

A unique resource to help high schools and colleges provide students with comprehensive financial aid information

COLLEGE COST EXPLORER
FUND FINDER™

This software program was developed by the College Board in collaboration with American Student Assistance (ASA) and The Education Resources Institute (TERI) to ensure that all students have the facts they need about how to pay for college.

FUND FINDER stands out because it is:

▶ *Authoritative* — all scholarship and college information collected exclusively from primary sources; accuracy of all facts assured.

▶ *Simple to use* — easy access to entire program from any screen. On-screen instructions permit independent student use. All information can be viewed on screen or printed out in seconds.

▶ *Expandable* — the Local Scholarship Entry Program lets administrators customize the data base by adding local sources of funding not available in any national or state data base.

Building on the award-winning College Cost Explorer program, FUND FINDER is a total resource that provides:
▶ lists of scholarships matched to students' specific eligibility
▶ data base of 3,000 sources of private and public scholarships, internships, and loans
▶ separate data base of 1993-94 financial aid availability at 2,900 two- and four-year institutions, plus up-to-date college costs
▶ interactive electronic work sheets that let dependent and independent students calculate expected family contribution, using the new Federal methodology

Other special features include: electronic bulletin board for posting messages to students, on-screen calculator and guidance information to help students develop and understand various options for loan repayment, on-screen glossary of financial aid terms, list of authoritative books on financial aid.

FUND FINDER is affordable. For a license fee of only $495 and a 25% discount for annual renewal, guidance counselors and financial aid officers can provide students and families with complete college funding information at no cost to them.

MS-DOS 3.5" disks (5.25" disks for high density drives on request).
Requirements: 512K RAM, PC-DOS 2.1 or higher, MS-DOS 3.2 or higher; hard drive with 2 MB of free space plus 1 MB for local data base; at least a CGA or (for monochrome monitors) a Hercules card.

Under the terms of the College Board license agreement, students may not be charged for the use of the *College Cost Explorer FUND FINDER* program.

For further information about FUND FINDER and its license options, please write or FAX: Publications Customer Service, The College Board, 45 Columbus Avenue, New York, New York 10023-6992; FAX: (212) 713-8143, or call (212) 713-8165, Monday through Friday, 9 a.m. to 5 p.m. (EST).

Order Form

Mail order form to: College Board Publications, Department T28, Box 886, New York, New York 10101-0886

Qty.	Item No.	Title	Price	Amount
____	004000	The College Board Guide to 150 Popular College Majors	$ 16.00	$_____
____	004795	The College Handbook, 1994	$ 20.00	$_____
____	004809	Index of Majors and Graduate Degrees, 1994	$ 17.00	$_____
____	004817	College Costs and Financial Aid Handbook, 1994	$ 16.00	$_____
____	239369	3-Book Set: College Handbook, Index of Majors/Graduate Degrees, College Costs and Financial Aid Handbook, 1994	$ 36.00	$_____
____	004825	The College Handbook for Transfer Students, 1994	$ 17.00	$_____
____	004833	The College Handbook Foreign Student Supplement, 1994	$ 16.00	$_____
____	004566	Introducing the New SAT	$ 12.00	$_____
____	003667	10 SATs. Fourth edition	$ 11.95	$_____
____	003942	The College Board Achievement Tests (rev. edition)	$ 12.95	$_____
____	004558	The Official Handbook for the CLEP Examinations	$ 15.00	$_____
____	004418	Breaking the Science Barrier: How to Explore and Understand the Sciences	$ 14.00	$_____
____	003543	The College Board Guide to Jobs and Career Planning	$ 12.95	$_____
____	003330	Choosing a College: The Student's Step-by-Step Decision-Making Workbook	$ 9.95	$_____
____	004280	Your College Application	$ 9.95	$_____
____	003276	Your College Application video cassette	$ 29.95	$_____
____	004299	Writing Your College Application Essay	$ 9.95	$_____
____	002601	Campus Visits and College Interviews	$ 9.95	$_____
____	002261	The College Admissions Organizer	$ 16.95	$_____
____	003047	College Bound: Getting Ready, Moving In, and Succeeding on Campus	$ 9.95	$_____
____	003357	Countdown to College: Getting the Most Out of High School	$ 9.95	$_____
____	003179	Campus Health Guide	$ 14.95	$_____
____	003349	Coping with Stress in College	$ 9.95	$_____
____	003837	Inside College: New Freedom, New Responsibility	$ 10.95	$_____
____	003535	The Student's Guide to Good Writing	$ 9.95	$_____
____	002598	Succeed with Math: Every Student's Guide to Conquering Math Anxiety	$ 12.95	$_____
____	003977	ABC's of Eligibility for College-Bound Student Athletes video cassette	$ 49.95	$_____
____	002075	The College Board Guide to Going to College While Working	$ 9.95	$_____
____	003055	How to Help Your Teenager Find the Right Career	$ 12.95	$_____
____	003160	The College Guide for Parents	$ 12.95	$_____
____		College Explorer, 1994 ____ 004647 (Apple II) ____ 004639 (MS-DOS)	$ 125.00	$_____
____		College Planner ____ 003683 (Apple II) ____ 003705 (MS-DOS)	$ 35.00	$_____
____		College Explorer Plus, 1993 ____ 004760 (MS-DOS)	$ 295.00	$_____

Payment must accompany all orders not submitted on an institutional purchase order or charged to a credit card. The College Board pays UPS regular ground postage to the 48 contiguous states on credit card and prepaid orders (orders to P.O. boxes, Alaska, and Hawaii ship via 4th class). Credit card and purchase orders must be for a minimum of $25. Postage is charged on all orders received on purchase orders or requesting faster shipment. Allow 7–10 working days from receipt of order for delivery.

CA residents, add 7.25% sales tax
PA residents, add 6% sales tax $_____
Subtotal $_____
Handling Charge $ 3.95
Total $_____

___ Enclosed is my check or money order made payable to the College Board
___ Enclosed is an institutional purchase order (orders for $25 or more), or
___ Please charge my ___ MasterCard ___ Visa. My credit card number is ___ ___ ___ ___/___ ___ ___ ___/___ ___ ___ ___/___ ___ ___ ___

Card expiration date: ___/___
                       month/year   Card holder's signature

Credit card holders only can place orders by calling toll-free 1-800-323-7155 Monday through Thursday from 8am to 12 midnight; Friday, 8am to 11pm EST. Please have your credit card number ready when you call and give operator the department number T28. For other information or assistance, call (212) 713-8165, Monday through Friday, 9am to 5pm EST, FAX (212) 713-8143.

Ship to:
Name _____   City _____

Street Address (**No P.O. Box numbers**) _____   State _____   Zip _____

_____   Telephone _____

MAKE YOUR MAJOR DECISION A WISE ONE

"This is an easy-to-use guide and contains very useful information." —*Voice of Youth Advocates*

"This unique book offers [students] information they need to make sound choices about bachelor's degree majors at 4-year colleges."
—*The International Educator*

"...presents a multitude of college majors."
—*Booklist*

The College Board Guide to 150 Popular College Majors is a unique guide that will help students and their parents make informed choices concerning college majors. It contains detailed, up-to-the-minute descriptions of the most widely offered undergraduate majors, each written by a leading professor in the field.

Majors are grouped into 17 fields ranging from the arts, business, and engineering to health services and the physical sciences.

Each entry in *The College Board Guide to 150 Popular College Majors*:

- describes the content of the major
- explains what a student will study
- lists related majors for a student to consider

In addition to an overview of the major, including new territory being explored, each description lists:

- interests and skills associated with success in the major
- recommended high school preparation
- typical courses in the major
- specializations within the major
- what the major is like
- careers the major may lead to
- where to get more information

The introduction provides authoritative advice on what a major is, how to choose a major, and the connection of majors to careers and further education. In an introductory chapter, college students tell how they chose their majors. 004000   ISBN: 0-87447-400-0, 1992, 328 pages, glossary, indexes, $16.00

Order Form

Mail order form to: College Board Publications, Department T28, Box 886, New York, New York 10101-0886

Qty.	Item No.	Title	Price	Amount
___	004000	The College Board Guide to 150 Popular College Majors	$ 16.00	$_____
___	004795	The College Handbook, 1994	$ 20.00	$_____
___	004809	Index of Majors and Graduate Degrees, 1994	$ 17.00	$_____
___	004817	College Costs and Financial Aid Handbook, 1994	$ 16.00	$_____
___	239369	3-Book Set: College Handbook, Index of Majors/Graduate Degrees, College Costs and Financial Aid Handbook, 1994	$ 36.00	$_____
___	004825	The College Handbook for Transfer Students, 1994	$ 17.00	$_____
___	004833	The College Handbook Foreign Student Supplement, 1994	$ 16.00	$_____
___	004566	Introducing the New SAT	$ 12.00	$_____
___	003667	10 SATs. Fourth edition	$ 11.95	$_____
___	003942	The College Board Achievement Tests (rev. edition)	$ 12.95	$_____
___	004558	The Official Handbook for the CLEP Examinations	$ 15.00	$_____
___	004418	Breaking the Science Barrier: How to Explore and Understand the Sciences	$ 14.00	$_____
___	003543	The College Board Guide to Jobs and Career Planning	$ 12.95	$_____
___	003330	Choosing a College: The Student's Step-by-Step Decision-Making Workbook	$ 9.95	$_____
___	004280	Your College Application	$ 9.95	$_____
___	003276	Your College Application video cassette	$ 29.95	$_____
___	004299	Writing Your College Application Essay	$ 9.95	$_____
___	002601	Campus Visits and College Interviews	$ 9.95	$_____
___	002261	The College Admissions Organizer	$ 16.95	$_____
___	003047	College Bound: Getting Ready, Moving In, and Succeeding on Campus	$ 9.95	$_____
___	003357	Countdown to College: Getting the Most Out of High School	$ 9.95	$_____
___	003179	Campus Health Guide	$ 14.95	$_____
___	003349	Coping with Stress in College	$ 9.95	$_____
___	003837	Inside College: New Freedom, New Responsibility	$ 10.95	$_____
___	003535	The Student's Guide to Good Writing	$ 9.95	$_____
___	002598	Succeed with Math: Every Student's Guide to Conquering Math Anxiety	$ 12.95	$_____
___	003977	ABC's of Eligibility for College-Bound Student Athletes video cassette	$ 49.95	$_____
___	002075	The College Board Guide to Going to College While Working	$ 9.95	$_____
___	003055	How to Help Your Teenager Find the Right Career	$ 12.95	$_____
___	003160	The College Guide for Parents	$ 12.95	$_____
___		College Explorer, 1994 ___ 004647 (Apple II) ___ 004639 (MS-DOS)	$ 125.00	$_____
___		College Planner ___ 003683 (Apple II) ___ 003705 (MS-DOS)	$ 35.00	$_____
___		College Explorer Plus, 1993 ___ 004760 (MS-DOS)	$ 295.00	$_____

Payment must accompany all orders not submitted on an institutional purchase order or charged to a credit card. The College Board pays UPS regular ground postage to the 48 contiguous states on credit card and prepaid orders (orders to P.O. boxes, Alaska, and Hawaii ship via 4th class). Credit card and purchase orders must be for a minimum of $25. Postage is charged on all orders received on purchase orders or requesting faster shipment. Allow 7–10 working days from receipt of order for delivery.

CA residents, add 7.25% sales tax
PA residents, add 6% sales tax $_____
Subtotal $_____
Handling Charge $ 3.95
Total $_____

___ Enclosed is my check or money order made payable to the College Board
___ Enclosed is an institutional purchase order (orders for $25 or more), or
___ Please charge my ___ MasterCard ___ Visa. My credit card number is ___ ___ ___ ___/___ ___ ___ ___/___ ___ ___ ___/___ ___ ___ ___

Card expiration date: ___/___
                    month/year   Card holder's signature

Credit card holders only can place orders by calling toll-free 1-800-323-7155 Monday through Thursday from 8am to 12 midnight; Friday, 8am to 11pm EST. Please have your credit card number ready when you call and give operator the department number T28. For other information or assistance, call (212) 713-8165, Monday through Friday, 9am to 5pm EST, FAX (212) 713-8143.

Ship to:
Name _____   City _____

Street Address (**No P.O. Box numbers**) _____   State _____ Zip _____

_____   Telephone _____

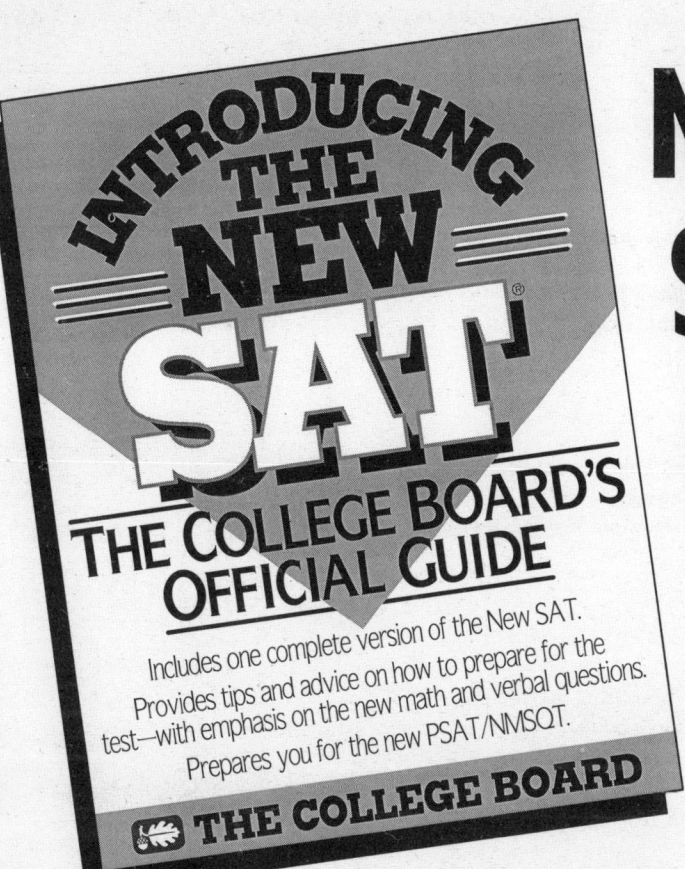

Now Students Can Get Expert Advice Firsthand

INTRODUCING THE NEW SAT
THE COLLEGE BOARD'S OFFICIAL GUIDE

Includes one complete version of the New SAT. Provides tips and advice on how to prepare for the test—with emphasis on the new math and verbal questions. Prepares you for the new PSAT/NMSQT.

THE COLLEGE BOARD

This is the *only official guide* to the new SAT, which students will take for the first time on March 19, 1994. Produced by the College Board, the sponsors of the SAT, the guide has been created to help all students prepare more effectively and confidently for the tests.

Written in a clear, lively style, *Introducing the New SAT: The College Board's Official Guide* provides expert advice and helpful test-taking strategies from the individuals who actually develop the test. It includes more than 80 practice questions *plus one complete practice test*.

Divided into four sections, the guide...

- explains what is different about the new SAT—and why;
- presents strategies to improve your scores, including pointers for educated guessing, hints on pacing, setting target scores, and general tips for both Verbal and Math sections;
- provides a complete practice test (SAT I);
- offers more than 80 additional sample questions designed to help you sharpen your skills.

004566 ISBN: 0-87447-456-6, 1993, 256 pages, $12.00

Purchase *Introducing the New SAT* using the order form at the back of this publication.

Order Form

Mail order form to: College Board Publications, Department T28, Box 886, New York, New York 10101-0886

Qty.	Item No.	Title	Price	Amount
____	004000	The College Board Guide to 150 Popular College Majors	$ 16.00	$_____
____	004795	The College Handbook, 1994	$ 20.00	$_____
____	004809	Index of Majors and Graduate Degrees, 1994	$ 17.00	$_____
____	004817	College Costs and Financial Aid Handbook, 1994	$ 16.00	$_____
____	239369	3-Book Set: College Handbook, Index of Majors/Graduate Degrees, College Costs and Financial Aid Handbook, 1994	$ 36.00	$_____
____	004825	The College Handbook for Transfer Students, 1994	$ 17.00	$_____
____	004833	The College Handbook Foreign Student Supplement, 1994	$ 16.00	$_____
____	004566	Introducing the New SAT	$ 12.00	$_____
____	003667	10 SATs. Fourth edition	$ 11.95	$_____
____	003942	The College Board Achievement Tests (rev. edition)	$ 12.95	$_____
____	004558	The Official Handbook for the CLEP Examinations	$ 15.00	$_____
____	004418	Breaking the Science Barrier: How to Explore and Understand the Sciences	$ 14.00	$_____
____	003543	The College Board Guide to Jobs and Career Planning	$ 12.95	$_____
____	003330	Choosing a College: The Student's Step-by-Step Decision-Making Workbook	$ 9.95	$_____
____	004280	Your College Application	$ 9.95	$_____
____	003276	Your College Application video cassette	$ 29.95	$_____
____	004299	Writing Your College Application Essay	$ 9.95	$_____
____	002601	Campus Visits and College Interviews	$ 9.95	$_____
____	002261	The College Admissions Organizer	$ 16.95	$_____
____	003047	College Bound: Getting Ready, Moving In, and Succeeding on Campus	$ 9.95	$_____
____	003357	Countdown to College: Getting the Most Out of High School	$ 9.95	$_____
____	003179	Campus Health Guide	$ 14.95	$_____
____	003349	Coping with Stress in College	$ 9.95	$_____
____	003837	Inside College: New Freedom, New Responsibility	$ 10.95	$_____
____	003535	The Student's Guide to Good Writing	$ 9.95	$_____
____	002598	Succeed with Math: Every Student's Guide to Conquering Math Anxiety	$ 12.95	$_____
____	003977	ABC's of Eligibility for College-Bound Student Athletes video cassette	$ 49.95	$_____
____	002075	The College Board Guide to Going to College While Working	$ 9.95	$_____
____	003055	How to Help Your Teenager Find the Right Career	$ 12.95	$_____
____	003160	The College Guide for Parents	$ 12.95	$_____
____		**College Explorer, 1994** ____ 004647 (Apple II) ____ 004639 (MS-DOS)	$ 125.00	$_____
____		**College Planner** ____ 003683 (Apple II) ____ 003705 (MS-DOS)	$ 35.00	$_____
____		**College Explorer Plus, 1993** ____ 004760 (MS-DOS)	$ 295.00	$_____

Payment must accompany all orders not submitted on an institutional purchase order or charged to a credit card. The College Board pays UPS regular ground postage to the 48 contiguous states on credit card and prepaid orders (orders to P.O. boxes, Alaska, and Hawaii ship via 4th class). Credit card and purchase orders must be for a minimum of $25. Postage is charged on all orders received on purchase orders or requesting faster shipment. Allow 7–10 working days from receipt of order for delivery.

CA residents, add 7.25% sales tax
PA residents, add 6% sales tax $_____
Subtotal $_____
Handling Charge $___3.95

Total $_____

___ Enclosed is my check or money order made payable to the College Board
___ Enclosed is an institutional purchase order (orders for $25 or more), or
___ Please charge my ___ MasterCard ___ Visa. My credit card number is ___ ___ ___ ___/___ ___ ___ ___/___ ___ ___ ___/___ ___ ___ ___

Card expiration date: ___/___   _____
                    month/year   Card holder's signature

Credit card holders only can place orders by calling toll-free 1-800-323-7155 Monday through Thursday from 8am to 12 midnight; Friday, 8am to 11pm EST. Please have your credit card number ready when you call and give operator the department number T28. For other information or assistance, call (212) 713-8165, Monday through Friday, 9am to 5pm EST, FAX (212) 713-8143.

Ship to:
Name _____   City _____

Street Address (**No P.O. Box numbers**) _____   State _____ Zip _____

_____   Telephone _____

ANNOUNCING

EXPLORER PLUS APPLICATION NETWORK™

...the all-new high school-based integrated guidance and application system

ExPAN is a comprehensive software program designed to provide students and counselors with an array of much-needed services, including:

- College search
- Student portfolio
- Financial aid worksheets
- Computerized Common Application
- Application tracking
- Counselor reports

ExPAN Helps Students

- Build a student portfolio
- Choose colleges
- Find out about financial aid
- Complete computerized applications and apply to college

ExPAN Saves Time for Counselors

Automatic record-keeping makes it easier and faster to monitor students' application status and obtain administrative reports. This easy-to-use Windows-based software comes with both Supervisor and Student Manuals.

New Features to Come

ExPAN is modular in design so new software programs may be added and integrated into a *total* system. Counselors will soon be able to add modules on careers, majors, scholarships, and decision-making skills.

Find out More about ExPAN

The license fee is $750, or $1,125 for network and multicomputer use. For further information about the program and license options, please write or FAX: Publications Customer Service, The College Board, 45 Columbus Avenue, New York, New York 10023-6992; FAX: (212) 713-8143, or call (212) 713-8165, Monday through Friday, 9 a.m. to 5 p.m. (EST).

Technical requirements

IBM or 100% compatible PC, 386 or better; Windows 3.1; 2 MB RAM; 20 MB hard drive recommended; VGA graphics; mouse; printer.

Order Form

Mail order form to: College Board Publications, Department T28, Box 886, New York, New York 10101-0886

Qty.	Item No.	Title	Price	Amount
___	004000	The College Board Guide to 150 Popular College Majors	$ 16.00	$_____
___	004795	The College Handbook, 1994	$ 20.00	$_____
___	004809	Index of Majors and Graduate Degrees, 1994	$ 17.00	$_____
___	004817	College Costs and Financial Aid Handbook, 1994	$ 16.00	$_____
___	239369	3-Book Set: College Handbook, Index of Majors/Graduate Degrees, College Costs and Financial Aid Handbook, 1994	$ 36.00	$_____
___	004825	The College Handbook for Transfer Students, 1994	$ 17.00	$_____
___	004833	The College Handbook Foreign Student Supplement, 1994	$ 16.00	$_____
___	004566	Introducing the New SAT	$ 12.00	$_____
___	003667	10 SATs. Fourth edition	$ 11.95	$_____
___	003942	The College Board Achievement Tests (rev. edition)	$ 12.95	$_____
___	004558	The Official Handbook for the CLEP Examinations	$ 15.00	$_____
___	004418	Breaking the Science Barrier: How to Explore and Understand the Sciences	$ 14.00	$_____
___	003543	The College Board Guide to Jobs and Career Planning	$ 12.95	$_____
___	003330	Choosing a College: The Student's Step-by-Step Decision-Making Workbook	$ 9.95	$_____
___	004280	Your College Application	$ 9.95	$_____
___	003276	Your College Application video cassette	$ 29.95	$_____
___	004299	Writing Your College Application Essay	$ 9.95	$_____
___	002601	Campus Visits and College Interviews	$ 9.95	$_____
___	002261	The College Admissions Organizer	$ 16.95	$_____
___	003047	College Bound: Getting Ready, Moving In, and Succeeding on Campus	$ 9.95	$_____
___	003357	Countdown to College: Getting the Most Out of High School	$ 9.95	$_____
___	003179	Campus Health Guide	$ 14.95	$_____
___	003349	Coping with Stress in College	$ 9.95	$_____
___	003837	Inside College: New Freedom, New Responsibility	$ 10.95	$_____
___	003535	The Student's Guide to Good Writing	$ 9.95	$_____
___	002598	Succeed with Math: Every Student's Guide to Conquering Math Anxiety	$ 12.95	$_____
___	003977	ABC's of Eligibility for College-Bound Student Athletes video cassette	$ 49.95	$_____
___	002075	The College Board Guide to Going to College While Working	$ 9.95	$_____
___	003055	How to Help Your Teenager Find the Right Career	$ 12.95	$_____
___	003160	The College Guide for Parents	$ 12.95	$_____
___		College Explorer, 1994 ___ 004647 (Apple II) ___ 004639 (MS-DOS)	$ 125.00	$_____
___		College Planner ___ 003683 (Apple II) ___ 003705 (MS-DOS)	$ 35.00	$_____
___		College Explorer Plus, 1993 ___ 004760 (MS-DOS)	$ 295.00	$_____

Payment must accompany all orders not submitted on an institutional purchase order or charged to a credit card. The College Board pays UPS regular ground postage to the 48 contiguous states on credit card and prepaid orders (orders to P.O. boxes, Alaska, and Hawaii ship via 4th class). Credit card and purchase orders must be for a minimum of $25. Postage is charged on all orders received on purchase orders or requesting faster shipment. Allow 7–10 working days from receipt of order for delivery.

CA residents, add 7.25% sales tax
PA residents, add 6% sales tax $_____
Subtotal $_____
Handling Charge $ 3.95
Total $_____

___ Enclosed is my check or money order made payable to the College Board
___ Enclosed is an institutional purchase order (orders for $25 or more), or
___ Please charge my ___ MasterCard ___ Visa. My credit card number is ___ ___ ___ ___/___ ___ ___ ___/___ ___ ___ ___/___ ___ ___ ___

Card expiration date: ___/___   _____
           month/year   Card holder's signature

Credit card holders only can place orders by calling toll-free 1-800-323-7155 Monday through Thursday from 8am to 12 midnight; Friday, 8am to 11pm EST. Please have your credit card number ready when you call and give operator the department number T28. For other information or assistance, call (212) 713-8165, Monday through Friday, 9am to 5pm EST, FAX (212) 713-8143.

Ship to:
Name _____   City _____

Street Address (**No P.O. Box numbers**) _____   State _____ Zip _____

_____   Telephone _____

A unique resource to help high schools and colleges provide students with comprehensive financial aid information

COLLEGE COST EXPLORER
FUND FINDER™

This software program was developed by the College Board in collaboration with American Student Assistance (ASA) and The Education Resources Institute (TERI) to ensure that all students have the facts they need about how to pay for college.

FUND FINDER stands out because it is:

▶ *Authoritative* — all scholarship and college information collected exclusively from primary sources; accuracy of all facts assured.

▶ *Simple to use* — easy access to entire program from any screen. On-screen instructions permit independent student use. All information can be viewed on screen or printed out in seconds.

▶ *Expandable* — the Local Scholarship Entry Program lets administrators customize the data base by adding local sources of funding not available in any national or state data base.

Building on the award-winning College Cost Explorer program, FUND FINDER is a total resource that provides:
- lists of scholarships matched to students' specific eligibility
- data base of 3,000 sources of private and public scholarships, internships, and loans
- separate data base of 1993-94 financial aid availability at 2,900 two- and four-year institutions, plus up-to-date college costs
- interactive electronic work sheets that let dependent and independent students calculate expected family contribution, using the new Federal methodology

Other special features include: electronic bulletin board for posting messages to students, on-screen calculator and guidance information to help students develop and understand various options for loan repayment, on-screen glossary of financial aid terms, list of authoritative books on financial aid.

FUND FINDER is affordable. For a license fee of only $495 and a 25% discount for annual renewal, guidance counselors and financial aid officers can provide students and families with complete college funding information at no cost to them.

MS-DOS 3.5" disks (5.25" disks for high density drives on request).
Requirements: 512K RAM, PC-DOS 2.1 or higher, MS-DOS 3.2 or higher; hard drive with 2 MB of free space plus 1 MB for local data base; at least a CGA or (for monochrome monitors) a Hercules card.

Under the terms of the College Board license agreement, students may not be charged for the use of the *College Cost Explorer FUND FINDER* program.

For further information about FUND FINDER and its license options, please write or FAX: Publications Customer Service, The College Board, 45 Columbus Avenue, New York, New York 10023-6992; FAX: (212) 713-8143, or call (212) 713-8165, Monday through Friday, 9 a.m. to 5 p.m. (EST).

Order Form

Mail order form to: College Board Publications, Department T28, Box 886, New York, New York 10101-0886

Qty.	Item No.	Title	Price	Amount
____	004000	The College Board Guide to 150 Popular College Majors	$ 16.00	$_____
____	004795	The College Handbook, 1994	$ 20.00	$_____
____	004809	Index of Majors and Graduate Degrees, 1994	$ 17.00	$_____
____	004817	College Costs and Financial Aid Handbook, 1994	$ 16.00	$_____
____	239369	3-Book Set: College Handbook, Index of Majors/Graduate Degrees, College Costs and Financial Aid Handbook, 1994	$ 36.00	$_____
____	004825	The College Handbook for Transfer Students, 1994	$ 17.00	$_____
____	004833	The College Handbook Foreign Student Supplement, 1994	$ 16.00	$_____
____	004566	Introducing the New SAT	$ 12.00	$_____
____	003667	10 SATs. Fourth edition	$ 11.95	$_____
____	003942	The College Board Achievement Tests (rev. edition)	$ 12.95	$_____
____	004558	The Official Handbook for the CLEP Examinations	$ 15.00	$_____
____	004418	Breaking the Science Barrier: How to Explore and Understand the Sciences	$ 14.00	$_____
____	003543	The College Board Guide to Jobs and Career Planning	$ 12.95	$_____
____	003330	Choosing a College: The Student's Step-by-Step Decision-Making Workbook	$ 9.95	$_____
____	004280	Your College Application	$ 9.95	$_____
____	003276	Your College Application video cassette	$ 29.95	$_____
____	004299	Writing Your College Application Essay	$ 9.95	$_____
____	002601	Campus Visits and College Interviews	$ 9.95	$_____
____	002261	The College Admissions Organizer	$ 16.95	$_____
____	003047	College Bound: Getting Ready, Moving In, and Succeeding on Campus	$ 9.95	$_____
____	003357	Countdown to College: Getting the Most Out of High School	$ 9.95	$_____
____	003179	Campus Health Guide	$ 14.95	$_____
____	003349	Coping with Stress in College	$ 9.95	$_____
____	003837	Inside College: New Freedom, New Responsibility	$ 10.95	$_____
____	003535	The Student's Guide to Good Writing	$ 9.95	$_____
____	002598	Succeed with Math: Every Student's Guide to Conquering Math Anxiety	$ 12.95	$_____
____	003977	ABC's of Eligibility for College-Bound Student Athletes video cassette	$ 49.95	$_____
____	002075	The College Board Guide to Going to College While Working	$ 9.95	$_____
____	003055	How to Help Your Teenager Find the Right Career	$ 12.95	$_____
____	003160	The College Guide for Parents	$ 12.95	$_____
____		**College Explorer, 1994** ____ 004647 (Apple II) ____ 004639 (MS-DOS)	$ 125.00	$_____
____		**College Planner** ____ 003683 (Apple II) ____ 003705 (MS-DOS)	$ 35.00	$_____
____		**College Explorer Plus, 1993** ____ 004760 (MS-DOS)	$ 295.00	$_____

Payment must accompany all orders not submitted on an institutional purchase order or charged to a credit card. The College Board pays UPS regular ground postage to the 48 contiguous states on credit card and prepaid orders (orders to P.O. boxes, Alaska, and Hawaii ship via 4th class). Credit card and purchase orders must be for a minimum of $25. Postage is charged on all orders received on purchase orders or requesting faster shipment. Allow 7–10 working days from receipt of order for delivery.

CA residents, add 7.25% sales tax
PA residents, add 6% sales tax $_____
Subtotal $_____
Handling Charge $___3.95
Total $_____

___ Enclosed is my check or money order made payable to the College Board
___ Enclosed is an institutional purchase order (orders for $25 or more), or
___ Please charge my ___ MasterCard ___ Visa. My credit card number is ___ ___ ___ ___/___ ___ ___ ___/___ ___ ___ ___/___ ___ ___ ___

Card expiration date: ___/___
    month/year   Card holder's signature

Credit card holders only can place orders by calling toll-free 1-800-323-7155 Monday through Thursday from 8am to 12 midnight; Friday, 8am to 11pm EST. Please have your credit card number ready when you call and give operator the department number T28. For other information or assistance, call (212) 713-8165, Monday through Friday, 9am to 5pm EST, FAX (212) 713-8143.

Ship to:
Name _____ City _____
Street Address (**No P.O. Box numbers**) _____ State _____ Zip _____
_____ Telephone _____